FEATURE	MENU SELECTIONS		
Document Summary	Layout ➤ Document ➤ Summary		
Double Indent	Layout ➤ Paragraph ➤ Double Indent	Ctrl+Shift+F7	107
Double Underline	Font ➤ Double Underline		146
Draft Mode	View ➤ Draft Mode	Ctrl+Shift+F3	88
Endnote	Layout ➤ Endnote➤Create		803
Equations	Graphics ➤ Equation		754
Exit WordPerfect	File ➤ Exit	Alt+F4	23
Export Text	File ➤ Save As ➤ Format		853
Figure Box	Graphics ➤ Figure ➤ Retrieve	F11	645
File Manager	File ➤ File Manager		415
Flush-Right Line	Layout ➤ Line ➤ Flush Right	Alt+F7	106
Font	Font ➤ Font	F9	138
Footers	Layout ➤ Page ➤ Footers	Alt+F9 F	254
Footnote	Layout ➤ Footnote ➤ Create		803
Force Odd/Even Page	Layout ➤ Page ➤ Numbering ➤ Odd *or* Even	Alt+F9 N (O *or* E)	259
Full Justification	Layout ➤ Justification ➤ Full	Ctrl+F	104
Generate	Tools ➤ Generate	Alt+F12	833
Go To	Edit ➤ Go To	Ctrl+G	33
Graphics Box	Graphics ➤ *box type* ➤ Create		641
Hanging Indent	Layout ➤ Paragraph ➤ Hanging Indent	Ctrl+F7	107
Hard Page Break	Layout ➤ Page ➤ Page Break	Ctrl+⏎	242
Headers	Layout ➤ Page ➤ Headers	Alt+F9 H	250
Help	Help	F1	62
Horizontal Line	Graphics ➤ Line ➤ Horizontal	Ctrl+F11	165
Hyphenation On/Off	Layout ➤ Line ➤ Hyphenation	Shift+F9 E	385
Indent	Layout ➤ Paragraph ➤ Indent	F7	107
Index Entry	Tools ➤ Mark Text ➤ Index	F12 I	819
Italic	Font ➤ Italic	Ctrl+I	146
Keyboard Layout	File ➤ Preferences ➤ Keyboard	Ctrl+Shift+F1 K	911
Left Justification	Layout ➤ Justification ➤ Left	Ctrl+L	103
Line (graphic)	Graphics ➤ Line		164
Line Draw	Tools ➤ Line Draw	Ctrl+D	162
Line Height	Layout ➤ Line ➤ Height	Shift+F9 H	735

Requires that text be selected

Continued on inside back cover

Computer users are not all alike.
Neither are SYBEX books.

We know our customers have a variety of needs. They've told us so. And because we've listened, we've developed several distinct types of books to meet the needs of each of our customers. What are you looking for in computer help?

If you're looking for the basics, try the **ABC's** series. You'll find short, unintimidating tutorials and helpful illustrations. For a more visual approach, select **Teach Yourself**, featuring screen-by-screen illustrations of how to use your latest software purchase.

Mastering and **Understanding** titles offer you a step-by-step introduction, plus an in-depth examination of intermediate-level features, to use as you progress.

Our **Up & Running** series is designed for computer-literate consumers who want a no-nonsense overview of new programs. Just 20 basic lessons, and you're on your way.

We also publish two types of reference books. Our **Instant References** provide quick access to each of a program's commands and functions. SYBEX **Encyclopedias** and **Desktop References** provide a *comprehensive reference* and explanation of all of the commands, features and functions of the subject software.

Sometimes a subject requires a special treatment that our standard series don't provide. So you'll find we have titles like **Advanced Techniques, Handbooks, Tips & Tricks,** and others that are specifically tailored to satisfy a unique need.

We carefully select our authors for their in-depth understanding of the software they're writing about, as well as their ability to write clearly and communicate effectively. Each manuscript is thoroughly reviewed by our technical staff to ensure its complete accuracy. Our production department makes sure it's easy to use. All of this adds up to the highest quality books available, consistently appearing on best-seller charts worldwide.

You'll find SYBEX publishes a variety of books on every popular software package. Looking for computer help? Help Yourself to SYBEX.

For a complete catalog of our publications:

SYBEX Inc.
2021 Challenger Drive, Alameda, CA 94501
Tel: (510) 523-8233/(800) 227-2346 Telex: 336311
Fax: (510) 523-2373

SYBEX is committed to using natural resources wisely to preserve and improve our environment. As a leader in the computer book publishing industry, we are aware that over 40% of America's solid waste is paper. This is why we have been printing the text of books like this one on recycled paper since 1982.

This year our use of recycled paper will result in the saving of more than 15,300 trees. We will lower air pollution effluents by 54,000 pounds, save 6,300,000 gallons of water, and reduce landfill by 2,700 cubic yards.

In choosing a SYBEX book you are not only making a choice for the best in skills and information, you are also choosing to enhance the quality of life for all of us.

MASTERING
WORDPERFECT 5.1 FOR WINDOWS

MASTERING
WORDPERFECT® 5.1
FOR WINDOWS™

Alan Simpson

SYBEX®

San Francisco • Paris • Düsseldorf • Soest

ACQUISITIONS EDITOR: *Dianne King*
DEVELOPMENTAL EDITOR: *Christian T. S. Crumlish*
EDITORS: *Richard Mills and Jeff Kapellas*
ASSISTANT EDITORS: *Janna Clark and Brendan Fletcher*
EDITORIAL ASSISTANT:*Molly Spofford*
TECHNICAL EDITOR: *Sheldon M. Dunn*
WORD PROCESSORS: *Ann Dunn and Susan Trybull*
BOOK DESIGNER: *Amparo del Rio*
PRODUCTION ARTISTS: *Lucie Živny and Alissa Feinberg*
SCREEN GRAPHICS: *Delia Brown, Thomas Goudie, Cuong Le, and Aldo Bermudez*
POSTSCRIPT ICON TYPEFACE *created with CorelDRAW by Len Gilbert*
DESKTOP PUBLISHING PRODUCTION: *Len Gilbert*
LEAD PROOFREADER: *Rhonda M. Holmes*
PROOFREADERS/PRODUCTION ASSISTANTS: *Janet K. Boone and Edith Rex*
INDEXER: *Nancy Anderman Guenther*
COVER DESIGNER: *Ingalls + Associates*
COVER PHOTOGRAPHER: *Mark Johann*

Library of Congress Card Number:91-66933
ISBN: 0-89588-806-8

Manufactured in the United States of America
10 9 8 7 6 5 4 3 2 1

To Susan, Ashley, and Egg #2

Acknowledgments

very book is a team effort, and this book is certainly no exception. The skills, talents, and hard work of many people brought this book from the idea stage into your hands.

On the publishing side, the following people were instrumental in creating this book: Christian Crumlish, developmental editor; Richard Mills and Jeff Kapellas, editors; Janna Clark and Brendan Fletcher, assistant editors; Molly Spofford, editorial assistant; Chris Meredith, scheduling manager; Mac Dunn and David Brown, technical reviewers; Ann Dunn and Susan Trybull, word processors; Amparo del Rio, book designer; Lucie Živny and Alissa Feinberg, production artists; Len Gilbert, desktop publishing specialist; Rhonda Holmes, Janet Boone, and Edith Rex, proofreaders; Delia Brown, Cuong Le, Thomas Goudie, and Aldo Bermudez, graphics technicians; and Nancy Guenther, indexer.

On the authorial side, talented writers Elizabeth Olson, David Browne, Gordon McComb, Pat Burns, Brett Kelts, Mary Taylor, Maxine Iritz, and Charlie Prael all contributed to chapters and lessons. Martha Mellor miraculously managed all that material.

Bill Gladstone and Matt Wagner of Waterside Productions handled business matters.

Susan and Ashley provided love, support, sustenance, comfort, and lots of patience.

TABLE OF CONTENTS

PART TWO

FORMATTING YOUR DOCUMENTS

Chapter 4

SPACING, ALIGNING, AND INDENTING TEXT **95**

Chapter 5

FONTS, LINES, AND SPECIAL CHARACTERS 131

Chapter 6
CREATING TABLES 175

Chapter 7

Chapter 8

MASTERING YOUR PRINTER 293

PART THREE

TOOLS TO SIMPLIFY YOUR WORK

Chapter 9

SEARCHING AND REPLACING 341

Chapter 13

PART FOUR

AUTOMATING YOUR WORK

Chapter 14

PART FIVE

OFFICE TOOLS

Chapter 16

FORM LETTERS, MAILING LABELS, AND OTHER MERGES 539

Chapter 17
SORTING AND SELECTING RECORDS 581

Chapter 18
PERFECT MATH 613

PART SIX

DESKTOP PUBLISHING

Chapter 19

Chapter 20

WORKING WITH COLUMNS AND TYPESETTING FEATURES 707

Chapter 21

ADDING EQUATIONS TO YOUR DOCUMENTS **753**

PART SEVEN

MANAGING THE BIG JOBS

Chapter 22

AUTOMATIC NUMBERING AND OUTLINING **775**

Chapter 23
AUTOMATIC REFERENCING 801

PART EIGHT

TECHNIQUES FOR POWER USERS

Chapter 25

Chapter 26

Chapter 27

PART NINE

HANDS-ON LESSONS

Lesson 1

Lesson 2

Lesson 3

Introduction

ordPerfect Corporation has taken all the best features of the graphical user interface of the 1990s, Windows, and incorporated them beautifully into their now legendary word processing program. Beginners and old hands alike will appreciate the intuitive, interactive means of creating and editing documents that WordPerfect for Windows brings to the personal computer.

This is a book about using WordPerfect for Windows. The purpose of the book is twofold. On the one hand, the book is designed to teach you how to use WordPerfect, productively and efficiently, even if you've never touched a computer in your life. On the other hand, the book serves as a reference to all the big features and little details when you just need a quick reminder.

WHOM THIS BOOK IS FOR

As a super-successful software product, WordPerfect has two kinds of users: throngs of newcomers who are finding out just what this terrific program has to offer and experienced users (several million of them!) requiring in-depth information on new and improved features. This book is designed to help both kinds of users.

ARE YOU NEW TO COMPUTERS OR WORDPERFECT?

One of the toughest parts of learning to use a computer or learning to use a program is just getting the basic "feel" of the thing. For this reason, this book includes ten hands-on lessons at the back, designed to help newcomers get up and running fast.

I've also avoided the buzzwords and techno-babble that often make the manuals that accompany software so incomprehensible. Even in the general chapters before the hands-on lessons, I offer clear, step-by-step instructions for using all of WordPerfect's many useful features.

ARE YOU AN EXPERIENCED WORDPERFECT USER?

If you are an experienced WordPerfect user but are new to WordPerfect for Windows, you'll appreciate the in-depth descriptions of important new features in WordPerfect for Windows, like the graphical user interface, the ruler, the Button Bar, and other changes and refinements that will make your job easier.

The section titled "Tips for Experienced Users" near the end of this Introduction summarizes the new features and points you toward specific chapters that you'll want to focus on if you're upgrading to WordPerfect for Windows.

If you're new to Windows, you may want to read Appendix B. There you can learn all the basic skills of using Windows and Windows applications.

FEATURES OF THE BOOK

This book is designed both as a tutorial and as a quick reference to the many features of WordPerfect for Windows. Special features of the book, designed to simplify and speed your mastery of WordPerfect, and to provide easy access to information when needed, include the following:

Endpapers Inside the front and back covers you'll find a quick reference to the techniques for performing common tasks.

Pullout Reference Card You'll find a handy tear-out desktop reference chart at the back of the book, which you can remove and keep by your keyboard as a quick reference to WordPerfect keystroke and menu features.

Margin Notes   Margin notes provide cross-references to where related features are covered in the book, "hot tips" for added insight on creative ways to use features, and cautions about problems that can occur when using a feature.

Fast Tracks   The Fast Tracks at the beginning of selected sections provide a quick summary of techniques for using a specific feature, when you just need a quick reminder rather than a lengthy explanation.

Pull-Down Menu Steps   WordPerfect offers two methods of accessing its features: You can use the menus, or you can use shortcut keys. This book covers both methods, and you can use whichever you feel most comfortable with.

Hands-On Lessons   Everyone knows that the best way to learn something is by doing it. If you want to get the feel of creating a document, or creating and using tables, graphics, styles, macros, or form letters, try the accompanying hands-on lessons near the back of the book (Part 9). The lessons also refer you to specific chapters where you can get additional information.

Optional Companion Disk   You can purchase a copy of the various sample documents, styles, and macros presented in this book in ready-to-use form on a disk. The disk is not required to use this book, but it may come in handy if you want to use some of the examples as a starting point for your own work, without having to key in everything from scratch. See the coupon near the back of the book if you're interested.

STRUCTURE OF THE BOOK

This book is designed to supplement the densely packed and somewhat technical manual that came with your WordPerfect package. The purpose of the WordPerfect manual is to document every available feature in great detail. The purpose of this book is to show you how to use WordPerfect and put it to work for your own purposes, whatever they may be.

To make things easier for you and to help you focus on information that's relevant to your own use of WordPerfect, I've divided the book into nine parts:

Part One: Getting Started   The first part covers all the basics of typing, editing, saving, and printing documents with WordPerfect. If you are a beginner, you'll find that this part will help you ease into WordPerfect and become comfortable with the differences between using WordPerfect and using a typewriter.

Part Two: Formatting Your Documents This part takes you beyond basic typing, editing, and printing skills, and teaches you how to start controlling the exact appearance of your documents.

Part Three: Tools to Simplify Your Work This part covers tools and techniques to make your work easier, such as searching and replacing, checking your spelling and hyphenating text automatically, managing your documents, and customizing WordPerfect for your own needs.

Part Four: Automating Your Work This part covers two of WordPerfect's more convenient features, designed to simplify your work and increase your productivity: styles and macros.

Part Five: Office Tools This part covers those features of WordPerfect that are particularly useful in business settings, including merges, which are useful for mass mailings and fill-in forms, and the handy Math feature, which is useful for invoices, financial statements, and other documents that require some calculations.

Part Six: Desktop Publishing Desktop publishing is the wave of the '90s, and this part covers all you need to know about using graphics, lines, and columns to produce documents that are visually exciting and interesting.

Part Seven: Managing the Big Jobs This part covers tools that help you to create and manage bigger projects that require multiple chapters or sections, cross-referencing, footnotes, outlines, and other advanced features.

Part Eight: Techniques for Power Users This part covers advanced topics for power users, including interacting with other programs, using advanced macro and merge commands, and customizing the keyboard layout.

Part Nine: Hands-On Lessons When you need a little extra help in getting started with a particular feature, refer to this part for the appropriate hands-on lesson, which will take you step by step through a practical application of the feature. This helps give you an edge in learning new skills.

Appendices Appendix A offers information on installing WordPerfect for Windows and advanced start-up options for system managers and others responsible for setting up software. Appendix B presents a Windows primer, which acts as a reference for both beginning and experienced Windows users. Appendix C has a list of all the hidden codes used by WordPerfect.

ADDITIONAL SUPPORT

Much of the success that WordPerfect Corporation enjoys is based on its dedication to customer support. Phone numbers for answers to specific questions are listed below:

Installation	(800) 228-6076
Features	(800) 228-1029
Graphics/Tables/Equations	(800) 228-6013
Macros/Merges/Labels	(800) 228-1032
Laser/PostScript Printers	(800) 228-1023
Dot Matrix/Other Printers	(800) 228-1017
Networks	(800) 228-6066

You should be at your computer when you place the call and should have your WordPerfect license number (included with your WordPerfect package) handy. You should also know the make and model of your printer.

In addition to *Mastering WordPerfect 5.1 for Windows* and WordPerfect Corporation's support lines, you have another resource for getting help with WordPerfect: the WordPerfect Support Group. This is a national user group that publishes *The WordPerfectionist,* a monthly newsletter that provides useful tips and keeps you posted on new developments at WordPerfect Corporation. The group also provides product discounts, disk subscription services, and a user's forum on CompuServe. For information about the group and subscription rates, contact

WordPerfect Support Group

Lake Technology Park

P.O. Box 130

McHenry, MD 21541

(800) USA-GROUP

INTERIM RELEASES

From time to time, WordPerfect Corporation provides interim releases of WordPerfect to members of their software subscription service (the phone number is (800) 321-4566). These releases include minor fixes and enhancements to previous releases.

The interim release date of your copy of Word-Perfect appears in the upper-right corner of the Help screen (press F1).

In some cases, WordPerfect Corporation may change the information presented on your screen, add a feature, or change a feature slightly. Though every attempt has been made to keep this book up to date, there may be slight variations between this book and the release you are using.

If you find a discrepancy between a figure in this book and what you see on your screen, chances are it's because of a change made in an interim release. If an option that appears on your screen is not mentioned in this book, your best bet for getting information on that new feature is simply to press F1.

TIPS FOR EXPERIENCED USERS

If you've worked with WordPerfect 5.1 for DOS and are upgrading to Word-Perfect 5.1 for Windows, you'll find that virtually all the features you've grown accustomed to are in the Windows version. But the way you go about using some of these features has changed. The following sections explain what special steps you'll need to take, if any.

CROSS-COMPATIBILITY

WordPerfect 5.1 for Windows and WordPerfect 5.1 for DOS documents are stored in the same format. If you use WordPerfect for Windows, and someone else in your office uses WordPerfect 5.1 for DOS, you can share documents without going through any special steps to convert file formats. Just open and save documents in either product normally.

KEYBOARD COMPATIBILITY

By default, WordPerfect for Windows uses Windows Common User Access (CUA) keystrokes instead of the shortcut keys you may be familiar with from previous versions of WordPerfect. This book assumes you are using the CUA keyboard.

As an alternative to learning these new keystrokes, you can use the optional WordPerfect for DOS keyboard that comes with your WordPerfect package. This keyboard offers *some* compatibility with earlier versions of WordPerfect. See Chapter 27 for more information.

MACRO COMPATIBILITY

 NOTE NOTE *Word-Perfect 5.1 for Win-dows and WordPerfect 5.1 for DOS merge commands are fully compatible; only the macro commands have changed.*

WordPerfect for Windows uses an entirely new macro language, which is incompatible with macros created in earlier versions of WordPerfect. There is, however, a macro conversion utility provided with WordPerfect for Windows to help you convert existing macros to the new format.

Also, Alt+*key* macros are not available in WordPerfect for Windows. You can, however, attach macros to the menus, Button Bar, and some other keystrokes. See chapters 15, 26, and 27 for more information.

SUMMARY OF NEW AND IMPROVED FEATURES

Table I.1 provides a quick summary of the main new and improved features of WordPerfect for Windows, and where you can get additional information.

TABLE I.1:
New and Improved Features of WordPerfect

NEW/ MODIFIED FEATURE	DESCRIPTION	SEE CHAPTER
Auto Code Placement	Automatically places certain formatting codes at the beginning of the paragraph or page, replacing the existing code. Reduces code clutter and problems caused by competing codes.	3
Button Bar	Lets you convert commonly used menu options and macros to buttons that are readily available on the screen.	3
Convert	More foreign file formats are supported; they can be handled while opening or saving a file without using an external conversion program.	25
Cut and Paste	Text to be moved or copied is passed to the Windows Clipboard. This makes it easier to cut and paste between documents, as well as between Windows applications.	2
Dynamic Data Exchange (DDE link)	Data and graphics from other Windows applications can be linked to a WordPerfect document, allowing you to easily update the linked data when information in the source application changes.	25

NEW/ MODIFIED FEATURE	DESCRIPTION	SEE CHAPTER
File Manager	Replaces List Files; can be used outside of WordPerfect anytime that Windows is running.	12
Font Selection	You can change the font of selected text without changing the base font for all text beyond the insertion point.	5
Fonts	You can use WordPerfect or Windows fonts.	8, Appendix A
Graphical User Interface	Graphics, graphic lines, fonts, and other features are now readily visible on-screen—you don't need to switch to View Document to see an accurate representation of your document (draft mode is available if you want to work with only text).	3
Graphics	You can interactively size and position graphics with your mouse.	19
Macros	Though Alt+*key* macros are no longer supported, you can attach macros to menus, the Button Bar, or certain keys.	15, 27
Multiple Documents	You can edit up to nine documents at once, each in a separate document window that can be moved, sized, opened, and closed with the usual Windows techniques.	3, Appendix B
Preferences	Replaces Setup as the means of changing defaults. You can also use screen colors defined in the Windows Control Panel.	13
Print Preview	Replaces View Document and is still required to see some formatting features, such as headers, footers, and footnotes.	3
Printer Control	Background printing is handled by the Windows Print Manager.	8

TABLE 1.1:

New and Improved Features of WordPerfect (continued)

NEW/ MODIFIED FEATURE	DESCRIPTION	SEE CHAPTER
Printer Drivers	You can use WordPerfect or Windows printer drivers.	8
Quick List	Lets you replace any DOS path name, like C:\WPWIN\LETTERS, with a plain English name, like *Letters and Memos*.	12
Retrieve	**File ➤ R**etrieve is now used to *combine* documents. **File ➤ O**pen is used to open an existing document in a new document window, and **File ➤ N**ew is used to start a new document.	2, 12
Ruler	Provides a more interactive and intuitive means of changing tab stops, margins, and columns. Also provides shortcuts for choosing fonts, styles, justification, and other features.	3
Special Characters	Can be selected from a menu, without knowing the character's code.	5
Select Text	The term *select* replaces *block*. You can use your mouse, the F8 key, or Shift+*arrow* keys to select text.	2
Undo	Undoes your most recent change to a document, including formatting changes.	2

TABLE 1.1:

New and Improved Features of WordPerfect (continued)

PART ONE

Getting Started

The first three chapters of this book are written specifically for beginners. You'll learn how to start WordPerfect for Windows on your computer, and how to create, edit, print, save, and open WordPerfect documents. You'll also learn some techniques and shortcuts that will help you get the most out of this versatile program. The skills you'll learn in these chapters are the most important and fundamental, because you'll use them in every document you create. They will also smooth the road to learning WordPerfect's more advanced features.

CHAPTER 1

Creating and Printing Your First Document

ordPerfect for Windows is a word processing program that helps you to create and edit *documents*. A document is anything you might type with a typewriter: a memo, letter, magazine article, newsletter, or even an entire book. If you do any kind of typing or writing, WordPerfect for Windows is sure to make your work easier and more productive.

Perhaps the single most important feature that WordPerfect for Windows offers can be summarized as simply this: *You can change anything in your document without retyping.* For example, you can do the following:

◆ Insert, delete, move, and copy words, sentences, paragraphs, and entire pages without retyping

◆ Change the spacing, margins, and format of your document without retyping

◆ Automatically check and correct your spelling in an entire document in a matter of seconds

- Print dozens or even hundreds of personalized form letters, mailing labels, and envelopes

- Embellish your documents with typefaces, tables, graphics, and multi-column layouts

 If you're an experienced Word-Perfect user, see the Introduction for a summary of what's new in WordPerfect for Windows.

But this is just the beginning. As you'll see, WordPerfect for Windows offers much more than can be summarized in a few sentences. And no matter what sizes, types, or formats of documents you create, WordPerfect for Windows is certain to make your work much easier.

In this chapter, you'll start learning the basics of WordPerfect for Windows so that you can start being more productive right away. You'll learn how to create and print a document, and how to save the document for future use.

INSTALLING WORDPERFECT FOR WINDOWS

 Windows 3.0 is a program that must be purchased separately and installed on your computer.

WordPerfect for Windows is a *computer program,* a set of instructions that tell your computer how to act. Like all programs, WordPerfect for Windows must be purchased separately and installed on your computer before you can use it. You need to install WordPerfect for Windows only once, not each time you want to use it.

There are two ways to know whether WordPerfect for Windows is already installed on your computer. You do *not* need to install WordPerfect for Windows if

- You share a computer with other people, and someone else is already using WordPerfect for Windows on that computer.

- You have already installed WordPerfect for Windows on your computer, or your computer dealer has done this for you.

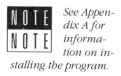 *See Appendix A for information on installing the program.*

If you are not sure whether WordPerfect for Windows is already installed on your computer, continue reading this chapter anyway. Doing so will help you to determine whether or not WordPerfect for Windows needs to be installed. (There's no harm in trying!)

GETTING STARTED

YOU MAY BE ABLE TO START WINDOWS 3 AND WORDPERFECT FOR WINDOWS

simply by typing *win wpwin* and pressing ↵ at the DOS command prompt. If so, you can skip to the section titled "The

. . . .

WordPerfect Document Window" later in this chapter.

If you don't know how to start your computer, refer to your computer manual or ask someone who knows.

In this section, you'll get Windows and WordPerfect up and running on your computer. I'll assume that you are already familiar with basic Windows operations and terminology. If you are not, or if you discover that you are having problems understanding or following the directions, you may need to backtrack a bit and invest some time in learning the Windows basics presented in Appendix B.

STARTING WINDOWS

> **TO START WINDOWS,**
>
> **you may be able to simply type *win* and press ↵ at the DOS command prompt.**

Depending on your computer's configuration, Windows may appear on the screen as soon as you start your computer. If it does, skip to the section titled "Starting WordPerfect for Windows" now.

If, on the other hand, you see a different DOS shell or the DOS command prompt (typically C>), follow these steps to start Windows:

1. If the DOS 4 or DOS 5 Shell appears, and you can run Windows from that shell, do so, and skip the steps below. If you cannot run Windows directly from that shell, exit that shell (typically by pressing F3) and continue with the steps below.

*Be sure to type **CD \WIN-DOWS**, not CD /WINDOWS, in step 3.*

2. If Windows 3 is not on the current drive, switch to the appropriate drive. For example, if Windows 3 is on drive C, type **c:** and press ↵.

3. Switch to the directory that Windows 3 is stored on. For example, if Windows 3 is stored in C:\WINDOWS, type

   cd \windows

   and press ↵ to get to that directory.

4. Type **win** and press ↵ to run Windows 3.

To double-click an icon, move your mouse until the pointer is on the icon you want, then rapidly click the left mouse button twice.

This should take you to Windows with the Program Manager window on the screen, as shown in Figure 1.1. If the Program Manager window is closed, double-click the Program Manager icon, most likely near the bottom-left corner of the screen.

Your screen may not look exactly like Figure 1.1. But all that matters is that the name *Program Manager* be displayed on the title bar of the current window on your screen.

STARTING WORDPERFECT FOR WINDOWS

WordPerfect

To start WordPerfect for Windows from the Windows Program Manager, follow these steps:

1. Double-click the group (document) icon for the program group that contains WordPerfect for Windows. Or, hold down the Ctrl key and press F6 until the group icon's name is highlighted, then release the Ctrl key and press ↵. Typically this icon is labeled simply *Word-Perfect,* as shown at left (also shown with its name highlighted in Figure 1.1).

WordPerfect

2. When the WordPerfect group window opens, you'll see the icons for several WordPerfect for Windows programs, as in the example shown in Figure 1.2.

3. Double-click the WordPerfect icon, or use the arrow keys to move the highlight to the WordPerfect icon, then press ↵.

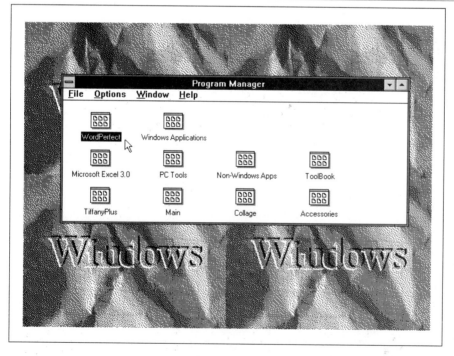

FIGURE 1.1:
The Windows 3 Program Manager window on the screen

This procedure takes you to the WordPerfect for Windows application. (Appendix A provides some start-up shortcuts and options for more experienced users.)

THE WORDPERFECT DOCUMENT WINDOW

When you first start WordPerfect for Windows, your screen will look like Figure 1.3. The large blank area is where you will do your typing and editing (it's like a blank sheet of paper). This area is a *document window,* also called the *Edit screen.* Other parts of the screen are described below.

THE TITLE BAR

The *title bar* at the top of the screen contains the title *WordPerfect* followed by *[Document1 - unmodified],* as well as the Control-menu box at the left and the Minimize and Restore buttons at the right (common to many Windows applications). These control the WordPerfect application window, as described in Chapter 3 and Appendix B.

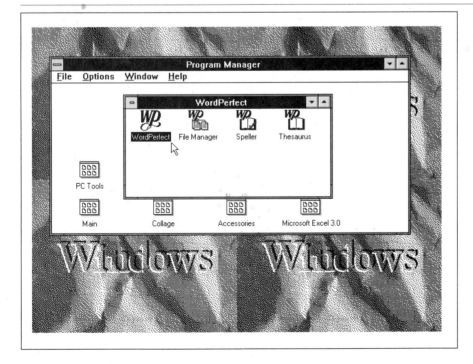

FIGURE 1.2:

The WordPerfect group window opened in the Program Manager

THE INSERTION POINT

The insertion point is the equivalent of the cursor in earlier versions of WordPerfect.

The *insertion point* is a small, blinking vertical bar that appears near the upper-left corner of your screen. It shows where the next character that you type will appear. As you'll see later, you can also move the insertion point through existing text without typing to position it before or after the letters or words that you want to change, delete, move, or insert.

THE I BEAM AND MOUSE POINTER

The *I beam* looks like a large, narrow uppercase I on the document screen. When you move your mouse, the I beam moves in the same direction. When you move the I beam into the title bar and menu areas near the top of the screen, it changes to an arrow (called the *mouse pointer*).

THE STATUS BAR

Fonts are explained in Chapter 5.

At the bottom of your screen is the *status bar,* which provides information about the current font (Courier 10cpi in Figure 1.3) and the position of the

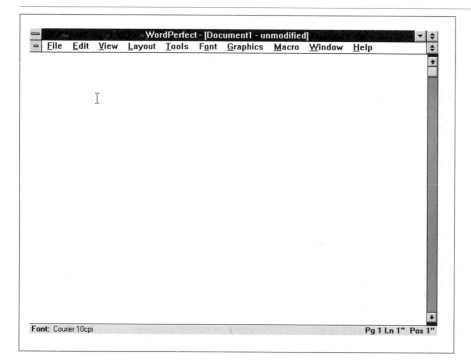

FIGURE 1.3:

The WordPerfect for Windows document window, ready for you to type in

insertion point on the screen in relation to its position on a printed sheet of paper, as summarized below:

Pg: shows which page you are currently typing or editing. In Figure 1.3 the Pg indicator shows *1,* because the insertion point is at the top-left of the first (currently blank) page.

Ln: shows which line you are currently typing or editing, as measured in inches from the top of the printed page. In Figure 1.3, the Ln indicator shows *1",* because the insertion point is automatically placed 1 inch below the top of the printed page. (Above the insertion point, there is an invisible 1-inch margin, which appears only on the printed copy of the document.)

Pos: shows the insertion point position, as measured in inches from the left side of the printed page. In Figure 1.3, the Pos indicator shows *1",* because the insertion point is in the leftmost screen position.

As you'll see later, the standard 1-inch margins can be changed at any time. WordPerfect for Windows uses 1-inch margins as *defaults* (predefined settings) for your convenience, since these are standard margin settings for many types of documents, such as letters and memos.

If you share a computer with others, someone may have changed the units of measurement from inches (") to centimeters (c) or some other scale. Don't worry about that.

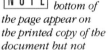

The margins at the top and bottom of the page appear on the printed copy of the document but not on-screen.

THE MENU BAR

The *menu bar* is directly beneath the title bar and displays the options File, Edit, View, and so forth. (Menu options are also called *commands.*) Choosing an option from the menu bar pulls down a menu. For example, Figure 1.4 shows the File pull-down menu after File has been chosen from the menu bar.

You use the usual techniques common to all Windows programs to choose menu options: just click any option with your mouse, or hold down the Alt key and press the underlined letter of the option you want. (See Appendix B if you are not already familiar with using menus.)

Pressing and releasing the Alt key without pressing another key will move the highlight into the menu area and temporarily disable the functions keys. Press Escape, or Alt again, to get back to normal.

To leave a pull-down menu without making a choice from it, move your mouse until the pointer is on some blank area of the screen outside the menu, then click the left mouse button again (or just press the Escape key twice).

Notice that there is also a Control-menu box and Restore button at the left and right of the menu bar, as well as a scroll bar running down the right edge of the screen. These features, common to all Windows applications, control the

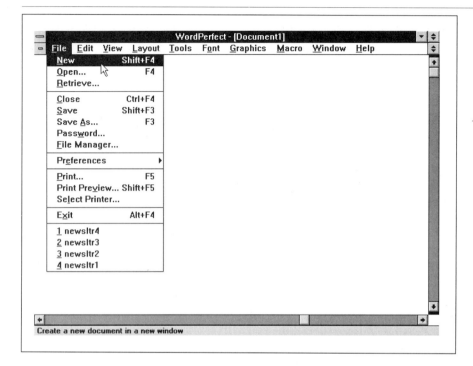

The File pull-down menu is displayed after clicking the File option on the menu bar or pressing Alt+F.

document window, or Edit screen, where you'll do your typing. You'll learn more about how to use them in Chapter 3.

USING YOUR KEYBOARD

If this is the first time you've used a computer, you'll undoubtedly notice that its keyboard is different from that of a standard typewriter. The computer keyboard is divided into four main areas:

◆ The function keys

◆ The typing keys

◆ The numeric keypad

◆ The arrow and other special keys

NOTE NOTE

For brevity, I'll refer to Word-Perfect for Windows as Word-Perfect from here on.

Figure 1.5 shows these areas on three popular computer keyboards.

The figure also points out the locations of the Tab, Backspace, Shift, and Enter (↵) keys. Before actually putting WordPerfect to work, let's take a look at a few special keys on your keyboard and how they work in WordPerfect.

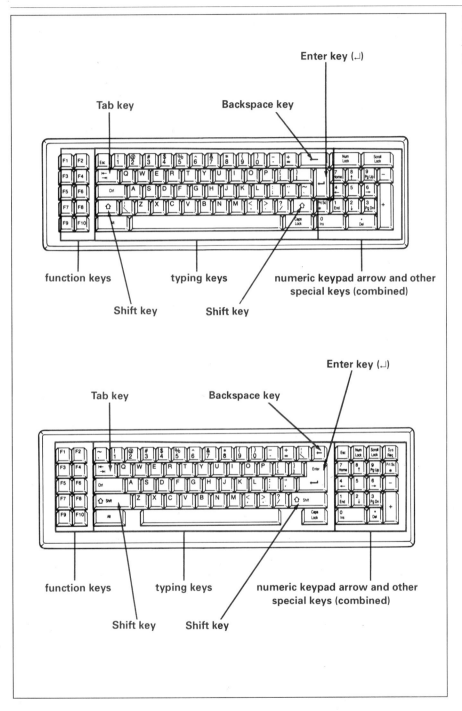

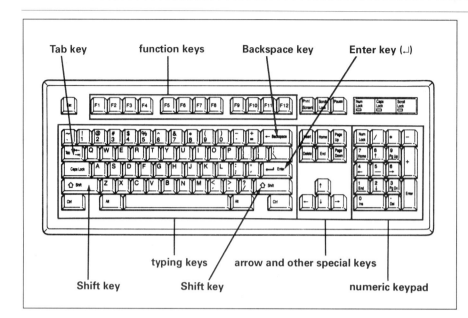

Be aware that different keyboards use different symbols for some keys. For example, the ↵ key is sometimes labeled *Enter* or *Return*. Refer to Figure 1.5 if you have trouble locating ↵, Tab, Shift, or Backspace.

THE NUM LOCK KEY

 *The arrow and other special keys don't do anything until you have typed some text on your screen.*

The Num Lock key has no equivalent on a typewriter. It determines whether numbers or other special keys are used when you press keys on the numeric keypad. When Num Lock is on, the number keys work. When Num Lock is off, the arrow and other cursor-movement keys work.

As you'll learn in Chapter 2, the arrow and other special keys are important because they allow you to edit existing text. The numbers on the numeric keypad are not so important, because you can use the numbers at the top of the typing area (as on a typewriter) to type numbers.

THE CAPS LOCK KEY

The Caps Lock key works in a way similar to most typewriters. If Caps Lock is on, letters are typed in uppercase (the Pos indicator on the status bar appears in all uppercase letters). If Caps Lock is off, letters are typed in lowercase (Pos appears with a capital *P* only). The Caps Lock key has no effect on numbers or punctuation marks.

THE SHIFT KEY

The Shift key serves the same purpose in WordPerfect as on a standard typewriter. It's used to type uppercase letters or other special characters. For example, to type a single capital letter *A,* you hold down the Shift key, type the letter *A,* and then release the Shift key. To type an asterisk (*), you hold down the Shift key and press the * key (the number 8). Unlike many typewriters, the function of the Shift key is reversed when Caps Lock is on: Letters are typed in lowercase.

THE TAB KEY

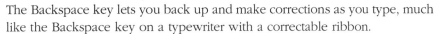

The Tab key works the same on the computer keyboard as it does on a typewriter: It indents to the next tab stop. Press Tab whenever you want to indent the first line of a new paragraph.

The Tab key is also very useful in controlling other types of indentation and alignments, as you'll learn in Chapter 4. You'll also learn to control how far the Tab key indents text, so you can gain more precise control over the appearance of your documents.

On some keyboards the Tab key is marked with two opposing arrows; it is usually to the left of the letter Q.

THE BACKSPACE KEY

The Backspace key lets you back up and make corrections as you type, much like the Backspace key on a typewriter with a correctable ribbon.

Don't confuse the Backspace key, which is in the typing-key area, with the ← key, which is one of the arrow keys. The Backspace key erases text to the left of the insertion point as the insertion point backs up. The ← key simply moves the insertion point back through existing text without erasing anything.

THE ENTER KEY

The Enter (↵) key is the computer's equivalent of the typewriter's carriage-return key (it is sometimes labeled *Return*). You press it when you've finished typing a line of text, or to choose a currently highlighted item.

When typing a document in WordPerfect, you use the ↵ key to end short lines of text, to insert blank lines, and to end paragraphs. Unlike with a typewriter, however, you do not need to press ↵ to end each line of text within a paragraph. I'll discuss this in more detail in "Typing with WordPerfect."

THE ESCAPE (OR CANCEL) KEY

The Escape key (labeled *Esc* or *Cancel* on some keyboards) is aptly named, because it lets you escape from unfamiliar territory back into more familiar territory. For example, if you inadvertently make a number of incorrect menu choices and end up at a menu or dialog box that you don't understand, you can usually press the Escape key (perhaps a few times) to work your way back to the more familiar document window, without making any choices from the menus or dialog boxes that appear.

COMBINATION KEYSTROKES

Upper- and lower-case letters don't matter in combination keystrokes. For example, to press Alt+F, hold down the Alt key and type either an uppercase or a lowercase F.

A plus sign (+) between two keys indicates a combination keystroke. For example, the instruction to press Shift+S means "hold down the Shift key, type the letter S, then release both keys." Ctrl+F5 means "hold down the Ctrl (Control) key, press the function key labeled *F5,* then release both keys." Alt+F7 means "hold down the Alt (Alternate) key, press F7, then release both keys."

Experimenting with these combination keystrokes may bring up menus you are not familiar with yet. Just press Escape to cancel the choice. As you may already know from previous Windows or WordPerfect experience, combination keystrokes can be used as shortcuts to using the menus.

TYPEMATIC KEYSTROKES

Unlike some typewriters, the computer's keys are *typematic.* This means that you can repeat a keystroke simply by holding down the key. You can see this for yourself by holding down any letter key on the keyboard for a few seconds. To erase the letters you typed, hold down the Backspace key for a few seconds.

TYPING WITH WORDPERFECT

TO TYPE A DOCUMENT WITH WORDPERFECT,

type as you normally would, except remember that when typing paragraphs, press ↵ only at the end of each paragraph, not at the end of each line.

Typing with WordPerfect is almost identical to typing with a regular typewriter, except for these three differences:

HANDS-ON

LESSON 1

If you want to get some quick, hands-on experience in typing and printing a WordPerfect document, see Lesson 1 in Part 9.

◆ Unlike typing with typewriters, you should not type the letter *l* in place of the number *1* and the letter *O* in place of the number *0*; they are not the same to a computer, and they do not look the same when printed by most printers.

◆ Because WordPerfect already assumes that 1-inch margins will be needed on the printed document, you need not do anything to add margins to your text.

◆ As you type past the right margin on your screen, WordPerfect automatically *word-wraps* text to the next line. The term *word wrap* means that when a line is filled with text, any following text is moved to the next line. You should only press the ↵ (Enter) key to end a short line that does not reach the right margin, to end a paragraph, or to add a blank line.

To add a blank line between two paragraphs, press ↵ twice at the end of the first paragraph.

This last difference between typewriters and WordPerfect is perhaps the hardest one for experienced typists to get used to. But it's important to let Word-Perfect handle the right margin automatically by not pressing ↵ until you've finished typing a paragraph. This gives you maximum flexibility to add, change, or delete words or sentences in the middle of the paragraph.

As an illustration, Figure 1.6 shows a sample printed business letter typed with WordPerfect. Figure 1.7 shows the same letter, but with ↵ keystroke symbols that show where you would press ↵ while typing that document.

HOW LARGE CAN YOUR DOCUMENTS BE?

Don't let the size of the WordPerfect document window fool you into thinking that you can create only small documents—this entire book was created with WordPerfect. As you'll see in the hands-on lessons in Part 9, WordPerfect automatically *scrolls* text to give you more room when you need it.

You can easily review and change text that has scrolled out of view by using the scroll bars or the various scrolling keys, such as ↑, ↓, Page Up (PgUp), Page Down (PgDn), and others.

One word of advice, though: the larger a document is, the longer it takes to perform basic operations like printing, saving, checking spelling, and so forth. Therefore, if you plan to create a *really* large document—like a book— it's best to treat each chapter as a separate document.

PRINTING A DOCUMENT

▌ **TO PRINT YOUR WORDPERFECT DOCUMENT,**
choose Print from the File pull-down menu, then click the Print button or press P.

You can print the document that you are working on at any time. Follow these steps:

1. Click the File option on the menu bar to access its pull-down menu (or press Alt+F).

January 7, 1992

Sidney R. Jackson, M.D.
Bayside Medical Group
5231 East Statton Drive, Suite 106
Los Angeles, CA 92312

Dear Dr. Jackson:

The update on your insurance policy is as follows. I am including a letter from the Regional Manager of Farmstead regarding the information specific to your occupational and medical concerns. Pending receipt of a referral letter from your previous doctor, this letter serves as an important part of your policy and should be safeguarded with your other documents.

I have turned over your policy to a full-time insurance agent, Bastien Cole. He will be able to serve you more adequately and provide the detailed information you may need for your specific problems. This will also allow me to relinquish my commissions in order to better serve you in a consultant capacity. In the meantime, however, you do have coverage in effect.

As indicated earlier by phone, I will be out of town for the next three weeks. Should you have any questions, please feel free to leave a message for me at my Florida office. I will be in contact with them daily for messages. Rest assured that I hope to continue to be of service to you.

Sincerely,

Edna R. Jones, M.D.

ERJ:ess

cc: Bastien Cole

FIGURE 1.6:
A sample business letter

2. Click the Print option to choose it (or press P). The Print *dialog box* shown in Figure 1.8 appears (with whatever text you may have typed visible in the background).

3. If the name of the printer that you want to print with appears under Current Printer near the top of the dialog box, skip to step 6.

To leave any dialog box without making a choice, click its Cancel button or press the Escape key. See Appendix B for more information on dialog boxes.

4. To choose a printer other than the one shown, choose the Select… button (move the mouse pointer to that button and click the left mouse button, or press S).

5. Click the name of the printer you want to use for printing, or press ↑ and ↓ until the name of the printer is highlighted. Then click the Select button or press ↵. (Choosing printer is discussed in more detail in Chapter 8.)

```
January 7, 1992↵
↵
↵
Sidney R. Jackson, M.D.↵
Bayside Medical Group↵
5231 East Statton Drive, Suite 106↵
Los Angeles, CA  92312↵
↵
↵
Dear Dr. Jackson:↵
↵
The update on your insurance policy is as follows.  I am
including a letter from the Regional Manager of Farmstead
regarding the information specific to your occupational and
medical concerns.  Pending receipt of a referral letter from your
previous doctor, this letter serves as an important part of your
policy and should be safeguarded with your other documents.↵
↵
I have turned over your policy to a full-time insurance agent,
Bastien Cole.  He will be able to serve you more adequately and
provide the detailed information you may need for your specific
problems.  This will also allow me to relinquish my commissions
in order to better serve you in a consultant capacity.  In the
meantime, however, you do have coverage in effect.↵
↵
As indicated earlier by phone, I will be out of town for the next
three weeks.  Should you have any questions, please feel free to
leave a message for me at my Florida office.  I will be in
contact with them daily for messages.  Rest assured that I hope
to continue to be of service to you.↵
↵
Sincerely,↵
↵
↵
↵
Edna R. Jones, M.D.↵
↵
ERJ:ess↵
↵
cc:  Bastien Cole
```

FIGURE 1.7:
The ↵ symbols show where you would press ↵ while typing the letter: at the ends of short lines, at the ends of paragraphs, and wherever you want a blank line.

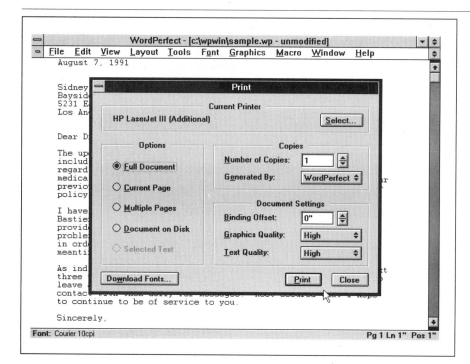

6. Under Options, click the Full Document option, or press Alt+F.

7. Click the Print button, or press P.

You'll see a brief message indicating the progress of the print job. If your printer is properly connected, turned on, online, and ready to accept output from the computer, your document should start printing soon.

When printing is complete, you'll be returned to the document window. But don't turn off your computer! You'll probably want to save your document for future use, and you should always *exit* WordPerfect before turning off your computer (this will be discussed in a moment).

PRINTER PROBLEMS

If WordPerfect prints gobbledygook, the printer may not be properly connected or installed. If you see a *message box* like the one below, click the OK button or press ↵ to remove the box. Then refer to Chapter 8 for additional information on printing.

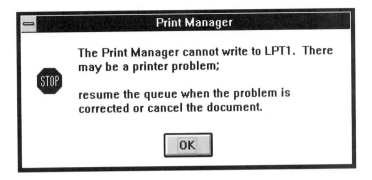

SAVING YOUR WORK

▌ **TO SAVE YOUR WORK,**

    **choose Save from the File pull-down menu (or press Shift+F3).
Type in a valid file name in the Save As text box (or use the suggested file name), and click Save (or press ↵).**

Chapter 12 discusses general file management techniques, including erasing files.

It's important to understand that the document in your WordPerfect document window is stored in the computer's *memory* (also called *RAM,* for *random access memory*). When you turn off your computer or exit WordPerfect, everything in memory is immediately and permanently erased.

Therefore, it's important to *save* a copy of your document in a file on your disk, in case you want to make changes to it later. Information stored on-disk is permanent—it is not erased when you turn off your computer. In fact, it is erased only when you take specific actions to erase it.

Before saving a document, you must first think up a *file name* for it, as discussed in the next section.

If you are not already familiar with the term "directory," don't worry about it. You'll learn more about directories in Chapter 12.

NAMING DOCUMENTS

Anything that you save on a hard or floppy disk, including a WordPerfect document, is considered to be a *file.* Individual files are often stored in groups, called *directories.* Every file in a given directory on the disk must have a unique name—that is, no two files in the same directory can have the same name.

The name you assign to a file must conform to the following rules and conventions:

◆ The name can be up to eight characters long and can contain letters, numbers, or both.

◆ The name can be followed by a period and an *extension* up to three characters long. The period that separates the file name from the extension is the only period allowed.

◆ Neither the name nor the extension can contain blank spaces.

◆ The name can contain underscores or hyphens, but none of the following characters: * ? + = [ ] : ; " / \ | > < .

◆ The name can be typed with upper- and lowercase letters (WordPerfect automatically converts all letters to lowercase.) Hence, the file names SMITH.LET, Smith.Let, Smith.let, and smith.let are all the same.

Examples of valid and invalid file names are shown in Table 1.1.

When deciding on a file name, try to use a descriptive name that will make it easy to find the file in the future. For example, the file name XXX tells you nothing about the contents of that file. But the file name SMITH (albeit brief) at least gives you a clue that the file contains something about somebody named Smith, perhaps a letter to that person.

NAME	VALID/INVALID
letter	Valid
letter.1	Valid
smith.let	Valid
1990tax.qt1	Valid
qtr_1.wp	Valid
qtr-1.wp	Valid
MyLetter.wp	Valid (but converted to myletter.wp)
qtr 1.Wp	Invalid (contains a blank space)
qtr1.w p	Invalid (extension contains a blank space)
12.1.90.wp	Invalid (too many periods)
MyFirstLetter.Txt	Invalid (too long)
done?.*	Invalid (contains punctuation marks)

TABLE 1.1:

Examples of Valid and Invalid File Names

Furthermore, although the extension to a file name is optional, it can be handy for remembering the type of information stored in the file. For example, you might want to use the extension .WP when saving WordPerfect documents, so that in the future you can tell which files on your disk are Word-Perfect documents simply by looking at the extensions.

SAVING THE CURRENT DOCUMENT

It's a good idea to save your work from time to time, even if you don't plan on exiting WordPerfect at the moment. That way, if a power outage or some other mishap suddenly shuts down your computer, only the work you've done since the last time you saved your document will be lost. To save a document without exiting WordPerfect, follow these steps:

As a shortcut for the first two steps, press Shift+F3.

1. Click the File option on the menu bar (or press Alt+F) to pull down the File menu.

2. Click Save or press S to choose Save. If you've never saved the current document before, you'll see the Save As dialog box, shown in Figure 1.9.

3. Type in a valid DOS file name, as described under "Naming Documents" earlier in this section.

4. Click the Save button, or press ↵. If you've previously saved this, or another, document with the name specified, you'll see a message box like the one below.

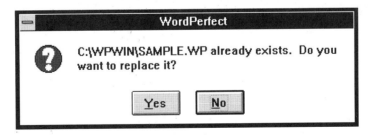

5. You have three choices at this point:

    ◆ If you want to replace the existing file with the document that's currently on your screen, answer Yes by clicking the Yes button or pressing Y. You would want to do this only in a situation where you don't care about saving the "old" existing file, such as when the document currently being saved is an improvement on the previous draft that already exists.

◆ If you don't want to replace the existing file with the one currently on your screen (or you're not sure), choose No by clicking the No button or pressing N. You'll be prompted to enter a different file name for this document. Repeat step 3, but enter a different name. This new document (or copy of the same document) will have the new name you provide; the original document (or previous draft) will retain its original name.

To save a copy of the current document with a new file name, choose the Save As option, rather than Save, from the File menu (or press F3). See Chapter 12 for more information on managing files.

After making your choice, you'll be returned to the Edit screen, where you can continue to work with your document. The name of the document now appears on the title bar, near the top of the screen.

In the future, if you want to save new additions or changes to the current document, use the same steps (choose Save from the File menu, or press Shift+F3). However, since you've already named the document, WordPerfect won't bother with displaying the dialog box or asking for the file name. Instead, it will simply save the document with the its current file name. All you'll see on the screen is a brief message on the status bar (near the lower-left corner of the screen) indicating that the document is being saved.

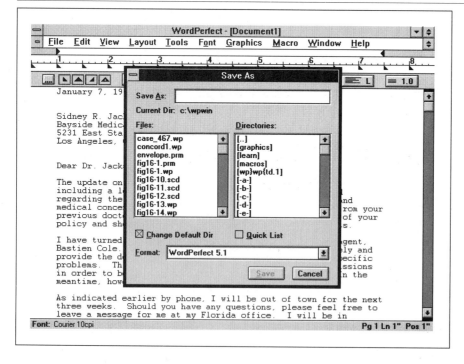

FIGURE 1.9:

The Save As dialog box

EXITING WORDPERFECT

When you've finished working with WordPerfect, you should always exit the program before turning off your computer, just to make sure all your work is saved. Follow these steps:

1. Click the File option on the menu bar to pull down its menu (or press Alt+F).

As a shortcut for steps 1 and 2, press Alt+F4.

2. Click Exit (or press X).

3. If you've made any changes to the current document since you last saved it, you'll see the message box below, asking whether you want to save those recent changes:

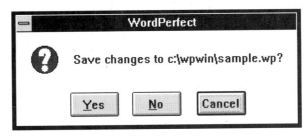

4. You can choose to save the current changes (by clicking the Yes button or pressing Y), or not to save them (by clicking the No button or pressing N). You'll be returned to the Windows Program Manager screen. Optionally, if you change your mind and don't want to exit WordPerfect after all, you can click the Cancel button (or press ↲).

If you want to close the WordPerfect group window, just click its Minimize button (the second button from the right on the WordPerfect title bar). If you plan to turn off your computer, it is also a good idea to exit Windows first, by choosing Exit from the Program Manager File pull-down menu or by pressing Alt+F4.

When you want to use WordPerfect for Windows again in the future, just follow the instructions presented at the beginning of this chapter for starting Windows and WordPerfect for Windows.

In this chapter you've learned how to start WordPerfect, type a document, print it, save it, and exit WordPerfect before turning off your computer. These are important basic skills that you'll use regularly in your work with WordPerfect, so you're off to a great start.

If you'd like some additional guidance on the topics covered in this chapter, you can get some hands-on experience in creating, printing, and saving a document in Lesson 1 in Part 9. Or, you can move on to Chapter 2 now, where I'll discuss editing a document.

CHAPTER 2

Editing Your Documents

LESSON 2

*Lesson 2 in
Part 9 provides
hands-on exer-
cises in editing
the document
you created in
Lesson 1.*

! n this chapter you'll learn how to edit a WordPerfect document by adding, changing, moving, and deleting text.
As you'll see, you can make any changes imaginable.
And you can edit a document at any time: while you are
creating it or long after you've printed and saved it.

If you have already saved your document and exited WordPerfect, you'll
need to do two things to get started:

◆ Start WordPerfect and get to the editing screen (if you've exited).

◆ *Open* the document you want to edit, as described in the next section.

Refer to Chapter 1 if you need a reminder on how to start WordPerfect.

OPENING A SAVED DOCUMENT

┃ TO OPEN A DOCUMENT,

click the name of the file that you want to open at the bottom
of the File menu (if it appears). Or choose Open from the File
pull-down menu (or press F4), then double-click its name

under Files in the dialog box, or type the name of the file you want to open and press ↵.

Every document you save is stored as a file on the disk. The File pull-down menu provides all the options you need for saving and opening files.

If you already saved a document, and no longer have it on your screen, you'll need to open that document before making any changes to it. If the document that you want to edit is currently on your screen, skip all steps below (the document is already open).

1. Click the **F**ile option on the menu or press Alt+F to pull down the File menu. The names of the last four documents you edited are listed at the bottom of the File menu. The names of all currently open documents appear at the bottom of the Window pull-down menu.

Unless your mouse is installed for left-hand use, use the left button to click, double-click, and drag.

2. If the name of the file you want to open appears at the bottom of the File menu, click the name once, and skip the remaining steps.

3. Click the **O**pen button, or press O to choose Open. You'll see the dialog box shown in Figure 2.1. (As a shortcut, you can also get to this dialog box by pressing F4.)

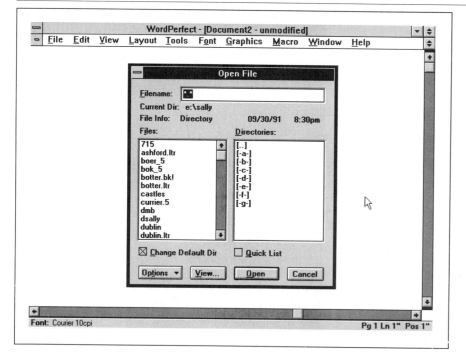

FIGURE 2.1:

The Open File dialog box on the screen

*The **Options** button in the Open File dialog box is discussed in Chapter 12.*

4. You now have several choices:

- ◆ Type the full name of the file you want to open, then press ⏎ (or click the **O**pen button).

- ◆ If the name of the file you want to open appears in the Files list box, double-click the name of the file you want to open. (If necessary, you can use the scroll bar on the right side of the Files box to locate the name of the file you want to open.)

- ◆ Press Tab until the highlight bar moves into the Files list box, then use the ↑, ↓, Page Up, and Page Down keys to highlight the name of the file you want to open and press ⏎.

The Open option on the File menu opens a document in its own document window. The Retrieve option is used to combine a document on the disk with the one in the current document window, as discussed in Chapter 3.

You can also change the drive and directory by clicking an option in the Directories list box to the right of the Files box. This is discussed in Chapter 12.

The file you choose appears in a document window, ready for editing. Its name appears on the title bar, near the top of the screen, as in the example shown in Figure 2.2.

WordPerfect lets you edit up to nine documents at once, each in its own document window. For now, however, I'll just talk about editing one document at a time.

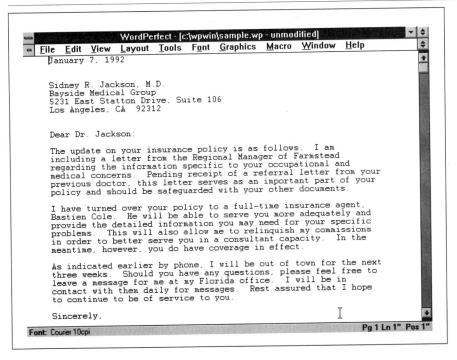

FIGURE 2.2:

A document named sample.wp opened and ready for editing

POSITIONING THE INSERTION POINT

TO MOVE THE INSERTION POINT TO ANY CHARACTER IN A DOCUMENT,

move the I beam to where you want to make changes, then click the left mouse button, or use the arrow and other special keys.

NOTE *Any editing you do, or text you type, happens at the insertion point, not at the I beam. So don't forget to click the mouse button after positioning the I beam to bring the insertion point to that position.*

You can position the insertion point anywhere in your document by placing the I beam wherever you want to make changes, then clicking the left mouse button.

As an alternative to the mouse, you can use the arrow and other special keys to position the insertion point, as listed in Table 2.1. Keep in mind the following points when trying to move the insertion point:

◆ You can move the insertion point through existing text only; that is, you cannot move down past the last character of the last line in a document (though you can press ↵ to *add* a line). Similarly, you cannot move past the end of a short line (though you can insert more spaces at the end of a line by pressing the spacebar).

◆ The arrow and other special keys on the numeric keypad work only if the Num Lock key is off. Also, these keys are typematic, so you can just hold them down to repeat them.

◆ Remember, a plus sign (+) indicates a combination keystroke. For example, Ctrl+→ means "hold down the Ctrl key and press →."

◆ A space between two keystrokes indicates separate keystrokes; for example, Home ← means "press and release the Home key, then press and release the ← key."

◆ WordPerfect for Windows offers two keyboard styles: Windows Common User Access (CUA) and WordPerfect for DOS. Throughout this book, I focus on the default CUA keyboard. (If the keys listed in Table 2.1 and other shortcut keys don't work as described, it may be that some keyboard other than the default Windows CUA keyboard is selected.)

If you press ← or → and the insertion point does not move immediately, it may not be a malfunction. Instead, WordPerfect may just be moving the insertion point through hidden codes that you cannot see at the moment. I'll discuss

TO MOVE	PRESS
To beginning of line (before codes)	Home Home or Home ←
To beginning of line (after codes)	Home
To bottom of document	Ctrl+End
To bottom of screen (then down one screen at a time)	Page Down
Down one line	↓
Down one paragraph	Ctrl+↓
To end of line (after codes)	End
Left one character	←
Left one word	Ctrl+←
Right one character	→
Right one word	Ctrl+→
To top of document (after codes)	Ctrl+Home
To top of document (before codes)	Ctrl+Home Ctrl+Home
To top of next page	Alt+Page Down
To top of preceding page	Alt+Page Up
To top of screen (then up one screen at a time)	Page Up
Up one line	↑
Up one paragraph	Ctrl+↑

TABLE 2.1:

Keys for Positioning the Insertion Point

those codes in the next chapter. Just keep pressing the arrow key until the insertion moves.

You can easily try most of the keys listed in Table 2.1 on your own, as long as there is text on your screen to move the insertion point through. A couple of general techniques are described in more detail below.

MOVING THROUGH PAGES

> **TO SCROLL THROUGH A DOCUMENT THAT IS LARGER THAN THE SCREEN,**
>
> use the scroll bar at the right of the document window, or the Page Up, Page Down, and other movement keys.

As you gain experience with WordPerfect, you'll undoubtedly create documents that are several pages long. As you continue to type past the bottom edge of the screen, the existing text will scroll off the top edge of the screen to make room for the new text.

When you get to the end of a page, a narrow gray line appears across your screen, indicating the start of a new page. The status bar indicates which page the insertion point is currently on. For example, in Figure 2.3, notice that the insertion point is below the page-break line and that the status line indicates that the insertion point is on page 2 (Pg 2).

The scroll bar at the right edge of the document window works like all Windows scroll bars, as summarized in Figure 2.4. To use the scroll bar to

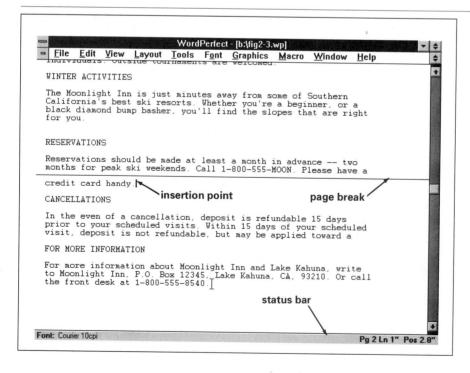

FIGURE 2.3:

The insertion point is on the second page of the document.

Clicking the scroll bar above or below the scroll box scrolls through the document about a screenful at a time.

After scrolling, don't forget to position the insertion point by clicking anywhere on the page before typing or editing.

scroll through a large document with many pages, you can drag the scroll box to any location on the bar, or you can move the mouse pointer to any position on the bar and click the left mouse button until the box reaches that position. For example, to move to the middle of a lengthy document, drag the scroll box to the middle of the scroll bar, or click repeatedly near the middle of the bar until the box reaches that destination.

When you scroll with the scroll bars, be aware that the insertion point does not move. To bring the insertion point to the current page, click anywhere on that page. At this point, the Pg indicator on the status bar will also reflect the current page number.

Of course, you can also use the Page Up, Page Down, and other keys listed in Table 2.1 to scroll through a lengthy document. When you use these keys to scroll, the insertion point *does* follow the scrolling, and the Pg indicator is updated each time you scroll to a new page.

MOVING TO A SPECIFIC PAGE

You can use the Go To feature to move the insertion point to a specific page. Follow the steps on the next page.

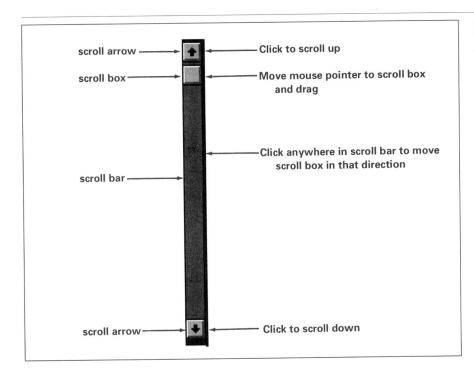

FIGURE 2.4:

A sample scroll bar and mouse techniques for using it

1. Click on **E**dit to pull down the Edit menu, then click on **G**o To (or just press the shortcut key, Ctrl+G). You'll see this dialog box:

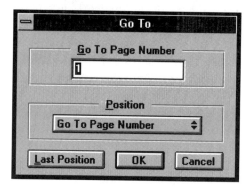

2. Do any of the following:

If you enter a page number that's larger than the highest-numbered page in the document, the insertion point moves to the last page in the document.

- ◆ Type the number of the page that you want to move the insertion point to, then click OK or press ↵.

- ◆ Move the mouse pointer to the Go To Page Number button, hold down the left mouse button, and drag the highlight to either the option **T**op of Current Page or **B**ottom of Current Page.

- ◆ Click on Last Position or press Alt+L to move the insertion point back to wherever it was before the last time you moved it.

MOVING TO SPECIFIC TEXT

If you want to move the insertion point to a specific character or phrase, use the Search feature as follows:

1. Click the **E**dit option on the menu bar, then click on **S**earch in the menu that appears (or just press F2). This dialog box appears:

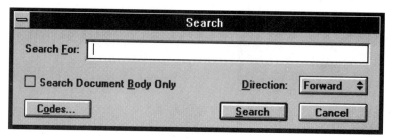

2. Type the character or phrase you want to move the insertion point to.

3. Note the direction next to the **D**irection prompt, which is either **For**ward or **B**ackward. If you want to change the direction of the search, move the mouse pointer to the button, hold down the left mouse button, move the pointer to the direction you want, and then release the mouse button.

4. Click the **S**earch button, or press ↵.

The insertion point moves to the last character or phrase you specified in step 2. If you want to search for the next occurrence of that character or phrase, choose Search Ne**x**t from the Edit pull-down menu (or press Shift+F2). If you want to search for the previous occurrence (above the current insertion point position), choose Search Pre**v**ious from the Edit menu (or press Alt+F2). (You'll learn more about the Search feature and the related Replace feature in Chapter 9.)

INSERTING AND REPLACING TEXT

TO SWITCH BETWEEN INSERT AND TYPEOVER MODES,

press the Insert (Ins) key.

INS

When editing a document, you can choose between two basic modes of adding text: *Insert mode* and *Typeover mode*.

◆ In Insert mode, new text is inserted between existing text.

◆ In Typeover mode, new text replaces (overwrites) existing text.

In the example below, three uppercase X's were inserted in the word *WordPerfect*, by placing the insertion point before the letter *P* and typing XXX in Insert mode:

WordXXXPerfect

In the next example, three letters were replaced by placing the insertion point before the letter *P*, switching to Typeover mode by pressing the Insert key, and then typing XXX:

WordXXXfect

Normally, WordPerfect is in Insert mode. To switch to Typeover mode, press the Insert key once. Notice that the word *Typeover* appears on the status bar, near the lower-left corner of the screen. To switch back to Insert mode, press the Insert key again, and the Typeover indicator disappears from the status bar. The Insert key acts as a *toggle;* that is, it switches between Insert mode and Typeover mode each time you press it.

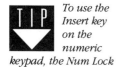

To use the Insert key on the numeric keypad, the Num Lock key must be off.

INSERTING TEXT, SPACES, AND LINES

To insert text (or spaces or lines) in a document, follow these basic steps:

1. Move the insertion point where you want to insert text, spaces, or lines.

2. Make sure you're in Insert mode (if "Typeover" appears in the lower-left corner of the screen, press the Insert key).

3. Type the text to be inserted as you normally would type (all other text will move to the right and down to make room).

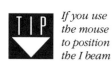

If you use the mouse to position the I beam where you want to insert text, don't forget to click the left mouse button before typing.

◆ To insert a blank space, press the spacebar.

◆ To insert text, just type your text.

◆ To insert a blank line or break a line into two pieces, press ↵.

If you make mistakes while inserting new text, you can make corrections as usual with the Backspace and Delete keys (described in more detail in a moment).

CHANGING TEXT AND LINES

If you want to change or replace existing text, follow these steps:

1. Move the insertion point where you want to replace existing text.

2. Make sure you're in Typeover mode (if "Typeover" does not appear in the lower-left corner of the screen, press the Insert key).

3. Type your new text—it will overwrite the existing text.

In many cases, you'll probably want to replace some text and insert other text. No problem—just press Insert when you want to switch from Insert mode to Typeover mode, or vice versa.

HOW INSERT AND TYPEOVER AFFECT BACKSPACING

There's a slight difference in the way the Backspace key operates in Insert mode and Typeover mode. In Insert mode, pressing Backspace deletes the character to the left of the insertion point and drags all characters to the right along with it (this fills in any holes that would otherwise be left by the deleted text). In Typeover mode, the Backspace key still deletes the character to the left, but does not drag the characters to the right with it. Instead, it leaves blank spaces in place of the characters it deleted.

SELECTING TEXT

TO SELECT TEXT,

move the I beam to the first character of text you want to select. Then hold down the left mouse button, and drag the I beam to the last character you want to select. Then release the mouse button.

You can select (or highlight, or block) any section of text that you want to work with in a document. That section of text can be as small as a single character, as large as the entire document, or any size in between. Once selected, the text is shown in reverse video or a different color, as in Figure 2.5.

Once you've selected text, you can perform many operations on it, including deleting, moving, copying, printing, and so forth.

SELECTING TEXT WITH THE MOUSE

To select text with your mouse, follow these steps:

1. Move the I beam to the first character of text that you want to select.

2. Hold down the left mouse button, and drag the I beam to the last character you want to select.

3. Release the mouse button when all the desired text is selected (highlighted).

4. If you decide to select more text after releasing the mouse button, move the I beam to where you want to extend the selection to, hold down the Shift key, and click the left mouse button.

If you want to select more text than is currently on the screen, just keep the mouse button depressed and roll the I beam right off the edge of the screen in the direction you want to keep going. As long as you keep the button depressed, text will scroll into the selection area. Release the mouse button when all the text is selected.

As an alternative to dragging the mouse pointer to select text, you can move the insertion point to the place where you want to start selecting text. Move the I beam to the end of the text you want to select. Then hold down the Shift key and click the left mouse button.

Finally, you can also select just a single word, sentence, or paragraph simply by rapidly clicking the left mouse button two, three, or four times, respectively.

SELECTING TEXT WITH THE KEYBOARD

If you prefer to use the keyboard instead of the mouse,

1. Move the insertion point to the first character of text that you want to select.

2. Hold down the Shift key, and press any keys listed in Table 2.1 to move the insertion point and extend the selection.

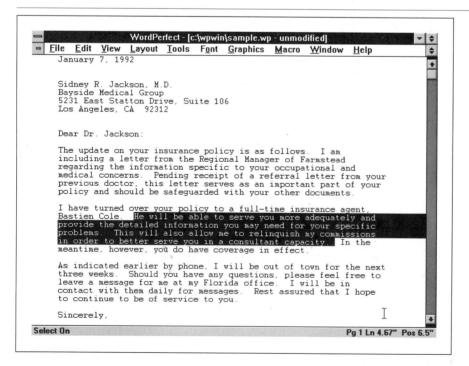

FIGURE 2.5:

An example of selected text

Optionally, if you don't want to hold down the Shift key while trying to press other combination keystrokes, you can do the following:

1. Move the insertion point to the first character of text that you want to select.

2. Press F8. The *Select Mode* indicator appears on the status bar, near the lower-left corner of the screen.

You can keep typing characters to which you want to extend the selection until all the text you want is highlighted.

3. Use the arrow and any other positioning keys listed in Table 2.1 to extend the selection over all the text you want to select. Optionally, type the character that you want to extend the selection to (for example, type a period to extend the selection to the end of the current sentence, or press ↵ to extend the selection to the end of the paragraph).

USING SEARCH TO SELECT TEXT

If you want to select a very large chunk of text, you can use the Search feature to extend the selection to any character or group of characters:

1. Move the insertion point to the beginning of the text you want to select.

2. Start the selection by holding down the left mouse button and moving the mouse, or by pressing F8. (If you're using the mouse, you can release the mouse button once you've gotten the selection started.)

The Search feature is discussed in detail in Chapter 9.

3. Press Search (F2), or select **S**earch from the Edit pull-down menu.

4. Type the character (or characters) you want to extend the selection to.

5. Click on **S**earch, or press ↵.

USING THE MENUS TO SELECT TEXT

You can also use the menus to select a single sentence or single paragraph of text. Follow these steps:

1. Move the insertion point anywhere into the sentence or paragraph you want to select.

2. Click the **E**dit option on the menu bar, or press Alt+E to pull down the Edit menu.

3. Click on **S**elect or press E.

4. Click on **S**entence (or press S) to select the current sentence. Or click on **P**aragraph (or press P) to select the current paragraph.

UNSELECTING TEXT

Many normal menu options are dimmed and unavailable when text is selected. You may need to unselect text to get the menus back to normal.

If you select some text, then realize you've made a mistake and want to start all over, you can easily "unselect" the currently selected text. You can use either your mouse or the keyboard:

◆ With the I beam positioned anywhere on the document window (*not* on the menu or title bar), click the left mouse button.

◆ Press the F8 key.

Now you can start over and select some other text if you wish.

SUMMARY OF OPERATIONS FOR SELECTED TEXT

Chapter 3 discusses abbreviated menu sequences, like Font ➤ Underline, in more detail.

Regardless of which technique you use to select text, as long as *any* text is selected on the screen, you can use a variety of WordPerfect features to manipulate that text. In the sections that follow, I'll discuss the more basic editing techniques, including moving, copying, deleting, and changing the case of selected text.

For future reference, Table 2.2 lists all the operations you can perform on selected text and includes a reference to where each of these operations is covered in more detail. Note that the ➤ symbol shows a sequence of menu choices. For example, F**o**nt ➤ **U**nderline means "pull down the Font menu and choose Underline."

MOVING AND COPYING TEXT (CUT AND PASTE)

TO MOVE OR COPY SELECTED TEXT,

select the text you want to move or copy. Then choose Cut or Copy from the Edit menu, or press Shift+Del (to move) or Ctrl+Ins (to copy). Finally, position the insertion point at the destination for the text, and choose Paste from the Edit pull-down menu (or press Shift+Ins).

One of the most common editing operations is moving text around to reorganize it. Copying is also fairly common. For example, when typing a list of names and addresses of people in the same neighborhood, you might want

ACTION	MENU CHOICES	SHORTCUT	SEE CHAPTER
Append to file	**Edit ➤ Append**		3
Boldface	**Font ➤ Bold**	Ctrl+B	5
Center	**Layout ➤ Line ➤ Center**	Shift+F7	4
Change appearance	**Font ➤** *choose appearance*	F9	5
Change case	**Edit ➤ Convert Case**		2
Change color	**Font ➤ Color**		5
Change font	**Font ➤ Font**	F9	5
Change size	**Font ➤ Size**	F9 or Ctrl+S	5
Comment	**Tools ➤ Comment ➤ Create**		3
Copy	**Edit ➤ Copy**	Ctrl+Ins	2
Delete		Delete	2
Flush right	**Layout ➤ Line ➤ Flush Right**	Alt+F7	4
Mark for reference	**Tools ➤ Mark Text**	F12	23
Move	**Edit ➤ Cut**	Shift+Del	2
Print	**File ➤ Print**	F5	8
Protect	**Layout ➤ Page ➤ Block Protect**		7
Replace	**Edit ➤ Replace**	Ctrl+F2	9
Reselect text	**Edit ➤ Go To**	Ctrl+G	2
Save	**File ➤ Save As**	F3	12
Sort	**Tools ➤ Sort**	Ctrl+Shift+F12	17
Spelling check	**Tools ➤ Speller**	Ctrl+F1	10
Style	**Layout ➤ Styles** ·	Alt+F8	14
Table	**Layout ➤ Tables**	Ctrl+F9	6
Underline	**Font ➤ Underline**	Ctrl+U	5

TABLE 2.2:

Operations That You Can Perform on Selected Text

HANDS-ON

LESSON 2

*Lesson 2 in
Part 9 provides
a hands-on ex-
ercise in
moving text.*

to copy just the street address, city, state, and zip code from one person to the next, without retyping. Or, you might want to copy certain passages, such as standardized paragraphs, from one document to another.

The basic steps for moving and copying are practically identical. The only difference, of course, is that *moving* text takes it from one place and puts it in another, as shown in figures 2.6 and 2.7. *Copying,* on the other hand, leaves the text in its original place, and places a copy of that text in a new location, as shown in figures 2.8 and 2.9.

To move or copy text, follow these steps:

1. Select the text you want to move or copy.

2. Click on **E**dit on the menu bar (or press Alt+E) to pull down the Edit menu.

3. If you want to move the selected text, click on Cu**t** or press T (the selected text disappears). If you want to copy the selected text, click on **C**opy (or press C).

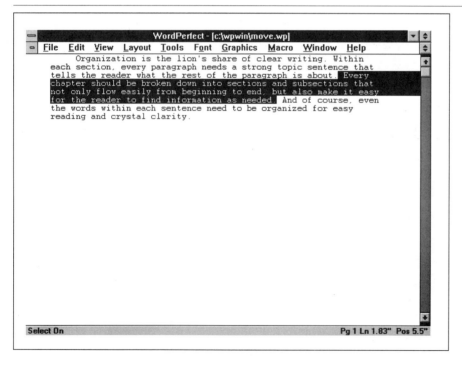

FIGURE 2.6:

*Selected text is
highlighted on the
screen.*

The selected text in Figure 2.6 has been moved up and is now the second sentence.

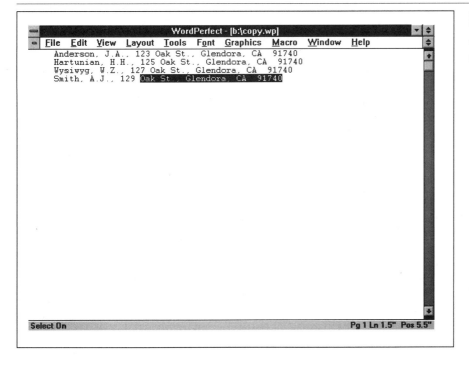

FIGURE 2.8:

Sample text selected on the screen

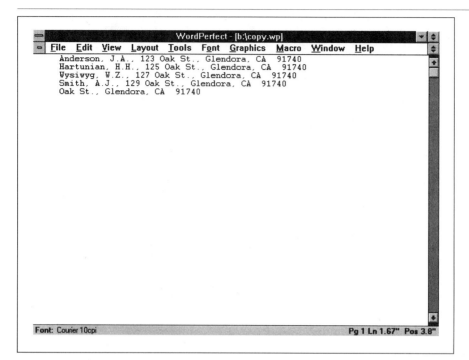

FIGURE 2.9:

The selected text in Figure 2.8 after being copied down to the next line

4. Move the insertion point wherever you want to move or copy the text to. (Don't forget to click the left mouse button if you use the mouse to first position the I beam.)

You can use the mouse, the scroll bar, any key listed in Table 2.1, Go To (Ctrl+G), or Search (F2) to help position the insertion point in step 4.

5. Click on **E**dit on the menu bar (or press Alt+E) to pull down the Edit menu, then click on **P**aste (or press P). (As an alternative to using the menu, you can just press Shift+Ins.)

As with most WordPerfect options, there are several shortcuts you can use to cut, copy, and paste selected text. You can use any of the shortcut keys listed below *after* selecting text in lieu of choosing options from the menu:

TO	PRESS	OR PRESS
Cut	Shift+Del	Ctrl+X
Copy	Ctrl+Ins	Ctrl+C
Paste	Shift+Ins	Ctrl+V

If you are trying to move the text to the end of the document, but cannot move the insertion point down to a new line, don't worry about it. Just move the insertion point as far down and to the right as you can (by pressing Ctrl+End or scrolling with your mouse), and press ↵ to insert as many blank lines as necessary, or press the spacebar to insert as many spaces as necessary. *Then* paste the selected text.

Note that the general steps above are useful for moving and copying text in normal, paragraph format. If you need to move a rectangular section of text, such as a column in a table, refer to chapters 4 and 6.

MAKING ADDITIONAL COPIES OF SELECTED TEXT

The Windows Clipboard is discussed in Chapter 25.

Whenever you choose Cut or Copy from the Edit menu, the selected text (or a copy of it) is stored in the Windows Clipboard and stays there until you cut or copy some other selected text. Therefore, if you want to paste additional copies of the text that you just pasted, you need not go through the bother of reselecting the same text. Instead, just move the insertion point to where you want to place another copy, and choose Paste from the Edit menu again, or press Shift+Ins.

SELECT AND GO TO

If text is selected, and you use the Go To option to position the insertion point, you'll see two additional options on the Go To Page Number menu when you move the mouse pointer to that option and hold down the left mouse button:

Beginning of Selection: moves the insertion point back to the beginning of the selected text (after clicking OK or pressing ↵ to leave the dialog box) and unselects the text.

Reselect Text: reselects the previous selection if you've already chosen Beginning of Selection.

DELETING TEXT

TO DELETE A CHARACTER,

move the insertion point to that character and press the Delete key.

As you'll see, you can easily delete blank spaces and lines, as well as text.

WordPerfect offers a great deal of flexibility in deleting text from a document. Of course, when deleting text, there is always the chance that you may delete the wrong letter, word, or group of words. For that reason, WordPerfect also lets you undelete the text you've just deleted. That way, you don't have to be nervous about deleting, because you can always bring back what you deleted.

You've already learned how to use the Backspace key to delete text to the left of the insertion point. This technique works pretty much the same way it does on a typewriter that automatically whites out text as you press Backspace. In this section, I'll look at other techniques for deleting text.

DELETING CHARACTERS

You can use the Delete key to delete an individual character or a group of characters. However, unlike the Backspace key, which deletes the character to the left of the insertion point, the Delete key deletes the character to the right of the insertion point.

The Delete key is abbreviated *Del* on many keyboards. To use the Delete key on the numeric keypad, the Num Lock key must be off (otherwise, pressing Del types a period (.) rather than deleting text). To delete text using the Delete key, follow these steps:

A blank space is simply a character in WordPerfect, so you can delete a space just like any other character.

1. Move the insertion point to where you want to start deleting characters.

2. Press the Delete key to delete the character at the insertion point.

You can press Delete repeatedly (or hold it down) to delete as many characters as you wish.

DELETING SELECTED TEXT

If you accidentally delete or replace selected text, choose Edit▸Undo to bring it back.

As an alternative to pressing Delete repeatedly, you can simply select any amount of text, then press Delete or the Backspace key once to delete that text.

1. Use the keyboard or mouse to select the text you want to delete.

2. Press Delete or Backspace, or choose Cu**t** from the **E**dit pull-down menu, or just start typing any new text that you want to replace the selected text with.

The selected text is removed from the screen, and surrounding text is reformatted to fill the gap left by the deletion. Figure 2.10 shows an example with text selected within a paragraph. Figure 2.11 shows that document after deletion of the selected text.

You may need to insert or delete blank spaces after deleting text if there are too many, or too few, blank spaces at the beginning and end of your

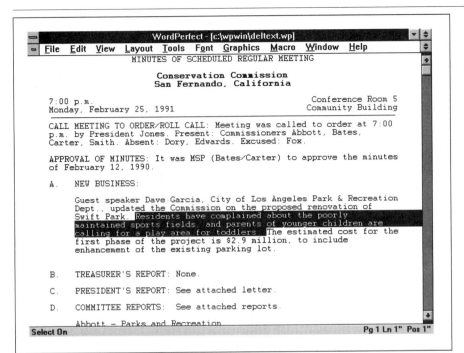

FIGURE 2.10:

*Selected text within a
paragraph*

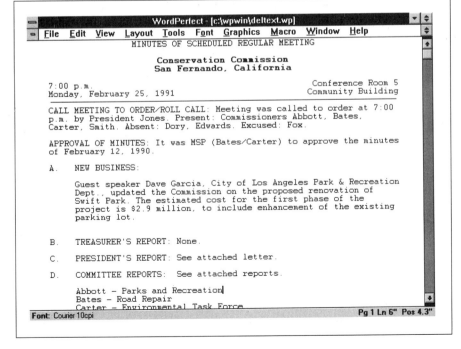

FIGURE 2.11:

*The document from
Figure 2.10 after
deletion of the selected
text*

selected text. For example, if you delete a word from the middle of a sentence, but don't delete either the blank space in front of or behind that word, two extra blank spaces will remain. Delete one of the extra spaces by moving the insertion point to it and pressing Delete.

Deleting a Word

As a shortcut to pressing the Delete key repeatedly (or holding it down), you can delete an entire word and the blank space that follows it:

1. Move the insertion point to the word you want to delete.

2. Press Ctrl+Backspace.

To delete several words, you can hold down the Ctrl key and press the Backspace key repeatedly.

Deleting a Blank Line

If you use the mouse to position the I beam, don't forget to click the left mouse button to bring the insertion point to the I beam before deleting.

If you press ⏎ to insert a blank line when typing your text and then decide to delete a blank line, follow these steps:

1. Move the insertion point to the blank line that you want to delete.

2. Press the Delete key.

That's all there is to it. However, if the blank line contains spaces, tabs, or other hidden codes (discussed in the next chapter), you may need to press Delete more than once to delete these invisible characters before the blank line disappears.

Deleting the Rest of a Line

Another shortcut to pressing the Delete key repeatedly to delete text is to delete the rest of a given line of text. Here's how:

1. Move the insertion point to where you want to start deleting text (or to the first character of a line to delete the entire line).

2. Press Ctrl+Delete.

The Ctrl+Del combination keystroke is often referred to as "Delete EOL," which stands for "Delete to End Of Line."

SUMMARY OF DELETION TECHNIQUES

Table 2.3 summarizes the keys used to delete text. Keep in mind that, in addition to, or as an alternative to, these techniques, you can simply select any text, then press Delete to delete it.

TO DELETE	POSITION INSERTION POINT AT	THEN PRESS
Character to right of insertion point	Character	Delete
Character to left of insertion point	Character	Backspace
Word	Word	Ctrl+Backspace
Blank line	Blank line	Delete
Rest of line	Start of deletion point	Ctrl+Del
Selected text		Delete or Backspace

TABLE 2.3:
Summary of Text Deletion Techniques

UNDELETING TEXT

TO UNDELETE ACCIDENTALLY DELETED TEXT,

press Alt+Backspace or Ctrl+Z immediately after realizing your mistake.

Now, let's suppose you delete some text, spaces, or lines, then suddenly realize, "Whoops! I deleted the wrong text!" (or too much text, or whatever). No need to panic—WordPerfect is quite forgiving. You can "undelete" text just as easily as you deleted it. There are a couple of methods you can use, all depending on how long ago you deleted the text.

UNDELETING TEXT IMMEDIATELY

If you delete some text and realize your mistake immediately (before making any other changes to the document), you can instantly undo the deletion. Do either of the following:

◆ Click on **E**dit or press Alt+E to pull down the Edit menu, then click on **U**ndo, or press U.

◆ Press Alt+Backspace or Ctrl+Z.

UNDELETING TEXT
AFTER MAKING OTHER CHANGES

 *As an alternative to using the menus in steps 2 and 3, press Alt+Shift+Backspace.*

If you delete some text but don't realize your mistake until after you've made other changes, the Undo feature will not restore the deleted text—it will just undo the most recent change. In such a case, follow these steps to undelete the deleted text:

1. Move the insertion point back to where you originally deleted the text.

2. Click on **E**dit or press Alt+E to pull down the Edit menu.

3. Click on U**n**delete or press N. The most recently deleted text reappears highlighted on the screen, along with this dialog box:

4. At this point, you have three options:

◆ If the highlighted text is indeed the text you want to undelete, click on **R**estore or press ↵.

◆ If the highlighted text is not the text you want to undelete, click on **N**ext (or press N), or click on **P**revious (or press P) to view previous deletions. The Undelete feature "remembers" your last three deletions, so if you don't see the text you want to delete after choosing Next or Previous a couple of times, the text you're looking for cannot be undeleted. If you see the text you want to undelete, click the **R**estore button (or press R).

◆ If you change your mind about undeleting, or you cannot find the text you want to undelete, click on Cancel or press Escape to clear the dialog box.

It's important to remember that WordPerfect only remembers your last three deletions and to realize that WordPerfect restores previously deleted text wherever the insertion point happens to be at the moment. (Undo restores deleted text to its original position.) So to avoid confusion, your best bet is to review the remaining text on your screen immediately after making a deletion (before you move the *insertion point*); if you change your mind, you can easily recover text simply by pressing Alt+Backspace.

SPLITTING AND JOINING PARAGRAPHS

The general techniques described so far make it easy to split one paragraph into two, or to combine two paragraphs into one. As any writer knows, these are pretty common tasks when editing the first draft of a document. The discussion of hidden codes in the next chapter will shed more light on these techniques and will help you solve other kinds of formatting problems.

SPLITTING ONE PARAGRAPH INTO TWO

If you decide that a single paragraph in your document is best split into two paragraphs, you can easily make that change:

1. Move the insertion point to the beginning of the sentence that you want to be the start of a new paragraph.

2. Press ↵.

3. If you want to insert a blank line above this new paragraph, press ↵ again. If you want to indent this paragraph, press Tab.

JOINING TWO PARAGRAPHS

If you accidentally break a line of text in the middle, or you want to combine two paragraphs into one, just delete the blank lines or spaces that separate the paragraphs:

1. Move the insertion point to the end of the upper line.

2. Press the Delete key until the lower paragraph reaches the insertion point.

3. If necessary, insert blank spaces by pressing the spacebar while in Insert mode, as necessary, to separate the sentences.

Figure 2.12 summarizes the basic techniques for joining and splitting text. In Chapter 3, you'll learn about the Reveal Codes feature, which gives you a behind-the-scenes view of why these techniques work and provides more flexibility in controlling the appearance of your text.

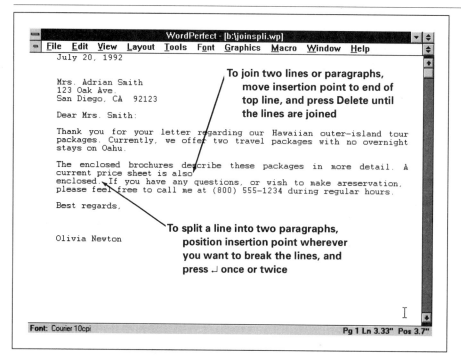

CHANGING UPPER- AND LOWERCASE

It's not uncommon to inadvertently type a long passage of text without realizing that Caps Lock is on, or to type something in lowercase and decide later to change it to uppercase. For this reason, WordPerfect offers a simple means of changing text from lowercase to uppercase, and vice versa:

1. Select the text that you want to change to upper- or lowercase.

2. Click on **E**dit or press Alt+E to pull down the Edit menu.

3. Click on C**o**nvert Case or press O.

4. If you want to convert to uppercase, click on **U**ppercase (or press U). To convert to lowercase, click on **L**owercase (or press L).

If you convert text to lowercase, the following words will remain capitalized:

◆ The word *I*, or any contraction (*I'm, I'll, I'd*).

◆ The first word at the beginning of a sentence (if the period or other exclamation point from the preceding sentence is included in the selected text).

Incidentally, the Convert Case option is fine for changing a single selection of text. But if you want to *globally* change case—for example change "Arco corporation" to "ARCO Corporation" everywhere in a document—use the Replace feature, described in Chapter 9. (The term *globally* means "throughout the entire document.")

SAVING YOUR CHANGES

It is important to keep in mind when you're editing a document that your changes are made to the copy of the document currently stored in the computer's memory (RAM), *but not to the copy stored on the disk*. If you turn off your computer (or if a power outage turns it off for you), your changes will not be saved on the disk, and they will be lost.

You can have WordPerfect automatically save your work every few minutes, as you'll learn in Chapter 13.

Therefore, it's important to save your work when you're editing an existing document. Remember, if you save your work every five minutes, the most work you stand to lose in the event of a mishap is five minutes' work. As discussed in Chapter 1, you can easily save your work from time to time, without exiting WordPerfect, simply by choosing the Save option from the File pull-down menu or by pressing Shift+F3.

Also, when you are finished with WordPerfect for the time being, don't forget to exit and save your work, using the Exit option on the File pull-down menu (or by pressing Alt+F4).

So now you're armed with two of the most important sets of skills for using WordPerfect: the ability to create (type) text, print it, and save it, and the ability to edit (change) existing text. If you need some additional guidance with some of the techniques described in this chapter, try taking Lesson 2 in Part 9.

Otherwise, you can forge ahead to Chapter 3 and learn a third set of basic skills: interacting with WordPerfect in general, including managing windows and multiple documents, getting on-screen help, and using handy options like the ruler and Button Bar.

CHAPTER 3

Getting the Most from WordPerfect

ow that you've had a chance to learn the basics of creating, editing, printing, and saving a document, you're ready to start moving into some of WordPerfect's more powerful features. As the sheer length of this book hints at, there are lots of them.

LESSON 3

For a hands-on lesson in using some of the features discussed in this Chapter, see Lesson 3 in Part 9.

But now that your basic typing and editing skills are in shape, you'll be able to pick and choose whatever features are relevant to your work. So don't think you need to read this book from cover to cover to become a WordPerfect whiz.

However, before you start picking and choosing specific features, you'd do well to spend some time learning about some of the more general features of WordPerfect that are relevant to all kinds of projects. These kinds of features are what this chapter is all about.

FOLLOWING MENU SEQUENCES

If you're familiar with Windows (or have read Appendix B) and the preceding chapters, you've no doubt seen that you can use all the same techniques to use the WordPerfect menus and dialog boxes that you can use in Windows 3 and all Windows applications. So rather than reiterate all the alternative techniques for choosing menu and dialog box options, I'll present a series of menu choices in an abbreviated format, where the symbol ➤ leads from one choice to the next.

For example, here's a sample instruction that you might encounter:

Choose Layout ➤ Line ➤ Flush Right (or press Alt+F7)

When you see this instruction, you can use either the menus or the shortcut key to follow the instruction. That is, you can do any of the following:

◆ Click on **L**ayout, then click on **L**ine, and then click on **F**lush Right.

◆ Press Alt+L then press L, then press F.

◆ Press and release Alt, then use the arrow keys to highlight **L**ayout and press ↵. Then use the arrow keys to highlight **L**ine and press ↵, and finally highlight **F**lush Right and press ↵.

◆ Press Alt+F7.

If a menu option described in this book isn't available on your menus, you may be using short menus. You can Choose View ➤ Short Menus to switch to full menus.

If a sequence of steps leads to a dialog box, just use the general Windows techniques presented in Appendix B to choose dialog box options. Don't forget, however, that after you've made your choices from a dialog box, you need to click OK (or press ↵) to activate those choices. Optionally, you can click Cancel (or press Escape) to leave the dialog box and cancel your current choices.

MANAGING WINDOWS AND DOCUMENTS

All the usual techniques for sizing, moving, opening, and closing windows described in Appendix B also work in WordPerfect for Windows. Notice, as pointed out in Figure 3.1, that there are separate buttons for the WordPerfect application window and the document window.

If your application and document windows are maximized, you'll see Restore buttons rather than the Minimize and Maximize buttons. You can click each Restore button to reduce each window's size, or you can use the Restore option on each window's Control menu (press Alt+spacebar and then R for the application window and Alt+− and then R for the document window).

You can edit up to nine documents at once in WordPerfect for Windows, each in a separate document window. In the next section, I'll explain how to open and close multiple documents.

OPENING AND CLOSING DOCUMENT WINDOWS

One key to opening and closing document windows, and keeping track of multiple documents, is understanding options for opening, closing, and saving documents on the File menu. The first few options on that menu are discussed in more detail below:

New: opens a new, empty document window, without affecting any currently open documents. Use this option when you want to start work on a new document.

Open: retrieves a saved document from disk, placing it in a new document window. Use this option whenever you want to edit an existing document.

Retrieve: retrieves a saved document from disk, placing it in the current document window. If the current document window already contains text, the incoming document is inserted in the current document at the insertion point. (However, you'll first see a message asking for permission to do this. Choose No if you don't want to combine the documents.) Use this option when you want to combine multiple documents in a single document window.

Close: saves the current document window and then closes it. If you've made changes since the last time the document was saved, a message box will appear asking whether you want to save those changes. Use this option when you've finished working on a document and no longer need to have immediate access to it. (To use the document again in the future, use File ➤ Open to reopen it.)

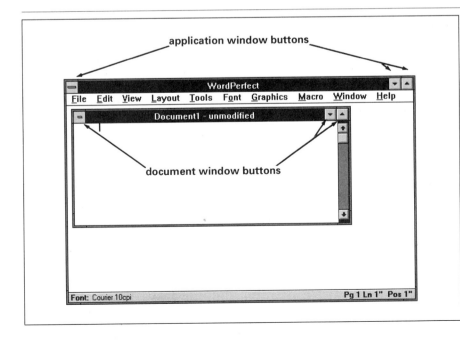

FIGURE 3.1:

Buttons for the WordPerfect application window and one document window

Save: saves the document in the current window, but leaves it on the screen for additional editing.

Save As: same as above, but lets you enter a new file name for the document.

VIEWING ALL OPEN DOCUMENTS

With the ability to have up to nine documents open on the screen at once, things can quickly become confusing, particularly since any one document window might obscure all the others. There are a few ways that you can get a quick look at what documents are currently open, by using the Window pull-down menu:

You can use File ➤ Preferences ➤ Display to display vertical and horizontal scroll bars on document windows (see Chapter 13).

◆ Choose **W**indow ➤ **C**ascade to cascade all open windows, so you can see the title bar of each, as in Figure 3.2.

◆ Choose **W**indow ➤ **T**ile to tile all the open documents (as in Figure 3.3).

Of course, you can organize your document windows however you wish, using the standard Minimize, Maximize, and Restore buttons, the title bar, and the Control menu on each window. For example, Figure 3.4 shows three document windows arranged such that minutes.wp is in the forefront (it's the active

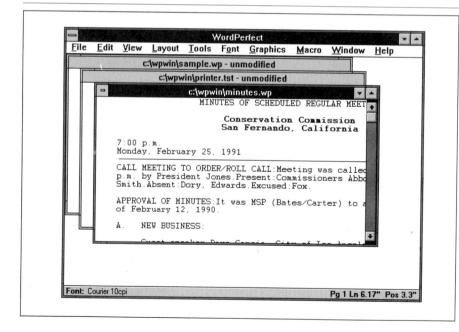

FIGURE 3.2:

Three document windows are cascaded on the screen. You can see the entire document window for the minutes.wp file but only the title bars for the printer.tst and sample.wp files.

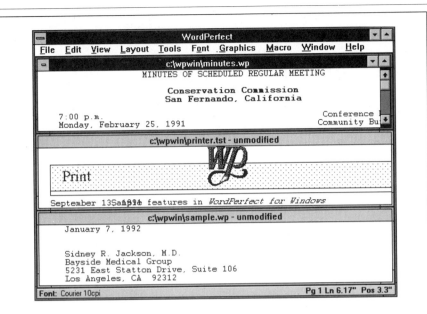

FIGURE 3.3:

Three document windows are tiled on the screen. You can see each document's window and a portion of the text in each document.

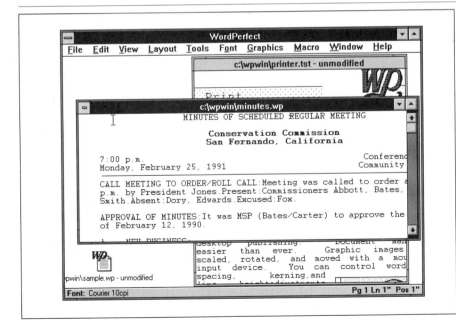

FIGURE 3.4:

Three document windows are on the screen. Minutes.wp is in the active window, printer.tst is in the background, and sample.wp is minimized to an icon.

window); printer.tst is largely obscured by minutes.wp, and sample.wp is shrunk to an icon (minimized) in the lower-left corner of the screen.

CHOOSING THE ACTIVE WINDOW

NOTE
NOTE

Even though you can edit only one document at a time, you can easily cut and paste between documents, as described later.

Even though you can have up to nine documents open at once, you can edit only the document in the *current* document window. It's easy to tell which window is the current one, because

◆ The title bar on the current document window is darkened (or colored differently).

◆ Only the current document window has a scroll bar, a Control-menu box, and Maximize, Minimize, and Restore buttons.

◆ The current document window overlaps any other open document windows.

There are several techniques that you can use to activate any open document window, even if it's entirely obscured by other windows. You can do any of the following:

◆ Click anywhere in the window you want to activate.

◆ Pull down the Window menu, then choose the document you want to work on (by clicking its name or typing the number next to its name).

◆ Press Next Document (Ctrl+F6) or Previous Document (Ctrl+Shift+F6) until the document window you want is active.

If you've minimized the document window to an icon, you can reopen it by using any of these methods:

◆ Double-click the document window's icon.

◆ Press Ctrl+F6 until the icon for the document you want is highlighted. Then press Alt+- and choose **R**estore.

◆ Choose **W**indow. You'll see a list of all open documents at the bottom of the menu. To choose one for editing, click its name or type the number next to the name.

CUTTING AND PASTING BETWEEN DOCUMENTS

One advantage of having multiple documents on the screen is that it makes it easy to move and copy text between documents. You use the same basic techniques you use for cutting and pasting within a single document:

◆   Select the text you want to move or copy.

◆   Choose **Edit ➤ C**opy (if you want to copy text) or **Edit ➤ C**ut (if you want to move the text). The selected text is copied or moved to the Windows Clipboard.

◆   Open the document you want to move or copy text to, or activate its window if it's already open.

◆   Position the insertion point where you want to place the text being moved or copied.

◆   Choose **Edit ➤ P**aste or press Shift+Ins.

Remember that once copied or cut, the selected text remains in the Windows Clipboard, even after pasting, until you cut or copy some other text. So if you want, you can paste that same text to any other document without reselecting it in the original document.

USING APPEND TO CUT AND PASTE

You can view the current contents of the Clipboard by using the Windows 3 Clipboard option in the Main group of the Program Manager. See Chapter 25.

There are a couple of alternatives to the technique described above that can help you cut and paste between documents. For one, you can *add* selected text to the Clipboard by choosing Edit ➤ Append (rather than Cut or Copy). This option lets you copy several sections of text to the Clipboard, which you can then paste wherever you wish.

You can also add selected text to the end of any existing document, even if that document is not open at the moment:

1.   Select the text that you want to copy to another document.

2.   Choose **File ➤ S**ave (or press Shift+F3).

3.   Type or choose the name of the file you want to add the selected text to (this cannot be the same name as the current document).

4.   Choose **S**ave.

5.   Choose **A**ppend.

If the file specified in step 3 does not exist on the specified drive and in the specified directory, WordPerfect creates it, then appends the text to it.

CLOSING A DOCUMENT WINDOW

Having lots of document windows open uses a lot of memory and can slow WordPerfect down. If you've finished working with a document, and you no longer want to keep it on the screen, you can close its document window. As usual, you can use any of several techniques. First, activate the document window (or highlight its icon if it's minimized) that you want to close, using any of the techniques just described. Then do one of the following:

◆ Choose **File** ➤ **C**lose (or press Ctrl+F4).

◆ Double-click the window's Control-menu box.

◆ Open the window's Control menu (press Alt+–) and choose **C**lose.

If you've made any changes to the document since it was last saved, you'll be given an opportunity to save those changes before the document window is removed from the screen.

In summary, keep in mind that whenever you use File ➤ New or File ➤ Open, you create a new document window. That document window remains on the screen until you take specific actions to close it. If several document windows are still open when you exit WordPerfect, you'll be given the opportunity to save any changes in each document window before the program ends.

GETTING HELP

TO GET QUICK, CONTEXT-SENSITIVE HELP,

press Help (F1).

When an open Help window is covered by some other window, use Alt+Tab or the Task List (Ctrl+Esc) to redisplay the Help window.

WordPerfect's built-in Help feature lets you see helpful advice and quick reminders on your screen without your having to refer to a book or manual. The help system is *context-sensitive,* which means that the help that appears is relevant to whatever you're trying to do at the moment. For example, if you've already worked your way to the Print dialog box (by choosing File ➤ Print), you'll see a window of help on that topic, as shown in Figure 3.5.

WordPerfect uses the Windows 3 help system, so all the usual techniques work for sizing and positioning the Help window. You can use the scroll bars to scroll through the help text, move the window by dragging its title bar, size the Help window from the borders or buttons, and so forth. For example, Figure 3.6 shows the Help window sized and positioned in the lower-left corner of the screen, with a sample WordPerfect document displayed behind it.

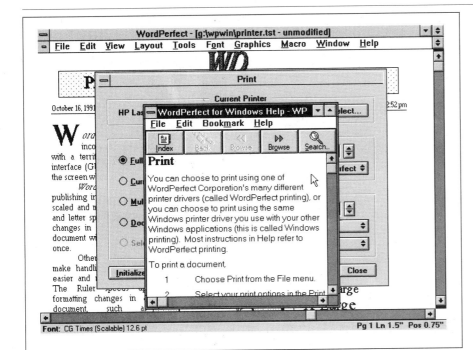

FIGURE 3.5:

A sample Help window, displayed after pressing F1 while the Print dialog box was displayed

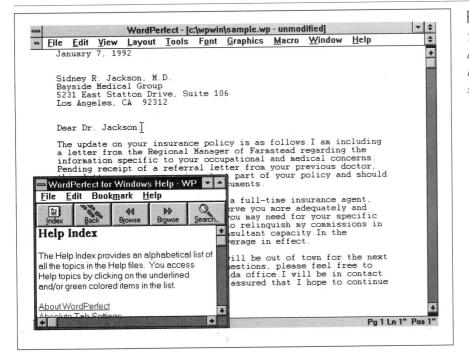

FIGURE 3.6:

The Help window sized and positioned in the lower-left corner of the screen

You can also use all the general help techniques described in Appendix B to use the WordPerfect help system. For example, you can use the various buttons to browse forward and backward, click on any underlined (or colored) "jump text" to get additional information on that topic, and so forth.

USING THE HELP MENU

As an alternative to using the F1 key for context-sensitive help, you can use the Help pull-down menu, provided there is no dialog box or other message currently on the screen. When you open this menu, by clicking the Help option or pressing Alt+H, you'll see these options:

Index: lists all help topics in alphabetical order. Click any option to choose it, or press Tab or Shift+Tab until the option you want is highlighted, then press ↵.

Keyboard: provides templates of both the default (Windows CUA) and DOS keyboards.

How Do I: presents a list of common tasks. Click any underlined option, or use the Tab and Shift+Tab keys to highlight an option, then press ↵.

Glossary: provides definitions of common terms. Move the mouse pointer to any option, and hold down the left mouse button to see the definition. Or, highlight any option with Tab or Shift+Tab, then hold down the ↵ key.

Using Help: presents instructions for using the help system.

What Is: changes the mouse pointer to a "What Is" icon, as an alternative technique for getting context-sensitive help (see "Using 'What Is'" below).

About WordPerfect: displays information about your version of WordPerfect, and your registration number. (Click OK or press ↵ when you're finished.)

USING BOOKMARKS

You can create your own index of help topics by using *bookmarks*. When you get to a help topic that you'd like to mark for future reference, choose Bookmark from the Help window menu bar. Then choose Define. The current index entry will appear in the text box under Bookmark Name.

If you wish, you can edit the entry, type a new one, or leave it as it is. Then choose OK (by clicking the OK button or pressing ↵). In the future, when you choose Bookmark from the Help window menu bar, your entry will appear on that menu. Just choose that option from the menu to jump to it.

If you later decide to delete a Bookmark entry, choose Bookmark ➤ Define from the Help window. Click the entry you want to delete (or press Tab until it's outlined and then press the spacebar), and click the Delete button (or press Alt+D).

ANNOTATING HELP

You can also annotate any help text to add your own comments. Choose **An**notate from the Help window's Edit pull-down menu. Then type your comments and click OK (or press ↵). A small "paper clip" icon appears next to the help topic title. In the future, whenever you want to review your annotation, just click the paper-clip icon.

COPYING HELP TEXT

You can also print any help topic simply by choosing File ➤ Print Topic from the Help window. Use File ➤ Printer Setup first if you need to select a printer.

You can copy any text from the Help window to the Windows Clipboard. From there, you can paste it into any WordPerfect document (or just about any Windows application screen, for that matter). Follow these steps:

1. When you get to the help topic that you want to copy, choose **Edit** ➤ **C**opy from the Help window (or press Ctrl+Ins).

2. Leave the help system by choosing **File** ➤ **E**xit (or by pressing Alt+F4).

3. Position the insertion point where you want to copy the help text to within your WordPerfect document.

4. Choose **E**dit ➤ **P**aste (or press Shift+Ins).

USING "WHAT IS"

One of the best techniques for getting help in WordPerfect is to use the "What Is" icon shown at left. There are two ways to get to this icon:

◆ If you're in a normal document window, choose **Help** ➤ **W**hat Is (or press Shift+F1).

◆ If you need help with a specific option in a dialog box or menu that is already visible on the screen, just press Shift+F1.

Once the icon appears, just move the mouse to move the icon to whatever item you need help with, then click the left mouse button. When you've chosen a valid option, the Help window displays the help text for that option.

EXITING HELP

When you've finished using the help system, you can close the Help window by using any of these techniques:

◆   Choose **File** ➤ **Ex**it from the Help window's menu bar.

◆   Double-click the Control-menu box in the upper-left corner of the Help window.

◆   Make sure the Help window is the currently active window, then press Alt+F4 (or Alt+F, then X).

 You can also minimize the help system to an application icon (shown at left) by clicking the Help window's Minimize button. To reopen the Help window, just double-click its icon, or press Alt+Tab until the icon is highlighted and then release the Alt key.

VIEWING THE RULER

The ruler, shown in Figure 3.7, is a handy device for viewing and changing tab stops, margins, and columns; it also provides shortcuts for various other features described in forthcoming chapters. To view the ruler (if it isn't currently visible in a document window):

◆   Choose **View** ➤ **R**uler (or press Alt+Shift+F3).

You can use the same method to remove the ruler if it's currently visible.

Each document window has a separate ruler. Initially, each new document window is displayed without the ruler. But you can easily turn on the ruler in each new document window with View ➤ Ruler. Optionally, you can have the ruler appear automatically in every new document by choosing File ➤ Preferences ➤ Environment ➤ Automatic Ruler Display (as discussed in Chapter 13).

I'll talk about techniques for using the ruler in later chapters. For now it's sufficient to know how to turn it on and off.

USING THE BUTTON BAR

TO VIEW THE BUTTON BAR,

choose View ➤ Button Bar.

If you're an experienced Word-Perfect user, you'll find the Button Bar to be a good alternative to the (now extinct) Alt-key macros.

The Button Bar is another handy tool, which allows you to access a series of menu choices by clicking a single button. To display the Button Bar,

◆ Choose **V**iew ➤ **B**utton Bar.

The default Button Bar is displayed beneath the menu bar, as shown in Figure 3.8. (If you want to get rid of the Button Bar, reselect **V**iew ➤ **B**utton Bar.)

To use the Button Bar, simply click any button. For example, once the Button Bar is displayed, you can just click the Open button (if one is available) to open a document, rather than go through the menus or use a shortcut key.

There may be more buttons than will fit across the screen on the Button Bar. To view additional buttons (if any), click on the left and right scroll arrows at the left side of the Button Bar.

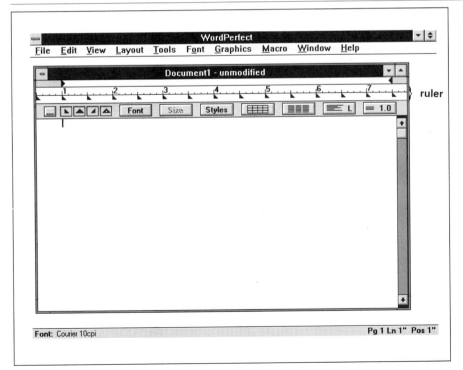

FIGURE 3.7:

The ruler displayed in an empty document window, after choosing View ➤ Ruler

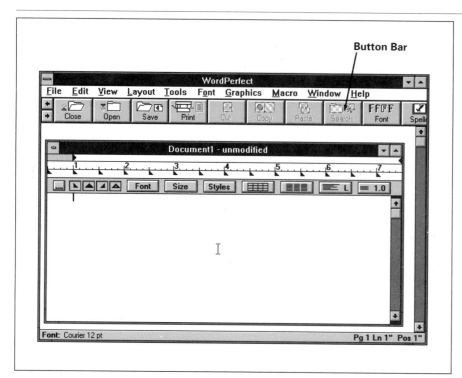

A sample Button Bar, displayed by choosing View ➤ Button Bar

CHANGING THE BUTTON BAR

You can also change the position and appearance of the Button Bar. To do so, Follow these steps:

1. Choose **V**iew ➤ Button Bar **S**etup ➤ **O**ptions. The dialog box shown below appears:

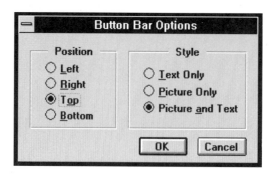

2. Choose any one of the available positions: **L**eft, **R**ight, **T**op, or **B**ottom.

3. Choose any available style, Te**x**t Only (no icons on the buttons), **P**icture Only (only icons on the buttons), or Picture **a**nd Text (the default; both text and an icon on each button).

4. Click OK or press ↵ to leave the dialog box.

The position and style of the Button Bar is simply a matter of personal preference, and you may want to experiment with different combinations to find one you like.

ADDING YOUR OWN BUTTONS TO THE BUTTON BAR

The default Button Bar provides some handy buttons, but you can easily create your own buttons. Basically, any menu selection that you find yourself repeating often is a good candidate for a button (I'll point out some good candidates in the chapters that follow). To add a button to the current Button Bar, follow these steps:

1. Choose **View** ➤ Button Bar **Setup** ➤ **E**dit. You'll see the dialog box shown below:

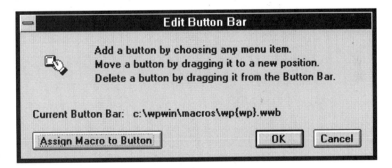

2. When you move the mouse pointer up to the menus, you'll notice that the pointer changes to the icon shown at left.

3. Choose whatever series of menu options you want to assign to the button, or press the appropriate shortcut key. The button is created when you've reached the end of a menu sequence (i.e., before you get to a dialog box).

4. If you want to add more buttons, repeat steps 2 and 3 as often as you wish. Otherwise, click OK or press ⏎ to save your buttons and remove the dialog box.

Each button you create will automatically be assigned a name and an icon.

If you want to create more complex buttons, such as buttons that can choose dialog box options or manipulate text, you'll need to record the keystrokes in a *macro,* then assign the macro to a button (see Chapter 15).

MOVING AND DELETING BUTTONS

As the Edit Button Bar dialog box indicates, you can also easily remove buttons or rearrange them:

1. If you are not already at the Edit Button Bar dialog box, choose **V**iew ➤ Button Bar **S**etup ➤ **E**dit.

2. To move a button, position the mouse pointer on it, hold down the left mouse button, and drag the button to the left or right. It will appear as a "ghost" button while you drag it. When you release the mouse button, the button you've been moving will be inserted in its new position.

3. To delete a button, drag it off the Button Bar.

4. When you've finished moving and deleting buttons, click OK.

CREATING A NEW BUTTON BAR

If you'd like to create a new Button Bar from scratch, choose **V**iew ➤ Button Bar **S**etup ➤ **N**ew. All the buttons in the current Button Bar will disappear, and you'll be taken to the dialog box for adding, moving, and deleting buttons.

You can add whatever buttons you wish to the Button Bar. When you're finished, click the OK button in the dialog box. You'll be prompted to enter a name for the new Button Bar. Type in a valid file name (up to eight characters, with no spaces or punctuation), but don't add an extension. WordPerfect will automatically add the extension .wwb (WordPerfect Windows Button) to whatever file name you provide. Click Save after typing the file name.

As an alternative to creating a new Button Bar from scratch, you can just modify any existing one. To save that Button Bar with a new file name, choose View ➤ Button Bar Setup ➤ Save As. Then type in the name and choose Save.

SELECTING A BUTTON BAR

After you've created your own Button Bars, you can choose one by following these steps:

1. Choose **V**iew ➤ Button Bar **S**etup ➤ **S**elect.

2. Choose one of the file names shown, using the usual techniques (i.e., double-click its name under Files, or type its name and press ↵).

The default sample button bar is named wp{wp}.wwb.

The Button Bar you chose will appear on the screen, replacing the existing bar (if any).

Later in this chapter, and later in the book as well, you'll see additional Button Bars that you can use with other specialized WordPerfect screens, including Print Preview, the Figure Editor, and the Equation Editor. I'll also suggest sample buttons you might want to create.

PREVIEWING YOUR PRINTED DOCUMENT

TO PREVIEW YOUR PRINTED DOCUMENT,

choose File ➤ Print Preview (or press Shift+F5).

A document window shows you only as much text as can fit within that window. If you'd like to get a preview of how the document will look when printed, you can use the Print Preview feature. This handy feature lets you see exactly how your document will look before you print it. To use Print Preview,

You cannot make any changes to a document while previewing it on the Print Preview screen.

◆ Choose **F**ile ➤ Print Pre**v**iew (or press Shift+F5).

You'll be taken to the Print Preview window, an example of which is shown in Figure 3.9. (You can size and position the Print Preview window, like any other window. But no other WordPerfect windows are available when Print Preview is open.) Notice that the window has its own menu bar, with the options File, View, Pages, and Help. The options on these menus are described below.

The Print Preview screen has its own Button Bar, offering shortcuts for menu selections that are in the Print Preview window. You can turn the Button Bar on or off by choosing View ➤ Button Bar. You can also add, move, and delete buttons by using the View ➤ Button Bar Setup options.

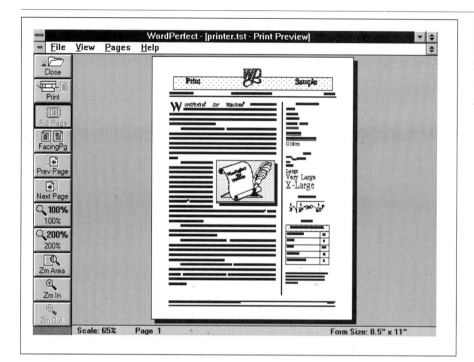

FIGURE 3.9:

The sample text on the Print Preview screen, after choosing File ➤ Print Preview

USING THE VIEW MENU OPTIONS

NOTE *The status bar at the bottom of the Print Preview screen shows the current magnification, page number, and page size (form size).*

You can view your document at several levels of magnification, using options on the View pull down menu (or equivalent buttons on the Print Preview Button Bar, as available). The options are the following:

100%	Letters shown at their actual printed size
200%	Letters displayed at twice their actual size, for a closer look
Zoom **In**	Increases current magnification by 25 percent, to a maximum of 400 percent
Zoom **Out**	Decreases the current magnification by 25 percent, to a minimum of 65 percent (Full Page)

Zoom Area	Lets you draw a frame around any area you want to magnify (move the mouse pointer to one corner of the area you want to magnify, then drag the pointer to the opposite corner and release the mouse button)
Zoom to **F**ull Width	Adjusts magnification to show the full width of the page
Reset	Restores the original magnification (as it was the last time you closed the Print Preview screen)

USING THE PAGES MENU OPTIONS

Depending on the resolution of your monitor, text may be converted to lines when the view is reduced to a small magnification.

The Pages menu also lets you view the document at various magnifications, and lets you go to a page as well. You options are the following:

Full Page	Displays the entire page (text that's too small to print is displayed as solid lines)
Fa**c**ing Pages	Displays facing pages with even-numbered pages on the left and odd-numbered pages on the right (if there is no facing page, such as when you're viewing page 1, no opposite page is shown)
Go to Page	Lets you enter a page number to view (Click OK or press ↵ after entering the page number)
Previous Page	Skips to the previous page (if any)
Next Page	Skips to the next page (if any)

If it's taking too long for Print Preview to draw a particular page, press Escape to cancel the redraw, then choose other options from the menus.

SCROLLING IN PRINT PREVIEW

While you're viewing a document at 100 percent or greater magnification, you can use the arrow, PgUp, and PgDn keys to scroll through the document. Use Ctrl+PgUp and Ctrl+PgDn to scroll left and right when the page is magnified wider than the screen. You can also use the scroll bars, when they appear, to scroll with your mouse.

When the document is highly magnified, the mouse pointer changes to the Move icon when it's on a page. When this happens, you can click the left mouse button to see a miniature page view. You can then drag the frame on this view to any location on the page, then release the left mouse button to magnify the framed area. To reduce the view again, choose any option from the View or Pages menu.

If you're viewing multiple pages, the mouse pointer changes to a magnifying glass when it's on a page. You can move this pointer to any page, then click the left mouse button to magnify that page.

CLOSING PRINT PREVIEW

When you're finished previewing the document,

◆ Choose **F**ile ➤ **C**lose (or press Ctrl+F4).

Optionally, if the Button Bar is displayed and there is still a Close button on it, just click that button.

WORKING WITH HIDDEN CODES

TO ACTIVATE OR DEACTIVATE REVEAL CODES,

drag the Reveal Codes bar to where you want to split the document window, or choose View ➤ Reveal Codes (Alt+F3).

All the formatting features that you use in a document, including hard returns (inserted when you press ↵), page breaks, and the many formatting features you'll learn about in future chapters, are controlled by hidden *codes* within the document. The reason these codes are initially hidden is simple: WordPerfect wants your document to look normal as you type and make changes. If your screen was cluttered with a bunch of strange-looking codes, your work would be much more complicated.

On the other hand, you can use the hidden codes to your advantage, particularly when you start using some of the more advanced WordPerfect features. For this reason, WordPerfect lets you view the codes so that you can see what's really going on behind the scenes in your document.

To view the hidden codes, you need to activate the Reveal Codes feature. You can use any one of the following techniques:

◆ Drag either of the Reveal Codes bars, located above and below the scroll bar (see Figure 3.10), to the pointwhere you want to split the document.

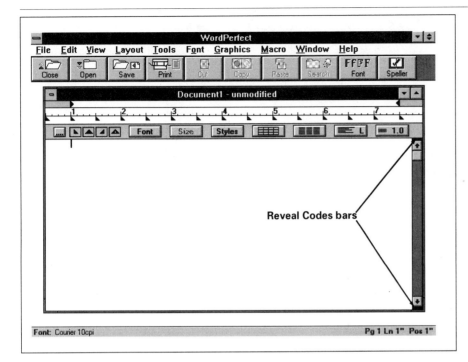

You can drag either the top or bottom Reveal Codes bar to open Reveal Codes in any document window.

If Reveal Codes shows nothing or is hard to read, you may need to change its colors by using File ➤ Preferences ➤ Display ➤ Reveal Codes Colors (see Chapter 13).

◆ Choose **View** ➤ **R**eveal Codes.

◆ Press Alt+F3.

Your document window will be divided into two sections: one shows the regular text, and the other shows roughly the same text, but with the codes visible. Figure 3.11 shows an example.

In Reveal Codes, the codes are enclosed in square brackets ([ ]) and are usually highlighted or colored differently. Figure 3.11 shows soft-return codes [SRt] where WordPerfect automatically word-wrapped a line and hard-return codes [HRt] where the author intentionally ended a line or added a blank line by pressing ⏎.

Although it's not necessary to memorize or even understand the role of every code to use Word-Perfect successfully, I've included a complete list for future reference in Appendix C.

PRACTICAL USE OF HIDDEN CODES

Every code plays some role in WordPerfect. For example, a single hard-return code, [HRt], tells WordPerfect and your printer to "end the line here, and go to the next line." In the document window, you see only the broken line, as in the split-paragraph example in Chapter 2. But in the Reveal Codes window you can actually see the [HRt] code.

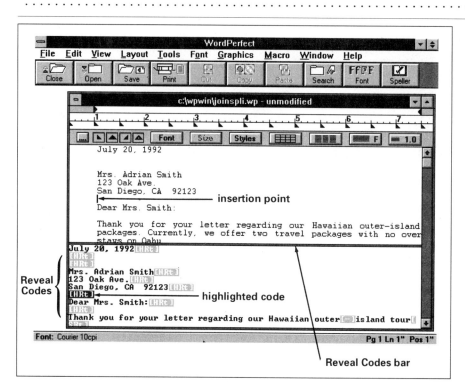

A sample document displayed with Reveal Codes on. You can drag the Reveal Codes bar separating the top and bottom portions of the document window to resize or close Reveal Codes.

If you move the highlight to that hidden code in Reveal Codes and press Delete to delete it, the [HRt] code disappears, and the line is no longer broken, as in the example of rejoining two lines of text in Chapter 2.

Although it's possible to split or join two lines of text without using Reveal Codes, you'll probably find it easier to do so with Reveal Codes turned on. In fact, when you start using the more advanced formatting features discussed in the chapters that follow, you'll probably find Reveal Codes to be an indispensable aid in troubleshooting formatting problems in your document.

About Single and Paired Codes

Most features in WordPerfect are controlled by a single code, such as [HRt] or [SRt]. As you'll see in future chapters, however, some features are controlled by *paired codes*. For example, if you boldface a block of text, the text appears in boldface on the screen. But in Reveal Codes, you actually see the hidden codes that are causing the text to be boldfaced:

[Bold On]This text is boldfaced, **[Bold Off]** and this is not.

In this case WordPerfect is using paired codes to activate and deactivate a specific printer feature, boldface print. The starting code, which activates the feature, contains the word "On" (e.g. [Bold On]) and the ending code, which deactivates the feature, contains the word "Off" (e.g., [Bold Off]). Hence, when you print the sentence shown above, the first part appears in boldface and the second part as normal text:

This text is boldfaced, and this is not.

About Hard and Soft Codes

In most cases, codes are inserted in a document when you press some key (such as ↵) or choose a formatting feature. In other cases, codes are inserted automatically, behind the scenes. For example, when you are typing a paragraph and type past the right margin, WordPerfect inserts a *soft-return* code ([SRt]) at the end of the uppermost line. This code tells WordPerfect and your printer to "end this line here and resume text on the next line."

Generally, codes that you insert yourself are referred to as *hard codes,* and codes that WordPerfect inserts for you are referred to as *soft codes.*

POSITIONING THE INSERTION POINT IN REVEAL CODES

You can also use the Search feature (Chapter 9) to locate a specific code in Reveal Codes.

When Reveal Codes is on, you can still use the mouse and insertion-point movement keys to move about the document, with the I beam in either the normal editing portion of the screen or the Reveal Codes portion.

When the insertion point lands on a hidden code rather than on some character, the entire character is highlighted in Reveal Codes. (As shown in Table 2.1 of Chapter 2, several keys are available for positioning the insertion point before or after the codes in a line or at the top of a document.) For example, in Figure 3.11, the insertion point is on the blank line above the salutation of the letter (*Dear Mrs. Smith*). But in Reveal Codes, you can see that the [HRt] code is highlighted.

EDITING CODES

You can delete, move, or insert codes in Reveal Codes by using the same basic techniques that you use in the editing portion of the screen. As you gain experience and read later chapters, you'll better appreciate this convenience. But for now, I'll just describe the general techniques for editing codes in Reveal

Codes. Feel free to refer back to this section if you later forget how to insert, delete, move, or copy codes.

Deleting Codes

Deleting one code in a paired-code set, such as [Bold On] and [Bold Off], automatically deletes the other code.

If you are having a problem with the format of your document, sometimes simply removing the code that's activating a feature that you no longer want to use will fix the problem. Figure 3.12 shows an example from Chapter 2, where a line was split in two at the word *also* in midsentence. With Reveal Codes on, it's easy to see the hard-return code ([HRt]) that's causing the line break. To fix the problem, you'd simply delete the [HRt] code.

Deleting a code works the same as deleting any other character on the screen:

NOTE NOTE

Soft codes that are placed automatically, such as a soft return ([SRt]), cannot be deleted.

1. If you have not already done so, turn on Reveal Codes.

2. Move the insertion point to the code you want to delete so that the entire code is highlighted in Reveal Codes.

3. Press Delete.

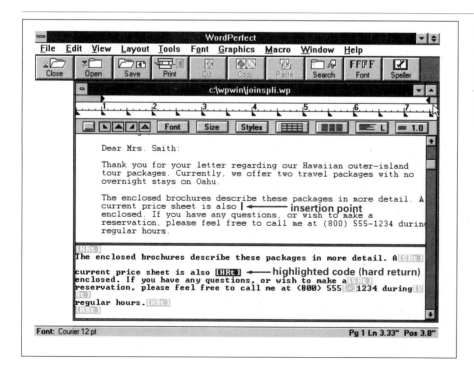

FIGURE 3.12:

A hard-return code ([HRt]), inserted by pressing ↵, causing a line to break in midsentence

As with text, if you delete a code by accident, you can immediately choose Edit ➤ Undo (or press Alt+Backspace) to undo the deletion. Or, if you've made additional changes since deleting the code, use Edit ➤ Undelete (Alt+Shift+Backspace) to restore the code at the current insertion-point position.

Deleting Codes without Reveal Codes

When Reveal Codes is turned off, many codes can still be deleted with the normal text-deletion techniques. For example, if you move the insertion point to a blank line, and press Delete, the hard-return code that's causing the blank line is deleted. Similarly, if you select and delete a section of text, any codes that were in that selected text are also deleted, whether or not Reveal Codes is on.

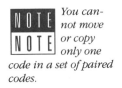

You cannot move or copy only one code in a set of paired codes.

Some codes, however, cannot be deleted when Reveal Codes is off. This prevents you from accidentally deleting a code that you cannot see when the insertion point appears to be on a regular character or space. If you decide that you would prefer to be able to delete hidden codes, even when Reveal Codes is not active, you can activate Confirm on Delete (choose File ➤ Preferences ➤ Environment ➤Confirm on Code Deletion). This option makes WordPerfect for Windows act more like earlier versions of WordPerfect, where if you attempt to delete a code from the regular Edit screen, you are prompted for permission first.

If you want to *globally* delete all the codes in a document, (for example, delete all the codes for boldface), you can use the Replace feature, discussed in Chapter 9.

Moving and Copying Codes

When you move or copy selected text that contains codes, the codes are moved or copied with the selected text. So rarely do you need to move or copy a single code or set of codes. However, once in a while you may want to move codes and not neighboring text, such as when you want to reposition a figure or footnote.

Moving a Single Code To move a single code, follow these steps:

1. If you have not done so already, activate Reveal Codes.

2. Move the insertion point to the code you want to move, so the entire code is highlighted.

3. Press Delete to delete the code.

4. Move the insertion point to the new location for the code.

5. Choose **E**dit ➤ U**n**delete (or press Alt+Shift+Backspace).

6. Choose **R**estore.

The code is inserted at the new insertion-point position.

Using Select to Move or Copy Codes If you want to copy a single code, or move or copy several codes, you can use the text selection feature:

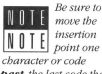

*Be sure to move the insertion point one character or code **past** the last code that you want to include in the selection.*

1. If you have not done so already, turn on Reveal Codes.

2. Move the insertion point to the first code that you want to move or copy, so the code is highlighted.

3. Press F8 and use the arrow keys to extend the selection, or move the insertion point to the last code, then hold down the Shift key and click the left mouse button. This can be tricky, because the selection area is not highlighted in Reveal Codes. However, the start of the selected area is marked by a [Select] code, and the current insertion-point position is highlighted in Reveal Codes. Just be sure that all the codes you want to move or copy are between the [Select] code and the highlight marking the end of the selection.

4. If you want to move the codes, choose **E**dit ➤ Cu**t**. Otherwise, to copy the codes, choose **E**dit ➤ **C**opy.

5. Move the insertion point to the new position for the codes, and choose **E**dit ➤ **P**aste.

CLOSING REVEAL CODES

To remove the Reveal Codes portion of a document window, do either of the following:

◆ Drag the Reveal Codes bar all the way to the top or bottom of the document window.

◆ Choose **V**iew ➤ **R**eveal Codes (or press Alt+F3) again.

USING AUTO CODE

Some codes are designed specifically to format an entire paragraph; some codes format an entire page. If you do not place these codes at the beginning of the appropriate paragraph or page, you may not get what you expect. To prevent such mishaps, WordPerfect offers Auto Code Placement.

NOTE *Line spacing is discussed in Chapter 4.*

Auto Code also prevents "code clutter" and competing codes that cancel one another out, common problems in earlier versions of WordPerfect. When Auto Code is on, codes inserted when you choose certain formatting features may not be placed at the exact insertion-point position, and new codes may automatically delete old codes. For example, suppose there's a [Ln Spacing:2] code at the beginning of a paragraph, for double spacing. If you change the line spacing to 3 anywhere in that paragraph, the new [Ln Spacing:3] code is automatically placed at the beginning of the paragraph and *replaces* the existing [Ln Spacing:2] code. The entire paragraph will be triple-spaced.

On the other hand, if Auto Code Placement is off when you insert the code for triple line spacing, the new code is inserted wherever the insertion point is at the moment, and the old [Ln Spacing:2] code remains in its original position. Any text between the [Ln Spacing:2] and [Ln Spacing:3] codes will be double-spaced. Text to the right of the [Ln Spacing:3] code (even within the same paragraph) will be triple-spaced.

Initially, the Auto Code feature is turned on when you first start Word-Perfect. You can activate or deactivate Auto Code Placement by using File ➤ Preferences ➤ Environment, as discussed in Chapter 13. When Auto Code Placement is off, WordPerfect for Windows code placement is identical to that of earlier versions of WordPerfect.

Table 3.1 lists the formatting features that are affected by Auto Code and where their codes are placed when Auto Code Placement is active.

USING DOCUMENT COMMENTS

TO INSERT A DOCUMENT COMMENT AT THE CURRENT INSERTION-POINT POSITION,

choose Tools ➤ Comment ➤ Create, type your comment, and click OK.

NOTE *A comment can contain up to 1024 characters.*

If you work in groups, or if you like to write notes to yourself as you write, or if you are one member of an author/editor team, you'll probably find *document comments* handy in your work. This feature lets you add notes to your

FEATURE	BEGINNING OF PARAGRAPH	BEGINNING OF PAGE
Columns	X	
Hyphenation Zone	X	
Justification	X	
Letter Spacing	X	
Line Height	X	
Line Numbering	X	
Line Spacing	X	
Margins (Left/Right)	X	
Margins (Top/Bottom)		X
Page Centering	X	
Page Numbering		X
Page Size	X	
Paragraph Numbering	X	
Suppress		X
Tab Set	X	
Word Spacing	X	
Word Spacing Justification Limits	X	

TABLE 3.1:

Where Formatting Codes Are Placed When Auto Code Placement Is On

document that stand out clearly from the rest of the text on your screen. Figure 3.13 shows an example in which a document comment has been used to drop a note to an author.

Another advantage of document comments is that they don't appear on the printed document. This allows you to review a clean copy of the manuscript without the distraction of the comments, then add or review comments on the screen, as required.

To add a comment to a document, follow these steps:

1. Position the insertion point where you want the comment to appear.

2. Choose **Tools** ➤ Comment ➤ Create. You'll see this dialog box:

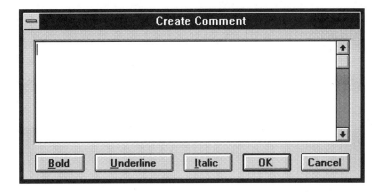

3. Type your comment, using the standard editing keys to make changes and corrections. If you want to break a line, press Ctrl+↵ rather than just ↵.

4. When you're finished, click the OK button.

The comment appears in the document window.

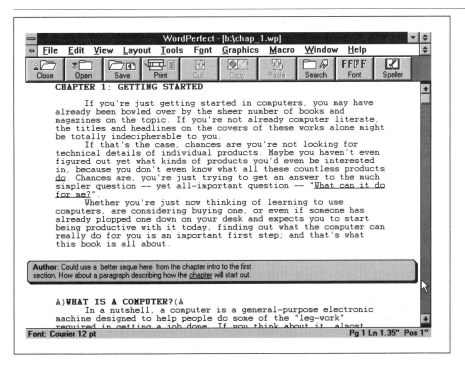

FIGURE 3.13:

A sample comment in the document window, inserted by selecting Tools ➤ Comment ➤ Create.

While typing your comment, you can activate and deactivate boldface, underline, or italics by clicking the appropriate button at the bottom of the dialog box. For example, to boldface a few words in the comment, click the Bold button, type the boldface text, then click the Bold button again to resume typing normal text. You can also select any existing text in the comment to make changes to it, using the usual text selection techniques.

CHANGING A DOCUMENT COMMENT

You can use the Search feature (Chapter 9) to locate comments easily.

If you need to change the text within a document comment,

1. Move the insertion point just below the comment you want to change.

2. Choose **Tools** ➤ Comment ➤ **Edit**. This takes you back to the same dialog box you used to create the comment.

3. Make whatever changes you wish with the usual editing keys and optional buttons.

4. Click the OK button.

MOVING, COPYING, OR DELETING A COMMENT

Each document comment you create is placed in a hidden [Comment] code at the insertion point. Like all codes, the [Comment] code is visible only in Reveal Codes. To move, copy, or delete a [Comment] code (and hence, the comment itself), use the techniques described in "Working with Hidden Codes" earlier in this chapter.

CONVERTING TEXT TO A COMMENT

You can convert any text in a document to a comment. This might come in handy if, say, you cannot decide whether or not to leave a particular passage in text, but don't want to delete it completely. Follow these steps:

1. Select the text that you want to convert to a comment (up to 1024 characters).

2. Choose **Tools** ➤ Comment ➤ **Create**.

The selected text will be displayed within a comment and removed from the regular text.

CONVERTING A COMMENT TO TEXT

If you want to convert a document comment to normal text within the document, follow these steps:

1. Move the insertion point just below the comment you want to convert to text.

2. Choose **Tools** ➤ Comment ➤ Convert to **Text**.

The text within the comment is converted to normal text, and the [Comment] code is removed. If necessary, add spaces or hard returns to blend the text correctly with existing text.

HIDING DOCUMENT COMMENTS

Comments do not appear on the Print Preview screen.

If you want to hide document comments on the screen so that you can focus on editing the regular text,

◆ Choose **View** ➤ Comments so that menu option is no longer checked.

To take the comments back out of hiding, reselect **View** ➤ Comments.

PRINTING DOCUMENT COMMENTS

There is no direct way to print a document comment within its box; you must convert it to text first. Optionally, you can display text in a framed graphic box (Chapter 19).

INSERTING A DATE

TO INSERT THE CURRENT DATE IN YOUR DOCUMENT WITHOUT HAVING TO TYPE IT,

choose Tools ➤ Date, then either Text or Code. Or press Ctrl+F5 for the date text, or Ctrl+Shift+F5 for the date code.

A simple, though handy, feature of WordPerfect is its ability to *date-stamp* a document. There are obviously lots of occasions for using dates in documents, such as the date at the top of a business letter or a memo, or perhaps a date used to indicate the current revision or printing of a document.

There are two types of dates you can type:

NOTE *The system clock is the calendar/ clock built into most computers. You can set the correct date and time by using the Windows Control Panel or the DATE and TIME commands in DOS.*

Date Text:types the current date, as determined by the system clock; the date never changes.

Date Code:enters a code that appears as the current system date; the date automatically changes when the system date changes.

Date Text is useful when you want to type a dated document and never want that date to change. Date Code is useful when you want the date to change. For example, if you plan to print multiple revisions of the same document, you might want to use the Date Code feature to always display the date of the most recent printing. If you plan to print a mass mailing that will take several days, you might want to use the Date Code feature to reflect accurately the date on which each letter is printed.

CHOOSING A DATE FORMAT

Regardless of whether you use Date Code or Date Text to enter the current date and time in your document, you can first define a format for displaying the date.

1. Choose **Tools** ➤ **Date** ➤ Format. You'll see this dialog box:

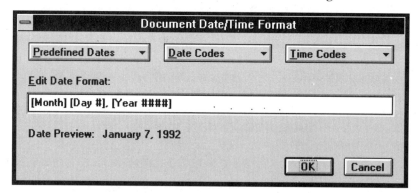

2. To choose a predefined date format, move the mouse pointer to the **P**redefined D**a**tes button. Hold down the left mouse button, move the highlight bar to the format you want, then release the mouse button. Optionally, use the **D**ate Codes and **T**ime Codes options, described a little later, to create your own date format.

3. When the sample date next to the Date Preview prompt shows the date format you want, click OK.

The date won't appear yet, but any dates that you insert in any document from this time forward will use the new date format (until, of course, you choose some other date format).

INSERTING THE DATE

1. Position the insertion point where you want to insert a date.

2. Choose **T**ools ➤ **D**ate.

3. Choose either **T**ext or **C**ode, depending on which kind of date you want to insert.

The date is displayed at the insertion-point position. If you chose Text, no codes are inserted, only the text of the code. If you chose Code, a [Date:] code, which includes the format of the date, is inserted in the document, though the date appears as normal text in the document window.

If you want to change the format of a date that's displayed with a [Date:] code, you first must delete the existing [Date:] code (you can use Reveal Codes to help with this). Then follow the procedures above to choose a new date format, and insert the date.

CREATING A CUSTOM DATE FORMAT

If none of the predefined date formats matches your needs, you can create your own date format:

1. Choose **T**ools ➤ **D**ate ➤ **F**ormat to get to the Document Date/Time Format dialog box shown earlier. Optionally, select a predefined date that most closely matches the date format you want, just to use it as a starting point.

2. Click the text box under **E**dit Date Format (or press Alt+E) to move the insertion point into that text box.

3. You can use the normal editing keys within the text box. For example, you can use the mouse or arrow keys to position the insertion point, select text or codes with the mouse or Shift and arrow keys, and delete text or codes with Delete or Backspace.

4. Move the insertion point to where you want to insert a date or time code, or text (including a blank space).

5. Type the text to insert, or press the spacebar to insert a space. Or, to insert a code, move the mouse pointer to the Date Codes button or

If you want your date format to include blank spaces between codes, be sure to insert those spaces in the date format with the spacebar.

Time Codes button, depending on which type of code you want to insert. Hold down the left mouse button, then move the mouse to highlight any one of the available options. (Table 3.2 shows examples of codes and sample date formats.) Release the mouse button when the option you want is highlighted.

The code is inserted in the text box, and the Date Preview example is updated to reflect the current format. You can repeat Steps 3–5 until the date is in the format you want. Then click OK or press ↵ to return to the document window.

CODES	EXAMPLE
[Month 0#]/[Day 0#]/[Year ##]	01/01/92
[Hour(12) #]:[Minute #] [AM/PM]	2:00 pm
[Abbr. Weekday], [Month #]/[Day #]	Tue, 12/31
[Weekday] at [Hour(12) #]:[Minute #]	Friday at 1:00

TABLE 3.2:

Examples of Custom Date and Time Formats

You'll notice that some date and time codes offer *zero* pad, and some offer *space* pad. This determines how single-digit numbers are padded, if at all. Examples are shown below:

1/1/92	No padding
1/ 1/92	Space pad
01/01/92	Zero pad

USING DRAFT MODE

As an alternative to using the graphical editing mode of WordPerfect, you can edit text in *draft mode*. In draft mode, graphics are displayed as empty boxes, and print attributes are colored rather than shown in WYSIWYG (What You See Is What You Get) fashion. For example, Figure 3.14 shows the sample printer.tst document, shown in earlier examples in this chapter, in draft mode.

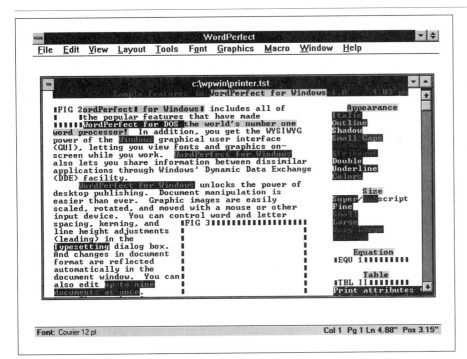

FIGURE 3.14:

Draft mode mimics the WordPerfect for DOS Edit screen. To switch between draft mode and the graphical mode, choose View ➤ Draft Mode.

Use File ➤ Preferences ➤ Display ➤ Draft Mode Colors to color the Draft Mode screen.

There are two reasons why you might want to use draft mode:

◆ If you are creating a complex document with graphics, and it takes too long to update the screen when scrolling, you can switch to draft mode to hide the graphics.

◆ If you are accustomed to earlier versions of WordPerfect (for DOS), you'll find the screen in draft mode to be nearly identical to the Edit screen.

To switch to draft mode (or from draft mode back to the graphical interface)

◆ Choose **View** ➤ **D**raft Mode.

USING THE SHORT MENUS

As an alternative to using the full menu system, you can use an abbreviated menu system that includes only the most commonly used WordPerfect features. To switch to short menus, or to switch from the short menus back to the full menus,

◆   Choose **View** ➤ Short **M**enus.

This chapter has presented a wide range of general features that can be useful in all types of work. If you're new to word processing (or Windows), all of this may seem a bit overwhelming at the moment. But remember, you can always refer back to this chapter when you need a reminder on how to use a specific feature. You can also take Lesson 3 in Part 9 to get some hands-on experience.

Chapter 4 will hone your typing and editing skills by teaching you basic document formatting, such as spacing, indenting, and aligning your text. You'll find many of the features that you learned about in this chapter useful along the way.

PART TWO

Formatting Your Documents

Part 2 builds upon the basic skills you learned in Part 1, giving you more control over the format and appearance of your printed documents. You'll learn to indent, align, and justify text; to embellish your document with fonts, lines, and special characters; to create tables and other multicolumn documents; and to format longer, multi-page documents. You'll also learn to take advantage of whatever features your printer offers. In the process, you'll not only refine your word processing skills but will also begin delving into the realm of desktop publishing.

CHAPTER 4

FEATURING

Spacing, Aligning, and Indenting Text

HANDS-ON
....
LESSON 4

For hands-on practice in using some of the features described in this chapter, see Lesson 4 in Part 9.

Many typing and writing tasks require spacing, justifying, indenting, and aligning text. As you'll discover in this chapter, WordPerfect offers much more flexibility in these areas than even the most sophisticated typewriter. As just one small example, on a typewriter, you must set your tab stops before you type. But with WordPerfect, you can change the tab stops *after* you've typed your text, and your text will adjust to the new stops.

ACTIVATING THE RULER

Many of the features and options described in this chapter are available from the ruler. You can turn the ruler on and off by selecting View ➤ Ruler from the menus or by pressing Alt+Shift+F3. Figure 4.1 shows the ruler and points out the locations of various buttons and icons used in this chapter.

CHANGING LINE SPACING

▌ TO CHANGE THE LINE SPACING,

position the insertion point where you want to change the spacing, click the Line Spacing button in the ruler, and choose one of the three spacing options in the list box. Or, select Layout ➤ Line ➤ Spacing, and enter the line spacing measurement you wish.

You can change the line spacing anywhere in your document and in as many different places as you want.

If you use a typewriter to type a single-spaced document, only to find that it should have been double-spaced, you have no choice but to retype the entire document. In WordPerfect, however, retyping isn't necessary. You can just click on a button or use the menus to change the line spacing to any measurement you wish.

1. Move the insertion point to the first character of the line where you want to change the line spacing (or to where you're about to type new text).

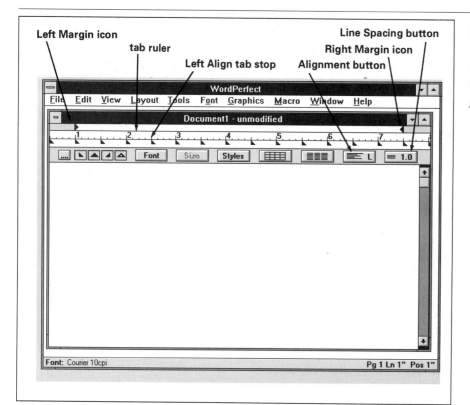

FIGURE 4.1:

The ruler, with buttons and icons that are relevant to this chapter pointed out

2. Click the Line Spacing button in the ruler (shown at left).

3. Drag the arrow to a new line-spacing selection in the list box.

As an alternative to using the ruler to adjust line spacing, you can choose Layout ➤ Line ➤ Spacing (or press Shift+F9 S) in step 2. You'll see the Line Spacing dialog box shown below. Click the up or down arrow button to move the line-spacing value higher or lower, or simply enter the value.

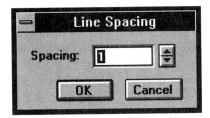

When entering a line-spacing value, you can enter fractions. For example, *1* is single spacing, *1.5* is one-and-a-half spacing, and *2* is double spacing. Figure 4.2 shows examples of all three. You can enter virtually any value when choosing your line spacing (e.g., *3* for triple spacing, *4* for quadruple spacing, *1.25* for one-and-a-quarter spacing, *1.10* for one-and-a-tenth spacing, and so on). Remember, your printer must be able to support the spacing values you enter. For example, dot-matrix printers may not be able to handle fractional spacing in smaller than half-line (.5) increments. If in doubt, refer to your printer manual.

The code on the Reveal Codes portion of the screen for a line-spacing change is [Ln Spacing:] followed by the current spacing (e.g., [Ln Spacing:2] for double spacing). When you change the spacing, all text to the right of and below the insertion-point position is spaced accordingly, up to the next [Ln Spacing:] code (if any) in the document.

TROUBLESHOOTING LINE-SPACING PROBLEMS

NOTE *When Auto Code Placement is on, the [Ln Spacing:] code is moved to the beginning of the current paragraph automatically, and replaces any [Ln Spacing:] code that might have already been there.*

If WordPerfect seems to ignore your request when you change the line spacing, it's probably because a previous [Ln Spacing] code is canceling the new one. Move the insertion point to the first character of the line where you chose a new line-spacing value. Open Reveal Codes by choosing View ➤ Reveal Codes (or pressing Alt+F3), and check for any multiple [Ln Spacing:] codes, like these:

[Ln Spacing:2][Ln Spacing:1]

Single spacing

Here is a paragraph that uses the default single spacing. To change the line spacing, position the cursor wherever you want to change the spacing (either before or after typing the text). Then use the Line Spacing button on the Ruler, or choose Layout ▸ Line ▸ Spacing from the menus. Choose or enter a number.

Double spacing

Here is a paragraph that uses the double spacing (2). To select

double spacing, position the cursor wherever you want to start

double spacing (either before or after typing the text). Then use

the Line Spacing button on the ruler, or choose Layout ▸ Line ▸

Spacing from the menus. Choose or enter **2**.

One-and-a-half spacing

You can enter fractions when defining your line spacing. For

example, this text uses one-and-a-half spacing, typed as either 1.5

or 1 1/2 when defining the line spacing. WordPerfect lets you set

the line spacing to just about any number - you're not at all

limited to 1, 1.5, and 2.

FIGURE 4.2:

Single (1), double (2), and one-and-a-half (1.5) spacing

In this example, the second code is canceling the first one, so if you wanted double spacing, you'd need to delete the [Ln Spacing:1] code. You can also undo a line-spacing change immediately by choosing Edit ➤ Undo from the Edit menu (or pressing Alt+Backspace).

If your printer prints at double the spacing you requested (e.g., you want single spacing, but it prints double), chances are the Auto Line-Feed or Auto LF setting on your printer is turned on. See your printer manual to learn how to turn this switch off.

CHANGING THE MARGINS

WordPerfect places a default 1-inch margin around every printed page of your document, as Figure 4.3 shows. But you can change the margins at any time, either before or after typing your document.

As with all formatting options, WordPerfect adjusts margins by inserting hidden codes at the current insertion point. Therefore, if you want to change

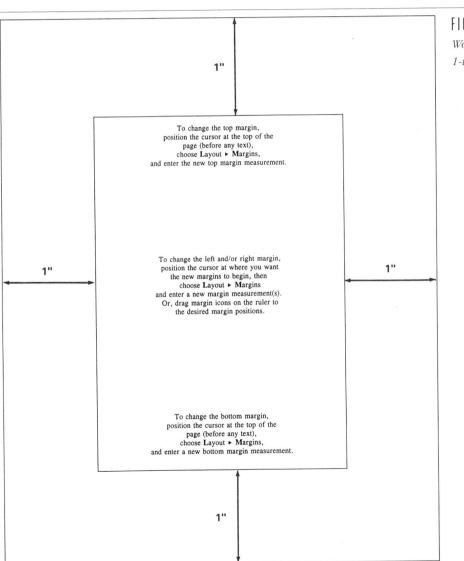

FIGURE 4.3:

WordPerfect's standard 1-inch margins

1"

1"

1"

1"

To change the top margin, position the cursor at the top of the page (before any text), choose **Layout ▸ Margins**, and enter the new top margin measurement.

To change the left and/or right margin, position the cursor at where you want the new margins to begin, then choose **Layout ▸ Margins** and enter a new margin measurement(s). Or, drag margin icons on the ruler to the desired margin positions.

To change the bottom margin, position the cursor at the top of the page (before any text), choose **Layout ▸ Margins**, and enter a new bottom margin measurement.

You don't need to change the margins to indent a single paragraph. You can use the indent keys instead, as discussed later.

the margins for an entire document, you should start by moving the insertion point to the top of the document (press Ctrl+Home), before you change the margin settings. If you want to change the margins for only a particular section of a document, move the insertion point to the top of that section before changing the margins.

CHANGING THE LEFT AND RIGHT MARGINS

TO CHANGE THE LEFT AND RIGHT MARGINS,

Move the insertion point to where you want to change the margins, and drag the Left and Right Margin icons in the ruler to the new margin positions, or choose Layout ➤ Margins (Ctrl+F8) to display the Margins dialog box. Enter new margin values in the Left and Right boxes, and click OK.

To use the ruler to change the left and right margins in a document, follow these steps:

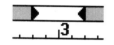

1. Position the insertion point where you want the new left and right margins to start.

2. Drag the Left and Right Margin icons to the new margin positions.

As an alternative to using the ruler, you can enter exact margin measurements by following these steps:

1. Move the insertion point to where you want to change the margin settings.

A quicker way to display the Margins dialog box is simply to double-click on either the Left or Right Margin icon in the ruler.

2. Choose **Layout** ➤ **Margins** (Ctrl+F8) to display the Margins dialog box.

3. Type a measurement for the left margin in inches, such as *2* for 2 inches or *1.5* for 1½ inches, then press Tab (or Alt+R).

4. Type a measurement for the right margin (again using a whole number or a decimal).

5. Choose OK or press ↵ to return to the document portion of the screen.

All text below the insertion-point position is automatically reformatted to fit in the new margins.

CHANGING THE TOP AND BOTTOM MARGINS

TO CHANGE THE TOP AND BOTTOM MARGINS,

move the insertion point to the top of the page where you want the new margins to take effect, and choose Layout ➤ Margins (Ctrl+F8) to display the Margins dialog box. Enter the new values for the top and bottom margins, and choose OK or press ↵.

To change the top and bottom margins on the printed page, follow these steps:

1. Position the insertion point at the top of the page where you want the new top or bottom margin to start (the insertion point must be placed before any text on the page).

2. Choose **L**ayout ➤ **M**argins (Ctrl+F8) to display the Margins dialog box.

3. Press Tab twice (or press Alt+T) to move to the Top margin box. Type a measurement for the top margin, such as *2* for 2 inches or *1.5* for 1½ inches, and press Tab (or Alt+B) to move to the Bottom margin box.

4. Type a measurement for the bottom margin (again using a whole number or decimal).

5. Choose OK or press ↵ to return to the document window.

You may want to check the Print Preview screen at Full Page size (Pages ➤ Full Page) to verify your change.

CHANGING OR DELETING MARGIN SETTINGS

If you have problems printing text within the margins, it may be because the paper is misaligned in your printer (see Chapter 8).

Sometimes, finding the best margins for printing a document involves a little trial and error. If you change your mind about the margin settings in a document, you can delete the hidden codes used to adjust the margins and replace them with new codes (by following the steps above to change the margins).

Reveal Codes shows the left and right margin settings as the code [L/R Mar:] followed by the left and right margin measurements. The code for the top and bottom margins appears as [T/B Mar:] followed by the top and bottom margin measurements.

To delete a margin code in Reveal Codes, follow these steps:

1. Position the insertion point in the general area of the margin change.

2. Choose **V**iew ➤ Reveal **C**odes (or press Alt+F3).

3. Move the insertion point as necessary to highlight the conflicting margin code (remember, if two codes are next to each other, the one to the right, or nearer to the following text, will be the controlling code).

4. Press the Delete key to delete the conflicting code.

TROUBLESHOOTING MARGIN PROBLEMS

When Auto Code Placement is on, the [L/R Mar.] code is moved to the beginning of the current paragraph automatically. The [T/B Mar.] code is automatically moved to the top of the page.

If WordPerfect seems to ignore your request for new margin settings, it may be that a previous [L/R Mar:] or [T/B Mar:] code is canceling your most recent request. For example, in the sequence of codes below, the code for using 0.75-inch left and right margins does nothing, because it's followed by a code that immediately changes the margins to 1.5 inches:

[L/R Mar:.75",.75"][L/R Mar:1.5",1.5"]Four score and

To use the 0.75-inch margins, you'd need to delete the [L/R Mar:1.5",1.5"] code.

Also, be aware that if WordPerfect encounters a [T/B Mar:] code in your document *after* it has already started printing the page, the new top and bottom margins will not take effect until the next page. This is why it's important to change the top and bottom margins at the very top of the page where you want the new margins to take effect.

Minimum Margin Widths

The "dead zone" is at the outer edges of the page, where the printer cannot print.

Laser and other printers that feed paper from a tray do so with small wheels that pull the paper by its edges through the printer. The outer edges of the page make up what is called the "dead zone," because the printer cannot print there. (If text were printed within the dead zone, the small wheels would likely smudge the printed text.)

You cannot set the margins to a value that falls within the dead zone. For example, if you try to set the margins to 0", WordPerfect automatically increases your margin measurement to compensate for the dead zone, typically a value between 0.20 and 0.30 inches.

ALIGNING AND JUSTIFYING TEXT

TO CHANGE THE ALIGNMENT OF A PARAGRAPH OR SELECTED TEXT,

move the insertion point to where you want to change the alignment, select the paragraph or text to be changed, click the Alignment button in the ruler, and choose the new alignment option, or choose Layout ➤ Justification ➤ Left (Crtl+L), Right (Ctrl+R), Center (Ctrl+J), or Full (Ctrl+F).

There are several ways to align and justify written text, as summarized below:

Left justification: Only the left margin is justified (smooth); the right margin is ragged.

Right justification: Text is smooth and flush against the right margin; the left margin is ragged.

Center justification: Text is evenly positioned between the left and right margins.

Full justification: Both the left and right margins are smooth.

Figure 4.4 shows examples of the various types of justification.

The basic steps for justifying text are as follows:

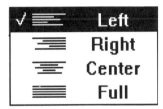

1. Position the insertion point where you want to change justification, whether it's at the first character of existing text or where you are about to start typing new text.

2. Click the Alignment button in the ruler, and choose the new justification. Or, choose **L**ayout ➤ **J**ustification from the pull-down menus and choose a justification style (**L**eft, **R**ight, **C**enter, or **F**ull).

At this point, all text to the right of and below the insertion point is justified according to your choice. However, you can repeat the steps above anywhere in the document to change to some other form of justification. I'll talk about each type of justification and some shortcuts in the sections that follow.

LEFT-JUSTIFYING TEXT

Left justification is the default justification option; that is, if you do not activate any other type of justification, your text will be left-justified. However, once you do activate some other form of justification, all text beneath that place in the document takes on the justification you specify.

If you want to return to left justification elsewhere in the document, you must position the insertion point where you want to reinstate left justification and follow the general steps for justifying text above to select left justification.

Left justification creates a typewritten look and is often used for form letters that are supposed to look as if they were typed personally. Left justification also removes the extra white space added between letters and words in full

*The jus-
tification
button's
appearance
will change only after
you have selected
another type of
justification.*

justification, thereby reducing the "rivers" of white space that often flow through text that's fully justified. Another way to reduce "rivers" of white space in fully justified text is with hyphenation (Chapter 11).

FULLY JUSTIFYING TEXT

Fully justifying text produces a smooth white margin and presents a word-processed or published look rather than a typewritten look. To smooth out the right margin, WordPerfect inserts space between words and letters, as required. The disadvantage of full justification is that it can cause loose lines

---

Full Justification_____

Unless you tell it otherwise, WordPerfect will print paragraphs with full justification, where both the left and right margins are smooth. Full justification is one of the hallmarks of documents created with a word processor instead of a typewriter. But in order to get both the left and right margins smooth, WordPerfect needs to add space between words and letters. This, in turn, can make the text look "gappy," and even produce rivers of white space running down the page in large documents.

Left Justification_____

Left justification produces a ragged-right margin, as in this example. This is often used to create a personalized "hand-typed" look. This justification method also removes the extra gaps between words and letters, and any rivers of white running down the page, because there's no need to add spacing text to reach the right margin.

Center Justification_____

An Example of Center-Justified Text
by
N.E. Buddee

August 18, 1991

Right Justification_____

Rightly Justified, Inc.
1234 Walla Walla Lane
P.O. Box 1234
Cucamonga, CA 91234

FIGURE 4.4:

Various types of justification

(extra white space between words and letters) and "rivers" of white space running down the page.

Automatic hyphenation (Chapter 11) can help reduce some of the white space caused by full justification. You can also change how WordPerfect places blank spaces between words and letters by changing the word-spacing justification limits, as described in Chapter 20.

CENTERING TEXT

Centering text is so common that there are actually a couple of ways to do it, either by justification, when you want to center several lines of text (such as all the text on a title page), or by alignment, when you want to center one or a few lines on a page. The result is the same: The text is centered between the margins. Choosing one technique over the other is simply a matter of deciding what's more convenient at the moment.

Centering a Short Line

If you want to center just a single short line, such as a title, follow these steps:

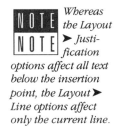

Whereas the Layout ➤ Justi-fication options affect all text below the insertion point, the Layout ➤ Line options affect only the current line.

1. Position the insertion point where you are about to type the short line or at the start of the short line if you've already typed it.

2. Choose **Layout ➤ Line ➤ Center** or press Shift+F7.

3. If you have not already done so, type your short text and press ↵. If you have already typed (and now centered) a short line, press the End key, then ↓ or ↵.

Following these steps centers only the current line, rather than all text beneath the insertion point. The hidden code for centering a single short line is [Center]. You can remove the code if you change your mind about centering the short line (or use Edit ➤ Undo if you change your mind immediately).

Centering Several Lines

Word-Perfect can also center text verti-cally, between the top and bottom margins, as you'll learn in Chapter 7.

If you want to center several lines of text, you may find it easier to turn on center justification above (or to the left of) the first line you want centered. Then, to reinstate some other form of justification, move the insertion point below (or to the right of) the last centered line, and activate some other form of justification.

The hidden code for activating centering for all text to the right and below is [Just:Center], which you can move or remove if you change your mind about center justification.

RIGHT-JUSTIFYING TEXT

Like centering, right justification (text is flush right) is pretty common, so WordPerfect offers an easy way to right-justify a single line, as well as groups of lines.

Right-Justifying a Short Line

If you just want to right-justify a single short line, follow these steps:

1. Position the insertion point where you are about to type the short line or at the start of the short line if you've already typed it.

2. Choose **L**ayout ➤ **L**ine ➤ **F**lush Right or press Alt+F7.

3. If you have not already done so, type your text and press ↵.

4. If you have already typed (and now right-justified) a short line, press the End key, then ↓ or ↵.

If you change your mind about a single right-justified line of text, remove the hidden [Flsh Rgt] code at the start of that line, using Reveal Codes (press Alt+F3). Optionally, if you just made the change, choose Edit ➤ Undo.

Right-Justifying Several Lines

When Auto Code Placement is on, it places the [Just:] code at the beginning of the current paragraph.

If you want to right-justify several lines of text, you may find it easier to turn on right justification at the point where you want it to begin (choose Layout ➤ Justification ➤ Right). This method inserts a hidden [Just:Right] code at the insertion-point position, right-justifying all text to the right of and below the insertion point. As usual, you can move or remove the [Just:Right] code should you later change your mind about right justification (or choose Edit ➤ Undo if you change your mind immediately).

A SHORTCUT FOR JUSTIFYING SELECTED TEXT

Chapter 2 has a complete discussion of techniques for selecting text.

Another quick way to center or right-justify several existing lines of text is to select them first, then choose the justification. This is especially handy because the justification only affects the selected lines. You save time because you don't have to change the justification for any text below the lines you justified. Follow these steps:

1. Select the lines you want to justify.

2. Choose **L**ayout ➤ **L**ine ➤ **C**enter to center the lines (Shift+F7) or **L**ayout ➤ **L**ine ➤ **F**lush Right to right-justify the lines (Alt+F7).

INDENTING PARAGRAPHS

TO INDENT OR HANG A PARAGRAPH,

move the insertion point to the start of the paragraph you want to indent or hang (or where you're about to type that paragraph), and press one of the following keys: Tab, Hanging Indent (Ctrl+F7), Margin Release (Shift+Tab), Indent (F7), or Double Indent (Ctrl+Shift+F7).

There are lots of ways to indent paragraphs, as demonstrated in Figure 4.5. All these indentations are easy to achieve with WordPerfect. Here are the general steps:

1. Move the insertion point to the point at which you want to start typing your paragraph, or if you've already typed the paragraph, move the insertion point to the first character in the paragraph.

2. Depending on what you want, do one of the following:

◆ To indent the first line of the paragraph, press Tab.

◆ To indent the entire left side of the paragraph, choose **L**ayout ➤ **P**aragraph ➤ **I**ndent or press F7.

◆ To indent both the left and right sides of the paragraph, choose **L**ayout ➤ **P**aragraph ➤ **D**ouble Indent or press Ctrl+Shift+F7.

◆ To indent all lines but the first line of the paragraph, called a *hanging* indent, choose **L**ayout ➤ **P**aragraph ➤ **H**anging Indent or press Ctrl+F7.

◆ To hang the first line of a paragraph into the left margin and align the remainder of the paragraph with the left margin (called an *outdent*), choose **L**ayout ➤ **P**aragraph ➤ **M**argin Release (Shift+Tab).

Regardless of how you indent or outdent a paragraph, you can change your mind and unindent or unoutdent the text.

Indenting with Tab

    If you just want to indent the first line of a paragraph, just press Tab before typing the first line. That's how you'd do it on a typewriter, and that's how it was done at the beginning of this paragraph. Of course, if you've already typed the entire paragraph, *then* later decide to indent the first line, just move the cursor to the start of that line and press Tab.

Indenting with Indent (F7)

    If you want to indent the entire left margin, move the cursor to the beginning of the paragraph you want to indent (or where you are about to type a paragraph), and press Indent (F7) as many times as necessary to get the level of indentation you want. The entire left margin of that paragraph will be indented, like this one (typed after pressing Indent twice).

Indenting with Double Indent (Ctrl+Shift+F7)

    If you want to indent both the left and right margins, as when typing a long quotation, move the cursor to the beginning of the paragraph you want to indent (or where you are about to type a paragraph), and press Double Indent (Ctrl+Shift+F7) as many times as necessary to get the level of indentation you want.

Hanging (outdenting) the First Line

If you want to indent all the lines *beneath* the first line in a paragraph, move the cursor to the beginning of that paragraph (or where you are about to start typing that paragraph), then press Hanging Indent (Ctrl+F7).

Hanging (outdenting) into the Left Margin

If you want to hang the first line of a paragraph out into the margin, move the cursor to the beginning of that paragraph (or where you are about to start typing that paragraph), then press Margin Release (Shift+Tab).

REMOVING INDENTS AND OUTDENTS

    If you change your mind about an indent or outdent in a paragraph, you can simply remove the hidden codes that are controlling the indent or outdent at

If you want to change the amount of indentation (or out-dentation), change the tab stops, as described later in this chapter.

the start of the paragraph. If you change your mind immediately, just choose Edit ➤ Undo. If it has been a while, follow these steps:

1. Move the insertion point to the start of the paragraph that you want to unindent or unoutdent.

2. Open Reveal Codes by choosing **V**iew ➤ Reveal **C**odes (or by pressing Alt+F3).

3. Delete the code controlling the indent or outdent.

The hidden codes for indentations are pretty obvious when you see them in Reveal Codes. They are listed below:

Tab	[Tab]
Indent	[Indent]
Double Indent	[Dbl Indent]
Hanging Indent	[Indent][Mar Rel]
Margin Release	[Mar Rel]

If your indents and outdents seem wildly out of control on the screen, you may just need to redraw the screen (press Page Down, then Page Up). If that doesn't clear things up, you'll need to use Reveal Codes to see whether any extraneous or missing codes are to blame.

TYPING LISTS

TO TYPE A BASIC NUMBERED (OR OTHER TYPE) OF LIST,

Type the number or special character that identifies the item in the list, press Indent (F7), type the text of that item, and press ↵ once or twice to start the next item in the list.

Bullets, pointing hands, and other special characters are described in more detail in Chapter 5.

Short lists are easy to type; Figure 4.6 shows some examples. Follow these steps to type each item in the list:

1. If you want to indent the item number or letter (or bullet, pointing hand, or check box) from the left margin, press Tab until you've indented far enough.

2. Type the item number, letter, bullet, or other special character.

Numbered List _____

1.   To type a numbered list, type the number (and perhaps a period) that identifies the item (e.g., 1. next to this item).

2.   Press Indent (F7) or Double Indent (Ctrl+Shift+F7) if you want to indent text from both sides.

3.   Type the text (this part).

4.   Press ↵ (once or twice) and repeat the steps above for the next item in the list.

Indenting the Entire List _____

1.   If you want to indent the entire list like this...

2.   Press Tab as many times as necessary to move the cursor out to the tab stop that you want the numbers aligned on, then type the number (e.g., 2.).

3.   Then press Indent (F7) or Double Indent (Ctrl+Shift+F7) and type the text next to the number, as usual.

Changing the Tab Stops _____

1. This list was typed exactly like the one above...

2. But then we changed the tab stops to narrow the gap between the left margin, each number, and its text, as described later in this chapter.

Bulleted List _____

• A bulleted list is the same as a numbered list...

• Except that you type a bullet (a special character) rather than a number to identify each item in the list.

Check List _____
☐ A check list is like any other list...
☐ Except that each item starts with a large hollow square (another special character).
☐ This example is also unique in that it's single-spaced by pressing Enter only once after typing each item.

Pointing List _____
☞ This list is just like any of those above...
☞ except it uses a different special character to the left.

FIGURE 4.6:
Examples of various lists

3. Press Indent (F7) or Double Indent (Ctrl+Shift+F7) if you want to indent the text from both sides.

4. Type the text of the item, and press ↵ (press ↵ twice if you want a blank line between items).

AUTOMATIC NUMBERING

Styles (Chapter 14) can also help you type lists, particularly ones that use special characters.

Rather than type each number in a numbered list or each letter in a lettered list (e.g., *A.*, *B.*, *C.*), you can use *automatic paragraph numbering* or *outlining* (see Chapter 22). These features offer a real advantage, because they automatically adjust all numbers (or letters) in the left column if you add, delete, or move items in your list.

CHANGING THE GAP

The gap between the number (or bullet or other special character) in each item in the list and the text of the item is controlled by the *tab stops*. To narrow or widen the gap, just change the tab stops, as described in the next section.

ABOUT TAB STOPS

You can see the current tab stops when the ruler is turned on.

WordPerfect automatically sets tab stops at every ½ inch, starting at the left margin. Because of this, if you do not change the tab stops, all indents and outdents created with the Tab, Margin Release, Indent, and Double Indent keys will initially be in ½-inch increments. That is, the first level of indentation will be ½ inch from the left margin, the next level will be 1 inch from the left margin, and so forth.

TAB ALIGNMENT

Not only can you change the position of tab stops but you can also determine how text is aligned at each tab stop. Your options are as follows:

 Left Align: Text typed at the tab setting is left-aligned at the tab stop (the usual method).

 Center: is centered at the tab stop.

 Right Align: Text is right-aligned at the tab stop.

 Decimal Align: Text is aligned on a decimal point or some other character.

Dot Leader Tabs: Empty space to the left of the tab stop is filled with dots (used in conjunction with any setting above).

I've already talked about left, center, and right justification in relation to paragraphs and short lines of text (which are really just very short paragraphs, since you end them with a ↵ keypress, like a paragraph). In terms of tab alignment, these same concepts apply to aligning text at the tab stop (or, in other words, to how text is aligned within tabular columns). Figures 4.7 through 4.9 show examples of left, center, right, and decimal alignment, as well as dot leaders. Notice the ruler, which was used to create each example. The next section explains how to change the tab stops with the ruler.

In all fairness, I should warn you that using tab alignments is just one way of typing text in tabular columns. A second, and often much easier method, is to use the Tables feature. (The Tables feature is covered in Chapter 6.) Nonetheless, you need to know some of the basics of using tab stops, even if it's just to control the amount of indenting and outdenting, or the gaps in lists.

TIP: To put the buttons above the ruler, so that your tab stops are closer to your text, choose File ➤ Preferences ➤ Environment, and then choose Ruler Button's on Top from the dialog box (see Chapter 13).

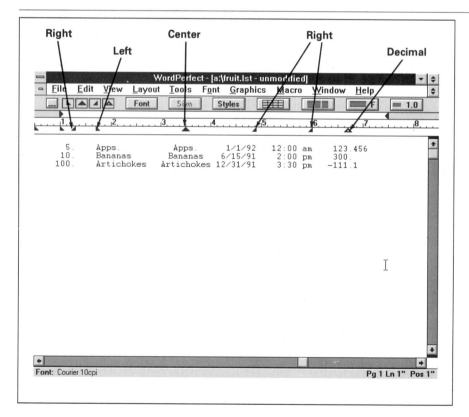

FIGURE 4.7:

Examples of various tab alignments

CHANGING TAB STOPS

TO CHANGE THE TAB STOPS,

move the insertion point above the text where you want to change the tab stops, move the pointer to the ruler, click on the tab stop you want to move, and drag it to its new position.

To change the tab stops using the Ruler, follow these steps:

1. Position the insertion point before the text that requires a different tab stop.

2. If the ruler is not already displayed, choose **View ➤ R**uler (Alt+Shift+F3) to display it.

3. Drag any tab-stop icons in the ruler to a new postition.

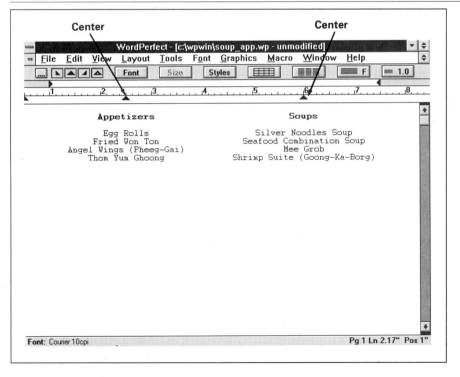

FIGURE 4.8:

An example of two center-aligned tab stops

As an alternative to using the ruler, you can use the menus to change the tab stops, by following these steps:

1. If you want to change tab stops in existing text, position the insertion point at the first character of (or just above) that text. Otherwise, position the insertion point wherever you're about to start typing new text.

2. Choose **L**ayout ➤ **L**ine ➤ **T**ab Set (or press Shift+F9 T). The Tab Set dialog box appears (see Figure 4.10).

3. Click the option button for the type of tab you want to set.

4. Type the number of inches for this tab location in the position box (you can use a decimal or a fraction).

5. Choose **S**et Tab to record the position in the vertical position list box. Optionally you can:

◆ Choose Clear **Ta**b immediately to unrecord the tab position you just set. Or, if you want to go back and change a position you set

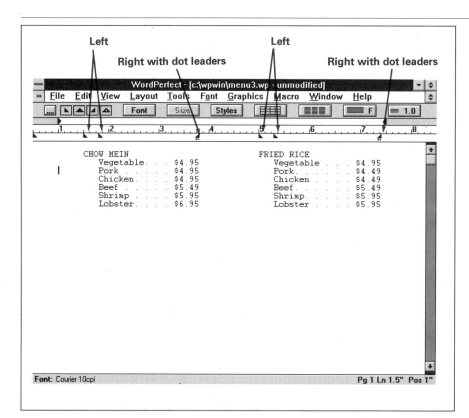

FIGURE 4.9:

An example of dot leaders

earlier, click on the up or down arrows, or scroll to the tab position, click to select it, and choose Clear T**a**b.

◆ Choose Clear Ta**b**s to clear all tabs in the ruler.

◆ Choose De**f**ault to set WordPerfect's default tab stops, a Left Align tab every ½ inch.

◆ If you want tab positions to be relative to the left edge of the paper, choose the Position From Left **E**dge option button. If you want tab stop positions to be relative to the left margin, choose the Position From Left **M**argin option button.

◆ Choose OK or press ↵ to return to the document.

The current tab stops appear in the ruler at the top of the screen. Figure 4.11 shows the default tab stops for WordPerfect. Notice that the ruler is marked in inches, with a larger vertical bar every half inch and smaller vertical ticks every eighth of an inch. Notice also that the ruler begins at 0 (the left edge of the page) and ends at 8½ (the right edge of the page). The tab stops, however, can be adjusted relative to either the left edge of the page or the left margin.

A careful look at Figure 4.11 shows the same text as Figure 4.9, but note that the text in Figure 4.11 is aligned differently and has a different tab line. That's because Figure 4.11 is the *before* shot, using the default tab settings

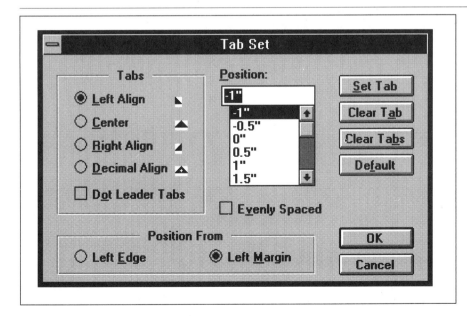

FIGURE 4.10:

The Tab Set dialog box

of ½ inch. Figure 4.9, on the other hand, shows the text alignment and tab ruler *after* finishing the setting of the tab stops.

To modify the tab ruler, you can do any of the following (in any order you wish):

As you adjust the tab ruler, your changes will be reflected in the text below the insertion point.

◆ Change a tab stop by clicking on any tab icon in the ruler and dragging it to a new position.

◆ Change the default Left Align tab to a Right Align tab, Center tab, or Decimal Align tab by clicking on the appropriate tab icon (to the left of the Font button) and dragging it to a new position.

You can select multiple tab stops on the ruler by dragging the mouse pointer through them and releasing the mouse button. Then you can drag the selected tab stops right or left, or delete them by dragging them off the ruler.

◆ Click on any tab icon and drag it down, off the ruler, to delete it. If you immediately change your mind, choose **E**dit ➤ **U**ndo (Alt+Backspace) to undo the deletion.

◆ Change the tab icons in the ruler to Dot Leader tabs by clicking on the Dot Leader box to the left of the icons. Now you can click on a Left Align dot-leader icon, Right Align dot-leader icon, Center dot-leader icon, or Decimal Align dot-leader icon and drag it to its new position in the ruler. Click on the Dot Leader box a second time to change the tab icons back to nonleader tabs.

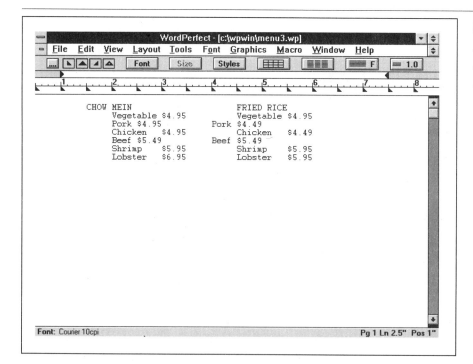

FIGURE 4.11:

Ready to change the tab stops, after choosing Layout ➤ Line ➤ Tab Set

LESSON 4

For a hands-on exercise in setting tabs, see Lesson 4 in Part 9.

Pressing the spacebar repeatedly accounts for the gap between "CHOW MEIN" and the next [Tab] code in the Reveal Codes portion of the screen in Figure 4.12.

When you've finished modifying the tab ruler, simply continue with your typing. All text following the new tab codes will reflect your changes. Text above the current insertion point position will not be affected at all.

USING TAB STOPS

Keep in mind that only the Tab, Margin Release (Shift+Tab), Indent (F7), Hanging Indent (Ctrl+F7), and Double Indent (Ctrl+Shift+F7) keys act on tab stops. The tab stop does nothing until you press one of these keys to move the insertion point to it. For example, to create the two-column menu shown in Figure 4.8, you would need to press Tab before typing the name of an appetizer or a soup to move the insertion point to the next tab stop.

In Figure 4.12, dot leaders do not appear unless you press Tab after typing a Chow Mein or Fried Rice entry. Also, to prevent dot leaders from appearing between the headings "CHOW MEIN" and "FRIED RICE," **CHOW MEIN** was typed, the spacebar was pressed until the insertion point was past the Right Align tab stop, and then Tab was pressed to move to the proper tab stop for aligning "FRIED RICE." Reveal Codes clearly shows these extra spaces before the tab.

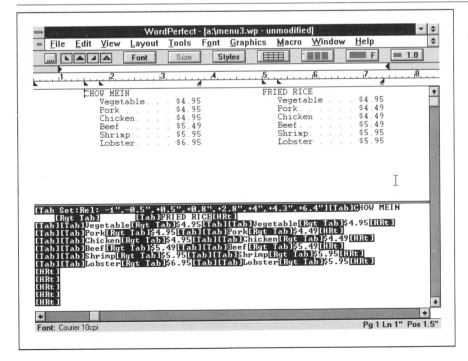

FIGURE 4.12:

The menu, with its final tab settings, as it appears in the Reveal Codes portion of the screen

Effects of Insert and Typeover on Tabs

When working with text that's already tabbed into place, keep in mind these two important points:

◆ When you are in Insert mode, pressing Tab inserts another [Tab] code in the text.

◆ When you are in Typeover mode, pressing Tab simply moves the insertion point to the next tab stop, without inserting a [Tab] code.

Therefore, when you are editing existing text that's already aligned on tab stops, you can press Insert to go to Typeover mode. Then you can press Tab or Shift+Tab to move from column to column without inserting extra tabs and margin releases (which would move the text out of alignment). Of course, you can also use the mouse or arrow keys to position the insertion point without inserting or deleting tabs or margin releases.

HIDDEN CODES FOR THE TAB RULER AND TAB STOPS

The Auto Code feature can help prevent code clutter and problems caused by multiple codes.

Whenever you change the tab stops in a document, WordPerfect inserts a hidden [Tab Set:] code, followed by *Rel* if you used a relative left margin or *Abs* if you used an absolute left margin, and then the position of each tab stop. Like all codes, [Tab] codes can be moved or deleted as you see fit by using Reveal Codes.

Codes appearing outside of the [Tab Set:] code indicate which kind of tab is controlling the position of the text. Normally, when you press the Tab key, a hidden [Tab] code is inserted in the document. This is the "normal" Left Align tab stop used by default.

When you use other types of tab stops, the hidden code inserted in the document depends on the type of tab stop the insertion point lands on when you press Tab, as listed below:

TAB STOP	HIDDEN CODE
Left	[Tab]
Right	[Rgt Tab]
Center	[Cntr Tab]
Decimal	[Dec Tab]

FIXING COMMON ALIGNMENT ERRORS

If you use the Tables feature (Chapter 6), you can avoid these alignment errors.

Three alignment errors are common when using tab stops to align text in columns:

◆ Lines between the columns are wavy instead of straight.

◆ Columns are misaligned because of missing or extra [Tab] (or other tab alignment) codes.

◆ Columns are misaligned because text in one or more columns is wider than the column itself.

Let's look at examples of each.

Fixing Wavy Columns

Figure 4.13 shows an example of printed text that's supposed to be evenly spaced in columns, but appears "wavy" instead. This problem is often caused by using blank spaces between columns (i.e., pressing the spacebar) instead of tabs. It is especially noticeable when you're using proportionally spaced fonts (described in Chapter 5). The only solution is to go back and replace all the blank spaces with tabs (or to start over using the Tables feature).

Fixing Column Misalignments

A second common error occurs when all the text lines up neatly into columns, but occasionally goes out of alignment, as in Davidson's street address and phone number in Figure 4.14.

If you look at the Reveal Codes portion of the screen in Figure 4.14, you'll notice two [Tab] codes in front of Davidson's address. These push the

Number	Date	Description	Deposit	Withdrawal
	8/1/91	Deposit	$1,000	
1001	8/1/91	Rent		$500.00
1002	8/1/91	Utilities		$75.00
1003	8/5/91	Water		$19
1004	8/14/91	Credit Card		$75.00
	8/15/91	Deposit	$1,000	
1005	8/16/91	Ray Co. (clothes)	$167.77	
1006	8/17/91	Dr. Dolittle	$88.00	
1007	8/20/91	WP Seminar	$250.00	

FIGURE 4.13:

Wavy columns caused by using spaces instead of tabs to separate columns

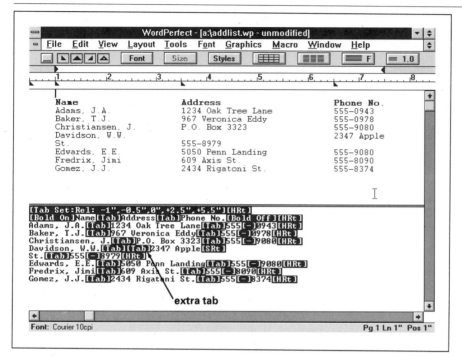

FIGURE 4.14:

*Columns out of
alignment because of
an extra [Tab] code*

address out to the second tab stop. The simple solution is to remove one of the [Tab] codes in front of the address.

Figure 4.15 shows another fairly common alignment problem, which at first glance looks a lot like the preceding problem. However, if you look at the Reveal Codes portion of the screen, you'll see that *every* address has only one [Tab] code in front of it.

So, if there are no extra [Tab] codes, what's causing Christiansen's address in the second column to shoot over to the third column? The answer is that the name in the first column is too wide for that column. Because the name extends past the first tab stop, the next [Tab] code in that column forces the address out to the second tab stop.

The only solution is to change the tab stops at the start of the list (but past the existing [Tab Set:] code) until the first column is wide enough to accommodate the longest (widest) name.

Checking the Tab-Stop Codes

If Auto Code Placement is off when you change the tab ruler, it's important to remember that WordPerfect does not change the existing [Tab Set:] code. Instead,

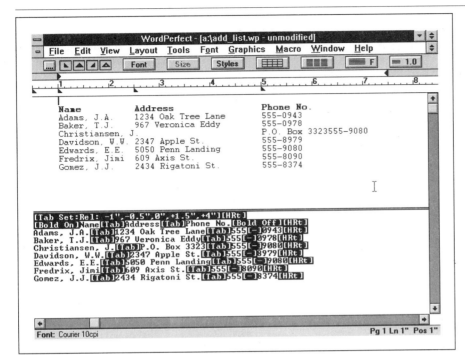

The first column spills into the second.

it inserts a *new* [Tab Set:] code. When two or more [Tab Set:] codes occur in succession in your document, only the tab stops in the *last* code are effective.

If you are having a problem with tab stops, use Reveal Codes to see whether there are multiple [Tab Set:] codes after the problem and delete any that are no longer needed. As discussed under "Refining Tab Stops," it's a good habit to delete an old [Tab Set:] code as soon as it is no longer needed, to prevent code clutter.

When Auto Code placement is on, inserting a [Tab Set:] code anywhere on a line places the code at the beginning of the line. Any subsequent tab-stop changes anywhere on the same line change only the one [Tab Set:] code. When Auto Code placement is off, each tab-stop change results in a new [Tab Set:] code.

Fixing Margin-Release Errors

If you press Margin Release (Shift+Tab) when the insertion point is in the middle of a line of text, some of your text may become garbled, because the back-shifted text overwrites existing text. To remedy this, open Reveal Codes and delete the [Mar Rel] code in the sentence.

Similarly, if you move text into the left margin inadvertently or change your mind about typing text in the left margin, use Reveal Codes to delete the [Mar Rel] code that's pushing the text into the margin.

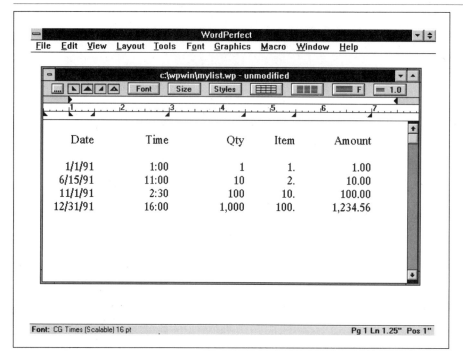

Examples of
right-aligned and
decimal-aligned text

Changing the Decimal Alignment Character

In general, dates, times, and numbers with equal (or no) decimal places look fine when right-aligned, as in Figure 4.16. However, if you right-align numbers with unequal decimal places, the decimal points won't line up vertically, as the left column in Figure 4.17 shows. To fix this problem, you need to decimal-align the numbers. For example, in the second column of Figure 4.17, the numbers are aligned on the decimal point.

You can change the alignment character and thousands separator to better align the British-style numbers. For example, the numbers in the third column in Figure 4.17 are aligned on the comma rather than on the decimal point. To make this change, follow these steps:

1. Move the insertion point just above the numbers you want to realign on a new decimal character or to where you are about to type the numbers you want aligned.

2. Choose **Layout** ➤ **Line** ➤ Special **Co**des (or press Shift+F9 O) to get to the Insert Special Codes dialog box, shown in Figure 4.18.

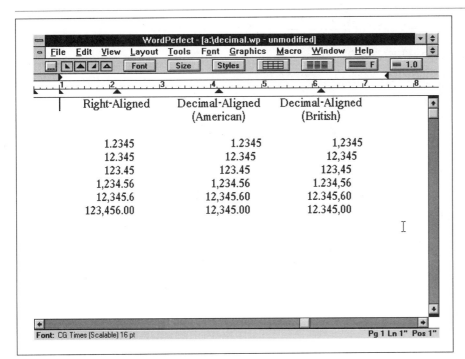

FIGURE 4.17:
Right-aligned numbers, American-style numbers aligned on the decimal point, and British-style numbers aligned on the comma

Right-Aligned	Decimal-Aligned (American)	Decimal-Aligned (British)
1.2345	1.2345	1,2345
12.345	12.345	12,345
123.45	123.45	123,45
1,234.56	1,234.56	1.234,56
12,345.6	12,345.60	12.345,60
123,456.00	12,345.00	12.345,00

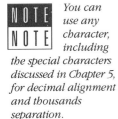

You can use any character, including the special characters discussed in Chapter 5, for decimal alignment and thousands separation.

3. In the Other Codes area, click the Decimal Align Character option button and type the character you want to use to align the numbers (for example, type a comma if you are using the British numbering system).

4. Optionally, press Tab and type the character to use for separating thousands in the number (for example, type a period if you are using the British numbering system).

5. Choose **I**nsert or press ↵ to return to the document window.

WordPerfect inserts a [Decml/Algn Char:] code at the current insertion-point position; all decimal-aligned numbers to the right of and beneath that position will then be aligned on whatever character you specified in step 3.

To return to American-style decimal alignment, repeat steps 1–5 wherever you want to resume that alignment style. If you want to use two different decimal alignment characters in side-by-side columns, you'll need to change the decimal alignment character at the start of each number. Look at Figure 4.19, which shows the Reveal Codes view of Figure 4.17. In the Reveal Codes part of the screen, you can see that the first tab stop is right aligned ([Rgt Tab]) and the next two are decimal-aligned ([Dec Tab]).

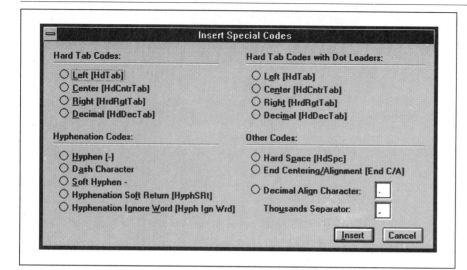

FIGURE 4.18:

The Insert Special Codes dialog box

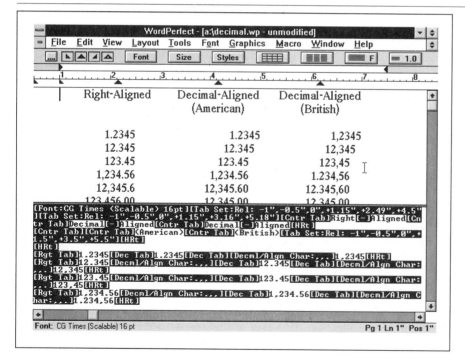

FIGURE 4.19:

American-style decimal-aligned numbers next to British-style decimal-aligned numbers

 *The Tables feature offers a simpler solution to using different decimal alignments in side-by-side columns.*

To switch back and forth between aligning on a period and a comma in the right two columns, the decimal alignment character had to be redefined several times, as evidenced by the many [Decml/Algn Char:] codes. If your work requires lots of unusual alignments like this, you probably should use the Tables feature, covered in Chapter 6.

CREATING DOT LEADERS ON THE FLY

> **TO CREATE DOT LEADERS WITHOUT CHANGING THE TAB STOPS,**
>
> **press Flush Right (Alt+F7) twice where you want to start the dot leaders.**

You can also add dot leaders to a column of text without changing the tab settings. This is particularly handy when you need a simple two-column list of items, like the menu in Figure 4.9. Simply type the text in the first column, choose Layout ➤ Line ➤ Flush Right twice or press Flush Right (Alt+F7) twice, and then type the text in the second column. The text will be right-aligned at the right margin. (If you want to narrow the gap between the two columns, adjust the left and right margins.)

MOVING, COPYING, AND DELETING TABULAR COLUMNS

As mentioned, using the Tables feature is the easiest way to create multi-column tables. However, if you use tabs instead and then decide to move, copy, or delete a particular column, you can do so by selecting. It can be a little tricky, so I recommend saving your document before trying this technique. Here are the general steps:

1. Move the insertion point to the top-left character in the column you want to move, copy, or delete.

2. Move the insertion point to the end of the column, highlighting the column. Initially, the highlight covers text in adjacent columns, as shown in Figure 4.20.

3. Choose **E**dit ➤ **S**elect ➤ **T**abular Column. Now only one column is highlighted, as shown in Figure 4.21.

4. To delete this column, choose **D**elete. Otherwise, choose **E**dit ➤ Cut (or press Shift+Del) or **E**dit ➤ **C**opy (or press Ctrl+Ins).

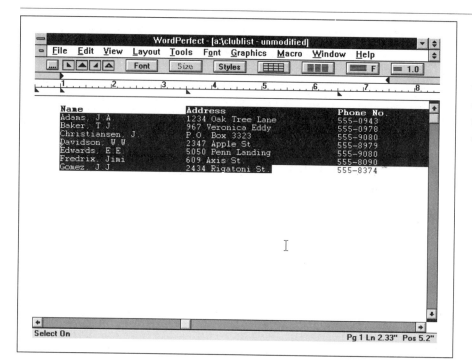

FIGURE 4.20:

Text from the top to the bottom of the second column is selected, but the highlighted area initially includes text in adjacent columns.

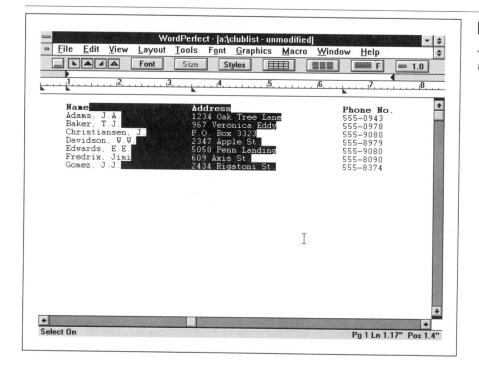

FIGURE 4.21:

A single column of text is selected.

5. If you chose Cut or Copy, move the insertion point to where you want the top-left corner of the moved or copied column to appear.

6. Choose **Edit ➤ P**aste (or press Shift+Ins).

If you change your mind after moving a column of text, choose Edit ➤ Undo (or press Alt+Backspace).

You may need to adjust the tab ruler to get exactly the effect you want after deleting, moving, or copying a column, using the general technique described in "Changing Tab Stops." If you make more of a mess than an improvement, and you'd like to undo the whole operation, just follow these steps:

1. Clear the screen by choosing **File ➤ C**lose or by pressing Ctrl+F4.

2. When asked about saving the *current* copy of the file, choose **N**o.

3. Choose **File ➤ O**pen (or press F4), choose or type the file name, and press ↵ to open the file as it was in step 1.

RELATIVE VS. ABSOLUTE TAB MEASUREMENT

As mentioned earlier in this chapter, you can choose between two types of tab measurement: relative and absolute. When you use relative measurement (the default setting in WordPerfect for Windows), tab stops are always measured from the left margin. In other words, the tab stops float with the left margin. For example, if you have relative tab stops at every $1/2$ inch and then move the left margin $1/4$ inch to the right, all tab stops also move $1/4$ inch to the right, so the first tab stop is still $1/2$ inch from the left margin.

When you use absolute measurement, tab stops are measured from the left edge of the page, without regard to the left margin; that is, they do not float with the left margin. For example, if you have absolute tab stops at every $1/2$ inch and then move the left margin $1/4$ inch to the right, the tab stops remain unchanged. Therefore, the first tab stop will be $1/4$ inch from the left margin, the second will be $3/4$ inch from the left margin, and so forth.

From a practical standpoint, relative tab stops are probably the easiest to get along with, because the various indent keys always have the same effect, regardless of where you've set the left margin. However, when you get into more advanced work involving graphics and multicolumn layouts (Part 6), you may prefer to use the absolute tab measurements so that you know the exact location of each tab stop.

HARD VS. SOFT TABS

One last tidbit of information about tabs is the difference between hard and soft tabs. Soft tabs are the "natural" tabs you get when you press the Tab key. They are called soft tabs because they change automatically if you change the alignment on the ruler. For example, if you change a center-aligned tab stop to right-aligned, any [Cntr Tab] codes at that tab stop (and below the tab ruler) are automatically changed to [Rgt Tab] codes.

If, for whatever reason, you do not want a tab code to change when the tab ruler changes, insert a hard tab by doing the following:

1. Position the insertion point where you want the hard tab.

2. Choose **L**ayout ➤ **L**ine ➤ Special C**o**des (or press Shift+F9 O) to display the Insert Special Codes dialog box.

3. Indicate which type of hard-tab code you want by clicking the appropriate option button.

4. Choose **I**nsert or press ↵ to insert the code (the code has *Hd,* for *hard,* in front of it).

WordPerfect's justification, indentation, and alignment options range from simple tabs to fancy indentations and every possible kind of text alignment. (In Chapter 6, you will learn about the Tables feature, which offers a more convenient means of typing text in tabular columns.) In the next chapter, you'll learn how to use fonts in your documents and how to produce lines and special characters.

CHAPTER 5

Fonts, Lines, and Special Characters

HANDS-ON
....
LESSON 4

For a hands-on lesson in using some of the techniques presented in this chapter, see Lesson 4 in Part 9.

ordPerfect lets you change the size, appearance, and typeface of printed text, and print special characters and lines that are not available directly from your keyboard. These capabilities can make your printed documents more attractive and visually interesting. For example, Figure 5.1 shows a sample document using plain text. Figure 5.2 shows the same document spruced up a bit with the kinds of features I'll be covering in this chapter.

WHAT CAN YOUR PRINTER DO?

Up to this point, every feature of WordPerfect that I've described in the book will work like a charm, regardless of your printer. But now we've come to a place where certain features of WordPerfect aren't really WordPerfect features at all. Instead, they are *printer-specific* features, which WordPerfect can use if (and *only* if) your printer is capable of producing them.

If you try using a special feature that is not available on your printer, WordPerfect will just ignore your request, making you feel as though *you* have done something wrong. So if you're not already sure of your printer's range of capabilities, you might want to take Lesson 4 in Part 9 to start getting a feel for your printer's capabilities.

ABOUT FONTS

Unless you're already familiar with computers or typesetting, the term *font*

```
                    Angela T. Joseph

18424 Mountain View Court Lake Meyer, Co.   93415     (319) 555-0938

    OBJECTIVE          Produce word processing and desktop
                       publishing documents on a freelance basis.


    EDUCATION          Bachelor of Arts, Business Administration,
                       State University of Colorado, Denver, 1980.


    EXPERIENCE         Sole Proprietor, Angela T. Joseph Word
                       Processing, Sturgeon Pond, Colorado.
                                             1985 to Present

                          Freelance secretary and home-based word
                          processing services.

                             Secretary for small office of architects
                             Freelance secretary for various offices
                             as temporary help

                       Clerk Typist II, Morgan T. Williams
                       Corporation, River Bend, Colorado
                                             1974 to 1985

                          Clerk typist and receptionist for the
                          general business office of a consulting
                          firm.

                             Process and type forms and reports from
                             outside consultants
                             Compile and ensure accuracy of monthly
                             statistical reports
                             Perform general duties including heavy
                             typing and filing

    PROFESSIONAL       Chamber of Commerce, Denver, Colorado
    ORGANIZATIONS      Business & Professional Association of Lake
                       Meyer, Colorado


    REFERENCES         Available upon request
```

FIGURE 5.1:

A plain document without fonts, lines, or special characters may be new to you. A font is basically a combination of three things:

◆ A typeface (sometimes called a *typestyle* or a *face*)

◆ A weight, such as **boldface**, *italic,* or roman (regular, like this)

◆ A size, measured in *points* or characters per inch (cpi)

Angela T. Joseph

| 18424 Mountain View Court | Lake Meyer, Colorado 93415 | (319) 555-0938 |

OBJECTIVE   Produce word processing and desktop publishing documents on a freelance basis.

EDUCATION   Bachelor of Arts, Business Administration, State University of Colorado, Denver, 1980.

EXPERIENCE   Sole Proprietor, *Angela T. Joseph Word Processing*, Sturgeon Pond, Colorado.   1985 to Present

Freelance secretary and home-based word processing services.

- Secretary for small office of architects
- Freelance secretary for various offices as temporary help

Clerk Typist II, *Morgan T. Williams Corporation*, River Bend, Colorado   1974 to 1985

Clerk typist and receptionist for the general business office of a consulting firm.

- Process and type forms and reports from outside consultants
- Compile and ensure accuracy of monthly statistical reports
- Perform general duties including heavy typing and filing

PROFESSIONAL   Chamber of Commerce, Denver, Colorado
ORGANIZATIONS   Business & Professional Association of Lake Meyer, Colorado

REFERENCES   Available upon request

FIGURE 5.2:

The document in Figure 5.1 spruced up with fonts, lines, and special characters

TYPEFACES

Figure 5.3 shows examples of various typefaces. Different occasions call for different typefaces. For example, Courier is a typewriter font, good for printing documents that you want to look typed. Times is a *serif* font—a serif is the little curlicue or tail at the top and bottom of each letter. Serif fonts are often used for small- to medium-size print, because the serifs help your eyes move through the text and read more easily.

Helvetica is a *sans-serif* font, so called because the letters have no tails. Sans-serif fonts are mainly used for large text, anywhere from the headlines in newspapers to the messages on street signs (as a glance at any road sign will prove).

Courier
Times
Helvetica
Blippo Black
Britannic
Broadway
Brody
Brush Script
Century Schoolbook
Chaucer
Clarendon
Clearface
Cooper Black
COPPERPLATE
Eurostile
Flange
Goudy

Hobo
Garamond
Korinna
New Baskerville
Souvenir
Zapf Chancery
Kaufmann Bold
Mariage
Murray Hill
Old Towne
Optimum
Palatino
Park Avenue
Serpentine
Square Serif
University
Vivaldi

FIGURE 5.3:

Examples of different typefaces

Decorative fonts, such as Chaucer (also called Cloister), are strictly for decoration. They are not particularly easy to read (especially in smaller sizes), but look nice and are often used to draw attention or create a mood. Examples abound all around you, from the elegant grace of a wedding invitation to the casual zaniness of a humorous greeting card. But overall, decorative fonts are best reserved for special occasions and should be used sparingly.

WEIGHTS

Figure 5.4 shows a single typeface, Times, in a variety of weights. Boldface (or bold) is thicker than the regular roman weight. Italic (also called *oblique*) is generally lighter and slanted. As you'll learn a little later, there are additional ways to change the appearance of text, regardless of its weight.

SIZES

N O T E
N O T E

See Chapter 20 for more information on Zapf Dingbats and other specialty fonts.

Figure 5.5 shows a single typeface and style (Times Roman) in a variety of sizes. A point is roughly $\frac{1}{72}$ of an inch, so 72 points is about 1 inch tall, 36 points is about $\frac{1}{2}$ inch tall, and so forth.

Finally, Figure 5.6 shows a variety of fonts. Each font is described in terms of its typeface, weight (if any), and size—for example, Courier 10cpi, Times Roman Italic 12pt, Helvetica Bold Oblique 20pt, and so forth. (Many decorative and specialty fonts, such as Zapf Dingbats and Vivaldi, are only available in a single weight—there is no bold or italic version.)

Keep in mind that WordPerfect cannot *create* fonts for you. Instead, it can only use whatever fonts are available from your printer. If your font selection is limited, chances are you can buy additional fonts for use with Word-Perfect and your printer. For more information on purchasing and installing additional fonts, see Chapter 8.

Times Roman
Times Bold
Times Italic
Times Bold Italic

FIGURE 5.4:

Examples of various weights

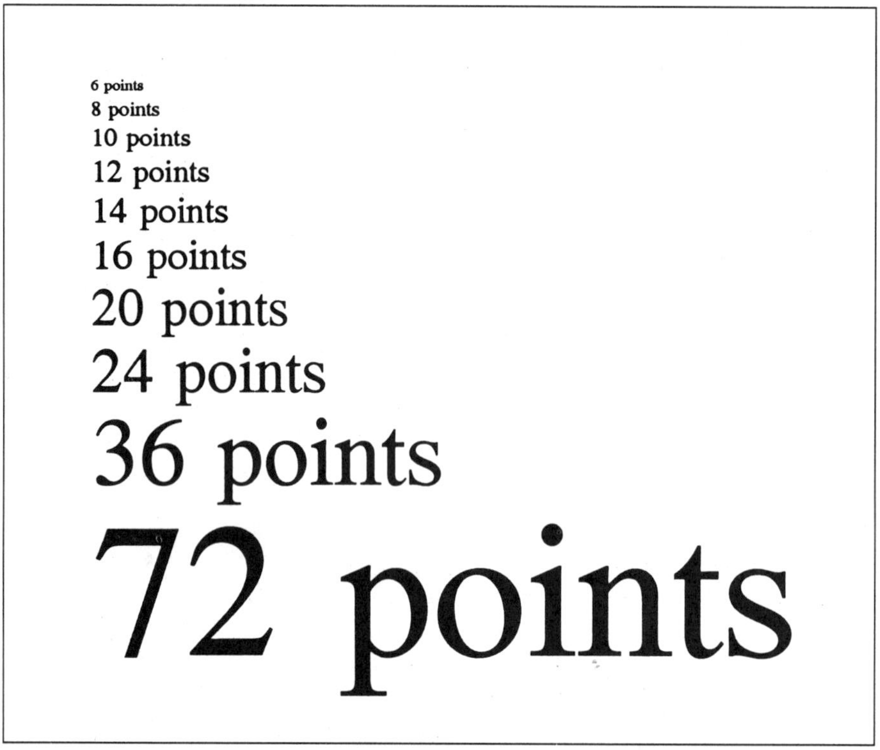

6 points
8 points
10 points
12 points
14 points
16 points
20 points
24 points
36 points
72 points

FIGURE 5.5:
*Examples of various
type sizes*

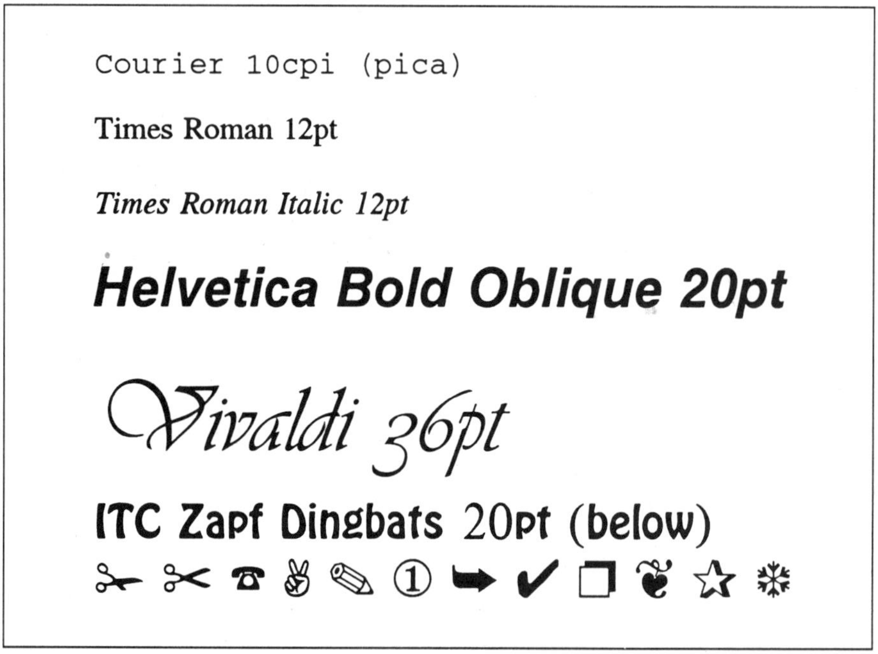

Courier 10cpi (pica)

Times Roman 12pt

Times Roman Italic 12pt

Helvetica Bold Oblique 20pt

Vivaldi 36pt

ITC Zapf Dingbats 20pt (below)

FIGURE 5.6:
*Examples of various
fonts*

PROPORTIONAL VS. MONOSPACED FONTS

As mentioned earlier, some fonts are measured in points, and others are measured in characters per inch. The reason is that there are two different ways of spacing characters horizontally along a line:

Monospacing: Every character takes up the same space; for example, an *i* is just as wide as a *w*.

Proportional spacing: Every character takes up only the space it needs; for example, an *i* does not take up as much space as a *w*.

Figure 5.7 illustrates this difference with a string of the letters *i* and *w*, in a monospaced font (Courier) and a proportionally spaced font (Times). The letters are the same width in the monospaced font, but the *i* is narrower than the *w* in the proportional font, so the letters appear more tightly packed together.

Because each character in a monospaced font takes up the same space, its size can be measured in characters per inch (abbreviated *cpi*). Two well-known Courier sizes are pica (10 cpi) and elite (12 cpi).

Proportionally spaced fonts cannot really be measured in this manner because the characters have different widths. Hence, these fonts are measured in terms of *height,* in points. The two different measuring systems can be a little confusing at first, but they are easy to get used to with a little practice. (Actually, the point size of a character usually includes a little blank space, called *leading,* at the top, as discussed in Chapter 20.)

> **NOTE** *A 10-cpi monospaced font is about the same size as a 12-point proportional font. The term "pitch" is sometimes used in place of cpi.*

SCALABLE VS. NONSCALABLE FONTS

Some fonts are *scalable* (also called *outline* fonts), which means that you can choose a size "on the fly," even in unusual increments (such as 10.5 points). PostScript printers, the Hewlett-Packard LaserJet III series, and many other laser printers offer scalable fonts.

```
iwiwiwiwiwiwiwiw
```
In a monospaced font, like Courier, every letter is the same width.

iwiwiwiwiwiwiwiw

In a proportionally spaced font, like Times, each letter uses only the space it needs.

FIGURE 5.7:

The difference between monospaced and proportionally spaced fonts

Nonscalable fonts only let you choose from a predetermined selection of sizes. The Hewlett-Packard LaserJet II series, and many dot-matrix printers, offer only nonscalable fonts. Some printers also offer a combination of fonts, where some font choices are scalable and others are not.

CHOOSING A FONT

TO CHOOSE A FONT,

position the insertion point where you want the new font to begin, or select text whose font you want to change. Choose Font ➤ Font, then choose the font you want. Then click the OK button.

If you have several printers, choose the printer you plan to print with by choosing File ➤ Select Printer before choosing fonts (see Chapter 8).

Fortunately, using fonts in WordPerfect is much simpler than learning all the terminology. Here's how you choose a font:

1. Move the insertion point to where you want to switch to the new font, either before existing text or where you want to start typing new text.

2. If you want to change the font for only a portion of existing text, select that text.

3. Choose Font ➤ Font (or press F9, or click the Font button on the Button Bar). The dialog box shown in Figure 5.8 appears (though the list of available fonts depends on your printer and current font collection). The current font is highlighted.

4. Move the highlight to the font you want to choose. You can scroll through typefaces by using the scroll bar to the right of the font list, by pressing ↑, ↓, PgUp, and PgDn, or by typing the name of the font you want to look for. An example of text in the currently highlighted font appears below the list.

The ability to see a font before choosing it is new to WordPerfect for Windows and has been dubbed WYSBYGI (pronounced "whiz biggie"), for "What You See Before You Get It."

5. If the currently highlighted font is scalable, a list of available point sizes appears next to the font list. Click the point size you want, or press Tab and then type the point size. (If the current font isn't scalable, skip this step.)

6. Optionally, choose an appearance or any combination of appearances in the Appearance area, either by clicking with your mouse or using the Tab and spacebar keys. Optionally, choose a relative size (appearances and sizes are discussed in more detail below).

7. When you are satisfied with your choice, click on OK or press ↵ (or click on Cancel or press Escape to abandon the current choices).

You are returned to the document window. If you did not select any text in step 2 above, all text past the insertion point (up to any previous font selections) is displayed in the chosen font. Similarly, any new text that you type will be displayed in that font.

If you did select text in step 2, that selected text is displayed in the new font, and the text remains selected. (The status bar near shows the name of the font at the insertion point position.) You can choose additional options for the selected text, or unselect it by clicking the left mouse button or pressing F8.

HIDDEN CODES FOR FONTS

When you change the font in a document, WordPerfect inserts a hidden [Font:] code, which includes the font name and size, at the insertion-point position. If you change the font of selected text, WordPerfect also inserts a [Font:] code at the end of the selected area to switch back to the original font.

As with all formatting features, you can use Reveal Codes (View ➤

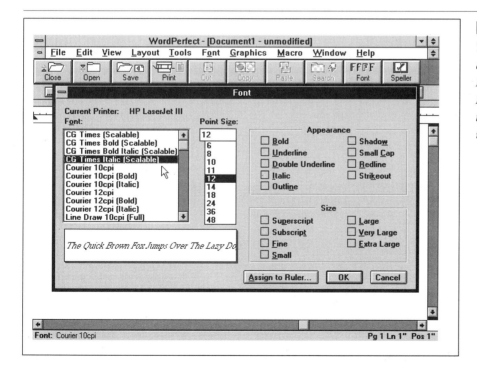

FIGURE 5.8:

The Font dialog box, accessed by choosing Font ➤ Font, pressing F9, or double-clicking the Font button on the ruler

Reveal Codes) to view the codes, and optionally delete any codes that may be causing an unwanted font change.

TROUBLESHOOTING FONT PROBLEMS

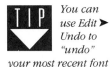

You can use Edit ➤ Undo to "undo" your most recent font change.

If you change the font in a document and nothing seems to happen, chances are there's a competing [Font:] code right after your new code. For example, suppose your text is currently shown in Times Roman and you change it to Helvetica, but nothing happens. If you leave the insertion point near where you changed the font, and turn on Reveal Codes, you'll see that the original Times Roman font is after the new Helvetica font, like this:

[Font:Helvetica 18pt][Font:Times Roman 18pt]

To fix this problem, you need to move the highlight to the [Font: Times Roman] code, and press Delete to delete it.

USING THE RULER TO CHOOSE A FONT

The ruler offers an optional shortcut for choosing a font:

1. If the ruler isn't displayed, choose **V**iew ➤ **R**uler (or press Alt+Shift+F3) to turn it on.

2. Position the insertion point where you want to change the font, or select the text whose font you want to change.

Font

3. Move the mouse pointer to the Font button, hold down the left mouse button, move the highlight to the font you want, then release the mouse button.

ADDING FONTS TO THE RULER

Initially, the Font button on the ruler may offer only a small selection of fonts. But you can add more fonts to the button by following these steps:

1. Double-click the Font button on the ruler (or choose **F**ont ➤ **F**ont, or press F9).

2. Click the **A**ssign to Ruler button (or press Alt+A). The dialog box shown in Figure 5.9 appears.

3. Highlight whatever font you'd like to add to the ruler, then click the Add button (or press Alt+A). Repeat this step to add as many fonts as you wish.

4. If you change your mind about a font and wish to delete it from the ruler button, highlight the font in the Fonts on **R**uler list (by clicking the name, or by pressing Alt+R then using the ↑ and ↓ keys). Then click the Clear button (or press Alt+C).

5. Click OK (or press ↵) to leave the dialog box.

6. Click Cancel or press Escape to leave the Font dialog box.

The next time you use the ruler, the fonts you chose will be available when you use the Font button. When you use the ruler to choose a scalable font, the text will be sized automatically to match the size of the text to its left (or the current point size). However, you can resize the text, as described in the next section.

USING THE SIZE BUTTON

If you want to change the size of the current font, you can use the Size button on the ruler. This option gives you only a limited selection of point sizes, but

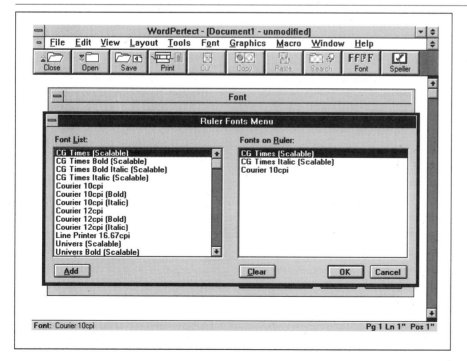

FIGURE 5.9:

The Ruler Fonts Menu dialog box.

it is a handy alternative to reselecting the font and size by using the Font menu. Here's how to use the button:

1. Move the insertion point to the place where you want to change the point size of the current font or select the text for which you want to change the point size.

2. Move the mouse pointer to the Size button, hold down the left mouse button, move the highlight to the point size you want, then release the left mouse button. The Size button is shaded and unavailable if the font at the insertion-point position is not scalable.

The selected text, or all text up to the next [Font:] code, is displayed in the new point size.

USING RELATIVE TYPE SIZES

TO CHANGE THE RELATIVE SIZE OF TEXT,

position the insertion point at the place where you want to change the size, or select text whose size you want to change. Then choose Font from the menu (or press Ctrl+S), then choose Subscript, Superscript, or Size for some other relative size.

If you want to change only the size of the current font, it's not necessary to choose a different font. You can just choose a size in relation to the current size. One advantage of a relative type size is that the relatively sized text changes if you change the point size of the current font.

For example, if you use subscripts and superscripts in your work, you always want them to be a bit smaller than adjacent text. Now, suppose you "manually" chose 12 points for all your regular text, then chose 10 points for superscripts and subscripts. If you later changed your mind and made all the regular text 10 points, your superscript and subscript text would no longer be smaller than the regular text. You would need to go back and manually change all the 10-point superscripts and subscripts to 8-point size. But if you chose the "relative" subscript and superscript sizes, you wouldn't need to bother. These size options will display the superscripts and subscripts at 60 percent of the size of the current font.

Figure 5.10 shows examples of the relative sizes available to you. Each size is a percentage of the size of the current font, as shown in Table 5.1.

If your printer has scalable fonts, WordPerfect calculates the relative type size mathematically, since "anything goes" with scalable fonts. However, if your printer does not offer scalable fonts, WordPerfect chooses whatever font is available that best approximates the size you've requested. Therefore, if your printer has a limited choice of fonts, the sizes may not match the percentages listed in the table.

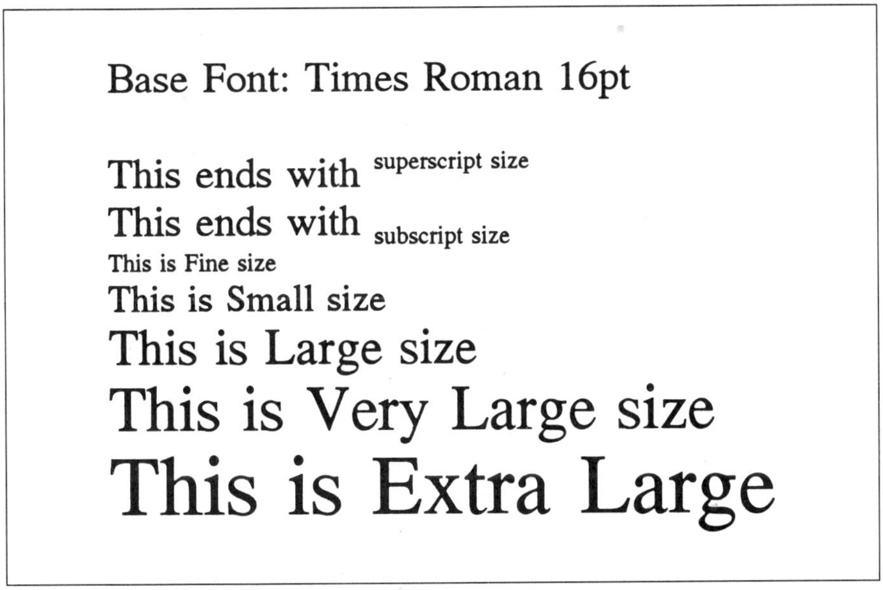

Base Font: Times Roman 16pt

This ends with superscript size

This ends with subscript size

This is Fine size

This is Small size

This is Large size

This is Very Large size

This is Extra Large

FIGURE 5.10:

Examples of sizes in relation to a 16-point font

SIZE	PERCENTAGE OF CURRENT FONT SIZE
Fine	60
Small	80
Large	120
Very Large	150
Extra Large	200
Superscript	60 (raised)
Subscript	60 (lowered)

TABLE 5.1:

Ratio of Print Sizes to Base Font

You can change the relative size of the current font either before or after typing the text, as discussed in the sections that follow.

CHANGING THE RELATIVE SIZE BEFORE YOU TYPE

To change the relative size of text before you type it, follow these steps:

1. Position the insertion point wherever you are about to type your new text.

2. Choose Font, then Subscript, Superscript, or Size and one of the sizes presented. Optionally, you can choose a size from the Font dialog box after choosing Font ➤ Font or double-clicking the Font button in the ruler. (If you use the dialog box, remember to click OK after choosing a size.)

3. Type whatever text you want displayed at the selected size.

4. When you want to start typing at the original size, press → then resume typing.

 *The shortcut key for the Size menu is Ctrl+S and for the Font dialog box is F9.*

CHANGING THE RELATIVE SIZE OF EXISTING TEXT

If you've already typed your text, changing its size is as simple as selecting the text and choosing a new size.

1. Select the text for which you want to change the relative size.

2. Choose Font, then either Subscript, Superscript, or Size and one of the sizes presented. Optionally, you can choose a size from the Font dialog box after choosing Font ➤ Font or double-clicking the Font button in the ruler. (If you use the dialog box, remember to click OK after choosing a size).

HIDDEN CODES FOR SIZE CHANGES

Relative font sizes are controlled by paired codes in Reveal Codes. The code that starts the size change contains the word *On*, the code that ends the size change contains *Off*, as listed in Table 5.2. Remember that only text between the starting and ending codes is displayed at the specified size. Text after the ending code is displayed at the original size.

SIZE	STARTING CODE	ENDING CODE
Fine	[Fine On]	[Fine Off]
Small	[Small On]	[Small Off]
Large	[Large On]	[Large Off]
Very Large	[Vry Large On]	[Vry Large Off]
Extra Large	[Ext Large On]	[Ext Large Off]
Superscript	[Suprscpt On]	[Suprscpt Off]
Subscript	[Subscpt On]	[Subscpt Off]

TABLE 5.2:

Paired Codes for Print Sizes

CHANGING THE SIZE RATIOS

The ratios of relative text sizes listed in Table 5.1 are not etched in granite; they are simply the defaults that WordPerfect uses for convenience. In some situations, you may want to specify a different ratio—for example, to make your superscripts and subscripts a little smaller or to make your extra-large sizes a little larger. You can do so quite easily with a little customization, by choosing File ➤ Preferences ➤ Print, as described in Chapter 13.

But be aware that, like all customization features on the Preferences menu, changing the size ratios affects the entire current document and all future documents (until the time that you change the size ratios again).

CHANGING THE DOCUMENT INITIAL FONT

Normally the initial starting font for a document is whatever font is chosen as the default font for the printer (see Chapter 13). If you want to use a different starting font (also called the *base* font) for a document, choose Layout ➤ Document ➤ Initial Font. Then choose a font from the list of available fonts. All text up to the first [Font:] code (if any) in the document will be displayed in the selected font.

This feature is especially handy when used in conjunction with relative sizes. For example, suppose you will be printing a document in a very small print size, but want to see it on your screen with larger letters. You could start by choosing a large print size as the document initial font.

A [Font:] code in the document always takes precedence over the document initial font.

As you type the document, use only relative sizing to change print sizes. Then, before printing your document, change the document initial font to the smaller size at which you want to print. As long as you didn't insert any [Font:] codes in the document, all the text will be resized accordingly.

CHANGING THE APPEARANCE OF TEXT

TO CHANGE THE APPEARANCE OF TEXT,

position the insertion point where you're about to type, or select existing text, and choose Font ➤ Appearance and then any available appearance.

You can change the appearance of text without choosing a new font. This is particularly useful for occasional boldfaced, italicized, and underlined text. Figure 5.11 shows examples of available appearances and some combined appearances.

Be aware, however, that not all printers support the full range of appearances. For example, Outline is available only on PostScript and Hewlett-Packard LaserJet III printers. Redline and Shadow tend to look different on different printers. You may need to experiment to find out how the various appearances will look on your printer.

CHOOSING TEXT APPEARANCES

The steps for changing the appearance of text are virtually identical to those for changing the relative size:

1. Position the insertion point wherever you are about to type your new text, or select the text whose appearance you want to change.

2. Pull down the Font menu and choose an attribute, or press any of the shortcut keys listed in Table 5.3. Optionally, choose Font ➤ Font, or double-click the Font button on the ruler, then choose any combination of appearances from the Font dialog box. (If you use the dialog box, don't forget to click OK after making your choices.) If you changed the appearance of selected text, skip the remaining steps.

3. Type the text that you want to display with the selected attribute.

Normal

Bold

Underline

Double Underline

Italic

Outline

Shadow

SMALL CAP

Redline

~~Strikeout~~

Shadow and Outline

ITALIC, SMALL CAP, UNDERLINE

Italic, Shadow, Double Underline

FIGURE 5.11:

Examples of appearance attributes

APPEARANCE	SHORTCUT
Bold	Ctrl+B
Italic	Ctrl+I
Underline	Ctrl+U
Normal	Ctrl+N

TABLE 5.3:

Shortcuts for Commonly Used Font Attributes

4. Press → as necessary, or End, when you're ready to resume typing normal text without the chosen attribute.

The change is apparent immediately on your screen or as soon as you start typing. Remember that not all appearances are available on all printers. Word-Perfect may ignore a requested appearance if it's not available on your printer, or select a different font to mimic the appearance.

HIDDEN CODES FOR APPEARANCES

Changes to the appearance of text are controlled by the codes listed in Table 5.4. Remember that only the text between the starting and ending codes is displayed with the specified appearance. Text after the ending code is displayed with the original appearance defined by the current font.

If you combine several appearances before typing text, the codes for all attributes will be combined, as in the example below:

[Bold On][Italc On][Italc Off][Bold Off]

As you type with the insertion point in the middle of the codes, the two Off codes will move to the right, and your text will have the combined attributes boldface and italics.

To resume typing normal text in this example, you would first need to press → twice—once to move the insertion point past the [Italc Off] code and

APPEARANCE	STARTING CODE	ENDING CODE
Bold	[Bold On]	[Bold Off]
Underline	[Und On]	[Und Off]
Double Underline	[Dbl Und On]	[Dbl Und Off]
Italic	[Italc On]	[Italc Off]
Outline	[Outln On]	[Outln Off]
Shadow	[Shadw On]	[Shadw Off]
Small Cap	[Sm Cap On]	[Sm Cap Off]
Redline	[Redln On]	[Redln Off]
Strikeout	[Stkout On]	[Stkout Off]

TABLE 5.4:

Codes for Controlling Text Appearance

a second time to move it past the [Bold Off] code. You can use Reveal Codes to keep track of the insertion-point position in relation to size and appearance attribute codes.

COMBINING SIZES AND APPEARANCES

NOTE *You may want to turn on Reveal Codes when combining sizes and appearances so that you can see where the insertion point is in relation to the codes.*

You can combine a size and any combination of appearances to get any look you want. Figure 5.12 shows some examples.

A behind-the-scenes look at a couple of examples will show how they were created. The "e=mc^2" example looks like this in Reveal Codes:

[Italc On]Italic sentence with[Bold On]e=mc[Suprscpt On]2[Suprscpt Off][Bold Off]in bold with superscript[Italc Off]

Notice that the starting and ending codes for each size and appearance correspond directly to how the example is printed.

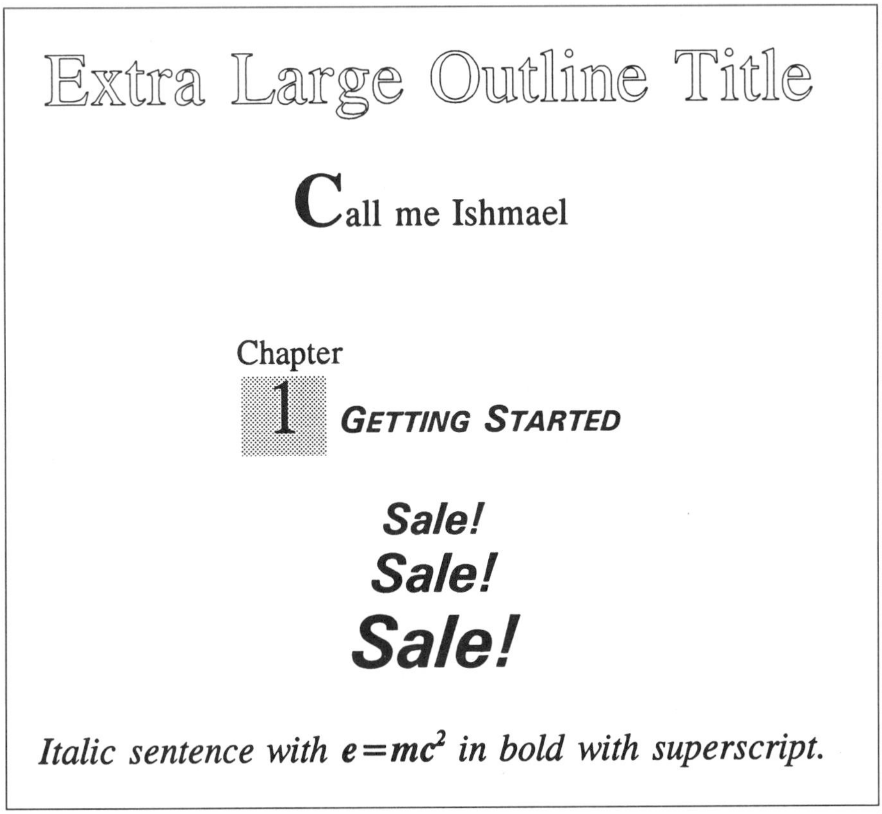

FIGURE 5.12:
Examples of combined sizes and appearances

NOTE NOTE *The "Chapter 1" example requires a printer that prints redline with a grayed background.*

The "Chapter 1" example looks like this in Reveal Codes:

[Small On]Chapter[Small Off][HRT]
[Ext Large On][Redln On] 1 [Redln Off][Ext Large Off] [Font: Helvetica Bold Italic 16pt][Sm Cap On]Getting Started[Sm Cap Off]

UNDOING SIZE AND APPEARANCE CHANGES

To undo a size or an appearance change, move the insertion point to the approximate position of the change, turn on Reveal Codes, and delete either the On or Off code for the appearance you want to eliminate.

Optionally, you can remove a size or an appearance change by selecting the text, then pulling down the Font menu or going to the Font dialog box (Font ➤ Font.) The sizes and appearances for the selected text are already chosen in the menu, or shaded in the dialog box. Choose whichever options you want to turn off.

If you want to remove all size and appearance options, you can select the text, then choose Font ➤ Normal or press Ctrl+N.

TROUBLESHOOTING SIZE AND APPEARANCE PROBLEMS

Sometimes it's the little things in word processing that drive you batty. For example, suppose you type and underline some text as shown below:

<u>"Whoops," </u>she cried.

Then, you decide that you don't want to underline the comma and quotation marks, only the word *Whoops*.

There are a couple of ways to fix this problem. But your best starting point is to move the insertion point to the general vicinity of the word, then turn on Reveal Codes. This gives you a bird's-eye view of the problem:

[Und On]"Whoops,"[Und Off] she cried.

Here it's obvious that the problem is that the comma and quotation mark are inside the [Und On] and [Und Off] codes. One way to fix the problem is simply to delete the existing [Und On] or [Und Off] code, select only the word *Whoops,* and then turn underlining back on. Or you could leave the codes in place, delete the comma and quotation marks, then retype them outside the

NOTE NOTE *Word-Perfect does not allow you to move or copy paired codes.*

[Und] codes. Either way, you want to end up with this arrangement:

"[Und On]Whoops[Und Off]," she cried.

The printed text will then look like this:

"Whoops," she cried.

UNDERLINING BLANK SPACES AND TABS

TO CHANGE THE UNDERLINE METHOD,

position the insertion point and choose Layout ➤ Typesetting.

The Underline and Double Underline appearances normally underline words and blank spaces between words. But you can choose whether or not to have WordPerfect underline spaces and tabs. Figure 5.13 shows examples of your options, where tabs are used to separate Name, Address, and City; and spaces separate City, State, and Zip.

To control the underlining method, follow these steps:

1. Move the insertion point to the first character or blank space where

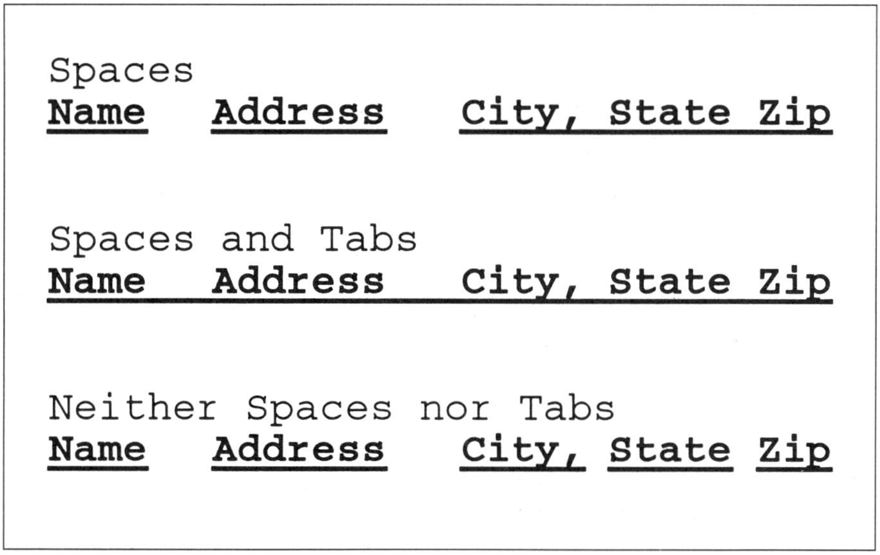

NOTE *The underline styles described here also affect text that you've underlined with Ctrl+U.*

Spaces
Name   Address   City, State Zip

Spaces and Tabs
Name   Address   City, State Zip

Neither Spaces nor Tabs
Name   Address   City, State Zip

FIGURE 5.13:

Optional underlining methods, available for both single underlining and double underlining

you want to change the underlining method.

2. Choose **L**ayout ➤ Typesetting.

3. In the Underline section of the dialog box, choose whichever options you want. If you leave both Underline Spaces and Underline Tabs unselected, neither spaces nor tabs will be underlined.

4. Click OK or press ↵ to return to the document.

All underlined and double-underlined text past the insertion point will adhere to the new underlining method. To change the underlining method elsewhere, simply repeat the steps in the appropriate section of the document.

SPECIAL TECHNIQUES
FOR REDLINE AND STRIKEOUT

Redline and strikeout are often used to denote changes in contracts and other legal documents. Redline indicates suggested additions to the original document, and strikeout indicates suggested deletions, as shown in the example in Figure 5.14.

On some printers, WordPerfect prints redline text as a grayed shade. On other printers, redline text is printed with a shaded background or with dots beneath the characters. On color printers, redline text is printed in red. You can change the appearance of redline text if you wish. To do so, choose File ➤ Preferences ➤ Print. This will take you to the Print Settings dialog box (discussed in Chapter 13). You can choose any one of the redlining methods in the dialog box, as described below:

Printer   Redline is printed as dictated by your
Dependent   particular printer.

THE PURCHASE PRICE INCLUDES: All tacked down carpeting, ~~all existing window treatments,~~ all existing window and door screens, all built-in appliances, television antennas, garage door opener and controllers, all ~~fixtures,~~ shrubs, trees and items permanently attached to the real property, all window treatments excluding the wooden louvers in the dining room, and all fixtures excluding chandelier in the dining room. Pool and spa equipment, if any, is also to be included.

FIGURE 5.14:

Redline and strikeout in a sample document

Mark **Left** Margin	Redline text is marked in the left margin by a character of your choosing.
Mark **A**lternating Margins	Redline text is marked by a character in the left margin on even-numbered pages and a character in the right margin on odd-numbered pages.

If you choose Left or Alternating, you can also choose a character to use as the redline mark. Normally, WordPerfect uses a vertical bar (|). To change that character, choose Redline Character, by clicking its box or pressing R.). Delete the old character and type any single character to use as the redline mark. Or press Ctrl+W and choose a special character from the available character sets (described a little later in this chapter). Click Insert and Close to return to the document.

You can remove all the redline markings and strikeout text from a document with a single command. This is useful for printing a final draft of the document, after you are certain that you no longer need the redline markings or the text that has been struck out. Follow these steps:

1. Choose **T**ools ➤ Do**c**ument Compare ➤ **R**emove Markings. The dialog box shown below appears.

2. If you want to delete just the strikeout text but leave in the redline markings, choose Leave **R**edline Marks. (Otherwise, both the strikeout text and the markings for the redline text will be removed.)

3. Click OK.

See Chapter 23 for information on comparing documents and automatically inserting redline and strikeout.

The strikeout text is removed from the document, and (depending on your choice in step 2), redline markings are removed. If you want to save the original copy of the document with redlining and strikeout still intact, be sure to save this copy of the document with a new file name, using the File ➤ Save As options.

PRINTING SPECIAL CHARACTERS

TO TYPE A SPECIAL CHARACTER,

choose Font ➤ WP Characters (or press Ctrl+W), choose a character set and character, then choose Insert and Close.

Your keyboard lets you type all the letters, numbers, and punctuation marks needed for most documents. But many situations call for special characters, like bullets, copyright marks such as © and ™, foreign-currency signs, and the ↑, ↓, →, ←, and ↵ characters used in this book.

WordPerfect offers over 1400 special characters for many different applications, including foreign-language characters, mathematical equations, scientific symbols, and more. There is also a Greek alphabet (both ancient and modern), as well as Hebrew, Russian, and Japanese alphabets.

If you have a graphics printer, you'll be able to print all the special characters that WordPerfect offers. If you don't have a graphics printer, you'll probably still be able to print quite a few of these symbols.

Follow these steps to insert a special character in your document:

If Word-Perfect cannot find a special character in the current font, it draws the character graphically.

1. Position the insertion point where you want to type the special character.

2. Choose Font ➤ **WP** Characters, or press Ctrl+W. The WordPerfect Characters dialog box appears (Figure 5.15).

If you know the number code of the character you want, you can type that number (including the comma) under Number in the dialog box, then press ↵.

3. To choose a different character set, move the mouse pointer to the box under **S**et, hold down the left mouse button, move the highlight to the character set you want, then release the left mouse button. Or, press Alt+S then use the ↑ and ↓ keys to scroll to a character set.

4. When the character set you want appears, use the scroll bar to scroll through available characters, or press Alt+C and use the arrow, PgUp, and PgDn keys to scroll.

5. When the character you want is selected, you can choose **I**nsert to insert that character and continue selecting more characters, or choose Insert **a**nd Close to insert the current character and leave the dialog box.

6. If you didn't choose Insert and Close in the preceding step, you can click the Close button to close the dialog box and return to the document.

The special character you've requested will appear on the document window. In Reveal Codes, the character appears, followed by its code if you highlight it.

You can leave the WordPerfect Characters dialog box on the screen to simplify adding special characters throughout the document. While the dialog box is displayed, you can move it wherever you wish as you would any other dialog box or window: by dragging its title bar or by using the Move option on its Control menu (Alt+spacebar). Then you can move back to the document by clicking the mouse pointer anywhere in the document. Position the insertion point where you want to insert another character, then choose a character set or character from the dialog box whenever you're ready. When you've finished with the dialog box, just click its Close button.

For future reference, Figure 5.16 shows some of the more commonly used special characters and the optional codes used to type each one. You can also tell which character set each special character belongs to by the first number in the code, as follows:

4	Typographic Symbols
5	Iconic Symbols
6	Math/Scientific

SHORTCUTS FOR COMMONLY USED SPECIAL CHARACTERS

As with most other WordPerfect features, there is yet another shortcut for

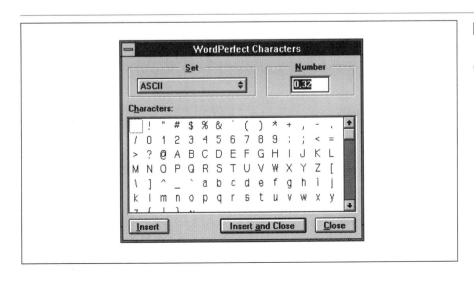

FIGURE 5.15:

The WordPerfect Characters dialog box

Bullets/List Items

●	4,0	Bullet
○	4,1	Hollow Bullet
■	4,2	Square Bullet
•	4,3	Small Bullet
○	4,37	Large Hollow Bullet
□	4,38	Large Hollow Square
●	4,44	Large Bullet
○	4,45	Small Hollow Bullet
■	4,46	Large Square Bullet
■	4,47	Small Square Bullet
□	4,48	Hollow Square Bullet
□	4,49	Small Hollow Square
☞	5,21	Right Pointing Index
☜	5,22	Left Pointing Index
✓	5,23	Check Mark
☐	5,24	Empty Ballot Box
☒	5,25	Marked Ballot Box

Currency

£	4,11	Pound/Sterling
¥	4,12	Yen
Pt	4,13	Pesetas
ƒ	4,14	Florin/Guilder
¢	4,19	Cent
¤	4,24	General Currency
$	4,57	Milreis/Escudo
₣	4,58	Francs
₢	4,59	Cruzado
₠	4,60	European Currency
₤	4,61	Lire

Foreign Language

¡	4,7	Inverted Exclamation
¿	4,8	Inverted Question Mark

Graphic

♥	5,0	Heart
◇	5,1	Diamond
♣	5,2	Club
♠	5,3	Spade

Fractions

½	4,17	1/2
¼	4,18	1/4
¾	4,25	3/4
⅓	4,64	1/3
⅔	4,65	2/3
⅛	14,66	1/8
⅜	4,67	3/8
⅝	4,68	5/8
⅞	4,69	7/8

General

¶	4,5	Paragraph Sign
§	4,6	Section Sign
®	4,22	Registered Trademark
©	4,23	Copyright
'	4,27	Left Single Quote
'	4,28	Right Single Quote
'	4,29	Inverted Single
"	4,30	Left Double Quote
"	4,31	Right Double Quote
"	4,32	Inverted Double Quote
–	4,33	En Dash (width of n)
—	4,34	Em Dash (width of m)
†	4,39	Dagger
‡	4,40	Double Dagger
™	4,41	Trademark
℠	4,42	Servicemark
℞	4,43	Prescription (Rx)
…	4,56	Em Leader (Ellipsis)
℅	4,73	Care of
‰	4,75	Per Thousand
№	4,76	Number (No.)
°	6,36	Degree
★	6,112	Solid Star
◀	6,28	Solid Triangle Left
▲	6,29	Solid Triangle Up
▼	6,30	Solid Triangle Down

FIGURE 5.16:

Examples of special characters not found on the keyboard but available through Font ➤ *WP Characters (Ctrl+W)*

♂	5,4	Male	**Math**			
♀	5,5	Female	√	5,14	Bent Radical	
✪	5,6	Compass	–	6,0	Minus	
☺	5,7	Happy Face	±	6,1	Plus or Minus	
☻	5,8	Dark Happy Face	≤	6,2	Less Than/Equal	
☹	5,26	Sad Face	≥	6,3	Greater Than/Equal	
☎	5,30	Telephone	∝	6,4	Proportional	
☻	5,31	Clock	÷	6,8	Division	
⌛	5,32	Hourglass	|	6,9	Absolute Value	
			{	6,18	Summation	
Keyboard/Computer			Σ	6,19	Infinity	
↵	5,20	Enter	∫	6,40	Integral	
→	6,21	Right Arrow				
←	6,22	Left Arrow	**Music**			
↑	6,23	Up Arrow	♪	5,9	Eighth Note	
↓	6,24	Down Arrow	♫	5,10	Sixteenth Notes	
↔	6,25	Left and Right Arrow	♯	5,27	Sharp	
▶	6,27	Solid Triangle Right	♭	5,28	Flat	
			♮	5,29	Natural	

4, Typographic Symbols character set
5, Iconic Symbols character set
6, Math/Scientific character set

FIGURE 5.16:

Examples of special characters not found on the keyboard but available through Font
➤ *WP Characters (Ctrl+W) (continued)*

typing some special characters. You can use a two-letter code in place of the two-number code. To use a two-letter shortcut, choose Font ➤ WP Characters (or press Ctrl+W) as usual. Then, rather than searching around for the appropriate character, just type in the two-character combination shown in the middle column under each heading of Figure 5.17, and press ↵. For example, to type a small bullet, you can press Ctrl+W, type *. and press ↵.

SIZING SPECIAL CHARACTERS

The size of the current font determines the size of special characters. For example, the first list in Figure 5.18 uses special character 5,21 from the Iconic Symbols set to put a pointing hand at the start of each item in a list. The hands are the same size as the current font.

In the second list, each pointing hand was increased to the Large size.

Character	Shortcut	Code	Character	Shortcut	Code
Bullets and Fractions			**Foreign Language**		
●	*.	[4,3]	¡	!!	[4,7]
●	**	[4,0]	¿	??	[4,8]
○	*o	[4,45]	æ	ae	[1,37]
○	*O	[4,1]	Æ	AE	[1,36]
½	/2	[4,17]	å	ao	[1,35]
¼	/4	[4,18]	ĳ	ij	[1,139]
			Ĳ	IJ	[1,138]
Currency Symbols			œ	oe	[1,167]
¢	c/	[4,19]	Œ	OE	[1,166]
ƒ	f-	[4,14]	ß	ss	[1,23]
£	L-	[4,11]			
¤	ox	[4,24]	**Other Typographic**		
₧	Pt	[4,13]	«	<<	[4,9]
¥	Y=	[4,12]	»	>>	[4,10]
			©	co	[4,23]
Math/Scientific Symbols			—	m-	[4,34]
±	+-	[6,1]	—	–	[4,34]
≤	<=	[6,2]	–	n-	[4,33]
≠	/=	[6,99]	¶	P|	[4,5]
≡	==	[6,14]	®	ro	[4,22]
≥	>=	[6,3]	℞	rx	[4,43]
≈	~~	[6,13]	SM	sm	[4,42]
			TM	tm	[4,41]

FIGURE 5.17:

Two-letter shortcuts for common special characters

To change the size of a special character, follow these steps:

1. Move the insertion point to the left of the special character you want to resize.

2. Select that character either by dragging the mouse button one character to the right or by pressing Shift+→.

3. Choose a relative size, as described earlier, from the Font pull-down menu or Font dialog box.

In the third example of pointing hands in Figure 5.18, the hands line up better with the text to the right. That's because the Advance feature (described in Chapter 20) was used to print each hand 8 points lower than the text next to it—a good trick to know if you're going to be combining text sizes!

You can also change the size of a special character by changing the font (Font ➤ Font) just to the left of the character. For example, the happy face in Figure 5.18 is special character 5,7 from the Iconic Symbols set, printed in a 140-point font (though reduced to fit into the book).

PRINTING TWO CHARACTERS IN ONE SPACE

If you can't find a special character or symbol that you need, you may be able

☞ Complete the order form

☞ Include your check or money order

☞ And mail it today!

☞ Complete the order form

☞ Include your check or money order

☞ And mail it today!

☞ Complete the order form

☞ Include your check or money order

☞ And mail it today!

FIGURE 5.18:

Examples of sized special characters

to create it by typing two or more characters in a single space with the Overstrike feature.

1. Move the insertion point to where you want to type the multiple characters.

2. Choose F**o**nt ➤ **O**verstrike ➤ **C**reate. This dialog box appears.

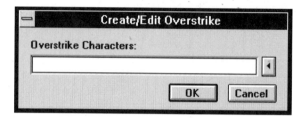

3. If you want to choose size and appearance attributes for the characters, move the mouse pointer to the button with the left-pointing triangle character in it, hold down the mouse button, highlight the size or appearance you want, then release the mouse button. You can repeat this step to combine a size and any number of appearances.

4. Type the characters that you want to overstrike. For example, typing O/ will produce Ø in the document.

5. Click OK or press ↵ when you're finished.

The characters appear in the same space in the document window. In Reveal Codes, the characters are displayed in an [Ovrstk:] code.

Changing an Overstrike

If you need to change an overstrike character, follow these steps:

1. Position the insertion point just past the overstrike characters you want to change.

2. Choose F**o**nt ➤ **O**verstrike ➤ **E**dit.

3. Use the normal editing keys to make changes, including Delete or Backspace to delete text or codes, and the left-pointing triangle button to choose size and appearance options.

4. Click OK.

If you want to delete an overstrike character altogether, turn on Reveal Codes and delete the [Ovrstk:] code.

Typing Diacritical Marks

A diacritical mark is a type of overstrike used to represent certain phonetic values, such as the acute and grave accents used in French.

There are also many *diacritical marks* available in the WordPerfect Characters Multinational 1 character set. As with other special characters, you can choose these from the WordPerfect Characters dialog box or by typing the two-number or two-letter code into the window. Figure 5.19 shows some examples. For example, pressing Ctrl+W, typing **'i**, and pressing ↵ produces an accented *i* (special character 1,49).

Multi-column layouts, like the one shown in Figure 5.20, are covered in Chapter 20.

DRAWING LINES

Using lines is a great way to spruce up a document, as in the sample document shown in Figure 5.20. (You'll learn to create complex documents like this in Part 6 of this book; for now, just notice that various types of lines are used in the document.)

FIGURE 5.19:

Sample diacritical marks

Diacritical	Mark	Shortcut	Code
Acute	í	'i	[1,49]
Caron	ž	vz	[1,207]
Cedilla	ç	,c	[1,39]
Centered Dot	l	:l	[1,151]
Circumflex	â	^a	[1,29]
Crossbar	ŧ	-t	[1,187]
Dot Above	ċ	.c	[1,103]
Grave	è	'e	[1,47]
Macron	ū	_u	[1,193]
Ogonek	ą	;a	[1,95]
Ring Above	å	@a	[1,35]
Slash	ø	/o	[1,81]
Stroke	ł	\l	[1,153]
Tilde	ñ	~n	[1,57]
Umlaut	ü	"u	[1,71]

There are actually several ways to add lines to a document:

◆ The *Underline* and *Double Underline* appearances described earlier can be used to underline text, spaces, and tabs.

◆ *Line Draw* can be used to draw a variety of line styles and can be used with any printer. The double underline beneath the nameplate in Figure 5.20 was created using Line Draw.

◆ *Graphic lines* work only with graphics printers. You can control the thickness, shading, and exact position of the lines. The vertical lines separating the columns in Figure 5.20 are graphic lines.

◆ The *Tables* (Chapter 6) and *Graphics* (Chapter 19) features, which also require a graphics printer, are ideal tools for drawing boxes around text, like the box surrounding the text in the middle of the document shown in Figure 5.20.

USING LINE DRAW

TO USE LINE DRAW TO DRAW LINES INTERACTIVELY,

press Ctrl+D to call up the Line Draw dialog box. Choose a character to use for drawing, then use the arrow keys to draw, move, and erase lines. Choose Close to close the dialog box.

Line Draw lets you interactively draw character-based lines, which you can print with a nongraphics printer. It's also useful for drawing lines in documents that you might plan on exporting to another word processor or text editor that does not offer graphic lines.

For Line Draw to work properly, you should use a monospaced font that includes line-drawing characters, such as Courier Line Draw. Proportional fonts make line drawing difficult. Also, use left justification to prevent characters in the lines from being spread across the margins.

When you use Line Draw, WordPerfect automatically switches to draft mode so that the lines appear correctly on the screen. It also switches to Typeover mode, so any text or lines you draw over will be replaced by the characters in the lines. To use Line Draw, follow these steps:

1. Position the insertion point where you want to start drawing a line or box.

Before using Line Draw to create a complex document, you might want to check out some of the examples created with the Tables feature at the end of Chapter 6.

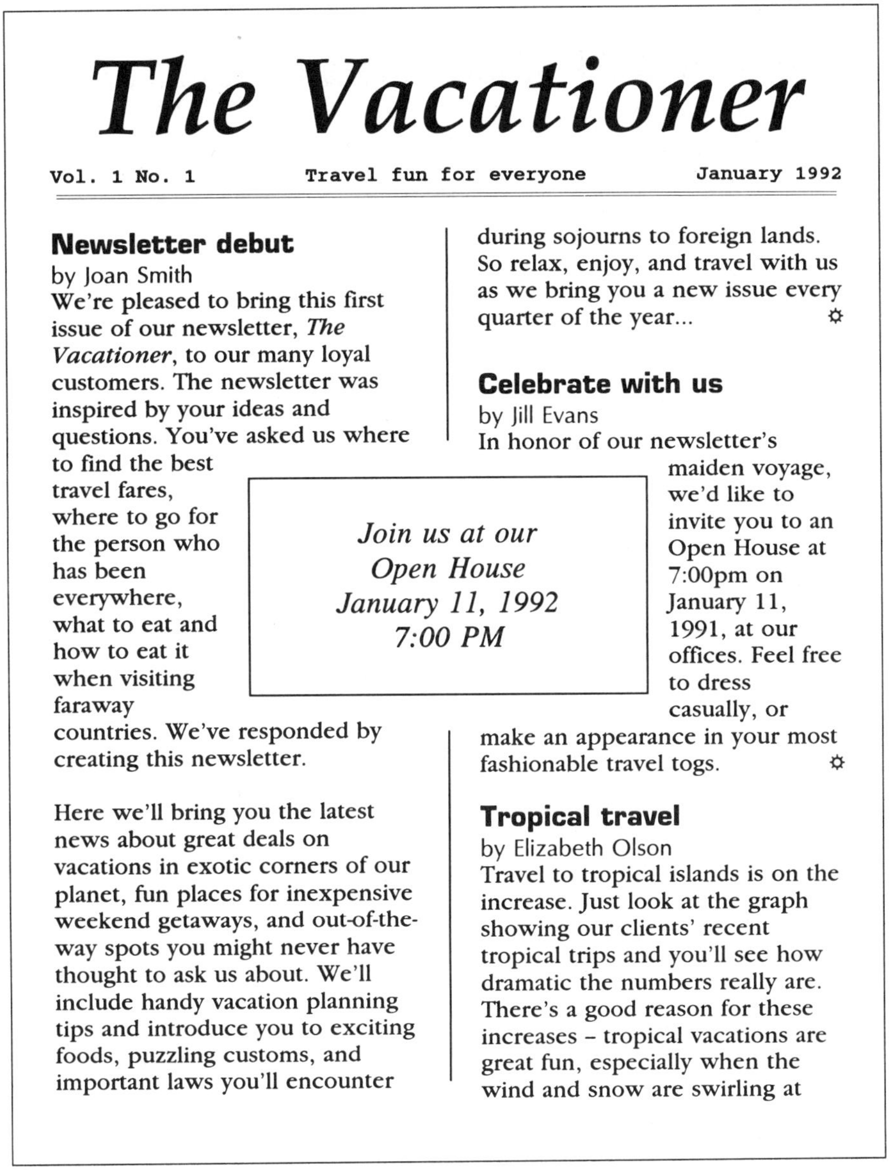

FIGURE 5.20:

*A sample document
with some lines added*

The Vacationer

Vol. 1 No. 1   Travel fun for everyone   January 1992

Newsletter debut
by Joan Smith

We're pleased to bring this first issue of our newsletter, *The Vacationer*, to our many loyal customers. The newsletter was inspired by your ideas and questions. You've asked us where to find the best travel fares, where to go for the person who has been everywhere, what to eat and how to eat it when visiting faraway countries. We've responded by creating this newsletter.

Here we'll bring you the latest news about great deals on vacations in exotic corners of our planet, fun places for inexpensive weekend getaways, and out-of-the-way spots you might never have thought to ask us about. We'll include handy vacation planning tips and introduce you to exciting foods, puzzling customs, and important laws you'll encounter during sojourns to foreign lands. So relax, enjoy, and travel with us as we bring you a new issue every quarter of the year...   ✿

*Join us at our
Open House
January 11, 1992
7:00 PM*

Celebrate with us
by Jill Evans

In honor of our newsletter's maiden voyage, we'd like to invite you to an Open House at 7:00pm on January 11, 1991, at our offices. Feel free to dress casually, or make an appearance in your most fashionable travel togs.   ✿

Tropical travel
by Elizabeth Olson

Travel to tropical islands is on the increase. Just look at the graph showing our clients' recent tropical trips and you'll see how dramatic the numbers really are. There's a good reason for these increases – tropical vacations are great fun, especially when the wind and snow are swirling at

2. Choose your monospaced font for drawing lines, using Font ➤ Font.

3. Press Ctrl+D to bring up the Line Draw dialog box:

4. Choose any one of the 11 characters shown. Or click the **C**haracter button, delete the existing character, and either type the character you want to draw with or press Ctrl+W and insert whatever special character you want to draw with.

5. Use the ↑, ↓, ←, and → keys to draw lines. You can also use Home (draw to left margin), End (draw to right margin), Ctrl+↑ (draw to top margin), and Ctrl+↓ (draw to bottom margin).

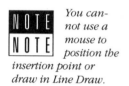

You cannot use a mouse to position the insertion point or draw in Line Draw.

6. If you need to move the insertion point without drawing, choose **M**ove from the Line Draw dialog box and position the insertion point. If you need to erase lines, choose **E**rase from the Line Draw dialog box, and move the insertion point over existing lines.

7. Repeat steps 3–5 as often as necessary to complete your drawing.

8. When you've finished drawing, choose the Close button from the dialog box.

When a character created with Line Draw is highlighted in Reveal Codes, that character's code appears (e.g., [3,22]).

Depending on what character you use to draw the line, you may notice a small arrow at the beginning and end of the line. That arrow will not appear in the printed document. Instead, it simply indicates the direction that you are going at the moment and also marks the end of the line. Any arrows that remain at the ends of lines will appear as half-space lines in the printed document (and on the Print Preview screen), not as arrows. Nonetheless, you can prevent the appearance of the little arrow by pressing Alt+End when you've finished drawing a line or by moving the insertion point to the arrow and pressing Delete.

DRAWING GRAPHIC LINES

TO DRAW GRAPHIC LINES,

position the insertion point and choose Graphics ➤ Line, choose either Horizontal or Vertical, and then define the line in the dialog box that appears.

Graphic lines are independent of the current font, so they don't pose any problems when used with proportionally spaced fonts. However, you need a graphics printer to print graphic lines.

Drawing Horizontal Graphic Lines

To draw a horizontal graphic line in a document, follow these steps:

1. Move the insertion point to the approximate location for the line.

2. Choose **G**raphics ➤ **L**ine ➤ **H**orizontal (or press Ctrl+F11). You'll see the dialog box shown in Figure 5.21.

3. Move the mouse pointer to the box under **H**orizontal Position (it has an up and a down arrow along its right side) or press Alt+H. Hold down the left mouse button, move the highlight to one of the options (described below), then release the mouse button (or scroll through the options with the ↑ and ↓ keys):

Left	The line extends from the left margin.
Right	The line extends from the right margin.
Center	The line is centered between the left and right margins (its length determined below).
Full	The line extends from the left margin to the right margin.
Specify	You enter the starting point, in inches, in the **Po**sition text box beneath the button, measured from the left edge of the page (e.g., entering *2* starts the line 2 inches from the left edge of the paper, 1 inch from the left margin).

4. If you do not want the line drawn at the current insertion-point position, choose the **V**ertical Position box, then one of these options:

Specify	Choose this option, then change the entry in the Position text box to reflect the vertical distance from the top of the page where you want the line drawn. For example, entering *2* draws the line two inches from the top of the page, one inch below the top margin.
Baseline	This option draws the line along the same line that the insertion point is on.

5. Optionally, choose **L**ength, then type in the length in inches (e.g., *3.5* for a $3\frac{1}{2}$-inch line). This option is shaded and unavailable if you chose Full as the horizontal position.

6. Optionally, choose **T**hickness, and type in the thickness in inches (some examples are shown in Figure 5.22).

7. Optionally, choose **G**ray Shading, and enter a value between 0 (no shading, pure white) and 100 (pitch black).

8. Choose OK to leave the menu and return to your document.

The line appears in the document window. Keep in mind that unless you specify otherwise, the line is drawn from the chosen margin to the current insertion-point position. For example, if you want to run a line from the end of the current word to the right margin, first make sure that the insertion point is at the end of that word. Then choose Graphics ➤ Line ➤ Horizontal. Choose Right as the line's horizontal position, then click OK.

Drawing Vertical Graphic Lines

Multi-column layouts are described in detail in Chapter 20.

The steps for creating a vertical line are about the same as those for creating a horizontal line. You can position the insertion point where you want the line to appear, or you can type in an exact measurement. If you want to place a line between columns created with the multicolumn layout features, first place the insertion point anywhere within a column (the insertion point must be below or to the right of the hidden [Col On] code that activates the columns). Then follow these steps:

1. Choose **G**raphics ➤ Line ➤ **V**ertical (or press Ctrl+Shift+F11).

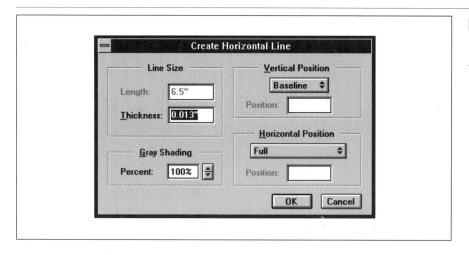

FIGURE 5.21:

The Create Horizontal Line dialog box

2. Choose one of the options below from the box under **H**orizontal Position:

Left Margin	The line is printed along the left margin.
Right Margin	The line is printed along the right margin.
Between Columns	This option displays the Right of Column text box, allowing you to specify which column to place the line in. For example, in a three-column document, entering *2* would place the line between the second and third columns.
Specify	If you choose this option, you can use the Position text box to type the distance from the left edge of the page at which to place the line (e.g., *4.25* is the center of an 8½-inch-wide page).

Examples of various graphic line widths

.013"

.026"

.039"

.052"

.063" (1/16 inch)

.078"

.091"

.104"

.117"

.125" (1/8 inch)

.188" (3/16 inch)

.25" (1/4 inch)

3. From the **V**ertical Position box, choose one of these options:

Full Page	The line runs the full length of the page, from the top margin to the bottom margin.
Top	The line starts at the top margin.
Center	The line is centered between the top and bottom margins.
Bottom	The line starts at the bottom margin.
Specify	Enter the distance, in inches, from the top edge of the page to start the line.

4. Optionally, choose **L**ength, type in the length of the line in inches (for example, *4 1/2* or *4.5)*, and then press ↵.

5. Optionally, choose **T**hickness, and type in a thickness (see Figure 5.22 for examples).

6. Optionally, choose **G**ray Shading and enter a value between 0 (for no shading, pure white) and 100 (pitch black), and press ↵.

7. Choose OK to leave the dialog box and return to your document.

The graphic line appears in the document. WordPerfect places a code in the document: [VLine:] for vertical lines and [HLine:] for horizontal lines. The code also includes the measurements that define the line.

CHANGING GRAPHIC LINES WITH YOUR MOUSE

Once you've created a graphic line, you can move it or change its thickness by using your mouse. Follow these steps:

1. Move the I beam to the line until the I beam changes to the pointer.

2. Click the left mouse button. The mouse pointer changes to the Move icon, and the line appears jagged, with square sizing handles interspersed along the line (you may need to scroll to see the sizing handles on a vertical line).

3. To move the line, hold down the left mouse button, and drag the Move icon to the line's new location. Then release the mouse button.

4. To change the thickness of the line, move the mouse pointer to a sizing handle. The pointer changes to a two-headed arrow when it is properly positioned (as at left). Hold down the left mouse button, and drag the icon until the line is the thickness you want.

5. Optionally, click the right mouse button, then click the Edit Line option to return to the line's dialog box, and make changes there.

To unselect a line and resume normal typing and editing, click anywhere outside the line.

CHANGING GRAPHIC LINES WITHOUT A MOUSE

As an alternative to using the mouse, you can edit any graphic line by returning to its dialog box:

1. Position the insertion point just to the right of the line you want to edit (you may want to use Reveal Codes to help position the insertion point at the exact [HLine:] or [VLine:] code for the line you want to change).

2. Choose **G**raphics ➤ Line, then either Edit **H**orizontal or Edit **V**ertical, depending on which type of line you want to edit.

You'll return to the line's dialog box, where you can make choices as described earlier in "Drawing Graphic Lines."

DELETING GRAPHIC LINES

If you want to change or delete a graphic line, follow these steps:

If the line stays on your screen after deleting its code, press Redisplay (Ctrl+F3) to redraw the screen.

1. Move the insertion point to about the place where you created the line.

2. Turn on Reveal Codes (**V**iew ➤ Reveal **C**odes or Alt+F3).

3. In Reveal Codes, move the highlight to the [HLine:] or [VLine:] code that defines the line you want to delete.

4. Press Delete to delete the code.

You'll see more examples of graphic lines in Part 6; all of them were created using the steps described in this section.

COLORING YOUR TEXT

TO CHANGE THE PRINT COLOR OF TEXT,

position the insertion point where you want to change the color, or select the text you want to color. Then choose Font ➤ Color and the color you want to print in.

If you are one of the fortunate few who own a color printer, you can easily color your printed text. But even if you don't own a color printer, your local print shop can probably print your documents in color for you. Use the techniques presented here to choose print colors, then refer to Chapter 20 for information on preparing your document for professional typesetting.

CHOOSING A PRINT COLOR

To change the print color of text, follow these steps:

The File ➤ Preferences ➤ Display options may affect the print color of text on your screen. See Chapter 13.

1. Move the insertion point to where you want to change the print color (either before existing text or where you're about to type). Or, if you want to change the color of a portion of existing text, select that text.

2. Choose Font ➤ **C**olor. The Select Text Color dialog box, shown in Figure 5.23 appears.

3. Choose a print color from the **P**redefined Colors box or from either spectrum, or define a color by using the options in the Color Options area (see below).

4. Click OK to return to your document.

If you selected text in step 1, that text is displayed in the selected color. If you did not select text, all new and existing text to the right of the insertion point and up to the next color change (if any) is displayed in the new color. Text color changes are controlled by [Color:] codes visible in Reveal Codes. The codes, of course, can be moved or deleted like any other.

CHOOSING A PREDEFINED COLOR

You can choose from among several commonly used colors. They appear in the Predefined Colors box in the Select Text Color dialog box.

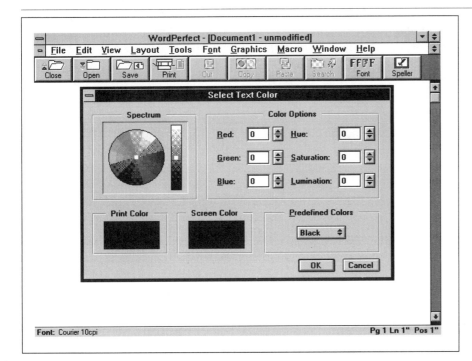

FIGURE 5.23:

Select Text Color dialog box appears when you choose Font ➤ Color.

1. Move the mouse pointer to the box under **P**redefined Colors, or press Alt+P.

2. Hold down the left mouse button and move the highlight to the color you want (other than Custom), then release the mouse button. Optionally, use the ↑ and ↓ keys to scroll to the color you want.

The Print Color and Screen Color boxes in the dialog box change to show you how the color will look when printed and on the screen. Click OK or press ↵ after choosing your predefined color.

The vertical spectrum affects lumination without changing hue or saturation.

CHOOSING A COLOR FROM THE SPECTRUMS

You can also choose a custom color from either the round or vertical-bar spectrum, near the upper-left corner of the Select Text Color dialog box. Click anywhere in either spectrum, or drag the small cursor within either spectrum to the color you want.

The options in the Color Options area change to reflect the chosen color. The Print Color and Screen Color boxes in the lower-left corner also change to show you how the color will look when printed and on the screen. Click OK or press ↵ to choose the current color and return to your document.

DEFINING A COLOR NUMERICALLY

You can also define a color numerically, or fine-tune the currently chosen color, by using the options under Color Options in the dialog box. Use the arrows next to each item to increase or decrease the value in the box. Or use the Tab and Shift+Tab keys to scroll from item to item, and the usual keys to delete and type in new values.

The Red, Green, and Blue options can be any value in the range of 0 to 255; 0 represents a complete lack of that color. The Hue can be any value in the range of 0 to 360. The Saturation and Lumination options can be any value in the range of 0 to 100. The effects of these various options will be apparent in the Print Color and Screen Color boxes and on the spectrums.

PRINTING SHADES OF GRAY

If you don't have a color printer, you can still print text in shades of gray. Use the same techniques described above to bring up the Select Text Color dialog box, then use the (vertical) spectrum to choose a gray shade. Optionally, choose Black as the predefined color, then change the Lumination option. The higher the lumination value, the lighter the text.

Different printers interpret gray shades and colors differently, so you may need to experiment to find just the right shades for your printer. As an example, Figure 5.24 shows gray shades and colors as printed by a PostScript printer and the Hewlett-Packard LaserJet III. The percentage values indicate the Lumination setting with a print color initially defined as Black.

In this chapter you've learned about a number of techniques for sprucing up the appearance of a document, including using fonts, print sizes and appearances, special characters, and lines. In Part 6 you'll round out these skills with more advanced *desktop publishing* features, which are similar to those presented here.

In the next chapter, you'll learn about one of WordPerfect's most powerful yet easy tools for organizing text into columns, the Tables feature.

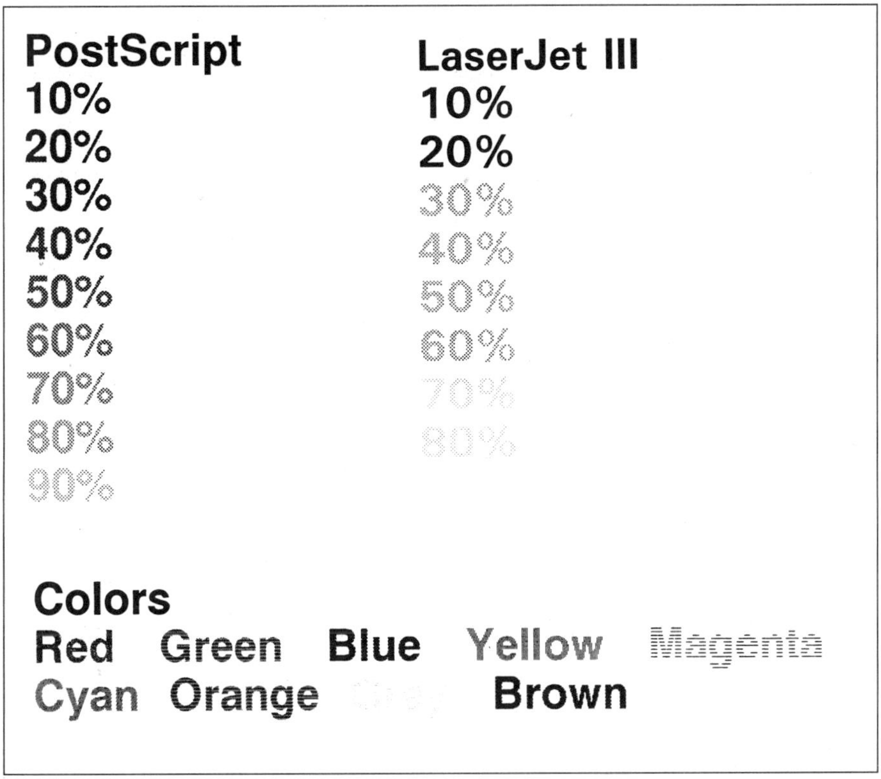

PostScript
10%
20%
30%
40%
50%
60%
70%
80%
90%

LaserJet III
10%
20%
30%
40%
50%
60%
70%
80%

Colors
Red   Green   Blue   Yellow   Magenta
Cyan   Orange   Brown

FIGURE 5.24:

Examples of using Lumination values with an initial print color of Black to print gray shades, and how various colors might look when printed with a noncolor printer

CHAPTER 6

Creating Tables

The Tables feature lets you type text into columns that you can later widen, narrow, or rearrange without ever changing a tab stop. It can be used to type *any* kind of document that involves columns, be it a simple list of names and addresses, a financial statement, an itinerary, or whatever.

About the only type of column that the Tables feature is *not* particularly good for is the newspaper-style, where you read down one column and then resume reading at the top of the next one. For this, a multicolumn layout (Chapter 20) is better.

HANDS-ON
....
LESSON 5

For a hands-on lesson in creating a table, see Lesson 5 in Part 9.

USES OF THE TABLES FEATURE

The Tables feature can be used to type any short passage or document that requires multiple columns. It is especially useful for creating small tables, like the example shown in Figure 6.1.

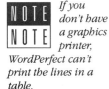
If you don't have a graphics printer, WordPerfect can't print the lines in a table.

But this feature is great for creating *any* short multicolumn document, even if you don't want to draw lines in the document. Figures 6.2 through 6.4 show how you might use the Tables feature to create an itinerary with parallel columns. Figure 6.2 shows the first draft of the itinerary, with the Tables feature used to organize some of the text into columns.

Destination	Arrives	Ticket Price
Oceanside	8:30 am	$12.50
San Clemente	9:00 am	$17.50
Santa Ana	10:00 am	$37.50
Anaheim	10:30 am	$40.00
Los Angeles	11:45 am	$55.00
Malibu	1:00 pm	$70.00

FIGURE 6.1:

A sample table created with the Tables feature

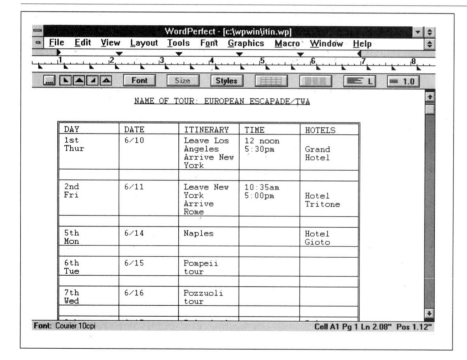

FIGURE 6.2:

The first draft of an itinerary in the document window

At any time, you can widen or narrow columns and join and split cells to get exactly the appearance you want. Text within each cell will automatically be wrapped to fit within that cell, and you can see your changes right on the screen as you make them. For example, Figure 6.3 shows the sample

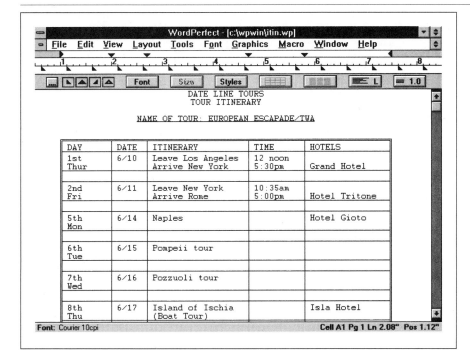

The second draft of the itinerary, after changing some column widths

A "cell" is the place where a row and column meet.

itinerary after column widths within the table have been adjusted to better accommodate the text inside the cells.

When everything looks good, you can easily change or remove any of the lines to get exactly the look you want. For example, Figure 6.4 shows the complete printed itinerary after removing most of the lines from the table. This presents text neatly placed into columns without an abundance of lines.

In a nutshell, the Tables feature lets you easily create and refine *any* multicolumn document. Later in this chapter, I'll show you some innovative and productive ways of using Tables to create some truly dazzling documents.

TABLES TERMINOLOGY

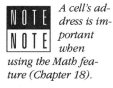

A cell's address is important when using the Math feature (Chapter 18).

The Tables feature has some terminology of its own. Basically, a table consists of *rows* and *columns*. The place where a row and column meet is a *cell*. Each cell has an *address* that indicates its position in the table. Whenever the insertion point is inside the table, the current cell's address appears on the status bar as you move the insertion point from cell to cell (see Figure 6.5).

The columns are labeled alphabetically from left to right, and the rows are numbered from top to bottom, so the cell in the upper-left corner is always cell A1, the cell to the right of that is cell B1, and so forth. Beneath cell A1 are cells A2, A3, and so forth.

CREATING A TABLE

TO CREATE A TABLE,

position the insertion point where you want to place the table in your document. Click the Tables button on the ruler, and drag the table symbol to the size of the table you want to create. Or choose Layout ➤ Tables ➤ Create (Ctrl+F9 C), and specify the size of the table you want to create.

DATE LINE TOURS
TOUR ITINERARY

NAME OF TOUR: EUROPEAN ESCAPADE/TWA

DAY	DATE	ITINERARY	TIME	HOTELS
1st Thur	6/10	Leave Los Angeles Arrive New York	12 noon 5:30pm	Grand Hotel
2nd Fri	6/11	Leave New York Arrive Rome	10:35am 5:00pm	Hotel Tritone
5th Mon	6/14	Naples		Hotel Gioto
6th Tue	6/15	Pompeii tour		
7th Wed	6/16	Pozzuoli tour		
8th Thu	6/17	Island of Ischia (Boat Tour)		Isla Hotel
9th Fri	6/18	Sorrento		
10th Sat	6/19	Leave Rome Arrive New York	1:15pm 4:20pm	
11th Sun	6/20 6/27	Leave New York Arrive Los Angeles	7:30pm 10:30pm	

FIGURE 6.4:

The sample itinerary, with most of the lines removed

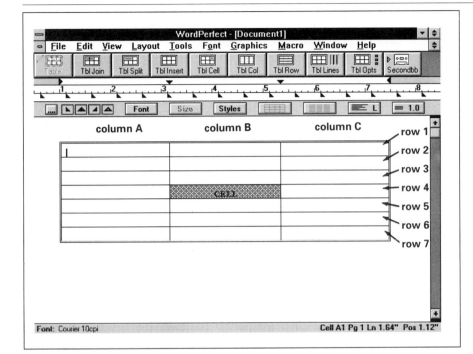

FIGURE 6.5:

Columns, rows, and a cell in a table

To work with tables, you must first create an empty table, which you can fill with information. You can use either the Tables button on the ruler or the menus to create an empty table, as described in the following sections.

CREATING A TABLE FROM THE RULER

WordPerfect offers a handy technique for creating an empty table, using the mouse and the ruler. Follow these steps:

1. Move the insertion point to wherever you want the table to appear in your document.

2. If the ruler isn't on, choose **View** ➤ **R**uler (or press Alt+Shift+F3) to display it.

3. Move the I beam to the Tables button (shown at left), and hold down the left mouse button. A grid representing an empty table appears, as in Figure 6.6.

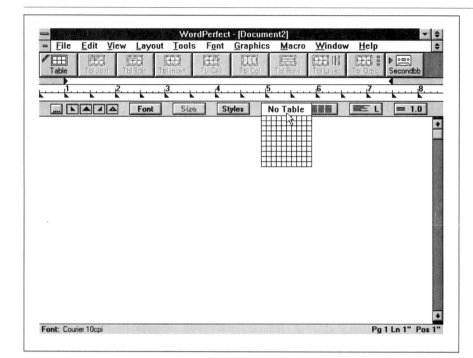

FIGURE 6.6:

The table symbol appears when you click the Tables button on the ruler.

4. Keep the mouse button depressed, and drag the mouse up or down to increase or decrease the number of rows in the table. Drag the mouse left or right to increase or decrease the number of columns in the table. The table symbol grows if necessary to accommodate more than 10 rows or columns, and the number of rows and columns in the current table is indicated on the bar at the top of the table symbol.

5. Release the mouse button when the table is the size you want. An empty table appears at the insertion point, equal in size to the table you specified with your mouse.

The triangular icons on the bar above the ruler represent column widths. You can widen or narrow a column by dragging any of these icons.

CREATING A TABLE FROM THE MENUS

You can also create a table from the menus. Follow these steps:

1. Move the insertion point to where you want to place the table in your document.

2. Choose **L**ayout ➤ **T**ables ➤ **C**reate (or press Ctrl+F9 C). You'll see this dialog box:

The largest possible table size is 32 columns by 32,756 rows.

3. Type the number of columns you want in your table in the **C**olumns text box (though you can add and delete columns later, if you wish), or just leave the suggested number, *3*.

4. Type the number of rows you want in the **R**ows text box (you can change your mind later), or just leave the suggested number, *1*.

5. Choose OK or press ↵ to leave the dialog box.

WordPerfect creates an empty table with the number of rows and columns you specified.

MOVING THROUGH A TABLE

One of the first things you'll need to know about using tables is how to move the insertion point to a specific cell.

One of the easiest ways to move to a specific cell is by using your mouse:

1. Move the I beam to the cell where you want the insertion point.

2. Click the left mouse button.

WordPerfect also offers many keyboard shortcuts for moving through a table, as listed in Table 6.1.

USING THE GO TO COMMAND

You can go to a specific cell by placing the insertion point anywhere within a table, then using the Go To dialog box.

1. Position the insertion point anywhere within the table.

TO MOVE	PRESS
Up one row	Alt+↑
Down one row	Alt+↓
Left one column	Alt+←
Right one column	Alt+→
To top of current cell	Alt+Home
To bottom of current cell	Alt+End
To next cell	Tab
To previous cell	Shift+Tab
To first cell in row	Home Home
To last cell in row	End End

TABLE 6.1:

Shortcut Keys for Moving in Tables

2. Choose **E**dit ➤ **G**o To (or press Ctrl+G). The Go To dialog box will appear.

3. Move the mouse pointer to the button under Position, click the button, and drag the highlight to any listed location.

4. If you chose Go To Cell in step 3, the insertion point will be in the Go To Cell text box. Type in the cell address you want and press ↵.

If the table is too big to fit in the document window, you can scroll through it with your mouse. Just click the left mouse button, and then drag the mouse in the direction you want to scroll. This will select the cells as you move through the table, but you can easily unselect them by clicking in a single cell when you have reached the area of the table you want to be in.

You can also use the scroll bars to the right and bottom of the document window to move through the text. When you use the scroll bars, note that you do not move the insertion point within the table; only your view of your table changes. To move the insertion point, simply click in the cell that you want to be in.

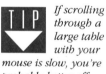 *If scrolling through a large table with your mouse is slow, you're probably better off using the Go To dialog box.*

TYPING AND EDITING TEXT IN A TABLE

TO TYPE OR EDIT TEXT IN A TABLE,

move the insertion point to where you want to type or edit the text, then type or edit as you normally would.

Once you've created an empty table, it's easy to type and edit text in it:

1. Move the insertion point to the cell in which you want to type text or change existing text.

2. Type your text as you normally would, or use any WordPerfect editing technique to make changes.

You can also use WordPerfect formatting features when typing or changing text in a cell. For example, you can press Shift+F7 to center text in a cell, or press Ctrl+B to boldface text or Ctrl+U to underline it. However, since Tab and Margin Release (Shift+Tab) are used to move from cell to cell, you can't use these keys to indent and outdent within a cell. But you can press Ctrl+Tab to indent or Ctrl+Shift+Tab to outdent. You can also change the ruler while in any cell. This affects all indents and outdents in the current cell and all cells to the right and below.

If the text you type is too wide for the cell, WordPerfect will word-wrap the text as though the cell were a page and will expand the height of the entire row to accommodate the text in that cell. (You can later widen or narrow the cell to change the word wrap within it.)

If you are accustomed to ending a paragraph by pressing ↵, you'll probably inadvertently press ↵ after filling a cell. There's no harm in doing so, but it causes the row to expand in height to accommodate the new line created; you probably will not want this extra blank line across the row. If you press ↵ by mistake, just press Backspace. You can also open Reveal Codes to locate and delete any extra [HRt] codes.

CHANGING A TABLE'S STRUCTURE

TO WORK WITH CELLS, COLUMNS, ROWS, OR THE TABLE STRUCTURE AS A WHOLE,

move the insertion point into the table first.

The Tables Button Bar offers several shortcuts for changing a table's structure.

You can modify an existing table in almost any way imaginable, even if you've already entered text in the table. The sections that follow describe the many ways to alter a table. First, I need to talk about ways in which you can select cells in a table, which will let you work with multiple cells or multiple columns while refining the structure of your table.

USING THE MOUSE TO SELECT TABLE CELLS

As with any text in your document, you can select a group of cells or columns that you want to work with. Follow these steps:

1. Move the I beam to the cell, row, or column you want to work with, near a line.

- ♦ If the I beam is at the left vertical line of a cell, row, or column, it changes to a left arrow. You will want the I beam to display a left arrow when selecting a row in step 2.

- ♦ If the I beam is at the top horizontal line of a cell, row, or column, it changes to an up arrow. You will want the I beam to display an up arrow when selecting a column in step 2.

2. Click the left mouse button once to select a cell, twice to select a row or column, or three times to select the entire table.

3. To select more than one row or column, click once when the mouse appears as an arrow, and hold down the mouse button while dragging into the next column or row. When the desired number of columns or rows has been selected, release the mouse button.

4. To select multiple cells, simply hold down the mouse button and drag across the desired cells.

Figure 6.7 shows a table with a row selected. The mouse again appears as an I beam or arrow when you have finished your selection, depending on the position of the mouse.

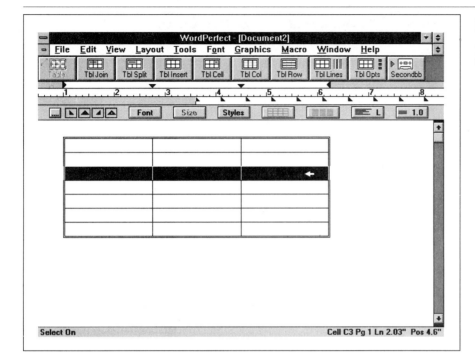

USING THE KEYBOARD TO SELECT TABLE CELLS

As an alternative to using the mouse, you can use the keyboard to select table cells. Follow these steps:

1. Move the insertion point to the cell where you want to begin the selection.

2. Hold down the Shift key while pressing ↑, ↓, →, or ← to extend the selection in whatever direction you want to go.

Be aware that if a cell already contains text, the selection will move through that text before it starts moving through cells. If you plan on selecting many cells, you may want to start by pressing Shift+↑ or Shift+↓ to begin selecting entire cells. Table 6.2 lists some additional shortcut keys that you can use to select cells.

TO SELECT	PRESS
Adjoining cells	Shift+*arrow key*
From current cell to first cell in row	Shift+Home Shift+Home
From current cell to last cell in row	Shift+End Shift+End
Current cell and one above	Alt+Shift+↑
Current cell and one below	Alt+Shift+↓
Current cell and one to left	Alt+Shift+←
Current cell and one to right	Alt+Shift+→

TABLE 6.2:

Shortcut Keys for Selecting Table Cells

RESIZING COLUMNS

TO CHANGE A COLUMN WIDTH BY USING THE RULER,

position the insertion point anywhere in the table, then drag the triangular icon in the ruler to widen or narrow the cell.

You can use the ruler to change the width of any column in the table. Follow these steps:

1. Move the insertion point anywhere into the table.

2. If the ruler is not already displayed on your screen, choose **V**iew ➤ **R**uler or press Alt+Shift+F3. You will see triangular icons above the ruler indicating the width of each column, as shown below.

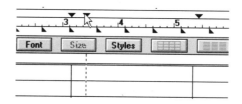

*If you have
more than
one table
on-screen,
make sure you move
the insertion point
into the one you want
to work with before
choosing the trian-
gular icons above the
ruler.*

3. Drag the triangular icon for any column to resize the column. (Columns to the right will be resized accordingly.)

You cannot widen a table beyond the width of the page. Therefore, if a table already extends to the right margin, and you widen a column that has other columns to the right of it, these columns will shrink accordingly. Once the table has reached the right margin, and the columns to the right have shrunk to the minimum width of one space, dragging the triangular icons farther to the right becomes impossible.

Figure 6.8 shows a small sample table before and after sizing the columns. As you can see, widening and narrowing columns helps you control word wrap within each column, the row height, and the distance between the text in the columns.

FIGURE 6.8:

A sample table before and after changing column widths

Original table, before sizing columns...

Item No.	Description	Size	Qty	Price
BW-111	Boy's Bermuda Short	22	1	$29.95
BW-204	Boy's Tank Top	12	1	$19.95
BW-607	Boy's Polo Shirt	12	1	$24.95

The same table as above after sizing the columns to better fit the text within each column...

Item No.	Description	Size	Qty	Price
BW-111	Boy's Bermuda Short	22	1	$29.95
BW-204	Boy's Tank Top	12	1	$19.95
BW-607	Boy's Polo Shirt	12	1	$24.95

And finally, the same table after realigning text, changing lines, and shading to give it a more polished look...

Item No.	Description	Size	Qty	Price
BW-111	Boy's Bermuda Short	22	1	$29.95
BW-204	Boy's Tank Top	12	1	$19.95
BW-607	Boy's Polo Shirt	12	1	$24.95

If changing a table's structure suddenly widens the table, you can redraw the table by pressing Ctrl+F3.

This convenient feature takes the guesswork out of figuring out tab stops and column widths before typing text into columns. Instead, you can just figure out how many columns you need, type text into each column, then easily adjust the column widths to best fit the text within each column. As you'll see, you can also align text within columns, use shading and text appearances, and change lines to further improve the appearance of your tables, as the bottom example in Figure 6.8 shows.

Sizing Columns to a Specific Width

When selecting columns rather than individual cells, you need only have the insertion point in one cell, or select one cell from each column, not every cell in every column.

If you want to set a column or group of columns to a specific width, such as 2.5 inches, follow these steps:

1. Move the insertion point anywhere in the column you want to resize. If you want to set the width of more than one column, select the columns whose width you want to change, as described earlier in this chapter.

2. Choose **L**ayout ➤ **T**ables ➤ Col**u**mn, or press Ctrl+F9 U. You'll see this dialog box:

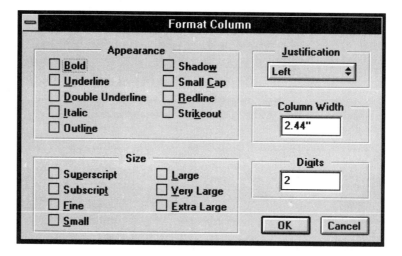

3. Choose C**o**lumn Width, and type the column width (e.g., **2.5** or **2½** for 2½ inches, or **90p** for 90 points) in the text box.

4. Choose OK or press ↵ to return to the document window.

JOINING CELLS

TO JOIN TWO OR MORE CELLS,

**select the cells you want to join, then choose Layout ➤ Tables
➤ Join (Ctrl+F9 J).**

When you *join* cells, you remove the boundaries (lines) between them. You can join any number of adjacent cells to form a single cell. Follow these steps:

1. Move the insertion point into the table, and select all the cells that you want to join to form a single cell.

2. Choose **L**ayout ➤ **T**ables, or press Ctrl+F9.

3. Choose **J**oin. The cells will be joined to form one larger cell.

Figure 6.9 shows an example of cells in the top row of a table before, during, and after the joining of the cells and the centering of the text within the cell; in this figure, the shading in step 2 indicates selected (highlighted) cells. This, of course, is just one example; you can join *any* group of adjacent cells in a table (you'll see additional examples later in this chapter).

Incidentally, if you join cells that already contain text, the text in those cells will be separated by tabs ([HdTab] codes), which you can remove in Reveal Codes if you wish.

SPLITTING CELLS

NOTE *If you change your mind immediately about joining cells, you can choose Edit ➤ Undo or press Alt+Backspace to resplit them.*

When you *split* cells, you add boundaries between them. You can resplit cells you've joined, or you can split a cell to type text in two or more rows or columns within the cell. The basic steps for splitting cells are almost the same as for joining them:

1. Move the insertion point into the table, and select all the cells that you want to split.

2. Choose **L**ayout ➤ **T**ables ➤ **S**plit, or press Ctrl+F9 S. You'll see this dialog box:

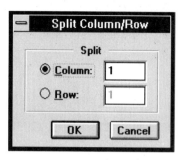

3. Choose either **C**olumn or **R**ow, depending on whether you want to split the cell into rows or columns.

4. WordPerfect will prompt you with a number indicating how many cells are in the adjacent row or column. Press ↵ to accept this number, or type in a new number and press ↵.

If you are using the Split option to undo the effects of a previous joining operation, WordPerfect will place the cell boundaries so that they line up with existing boundaries. If you split a single cell into two or more cells, WordPerfect will create equal-size rows or columns within the cell. The new columns or rows will have the same formatting as the original cell. Figure 6.10 shows an example of a single cell before and after being split into three columns.

CHANGING THE LINES IN A TABLE

TO ALTER OR REMOVE THE LINES IN A TABLE,

select the cells whose lines you want to change, and choose Layout ➤ Tables ➤ Lines. Choose the new line style for each of the lines you want to alter.

You can change or remove the lines in any single cell or group of selected cells. Follow these steps:

1. If you want to change the lines for a single cell, move the insertion point to that cell.

Joining cells to create a table title

Train Schedule		
Destination	Arrives	Price
Oceanside	8:30 am	$12.50
San Clemente	9:00 am	$17.50
Santa Ana	10:00 am	$37.50

Step 1: Move the insertion point to the leftmost cell that you want to join (cell A1 in this example).

Train Schedule		
Destination	Arrives	Price
Oceanside	8:30 am	$12.50
San Clemente	9:00 am	$17.50
Santa Ana	10:00 am	$37.50

Step 2: Select the cells to be joined (in this example, by dragging the mouse pointer across all three columns, or by holding down Shift and pressing End twice).

Train Schedule		
Destination	Arrives	Price
Oceanside	8:30 am	$12.50
San Clemente	9:00 am	$17.50
Santa Ana	10:00 am	$37.50

Step 3: Select Layout ▸ Tables ▸ Join to join the selected cells, as shown.

Train Schedule		
Destination	Arrives	Price
Oceanside	8:30 am	$12.50
San Clemente	9:00 am	$17.50
Santa Ana	10:00 am	$37.50

Step 4: Optionally, if you want to center text in the current cell, choose Layout ▸ Tables ▸ Cell ▸ Justification ▸ Center.

2. If you want to change the lines surrounding multiple cells (or the whole table), select the cells whose lines you want to change.

A table with three columns, and two rows...

The same table as above after splitting cell B1 (center of top row) into three columns...

3. Choose **L**ayout ➤ **T**ables ➤ **L**ines. You'll see the Table Lines dialog box, which lets you choose specific lines to alter:

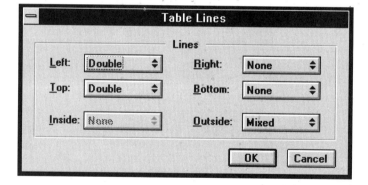

Left	Changes the line at the left edge of the cell or selected cells
Right	Changes the line at the right edge of the cell or selected cells
Top	Changes the line at the top of the cell or selected cells

Bottom	Changes the line at the bottom of the cell or selected cells
Inside	Changes lines inside the selected cells
Outside	Changes lines along the outside border of the selected cells

4. Choose an option from the dialog box. The various line styles are illustrated in Figure 6.11. (Notice the combined use of single lines at the left and top of a cell and thick lines at the right and bottom of a cell to create a "drop-shadow" appearance.)

The dot leaders in Figure 6.12 were created by pressing Alt+F7 twice after typing the text that precedes the dots.

As an example of changing the lines in a table, Figure 6.12 shows you the steps required to remove all the lines from a sample table and to place single lines around the outside border. Note, however, that after removing all the lines (step 2), the document appears to have been created by using tab stops only. This shows how the Tables feature can be used to create multicolumn tables without table lines, and without the hassle of setting tab stops on the ruler.

Changing the line style can be a tad tricky. For example, look at cells A1 and A2, where A2 is beneath cell A1, and a single line separates the two cells. Is that single line on the bottom of cell A1 or the top of cell A2? The answer to this question is relevant, because if cell A1 has a single line at the bottom and cell A2 has a double line at the top, all three lines will be printed, causing an extra thick line to appear, as Figure 6.13 shows.

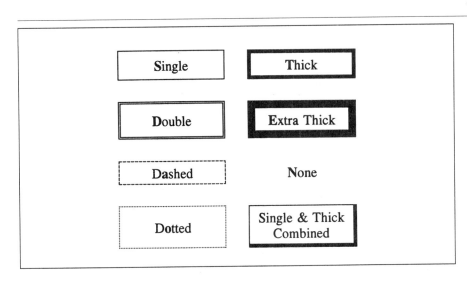

FIGURE 6.11:

Examples of various line styles, and a combination of single and thick lines in a single cell to create a "drop-shadow" appearance

Table of Contents	
Introduction	1
Experimental Design . .	3
Results	4
Conclusion	6

Step 1: The entire table is created, and all cells are selected by moving the I beam near any cell edge and rapidly clicking the left mouse button three times.

Table of Contents	
Introduction	1
Experimental Design . .	3
Results	4
Conclusion	6

Step 2: All lines are removed from the table by choosing **Layout** ▸ **Tables** ▸ **Lines** then choosing None for both Outside and Inside.

Table of Contents	
Introduction	1
Experimental Design . .	3
Results	4
Conclusion	6

Step 3: The entire table is reselected by moving the I beam to any cell edge and rapidly clicking the left mouse button three times.

Table of Contents	
Introduction	1
Experimental Design . .	3
Results	4
Conclusion	6

Step 4: A single line is drawn around the table after selecting **Layout** ▸ **Tables** ▸ **Lines** ▸ **Outside** ▸ **Single**.

Table of Contents	
Introduction	1
Experimental Design . .	3
Results	4
Conclusion	6

Step 5: For the finale, the lines at the right and bottom of the table are changed to Thick, giving a drop-shadow appearance. To get some extra space at the bottom of the table, the insertion point is moved past the number 6 at the bottom of the table, and ↵ is pressed to heighten that row.

FIGURE 6.12:

Examples of changing lines in a sample table

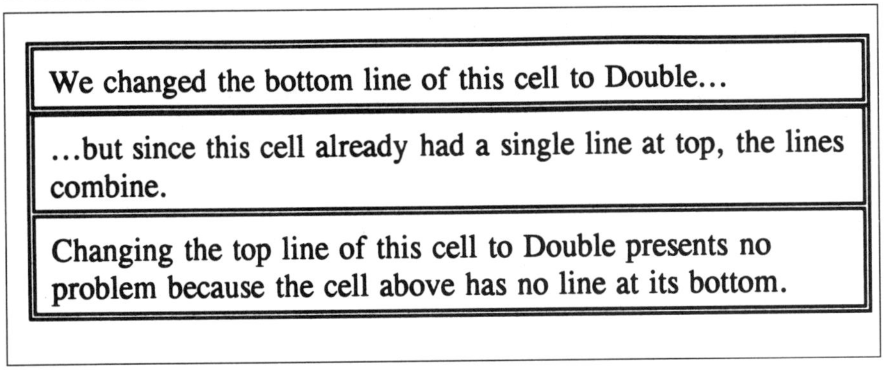

FIGURE 6.13:

Doubling of lines at the bottom of the top cell

There are two ways to avoid this problem. One is to be aware of how WordPerfect sets up the lines between interior cells when you first create a table, as listed below:

NOTE
NOTE

The outer-most cells in a table obviously have double lines at one or two borders when you first create the table.

Top border	Single line
Left border	Single line
Right border	None
Bottom border	None

In other words, you can change the top or left line of an interior cell without worrying about doubling the lines. However, if you want to change the right line of a particular cell, you should move one cell to the right and change that cell's left line. Or, if you want to change the bottom line of a cell, you should move to the cell beneath that one and change its top line.

You can also tell how the lines are currently defined in a cell simply by looking at the existing settings for Left, Right, Top, and Bottom in the Table Lines dialog box.

SHADING CELLS

TO SHADE CELLS,

select the cells you want to shade, then choose Layout ➤ Tables ➤ Cell, and click the Shading check box.

Shading can enhance the appearance of a cell to call attention to it. Shading is also an alternative to using lines to separate cells, rows, or columns. Figure 6.14 shows an example where every other row is shaded.

To shade a cell or group of cells, follow these steps:

1. Move the insertion point to the cell you want to shade or to the cell in the upper-left corner of the group of cells you want to shade.

2. If you want to shade more than a single cell, select the group of cells you want to shade.

3. Choose **L**ayout ➤ **T**ables ➤ **C**ell, or press Ctrl+F9 E.

4. Choose **Sh**ading by marking the check box.

By default, the cell shading is 10 percent of black. You can lighten or darken the shading by choosing Layout ➤ Tables ➤ Options and typing a number in the Shading text box, as discussed later in this chapter.

INSERTING ROWS AND COLUMNS

TO INSERT A ROW OR COLUMN,

position the insertion point, and choose Layout ➤ Tables ➤ Insert. Type the number of rows or columns you want to insert.

You can insert new rows or columns in a table at any time. This is handy if you accidentally skip a row when typing your text, or if you need to add

Milk	A	B$_1$	B$_2$	B$_6$	B$_{12}$
		Vitamin (mg)			
Whole	307	.093	.395	.102	.871
Lowfat (2%)	500	.095	.403	.105	.888
Skim	500	.088	.343	.098	.926
Buttermilk	81	.083	.377	.083	.537
Condensed	1004	.275	1.27	.156	1.36
Evaporated	306	.059	.398	.063	.205
Chocolate	302	.092	.405	.1	.835

FIGURE 6.14:
Shading used as an alternative to lines

 *If you want to add new columns or rows to the right or bottom of the table, see "Changing the Table Size" later in this chapter.*

another row or column between existing ones. Follow these steps:

1. Move the insertion point to the right of or below where you want to insert a new row or column. (New rows are added above the current row, and new columns are added to the left of the current column.)

2. Choose **L**ayout ➤ **T**ables ➤ **I**nsert, or press Ctrl+F9 I. You'll see this dialog box:

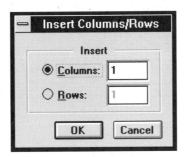

3. Choose either **R**ows (to insert rows) or **C**olumns (to insert columns). You can only insert rows or columns, not both.

4. If you want to insert one row or column, just press ↵. Otherwise, move the insertion point into the appropriate text box, type the number of rows or columns you want to add, and press ↵.

The new rows or columns are inserted, and you return to the document window.

When you insert rows, the rows at the bottom of the table are moved down to make room. However, if you insert a column in a table that's already as wide as the page, WordPerfect splits the current column into two columns. You can then resize the columns as necessary by using the triangular icons above the ruler, as described earlier in this chapter.

You can use a shortcut technique to insert a row. Rather than use the pull-down menus, position the insertion point, and press Alt+Insert to insert a row above, or Alt+Shift+Insert to insert a row below.

Incidentally, you can use blank rows and columns to add space between rows and columns if you wish. For example, Figure 6.15 shows a document with a blank column separating the two columns of text and a blank row separating each section of text. Figure 6.16 shows the same document with the lines removed. The blank column and blank rows become extra blank space in the finished document.

MINUTES OF SCHEDULED REGULAR MEETING

**Conservation Commission
San Fernando, California**

7:00 p.m.   Conference Room 5
Monday, February 25, 1992   Community Building

CALL MEETING TO ORDER/ROLL CALL	Meeting was called to order at 7:00 p.m. by President Jones. Present: Commissioners Abbott, Bates, Carter, Smith. Absent: Dory, Edwards. Excused: Fox.
APPROVAL OF MINUTES	It was MSP (Bates/Carter) to approve the minutes of February 12, 1992.
NEW BUSINESS	Guest speaker Dave Garcia, City of Los Angeles Park & Recreation Dept., updated the Commission on the proposed renovation of Swift Park. The estimated cost for the first phase of the project is $2.9 million, to include enhancement of the existing parking lot.
COMMITTEE REPORTS	See attached reports. Abbott - Parks and Recreation Bates - Road Repair Carter - Environmental Task Force
OLD BUSINESS	Abbott handed out sample letters to elected officials for the letter-writing campaign. Bates reported on the meeting he attended with the Condo Association.
STAFF REPORT	Mr. Smith reported that the next meeting of the Planning Group will include a public hearing on the proposed freeway.
ADJOURNMENT	The meeting was adjourned at 8:00 p.m. to the next meeting of Monday, March 25, 1992.

FIGURE 6.15:
A blank column and blank rows used for extra spacing in a table

MINUTES OF SCHEDULED REGULAR MEETING

**Conservation Commission
San Fernando, California**

7:00 p.m.   Conference Room 5
Monday, February 25, 1992   Community Building

CALL MEETING TO ORDER/ROLL CALL	Meeting was called to order at 7:00 p.m. by President Jones. Present: Commissioners Abbott, Bates, Carter, Smith. Absent: Dory, Edwards. Excused: Fox.
APPROVAL OF MINUTES	It was MSP (Bates/Carter) to approve the minutes of February 12, 1992.
NEW BUSINESS	Guest speaker Dave Garcia, City of Los Angeles Park & Recreation Dept., updated the Commission on the proposed renovation of Swift Park. The estimated cost for the first phase of the project is $2.9 million, to include enhancement of the existing parking lot.

COMMITTEE REPORTS	See attached reports.
	    Abbott - Parks and Recreation
	    Bates - Road Repair
	    Carter - Environmental Task Force

OLD BUSINESS	Abbott handed out sample letters to elected officials for the letter-writing campaign. Bates reported on the meeting he attended with the Condo Association.
STAFF REPORT	Mr. Smith reported that the next meeting of the Planning Group will include a public hearing on the proposed freeway.
ADJOURNMENT	The meeting was adjourned at 8:00 p.m. to the next meeting of Monday, March 25, 1992.

FIGURE 6.16:

The document shown in Figure 6.15 with the lines removed from the table

DELETING ROWS AND COLUMNS

▌ **TO DELETE A ROW OR COLUMN,**

position the insertion point and choose Layout ➤ Tables ➤ Delete, or press Alt+Delete.

You can delete an entire row or column as easily as you can insert one. Follow these steps:

1. Move the insertion point to the row or column that you want to delete.

2. Choose **L**ayout ➤ **T**ables ➤ **D**elete, or press Ctrl+F9 D. You'll see this dialog box:

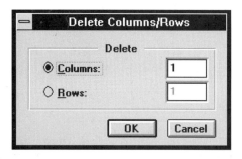

3. Choose either **R**ows (to delete rows) or **C**olumns (to delete columns).

4. To delete one row or column, press ↵. Otherwise, move the insertion point into the appropriate text box, type the number of rows or columns you want to delete, and press ↵.

Be careful when deleting multiple rows and columns. If you delete multiple rows, remember that the current row and the rows beneath it are deleted. If you delete multiple columns, the current column and the columns to the right are deleted.

One way to exercise caution is to select exactly the rows or columns you want to delete. Then choose Layout ➤ Tables ➤ Delete. WordPerfect will delete only the selected rows or columns.

If you make a mistake or change your mind about deleting rows or columns, you can undelete rows or columns by choosing Edit ➤ Undo (Alt+Backspace).

You can use a shortcut technique to delete a row. Rather than go through the pull-down menu options, just move the insertion point to the row you want to delete, and press Alt+Delete.

You can only restore the most recent row or column deletion; you cannot restore any previous deletions.

Note that these commands delete an entire row or column. If you simply want to delete the text within a row or column, you should move the insertion point to the cell that contains the text you want to delete, and use the standard deletion keys.

Table 6.3 summarizes the shortcut keystrokes for modifying the structure of tables.

TO	PRESS
Insert a row above the current row	Alt+Insert
Insert a row below the current row	Alt+Shift+Insert
Delete the current row	Alt+Delete
Insert a tab	Ctrl+Tab
Insert a margin release	Shift+Ctrl+Tab
Insert a hard row (row + page break)	Ctrl+↵

TABLE 6.3:

Shortcut Keys for Editing the Structure of Tables

EMPTYING CELLS

TO DELETE THE CONTENTS OF CELLS WITHOUT CHANGING THE SIZE OF THE TABLE,

select the cells containing the text you want to erase, and press Delete.

If you want to delete text from several cells, leaving the cells empty, select the cells you want to empty, then press Delete. If you've selected an entire column or row, a dialog box like the one below will appear.

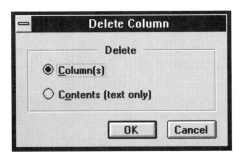

Choose Contents (text only) and press ↵. Only the contents of the selected cells are deleted, but the empty cells remain in the table.

CHANGING THE TABLE SIZE

If you run out of room in a table and need to add new rows at the bottom or new columns to the right, follow these steps:

NOTE *If you decrease the number in the text box, WordPerfect deletes columns or rows to size the table accordingly. You can't correct this mistake with the Escape key—you must use Edit ➤ Undo (Alt+Backspace).*

1. Move the insertion point into the table, and choose **L**ayout ➤ **T**ables ➤ **O**ptions. You'll see the Table Options dialog box, shown in Figure 6.17.

2. In the Table Size area, choose either **C**olumns or **R**ows, depending on which you want to add.

3. The number of columns and rows currently in the table is shown. Type in the *total* number of rows or columns that you want in the table. For example, if the text box shows that there are currently 15 rows in the table, and you want to add 5 rows, type **20.**

4. Choose OK or press ↵ when you're finished.

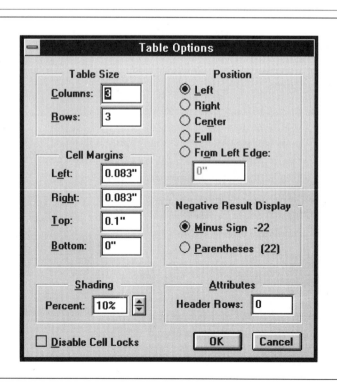

FIGURE 6.17:

The Table Options dialog box

If you increase the number of columns in a table that is already as wide as the margins allow, columns to the left of the new column will be resized to make room for the new columns. As always, you can use the triangular icons above the ruler to resize the columns.

MOVING AND COPYING IN TABLES

There are two basic ways to move or copy information in a table: The first way is to move or copy entire rows or columns, which often changes the actual structure of the table. For example, when you copy an entire row, the copied row is added to the table, so the table becomes one row larger. The second way is to move or copy text (the contents of cells) only. This type of move is called a *block* move and does not change the structure of the table. For example, when you block copy the contents of one row to another, the contents of these rows will match; however, WordPerfect does not add a new row to the table. Figure 6.18 illustrates the difference.

You use regular moves when you want to copy an entire row or column; you use block moves when you want to move or copy only some of the cells in a row or column to existing rows or columns. Note that you cannot

Apples	Bananas	Cherries

The first row is selected.

Apples	Bananas	Cherries
Apples	Bananas	Cherries

Copying text as a block, using **Edit** ▸ **Copy** ▸ **Selection**, then pasting to another row (**Edit** ▸ **Paste**), copies only the cell text; no new row is added.

Apples	Bananas	Cherries
Apples	Bananas	Cherries

Copying text as a block, using **Edit** ▸ **Copy** ▸ **Row(s)**, then pasting to another row (**Edit** ▸ **Paste**), copies the entire row, inserting a new row at the paste position.

FIGURE 6.18:
Copying a row vs. copying a block

transpose rows or columns while moving or copying; that is, you cannot copy a row to a column or vice versa. The two types of moving and copying are discussed in separate sections that follow.

Moving or Copying a Row or Column

To move or copy a row or column in a table, follow these steps:

1. Select the rows or columns you want to move or copy.

2. Choose **Edit** ➤ Cu**t** (or press Shift+Delete), or choose **Edit** ➤ **C**opy (or press Ctrl+Insert). (If you choose Cut, the row or column temporarily disappears.) This dialog box will appear:

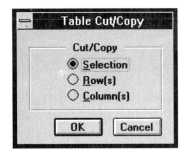

3. Select **R**ow(s) or **C**olumn(s) to move or copy the entire row or column. Choose OK or press ↵.

4. Move the insertion point to the row or column you want to move or copy to, and click the left mouse button (a moved or copied row will be positioned above the insertion point, and a moved or copied column will be positioned to the left of the insertion point).

5. Choose **Edit** ➤ **P**aste, or press Shift+Insert.

Because WordPerfect always moves or copies to the row above, or to the column to the left of, the current one, you cannot directly move or copy to the last column or row of a table. (For example, if you specify the last column of a table as the place to copy a column, the copied column will be one column to the left of the last column.)

To get around this, you need to move or copy the row or column as close to the last row or column as you can get. Then you can move the last column one column to the left, or move the last row one row up, to get things positioned the way you want them.

Moving or Copying the Contents of Cells

When moving or copying a block (i.e., the contents of cells) in a table, you must make sure that a sufficient number of rows and columns are available to accept the moved or copied data. For example, you cannot move or copy three rows into only one row. (If you try to do this, WordPerfect will move only as much of your text as will fit into available rows and columns.) If necessary, add some new rows or columns first.

To move or copy a block of selected text in a table, follow these steps:

 The steps for moving or copying a block are almost the same as for moving or copying a row or column. The only difference is that you choose Selection instead of Row(s) or Column(s).

1. Select the text that you want to move or copy.

2. Choose **E**dit ➤ Cu**t** (or press Shift+Delete) or choose **E**dit ➤ **C**opy (or press Ctrl+Insert). If you choose Cut, your text will disappear temporarily.

3. You will see the Table Cut/Copy dialog box. Choose Selection. Choose OK or press ↵.

4. Move the insertion point to the destination cell.

5. Choose **E**dit ➤ **P**aste (or press Shift+Insert).

You can use this general technique to copy text from within a table to the outside of table, to copy text from outside of a table to the inside of the table, or to copy text from one part of a table to another part. If you select a block of text outside of a table and then move or copy that text into a table cell, the entire block is placed in a single cell.

REPEATING A TABLE HEADER ON MULTIPLE PAGES

A *header* is a row or group of rows in a table that is repeated on each page where the table is printed. Headers are very useful when your table spans several pages of text and you want the table title or column titles to appear at the top of the table on each printed page.

You can use any number of rows at the top of the table for a header. Follow these steps:

1. Move the insertion point into the table, and choose **L**ayout ➤ **T**ables ➤ **O**ptions or press Ctrl+F9 O. You'll see the Table Options dialog box, which you saw earlier in this chapter.

2. Move the insertion point to the Header Rows text box in the **A**ttributes area.

3. Type the number of rows you want to repeat on each page, counting from the top of the table (e.g., **2** to repeat the first two rows).

4. Choose OK or press ⏎.

The heading rows won't be repeated in the document window, but you will see an asterisk next to the cell address on the status bar when your insertion point lands in a cell in a heading row. For example, you'll see a message like this one:

Cell A1* Doc 1 Pg 1 Ln 1.14" Pos 1.12"

You'll need to go to the Print Preview screen (press Shift+F5) if you want to see the heading rows repeated on subsequent pages of a multipage table.

If you change your mind about the headers, just choose Header Rows again, type **0**, and press ⏎.

FORMATTING TEXT IN A TABLE

TO CHANGE THE SIZE OR APPEARANCE OF ALL THE TEXT IN ONE OR MORE CELLS,

move the insertion point to any single cell, or select a group of cells or columns. Choose Layout ➤ Tables, then Cell or Column, then Size or Appearance.

Formatting helps you improve the appearance of text within a table. You can format a single cell, a group of cells, a column, or several columns in a single operation. Several formatting techniques were used to create the table shown in Figure 6.19:

◆ The top title is in large size, boldfaced, and italicized.

◆ The column titles are boldfaced.

◆ The row titles are italicized.

◆ All numbers are right-aligned in their columns.

COMPARATIVE OPERATING EXPENSES			
Division	1990	1991	% Change
North	1,980,870	2,780,870	40.4%
South	987,750	760,080	-23.1%
East	986,500	1,100,000	11.5%
West	1,275,000	987,000	-22.6%
Total	5,230,120	5,627,950	7.6%

FIGURE 6.19:
A formatted table

To access the formatting options, choose Layout ➤ Tables, then Cell or Column, from the pull-down menus. To get started with formatting text in a cell or column, follow these steps:

1. Move the insertion point into the table, and choose the cells you want to format.

   ◆ If you want to change the format of a single cell or column, move the insertion point to that cell or column.

   ◆ If you want to change the format of a group of cells, select those individual cells.

   ◆ If you want to change the format of several columns, select those columns.

2. Choose **Layout** ➤ **T**ables, or press Ctrl+F9.

   ◆ If you are formatting a single cell or a group of selected cells, choose **C**ell. You'll see the Format Cell dialog box, shown in Figure 6.20.

   ◆ If you are formatting a column or a group of selected columns, choose Col**u**mn. You'll see the Format Column dialog box, shown in Figure 6.21.

The sections that follow describe the options in these dialog boxes.

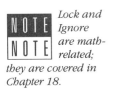

Lock and Ignore are math-related; they are covered in Chapter 18.

CHANGING TEXT APPEARANCE

The print appearances in the Format Cell and Format Column dialog boxes are described in Chapter 5. Be aware that these options are cumulative. For example, if you assign the Outline appearance to some cells and then assign the Bold appearance to any of the same cells, the result is Bold and Outline combined.

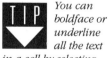

FIGURE 6.20:

The Format Cell dialog box

Format Cell

Appearance
- Bold
- Underline
- Double Underline
- Italic
- Outline
- Shadow
- Small Cap
- Redline
- Strikeout

Cell Attributes
- Shading
- Lock
- Ignore Cell When Calculating

Justification: Left
Alignment: Top

Size
- Superscript
- Subscript
- Fine
- Small
- Large
- Very Large
- Extra Large

☒ Use Column Justification
☒ Use Column Size and Appearance

OK   Cancel

FIGURE 6.21:

The Format Column dialog box

Format Column

Appearance
- Bold
- Underline
- Double Underline
- Italic
- Outline
- Shadow
- Small Cap
- Redline
- Strikeout

Justification: Left

Column Width: 2.44"

Size
- Superscript
- Subscript
- Fine
- Small
- Large
- Very Large
- Extra Large

Digits: 2

OK   Cancel

> **TIP**
> *You can boldface or underline all the text in a cell by selecting that cell and pressing Ctrl+B or Ctrl+U.*

To undo the appearance attributes of a cell or column, you must unmark the check box in front of the option. You can also choose Edit ➤ Undo (Alt+Backspace) if you change your mind immediately after making a change. Another option for returning the text to normal is to select the text and choose Font ➤ Normal (Ctrl+N).

If you want to change the appearance of only part of the text in a cell (for example, double-underline a single word), do so while typing or after selecting the text in the document window. Select one of the appearance options from the Font pull-down menu, or press a shortcut key.

CHANGING TEXT SIZE

Choosing a Size option from the dialog box changes the size of the text in the specified cell or column. Text outside the cells or columns remains unchanged. However, be aware that the actual printed size is determined entirely by your printer, not by WordPerfect.

If you choose a large size, the height of the entire row in the table is expanded to accommodate the new size. If you choose a small size for all the cells across a row, the height of the row is *not* decreased. (But you can use the Row feature, discussed later, to change the height of the row.)

If you want to change the size of part of the text in a cell, do so while typing or after selecting text within the cell, with the Font ➤ Size option (Ctrl+S).

APPLYING SHADING

The Cell Attributes area of the Format Cell dialog box lets you apply shading to a cell or group of cells. (Lock and Ignore Cell When Calculating are discussed in Chapter 18.) When you choose the Shading option, the cell or group of selected cells will have background shading applied to them.

The shading will look like a bunch of small dots on the screen, but will print out as a gray tone on most laser printers. The actual resolution and evenness of shading is printer-dependent.

CHANGING JUSTIFICATION

The Justification option in the Format Cell and Format Column dialog boxes lets you determine how text in a cell or column is justified. When you click on the button and hold down the mouse button, you'll see the following pop-up list:

Figure 6.22 shows examples of the various types of column and cell justification. The Left, Full, Center, and Right options work the same way they do when you justify paragraphs (discussed in Chapter 4). The Decimal Align option is used to align numbers on a specific character (typically the decimal point), as in the tabular columns described in Chapter 4.

The Mixed option appears when you have selected a group of cells that do not have the same settings. For example, the group of selected cells might contain one cell that is centered and other cells that are left-justified.

For the most part, you'll probably use center alignment for column titles, left alignment for text, and right alignment for numbers, dates, times, and so forth. However, if you want to display numbers with decimal points (especially when some numbers have more digits than others to the right of the decimal point), or if you want to display negative numbers in parentheses, you'll probably want to use decimal alignment (the numbers will align on the decimal point).

If you use a non-American numbering system that aligns numbers on something other than a period, such as the comma in British format (e.g., *123.456,78*), change the alignment character anywhere above and to the left of (or even outside of and above) the decimal-aligned column. Choose Layout ➤ Line ➤ Special Codes, and change the Decimal Align character (see Chapter 4).

If you want to justify only a portion of the text in a cell, do so while typing text in the cell or editing text. For example, you can press Shift+F7 to center part of the text in a cell.

To correctly decimal-align numbers with more than two decimal places or with negative numbers displayed in parentheses, you must change the Digits setting for that column by choosing Layout ➤ Tables ➤ Column and entering the correct number in the Digits box.

CONTROLLING ALIGNMENT

The Alignment option in the Format Cell dialog box is generally used to control how text is vertically aligned in a cell that is several lines tall. When you

Left	Full	Center	Right	Decimal
ABC Corp.	ABC Corp.	ABC Corp.	100.00	.123
Acme Rentals	Acme Rentals	Acme Rentals	1,000.00	123.45
Digital, Inc.	Digital, Inc.	Digital, Inc.	10,000.00	(1,234.56)
SYBEX, Inc.	SYBEX, Inc.	SYBEX, Inc.	100,000.00	99,999.99
Ann Nye Chiropractic	Ann Nye Chiropractic	Ann Nye Chiropractic	900,000.00	0.001

FIGURE 6.22:
Examples of types of column justification

choose Alignment, you'll see this pop-up list:

Figure 6.23 shows how you could use the options on the list to control vertical alignment in a table.

USE COLUMN JUSTIFICATION

The Use Column Justification option is available only when you are formatting cells. Use this option to reset the justification of the cell or selected cells to match the justification of the rest of the column.

USE COLUMN SIZE AND APPEARANCE

The Use Column Size and Appearance option is available only when you are formatting cells. Use this option to reset the size and appearance of the cell or selected cells to match the size and appearance of the rest of the column.

CHANGING COLUMN WIDTH

The Format Column dialog box includes a Column Width option. The current width of the columns displayed is in the Column Width text box.

You can type in a new width in inches (e.g., **1.5** for 1½ inches) and then choose OK or press ↵. WordPerfect will adjust the widths of other

Top Vertical Alignment	This cell contains enough text to extend through three lines
Center Vertical Alignment	This cell contains enough text to extend through three lines
Bottom Vertical Alignment	This cell contains enough text to extend through three lines

FIGURE 6.23:

Examples of vertical alignments in cells

columns if necessary, as when you widen and narrow columns with the triangular icons above the ruler.

You'll probably find that changing column widths interactively with the triangular icons is easier than using the Column Width option. But if you want several columns to have the same width, you can select all these columns, choose Layout ➤ Tables ➤ Columns, and set the width for all the columns.

DETERMINING THE NUMBER OF DECIMAL PLACES

The Digits option is very useful when doing math in tables, as discussed in Chapter 18.

The Digits option is available when you are formatting columns. It lets you determine how many decimal places are displayed to the right of the decimal point. If left unchanged, WordPerfect uses two decimal places.

If your numbers have more than two decimal places of accuracy in a column, and they are decimal-aligned, you should choose the Digits option and indicate the correct number of decimal places to show for each number. Otherwise, the numbers will not be wrapped correctly in their cells. If you are displaying negative numbers in parentheses, add an extra digit in Digits for the closing parenthesis.

ADJUSTING THE ROW HEIGHT

TO ADJUST THE HEIGHT OF A ROW IN A TABLE,

move the insertion point anywhere in the row, or select the rows you want to change, then choose Layout ➤ Tables ➤ Row, and change the settings.

If you want to decrease or increase the distance between rows in a table, choose Cell Margins from the Table Options dialog box, described later in this chapter.

The Layout ➤ Tables ➤ Row option affects the row that the insertion point is currently in or any number of rows that you have selected.

Normally, WordPerfect determines the height of a row based on the height of the text printed in that row and the space allotted between rows (as set in the Table Options dialog box, discussed later). To change the row height, follow these steps:

1. Move the insertion point into the table, and choose the rows whose height you want to change.

 ◆ If you want to change the height of a single row, move the insertion point to that row.

♦ If you want to change the height of more than one row, select those rows.

2. Choose **L**ayout ➤ **T**ables ➤ **R**ow. You'll see the following dialog box:

3. Choose **S**ingle Line or **M**ulti Line for the number of lines per row.

4. Choose **A**uto or **F**ixed for the row height. If you chose Fixed, type a fixed row height in the text box.

5. Choose OK or press ↵ to return to the document window.

By default, all rows are defined as Multi Line and Auto. This means that a single row can contain multiple lines of word-wrapped text and that Word-Perfect will determine the height of each line automatically.

If you change the setting to Single Line, cells in that row can no longer support multiple lines of text. Any text that would normally be word-wrapped within a cell is simply cut off and becomes invisible. (However, WordPerfect "remembers" the wrapped text, so if you change the setting back to Multi Line, the text reappears in the cell.)

If you change the height method from Auto to Fixed, the current row height will be displayed, and you can type in a new row height and press ↵.

Note that if you use Single Line and Fixed, and the row height you specify is not tall enough to display the text within the row, that text will not appear in the cell. You'll want to use this option only to increase the row height.

If you assign Multi Line and Fixed to a row, then all the lines of text within a cell in that row must fit within the row height you specify. Any lines of text that do not fit within the fixed row height you determine will not be visible. Once again, this option is best used for increasing the row height.

The progress chart in Figure 6.35 shows a practical example of changing the row height.

TROUBLESHOOTING FORMAT PROBLEMS

Embedded text-appearance codes are not necessarily overridden by menu choices. For example, if a cell contains [Bold On] and [Bold Off] codes, and you use Format ➤ Cell to italicize that cell, the result is bold and italics combined (unless you delete the [Bold] codes from the cell).

If you change the format of a group of cells or a column, and some (or all) cells ignore the change, it's probably due to the way WordPerfect prioritizes formatting changes (it's not a malfunction). Here's how these priorities work:

◆ Formatting options activated after choosing Layout ➤ Tables ➤ Cell get first priority and override choices made by choosing Layout ➤ Tables ➤ Column and choices made while you are entering text.

◆ Formatting codes entered when you are entering or editing text in the table get second priority and override only those choices made by choosing Layout ➤ Tables ➤ Column.

◆ Formatting options activated by choosing Layout ➤ Tables ➤ Column get lowest priority and override neither of the above.

For example, if you center text in a cell with Shift+F7 while typing text in a cell, that text will remain centered unless the cell is formatted with Layout ➤ Tables ➤ Cell.

Similarly, if you use Layout ➤ Tables ➤ Cell to format a particular cell, and then use Layout ➤ Tables ➤ Column to reformat that entire column, the previous Cell choices remain in effect. To reset the cells to match the format of the column, reselect the "faulty" cells, choose Layout ➤ Tables ➤ Cell, and then choose either Use Column Justification or Use Column Size and Appearance to undo the previous choices.

You can use this built-in prioritization to your advantage. For example, each column in Figure 6.22 has a different type of alignment, and each was aligned by choosing Layout ➤ Tables ➤ Column to justify the cells. But the title (top) cell of each column contains centered text. That's because all the cells in the top row were selected first, then centered, using Layout ➤ Tables ➤ Cell, with justification set to Center. Hence, all the cells share center alignment of text, overriding the alignment assigned to the column as a whole.

USING FONTS IN A TABLE

Changes to the font in a table act like changes to the font in the normal document window; that is, all text (in all cells) to the right of and below a font change (i.e., a hidden [Font] code) is changed to the specified font.

If you want to set the font for the entire table, move the insertion point outside of and just above the start of the table (so that the insertion point is

Fonts are discussed in Chapter 5.

on, or to the left of, the [Tbl Def:] code that starts the table), and specify your font by choosing Font ➤ Font (or pressing F9).

To change the font for text in a given cell, move the insertion point to the first character of text in that cell, and choose Font ➤ Font (or press F9). All cells to the right of and below the insertion point will be affected. Then, if necessary, change the font at the beginning of any cell to the right of or below the current one to initiate a different font.

POLISHING THE APPEARANCE OF A TABLE

NOTE NOTE	*Options you choose from the Table Op-*

tions dialog box apply to the entire table (but don't affect any other tables in your document).

You can use the Table Options dialog box to refine the appearance of your tables by following these steps:

1. Move the insertion point to any cell in the table.

2. Choose **L**ayout ➤ **T**ables ➤ **O**ptions, or press Ctrl+F9 O. You'll see the Table Options dialog box, shown earlier in the chapter in Figure 6.17.

3. Make your choices as discussed in the sections that follow.

4. Choose OK or press ↵ to return to the document window.

CHANGING TABLE SIZE

As discussed earlier in this chapter, you can change the size of the entire table by changing the number of columns and rows. You can also add rows and columns to the end of the table rather than to its interior.

CHANGING CELL MARGINS

The options in the Cell Margins area let you control the distance between the lines that surround the cells and the text within the cells. Figure 6.24 shows examples of cell margins, using both left-aligned and right-aligned text examples.

These options are especially useful when you want to print your table without any lines and need to control the line spacing and the spacing between columns. For example, the bottom half of Figure 6.24 shows a table printed with lines removed and the default cell-margin settings, and the same table after reducing the Top cell margin from the default of 0.1 inch to 0.028 inches.

Examples of Cell Margins (Left-justified text)

Default cell margins are shown here

Cell Margins: Left=0, Right=0, Top=0, Bottom=0

Cell Margins: Left=.1, Right=.1, Top=.07, Bottom=.03

Cell Margins: Left=.25, Right=.25, Top=.25, Bottom=.25

Examples of Cell Margins (Right-justified text)

Default cell margins are shown here

Cell margins: Left=0, Right=0, Top=0, Bottom=0

Cell margins: Left=.1, Right=.1, Top=.07, Bottom=.03

Cell margins: Left=.25, Right=.25, Top=.25, Bottom=.25

Table with default Cell Margins, and no lines...

Wanda Carneros	(123)555-0123
Tersha d'Elgin	(818)555-0987
Victoria Dumplin	(313)555-0385
Ambrose Pushnik	(714)555-5739
Frankly Unctuous	(414)555-0312

Same table as above after changing the Cell Margins at the Top to 0.028...

Wanda Carneros	(123)555-0123
Tersha d'Elgin	(818)555-0987
Victoria Dumplin	(313)555-0385
Ambrose Pushnik	(714)555-5739
Frankly Unctuous	(414)555-0312

CONTROLLING SHADING

The Shading option lets you determine the darkness of the shading in table cells where shading is turned on by using **L**ayout ➤ **T**ables ➤ **L**ines ➤ **C**ell (see "Shading Cells" earlier in this chapter). By default, WordPerfect uses a light shading, 10 percent of black.

After choosing this option, enter a value between 0 (no shading) and 100 (100 percent shading, which is black) and choose OK or press ↵.

CHANGING POSITION

If your table is narrower than the width of the margins on the page, you can choose an option in the Position area to determine how your table is positioned between the margins:

Left	The left edge of the table is aligned at the left margin.
Right	The right edge of the table is aligned at the right margin.
Ce**n**ter	The table is centered between the two margins.
Full	The table is sized to fit between the margins.
Fr**o**m Left Edge	Lets you align the left edge of the table a specific distance from the left edge of the page. For example, if you enter .5, the left edge of the table is printed ½ inch from the left edge of the page.

See "Making More Room in a Table" later in this chapter for information on creating and printing wide tables.

If you use the From Left Edge option, be careful to leave enough room for the table to be printed. For example, if there are 6.5 inches of space between the margins on your page, and your table is 5 inches wide, you have 1.5 inches of "play" between the table and the margins. If, however, you set the position of the left edge of the table to 2 inches, the rightmost 0.5 inch of the table will not be printed.

The Left, Right, and Center options only affect tables that are narrower than the distance between the margins. Since WordPerfect automatically creates tables to fill the space between the margins, you must narrow one or more columns before any of these options will have an effect.

DISPLAYING NEGATIVE RESULTS

The options in the Negative Result Display area let you determine whether table calculations that result in negative numbers are displayed with a leading minus sign or in parentheses. See Chapter 18 for more details.

CHANGING ATTRIBUTES

Under Attributes, you can choose the number of header rows for a table, as discussed earlier in this chapter in "Repeating a Table Header on Multiple Pages."

UNLOCKING CELLS

The Disable Cell Locks option enables you to unlock cells that you have locked previously. This is generally done to protect information, such as formulas when creating math tables. For a full description, see Chapter 18.

MANAGING TABLES

This part of the chapter discusses general topics concerning tables and how to use tables in combination with other features of WordPerfect. Chapter references to these related features are also provided.

HIDDEN CODES FOR TABLES

When you create a table, WordPerfect stores hidden codes in the document, starting with [Tbl Def:] and ending with [Tbl Off]. Between these, each [Row] code marks the beginning of a new row in the table. The contents of a cell are preceded by the [Cell] code.

Graphics boxes are covered in Chapter 19.

A cell cannot contain another table; that is, it cannot contain [Tbl Def:] and [Tbl Off] codes. But it can contain a code to display a graphics box that contains a table. So technically, it is possible to display a table within a table (though you may be hard-pressed to think of a practical application for this).

MOVING OR COPYING TABLES

If you ever need to move or copy a table in a document, open Reveal Codes. Then select the entire table, including the [Table Def:] and [Tbl Off] codes. You can then move or copy the table as you would any other selected text, by choosing Edit ➤ Cut (Shift+Delete) or Edit ➤ Copy (Ctrl+Insert).

You can't cut or copy the table if you select the table by clicking the mouse rapidly three times. If you use this method, WordPerfect presents the dialog box for moving and copying blocks, rows, or columns. Since you can't select both rows and columns, you can't move or copy the table this way.

MOVING OR COPYING TEXT BETWEEN TABLES

If your document contains two or more tables, you can move or copy text between them quite easily:

1. Move the insertion point into the table that contains the text you want to move or copy.

2. Select the text that you want to move or copy.

3. Choose **E**dit ➤ **C**ut (Shift+Delete) or **E**dit ➤ **C**opy (Ctrl+Insert). The dialog box for moving/copying selections, rows, or columns will appear.

4. Choose **S**elect.

5. Choose OK or press ↵ to return to the document window.

6. Move the insertion point into the cell in the other table where you want to move or copy the text to (i.e., the destination cell).

7. Choose **E**dit ➤ **P**aste (Shift+Insert). The text will be moved or copied.

DELETING A TABLE

To delete an entire table, including all its contents, follow these steps:

When deleting a table, you can move the insertion point to any cell in the table and click rapidly three times to select the entire table.

1. Select all the cells in the table, or in Reveal Codes, select the [Tbl Def:] code.

2. Press Delete. You'll see this dialog box:

♦ Choose **E**ntire Table to delete the table and its contents.

♦ Choose **C**ontents (text only) to delete the text and leave the table structure intact.

♦ Choose **T**able Structure (leave text) to delete the table structure and leave the text. If you choose this option, the text will be separated by tabs when you return to the document window.

3. Choose OK or press ↵ after you have made your choice.

CONVERTING A TABLE TO TEXT

You can use the Tables feature to organize your text, and then convert the table to standard text if you wish. This is sometimes handy when exporting a document to another word processor or typesetting machine that cannot interpret WordPerfect codes.

To convert a table to text, follow the steps in the preceding section, choosing Table Structure in the Delete Table dialog box. WordPerfect immediately converts [Cell] codes to [Tab] codes; the spacing of the table depends on the current tab settings. Most likely, you will need to change the tab settings above the text to get it properly aligned and to get exactly the spacing you want.

In Figure 6.25, the top example shows text that was initially entered in a table. The middle example shows the table just after the [Tbl Def:] code was removed. The phone numbers are out of alignment because the current tab stops weren't properly set. The bottom example shows the table after the tab stops were changed to better align the text.

A sample table...

Wanda Carneros	(123)555-0123
Tersha d'Elgin	(818)555-0987
Victoria Dumplin	(313)555-0385
Ambrose Pushnik	(714)555-5739
Frankly Unctuous	(414)555-0312

Same table as above after removing the table structure, leaving just the text...

```
Wanda Carneros   (123)555-0123
Tersha d'Elgin     (818)555-0987
Victoria Dumplin       (313)555-0385
Ambrose Pushnik        (714)555-5739
Frankly Unctuous            (414)555-0312
```

Same as above after changing the tab stops...

```
Wanda Carneros         (123)555-0123
Tersha d'Elgin         (818)555-0987
Victoria Dumplin       (313)555-0385
Ambrose Pushnik        (714)555-5739
Frankly Unctuous       (414)555-0312
```

FIGURE 6.25:

Converting a table to text

CONVERTING TEXT TO A TABLE

If you have text that is organized into columns with [Tab] codes and want to convert it to a table, follow these steps:

1. Move the insertion point to the first character of text that you want to put into a table.

2. Select the text you want to convert to a table.

3. Move the insertion point to the [HRt] code after the last character of text that you want to put into the table. Make sure that all the text is selected (in the document window) and that only the single, last [Hrt] code is selected (in Reveal Codes).

4. Choose **L**ayout ➤ **T**ables ➤ **C**reate, or press Ctrl+F9 C. You'll see this dialog box:

5. If you are creating the table from text organized with tabs, choose the first option. If you've defined parallel columns, choose the second option.

The table will be created, and you can use the techniques described in this chapter to make changes if you wish.

The procedure can be tricky if you did not modify the tabs on the ruler before initially typing your columnar table, because WordPerfect interprets each [Tab] (or similar) code as a cell when converting text to a table. For example, Figure 6.26 shows text in the document window neatly arranged into columns. However, the original tab settings were used, so in some cases it required two or more [Tab] codes to move text over to the appropriate tab stop (as you can see in Reveal Codes).

If you were then to select that text and create a table, you'd end up with a pretty messy table, as shown in Figure 6.27.

Rather than try to fix the table, you'll probably find it easier to convert such a table back to text by using the methods discussed earlier. Then remove

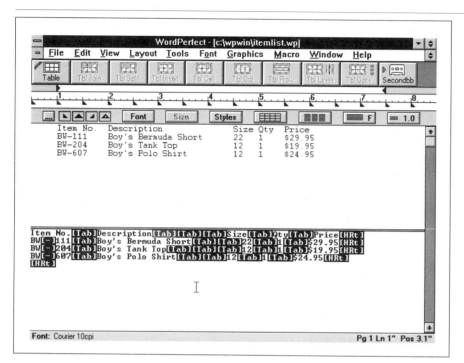

Columns typed using the initial ½-inch tab stops

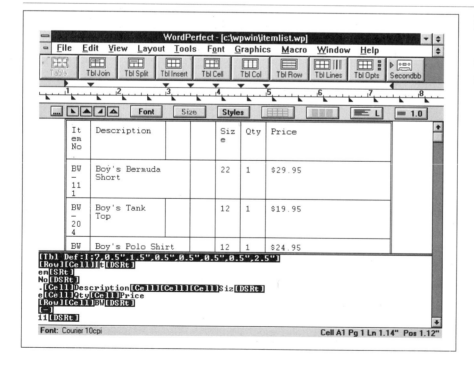

The result of converting the text shown in Figure 6.26 to a table

If your table seems to disappear while changing from table to text or vice versa, check the scroll bar. The table or text may have scrolled out of view.

any multiple [Tab] codes so that only one [Tab] code separates each column. Next, move to the top of the columns and adjust the tabs (use the ruler or choose Layout ➤ Line ➤ Tab Set) so that the text is neatly aligned, as in Figure 6.28.

Now you can reselect the text you want to move into a table, and create a table. The result is a much neater and more manageable table, as shown in Figure 6.29.

MAKING MORE ROOM IN A TABLE

One of the most common problems with tables is not having enough space on the page to get all the information you need into the table. There are four ways to solve this problem:

◆ Change to a font with a smaller point size (see Chapter 5) just to the left of the [Table Def:] code. The entire table will use the new font, so more characters can fit in each cell.

◆ If your printer can do it, print the table sideways on the page by changing the code for paper size and type to landscape format (Chapter 7).

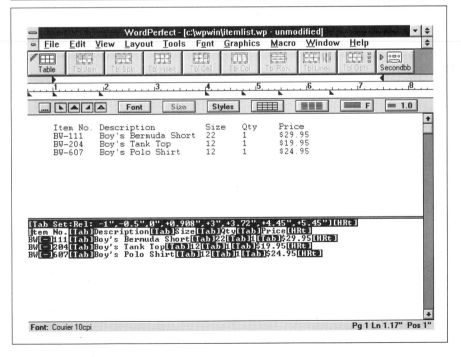

FIGURE 6.28:

The text shown in Figure 6.26 after removing multiple [Tab] codes and adjusting tabs on the ruler

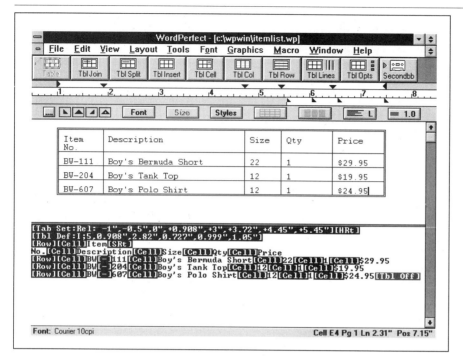

FIGURE 6.29:

The result of converting the text shown in Figure 6.28 to a table

After you've changed the paper size, you can add more columns to the new page width or widen existing columns.

◆ Reduce the cell margins in the Table Options dialog box (described earlier in this chapter).

◆ Reduce the left and right margins just above the table so that the table is printed within the narrower margins.

Of the four options, printing the table sideways on the page, in landscape format, gives you the greatest overall width without reducing the type size.

WRAPPING TEXT AROUND A TABLE

NOTE
NOTE

You could place a table in any of the graphics boxes shown in Figure 6.30, as you'll learn in Chapter 19.

If you want to print a table so that text wraps around it, or if you want to display two or more tables side by side, you must place the table in a graphics box. For example, the table in the lower-right corner of Figure 6.30 is in a page-anchored graphics box, so text and columns outside the box flow around it.

In Chapter 20, you'll learn how to create complex documents like the one shown in Figure 6.30.

Examples of Graphic Boxes

CHECK BOX
We start with a small graphic image that is anchored to this paragraph (the box's hidden code is just before the first character of this paragraph.

The box is sized small, and the text of the paragraph wraps around it.

DIPLOMA
Another case for anchoring a figure to a paragraph is when you want a figure to closely follow its callout in text.

For example, Figure 1 shows a diploma. To keep that figure near, but below, it's anchored to the top of the next paragraph. Its width is the full width of this column.

Figure 1.

Because the box is as wide as this column, no text wraps around the side of the box.

TEXT BOX
The text box in the center of the page is anchored to the page. Its hidden code is at the top of the page. All text wraps around it. Page anchoring is the only way to create boxes that cross columns.

TABLE BOX
The Table box in the lower right corner of the page is also anchored to the page

WordPerfect has lots of tools for aligning graphic boxes in columns

(bottom right corner). Page anchoring was required here because we needed the table to be wider than one column.

FOOTER
The star symbol at the lower left corner of the page is actually in a footer. It's character-anchored, because that's the only anchor type allowed

in headers and footers.

IN-LINE GRAPHIC
Next we have a small graphic mouse 🐭 in text. The mouse graphic is in a character anchored User Box, and is sized small enough to fit on a line of text.

Small character-anchored graphics like that can be used as icons in text, margins, or in margin notes -- or perhaps for amusing pictures in children's books.

COLUMNS & LINES
The columns in this example are newspaper columns with a distance of .4" between them. Chapter 20 discusses multi-column layouts in detail.

The lines are all graphic lines with the Graphics ▸ Line menu options.

The table below shows the Column (horizontal) and Vertical position, as the length, of each vertical line.

Line	1st	2nd	3rd	4th
Column	1	2	1	2
Vertical	1.51	1.51	6.35	6.35
Length	2.63	2.63	3.45	2.08

FIGURE 6.30:

A table in a graphics box in the lower-right corner of a sample document

PREVENTING PAGE BREAKS

If you want to ensure that a small table is never split across two pages in your document, your best bet is to place the table in a graphics box and reference the table by its number. This is the most common method used in larger documents; for example, the text may refer the reader to "Table 2.1," and Table 2.1 is placed as close to the reference as possible, without being split across two pages.

REFERENCING TABLES AUTOMATICALLY

You'll learn about automatic referencing in Part 7.

The other advantage of placing tables in graphics boxes is that you can use *automatic referencing:* If you add or delete a table, all the table numbers are adjusted automatically, as are the references in text to those tables. So you don't need to manually renumber all the tables and the references to them.

SORTING OR ALPHABETIZING TEXT IN A TABLE

If you want to sort (or alphabetize) the contents of a table, use the sorting and selecting options discussed in Chapter 17.

CREATING ADVANCED DOCUMENTS

The Tables feature is a great tool for typing text into tables, but as you've seen, it's also a great tool for typing any kind of multicolumn text, such as the sample itinerary shown earlier in this chapter. With a little ingenuity, you can use the Tables feature to create some extraordinary documents, such as those normally produced by graphic arts departments. The following sections present some examples that you can use as food for thought in creating your own advanced documents.

CALENDAR

The school lunch calendar shown in Figure 6.31 was created with the Tables feature. All the cells in the top row are joined, and the month name (November) is centered and displayed in a 30-point font with small caps. Each day name is centered and italicized in its cell. Within each date, the number is in the 20-point bold, italic, Univers font (similar to Helvetica).

			NOVEMBER			
Sun	Mon	Tue	Wed	Thu	Fri	Sat
				1 Hot dogs n' bananas	**2** Peaches in spinach	**3**
4	**5** Ice cream pasta	**6** Vermicious Knids	**7** Homemade Wangdoodle	**8** Liver and Jujubes	**9** Sweet n' Sour sundae	**10**
11	**12** Deep fried loquat	**13** Pepperoni in potatoes	**14** Macaroni n' liverwurst	**15** Marshmallows in pea soup	**16** Cosmic Sustenance	**17**
18	**19** Day-old nachos	**20** M&M's in Brie cheese	**21** Mushrooms in caramel sauce	**22** MSG-caked doughnuts	**23** Cream puff on a stick	**24**
25	**26** Peanut butter n' bacon bits	**27** Steamed head cheese	**28** Big Hunk omelette	**29** Wholly Macaroni	**30** Cajun-style caviar	

ORG CHART

Tables are a great way to create org (organizational) charts, like the one shown in Figure 6.32. Figure 6.33 shows the org chart after joining and filling cells, but before removing any lines.

Notice in the bottom row of the chart that you need to join a pair of cells to create one box. This is necessary to get the centered vertical line to come out of the top of the box. You also need at least one blank cell separating each box. The drop-shadow appearance of the topmost cell was created by setting the top and left lines to Single, and the right and bottom lines to Thick.

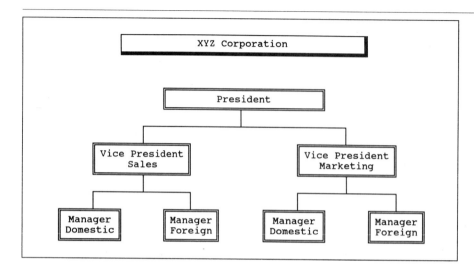

FIGURE 6.32:

A sample org chart

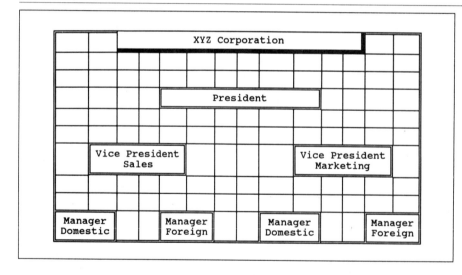

FIGURE 6.33:

The org chart before removing table lines

PROGRESS CHART

Figure 6.34 shows a progress chart created with the Tables feature. The chart is printed sideways on the page (landscape format). Figure 6.35 shows the chart before removing any lines from the table.

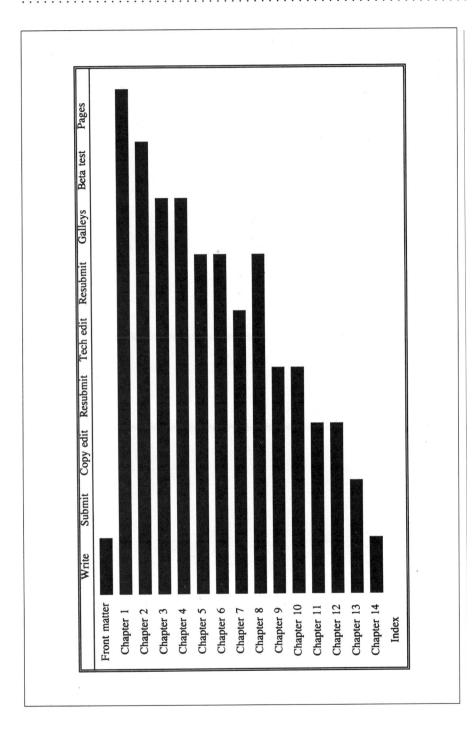

FIGURE 6.34:

A sample progress chart

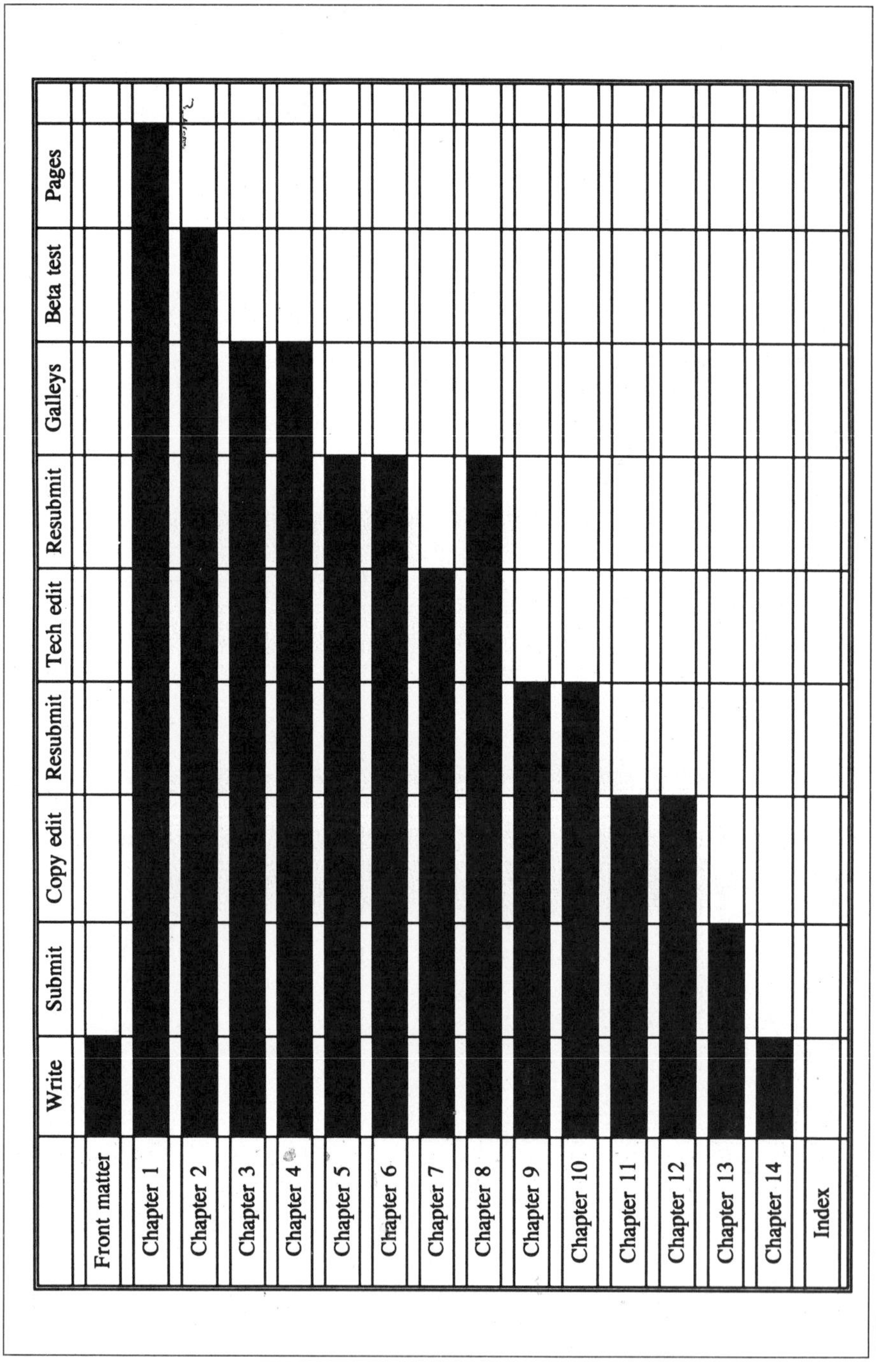

	Write	Submit	Copy edit	Resubmit	Tech edit	Resubmit	Galleys	Beta test	Pages
Front matter	█								
Chapter 1	█	█	█	█	█	█	█	█	█
Chapter 2	█	█	█	█	█	█	█	█	
Chapter 3	█	█	█	█	█	█	█		
Chapter 4	█	█	█	█	█	█	█		
Chapter 5	█	█	█	█	█	█			
Chapter 6	█	█	█	█	█	█			
Chapter 7	█	█	█	█	█				
Chapter 8	█	█	█	█	█	█			
Chapter 9	█	█	█	█					
Chapter 10	█	█	█	█					
Chapter 11	█	█	█						
Chapter 12	█	█	█						
Chapter 13	█	█							
Chapter 14	█								
Index									

FIGURE 6.35:
A sample progress chart before removing the table lines

Two tricks were used to create the progress chart: First, every other row, starting at the second row, was narrowed to 0.1" inches by choosing Layout ➤ Tables ➤ Row and selecting Fixed. This was necessary to reduce the gaps between the bars in the chart. Second, the bars were drawn by setting the gray shade to 100 percent (pure black), selecting the cells to darken, and selecting shading.

PLAY-OFF CHART

Figure 6.36 shows a sample play-off chart created with Tables. The chart is printed sideways on the page (landscape format). Figure 6.37 shows the chart before removing any table lines.

The design of the play-off chart is fairly simple: Each box is actually two cells (one atop the other), joined so that the centered line comes out of the right side of the box.

FILL-IN FORMS

Tables are also great for creating your own company fill-in forms, like the invoice shown in Figure 6.38. This invoice is actually a collection of three tables on a single page, as you can see in Figure 6.39. This figure shows the invoice after joining cells and filling them with text, but before shading cells and removing table lines.

Actually, one of the trickiest parts of creating this form was getting the company name and address to align next to the table. To accomplish this, the text was put in a User box (Chapter 19) that was anchored to the upper-right corner of the page, with Wrap Text Around Box set to No.

TEXT FRAMES

Figure 6.40 shows a sample menu from a Mexican fast-food stand: framed text, with the lines running into the title. Figure 6.41 shows the menu before removing table lines and changing the fonts.

Notice how the table started out as three columns (across the bottom row). To get the run-in line effect, the top two rows were split into three columns each, then the pair of cells in the middle were joined. Then the title was typed into this joined cell (e.g., "Burritos") and centered vertically within its cell.

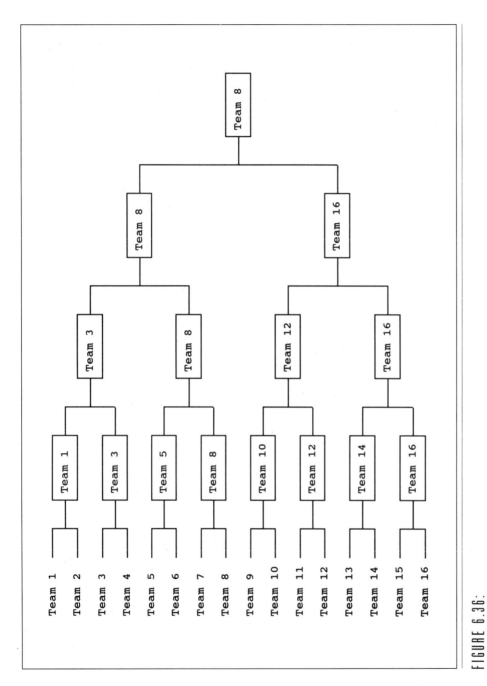

FIGURE 6.36:

A sample play-off chart

Team 1	Team 1					
Team 2						
Team 3	Team 3	Team 3				
Team 4						
Team 5	Team 5		Team 8			
Team 6		Team 8				
Team 7	Team 8					Team 8
Team 8				Team 8		
Team 9	Team 10					
Team 10		Team 12				
Team 11	Team 12					
Team 12			Team 16			
Team 13	Team 14			Team 16		
Team 14		Team 16				
Team 15	Team 16					
Team 16						

FIGURE 6.37:

The play-off chart before removing table lines

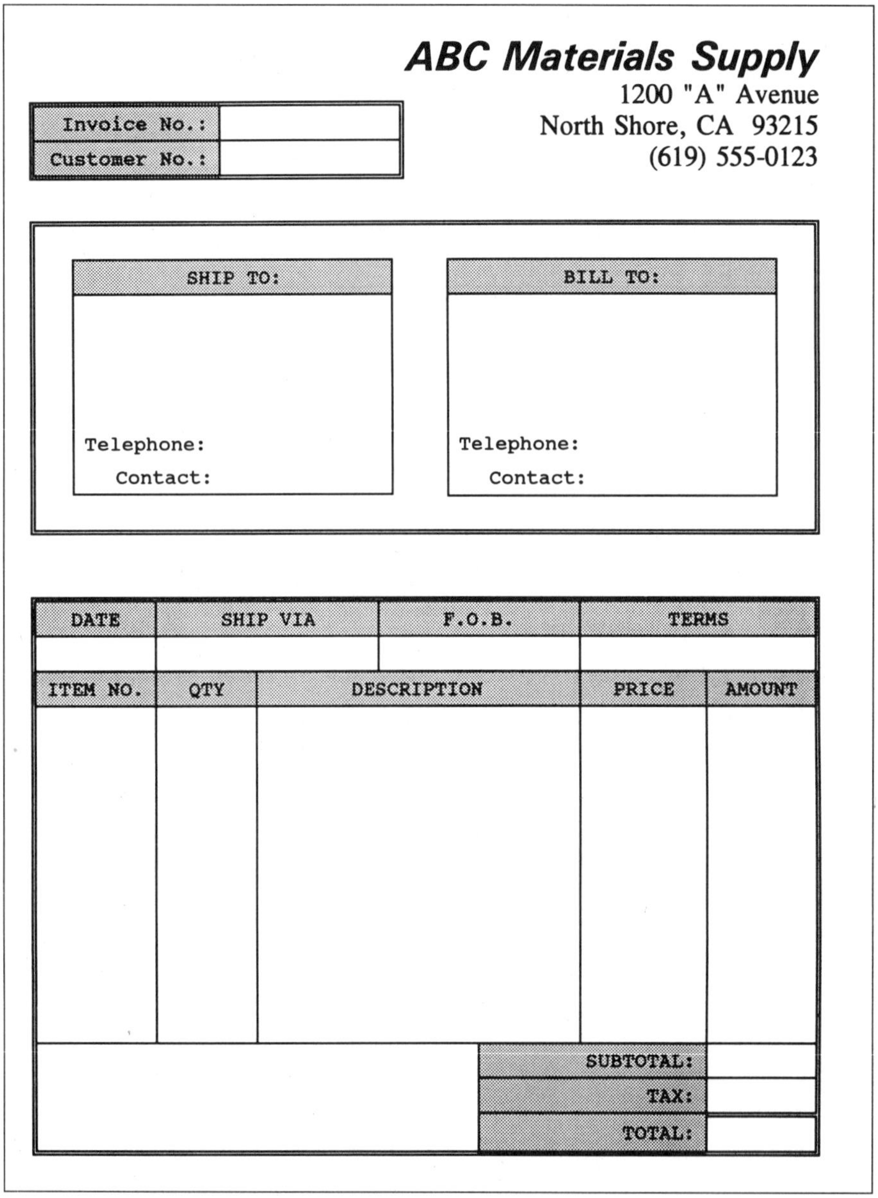

Invoice No.:	
Customer No.:	

ABC Materials Supply
1200 "A" Avenue
North Shore, CA 93215
(619) 555-0123

SHIP TO:	BILL TO:
Telephone:	Telephone:
Contact:	Contact:

DATE	SHIP VIA	F.O.B.	TERMS

ITEM NO.	QTY	DESCRIPTION	PRICE	AMOUNT
			SUBTOTAL:	
			TAX:	
			TOTAL:	

FIGURE 6.38:

A sample fill-in form

ABC Materials Supply
1200 "A" Avenue
North Shore, CA 93215
(619) 555-0123

| Invoice No.: | |
| Customer No.: | |

	SHIP TO:		BILL TO:	
Telephone:		Telephone:		
Contact:		Contact:		

DATE	SHIP VIA	F.O.B.	TERMS	

ITEM NO.	QTY	DESCRIPTION	PRICE	AMOUNT
			SUBTOTAL:	
			TAX:	
			TOTAL:	

FIGURE 6.39:

The fill-in form before removing lines from the three tables

Burritos			Tacos	
Carne Asada	**$2.40**		**Folded:**	
Machaca	**$2.10**		**1 Beef . . . .**	**$1.60**
Chorizo	**$2.10**		**1 Chicken . . . .**	**$1.60**
Mixed	**$2.10**		**1 Carne Asada . . .**	**$2.00**
Beef	**$2.00**		**Rolled:**	
Chicken	**$2.00**		**1 Rolled Taco . . . .**	**$ .50**
Bean	**$1.60**		**w/ Guacamole**	**$ .60**
			3 Plain w/ Cheese	**$1.30**
			w/ Guacamole	**$1.80**

FIGURE 6.40:

A sample menu

Burritos			Tacos	
Carne Asada	$2.40		Folded:	
Machaca	$2.10		1 Beef	$1.60
Chorizo	$2.10		1 Chicken	$1.60
Mixed	$2.10		1 Carne Asada . . .	$2.00
Beef	$2.00		Rolled:	
Chicken	$2.00		1 Rolled Taco . . .	$ .50
Bean	$1.60		w/ Guacamole .	$ .60
			3 Plain w/ Cheese .	$1.30
			w/ Guacamole .	$1.80

FIGURE 6.41:

The sample menu before removing table lines and changing fonts

The Tables feature is so powerful, and so useful, that it's practically a product in itself. And I haven't even touched on its math capabilities (Chapter 18), which are perfect for typing financial reports, invoices, and more.

In Chapter 7, you'll learn about some general techniques for formatting pages and entire documents, including numbering pages, printing headers and footers on every page, printing on nonstandard paper sizes (such as labels and envelopes), and much more.

CHAPTER 7

Formatting Your Pages

hapter 4 introduced several features that control the general appearance of text on a page, including indenting and aligning text, and setting margins. This chapter discusses additional ways to format your printed pages, particularly when you have documents that are more than a page or two in length. Topics include creating title pages, numbering pages, controlling how and when WordPerfect starts printing on a new page, protecting selected text from being split across two pages, and using nonstandard paper sizes like envelopes, mailing labels, and more. You'll find these features on the Layout ➤ Page pull-down menu.

HANDS-ON
....
LESSON 7

For a hands-on lesson in commonly used page-formatting techniques, see Lesson 7 in Part 9.

VERTICAL CENTERING

TO VERTICALLY CENTER ALL THE TEXT ON A PAGE,

move the insertion point to the top of the page where you want to center the text, then choose Layout ➤ Page ➤ Center Page.

Title pages and some other documents often require that text be centered both horizontally (from left to right) and vertically (from top to bottom) on the page. Figure 7.1 shows an example in which the text on a title page is centered both horizontally and vertically.

To center text vertically on the page, you can use the Center Page option on the Page submenu. (You've already seen how to center text horizontally in Chapter 4.) Follow these steps:

When Auto Code Placement is on (Chapter 13), the insertion point can be anywhere on the page: WordPerfect will automatically move the [Center Pg] code to the top of the page, before all text.

1. Move the insertion point to the top of the page where you want to center text vertically (the insertion point must precede all text on that page).

2. Choose **L**ayout ➤ **P**age ➤ **C**enter Page (or press Alt+F9 C).

Vertical centering affects all the text on the current page only; it is typically used to center all the text on a title page (though it can be used to center text on any single page that would look better with identical top and bottom margins, such as very brief letters, memos, invitations, and so forth).

To prevent text beyond the centered page from being vertically centered as well, add a hard page break (discussed in "Starting Text on a New Page") just below the last line of text on the centered page.

As with most page-formatting features, vertical centering will not be obvious in your document window. To see it, you'll need to switch to the Print Preview screen (Shift+F5) or print your document.

UNCENTERING A CENTERED PAGE

If you *immediately* change your mind about centering the text on a page, choose Edit ➤ Undo (or press Alt+Backspace). If you have performed other editing tasks since you centered the text on a page, move the insertion point to the top of the centered page, open Reveal Codes (by choosing View ➤ Reveal Codes or by pressing Alt+F3), and delete the [Center Pg] code.

If Auto Code Placement is on, you can also uncenter a page by moving the insertion point to that page; then choose Layout ➤ Page ➤ Center Page or press Alt+F9 C again.

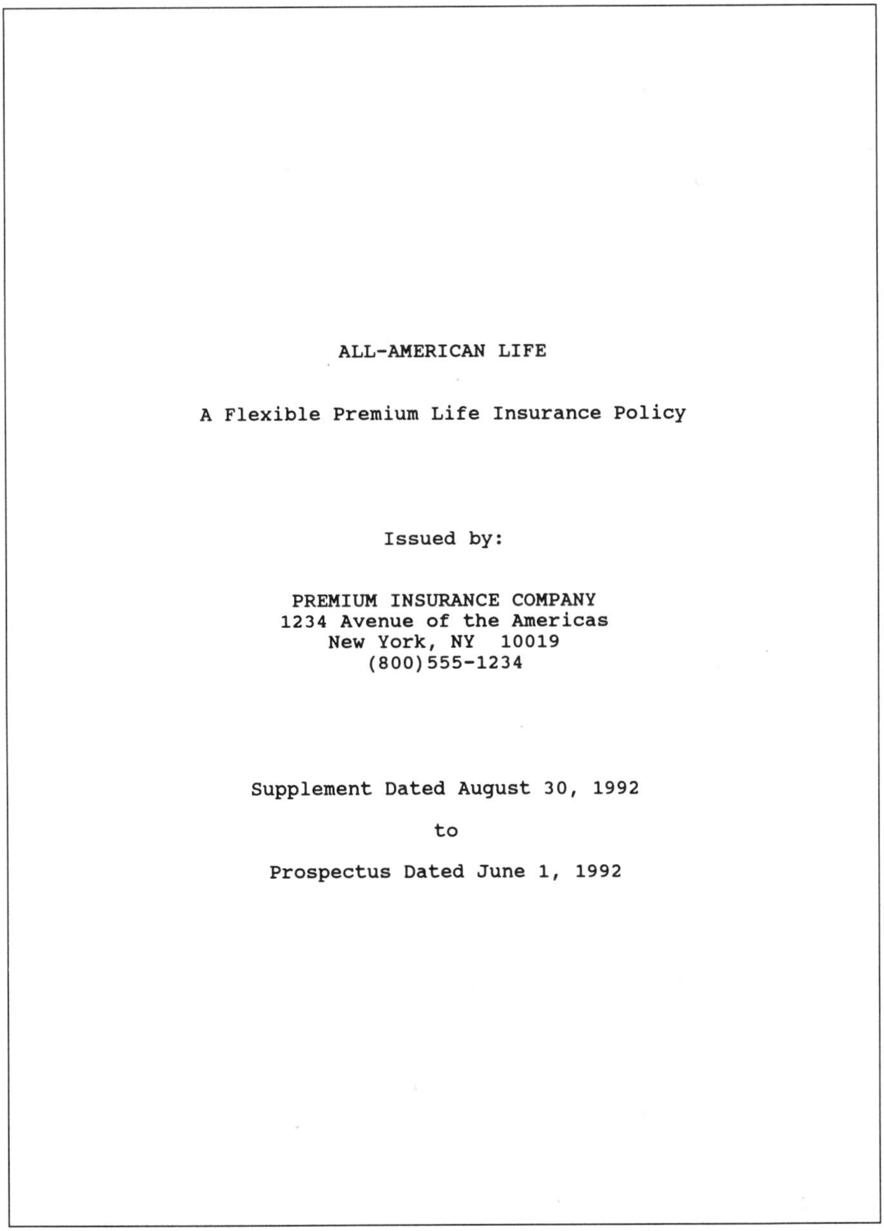

```
                    ALL-AMERICAN LIFE

        A Flexible Premium Life Insurance Policy




                        Issued by:


              PREMIUM INSURANCE COMPANY
              1234 Avenue of the Americas
                 New York, NY  10019
                   (800)555-1234




            Supplement Dated August 30, 1992

                           to

            Prospectus Dated June 1, 1992
```

FIGURE 7.1:

A sample page with text centered horizontally and vertically

STARTING TEXT ON A NEW PAGE

TO INSERT A HARD PAGE BREAK,

position the insertion point and choose Layout ➤ Page ➤ Page Break or press Ctrl+⏎.

WordPerfect automatically breaks a long document into separate pages. That is, as you type beyond the length of a page, WordPerfect inserts a *soft page break,* which appears on the screen as a long horizontal line. It's called a soft page break because WordPerfect can automatically adjust it as you add and delete text in your document. For example, if you add another paragraph to a page that is already filled with text, WordPerfect will automatically move some of the text on the current page down to the next page.

For the most part, you should allow WordPerfect to handle page breaks automatically—this gives you the most flexibility for adding and deleting text in a long document. However, in some situations, you may want to force WordPerfect to start a new page at a certain point in your document. For example, if your document starts with a title page, any text that you type beneath the title page should start on a new page.

To force WordPerfect to start printing on a new page, you need to insert a *hard page break:*

1. Position the insertion point at the location where you want to end the current page.

2. Choose **L**ayout ➤ **P**age ➤ **P**age Break, or press Ctrl+⏎.

You will see a long double line indicating where the page will break, as in the example in Figure 7.2. As you move the insertion point above or below the hard page break, using the mouse or arrow keys, the status bar shows the page number that the insertion point is on.

DELETING A HARD PAGE BREAK

If you change your mind about adding a hard page break, you can delete the [HPg] code that's forcing the page break from the Reveal Codes portion of the screen. Or, if you change your mind *immediately* after adding the page break, you can choose Edit ➤ Undo or press Alt+Backspace to remove it. In Reveal Codes, a soft page break appears as [SPg], and a hard page break appears as [HPg]. You never need to delete a soft page break.

OTHER LINE AND PAGE BREAK CODES

While I'm on the subject of codes, I might as well briefly mention a few of the more obscure codes that you might discover in Reveal Codes. WordPerfect automatically takes care of creating these codes and converting them into other types of codes when necessary, so you needn't be too concerned about them. The codes are the following:

[DSRt]: A *deletable soft return* is inserted when automatic hyphenation is turned off and WordPerfect needs to break a word that's wider than the margins (or column). You'll learn about hyphenation in Chapter 11.

[HRt-SPg]: This code will appear if a soft-page code ([SPg]) was originally a hard-return code ([HRt]).

[Dorm HRt]: A *dormant hard return* is created automatically when a hard-return code ([HRt]) appears alone on a line at the top of a page that is started by a soft page break ([SPg]). WordPerfect creates this code to prevent unwanted blank lines at the top of a page. It will change the code back to [HRt] if the code moves from the top of the page as a result of additions or deletions of text above it.

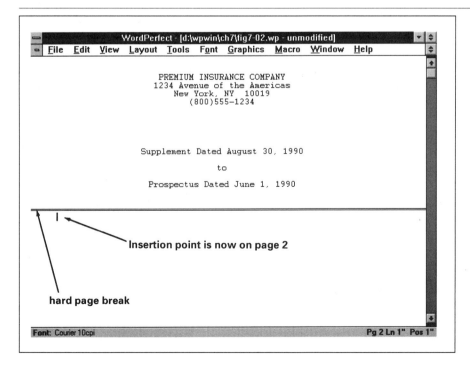

FIGURE 7.2:

A hard page break at the bottom of a title page

AUTOMATIC PAGE NUMBERING

┃ TO ACTIVATE AUTOMATIC PAGE NUMBERING,

position the insertion point at the top of the page where page numbers should begin printing, and choose Layout ➤ Page ➤ Numbering (or press Alt+F9 N). Then open the Position pop-up list, choose any one of the nine suggested positions, choose additional numbering options as needed, and choose OK or press ↵.

You never need to type page numbers in a WordPerfect document, because WordPerfect can automatically number the pages for you. The advantage of automatic page numbering is that no matter how much text you add, change, or delete in a document, the page numbers will always be in proper sequence and in the right place on each printed page. You'll need to print the document or go to the Print Preview screen to see the page numbers.

As you may have guessed by now, WordPerfect uses hidden codes to control page numbering. Therefore, before choosing the menu options to display the page numbers, be sure to position the insertion point before any text at the top of the first page where you want the numbering to start.

When Auto Code Placement (see Chapter 13) is on, the insertion point can be anywhere on the page; WordPerfect automatically moves the [Pg Numbering] code to the top of the page, before all text.

The Page Numbering dialog box lets you set the options for automatic page-numbering either all at once or one at a time, though setting all the features at once is probably the easiest method. Follow these steps:

1. Move the insertion point to the top of the page (before any text) where you want page numbering to start. For example, to start numbering from the first page of a document, press Ctrl+Home.

2. Choose **L**ayout ➤ **P**age ➤ **N**umbering (or press Alt+F9 N). You will see the Page Numbering dialog box, shown in Figure 7.3.

3. Choose one or more page-numbering options from the dialog box, as described below.

4. Choose OK or press ↵ to return to the document window.

The following sections explain the individual page-numbering options, but keep in mind that you can easily make all your page-numbering decisions at once. As always, you can specify new settings at a later time if you change your mind.

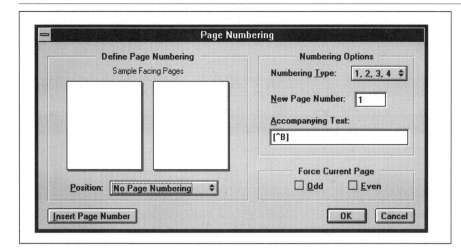

POSITIONING THE PAGE NUMBERS

NOTE *Like all pop-up lists, you can choose an option from the Position pop-up list by clicking its button with your mouse and dragging the highlight to the option you want. Or, press Alt and the underlined key (Alt+P in this example) and using the ↑ and ↓ keys to choose an option.*

You can have WordPerfect display page numbers anywhere in your printed document. To print page numbers, follow these steps:

1. Move the insertion point to the top of the page (before any text).

2. Choose **L**ayout ➤ **P**age ➤ **N**umbering (or press Alt+F9 N). The Page Numbering dialog box will appear.

3. Open the **P**osition pop-up list, and choose a page number position: **N**o Page Numbering, Top **L**eft, Top **C**enter, Top **R**ight, **A**lternating Top, **B**ottom Left, Bo**t**tom Center, Bo**t**tom Right, or Alt**e**rnating Bottom. The Sample Facing Pages diagram in the dialog box will display sample page numbers in the position you chose and in the style specified in the Numbering Type, New Page Number, and Accompanying Text options described later.

4. Choose OK or press ↵ to return to the document window.

The Top Left, Top Center, Top Right, Bottom Left, Bottom Center, and Bottom Right options in the Position pop-up list position the number in the same place on each printed page. For example, if you choose Top Left, the page number will appear in the upper-left corner of each printed page. If you choose Bottom Center, the page number will be centered at the bottom of each page.

The Alternating Top and Alternating Bottom options in the Position pop-up list are for placing page numbers on alternating pages. These are used in documents that are bound like a book. If you choose Alternating Top, the page number appears in the upper-left corner of even-numbered pages and in the upper-right corner of odd-numbered pages. If you choose Alternating Bottom, the page number appears in the lower-left corner of even-numbered pages and in the lower-right corner of odd-numbered pages.

You can also place page numbers in headers and footers, as described later in this chapter.

The No Page Numbering option in the Position pop-up list omits page numbers for the current page and all pages that follow, regardless of any other settings in the dialog box. Therefore, if you want to print automatic page numbers, be sure to choose a Position option other than No Page Numbering, which is the initial setting.

RESTARTING THE PAGE-NUMBERING SEQUENCE

Normally, WordPerfect automatically keeps track of page numbers based on the order in which they will be printed, with the first page being page 1. However, you might need a different starting page number.

For example, if your document begins with a title page and other front matter (any material that precedes the main text of a book), you don't normally number those pages. Instead, page 1 is probably the first page of body text (e.g., the first page of Chapter 1), even though that page is not actually the first page that's printed.

Therefore, if you turn on page numbering on the third page of the document, its page number will still be 3. (In other words, WordPerfect knows that this is the third printed page, even though it did not print page numbers on any of the preceding pages.)

To get around this problem, you need to restart the page number sequence by following these steps:

1. Move the insertion point to the top of the page, before any text, where you want to restart the numbering sequence.

2. Choose **Layout** ➤ **Page** ➤ **N**umbering (or press Alt+F9 N). You'll see the Page Numbering dialog box.

3. Choose **N**ew Page Number (or press Alt+N) and type the new page number for the current page in the text box.

4. Choose OK or press ↵ to return to the document window.

Page numbering will start at whatever number you entered in step 3, and all subsequent pages will be numbered accordingly (assuming, of course, that you also remember to turn on page numbering so that the numbers are printed).

USING ROMAN NUMERALS FOR PAGE NUMBERS

 If you want to see examples of Roman-numbered pages, look through the first few pages of this book.

You can number your WordPerfect documents with Roman numerals (e.g., *i, ii, iii*) instead of the usual Arabic numbers (e.g., *1, 2, 3*). Just follow these steps:

1. Place the insertion point before any text at the top of the page where you want Roman numerals.

2. Choose **Layout** ➤ **Page** ➤ **Numbering** (or press Alt+F9 N). The Page Numbering dialog box will appear.

3. Open the Numbering **Type** pop-up list, and choose one of the options for using Roman numerals. Choosing *i, ii, iii, iv* sets page numbering to lowercase Roman numerals; choosing *I, II, III, IV* sets page numbering to uppercase Roman numerals.

4. Choose OK or press ↵ to return to the document window.

To return page numbering to Arabic numerals, choose *1, 2, 3, 4* from the Numbering Type pop-up list.

When you choose a Roman-numeral numbering type, page numbering starts at the new page number, but uses the appropriate style of Roman numerals. For example, if you choose *3* as the starting page number for a page and *i, ii, iii, iv* for Numbering Type, WordPerfect automatically numbers that page as *iii* and the pages that follow as *iv, v, vi* and so forth.

CHANGING THE APPEARANCE OF PAGE NUMBERS

 See Chapter 23 for information on printing dual page numbers, such as "Page 2 of 20."

Initially, page numbers include just the number itself, but you can change the appearance to include other characters. The page number is represented by a code, which shows up as *[Pg NumStyle:^B]* in Reveal Codes, and as *[^B]* below the Accompanying Text option in the Page Numbering dialog box. For example, you can print page numbers in the format *Page 1* or *-1-*. To do this, you need to include the text and a page-numbering code, to indicate exactly where you want the page number to appear. Thus, the first example would be represented in the document window as *Page ^B* and the second as *-^B-*.

Here are the steps for adding text to the page-numbering code (assuming that you've already specified that page numbers should be printed):

1. Position the insertion point before any text at the top of the page where you want accompanying text to be displayed along with the page number.

2. Choose **Layout** ➤ **Page** ➤ **Numbering** (or press Alt+F9 N). The Page Numbering dialog box will appear.

3. Move the insertion point to the text box below the **A**ccompanying Text option.

4. Type in whatever text should appear before and after the page-numbering code, which is displayed in the box as *[^B]*. Make sure that the [^B] code appears where you want the actual page number to appear—for example, *- [^B] -* or *Page [^B]*.

5. Choose OK or press ↵ to return to the document window.

Be sure to include blank spaces in step 4 if required. For example, if you type *Page* in front of the [^B] code without pressing the spacebar to separate the two, your page number will appear as *Page[^B]* in the Accompanying Text portion of the Page Numbering dialog box, as *Page^B* in the document window, and as *Page1* on the first printed page or the Print Preview screen.

The maximum length of the text and page number is 30 characters. You can include WordPerfect special characters entered by choosing Font ➤ WP Characters from the document window or by pressing Ctrl+W, as described in Chapter 5.

WordPerfect will add a hidden [Pg Num Style:] code to your document at the insertion point. As usual, if you change your mind about the new page-numbering style, or you end up with competing codes, you can use Reveal Codes to delete the hidden code. If you change your mind *immediately* after inserting the page-numbering style, you can remove it by choosing Edit ➤ Undo (Alt+Backspace).

PRINTING A PAGE NUMBER IN TEXT

If you want to print the current page number somewhere within the body of your text (as opposed to above or below the text), move the insertion point wherever you want the page number to appear, choose Layout ➤ Page ➤ Numbering (or press Alt+F9 N), and then choose Insert Page Number in the dialog box and press ↵.

For example, suppose you want to include the line

This page (24) intentionally left blank

in a document, but want to ensure that the page number shown in parentheses is indeed the current page number, regardless of any later editing. To do so, position the insertion point wherever you want that line of text to appear, type *This page (,* choose Layout ➤ Page ➤ Numbering, choose Insert Page Number, press ↵, then type *) intentionally left blank.*

WordPerfect displays ∧B and any accompanying text you added in the document window as the page number (again, just switch to the Print Preview screen to see the actual page number). It also inserts a hidden code, [Insert Pg Num], in your document, which you can see in Reveal Codes.

HIDING THE PAGE NUMBER ON A PAGE

In some situations, you might not want to print the page number on a specific page in a document. For example, you might want to omit the number from a page that shows a full-page illustration. To hide the page number on a particular page, without disrupting the numbering sequence, follow these steps:

1. Place the insertion point before any text at the top of the page where you want to hide the page number.

2. Choose **Layout** ➤ **P**age ➤ S**u**ppress, or press Alt+F9 U. You will see the Suppress dialog box:

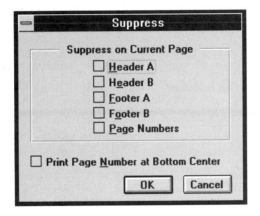

3. Check the **P**age Numbers box.

4. Choose OK or press ↵ to return to the document window.

The page number will be deleted from the current page, but subsequent pages will be numbered in correct sequence.

PRINTING PAGE HEADERS AND FOOTERS

TO PRINT A PAGE HEADER OR FOOTER ON PRINTED PAGES IN A DOCUMENT,

1. Position the insertion point at the top of the page where you want the headers or footers to start.

2. Choose Layout ➤ Page (or press Alt+F9).

3. Choose either Headers or Footers, either A or B, and the frequency of the header or footer.

4. Choose Create and create the header or footer.

5. Choose Close when you're finished.

You will see page headers and footers when you print the document and on the Print Preview screen, but not in the normal document window. The hidden codes are [Header A:], [Header B:], [Footer A:], and [Footer B:].

Alternating right and left page headers are called the "recto head" and "verso head" in publishing. Recto means right, verso means left.

With WordPerfect, you can define a *page header,* which is automatically printed at the top of each page, and a *page footer,* which is automatically printed at the bottom of each page. If you've ever had to type a document where you needed to include a header and footer on every page, you're sure to love this feature, because you have to type the header or footer only once. From that point on, WordPerfect will print it on every page (or alternating pages, if you request it), regardless of whether you add or delete paragraphs.

Page headers and footers can be up to a page in length, but generally a line or two line is sufficient, since you'll rarely need to repeat several lines of text on every page in a document. You can also include page numbers, the current date, lines, special characters, graphic boxes, and other formatting features in a header or footer. Figure 7.4 shows an example where the header has a graphic line at the bottom, and the footer has one at the top, to better set off the header and footer from the rest of the text.

You might want to print different headers and footers on alternating pages. For example, you might want to print Header A on even-numbered pages and Header B on odd-numbered pages. This is the standard format used in books and other documents. Figure 7.5 shows two pages from a sample document with this header format.

CREATING A PAGE HEADER

Follow these steps to add a page header to a document:

1. Place the insertion point before any text at the top of the page where you want the header to start printing.

Thatcher History   First Draft
_____

   The British Conservative Party has been in trouble as of
late. Their woes appear related to their leadership crisis.
Margaret Thatcher has been a dynamic Prime Minister in her years
in office. However, it is this uncompromising nature of hers
which has been as a spot on an otherwise spotless career. Lately
this attitude has cost her dearly with back benchers and cabinet
members alike. Her "public approval rating at 24% is lower than
any other Prime Minister since the polling has been conducted."

   With the Conservative Party running 19 percentage points
behind Labour, questions have arisen as to which direction the
Tory Party should take, more precisely who shall be chosen as its
director. However, neither will out-and-out declare their
candidacy in fear that voters would see it as back-stabbing the
"Iron Lady." They too fear a confrontation with Thatcher
herself. "When Maggy bites she finds it a bit rough to let go."

   In estimating these possible candidates chances of gaining
the Tory leadership, it is first important to demonstrate there
is a crisis which would, or rather could, dictate a change in
leadership. Thus, it must be shown that Margaret Thatcher does
not have a monopoly on Tory future leadership. One member of
Parliament was quoted as saying, "In '84 she could have pushed

_____

Date Printed: August 16, 1991   Page: 6
File Name: Thatcher.wp   ☼

FIGURE 7.4:

A sample page header and footer with graphic lines

Header A (even pages)   **Header B (odd pages)**

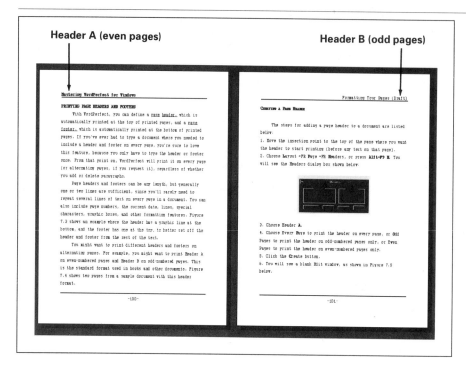

FIGURE 7.5:

Two different headers, one for even-numbered pages and one for odd-numbered pages

2. Choose **Layout** ➤ **P**age ➤ **H**eaders, or press Alt+F9 H. You will see the Headers dialog box:

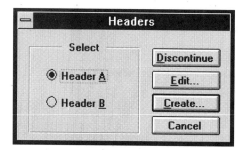

3. Choose Header **A**.

4. Choose **C**reate. You will see a blank document window, as shown in Figure 7.6.

5. Choose Placement (by clicking the button or pressing Alt+P). Then choose Every **P**age to print the header on every page, **O**dd Pages to print the header on odd-numbered pages only, or E**v**en Pages to

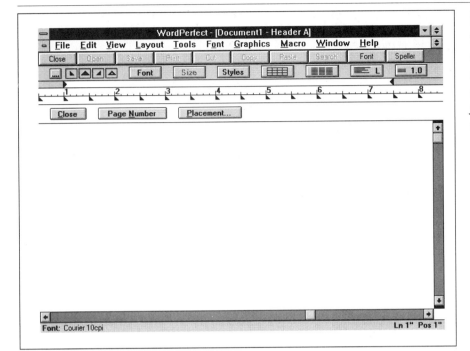

FIGURE 7.6:

This is the window for creating or changing a header (or footer). Editing a header or footer is the same: Only the title bar differs.

print the header on even-numbered pages only. Choose OK or press ↵ when done.

6. Type the header, which can contain up to a page of text. You can design your page header by using any of the undimmed pull-down menu options and shortcut keys, including Center (Shift+F7) and Flush Right (Alt+F7), graphic lines (**G**raphics ➤ **L**ine), WordPerfect special characters (Ctrl+W), and any size, appearance, or font options on the **Fo**nt pull-down menu (F9). If you want to include a page number, position the insertion point where you want the page number to appear and choose **P**age Number. (The page number will appear as ∧*B*.)

7. If you want to print more than one blank line beneath the header, press ↵ once for each additional blank line.

8. Choose Close when you've finished typing the header.

If you want to create a second header, repeat the steps above again, but choose Header B instead of Header A in step 3. Repeat the steps for choosing a position for the header (e.g., odd-numbered pages or even-numbered pages). Then type the second header, and choose Close to return to the document window.

If you print both Header A and Header B on every page, one may print over the other, unless you carefully align text in each header to prevent this (e.g., center the text in one header and right-align text in the other). You can switch to the Print Preview screen (Shift+F5) to verify the alignment.

CREATING A PAGE FOOTER

The steps for creating page footers are almost identical to those for creating page headers; the only real difference is that you choose *Footers* instead of *Headers* on the Page menu.

1. Place the insertion point before any text at the top of the page where you want the footer to start printing.

2. Choose **Layout ➤ P**age **➤** Footers, or press Alt+F9 F. You will see the Footers dialog box, which looks just like the dialog box for headers, except that its title bar says "Footers" instead of "Headers."

3. Choose Footer **A**.

4. Choose **C**reate. You will see a blank document window, which is the same as the one shown in Figure 7.6, except that its title bar says "Footer A" instead of "Header A."

5. Use the **P**lacement button to choose **E**very Page to print the footer on every page, or **O**dd Pages to print the footer on odd-numbered pages only, or E**v**en Pages to print the footer on even-numbered pages only.

6. Type your footer, using any of the document window techniques described in "Creating a Page Header" to format the text. As with headers, footers can contain up to a page of text.

7. Choose **C**lose when you've finished typing the footer.

Since headers and footers can contain more than one line, there's really no need to create two separate headers or footers to be printed on every page, unless you want to suppress only one of them on certain pages.

If you want to create a second footer, repeat the steps above again, but choose Footer B instead of Footer A in step 3. Repeat the steps for choosing a position for the footer (e.g., odd-numbered pages or even-numbered pages), and create your second footer. As mentioned earlier, if you want both Footer A and Footer B to be printed on every page, be sure to align the text in each footer so that one doesn't overwrite the other.

CHANGING AN EXISTING HEADER OR FOOTER

If you want to change an existing header or footer without retyping it, follow these steps:

1. Position the insertion point just to the right of the header or footer you want to change (open Reveal Codes by choosing **V**iew ➤ Reveal **C**odes or pressing Alt+F3 to do this more easily).

2. Choose **L**ayout ➤ **P**age, or press Alt+F9.

3. Choose either **H**eaders (to change an existing header) or **F**ooters (to change an existing footer).

4. Using the dialog box that appears, choose the header or footer you want to change (either **A** or **B**).

5. Choose **E**dit.

At this point, the existing header or footer appears in an otherwise blank document window. You can use all the usual WordPerfect editing techniques to change the header or footer, including opening Reveal Codes to view blank lines beneath a header (these appear as [HRt]). When you've finished making your changes, choose Close to return to the document window.

INCLUDING PAGE NUMBERS IN HEADERS AND FOOTERS

To include a page number in a header or footer, you must first go through the steps to create or edit the header or footer, as described above. When you get to the window for editing the header or footer, choose Page Number where you want the page number to appear. Although the screen will show ∧B, this symbol will be replaced by the correct page number when you print the document or preview it on the Print Preview screen.

Be sure to include any necessary blank spaces when typing a page header or footer that includes a page number. For example, if you want a page number to appear as *Page 1* on the first page, type the word *Page,* press the spacebar, and then choose Page Number, so the number appears as *Page* ∧B on the screen.

Also, if you include page numbers in a header or footer, you should turn off automatic page numbering—that is, choose No Page Numbering from the

Position option pop-up list in the Page Numbering dialog box—for all pages that will show the header or footer. Otherwise, the page number will appear twice on each page: once in the position dictated by automatic page numbering and then again in the header or footer.

Any changes you make by choosing Layout ➤ Page ➤ Numbering (Alt+F9 N) and specifying any of the numbering options (Numbering Type, New Page Number, or Accompanying Text) will also affect page numbers that appear in headers and footers.

INCLUDING THE DATE AND TIME IN A HEADER OR FOOTER

If you plan to print multiple revisions of a document, it's a good idea to *date-stamp* each printed copy, so you can see at a glance how recent it is. Figure 7.4 showed an example where the page footer included the date of the current printing.

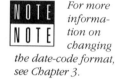

For more information on changing the date-code format, see Chapter 3.

To include the current date or time in a header or footer, go through the usual steps to create or edit the header or footer. Then position the insertion point wherever you want the date or time to be displayed in the header or footer, choose Tools ➤ Date ➤ Format, and define a format for the date or time. Then choose Tools ➤ Date ➤ Code (or press Ctrl+Shift+F5) to insert the date or time.

HIDING HEADERS AND FOOTERS ON A PAGE

You can hide the headers or footers on any single page in your document. For example, you may want to omit headers and footers from pages that have full-page graphics or from blank pages that you've intentionally included for back-to-back printing or binding. To omit all, or some, headers and footers on a single page, follow these steps:

1. Move the insertion point to the top of the page where you want to hide headers or footers.

2. Choose **L**ayout ➤ **P**age ➤ S**u**ppress, or press Alt+F9 U.

At this point, the Suppress dialog box appears on your screen. This is the same dialog box you saw earlier in the discussion on hiding a page number on a page.

The dialog box options let you suppress—on the current page only—Header A, Header B, Footer A, Footer B, and automatic page numbering (as described earlier in this chapter). You can choose any combination of options by clicking in their check boxes. For example, you can suppress Header A and Footer A, or all headers, or all footers, or automatic page numbers.

The Suppress dialog box also provides the Print Page Number at Bottom Center option for printing a page number at the bottom center of a page. This option is handy if you've suppressed a footer (or header) that includes a page number, haven't defined automatic page numbers, but still want a page number to print on the current page.

After you've defined the features you want to suppress on the current page, or chosen to print the page number at the bottom center of the page, choose OK or press ↵ to return to the document window.

DISCONTINUING HEADERS AND FOOTERS

In the preceding section, you learned how to temporarily suppress page headers and footers on a specific page. You can also turn off, or discontinue, headers and footers to suppress them on the current page and all pages that follow. Follow these steps:

Discontinuing headers and footers does not discontinue automatic page numbering (if you've chosen to number your pages automatically, instead of in a header or footer). To discontinue automatic page numbering, choose Layout ➤ Page ➤ Numbering (or press Alt+F9 N P), open the Position pop-up list, and choose No Page Numbering.

1. Move the insertion point to the top of the page where you want to discontinue a page header or footer (or anywhere beneath the first line of the preceding page).

2. Choose **L**ayout ➤ **P**age, or press Alt+F9.

3. Choose **H**eaders to discontinue page headers, or choose **F**ooters to discontinue page footers.

4. Choose the header or footer that you want to discontinue (**A** or **B**) from the dialog box.

5. Choose **D**iscontinue.

6. Repeat steps 2–5 for each header and footer that you want to discontinue.

TROUBLESHOOTING HEADER AND FOOTER PROBLEMS

Headers and footers can be a bit troublesome when you're first trying to get the hang of them, so let's look at some common problems and their solutions.

Refining the Position of Headers and Footers

Neither headers nor footers are printed within the top and bottom margins. Instead, the first line of the header is always printed as the first line below the top margin, and the bottom line of the footer is always printed as the last line above the bottom margin. WordPerfect automatically leaves one blank line between the text and the header or footer, but you can press ↵ to add more blank space after typing a header or before typing a footer.

If you want your headers or footers to appear "in the margins," you must change the margin settings. For example, suppose you want the header to be printed ½ inch from the top of the page and the footer to be printed ½ inch from the bottom of the page. You must change the top and bottom margins to 0.5 inches by using the techniques described in Chapter 4 for changing margins (that is, choose Layout ➤ Margins, or press Ctrl+F8, and type the new margin settings). Make sure the [T/B Margin:] code that defines the new top and bottom margins precedes the codes that define the header and footer.

Disappearing Headers and Footers

When WordPerfect prints a page, it first plans the page by observing the formatting codes at the top of that page. If any text on that page precedes a [Header] or [Footer] code, the code is ignored until the next page is about to be printed.

Techniques for moving codes from one place to another are covered in Chapter 3.

Therefore, if you place [Header] and [Footer] codes in or after the first line of text on a page, or they get moved away from the top of the page when you insert new text, the headers and footers will not be printed until the next page. If this is a problem, you can use Reveal Codes to move the [Header] and [Footer] codes to the top of the page where you want the headers and footers to begin.

FORMATTING FOR BINDING

In many situations, you will want to ensure that a particular page is printed as an odd-numbered page. For example, for documents containing chapters, it's common practice to start each new chapter on an odd-numbered page. If you are printing a brochure with a mail-in coupon attached, you might want to ensure that the coupon is printed as an odd-numbered page, so it won't be on the back of another page.

When writing a manuscript with lengthy chapters or sections, you may find it easier to store each chapter or section in a separate file. The Styles (Chapter 14) and Master Document (Chapter 24) features can help you better manage large documents.

If you are certain that you want a particular page to be printed as an odd- or even-numbered page, you can inform WordPerfect of this by following these steps:

1. Move the insertion point to the top of the page that should have an odd or even page number.

2. Choose **Layout ➤ Page ➤ Numbering**, or press Alt+F9 N. You'll see the Page Numbering dialog box shown earlier.

3. Put an *X* in the **O**dd or **E**ven check box below the Force Current Page option.

4. Choose OK or press ↵.

In the document window, you may see that WordPerfect has inserted a soft page break (if necessary) to ensure that the page begins on either a new odd- or even-numbered page. If you look at the page in Reveal Codes, you'll see the [Force:Odd] or [Force:Even] code at the top of the page. You may also see the soft-page-break code ([SPg]), indicating the location of the soft page break.

ENSURING A NEW ODD-NUMBERED PAGE

Keep in mind that forcing text to be printed on an odd- numbered page does not guarantee that the text will be printed on a *new* page. Instead, it only guarantees that the text will start on a new page if the page currently being printed is even- numbered. If you need to ensure that text starts on a new odd-numbered page (like a chapter heading or a full-page coupon), you should first insert a hard page break at the top of the page (by choosing Layout ➤ Page ➤ Page Break or pressing Ctrl+↵). Then, insert the [Force:Odd] code at the top of that page, using the steps listed above.

When you print the document, if the page before the new odd-numbered page is itself an odd-numbered page, WordPerfect will print a blank, even-numbered page and then the new odd-numbered page. If you then copy the pages back to back on a copy machine (including the blank even-numbered page), the odd-numbered page will appear on a page by itself; it won't be attached to the back of an even-numbered page.

When copying back to back, you always need to place an even number of pages in the copy machine (for example, insert four, not three, pages in the machine). Therefore, you may need to add a blank piece of paper after your coupon if it is currently the last (odd-numbered) page of your document.

KEEPING TEXT TOGETHER

WordPerfect offers two techniques to ensure that selected text stays together on one page: *Block Protect* and *Conditional End of Page*. Block Protect is generally used to prevent passages of text, such as a quotation, sidebar, or columnar table, from being split across two pages. Conditional End of Page is generally used to keep section headings and the text that follows from being split across two or more pages.

USING BLOCK PROTECT TO KEEP TEXT TOGETHER

The Block Protect feature is best used when you want to keep selected text (which can include hidden formatting codes) together on a page. These are the general steps for protecting selected text:

Chapter 2 has a complete discussion of techniques for selecting text.

1. Select the lines of text you want to keep together on a page. The selected text must be less than a full page in length, but you can select text that crosses a page break.

2. Choose **Layout ➤ P**age **➤ B**lock Protect, or press Alt+F9 B.

When you print the document (or preview it on the Print Preview screen), WordPerfect will calculate the number of lines available on the current page before printing the protected block. If there isn't enough room to print the protected block, it will skip to the next page before printing it.

You can move or copy existing text or tables to graphic boxes.

A disadvantage of this technique is that the page preceding the protected block may end with too many blank lines, since WordPerfect skips to the next page prematurely to prevent splitting the protected block of text.

Graphic boxes offer a better solution to this problem, particularly if you're concerned about splitting a table. If you place a table in a graphic box (and the table can fit on one page), WordPerfect will not break the table across two pages and will not leave a gap at the end of the page preceding the table. See Chapter 19 for more information on graphic boxes.

Removing Block Protection

If you protect a block of selected text, then change your mind and decide to unprotect it, use the same general technique that you use to turn off most other formatting features: Delete the hidden code that activates that feature.

1. Move the insertion point to the upper-left corner of the protected block.

2. Open Reveal Codes by choosing **V**iew ➤ Reveal **C**odes or by pressing Alt+F3.

3. Move the Reveal Codes highlight to the [Block Prot:On] code and press Delete.

USING CONDITIONAL END OF PAGE TO KEEP LINES TOGETHER

You may also want to keep certain lines of text together on a page in a document. For example, if your document uses section headings, you might want to ensure that the heading does not end up at the bottom of one page, with its related paragraph at the top of the next page.

You can define a *conditional end of page* to prevent two or more specific lines of text from being broken across two pages. To do this, you need to count the number of lines that must be kept together, including any blank lines. For example, if you have a heading, followed by a blank line, followed by the first line of text of the paragraph beneath that heading, as in Figure 7.7, you can specify three lines for a conditional page break to prevent the heading and paragraph from being split across two pages.

When you've determined how many lines of text need to be kept together on the page, follow these steps to insert the conditional end of page:

1. Move the insertion point to the line *above* the lines that you want to keep together (even if that line contains text).

2. Choose **Layout** ➤ **Page** ➤ Conditional **E**nd of Page, or press Alt+F9 E.

3. Include the number of lines below the insertion point that should be kept together.

4. Choose OK or press ↵ to return to the document window.

These commands insert a hidden code indicating how many lines beneath the code's position are to be kept on a single page. For example, if you specify

---

Work Avoidance

Sometimes work itself can be a form of work avoidance. Recently, while writing an article that absolutely had to be done by 3:00, I suddenly had the urge to vacuum my closet. While waving the vacuum nozzle around without paying attention, I (or rather, the vacuum cleaner) sucked some ties off my tie rack. They came out of the vacuum cleaner hose looking like little silk prunes. So now there was another job to do -- iron some ties.

FIGURE 7.7:

Conditional End of Page can prevent the heading from ending up alone at the bottom of a page.

three lines, the inserted code is [Cndl EOP:3]. When WordPerfect encounters this code in a document, it counts the number of blank lines available on the page currently being printed. If there isn't enough space to print the number of lines that must be kept together (three in this example), it skips to the next page before printing the lines.

Many people ask why WordPerfect has both Block Protect and Conditional End of Page. After all, they seem to serve the same purpose. But there is a subtle difference. Block Protect works by placing a [Block Prot:On] code at the top and a [Block Prot:Off] code at the bottom of the protected block. Any changes that you make to the protected block, including the addition or deletion of lines, still keep the entire block protected.

 *Soon you'll learn about widow and orphan protection, yet another technique for keeping lines together.*

On the other hand, Conditional End of Page inserts only one hidden code, [Cndl EOP:*n*], in a document, which tells WordPerfect to skip to the next page if there is not enough space to print at least *n* lines. Whether the text beneath the [Cndl EOP:] code grows or shrinks is irrelevant, because the idea is simply to keep a few lines from being split, not a whole body of text.

Removing a Conditional End of Page

If you change your mind *immediately* about using Conditional End of Page in a document, choose Edit ➤ Undo (Alt+Backspace). Alternatively, if you've made other changes since adding the conditional end of page, move the insertion point wherever it was when you chose the commands to insert the conditional end of page. Then open Reveal Codes and delete the [Cndl EOP:] code that's keeping the lines together.

PREVENTING WIDOWS AND ORPHANS

In WordPerfect terminology, a *widow* is the first line of a paragraph, printed on the last line of a page. An *orphan* is the last line of a paragraph, printed on the first line of a new page. Figure 7.8 shows an example of a page with both a widow and an orphan.

You can have WordPerfect automatically prevent widows and orphans in a printed document. To prevent a widow, WordPerfect moves the first line of a paragraph to the top of the next page. To prevent an orphan, WordPerfect moves the next-to-last line of a paragraph to the top of the next page.

Follow these steps to invoke widow/orphan protection:

1. Move the insertion point to the top of the document (or to the place where you want to begin protecting against widows and orphans).

2. Choose **Layout** ➤ **Page** ➤ **W**idow/Orphan, or press Alt+F9 W.

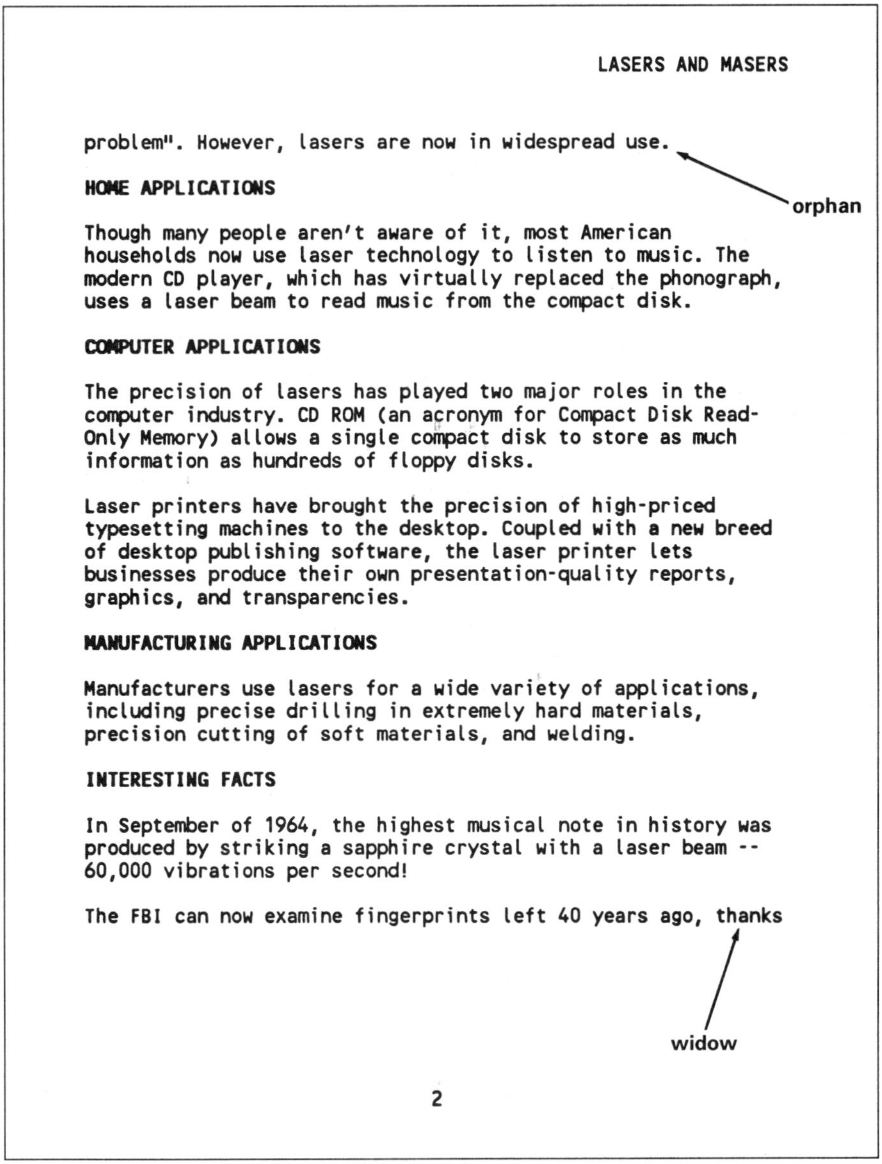

FIGURE 7.8:

A page with both a widow and an orphan

LASERS AND MASERS

problem". However, lasers are now in widespread use.

HOME APPLICATIONS

Though many people aren't aware of it, most American households now use laser technology to listen to music. The modern CD player, which has virtually replaced the phonograph, uses a laser beam to read music from the compact disk.

COMPUTER APPLICATIONS

The precision of lasers has played two major roles in the computer industry. CD ROM (an acronym for Compact Disk Read-Only Memory) allows a single compact disk to store as much information as hundreds of floppy disks.

Laser printers have brought the precision of high-priced typesetting machines to the desktop. Coupled with a new breed of desktop publishing software, the laser printer lets businesses produce their own presentation-quality reports, graphics, and transparencies.

MANUFACTURING APPLICATIONS

Manufacturers use lasers for a wide variety of applications, including precise drilling in extremely hard materials, precision cutting of soft materials, and welding.

INTERESTING FACTS

In September of 1964, the highest musical note in history was produced by striking a sapphire crystal with a laser beam -- 60,000 vibrations per second!

The FBI can now examine fingerprints left 40 years ago, thanks

widow

2

All text to the right of and below the insertion point in the current document will be reformatted to prevent widows and orphans. For example, Figure 7.9 shows the same page as Figure 7.8, but printed with widow/orphan protection.

```
                      LASERS AND MASERS


Initially, the laser was viewed as "solution looking for a
problem". However, lasers are now in widespread use.
                                                          no orphan
HOME APPLICATIONS

Though many people aren't aware of it, most American
households now use laser technology to listen to music. The
modern CD player, which has virtually replaced the phonograph,
uses a laser beam to read music from the compact disk.

COMPUTER APPLICATIONS

The precision of lasers has played two major roles in the
computer industry. CD ROM (an acronym for Compact Disk Read-
Only Memory) allows a single compact disk to store as much
information as hundreds of floppy disks.

Laser printers have brought the precision of high-priced
typesetting machines to the desktop. Coupled with a new breed
of desktop publishing software, the laser printer lets
businesses produce their own presentation-quality reports,
graphics, and transparencies.

MANUFACTURING APPLICATIONS

Manufacturers use lasers for a wide variety of applications,
including precise drilling in extremely hard materials,
precision cutting of soft materials, and welding.

INTERESTING FACTS

In September of 1964, the highest musical note in history was
produced by striking a sapphire crystal with a laser beam --
60,000 vibrations per second!



no widow
```

Two lines from the paragraph at the end of the previous page are now printed at the top of the current page. The first line of the last paragraph is no longer on this page; instead, it's printed as the first line on the next page (not shown).

Disabling Widow/Orphan Protection

If you change your mind immediately after adding widow/orphan protection, you can choose Edit ➤ Undo (Alt+Backspace) to undo the protection.

To disable widow/orphan protection at a particular place in your document (so that later pages are not protected), move the insertion point to where you want to turn off widow/orphan protection. Then repeat the steps described in the preceding section. This will remove the check mark next to the Widow/Orphan option on the Page menu, indicating that protection is now turned off.

If you want to disable widow/orphan protection altogether, first position the insertion point where you initiated protection, then use Reveal Codes to locate and delete the [W/O On] code.

KEEPING WORDS TOGETHER ON A LINE

You can also prevent a particular pair of words from being separated and placed on two lines by inserting a *hard space* between the words. For example, when printing a document that contains phone numbers with area codes, like (415) 555-8233, you might want to prevent WordPerfect from putting the area code on one line and the rest of the phone number on the next line or page.

To insert a hard space between two words while typing them, follow these steps:

1. Type the first word (without typing a space after it).

2. Choose **L**ayout ➤ Line ➤ Special Co**d**es (or press Shift+F9 O).

3. Choose Hard S**p**ace (located under Other Codes in the Insert Special Codes dialog box).

4. Press ↵ or choose **I**nsert.

5. Type the second word.

The space looks like any other normal blank space in the document window. In Reveal Codes, however, it appears as [HdSpc].

If you want to insert a hard space between two words that are already separated by a normal space, move the insertion point between the two words, follow steps 2–4 above, then press the Delete key to delete the regular space.

PRINTING ON NONSTANDARD PAGE SIZES

TO PRINT ON PAPER OTHER THAN THE STANDARD 8½" × 11" SIZE,

position the insertion point at the top of the page where the new paper size should begin. Choose Layout ➤ Page ➤ Paper Size (or press Alt+F9 S), and choose the size you want to use.

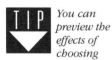

You can preview the effects of choosing nonstandard page sizes on the Print Preview screen.

By default, WordPerfect assumes that you will print your document on the *standard* page size, which is 8½ " × 11" in the United States. But many documents call for other page sizes, such as legal documents that must be printed on 8½ " × 14" paper or labels that are only a few inches wide and high. Many preprinted forms, such as invoices and packing slips, also require unusual paper sizes.

Whether you can print text on nonstandard page sizes depends largely on your printer. For example, most laser printers require a special sheet feeder for legal-size paper. On many dot-matrix and other tractor-fed printers, you can only print sideways on the page if the platen is wide enough to accommodate 11-inch wide paper. (As discussed in Chapter 8, laser printers can print sideways on a page even though the paper is fed normally.)

If you have any problems using the techniques described in this section, you should study printing in general (see Chapter 8) and perhaps learn more about your particular printer by referring to its manual.

CHOOSING A PAPER SIZE

Installing a printer for use with Word-Perfect is covered in Appendix A.

Whenever you install a printer for use with WordPerfect, the installation program creates a *printer resource file* (which has the file-name extension .PRS) containing information and options for that printer. Included in this file are some paper sizes and types commonly used with that printer. To use one of these predefined paper sizes, choose the printer you want to use (see Chapter 8), then follow these steps:

1. Position the insertion point before any text at the top of the first page that will be printed on the page with the new size.

2. Choose **L**ayout ➤ **P**age ➤ Paper **S**ize, or press Alt+F9 S. An alphabetical listing of the currently available paper sizes appears in the Paper Size dialog box, shown in Figure 7.10 (the paper sizes displayed depend on your printer and the paper sizes you've created). The currently selected paper size is highlighted in the dialog box. (If you don't see the paper size you need, you can add it, as described later in this chapter.)

3. Choose the paper size you want, either by double-clicking on it with your mouse or by moving the highlight to it and choosing **S**elect. A quick way to move the highlight is to begin typing the name of the paper size you want. For example, type the first character (or characters) of the word *Envelope* to quickly move the highlight to the Envelope paper size (assuming one exists).

NOTE *If you select a Windows printer driver in the Select Printer dialog box, you can only choose one paper size for your entire document. See Chapter 8 and "Using Windows Printer Drivers" later in this chapter for more information.*

WordPerfect puts a hidden [Paper Sz/Typ] code in your document, indicating the size of paper to be used for printing. When Auto Code Placement is on, the [Paper Sz/Type] code is automatically inserted at the top of the current page and replaces any existing [Paper Sz/Type] code on that page. When Auto Code Placement is off, only text to the right of and below the insertion point is printed on the paper with the new size. Hence, if any text precedes the [Paper Sz/Typ] code on the page, the code will be ignored until the next printed page.

As usual, if you change your mind about the currently chosen page size, you can return to the normal size by deleting the hidden [Paper Sz/Typ] code. (If you change your mind immediately after changing the paper size, you can choose Edit ➤ Undo (Alt+Backspace) to undo the selection.) If you need to change a chosen page size, delete the existing [Paper Sz/Typ] code so that it does not override the new code, or make sure that Auto Code Placement is on.

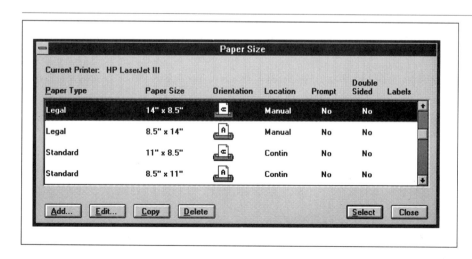

FIGURE 7.10:
The Paper Size dialog box

In the following sections, I'll talk about printing on some common paper sizes. Remember, if a particular paper size is not currently available for your printer, you can probably just add that paper size, as discussed later in this chapter.

PRINTING SIDEWAYS ON THE PAGE

In some situations, you might want to print a document sideways. Sideways printing is often called *landscape* printing, because the text or graphic is printed *across* the long edge of the page (the way landscapes in art are usually painted). The printing mode used with most documents is called *portrait* printing, because the text is printed *down* the long edge of the page (the way portraits are usually painted).

Printing in landscape mode is useful for many types of documents, particularly large, lengthy tables. Figure 7.11 shows a printed table at arm's length in portrait mode and in landscape mode. As you can see by the number of rows and the amount of white space on the pages, landscape mode offers much better use of the available space on the page. How you go about printing in landscape mode depends on what kind of printer you have.

Printing Sideways with a Laser Printer

*To print sideways when using a Windows printer driver, choose **F**ile ➤ **P**rint ➤ **S**elect ➤ **S**etup ➤ **L**andscape first. Then work your way back to the Print dialog box, and choose **P**rint.*

To print sideways on a standard-size page with a laser printer, you must first choose a landscape paper size. You can identify a landscape size by the small rotated *A* lying on its side in the printer button for that size. (The second "Legal - Dup Short" paper type in the Paper Size dialog box shown earlier shows an example.) Follow the steps above to choose the landscape size.

When it's time to actually print the document, just choose File ➤ Print (F5), then Full Document. You do not need to change the direction of the paper in the printer—the laser printer will automatically print sideways on the page, even though the paper is fed into the printer normally.

Printing Sideways with a Nonlaser Printer

See your printer manual for information about printing in landscape mode.

If you want to print sideways on a nonlaser printer, you must first inform WordPerfect by choosing a landscape paper size.

When you're ready to actually print the document, you will probably need to feed the paper into the printer sideways, as shown in Figure 7.12. The platen (the paper roller) must be wide enough to accommodate the page. For example, you can only print sideways on an $8\frac{1}{2}$ " $\times$ 11" page if your printer can accept 11-inch-wide paper.

FIGURE 7.11:

A large table printed in portrait mode and landscape mode (continued on next page)

If you need to...	Choose	Notes
Change the top and bottom margins	Layout ▸ Margins	If Auto Code Placement is not turned on, be sure to first position the insertion point to the top of the page where you want to change the margins. Otherwise, new margins won't take effect until the next page.
Center text on the page	Layout ▸ Page ▸ Center Page	After choosing these options, place a hard page break at the bottom of the text by positioning the insertion point and pressing Ctrl+↵.
Number pages	Layout ▸ Page ▸ Numbering	The Page Numbering dialog box lets you define the position, type, starting number, and style of the page number. You can also force the page to be odd- or even-numbered from this same dialog box.
Choose a paper size	Layout ▸ Page ▸ Center Page	If the paper size you want isn't listed in the Paper Size dialog box, you can create it using the Add button. However, be sure to define only paper sizes that are within the capabilities of your printer.

Portrait

Once you've chosen the paper size and placed the paper properly in the printer, you can go ahead and print the document by choosing File ➤ Print (F5), then choosing Full Document. If WordPerfect expects manually fed pages at this point, you'll need to insert the paper a page at a time (as described in "Location" and "Prompt to Load Paper" in "Adding a Paper Size" later in this chapter).

If you need to...	Choose	Notes
Change the top and bottom margins	Layout ▶ Margins	If Auto Code Placement is not turned on, be sure to first position the insertion point to the top of the page where you want to change the margins. Otherwise, new margins won't take effect until the next page.
Center text on the page	Layout ▶ Page ▶ Center Page	After choosing these options, place a hard page break at the bottom of the text by positioning the insertion point and pressing Ctrl+↵.
Number pages	Layout ▶ Page ▶ Numbering	The Page Numbering dialog box lets you define the position, type, starting number, and style of the page number. You can also force the page to be odd- or even-numbered from this same dialog box.
Choose a paper size	Layout ▶ Page ▶ Center Page	If the paper size you want isn't listed in the Paper Size dialog box, you can create it using the Add button. However, be sure to define only paper sizes that are within the capabilities of your printer.
Change the document initial codes	Layout ▶ Document ▶ Initial Codes	The document initial codes area is a prime choice for codes that affect the entire document, because the codes are above all text and outside the document window. This is especially useful in primary merge files for labels and other non-standard paper sizes.

Landscape

FIGURE 7.11:

A large table printed in portrait mode and landscape mode (continued)

PRINTING ON LETTERHEAD

Most businesses use letterhead stock to print letters. Typically, only the first page of a multipage letter is printed on letterhead; any pages that follow are printed on plain sheets. Therefore, there's no need to adjust the margins to print beneath the letterhead. Instead, you just need to make sure that the first line of the letter on the first page will be printed beneath the letterhead. To do so, first measure the distance from the top of the page to where you want the first line of the letter to be printed, as shown in Figure 7.13.

When you're ready to create your letter, start with a clear document window and look at the Ln (line) measurement in the lower-right corner of your screen. Press ↵ until that measurement is set about where you want to print the first line, as in Figure 7.14. Then just type your entire letter (and save it in case you want to use it again).

With a tractor-fed printer, you might have to reposition the tractors to insert the paper; consult your printer manual.

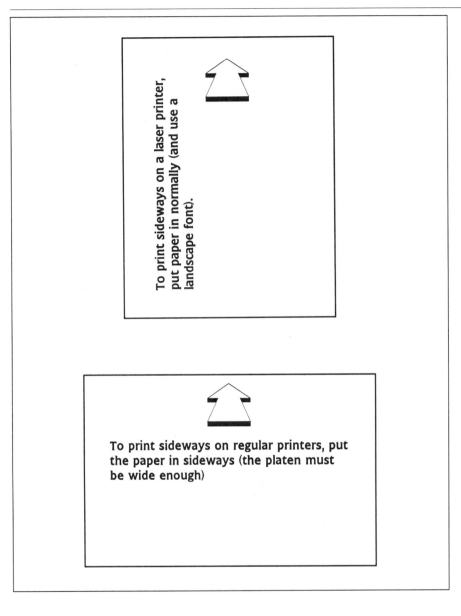

When you're ready to print your letter, put the letterhead page into the printer. If you are using a printer that is fed from a tray, put as many blank letterhead bond pages in the bin as necessary to print all the pages after the first. Then put the letterhead page on top of those pages. If you're using a tractor-fed printer, put the letterhead page in the printer, positioning the top of the page just slightly above the print head.

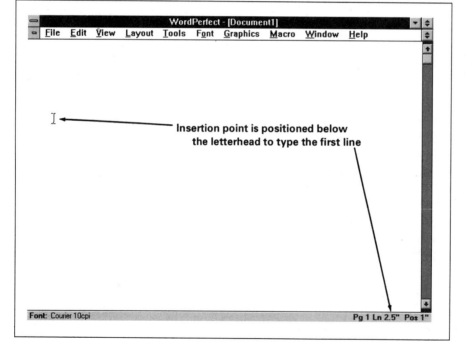

FIGURE 7.13:

The distance from the top of the page to the first line on letterhead stock

```
T
E
K                    About 2½ inches
K
```

Tekk Inc.
1212 Incumbency Dr.
Suite 200
Alameda, CA 94501

(415) 555-2582

January 31, 1991

Alex T. Wannamaker
ABC Corporation
12345 Bayside Dr.
Alameda, CA 94501

Dear Mr. Wannamaker:

FIGURE 7.14:

The insertion point positioned to type the first line of a letter

WordPerfect - [Document1]

File   Edit   View   Layout   Tools   Font   Graphics   Macro   Window   Help

I ←——————— **Insertion point is positioned below the letterhead to type the first line**

Font: Courier 10cpi   Pg 1 Ln 2.5" Pos 1"

Then print as you normally would (choose File ➤ Print, and then choose Full Document). That's about all there is to it, though there may be one additional catch if you are using a tractor-fed printer that is not giving you ample time to load additional pages after the first printed page. You may want to use (or create) a paper size that pauses before printing each page, so you have time to load each sheet individually. To do so, you'll need to set the Location of Paper option to Manual, as described in "Adding a Paper Size" later in this chapter.

PRINTING ON ENVELOPES

Check your printer manual for additional information on how to load envelopes into your particular printer.

To print on legal-size (9½ " × 4") envelopes, you need a laser printer that can handle envelopes or a dot-matrix or other type of printer that can handle 9½ -inch-wide paper. Then you have to choose the paper size for printing on envelopes, as discussed earlier in "Choosing a Paper Size." The size to choose (or create, if it's not already available) is 9½ " × 4", often named *Envelope* with printers that have predefined this size for you.

After you've chosen that paper size, be sure to reduce the top and left margins to about 0.3 inch each if you want to type a return address on the envelope. You may also want to adjust the ruler so that there is only one tab stop, at about the 3.25-inch mark.

Now type the return address (if any), then press ↵ about seven times to add some blank lines. Finally, type the recipient's name and address, remembering to tab to about the 3.5-inch mark before typing each line. Figure 7.15 shows an example of an envelope in the document and Reveal Codes portions of the screen. Figure 7.16 shows the sample envelope after printing. Before printing the envelope, you can preview it on the Print Preview screen and make adjustments in the document window, if necessary.

If you want to print more than two or three envelopes, look into the Merge feature (Chapter 16).

If you want to type multiple envelopes before printing them, add a hard page break (by choosing Layout ➤ Page ➤ Page Break or pressing Ctrl+↵) before typing each envelope; this ensures that the previous, complete envelope is ejected from the printer before text for the next envelope is printed. If your printer cannot handle a stack of envelopes, make sure your envelope paper size's paper location is set to Manual so that you have time to feed each envelope individually. (See the sections on adding and changing a paper size later in this chapter.)

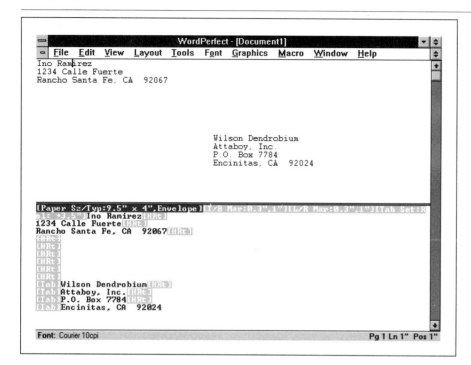

An example of an envelope in the document and Reveal Codes portions of the screen

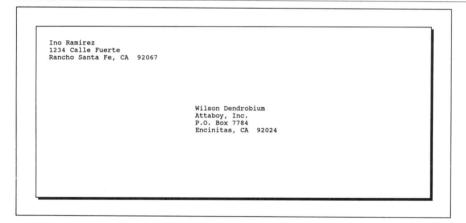

FIGURE 7.16:

A sample printed envelope

PRINTING ON LABELS

Most printers can print directly on labels. With laser printers, you need to purchase special sheet-fed labels that are specifically designed to tolerate the high heat generated by laser printers. Avery offers a wide variety of laser-printer labels. Figure 7.17 shows an example of some printed sheet labels (though the sheets are generally 11 inches long and can accommodate six or seven rows of labels).

Dot-matrix and similar printers use tractor-fed labels. These are often single-column labels, on long continuous rolls (or connected sheets) of paper, with holes on both edges for feeding through the printer tractor. Figure 7.18 shows an example of some printed tractor-fed labels.

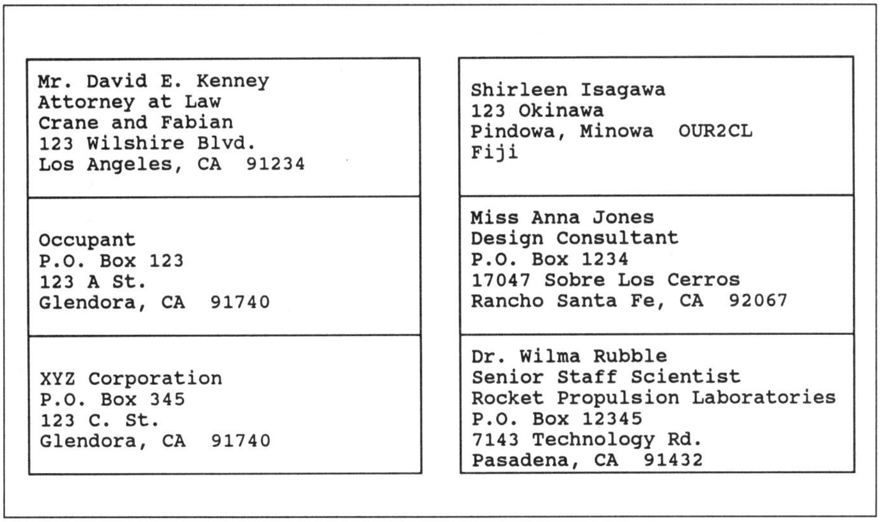

FIGURE 7.17:

An example of printed sheet-fed labels

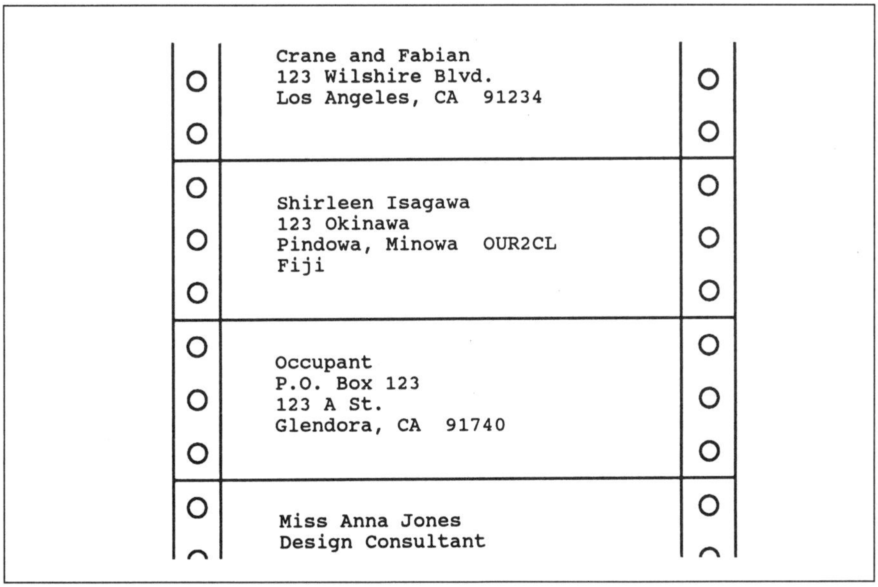

```
Mr. David E. Kenney
Attorney at Law
Crane and Fabian
123 Wilshire Blvd.
Los Angeles, CA  91234
```

```
Shirleen Isagawa
123 Okinawa
Pindowa, Minowa   OUR2CL
Fiji
```

```
Occupant
P.O. Box 123
123 A St.
Glendora, CA   91740
```

```
Miss Anna Jones
Design Consultant
P.O. Box 1234
17047 Sobre Los Cerros
Rancho Santa Fe, CA  92067
```

```
XYZ Corporation
P.O. Box 345
123 C. St.
Glendora, CA   91740
```

```
Dr. Wilma Rubble
Senior Staff Scientist
Rocket Propulsion Laboratories
P.O. Box 12345
7143 Technology Rd.
Pasadena, CA  91432
```

FIGURE 7.18:

An example of printed tractor-fed labels

```
Crane and Fabian
123 Wilshire Blvd.
Los Angeles, CA  91234
```

```
Shirleen Isagawa
123 Okinawa
Pindowa, Minowa   OUR2CL
Fiji
```

```
Occupant
P.O. Box 123
123 A St.
Glendora, CA   91740
```

```
Miss Anna Jones
Design Consultant
```

Both types of labels are generally available at any office- supply or computer-supply store.

To print on labels, you first must choose the appropriate label size at the top of the document by choosing Layout ➤ Page ➤ Paper Size Options. (The last column of the Paper Size dialog box, Labels, displays the number of columns and rows of labels per page, if the paper size is indeed designed to print labels.) If the size you want is not listed, you'll need to create it first (see "Creating a Paper Size for Labels" later in this chapter), then choose that size.

Once you've chosen the paper size for printing on labels, you can think of each label as a page of text, because typing on individual labels is pretty much the same as typing on individual pages. Here are some tips:

If you want to print more than a few labels, look into the Merge feature (Chapter 16).

◆ If you want to center text horizontally on each label, choose (just once) **L**ayout ➤ **J**ustification ➤ **C**enter (or press Ctrl+J) before typing the first label. If you want to center only a few lines in each label, choose **L**ayout ➤ **L**ine ➤ **C**enter (Shift+F7) (once for each line you want to center).

◆ If you want to center text vertically on each label, choose **L**ayout ➤ **P**age ➤ **C**enter Page (or press Alt+F9 C) at the top of each label.

◆ When you've finished typing one label and are ready to type the next, insert a hard page break (choose **L**ayout ➤ **P**age ➤ **P**age Break or press Ctrl+↵) to move to the next "page" (label).

◆ To see how your labels will look when printed, switch to the Print Preview screen (choose **F**ile ➤ Print Pre**v**iew or press Shift+F5).

Because Word-Perfect treats each label as a separate page, choosing File ➤ Print then choosing Current Page from the Print dialog box prints a single label only (whichever label the insertion point is on at the moment).

Figure 7.19 shows some sample names and addresses typed in the document window for printing on labels. In Reveal Codes, notice that the [Paper Sz/Typ] code for labels is the first code in the document. Each label starts with a [Center Pg] code to vertically center text on the page, and each label ends with a hard page break ([HPg]), typed by pressing Ctrl+↵. This is the exact document window used to print the labels shown in Figure 7.17.

After typing your label text, load your labels into the printer. If you are using a dot-matrix printer, align the paper so that the print head is positioned where you want to start printing the first label. Then print as you normally would. If you have problems aligning text in each label, it may be that you've simply misaligned the labels in your printer, or you may need to modify (edit) the label's paper size, as described later in this chapter.

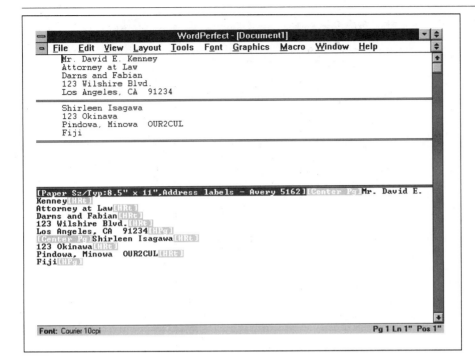

Sample labels in the document and Reveal Codes portions of the screen

---

ADDING A PAPER SIZE

▌ **TO ADD (CREATE) A NEW PAPER OR LABEL SIZE,**

choose Layout ➤ Page ➤ Paper Size. Choose Add, then choose the options that define your page or label size.

> **NOTE** *If you've installed Word-Perfect for use with multiple printers, be sure to choose the appropriate printer before defining a page size, using File ➤ Select Printer (Chapter 8).*

If the paper size you need is not available when you get to the Paper Size dialog box, you can add your own. You only need to define a new size once. In the future, you can choose that size whenever you want, using options on the Layout menu (as explained later). Before defining the paper size, of course, you must measure the width and length of the paper, or each label on the paper. Then follow these steps to create your paper size:

1. Choose **L**ayout ➤ **P**age ➤ Paper **S**ize, or press Alt+F9 S.

2. Choose **A**dd. You will see the Add Paper Size dialog box, shown in Figure 7.20.

3. Choose options in the dialog box to define more information about your paper, as described in the sections that follow.

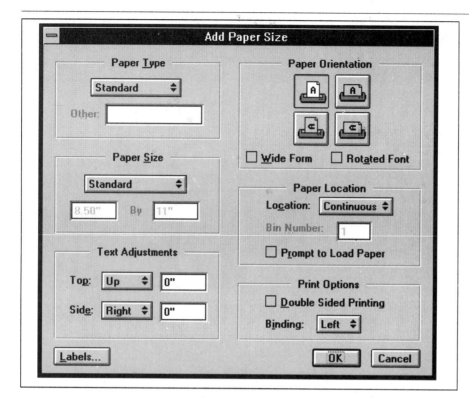

FIGURE 7.20:

The Add Paper Size dialog box

4. Choose OK or press ↵ when you've finished defining the paper size. Your new paper size will be included in the list of available sizes. To use your new size, choose it as you would any other paper size on the list.

The discussion here assumes you chose a WordPerfect printer driver from the File ➤ Select Printer dialog box. If you chose a Windows printer driver, the Edit Labels dialog box, not the Add Paper Size dialog box, appears when you choose Add. See "Using Windows Printer Drivers" later in this chapter for more information.

MAKING SENSE OF THE OPTIONS IN THE ADD PAPER SIZE DIALOG BOX

The Add Paper Size dialog box has options for changing paper type and size, adjusting text on the printed page, defining the paper orientation and location, printing on one or both side of the page, and setting the binding edge. The same dialog box appears when you edit an existing paper size; the only difference is that the menu bar says "Edit Paper Size" instead of "Add Paper Size."

Paper Type   The Paper Type option lets you define the *name* of the paper size; this choice is just the name used to describe the paper type in the Paper Size dialog box shown earlier. It has no effect on how WordPerfect or your printer operates.

To define the paper type, open the pop-up list below the Paper Type option and choose a general paper type. You can choose Other from this pop-up list, then type any name you want, such as *Address labels,* rather than choose one of the suggested names.

Paper Size   When you open the pop-up list below the Paper Size option, you'll see many common paper sizes, including standard (8½" × 11"), legal (8½" × 14"), envelope (9½" × 4"), and a few others. If the paper size you want is not displayed, you can choose Other and enter your own width and height measurements.

Text Adjustments   The Text Adjustments options let you handle situations in which different types of paper are loaded into the printer differently. For example, if you set the margins to 1 inch all the way around a page, but then find that some of the margins are not exactly 1 inch, you can adjust the overall placement of text on the page with this option.

Suppose you consistently load paper into your printer with the left edge of the page as far to the left as it can go in the printer; but when printing pages with a 1-inch left margin specified, you still end up with only a ¾-inch left margin. To shift all the text ¼ inch to the right on the page, open the pop-up list next to the Side Text Adjustments option, choose Right, and type ¼ (or .25). Your 1-inch margins will be correct in future printings.

You can open the Top pop-up list, choose Up or Down, and then type an adjustment to move the text up or down; likewise, you can open the Side pop-up list, choose Left or Right, and then type an adjustment to move the text to the left or to the right. If you change your mind about any text adjustment and you want to reset the adjustment to 0 inches, just choose the appropriate option in the Top or Side pop-up list and type **0** for the adjustment. To reset *all* text adjustments to 0, repeat these steps for each option in both the Top and Side pop-up lists.

Paper Orientation   The Paper Orientation option lets you choose how you want to feed the paper into the printer (short or long edge first) and whether you want to rotate the font (landscape printing). The standard orientation is to feed the short edge first and not to rotate the text (portrait printing). You can either click an appropriate printer button or use the Wide Form and Rotated Font check boxes to choose the form direction and font rotation.

Don't use the Text Adjustments feature to try to create margins on your pages. Use it only to make adjustments when your margin measurements don't come out right on your printed pages.

Do not choose one of the rotated font orientations if you have a printer that cannot rotate its fonts (or print the font sideways), such as a dot-matrix or daisywheel printer—your document will not print correctly.

The printer buttons are as follows:

Top left

Chooses the normal portrait form, where you feed in the short end of the form first and do not rotate the text. In this mode, text is printed across the page, top to bottom.

Bottom left

Also selects a portrait form, where the short end is fed in first, but here the font is rotated (landscape). Landscape fonts are printed sideways on the page, even though the page is inserted normally into the printer. Notice how the letter *A* on the button is rotated on its side.

Top right

Chooses a wide form, where you feed the wide end of the form first and do not rotate the text. As with the top-left button, text is printed across the page, top to bottom.

Bottom right

Chooses a wide form and rotates the font.

As an alternative to using the printer buttons, you can place an *X* in either the Wide Form or Rotated Font check box, or both. Filling in these check boxes automatically chooses the equivalent printer button, as listed here:

◆ Leave both check boxes empty: equivalent to choosing the top-left button.

◆ Choose Rotated Font only: equivalent to choosing the bottom-left button.

◆ Choose **W**ide Form only: equivalent to choosing the top-right button.

◆ Choose **W**ide Form and Rotated text: equivalent to choosing the bottom-right button.

Location   The Location option lets you define where and how the paper is loaded into the printer. When you open the pop-up list next to this option, you are given three options:

Continuous

Choose this option if the paper is fed continuously through a tractor or from the standard bin (sheet feeder) on a laser printer.

Manual

Choose this option if you want to feed sheets one at a time and have WordPerfect pause after printing each page.

Bin Number   Choose this option if the paper is fed from a bin other than the standard bin. For example, if your printer lets you feed standard-size paper from one bin and legal-size from another, choose this option and then type the bin number for the paper size you are currently defining.

If you choose Continuous or Bin Number and then print using that paper size, WordPerfect prints normally. If you choose Manual and later print a document using that paper size, here's what happens instead:

Different printers may react slightly differently to the Location and Prompt to Load Paper settings.

◆ If you did not fill in the Prompt to Load Paper check box, neither the printer nor the screen do anything right away. The printer waits for you to insert a sheet of paper before it starts printing (some printers may flash a message, such as "LOAD LETTER," while waiting for you to insert a sheet of paper). After printing a page, WordPerfect again waits for you to insert the next page before resuming printing.

◆ If you marked the Prompt to Load Paper check box with an *X,* basically the same things happen as above, except that after you send the document to the printer your computer will beep once and wait for you to switch to the Windows Print Manager (press Ctrl+Esc and then double-click Print Manager on the Task List). After you switch to the Print Manager, you will see the message "Insert the first page in the printer." Insert the first page in the printer, then choose OK. After feeding each page into the printer, you can switch back to Word-Perfect.

There's really no need to choose both Manual and Prompt to Load Paper, because when you choose Manual, WordPerfect waits for each sheet to be fed before printing.

Prompt to Load Paper   The Prompt to Load Paper option lets you determine whether WordPerfect will beep and wait before printing a document. If you leave the check box next to this option empty, printing starts immediately after you choose any File ➤ Print option, such as Full Document, that prints a document.

If you choose the check box next to this option, WordPerfect will beep and pause before printing the first page of your document. This is useful if you are defining a nonstandard paper size and want to be reminded to insert that paper before printing.

Double Sided Printing If you have a duplex printer (a printer that can print on both sides of a piece of paper page), such as the LaserJet IID or IIID, you can mark the Double Sided Printing check box to activate this capability for the page size you are currently defining. If you choose this option, but your printer cannot print on both sides of the page, the choice will be ignored.

Binding You can open the pop-up list next to the Binding option to determine how the pages are printed:

Top	Pages will be printed for binding at the top.
Left	Pages will be printed for binding along the left side.

If you have a non-duplex printer, see Chapter 8 for help with printing on both sides of the paper.

The amount of space allowed for binding is determined by the Binding Offset choice on the Print menu (choose File ➤ Print, then choose Binding Offset in the dialog box). For more information on binding, see Chapter 8.

If you have a duplex printer and have chosen Double Sided Printing, the Binding option has a more pronounced effect. With Top chosen as the binding edge, every other page is printed upside down so that the pages read normally when bound at the top. With Left chosen, the binding edge is at the right margin on even-numbered pages and at the left margin on odd-numbered pages. (Your duplex printer's manual may provide additional examples of double-sided printing and binding.)

Labels Choose Labels in the Add Paper Size dialog box (in the bottom-left corner) only if the paper size you are defining is to be used for printing on labels.

CREATING A PAPER SIZE FOR LABELS

Some companies include specific instructions right in the box for using their labels with Word-Perfect.

You can create a paper size for labels by going through the same techniques described in "Adding a Paper Size." To define your own size, you first need the exact measurements of your labels. Typically, these measurements are printed on the box containing the labels. If not, you can break out your trusty ruler and measure the labels yourself. Most important, you need to know the label height and width. Figure 7.21 shows the measurements that WordPerfect will ask you about.

Note that the exact steps for defining *sheet-fed* labels (those that are on separate sheets) and for defining *tractor-fed* labels (those on a continuous roll,

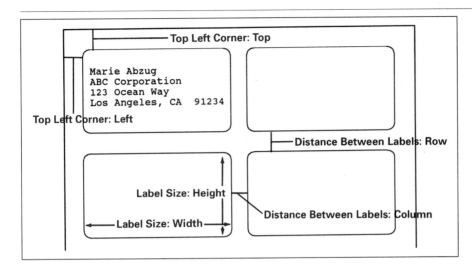

Label measurements on sample labels

used with nonlaser printers) vary slightly. You may need to make some adjustments to print properly on tractor-fed labels. But regardless of which type of label you're using, the basic steps are similar to creating any other paper size:

1. Start in the WordPerfect document window (position the insertion point at the top of the document if you already have labels on-screen).

2. If you've installed multiple printers, choose **File** ➤ Se**l**ect Printer and highlight the printer you want to use. Then choose **S**elect or press ↵ to get back to the document window.

3. Choose **L**ayout ➤ **P**age ➤ Paper **S**ize (or press Alt+F9 S).

4. Choose **A**dd. The Add Paper Size dialog box appears.

5. Open the Paper **T**ype pop-up list and choose **L**abels, or choose **O**ther and type in a name that describes your labels (for example, *Address Labels* or *3.5" Disk Labels*).

6. Open the Paper **S**ize pop-up list. If you are defining a paper size to print sheet (laser printer) labels, choose Standard (8½" × 11") as the paper size—the size of the entire sheet of labels. If you are defining a paper size for tractor-fed labels, choose **O**ther and enter the combined width of the labels (and any space between them) for Width, and enter the height of a single label for Height. For example, if you want to print on two-across labels on a dot-matrix printer, where

each label is 4 inches wide and 1¹⁵⁄₁₆ inches tall, with ¹⁄₁₆ inch of space between each row of labels, enter *8* (or *8.5"*) as the page width and *2* as the page height.

7. If you want WordPerfect to pause to allow you to feed sheets of labels individually into your laser printer, open the Location pop-up list and choose **M**anual.

8. If you want WordPerfect to beep to remind you to load tractor-fed labels into the printer before it starts printing them, mark the **Pr**ompt to Load Paper check box.

9. Choose **L**abels. The Edit Labels dialog box, shown in Figure 7.22, appears. Use Figure 7.21 and the sections that follow to define the size of your labels.

10. Change the label settings as described in the following sections, then choose OK or press ↵ to return to the Add Paper Size dialog box.

11. Choose OK or press ↵ to return to the Paper Size dialog box.

12. If you want to select the label paper size now, choose **S**elect (if not, choose **C**lose). You will return to the document window.

You can use your new label format (with the current printer) at any time in the future simply by positioning the insertion point at the top of the document and choosing Layout ➤ Page ➤ Paper Size (or by pressing Alt+F9 S), highlighting the name of your new format, and choosing Select or pressing ↵.

| NOTE | *If you want to remove the label settings but retain the other information you set in the Add Paper Size dialog box, choose Remove Labels instead of OK.* |

FIGURE 7.22:
The Edit Labels dialog box

The following sections describe each option in the Edit Labels dialog box.

Label Size   In the Label Size area, you define the width and height of a single label. Type in the width of a single label in the Width text box. Enter the height of a single label in the Height text box. If you are defining tractor-fed labels, include the distance between labels in the label width and height. For example, if the labels are $2^{15}\!/_{16}$ inches tall with $\frac{1}{16}$ inch of space in between each row, define the label height as 3 inches.

Labels Per Page   In the Labels Per page area, you define the number of labels across the page and the number of labels down one column on a sheet. Type the number of labels across the page in the Column text box. Next, if you are using sheet labels, enter the number of labels down one column on a sheet in the Row text box. If you are using continuous (tractor-fed) labels, enter *1* in the Row text box.

Top Left Label   In the Top Left Label area, you tell WordPerfect where to find the top-left label on the sheet. In the Top Edge text box, enter the distance from the top of the page to the top of the first label, as shown in Figure 7.21. In the Left Edge text box, enter the distance from the left edge of the page to the first label. If you are using tractor-fed labels, you can set both of these measurements to 0 inches. But, before printing labels, you'll need to position the first label in the printer so that the print head is exactly where you want to print the first character of the label.

When printing tractor-fed labels, remember that the left-right position of the tractors and the vertical position of the print head on the first label before printing will greatly affect how text is printed on each label. WordPerfect doesn't know how you've aligned the labels in your printer; it just starts printing at the current print-head position. See Chapter 16 for more information.

Distance Between Labels   In the Distance Between Labels area, you define the spacing between columns and rows of labels. The distance between labels is difficult to measure exactly, but it is typically 0 inches (no space), $\frac{1}{16}$ inch, $\frac{1}{8}$ inch, or perhaps $\frac{1}{4}$ inch. Type the distance between columns (the physical space between adjacent labels) into the Column text box. If you are using tractor-fed labels, enter this distance as *0*, regardless of the actual distance between two or more labels. Next, type in the distance between two rows or, if you are using tractor-fed labels, type *0* into the Row text box (you've already accounted for the distance between labels in your height measurement; e.g., when you typed *3"* for $2^{15}\!/_{16}$-inch labels with $\frac{1}{16}$ inch between labels).

Label Margins   In the Label Margins area, you specify the margins used on a single label. Typically, you do not want the contents of mailing labels to be word-wrapped, so you should leave all these choices set to 0.

However, if you want to ensure that text on each label is not too close to the left edge of the label, you might want to specify a small left margin, of about ¼ inch or so. Or, if you will be printing on labels that already have your company logo and return address printed at the top, you can specify a top margin equal to the height of the preprinted return address. This way, the text will always print below the return address.

Similarly, when printing 3½-inch disk labels, leaving a top margin of about 0.68 inch prevents text from being printed on the part of the label that wraps to the back of the disk; it also helps you to vertically center text on the front of the label.

CHANGING A PAPER SIZE DEFINITION

The Auto Code Placement feature (Chapter 13) can help prevent code clutter and problems caused by multiple codes.

If you define and use a paper (or label) size and find that it needs some fine-tuning, follow these steps to make changes:

1. If the document you're using at the moment uses the paper size you're about to change, delete the existing [Paper Sz/Typ] code in Reveal Codes (to prevent code clutter or confusion).

2. Choose **L**ayout ➤ **P**age ➤ Paper **S**ize, or press Alt+F9 S.

3. Move the highlight to the paper size you want to change.

4. Choose **E**dit.

5. Make your choices in the Edit Paper Size dialog box (just as when you initially created the paper or label size).

6. Choose OK or press ↵ until you return to the Paper Size dialog box.

7. If you want to use the newly modified paper size now, choose **S**elect to return to the document window. (If you don't want to use the newly edited paper size right now, just choose **C**lose.)

DELETING, COPYING, AND FINDING PAPER SIZES

If you look at the bottom of the Paper Size dialog box, you'll also see these option buttons:

Copy   Makes an exact copy of the currently highlighted paper size definition. The copy can be used as the starting point for creating a similar paper size.

Delete   Deletes the currently highlighted paper size definition. Choose **D**elete, then choose **Y**es to delete the definition.

THE "ALL OTHERS" PAPER SIZE

The [ALL OTHERS] paper size that appears in the Paper Size dialog box and elsewhere is confusing for many people. Basically, it's a catchall category for invalid paper sizes. For example, suppose a friend creates some disk labels, using a paper size for printing on Avery 5197 (5¼-inch disk) labels. She gives you a copy of the document, and you use the usual File ➤ Open command (F4) to open the file.

If you do not have the Avery 5197 label size defined for your printer, WordPerfect automatically assigns the [ALL OTHERS] paper size to that document. Typically, the paper size is simply the standard 8½ " × 11" page.

You can change the [ALL OTHERS] size if you want (though offhand I can't think of any practical reasons for doing so, since it is just a catchall for invalid paper sizes). To change the [ALL OTHERS] paper size, choose Layout ➤ Page ➤ Paper Size (or press Alt+F9 S), highlight [ALL OTHERS], and choose **E**dit. A dialog box with options similar to those for creating normal paper sizes appears. Make your choices as usual.

USING WINDOWS PRINTER DRIVERS

To use a Windows printer driver, choose File ➤ Select Printer, choose the Windows, and then press ↵. See Chapter 8 for more information on selecting printers and printer drivers.

Earlier in this chapter I mentioned that your options for defining and using paper sizes are more limited when you use a Windows printer driver than when you use a WordPerfect printer driver. When using a Windows driver, you'll notice the following limitations and differences:

◆ You can choose only one paper size throughout your document; this preselected paper size is named *Current Windows Form* in the Paper Size dialog box, and you cannot copy, edit, or delete this paper definition.

◆ If you want to change the Current Windows Form for a Windows printer driver, you must choose **F**ile ➤ Se**l**ect Printer, then choose **S**etup, or use the Control Panel in Windows. For more information, see the section on configuring your printer in your Windows manual.

◆ Although you are limited to one paper size definition per document and cannot alter the Current Windows Form using WordPerfect, you *can* add new definitions for printing labels. Just choose Layout ➤ **P**age ➤ Paper **S**ize (Alt+F9 S), then choose **A**dd. This takes you directly to the Edit Labels dialog box, where you can create several different label definitions by following the steps described earlier; you can copy, edit, or delete these definitions. Once created, these label definitions are available for every Windows printer you have installed.

PROTECTING YOUR FORMATTING CODES

As I've mentioned repeatedly throughout this chapter, many formatting codes must be at the top of the page where you want them to take effect, before any text on that page. However, as I've also mentioned repeatedly, the Auto Code Placement feature can make the use of page-formatting codes much easier, since it places these codes at the top of the current page and deletes any competing codes automatically.

CHOOSING AN INITIAL FORMAT

You'll learn more about combining documents in Chapter 12.

If you want to use a certain format throughout a document, such as printing every page in landscape mode, you can place the formatting codes in an area typically called Document Initial Codes (so called because it contains codes used to format the entire document). Placing formatting codes in this area offers two advantages:

◆ Because the codes are outside of and before all the text in the document, you need not be concerned about inadvertently inserting text before the codes or inadvertently moving the codes to another place in the document.

◆ When you use **File ➤ Retrieve** or **File ➤ File** Manager to combine documents, only the Document Initial Codes for the first document are retained. The initial codes from files retrieved subsequently are ignored, thereby giving all the combined files the same set of initial formatting codes.

To place formatting codes in the Document Initial Codes area, follow these steps:

1. Choose **Layout ➤ D**ocument ➤ Initial **C**odes, or press Ctrl+Shift+F9 C. The Reveal Codes window appears in the document window, as shown in Figure 7.23.

2. Choose your formatting options from the **Layout ➤ P**age (Alt+F9) or Layout ➤ Line (Shift+F9) menus. (A particular request will be ignored if that option is not allowed in Document Initial Codes.)

3. Choose **Close** or **File ➤ Close** (Ctrl+F4) to return to the normal document window.

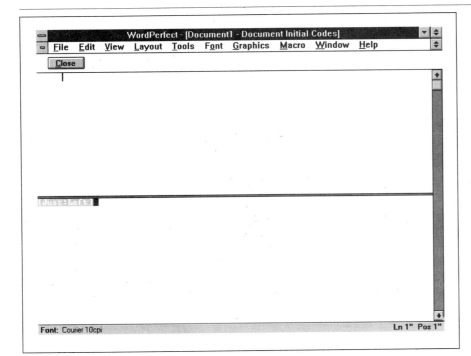

The codes will not appear in the document but will affect all the text (up to a competing formatting code) in the document. Check the Print Preview screen if necessary to make certain.

If you later change your mind about the Document Initial Codes, use the same basic steps to return to the Initial Codes screen and make new choices or delete old ones, as necessary. You can delete any code by highlighting it in Reveal Codes and pressing Delete.

If you forget to exit from the Initial Codes screen before typing text, simply select all the text that you typed accidentally. Then choose Edit ➤ Cut or press Shift+Del. Choose Close to leave the screen. Finally, position the insertion point where you want to insert the text in the actual document, and choose Edit ➤ Paste or press Shift+Ins to retrieve the text.

CHOOSING AN INITIAL FONT

You can also choose an initial font for the document by using a similar technique. As with formatting codes, the selected font affects all the starting text in the document (up to the next [Font] code—it is ignored if the document is retrieved into an open document that uses a different font).

Chapter 5 has a complete discussion of fonts and how to choose them.

To change the initial font of a document, follow these steps:

1. Choose **Layout** ➤ **Document** ➤ Initial **Font**, or press Ctrl+Shift+F9 F.

2. Highlight the font you want, using your mouse or the ↑ and ↓ keys, or type the first few letters of the font name.

3. If you've chosen a scalable font, highlight the point size with your mouse or type in a point size.

4. Choose OK to press ↵ to return to the document window.

If you want to change the initial font again in the future, follow the same steps.

In the next chapter, you'll learn how to gain more control over your printer and learn more about its capabilities.

CHAPTER 8

Mastering Your Printer

This chapter is about using your printer effectively. After all, the goal of any word processing project is to produce a neatly printed *hard copy* (paper copy) of your document. So here I'll talk about keeping text aligned on pages, printing multiple copies, printing specific pages from a document, expanding your font collection, and basic troubleshooting.

KEEPING PAGES ALIGNED WHEN PRINTING

TO ENSURE THAT TEXT IS ALIGNED PROPERLY WHEN PRINTING WITH DOT-MATRIX OR DAISY-WHEEL PRINTERS,

align a page perforation just above the print head before turning on the printer.

 If you have a printer that prints from sheets in a tray or requires you to load sheets individually, you can skip this section.

If your printer uses continuous-form (also called tractor-fed) paper, your first step in printing a document should be to avoid the common text-over-the-page-break syndrome. This occurs when text that's supposed to be together on a page is split across two pages, as in Figure 8.1 (the grayed area

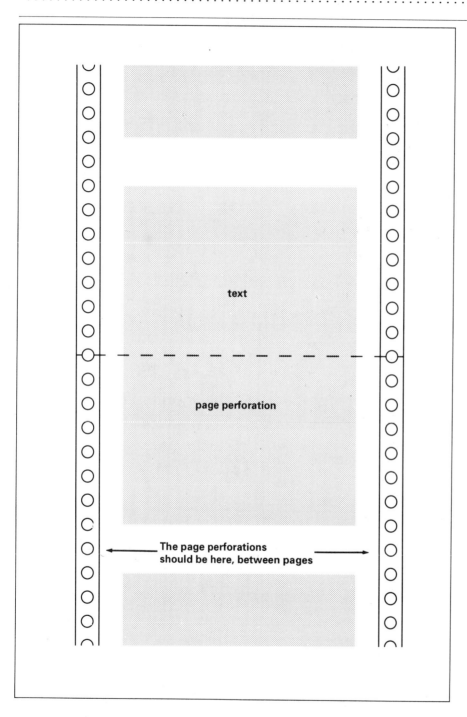

Pages that are not aligned properly

represents printed text, the white area represents margins). You can easily avoid this problem once you understand how tractor-feed printers work.

Your computer and WordPerfect assume that when you first turn on the printer, a page perforation is just above the print head so that the printer is ready to print the first page. This place is called the *top of form,* and your computer keeps track of it by counting how many lines are printed.

If you turn on your computer with the print head somewhere near the middle of the page, you've inadvertently chosen *that* position as the top of the page. Hence, when you print, the top of your text will start printing in the middle of the page, and you'll end up with the situation shown in Figure 8.1.

But even if you do turn on your printer with the page perforation properly aligned, you may still end up with this problem. WordPerfect knows the paper has been moved when *it* moves the paper, but does not know the paper has been moved when *you* move it. So, if you manually crank a sheet of paper through the printer after you've turned it on, future printed pages will be misaligned.

The general rules of thumb to follow are these:

Not only does manually cranking the paper through a printer mess up the page alignment, it can also damage your printer if the power is turned on.

◆ If your pages are misaligned, turn off the printer and manually crank the paper through until there's a page perforation just above the print head, then turn the printer back on.

◆ Once the paper is aligned properly and the printer is turned on, do not crank the paper manually through the printer. Instead, use the printer's *form-feed* or *line-feed* button (see your printer manual for more information).

STARTING PRINTING

TO PRINT A COPY OF THE DOCUMENT CURRENTLY BEING EDITED,

choose File ➤ Print ➤ Print (or press F5 P, or press Ctrl+P).

You've already learned how to start printing a document by choosing File ➤ Print ➤ Print. In this chapter, you'll learn some new ways to print a document. You'll find the printer commands on the File pull-down menu. Regardless of which techniques you use, a couple of general points are worth keeping in mind about printing.

First, be aware that WordPerfect may not start printing your document right away. That's because WordPerfect creates a print file containing the text to be printed and sends the file to the Windows Print Manager for printing. WordPerfect displays the status of this file creation operation inside the Current Print Job dialog box. (After printing is complete, WordPerfect automatically deletes the print file.) This process may take a minute or more depending on your computer, your printer, and the size of your document. So if you start printing and nothing happens immediately, be patient.

On the other hand, if the printer doesn't start printing for a long time, or if you see the message "Cannot print," you should check to be sure that your printer is properly connected to your computer, that it is turned on, and that the printer is online. Or, check the Windows Print Manager for more information (see "Controlling Print Jobs" later in this chapter.)

WordPerfect uses a technique called *background printing* to print your documents. This means that once you tell WordPerfect to start printing something, it performs that job "in the background" so that you can continue editing other documents or choose other documents to print. As soon as WordPerfect sends the print file to the Print Manager, it removes the Current Print Job dialog box from your screen and permits you to continue working with the current document.

CHOOSING FROM MULTIPLE PRINTERS

IF YOU'VE INSTALLED MULTIPLE PRINTERS FOR USE WITH WORDPERFECT,

choose File ➤ Select Printer and choose one to work with from the Available Printers list.

WordPerfect lets you install as many printers as you wish. You can even install printers that you don't own (such as a PostScript printer) to develop a document that you'll be typesetting later.

Keep in mind that every installed printer has its own set of fonts and paper sizes. Therefore, before you even start typing a document, you should probably choose the printer you plan to use to print that document. Here's how:

If you want to install additional printers for use with WordPerfect, see Appendix A.

1. Choose **File** ➤ Select Printer. A list of available, installed printers appears in the Select Printer dialog box, shown in Figure 8.2 (your screen will show the printers available to you).

2. Choose either **W**ordPerfect or Wi**n**dows from the Printer Drivers options near the bottom of the dialog box, depending on which type of driver you prefer to use (differences are discussed a little later in the chapter).

3. Double-click on the name of the printer you want to use, or use the ↑ and ↓ keys to highlight the printer you want, then choose **S**elect.

NOTE *Choosing File ➤ Preferences ➤ Environment ➤ Format Retrieved Documents for Default Printer controls whether WordPerfect will use the default printer to format documents or will try to use the printer that was in use when you saved the document.*

When you save a document, WordPerfect also saves the name of the printer that was selected at that time. If, in the future, you open or retrieve that document with a different printer in use, you may see the message "Formatting for default printer" near the lower-left corner of the window. WordPerfect is choosing whatever fonts and paper sizes in the currently selected printer best match the ones you chose when first developing the document with a different printer selected.

If you later look at the document in Reveal Codes, you'll see that many of the [Font:] codes include an asterisk (*), indicating that WordPerfect will use the available font shown, rather than the one you originally chose.

To revert to your original font choices, reuse the same printer: Choose File ➤ Select Printer, then choose the printer originally used to create the document.

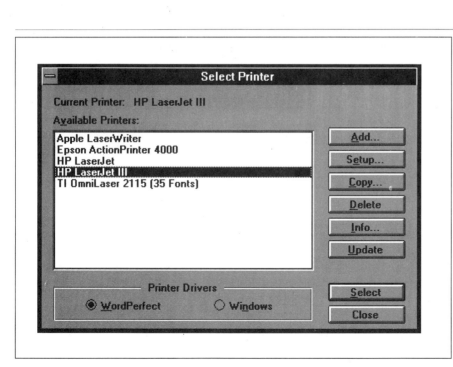

FIGURE 8.2:

The Select Printer dialog box

ABOUT WORDPERFECT
AND WINDOWS PRINTER DRIVERS

As mentioned previously, you can choose either a Windows printer driver or WordPerfect driver when selecting a printer. Some of the differences between the two types of drivers are summarized in the following sections.

WINDOWS PRINTER DRIVERS

Windows printer drivers

To learn more about Windows printer drivers, see your Windows documentation.

◆ Are installed by using the Printers option in the Windows Control Panel (in the Main group of the Windows Program Manager)

◆ Offer better color PostScript support than WordPerfect drivers

◆ Support Windows System Fonts and Type Manager

One disadvantage to Windows printer drivers is that you can use only one paper size and orientation per print job. Furthermore, when creating new paper sizes for a Windows printer driver (as discussed in Chapter 7), you can only define label sizes.

When a Windows printer driver is selected, choosing File ➤ Select Printer ➤ Setup, and then Options, takes you to the standard Windows dialog boxes for choosing options, as shown in Figure 8.3.

You can use the options on these menus to choose a paper source and size, orientation (portrait or landscape), default margins, scaling, destination (printer or file), and so forth, as available for your printer. You can use these options in lieu of the Layout ➤ Page ➤ Paper Size options described in Chapter 7 and Print to Disk options when using a Windows printer driver.

WORDPERFECT PRINTER DRIVERS

WordPerfect printer drivers are

◆ Installed via the WordPerfect installation program

◆ Offer multiple orientations (both landscape and portrait) during a single print job

◆ Offer multiple bins (e.g., both letters and envelopes) during a single print job

◆ Generally faster than Windows printer drivers

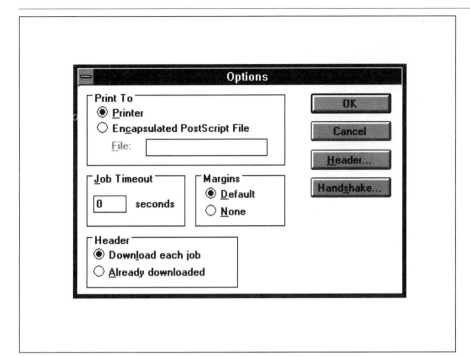

FIGURE 8.3:

Options available after choosing File ➤ Select Printer ➤ Setup, and Options, with a Windows printer driver

The main tool that WordPerfect offers for printing multiple orientations and paper sizes during a single print job is the Layout ➤ Page ➤ Paper Size options (described in Chapter 7), which you can use throughout your document to change paper sizes.

For the most part, this book assumes you are using WordPerfect printer drivers, except where explicitly stated otherwise. If you need to install additional WordPerfect printer drivers, use the WordPerfect installation program (described in Appendix A) and the printer disks that came with your Word-Perfect package, or additional printer disks purchased from WordPerfect Corporation.

PRINTING THE DOCUMENT ON THE SCREEN

I've already covered the steps required to print the document currently on your screen. You start by choosing File ➤ Print or pressing F5 to get to the Print dialog box, shown in Figure 8.4. Choose Full Document in the Options area when you want to print the entire document that's currently on your

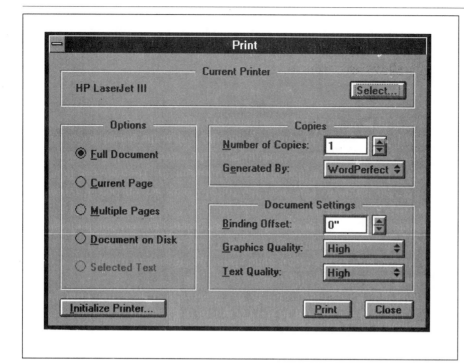

screen, and then choose Print to print the document and return to the current document window. (Any changes you make to the current document while it is being printed will *not* be incorporated into the current printing.)

PRINTING A PAGE

Sometimes after typing a long document, you discover a mistake on a particular page. To save time and paper, you can simply correct the error and reprint that page only. (This assumes, of course, that your changes do not alter the number of lines on the page.) To print a particular page in your document, follow these steps:

1. Move the insertion point to the page of the document that you want to print.

2. Choose File ➤ Print (or press F5).

3. Choose the **C**urrent Page option in the Options area.

4. Choose **P**rint or press ↵ to begin printing.

After the page is printed, compare it to the previous copy of the page to make sure that the new copy starts and ends with the same words. If not, you'll need to reprint all pages that follow the page you just printed.

PRINTING SELECTED TEXT

You can print any block of text in your document by selecting the text with your mouse and choosing File ➤ Print or pressing F5. In the Print dialog box, notice that WordPerfect automatically chooses the Selected Text option in the Options area. Choose Print to begin printing the document.

PRINTING A DOCUMENT STORED ON DISK

TO PRINT A DOCUMENT THAT IS STORED ON DISK,

choose File ➤ Print (F5). Choose Document on Disk in the dialog box, and choose Print. Then enter the name of the file you want to print.

It's not necessary to open a saved document in an empty document window to print it. You can print a document directly from disk, so long as you know its location and file name. Follow these steps:

1. Choose **F**ile ➤ **P**rint (or press F5).

2. Choose **D**ocument on Disk in the Options area of the Print dialog box.

3. Choose **P**rint.

4. Type the complete file name of the document you want to print, or click the button next to the Filename option to choose a file to print.

5. Choose **P**rint (or press ↵) to print the entire document, or specify pages to print in the **R**ange text box (as discussed in the next section).

The File Manager feature, discussed in Chapter 12, provides an easier way to print documents from the disk.

WordPerfect will begin printing the document you've named, unless you've made a mistake. For example, if you mistyped the file name or typed the name of a file that is not available on the current disk and directory, WordPerfect displays the message "File not found." Choose OK to continue, and try again by typing the file name correctly and pressing ↵ or by choosing a file by clicking the File button to the right of the text box. Or, cancel the operation by choosing Cancel or pressing Escape.

If the document was formatted for a printer other than the currently selected printer, you'll see the message "Document not formatted for current printer. Continue?" If you choose Yes, WordPerfect will print the document, using the currently selected printer. However, the document will be printed with whatever fonts most closely match your originally selected fonts. If you don't want to print the document with the current printer, choose No. Then choose the printer you want, and choose File ➤ Print ➤ Document on Disk ➤ Print (or press F5 D P) to print the document.

PRINTING SPECIFIC PAGES

TO PRINT SELECTED PAGES FROM A DOCUMENT,

choose File ➤ Print ➤ Multiple Pages ➤ Print (or press F5 M P), enter the page or range of pages you want to print, then choose Print to begin printing.

You can print a specific page or groups of pages from any document, whether you choose File ➤ Print ➤ Multiple Pages (F5 M) or File ➤ Print ➤ Document on Disk (F5 D). To print a specific page, simply enter the page number in the Range text box after choosing the Print command. You can combine the page choice styles if you wish. For example, entering **5,7,9,15-20** prints pages 5, 7, and 9, and then pages 15 through 20. Entering **1-3 7-9** prints pages 1 through 3, then pages 7 through 9. Entering **-10 90-** prints the first 10 pages of the document, then skips to page 90 and prints the rest of the document (that is, page 90 and all pages that follow). Choose Print or press ↵ when you're finished.

You can also print odd-numbered pages (for example, the first, third, and fifth) and even-numbered pages (for example, the second, fourth, and sixth), using the options in the Odd/Even Pages pop-up list in the Multiple Pages dialog box. Be aware, however, that these are *physical* pages and don't necessarily adhere to page numbering you've defined with Layout ➤ Page ➤ Numbering ➤ New Page Number (Alt+F9 N N). To ensure that odd-numbered and even-numbered pages are printed in proper sequence when using this feature, you should choose Layout ➤ Page ➤ Numbering and then Odd or Even in the Force Current Page area to make sure that a page-numbering change also forces an odd/even page break when required.

 *A document summary contains the file's name, type, and creation date. You can add more information, such as the subject of your file and an abstract of its contents.*

You can also choose File ➤ Print ➤ Multiple Pages ➤ Print, and then Logical Odd or Logical Even from the Odd/Even Pages command button to print odd and even *logical pages,* which are labels on a sheet. The sheet of paper is always considered a physical page, whereas each label on a sheet is a logical page. Logical pages are numbered from left to right starting at the top of the sheet. So if you print the Logical Odd labels, WordPerfect will print the first, third, fifth, and following odd labels. If you print the Logical Even labels, Word-Perfect will print the second, fourth, sixth, and following even labels.

You can also mark the Document Summary check box in the Multiple Pages dialog box to print the document summary (Chapter 12). Examples of pages to print are presented in Table 8.1.

PRINTING PAGES FROM SECTIONS

If your document is divided into sections or chapters, you may have numbered the first page of each section or chapter *page 1*. In addition, you may have numbered introductory pages with Roman numerals, like *i, ii, iii*. For example, suppose you've created a document consisting of a preface and three chapters, with the range of page numbers shown below:

Preface	i–ix
Chapter 1	1–15
Chapter 2	1–10
Chapter 3	1–20

To print specific pages from such a document, you can indicate a section by typing the section number, followed by a colon, followed by page numbers. For example, typing **2:10-15** will print pages 10 through 15 from Chapter 2. To print page 15 from Chapter 1, you would specify page **1:15.** To print pages i through iii of the preface, you would specify **i-iii.**

PRINTING BACK TO BACK
WITH NONDUPLEX PRINTERS

On most laser (and other sheet-fed) printers, you can print back to back simply by printing all the even-numbered pages, flipping the pages over, putting them back into the printer, and then printing the odd-numbered pages on the front of the even-numbered pages. When creating the document, however, be sure

ENTRY	WHAT IS PRINTED
5	Page 5 only
5,7	Pages 5 and 7, but no pages in between
5 7	Same as above (a blank space can be used in lieu of a comma)
5-	Page 5 and all pages that follow
5-7	Pages 5 through 7
-7	From the beginning of the document to page 7
S1-5	Document summary, followed by pages 1 through 5
S-	Document summary and entire document
S,5,7	Document summary, page 5, and page 7
O	All odd-numbered pages
E1-4	Even-numbered pages from 1 to 4 (pages 2 and 4)
LE	All even-numbered logical pages when a label paper size is in use (e.g., labels 2, 4, 6, 8, etc.)

TABLE 8.1:

Examples of Entries Used to Specify Multiple-Page Printing

Printing back to back with duplex printers like the HP LaserJet IID and IIID is simply a matter of choosing a back-to-back paper size (see Chapter 7).

that you force an odd/even page break wherever you start a new page number. Then you can follow these steps to print the document:

1. If possible, change your print collation so that the printer collates backward (i.e., pages come out face up with the first printed page at the bottom of the stack). See your printer manual for instructions on changing the collation.

2. With the document you want to print already in the current document window, choose **File** ➤ **Print** ➤ **Multiple Pages** ➤ **Print** (or press F5 M P).

3. Choose **Even** from the **Odd/Even Pages** pop-up list.

4. When the print job is finished, if you couldn't collate backward in step 1, reshuffle so that page 2 is on bottom, page 4 is on top of that, and so forth, until the last page is on top. (You may also want to wait a few minutes for the paper to dry out, and help uncurl it if possible, so it will feed better going back through the printer.)

5. Flip over the whole stack so that the back of page 2 is on top of the stack, and put the stack back into the printer.

6. Choose **F**ile ➤ **P**rint ➤ **M**ultiple Pages ➤ **P**rint (or press F5 M P).

7. Choose **O**dd from the **O**dd/Even Pages pop-up list.

As long as no paper jams cause problems on the paper's second pass through the printer, your back-to-back document should be complete.

PRINTING BACKWARD—LAST PAGE FIRST

Some sheet-fed printers *always* print pages face up, so the first printed page ends up at the bottom of the stack. Consequently, you must manually recollate all the pages top to bottom.

As an alternative, you can just print the entire document backward (from last page to first) so that the first pages (which get printed last) end up on the top of the stack, and all the pages that follow are in proper sequence.

Macros are introduced in Chapter 15.

Unfortunately, there's no simple way to do this in WordPerfect, but the macro shown in Figure 8.5 can handle the job quite easily. It works by moving the insertion point to the end of the document, printing that page, then moving the insertion point up a page, printing that page, and so forth. It stops when it gets to page 1.

To use the macro (after creating it), choose Macro ➤ Play (or press Alt+F10), type the macro name (such as *BACKPRIN*), then press ↵. Just make sure your printer is ready, and the macro will do the rest. (You'll hear two beeps when the macro is finished, indicating that you can use the keyboard again.)

PRINTING MULTIPLE COPIES

TO PRINT MULTIPLE COPIES OF A WORDPERFECT DOCUMENT,

choose File ➤ Print ➤ Full Document ➤ Number of Copies, type the number of copies to print, then choose Print to begin printing.

You can tell WordPerfect to print multiple copies of any document by following these steps:

1. Choose **F**ile ➤ **P**rint (or press F5).

```
Application (WP;WPWP;Default;"WPWPUS.WCD")
//*************************************** BackPrin.wcm
//*** Macro to print pages backwards (last page first.)

//*** Initialize PageNumber variable.
ASSIGN (PageNumber;999)

//*** Move insertion point to last page of document, and print.
PosDocBottom()
PrintPage()

//*** Print remaining pages, up to and including page 1.
WHILE (PageNumber > 1)
   PosPagePrevious()
   PrintPage()
   GetWpData(
      MacroVariable:PageNumber;
      SystemVariable:Page!)
ENDWHILE

//*** Sound two beeps, then end macro.
BEEP
WAIT (60)
BEEP
QUIT
```

FIGURE 8.5:

A macro that prints pages backward, from the last page to page 1.

2. Choose **F**ull Document, **C**urrent Page, **M**ultiple Pages, or **D**ocument on Disk, as described in preceding sections.

3. Choose **N**umber of Copies, and type the number of copies you want to print.

4. Choose **P**rint (or press ↵) to begin printing.

It's important to remember that once you change the number of copies to print, that setting stays in effect for the remainder of the current session. Therefore, if you will be printing other documents in the same session, be sure to change the number of copies, as required, for each document that you print. You can also change the default number of copies to print for all future sessions with WordPerfect (this holds true for print quality and binding offset, discussed later in this chapter).

Some printers can print multiple copies by themselves; WordPerfect merely has to tell the printer how many copies to print. Other printers, how-ever, do not have this capability, so WordPerfect must tell the printer to print one copy several times (that is, after the printer prints one copy, WordPerfect tells it to print the next copy).

Printing multiple copies is slightly faster if the printer handles the job by itself. To use this method with your own printer, choose File ➤ Print ➤ Mul-tiple Copies ➤ Generated By (or press F5 U E). Then choose Printer. If your printer cannot print multiple copies by itself, your choice will be ignored and WordPerfect will handle the multiple copies.

Incidentally, using the printer to print multiple copies may change how the printed pages are collated. If you set Generated By to WordPerfect (the default setting), and you print two copies of a five-page document, Word-Perfect will print the entire first copy, and then the entire second copy. But if you set Generated By to Printer, WordPerfect may print two copies of page 1, then two copies of page 2, and so forth.

CHOOSING A PRINT QUALITY

TO CHOOSE A PRINT QUALITY,

choose File ➤ Print, then choose either Graphics Quality or Text Quality.

The Document Settings area in the Print dialog box offers two options for controlling print quality: Text Quality and Graphics Quality. Both options offer the following four settings:

High   Uses the slow, high-quality print mode

Medium   Uses the medium-speed, medium-quality print mode

Draft   Uses the high-speed, draft-quality print mode

Do **N**ot Print   Prints no text or graphics

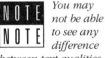

You may not be able to see any difference between text qualities on a laser printer, since it will always produce high quality output.

If your printer has only two print qualities, such as draft and high, then medium print quality will probably be the same as high quality. Usually, you will use draft or medium quality when you want a quick printing or a draft copy of your document. When ready to print the final document, you can use the high-quality mode, which will take longer.

To change the quality of text or graphics for a document, follow these steps:

1. Open the document in an empty document window by choosing **F**ile ➤ **O**pen (or pressing F4) and entering a file name.

2. Choose **F**ile ➤ **P**rint (or press F5).

3. Choose **T**ext Quality or **G**raphics Quality, depending on which you want to change.

4. Choose one of the options from the menu.

5. Repeat steps 3 and 4 if you want to change both the text and graphics quality.

Now you can choose Full Document and Print to print the document currently in the document window, or you can choose Document on Disk and Print to print a document stored on disk.

The Do Not Print option in the Graphics Quality and Text Quality pop-up lists is useful when you are printing a document that combines text and graphics. If you just want to review a printed copy of the text in a document, you can set the graphics quality to Do Not Print so that you don't have to wait for all the graphics to be printed.

These options can also come in handy if you run out of memory while trying to print a document that combines text and graphics. First, print the text only. Then run the same pages through the printer again, printing only the graphics.

Figure 8.6 shows examples of draft-, medium-, and high-quality graphics from a laser printer.

When you save a document, WordPerfect saves the text and graphics qualities you've specified with the document. If you print a document from disk, it will be printed with the stored print quality, regardless of the current settings on the Print menu. Therefore, to change the print quality of a document stored on disk, you must first open that document in the current document window and then change the print quality before printing the document.

EXITING WHILE PRINTING

You can exit Word-Perfect while the printer is running as soon as the Current Print Job dialog box disappears from the screen.

During a print operation, the Current Print Job dialog box remains on screen for as long as it takes WordPerfect to create a print file and send it to the Windows Print Manager. For small documents, this may be only a few seconds. During this time you cannot exit WordPerfect. As soon as the Print Manager receives the print file, the Current Print Job dialog box disappears and you are returned to the current document window. Depending on the size of the print file, you may be able to continue executing commands and working with documents while the printer is running.

Draft Quality

Medium Quality

High Quality

For more information on Windows, see Appendix B.

You can exit WordPerfect temporarily to run another program or enter a DOS command (by selecting the DOS Prompt icon from the Windows Main group window). This will not stop the printer from running the current print job. (Do not load any memory-resident (TSR) programs while temporarily in DOS. Otherwise, you may not be able to return to WordPerfect.)

You can (usually) flip back to Windows or to another running program by pressing Ctrl+Escape. To return to WordPerfect, double-click on its name in the Task List.

TESTING YOUR PRINTER'S CAPABILITIES

TO SEE HOW YOUR PRINTER HANDLES THE SAMPLE PRINTED DOCUMENT,

choose File ➤ Print ➤ Document on Disk ➤ Print, type PRINTER.TST as the name of the file to print, then choose Print to begin printing.

Your WordPerfect program includes a document named PRINTER.TST that demonstrates a wide range of your printer's current capabilities. (The word *current* is important here because, as you'll learn in a moment, you can expand the capabilities of many printers through the addition of extra fonts.) You can also use this document to test your printer's print qualities.

The PRINTER.TST file is copied to your \WPWIN directory by default during the WordPerfect installation process. Follow these steps to print the PRINTER.TST file:

1. If you have multiple printers, choose **File ➤ Se**l**e**ct Printer, and highlight a printer name in the Available Printers list.

2. Optionally, choose S**e**tup to select the printer features you want to test.

3. Choose **S**elect.

4. Choose **File ➤ Print ➤ D**ocument on Disk **➤ Print**, type **printer.tst**, and press ↵ to print all pages. (If WordPerfect displays the message "Document not formatted for the current printer. Continue?", select **Y**es to begin printing.)

Figure 8.7 shows how the document looks when printed on a HP LaserJet III printer, which handles a wide range of fonts, text sizes, and text appearances, and has full graphics capability. Comparing your printed copy to Figure 8.7 will help you see the capabilities and limitations of your own printer.

CONTROLLING PRINT JOBS

TO DELETE, RUSH, OR PAUSE A PRINT JOB,

first get to the Print Manager by choosing the Print Manager icon from the Windows Main group.

Whenever you tell WordPerfect to print a document, it treats your request as a *print job*. Rather than forcing you to wait for your entire document to be printed before you can resume your work, WordPerfect starts your print request and then returns control to you so that you can edit another document or choose other documents for printing.

Print		Sample

October 15, 1991 — WordPerfect for Windows 5.1 — 9:39 am

Wordperfect® *for Windows*™ combines the incomparable set of features WordPerfect is famous for with a terrific implementation of the Windows graphical user interface (GUI). You can view your fonts and graphics right on the screen while you work.

WordPerfect for Windows unlocks the power of desktop publishing in a word processor. Graphic images can be easily scaled and moved on the screen with a mouse. Kerning, word and letter spacing, and line height adjustments are a snap. And changes in document format are reflected automatically in the document window. You can also edit up to nine documents at once.

Other new features make handling documents easier and more efficient. The Ruler speeds up formatting changes in a document, such as margins, tabs, columns, and line spacing. The Button Bar™ lets you attach commonly used features  or macros to a button for instant access. And Quick List™ gives you swift and easy access to your most frequently used directories and files.

Tables are easy to create and edit. The Ruler provides a handy shortcut for creating tables by simply clicking and dragging to the desired size.

WordPerfect for Windows can use the same printer drivers and features that are available in WordPerfect for DOS. For instance, you can access all 1,500 characters in the WordPerfect character sets. Or, if you like, you can use the Windows system printer drivers.

For veteran WordPerfect users, *WordPerfect for Windows* provides a smooth step into the Windows world. Even for the novice, *WordPerfect for Windows* is the answer for the person looking for a powerful, reliable, and easy to use Windows word processor.

APPEARANCE

Italic
Outline
Shadow
SMALL CAPS
Redline
~~Strikeout~~
<u>Double Underline</u>
Color

SIZE

$^{Super}/_{Sub}$script
Fine
Small
Large
Very Large
X-Large

EQUATION

$$\frac{1}{Z} = \sqrt{\frac{1}{R^2} + (\omega C - \frac{1}{\omega L})^2}$$

TABLE

Graphic Characters	
International	‡
Legal	§
Math	≠
Scientific	Σ
Typographical	®

Print attributes (italic, shadow, font size, etc.) and quality of graphic characters are dependent upon the capabilities of each printer.

FIGURE 8.7:
The PRINTER.TST file printed on a HP LaserJet III, with Graphics Quality set to High

You can also print several files by marking their names in the File Manager window (see Chapter 12).

This comes in handy when you're printing many lengthy documents, because you can easily stack up a series of print jobs. For example, if you need to print several chapters from a book, you can repeatedly use the Document on Disk option of the Print command to specify several chapters to print. Then you can resume working on another document (or go to lunch) while WordPerfect prints all your documents.

Of course, WordPerfect lets you change your mind about printing a document or any series of documents. You can also stop the printer, or pause it, in case you need to start over (or change the printer ribbon). There are two ways you can control a print job: Use the Cancel Print Job command in the Current Print Job dialog box, or access the printer control commands in the Windows Print Manager.

THE CURRENT PRINT JOB DIALOG BOX

As soon as you select Print to start a new print job, WordPerfect displays the Current Print Job dialog box. This dialog box keeps you abreast of the print job currently being processed by WordPerfect.

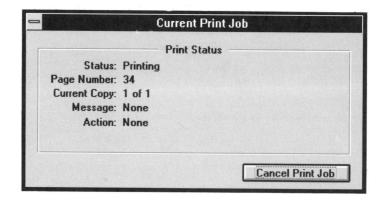

Status displays such messages as "Starting print job," "Printing," and "End of Job" to describe where WordPerfect is in the process of creating the print file.

Page Number is updated regularly to show you exactly how many pages have been transferred to the print file, such as "8" for pages 1 through 8.

Current Copy shows how many copies are being created for the current print job. When you choose to print multiple copies of a document, WordPerfect displays a message, such as "2 of 3," in this field to indicate which copy currently is being processed.

Message displays printer operation messages, such as "Completing line" when you cancel a print job. When WordPerfect requires that you perform an action to complete a print request, it displays the action you should take in the Action field.

Canceling the Current Print Job As long as the Current Print Job dialog box is visible on-screen, you can select Cancel Print Job to cancel the current print job. As soon as you do, WordPerfect stops creating the print file and the dialog box disappears.

Once the dialog box disappears, though, you can no longer cancel the print job from the Current Print Job dialog box—you must use the Windows Print Manager.

THE PRINT MANAGER

If your printer is attached to a network, bypass the Print Manager and allow your network print spooler to control the print jobs. When you deactivate the Print Manager from the Windows Control Panel, WordPerfect automatically passes print files to the printer via the network spooler.

As soon as WordPerfect creates the print file for a print job, it transfers the file to the Windows Print Manager. You probably can control the current print job by accessing the Print Manager, depending upon the size of the print file being sent. Follow these steps:

1. From the current document window, press Ctrl+Esc to display the Windows Task List.

2. If Print Manager does not appear in the list, highlight Program Manager and choose **S**witch To.

3. Choose the Print Manager icon from the Main group.

4. If Print Manager appears in the list, highlight it and choose **S**witch To.

The Print Manager window with some documents already queued for printing is shown in Figure 8.8.

The Print Manager window displays complete information about all current print jobs. Among other things, it tells you about the documents being printed, describes the printer currently connected to your computer, and lists the files that currently reside in the print queue.

The Print Manager window is divided into four sections: the menu bar, the Message box, the printer queue information line, and the file information line. Each of these is discussed in the following sections.

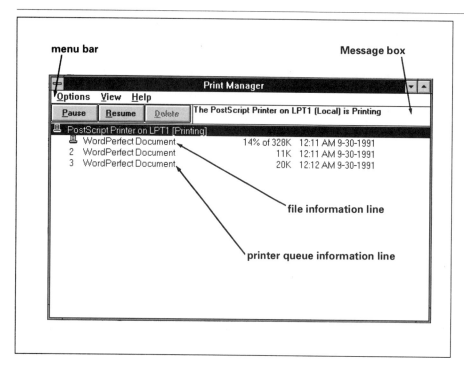

Printer Queue Information Line

The printer queue information line describes the documents currently being printed for the current print job. It shows the name of the printer, where the printer connects to your computer, and the current status of the printer.

If you have more than one printer connected to your computer, you'll see multiple printer queue information lines. Also, you might see a print queue for each printer.

If you are operating WordPerfect on a network, and you are connected to a network printer, this line also shows network-server connection information. (The Print Manager displays in the Message box any information that your network sends during a print operation. The amount of information and level of detail provided depend entirely on your network software.)

File Information Line

The file information line describes the title of the print job assigned by Word-Perfect, the file's position in the queue, or a printer icon if the file is printing.

Optionally, the file information line displays the size of the file in kilobytes, and the time and date WordPerfect sent to the Print Manager when you started the print operation.

If a file is currently printing, its information line also shows a percentage that tells you the amount of the file that has been printed so far.

The Message Box

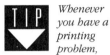

Whenever you have a printing problem, you should check the Message box to determine the problem.

The Message box provides information on what's happening with the printer. If WordPerfect is busy printing, the line may show a message such as "The PostScript printer on LPT1 (Local) is Printing." If there is a problem (for example, if the printer isn't plugged in, isn't properly connected to the computer, or isn't online), the Message box may show a message such as "The HP Laser-Jet III on LPT1 (Local) is STALLED." When you've corrected the problem, just choose Resume to continue printing.

SLAMMING THE BRAKES

Sometimes a page gets mangled while printing, or a label peels off and sticks to the platen, and yet the printer keeps trying to print. Depending upon how much of a print job has been completed, you can use one of two methods to cancel the current print job.

Press the online button to take the printer offline so that you can correct a printer problem without canceling the current print job. Once you correct the problem, put the printer back online to complete the current print job.

Recall that WordPerfect removes the Current Print Job dialog box from your screen as soon as it transfers the print file to the Windows Print Manager. At this time, you no longer can cancel the print job from the Current Print Job dialog box, so you must attempt to do so from the Print Manager (see the next section).

As a last resort, you can immediately stop all printing by turning off the printer. If you're using a tractor-feed printer, remember to align the top of the first page just above the print head before turning on the printer.

To resume printing, you'll need to go through the Print dialog box. If you don't want to start printing the document from page 1, use the Multiple Pages option in the Print dialog box to specify which pages to print.

CANCELING A SPECIFIC PRINT JOB

You can also cancel a specific print job without resetting the printer. You might want to do this if you are processing multiple print jobs, and discover that you selected the wrong document for printing or realize that you need to further edit a document before printing it. Follow these steps:

1. Choose the Print Manager icon from the Windows Main group.

2. Select the line in the print queue containing the print job you want to cancel.

3. Choose **D**elete.

4. When Windows prompts you to confirm the deletion, choose OK.

If you canceled the current print job, printing may not stop immediately, because your printer buffer already contains additional pages to be printed. When the buffer is empty, WordPerfect will advance the paper to the top of the next page and begin the next print job.

PAUSING AND RESUMING OPERATION OF THE PRINTER

If you just want to pause the printer temporarily while a document is being printed (for example, to change the ribbon or to make some other adjustment to your printer), follow these steps:

1. Choose the Print Manager from the Windows Main group.

2. Select the line in the print queue containing the print job you want to pause.

3. Choose **P**ause, and wait for the current page to finish printing. You'll see a message such as "The PostScript Printer on LPT1 (Local) is Paused" in the Message box.

4. Adjust the printer as necessary, then realign the top of the page (on a sheet-fed printer, use the form-feed or FF button; on a dot-matrix printer, turn off the printer, scroll the top of a page perforation up to the print head, then turn on the printer again).

5. When you are ready to resume printing, choose **R**esume.

WordPerfect will start printing again, beginning at the exact location where it ceased printing after you chose Pause.

PRINTING ONE PAGE AT A TIME

When using a printer that requires manual feeding or a paper size defined for manual feeding, WordPerfect will display the message "Insert the first page in the printer" when you tell it to print something. The message is your cue to insert the paper to print on.

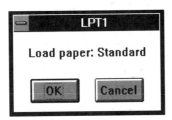

Follow these steps:

Turning the platen manually while the printer is on can damage some printers!

1. If you're using a dot-matrix printer, turn the printer off.

2. Insert the paper on which you want to print, making sure to align the top of the sheet just above the print head.

3. If you're using a dot-matrix printer, turn the printer back on and make sure it's online.

4. When you are ready to print, choose OK in the message box.

5. If there are additional pages to be printed, you'll see the same message box before the next page is printed, and the printer will stop. Insert another page, and choose OK again.

RUSHING A PRINT JOB

Suppose you stack up several lengthy print jobs but suddenly need to print a quick memo or letter. You need not cancel your existing print jobs. Instead, you can just rush the job that needs to be handled to the front of the print queue in the Print Manager. Follow these steps:

1. Choose the Print Manager icon from the Windows Main group.

2. Select the line in the print queue containing the print job you want to rush.

3. Drag the selected line to the top position in the print queue, and then release the mouse button. Alternatively, select the file, hold down the Ctrl key, and press ↑ or ↓ to move the file to a different position in the queue.

The Print Manager immediately renumbers the file information for each print job in the queue to reflect the change. If you want to rush a print job ahead of the job that is currently printing, you must cancel the current print job. Otherwise, you'll have to wait until WordPerfect is finished printing the current job.

PRINTING FOR BINDING

If your document will be printed (or copied) back to back and then bound like a book, you might want to leave some extra space for the right margin of even-numbered pages and the left margin of odd-numbered pages, as the example in Figure 8.9 shows. This will prevent text from running into the binding when the document is bound.

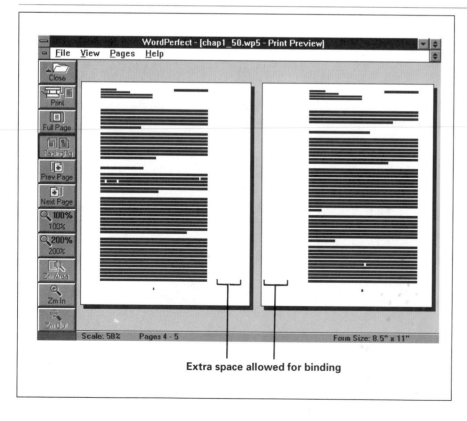

FIGURE 8.9:

Extra margin space allotted for binding

Extra space allowed for binding

To add space for binding (assuming the document you want to print is in the current document window), follow these steps:

1. Choose **File** ➤ **Print** ➤ **B**inding Offset (or press F5 B).

2. Type in the extra space you want to allot for binding (for example, type **.5** to leave an extra half-inch of space).

3. Choose **P**rint (or press ↵) to begin printing.

You will not see any obvious change in the current document window. However, you can preview the printed document on-screen by choosing File ➤ Print Preview (Shift+F5). In the Print Preview window, choose Pages ➤ Facing Pages (or click the FacingPg button) to display two pages side by side.

Changing the binding offset alone may not be sufficient for printing your document because it may decrease the right margin too much. You can even out the margins by cutting the desired binding offset in half and adding that value to both the left and right margins for the document.

For example, suppose you want a ½-inch binding offset and 1-inch margins on both sides of each printed page. The magic number for evening the margins is half of the desired binding offset (in this case, ¼ inch). When you've determined the magic number, follow these steps:

1. Choose **File** ➤ **Print** ➤ **B**inding Offset (or press F5 B).

2. Enter the magic number (one-half of the desired binding offset; in this example, the number is **0.25**).

3. Choose Close to return to your document.

4. Press Ctrl+Home to move the insertion point to the top of the document.

5. Choose **L**ayout ➤ **M**argins (Ctrl+F8).

6. Add the magic number to the left margin setting (for example, if you want a 1-inch margin with a ½-inch binding offset, type **1.25**). Then choose OK.

7. Repeat step 6 for the right margin.

8. Choose **P**rint (or press ↵) to begin printing.

You may want to view facing pages in the Print Preview window again, just to make sure that all is well. If you save the document after making these changes, the new binding offset is also saved with the document. Therefore, if you print the document from the disk (rather than from the screen), your binding offset will still be correct. On the other hand, if you want to change the binding offset of a file on disk, you must first open that file, and make the change while the document is in the current document window.

PRINTING TO DISK

> **TO PRINT A FILE TO DISK,**
>
> choose File ➤ Select Printer ➤ Setup ➤ Port ➤ File, and enter in the Filename text box a path and file name for the print file.

You can print a copy of your document directly to a disk in a format that can later be printed directly from DOS. This is handy if you want to print your document with a computer that does not have WordPerfect installed on it or with typesetting equipment.

For example, suppose your home computer has WordPerfect installed on it, but has no printer or just a so-so printer. However, your office has a computer that uses DOS (or Windows) and has a laser printer connected to it, but does not have WordPerfect installed on it.

To print your documents with the office printer, you first need to install the WordPerfect printer files on your home computer that match the printer at work, just as if that printer were attached to your home computer (you need do this only once). You can then create, edit, and save your documents in the usual manner. You might also want to format and label a floppy disk for storing the printed copy of your file (I'll refer to this disk as the *transfer* disk).

When you want to print a copy of your document to disk, so you can later print it on the office printer, follow these steps (they apply only when you choose File ➤ Select Printer and choose WordPerfect as the printer driver):

Appendix A discusses printer installation.

If you're using a Windows printer driver, choose File ➤ Select Printer ➤ Setup ➤ Options to print to disk.

1. If you have not done so already, open the file you want to print at the office by choosing **File** ➤ **O**pen (or pressing F4) and typing the file name.

2. Choose **File** ➤ **S**elect Printer, then move the highlight to the name of the office printer (the printer you'll actually use to print the document).

3. Choose Se**t**up ➤ **P**ort ➤ **F**ile.

4. Type the path and name for the file you'll use to store the "printed" document (e.g., MYDOC.PRN or A:\TRANSFER.PRN).

5. Choose OK (or press ↵) to return to the Select Printer dialog box.

6. Choose **S**elect.

7. If you named a floppy drive in step 4 above (e.g., *A:* or *B:*), insert a formatted disk in that drive. (You use DOS or the Windows File Manager, not WordPerfect, to format floppy disks.)

8. Choose **F**ile ➤ **P**rint (or press F5) to display the Print dialog box.

9. Check the **T**ext Quality and **G**raphics Quality options and make changes, if necessary.

10. Choose **F**ull Document (or whatever print option you prefer).

11. Choose **P**rint to begin printing.

You'll probably hear some whirring and buzzing, and see the drive light go on as WordPerfect prints your document to the disk. It may take a few seconds, or a few minutes. If you specified the hard-disk drive in step 4, be sure to copy the file named in step 4 to a floppy disk so that you can take that file to your office. You can use DOS, the Windows File Manager, or the Word-Perfect File Manager to make the copy.

To print the document on your office laser printer, follow these steps:

*If you're using Windows on your office computer, double-click on the DOS Prompt icon in the Main group in step 1. After completing step 4, type **EXIT** and press ↵.*

1. Get to the DOS command prompt (e.g., *C:>*).

2. Insert the transfer disk in drive A.

3. At the DOS command prompt, type **COPY** *filename* **/B PRN,** where *filename* is the path and name of the print file. For example, if you used A:\TRANSFER.PRN in step 4 above, and the disk you created in that step is now in drive A of the office computer, the actual command is **COPY A:\TRANSFER.PRN /B PRN**.

4. Press ↵. It may take a couple of minutes for the document to start printing.

Whenever you print a document on the home computer using the name of the printer from the office, the printout will go to the file that you specified as the port. You don't have to change the port again unless you want to print to a different file name in the future, or you want to resume printing to a real printer port.

Incidentally, if you are using this technique to print your document on a typesetting machine, you use the same first set of steps listed above for sending printed output to a file instead of a printer port. The only difference is that you'll probably want to choose a PostScript printer, such as the Apple Laser-Writer, after choosing File ➤ Select Printer.

To resume printing to a printer after printing to a disk, be sure to change the port back to its original setting: Choose File ➤ Select Printer ➤ Setup ➤ Port. Reset the port; typically you use the LPT 1 setting for parallel printers and the COM 1 setting for serial printers. Choose OK, then choose Select to save the new setting.

MAXIMIZING PRINTER SPEED

If you are not sharing printers with others on a network, and you are not using any third-party print spoolers, you can maximize printer performance by using the WordPerfect printer drivers instead of the Windows printer drivers. The increase in printer speed is especially evident when Windows uses a system (or raster) font, because these types of fonts are created graphically and require additional printing time.

If you use Windows printer drivers, be aware that you can control the speed at which the Print Manager transfers information to the printer port on your machine. Unfortunately, faster printer speeds use more of your machine's processor time, so also be aware that other Windows applications may operate more slowly as a result.

 *This assumes you're using a Windows printer driver.*

To select a print priority for future print jobs, choose the Print Manager from the Windows Main group. Choose Options and one of the following:

◆ **H**igh Priority, to increase printing speed and slow down applications

◆ **M**edium Priority, to share processing time equally between the Print Manager and other applications that are running

◆ **L**ow Priority, to increase application operating speed and slow down printing

CHOOSING A SHEET FEEDER

If your printer uses an oversize or multiple-bin paper feeder (excluding the regular paper bin or sheet feeder that came with your printer), you may need to inform WordPerfect that this new feeder is in use. Choose File ➤ Select Printer ➤ Setup ➤ Sheet Feeder.

Choose a sheet feeder from the list of available options (or **No Sheet Feeder** to use your regular, original sheet feeder). If you choose an option other than **No Sheet Feeder**, you can get more information about the feeder by choosing the Info button (as shown in Figure 8.10). Once you've selected your sheet feeder, choose Close, Select, or OK, as appropriate, from the various dialog boxes to work your way back to the document window.

Because custom sheet feeders can generally hold many types of paper (legal-size, letter-size, envelopes, and more), you'll want to change some of your existing paper size definitions to use the new sheet feeder:

1. Choose **L**ayout ➤ **P**age (or press Alt+F9).

2. Choose Paper **S**ize, and highlight (or create) any paper size, as discussed in Chapter 7.

3. Choose **E**dit ➤ Lo**c**ation ➤ **B**in, and enter in the Bin **N**umber text box the appropriate bin number for the paper size you're changing (or creating).

4. Choose OK (or press ↵) to return to the Paper Size dialog box, and choose **S**elect.

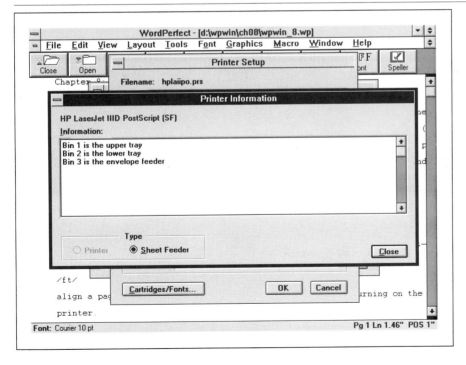

FIGURE 8.10:

Sample Printer Information dialog box after choosing a custom sheet feeder

EXPANDING YOUR FONT COLLECTION

TO INSTALL NEWLY ACQUIRED CARTRIDGE OR SOFT FONTS FOR USE WITH WORDPERFECT,

choose File ➤ Select Printer ➤ WordPerfect ➤ Setup ➤ Cartridges/Fonts.

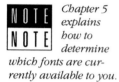
Chapter 5 explains how to determine which fonts are currently available to you.

It's important to understand that WordPerfect cannot actually *create* a font; WordPerfect can only *use* a font that your printer supports. There are several kinds of fonts:

Built-in fonts | Built-in (also called *resident*) fonts are built into your printer. If you have not installed any other fonts for use with WordPerfect, only the built-in fonts are available.

Cartridge fonts | You can add fonts to your printer with cartridges that you purchase separately. (Many printers require that you turn off the printer or take it offline before plugging in a cartridge. See your printer manual for instructions.)

Soft fonts | Soft fonts are stored on your computer's hard disk or a floppy disk and are *downloaded* (sent) to the printer as needed. Like cartridge fonts, soft fonts must be purchased separately. You also must copy the soft fonts onto your computer's hard disk and install them for use with WordPerfect before you can use them, as discussed later in this chapter.

PRINTERS AND FONTS

The range of fonts you can choose from is entirely dependent on your printer. There are four basic categories of printers; each supports different types of fonts:

Daisy-wheel printers: To change fonts on a daisy-wheel printer, you need to change the printing wheel (see your printer manual for instructions).

Dot-matrix printers: Some dot-matrix printers come with several built-in fonts and also let you add fonts with cartridges.

HP LaserJet and compatible printers: These printers offer very few built-in fonts, but you can expand your collection of fonts with cartridge fonts or soft fonts (or both).

PostScript printers: These printers usually come with about 35 built-in, scalable typefaces. In addition, you can purchase soft fonts, though not all soft fonts for PostScript printers are supported by WordPerfect.

If you have a laser printer that supports both cartridges and soft fonts, and you are thinking of buying your first set of fonts, consider a few points: Cartridge fonts are printed faster than soft fonts, because they need not be downloaded from the disk to the printer. On the other hand, soft fonts are cheaper than cartridge fonts and provide more flexibility in the long run, because you do not need to switch cartridges to change fonts.

If you have a laser printer and enough room on your hard disk, you might want to consider purchasing the Bitstream Starter Set, which includes three useful typefaces. The Starter Set also includes a program to help you add other Bitstream fonts that you might later decide to purchase (there are over 200 fonts to choose from).

The number to call for ordering your Bitstream Starter Set and descriptions of other font products you can order for use with WordPerfect are included in the documentation that came with your WordPerfect package. Remember, the Bitstream fonts can be used only with laser printers.

INSTALLING FONTS

This section shows how to install fonts for use with WordPerfect printer drivers. See your Windows manual to learn how to install fonts for use with Windows printer drivers.

Information about the fonts supported by your printer is stored in a WordPerfect file with the extension .ALL. For example, information about Hewlett-Packard fonts is stored in a file named WPHP1.ALL. Information about PostScript fonts is stored in a file named WPPS1.ALL. When you installed your printer, WordPerfect copied the appropriate .ALL file to the WordPerfect Corporation shared programs directory (typically C:\WPC) on your hard disk.

When you install fonts, you will see all the fonts supported by your printer; these are listed in the .ALL file. As you choose the fonts you own, WordPerfect will copy the names of chosen fonts to your printer resource file (.PRS). (In other words, the .ALL file contains data for all WordPerfect-supported printers; the .PRS file contains data for your particular printer, paper sizes, and fonts.) In the future, when you choose fonts for use in a document, only the fonts specified during the installation process will appear as valid options. This prevents you from inadvertently choosing fonts that you do not really own and have not specifically installed.

Installing a Font Cartridge

When you purchase a font cartridge for your printer, be sure to check the documentation that came with that cartridge for any additional information on installing it for use with WordPerfect.

Some font cartridges are available directly from your printer manufacturer; cartridges are also available from third-party vendors. For example, Hewlett-Packard offers a wide variety of cartridges for all their laser printers. Pacific Data Products also offers cartridges for use with HP LaserJet printers.

Before you buy a font cartridge from a third-party vendor, make sure that it's compatible with WordPerfect for Windows. (Compatible products are usually listed right on the cartridge packaging.) The manual that comes with a third-party cartridge should include specific instructions for updating the WordPerfect .ALL file. You should follow those instructions first, before proceeding with the steps below.

If you have a font cartridge that you want to use with WordPerfect, follow these steps to install the cartridge:

1. Starting from the current document window, choose **File** ➤ Select Printer.

2. Choose **W**ordPerfect for the printer driver. WordPerfect displays a list of installed printers in the Available Printers list.

3. If several printer names are shown, you can just click once on the name of the printer you want, or use the ↑ or ↓ key to move the highlight to the name of the printer for which you are installing fonts.

4. Choose **S**etup ➤ **C**artridges/Fonts.

These steps will bring you to the Cartridges and Fonts dialog box for installing cartridges and fonts, assuming that WordPerfect successfully located the .ALL file. If WordPerfect cannot find the .ALL file used to create the printer definition file, it will display a message box with a description of the problem. Choose OK to display the Directory List dialog box, and type the subdirectory where the .ALL files are located. If WordPerfect is unable to locate the .ALL file, you'll need to reinstall the printer.

The options shown in the Cartridges and Fonts dialog box depend on the printer you are using. If you have a printer that supports cartridge fonts but not soft fonts, this dialog box will display only the options Built-In and Cartridges. If your printer supports built-in, cartridge, and soft fonts, you'll see all three options on your screen, as shown below:

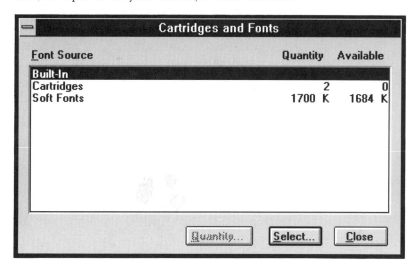

If you are installing a cartridge, choose Cartridges. You'll see the list of cartridges that WordPerfect supports—an example is shown in the Select Fonts dialog box below (though your screen may show completely different options, depending on the printer you are using):

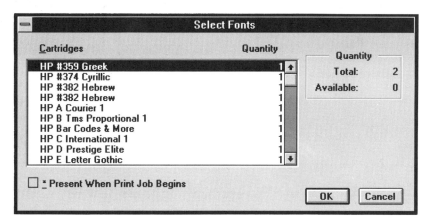

You can hold down the left mouse button as you drag it up or down through the list, or you can use the ↑, ↓, Page Up, and Page Down keys to scroll through the list.

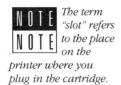

The term "slot" refers to the place on the printer where you plug in the cartridge.

In the upper-right corner of the window, notice that the Quantity area shows the total number of font cartridges in the printer and the number of slots available for installation. If you have more cartridges than slots and have already installed the maximum number of cartridges, you must unmark one of your installed cartridges by moving the highlight to one that is already marked with an asterisk (*), and then typing an asterisk. Then you can install a different cartridge for the slot you've made available. Remember, you may need to do this often if you use a wide variety of cartridge fonts (which is one of the disadvantages of cartridge fonts; with soft fonts you don't have to be concerned about available slots).

Follow these steps to proceed:

1. Click on the name of the cartridge you are installing, or use the movement keys to move the highlight to the name (press Page Up and Page Down to scroll through additional options, if any).

2. Type an asterisk (*) when the highlight is on the correct name for your cartridge.

3. Choose OK or **C**lose until you return to the current document window.

Now you can choose any fonts available on that cartridge by choosing Font ➤ Font (F9).

Installing Soft Fonts

To install soft fonts, follow these steps:

1. You must copy the fonts from the disks they were delivered on to a directory on your hard disk. Typically, the soft-font kit will include a program to simplify this process for you. It's important that all fonts be copied to the same directory. (This chapter assumes that all fonts are stored in a directory named C:\FONTS.)

Before purchasing a set of third-party soft fonts, make sure they're compatible with WordPerfect for Windows.

2. If you are using a third-party font, such as Bitstream, or the Adobe fonts designed for PostScript printers, you may first need to define your fonts, and then add them to the WordPerfect .ALL file. The soft-font package will provide instructions for doing so, if necessary.

3. Finally, you must inform WordPerfect that these fonts are now available for use as described in the next steps.

If you've completed the first two steps listed above, and you stored the soft fonts in the C:\FONTS directory, follow these steps:

1. Starting from the current document window, choose **File** ➤ Se**l**ect Printer.

2. Choose **W**ordPerfect for the printer driver. WordPerfect displays a list of installed printers in the Available Printers list.

3. If several printer names are shown, you can just click once on the name of the printer you want, or use the ↑ or ↓ key to move the highlight to the name of the printer for which you are downloading soft fonts.

4. Choose S**e**tup ➤ **C**artridges/Fonts.

These steps will bring you to the Cartridges and Fonts dialog box for installing cartridges and fonts, assuming that WordPerfect successfully located the .ALL file. If WordPerfect cannot find the .ALL file used to create the printer definition file, it will display a message box with a description of the problem. Choose OK to display the Directory List dialog box, and type the subdirectory where the .ALL files are located.

Defining Printer Memory Notice the Quantity and Available indicators at the right of the Cartridges and Fonts dialog box. The Quantity indicator lists the default amount of printer memory available for soft fonts. For example, many LaserJet printers come with half a megabyte (512K) of printer memory, 350K of which is available for soft fonts.

If you added memory to your laser printer when you purchased it, you should increase the Quantity value accordingly. For example, if you added a megabyte (about 1000K) of printer memory, bringing your total printer memory up to 1.5MB, you would choose Quantity, type in 1350 for the amount of memory available for soft fonts (adding the extra megabyte), and then choose OK.

Telling WordPerfect Which Fonts You Have Now you are ready to tell WordPerfect which soft fonts you have purchased and copied to your hard disk. Follow these steps:

1. Move the highlight to the Soft Fonts option, and choose **S**elect.

2. Depending on your printer, you may see a screen of font groups (such as the one shown below) identified by the manufacturer's part number—for example, AC and AD are part-number groups for Hewlett-Packard soft fonts, and FW is a part-number group for Bitstream fonts. Choose the part-number group that identifies your cartridge.

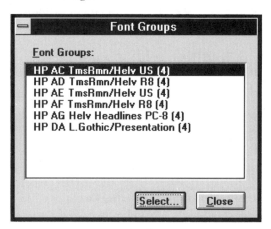

3. A list of all the *possible* fonts to choose from (including many that you may not have already purchased) appears. The Select Fonts dialog box below shows an example, but your screen may show other options; the options available depend on your printer.

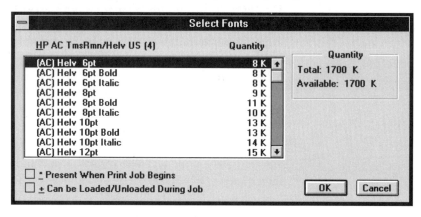

The example lists the Helvetica fonts from the Hewlett-Packard AC set. But the list of soft fonts for most printers is quite long. You can scroll through the entire list by holding the left mouse button as you drag up or down or by using the ↓, ↑, Page Down, and Page Up keys.

Choose only soft fonts that you have already purchased and copied to your disk.

As you scroll, you may notice that some fonts are categorized as *(Landscape)* or *(Land)*. You can choose these fonts for printing in landscape mode on HP LaserJet and compatible printers. Fonts that are not marked as *(Land)*, or are marked as *(Port)*, are for printing in normal portrait mode.

To tell WordPerfect that you have installed a soft font on your disk, move the highlight to the appropriate font and then type either + or *. Typing * tells WordPerfect that the font will already have been downloaded when printing begins. This requires an extra step (called *printer initialization*) before printing documents that use the font. You can only use the * to mark as many fonts as your printer can hold in memory. The Available memory indicator near the top of the window informs you of how much memory remains.

Typing + tells WordPerfect that the selected font will not be available when printing starts, and hence WordPerfect should copy the font to the printer before attempting to use it. This is the easiest way to use soft fonts, but it does slow down printing a bit.

Some printers let you mark fonts with both an asterisk and a plus sign (*+), which makes fonts "swappable." Such fonts are swapped out of printer memory, if necessary, to make room for additional fonts, then swapped back into the printer when the print job is complete. The Select Fonts dialog box below shows an example of soft fonts marked with both an asterisk and a plus sign.

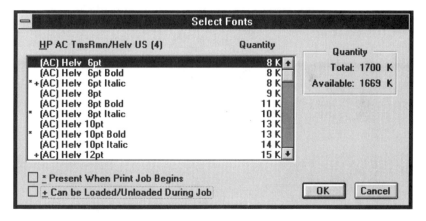

If erroneously you mark a font with +, *, or both, or you change your mind, move the highlight to that choice and type + or * again to remove the mark. Then you must complete two more steps:

1. Mark all fonts that you have copied to your hard disk and want to use in the future with *, +, or both (*+).

2. When you've finished marking your available soft fonts, choose OK or Close until you see the Printer Setup dialog box, shown in Figure 8.11.

Identifying the Fonts Directory Next, you need to tell WordPerfect where to find your soft fonts. If you've been following along, you should now be at the Printer Setup dialog box. (If you've already exited to the current

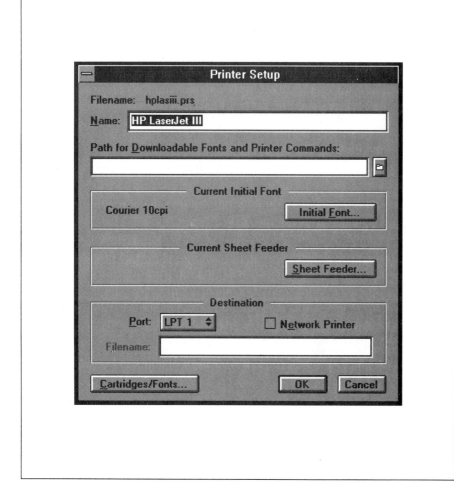

FIGURE 8.11:

The Printer Setup dialog box

document window, choose File ➤ Select Printer ➤ Setup.) Then follow these steps to specify your fonts directory:

1. Choose Path for **D**ownloadable Fonts and Printer Commands.

2. Type the name of the directory where your soft fonts are stored (earlier examples used C:\FONTS).

3. Press ↵.

4. Choose OK or Close to return to the current document window.

You must enter a valid drive and directory name in step 2; otherwise, WordPerfect rejects your entry with "Directory does not exist. Create directory?"

In the future, you can choose any of your newly installed soft fonts just as you did in Chapter 5, by choosing Font ➤ Font (or by pressing F9). However, don't forget that you'll need to complete one extra step if you choose a font marked only with an asterisk in the preceding section. This step is explained below in "Downloading Soft Fonts You Marked with an Asterisk."

CHOOSING AN INITIAL FONT FOR A PRINTER

Typically, WordPerfect uses a basic "typewriter" font (typically 10 cpi) if you choose to print a document without specifically choosing a different font within that document. If you'd like to change the initial font for your printer, follow these steps:

1. Choose **F**ile ➤ Se**l**ect Printer from the current document window.

2. Highlight the printer whose initial font you want to change.

3. Choose S**e**tup ➤ Initial **F**ont.

4. Highlight the new font, choose a point size for the font if this option is available, and then choose OK (or press ↵).

5. Choose OK or press ↵ until you return to the current document window.

Remember that the choice you make here is used only if you do not override the choice by changing the font within the document or the initial font for this particular document (by choosing Layout ➤ Document ➤ Initial Font or by pressing Ctrl+Shift+F9 F).

DOWNLOADING SOFT FONTS YOU MARKED WITH AN ASTERISK

If you marked any soft fonts with only an asterisk (*), you must download them to your printer before using them to print a document. Otherwise, Word-Perfect will substitute a font that has already been downloaded or a built-in font. Follow these steps:

1. Starting at the current document window, choose **File ➤ Print ➤** Download Fonts, or press F5 W.

2. When prompted, choose **Y**es.

The downloading is treated like any other print job, so you can monitor it from the Current Print Job dialog box. Once downloading is complete, the fonts will reside in the printer until you turn off the printer or choose File ➤ Print ➤ Download Fonts again. Therefore, any print jobs using those fonts will be completed quite quickly, because you don't need to wait for WordPerfect to re-download each font in the document every time you print the document.

TROUBLESHOOTING PRINTER PROBLEMS

In this section, I'll look at some common printer problems and give some suggestions for diagnosing and solving them.

THE PRINTER DOES NOT PRINT AT ALL

If the printer totally ignores your print request, ask yourself the following:

◆ Is the printer turned on and online?

◆ Is the printer cable properly connected at both ends?

◆ Is the printer waiting for you to insert paper? (Insert paper through the manual feed to find out.)

◆ Are instructions waiting in the Current Print Job dialog box or in the Print Manager? (If the Current Print Job dialog box is on-screen, look at the Message field. To check the Print Manager, choose the Print Manager icon in the Windows Main group.)

◆ Is the appropriate printer selected? (Choose **File ➤** Select Printer to find out.)

◆ Is the proper printer port selected? (Choose **File** ➤ Se**l**ect Printer ➤ **S**etup ➤ **P**ort to find out.)

◆ Does the printer work with other programs? If not, are you sure the printer has been properly installed according to the manufacturer's instructions?

TEXT DOES NOT ALIGN PROPERLY ON THE PAGE

If your printer prints, but the text is poorly aligned on the page, ask yourself the following:

◆ If you're using a dot-matrix printer, did you properly align the paper while the printer was off (as described near the beginning of this chapter)?

◆ Does your printer have buttons of its own for controlling page length, line length, number of lines per inch, and automatic line-feed? If so, are they set correctly?

◆ Did you choose the correct printer name? (Choose **File** ➤ Se**l**ect Printer to find out.)

THE WRONG FONT APPEARS ON THE PRINTOUT

If the wrong font appears on your printout, ask yourself the following:

◆ Are you using the same printer to print the document that you used when creating the document? (Choose **File** ➤ Se**l**ect Printer to find out.) WordPerfect can only use whatever fonts the current printer has available.

◆ Did you use a soft font marked with an asterisk during font installation but have not yet downloaded?

◆ If you're using downloadable soft fonts, is WordPerfect looking for them in the correct directory? (Choose **File** ➤ **P**rint Se**l**ect Printer ➤ **S**etup ➤ Path for **D**ownloadable Fonts and Printer Commands to find out.)

◆ If you're using cartridge fonts, have you installed them for use with WordPerfect yet? (See "Installing a Font Cartridge" earlier in this chapter.)

◆ Is a message waiting in the Current Print Job dialog box that will provide further information? (If the Current Print Job dialog box is on-screen, look at the Message and Action fields to determine the course of action you should take.)

This chapter completes Part 2, where you've covered a lot more of the meat of WordPerfect, giving you more control over the "day-to-day stuff" of using the program. Starting in Part 3, you'll learn about many techniques to make your work easier, especially when you start getting into larger jobs.

PART THREE

Tools to Simplify Your Work

Now that you've reached this part of the book, your word processing skills should be well honed, and your documents should have a more polished appearance. Here you'll learn about WordPerfect features designed to simplify your work and increase your productivity. You'll learn about searching and replacing, checking your spelling, using the Thesaurus, and using automatic hyphenation. You'll also learn about tools that help you manage your documents, and how to customize WordPerfect to better suit your own word processing needs.

CHAPTER 9

Searching and Replacing

Did you ever type a lengthy report, only to notice you'd made a critical mistake over and over? Maybe you used the word "Corp." instead of "Inc." in a company name, or used first names instead of last names.

One of the most powerful features of a word processor is its ability to search rapidly through a document for specific text, and optionally, to replace that text with something else. This chapter covers WordPerfect's powerful Search and Replace features, which you'll undoubtedly find to be two of your most indispensable word processing tools. You'll find the Search and Replace features on the Edit pull-down menu.

USING THE SEARCH FEATURE

TO SEARCH FOR TEXT IN A DOCUMENT,

choose Edit ➤ Search (F2), type the text you want to search for (if you want to search backward, choose Direction), then choose Search or press ↵ to begin the search.

The Search feature lets you locate a specific sequence of characters anywhere in your document. You tell WordPerfect what you're looking for, and WordPerfect finds it, moving the insertion point immediately past the last character in the sequence. To search for text, follow these steps:

1. Position the insertion point where you want to begin the search (such as, at the top of the document if you want to search the entire document).

2. Choose **E**dit ➤ **S**earch, or press F2. You'll see the Search dialog box:

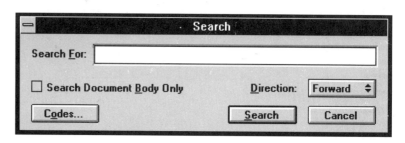

3. Type the characters you want to search for. (WordPerfect automatically places the insertion point in the Search **F**or text box.) You can type almost anything: single characters, words, partial sentences (up to 80 characters). What you type here is often referred to as the *search string,* because it's a string of characters.

4. Choose **S**earch to start the search.

Depending on the options you tions you set in Word- Perfect Preferences, your computer may beep if a search fails.

Once the search starts, WordPerfect scans your document from the insertion point down. If it encounters a matching piece of text, it stops searching and places the insertion point just to the right of the matching text. If WordPerfect cannot find the text you're looking for, it displays "String Not Found:" followed by the search string you entered, and then returns the insertion point to its original position.

WordPerfect always remembers a previous search. For example, suppose you search for the word *horse* and the insertion point lands at that word. If this is not the particular instance of *horse* you're looking for, you can just choose Edit ➤ Search Next (or press Shift+F2) to find the next occurrence of the word.

Of course, if you don't want to repeat your previous search, you can type new search text into the Search For text box after choosing Edit ➤ Search (F2).

To return the insertion point to its original position after a successful search, choose Edit ➤ Go To (or press Ctrl+G), and choose Last Position.

SEARCHING BACKWARD

Normally, Search searches from the insertion point down (forward) to the end of a document. However, sometimes you want to search from the insertion point backward, toward the beginning of your document. Follow these steps:

1. Position the insertion point where you want to begin your backward search.

2. Choose **E**dit ➤ **S**earch (**F2**). You'll see the Search dialog box.

3. Type the characters you want to search for in the Search **F**or text box, just as in a forward search.

4. Move the mouse pointer to the Direction box, hold down the left mouse button, and choose Backward. Or press Tab to move to the box and use the arrow keys to choose Backward.

5. Choose **S**earch (or press ↵) to start the search.

To search backward again for the same text, choose Edit ➤ Search Previous, or press Alt+F2.

EDITING THE SEARCH TEXT

As mentioned, WordPerfect always remembers the previous search string. When you begin a search and that "remembered" search string appears in the Search For text box, you can do one of three things:

◆ Leave the search text as it is to repeat the previous search, by choosing **S**earch.

◆ Enter new search text by simply typing it in the Search **F**or text box (WordPerfect selects all the text automatically, so the old search text disappears immediately as soon as you start typing).

◆ Edit the previous search text with the mouse or the usual editing keys.

If you choose the third option, it's important to start by pressing an editing key, such as ← or →, so that the existing search string is not erased. Here are the editing keys you can use, which work in virtually the same manner as in normal text editing:

Delete	Deletes the character to the right of the insertion point (however, if Delete is the first key pressed, you will delete the entire search string)

Backspace	Deletes the character to the left of the insertion point (however, if Backspace is the first key pressed, you will delete the entire search string)
End	Moves the insertion point to the end of the search string
Home	Moves the insertion point to the beginning of the search string
Ctrl+→	Moves the insertion point forward, to the beginning of the next word in the search string
Ctrl+←	Moves the insertion point backward, to the beginning of the previous word in the search string
Ctrl+Backspace	Deletes the word at the insertion point
→ ← Home End	Move the insertion point around the search string
Insert	Toggles between Insert mode and Typeover mode
Escape	Cancels any editing changes and exits Search without changing the search string

Editing the search string comes in handy when you're searching for text that's subtly different from what you had previously listed. You simply use the editing keys to change the search string, and then choose Search to start the search.

CASE SENSITIVITY IN SEARCHING

Normally, you wouldn't consider the difference between the words *Little* and *little* to be anything big. But Search is a little picky about case. If you tell it to locate *little,* it will find *Little,* as well as *little,* but if you tell it to locate *Little,* it won't find *little.* Here are the basic rules for using uppercase and lowercase letters in WordPerfect search strings:

◆ Search matches all lowercase characters in the search string with either uppercase or lowercase characters in the document.

◆ Search matches uppercase characters in the search string with only uppercase characters in the document.

For example, if you want to find the word *nirvana* and don't care what case it is, enter *nirvana* as the search text. If you want to find *Nirvana*—perhaps in a specific spot where you know it starts a sentence—enter *Nirvana* as the search text.

SEARCHING FOR WORDS

The Search feature cannot distinguish letter combinations from words. For example, if you tell it to search for the word *go,* it looks for the letters *g* and *o.* Therefore, it will find words like *go*tten, a*go*raphobia, Spa*go, Go*dzilla, and others.

If you want to search specifically for a word, you also need to search for the spaces surrounding the word. For example, to search for the word *go* (not the letters *g* and *o*), choose Edit ➤ Search (F2), position the insertion point in the Search For text box, press the spacebar, type *go,* press the spacebar again, and then choose Search to begin the search. WordPerfect looks for a space, followed by *go,* followed by another space.

Of course, it won't find *go,* (*go* followed by a comma) or *go.* (*go* followed by a period), because that's not the same as space-*go*-space. However, it will find these if you search for a space followed by *go* (without the additional space at the end). But of course, then it will also find *goofy, gone, gory,* and any other word beginning with *go,* since you're searching for a space followed by the letters *g* and *o.*

The bottom line is simply that spaces are characters, just like any letter, number, or punctuation mark. Therefore, you can use spaces in your search string to specify exactly what you're looking for.

SEARCHING FOR SPECIAL CHARACTERS

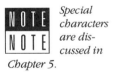

Special characters are discussed in Chapter 5.

You can also search for any special characters entered with Font ➤ WP Characters (Ctrl+W). You simply type the special character you're looking for in the Search For text box. For example, to search for a bullet you typed by using special character 4,0, start the search, move the insertion point to the Search For text box, and press Ctrl+W to display the WordPerfect Characters dialog box. Choose the WordPerfect character set that you want from the Set list box (in this example, you would scroll to the Typographical Symbols set), then choose and insert the bullet from the special characters display that appears (or type *4,0* and press ↵). The bullet appears as the search string. You can then type additional characters, or choose Search to begin the search.

USING WILDCARDS IN A SEARCH STRING

WHEREVER YOU WANT TO USE A WILDCARD IN YOUR SEARCH STRING,

choose Codes to display the Codes dialog box, and choose [Any Char].

What if you're not quite sure how you spelled a word in a document, or you're afraid it's spelled two different ways? This need not stymie your search efforts. WordPerfect lets you insert an *any-character* code in the search string to represent any single character, space, or tab in the search string.

For example, let's say you know you mentioned Carl Yastrzemski somewhere in your document, but you can never remember if the first *s* in his name should really be a *z*. In the Search For text box, you type *Ya*, choose Codes, choose and insert [Any Char], and type *trzemski*. The Search For text box looks like this:

Search For: Ya[Any Char]trzemski

If you spelled the rest of the name correctly, this search string will bring you to the right spot in your document.

SEARCHING FOR CODES

TO PUT FORMATTING CODES IN THE SEARCH STRING,

position the insertion point in the Search For text box, then choose Codes and scroll down the list of codes to find the code you want. Double-click on the code to put it in the search string.

To search for a code, such as [HRt], you must choose it from the Codes text box. If you simply type the characters in "[HRt]" as the text to search for, WordPerfect will not match them to a [HRt] code.

In addition to locating text in your document, you can also locate special characters and codes. In fact, nearly anything you type can be located in a document by searching for it.

As an example, consider [HRt], the special WordPerfect hard-return code inserted in a document whenever you press ↵. You can search for a hard return just as you search for any code or special character in a document: Simply choose it from the Codes menu.

To search for special characters, follow these steps:

1. Choose **E**dit ➤ **S**earch (F2).

2. Begin typing the search string in the Search **F**or text box.

3. Click the **C**odes button (or press Alt+C) to bring up the Codes dialog box.

4. If the Codes dialog box overlaps part of the Search **F**or text box, drag the Codes title bar to see both dialog boxes.

5. Highlight the code you want and choose **I**nsert or press ↵. Figure 9.1 shows the [Center] code highlighted in the Search Codes list box.

6. Insert as many codes, combined with any text, as you wish, up to a maximum of 80 characters ([Hrd] counts as five characters).

7. When you have finished inserting codes, choose **C**lose.

8. Optionally, choose **D**irection to search backward.

9. Choose **S**earch to start the search.

You can select any code from the Codes dialog box, including the On or Off code used in paired codes.

SEARCHING FOR FONTS AND STYLES

Like all formatting features, fonts (Chapter 5) and styles (Chapter 14) are controlled by codes, which you can search for like any other code. For example, to create the search string [Font], which searches for a font, choose Edit ➤ Search (F2), and then choose Codes. Scroll to the [Font] code and double-click on it to insert it in the Search For text box. To produce a [Style On] search

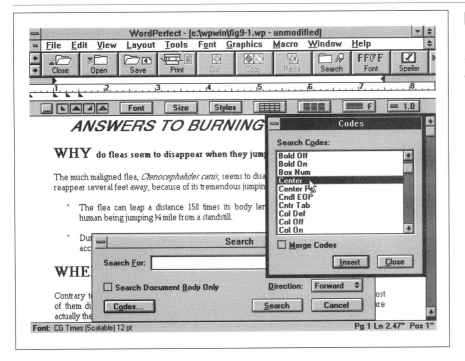

FIGURE 9.1:

The [Center] code highlighted in the Search Codes list box

string, which searches for a style, choose Edit ➤ Search (F2), then choose Codes. Scroll to the [Style On] code and double-click on it to insert it in the Search For text box.

When you perform the search, WordPerfect finds the nearest [Font] or [Style On] code. However, it won't let you search for a specific font (such as Courier 10-point) or a specific style.

LIMITED SEARCHES

> **TO LIMIT SEARCHES TO THE DOCUMENT BODY ONLY,**
>
> **choose Edit ➤ Search (F2), select Search Document Body Only, type in your search text as usual, and choose Search.**

A normal search looks through all the text in your document, including everything that will be printed as the final result, not just what is in the document window.

Normally, the Search feature looks for text and special codes in the main body of your document (including tables) as well as in headers, footers, footnotes, endnotes, graphic box captions, and text boxes. To restrict the search to the main body and tables only, you must perform a *limited search*.

A limited search works the same as a regular search, except that you must mark the Search Document Body Only check box in the Search dialog box, before proceeding with the search. To perform a limited search, follow these steps:

1. Choose **E**dit ➤ **S**earch (F2).

2. Mark the Search Document **B**ody Only check box with an *X*.

3. Type your search text, and then proceed with the search normally.

To continue a limited search, choose Edit ➤ Search Next (Shift+F2). To search backward to the previously found entry, choose Edit ➤ Search Previous (Alt+F2).

SEARCHING FOR A SPECIFIC PAGE

If you are using Roman page numbering, you should still type an Arabic-style number when using the Go To feature.

To move the insertion point quickly to a particular page in your document, use the Go To feature rather than Search: Choose Edit ➤ Go To or press Ctrl+G, then type the page number and press ↵. The Go To feature also remembers the last position of the insertion point before you moved it. To go to the insertion point's last position, choose Edit ➤ Go To (Ctrl+G) and choose Last Position.

USING SEARCH TO SELECT TEXT

The Search feature plays a helpful role in selecting text. When text is selected, WordPerfect uses the Search feature to extend the selection. This lets you extend the selected text to a specific word or phrase, rather than just a single character.

To use Search while selecting text, start the selection as you normally would, with the mouse or keyboard, then perform your search. Whether the search is forward or backward, the insertion point will land immediately *past* (to the right of) the first occurrence of the search string. Thus, if you use this technique for a backward search, the characters in the search string will *not* be highlighted as part of the selected text.

USING SEARCH TO FIND DOCUMENT BOOKMARKS

When WordPerfect loads a document, it places the insertion point at the very top of the first page. However, you may not have been at the top the last time you finished working with the document, especially if it's a long document that you've been working on over a number of days.

You can press Ctrl+End to get quickly to the end of the document. But suppose you were last working on text in the middle of the document. Or what if you wanted to go back to a few spots in the text where you weren't quite finished? How can you get there?

Two ampersands (&&) make a good bookmark because they are rarely used together in text.

The solution is to use an old word-processing device called a *bookmark*. A bookmark is simply a special character, pair of characters, symbol, or unique word you place in the text where you are working so that you can return to that place easily. To locate your place again, you can use the Search feature and enter your bookmark as the search string.

For example, suppose you are working in your document and suddenly remember that you need to move some text from another place in the document to where you are now. You can type two ampersands to mark your current spot, then go look for the text you want to move to that spot (of course, you can use the Search feature to look for this text). When you find the text you want to move, you can select it as usual, choose Edit ➤ Cut or press Shift+Del, choose Edit ➤ Search (F2), and type the && search string in the Search For text box. The insertion point will jump immediately to the destination, so you don't have to hunt around for it. You can choose Edit ➤ Paste (Shift+Ins) to complete the move.

Cut, Copy, Paste, and Select are discussed in Chapter 2.

Just remember to erase your bookmarks (&&) as soon as you've finished using them. Otherwise, you'll end up with a lot of double-ampersand characters throughout your document.

USING THE REPLACE FEATURE

TO REPLACE TEXT THROUGHOUT A DOCUMENT,

choose **Edit ➤ Replace (Ctrl+F2)**. Enter the text or codes you want to search for. Press Tab and enter the text or codes you want to replace the first ones with. Choose Replace All to replace all matching text and codes at once, or repeatedly choose Search Next then Replace to control each replacement.

Replace is a powerful WordPerfect operation that lets you choose any sequence of characters or codes and globally change it to something else. With one command you can change every *aunt* in your document to *uncle,* every *red* to *blue,* every *night* to *day.* As you'll see, you can also use Replace to make changes selectively rather than globally. Changing references to a location in a report, renaming characters in a play, and even changing the format of a document can be done easily with the Replace feature. The steps for using Replace are as follows:

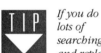 *If you do lots of searching and replacing, you might want to add buttons for Search, Search Next, Search Previous, and Replace to the Button Bar (see Chapter 3).*

1. To play it safe, save the entire document with **File ➤ Save** (Shift+F3). As you'll see, there is some risk of getting more than you bargained for when using Replace. Saving the document before you begin ensures that you'll be able to open the original if the operation doesn't go as planned.

2. Move the insertion point to where you want to begin the replacement operation (e.g., to the top of the document if you want to search and replace throughout the entire document). Like Search, Replace begins from the current position of the insertion point, not the top of the document.

3. Choose **Edit ➤ Replace**, or press Ctrl+F2. You'll see the Search and Replace dialog box:

Search and Replace

Search For:

Replace With:

☐ Search Document Body Only   Direction: Forward ⬍

Codes... Replace All Replace Search Next Close

4. Optionally, reset the direction of the replacement operation by choosing **D**irection.

5. Optionally, limit the replacement to the main body of the document by marking the Search Document **B**ody Only check box.

All the techniques described earlier for creating a search text string can be used while entering the Search For and Replace With text strings.

6. Enter the search string in the Search **F**or text box. This is the sequence of text or codes whose occurrences you want to change. Press Tab or click the Replace **W**ith text box.

7. Enter the *replacement string*—the text that will replace the search string at every occurrence—in the Replace **W**ith text box.

8. Choose Replace **A**ll to automatically replace all occurrences of the search string with the replacement string. Or choose Search **N**ext to find the next occurrence of the search string, then choose **R**eplace to replace it.

While Replace is working, the message "Please Wait..." appears at the bottom of the screen. If any text is replaced, the insertion point is positioned immediately after the first character of replaced text. If the text string is not found when you choose Replace All, WordPerfect may beep at you, but will display no message to that effect. If you choose Search Next, and the text string isn't found, WordPerfect will display "Next occurence not found." If the search string isn't found and no text is replaced, the insertion point will remain at its current position.

If you make a mistake and globally replace the wrong thing, you can undo it with the Undo command. Immediately after running Replace, select Edit ➤ Undo. All occurrences of the replaced text will be changed back to the original text. If you make a mistake with the Replace Next command, Undo will undo only the most recent occurrence of the replaced text.

Undo reverses only the most recent action.

If you cannot undo a replacement operation because you took some other action first, there's still a way of correcting the operation. If you saved your document for safety, as suggested earlier, you can simply close the document *without* saving it and reopen the copy of the document you saved before starting the replacement operation.

What kind of mistake might you make with the Replace feature? Let's say you type someone's name as *Simms* throughout a document, and you later learn that the person's name is spelled *Sims*. You could tell WordPerfect to replace *mm* with *m* at every occurrence, without confirmation. This will certainly do the job of changing *Simms* to *Sims,* but it will also change *hammer* to *hamer*, *summer* to *sumer*, and so on—not what you want, and potentially a real mess for your document.

You can stop the re-placement operation by choosing Close (or pressing Esc) at any time before choosing Replace All in the Search and Replace dialog box.

If you saved your document before the replacement operation, you can just close the fouled-up document without saving, and open the saved version from disk to try again. (This is also a good illustration of why it's important to make your search string as specific as possible in a Replacement operation. Specifying *Simms* as the search string and *Sims* as the replacement string in the earlier example would have avoided this problem altogether.)

Replace also allows you to restrict the search to the document and tables only, just as the Search feature does. Normally, WordPerfect will scan a document's headers, footers, captions, and so forth, as well as the main body of text. You can limit the replacement of text and codes to the body of the document only, by marking the Search Document Body Only check box in the Search and Replace dialog box.

When all text replacements have been made, the insertion point will be positioned after the first character of the last replacement made. To return the insertion point to its original position before Replace was started, choose Edit ➤ Go To (Ctrl+G) and choose Last Position.

CONTROLLING EACH REPLACEMENT

You can have WordPerfect automatically replace all occurrences of the search string with the replacement string. Alternatively, you can have it stop at each occurrence of the search string and do one of the following:

◆ Wait for you to replace the string

◆ Look for the next string without replacing this one

◆ Quit the replacement operation

If you choose Replace All in the Search and Replace dialog box, WordPerfect replaces every occurrence of the search string (starting at the current insertion-point position), without checking with you first.

If you choose Search Next, WordPerfect stops before making the replacement. You can then choose

◆ *Replace* to replace this occurrence of the search string

◆ *Search Next* to skip this occurrence (without replacing) and look for the next occurrence

◆ *Replace All* to go ahead and replace the remaining occurrences without waiting

◆ *Close* to stop the replacement operation altogether

If you are at all doubtful about the outcome of a replacement operation, it's probably a good idea to use Search Next followed by Replace, instead of Replace All.

REPLACING TEXT

Most often you'll use the Replace feature to change one word to another, often to fix a mistake. For example, if you find that you've inadvertently misspelled "Avco Corporation" as "Arco Corporation" in a document, you can use Replace to change every occurrence of *Arco* to *Avco*.

To save time, use abbreviations throughout your document, and then use Replace to expand them into complete words.

Besides fixing mistakes, Replace can also save you time. For example, suppose you have to type a long company name, like *Dendrobium Pharmaceuticals, Inc.,* throughout a document. To save some work, you can just type *XX* wherever you want that long company name to appear. Then, when you're finished, you can use Replace to change every occurrence of *XX* to *Dendrobium Pharmaceuticals, Inc.*

REPLACING CODES

As with the Search feature, you can use Replace to scan for formatting codes by choosing codes from the Codes dialog box. With Replace, you can both scan for the codes and replace them with other codes. (This procedure works for single codes, but not paired codes.)

You may need to manually delete the Tab in the first paragraph after completing the replacement.

For example, there are two common techniques for formatting paragraphs: You can type two hard returns at the end of a paragraph, or you can end a paragraph with a single hard return and start the next paragraph with a tab. Neither one is incorrect, they're just different.

As an example, let's suppose you type a document using a single hard return and tab to separate paragraphs, then decide to use double returns, without tabs, instead. To globally change to the new format, first position the insertion point at the top of the document. Then choose Edit ➤ Replace or press Ctrl+F2. When the insertion point is in the Search For text box, choose Codes to get to the Codes dialog box. Choose and insert the [HRt] and [Tab] codes. Then click the Replace With text box (or press Tab), and choose [HRt] codes from the Codes dialog box twice, so your Search and Replace dialog box looks like this:

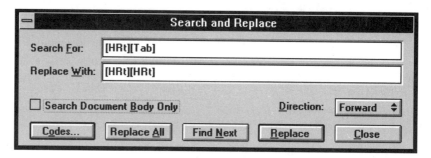

Finally, choose Replace All to replace all the old codes with the new ones.

As with Search, there are limitations in replacing formatting codes. For example, you can search for a generic [Ln Spacing:] code, but you cannot change all the single-spacing codes, [Ln Spacing:1], to double-spacing codes, [Ln Spacing:2]. Using the Styles feature (Chapter 14) is the best way to get around the limitations.

USING REPLACE IN PART OF A DOCUMENT

To limit replacement operation to a specific part of your document, follow these steps:

1. Select the text where you want to perform the search, using your mouse.

2. Choose **Edit** ➤ **R**eplace, or press Ctrl+F2.

3. Follow the usual steps for entering the text to search for and the text to replace it with.

4. Choose Replace **A**ll (or Search **N**ext followed by **R**eplace) to perform the replacement.

Only text within the selected block will be searched for and replaced. Any text outside the selected block will be ignored.

REPLACING CASE-SENSITIVE TEXT

Like Search, Replace observes differences between upper- and lowercase. Replace locates matching words based on the same rules that Search follows, but in making the replacement, it attempts to match the case of the text being replaced.

◆ Replace matches lowercase characters in the search string with either uppercase or lowercase characters in the document.

◆ Replace matches uppercase characters in the search string with only uppercase characters in the document.

Based on the cases of the replacement and search strings, WordPerfect guesses what case is needed in the replacement itself. In general, it replaces a capitalized word in the document with a capitalized version of the replacement. If a character in the replacement must always be uppercase, be sure to type it uppercase in the replacement string.

For example, suppose you're replacing *circle* with *square*. You enter *circle* as the search string, and Replace finds *Circle* (with an initial capital letter) in the text. It will replace *Circle* with *Square*.

Note that if Replace found *CIRCLE* (all caps), it would also replace it with *Square*—only the initial capital letter would be retained. Any other words in the replacement text remain lowercase when the search string is all lowercase.

Any capital letters in the replacement text will always remain capitalized. For example, if you are replacing *circle* with *SQUARE*, all replacement text will be capitalized in the document. That is, any instance of *circle*, with any mixture of upper- and lowercase letters, will be replaced with *SQUARE*.

USING REPLACE TO DELETE TEXT AND CODES

Use Search and Replace to find your bookmarks and replace them with nothing.

Replace can be used when you need to delete identical text repeatedly throughout your document. The procedure is simple: Don't supply a replacement string. Follow these steps:

1. To play it safe, save your document by choosing **File ➤ S**ave (Shift+F3).

2. Position the insertion point wherever you want the replacement operation to begin.

3. Choose **E**dit ➤ **R**eplace, or press Ctrl+F2.

4. Type the text or insert the codes you want to delete in the Search **F**or text box. Press Tab to move the insertion point to the Replace With text box.

5. If a text string is in the text box (from a previous Replacement operation), delete it by pressing Delete. Instead of entering a replacement string, choose Search **N**ext followed by **R**eplace (or choose Replace **A**ll). This causes Replace to change existing text to *nothing* (which is the same as deleting it).

It's generally a good idea to use Serach Next followed by Replace, instead of Replace All, when deleting text with the Replace feature. The only exception is when you're sure the search text is unique. Also, be doubly certain to save your document before you use Replace to delete text.

There is only one way to get the deleted text back. If you used the Replace All command to globally change the search string to nothing, you can undo all the changes by choosing Edit ➤ Undo (Alt+Backspace). However, if you used the Search Next command to individually replace the search string, Undo will undo only the last deletion.

A common use of Replace is to delete formatting codes. For example, you can strip out all the underlined text in your document simply by searching for the [Und On] codes and replacing them with nothing. When you delete the starting or ending code of a paired code, the other code is automatically deleted, so this operation deletes all the [Und Off] codes as well.

LIMITED REPLACING

As mentioned earlier, Replace works on text in the main body of your document as well as headers, footers, endnotes, footnotes, graphic-box captions, and text boxes. To limit the replacement to the main body of your document only, mark the Search Document Body Only check box in the Search and Replace dialog box. Then proceed as you normally would.

REPLACING PAIRED CODES

You can't use the Replace feature to change paired codes. For example, you can't change all italics to underline or all boldface to Large text. Similarly, you cannot change a specific font, such as Courier to Times Roman, because Replace can only find "generic" [Font] codes. The way to avoid this problem is to use styles (Chapter 14) rather than actual codes in your documents.

In the next chapter, you'll learn how to polish your finished documents by checking your spelling. You'll also learn how to use the WordPerfect Thesaurus.

CHAPTER 10

Checking Your Spelling and Finding the Right Word

nless you happen to be some kind of "human dictionary," you'll probably need to correct misspellings in your documents and go to the dictionary to find correct spellings. Let's face it, even human dictionaries make mistakes now and again. But with the help of WordPerfect, you can probably put away your dictionary once and for all and find the right spellings just by pressing a few keys.

Have you ever found yourself smack-dab in the middle of writing a sentence, only to discover that you're suddenly at a loss for words, or you've already overused a word like "exciting" and want to try something spicier like "delightful," "electrifying," "exhilarating," "inspiring," or "thrilling"? Even if you have the vocabulary of a verbal genius, you'll appreciate the convenience of having an online thesaurus that can not only suggest the right word to use but type it in for you as well.

This chapter discusses the Speller and the Thesaurus, two very handy tools for checking your spelling and finding just the right word for any occasion. You'll find both of them on the Tools pull-down menu.

ABOUT THE SPELLER

WordPerfect's Speller checks your document for misspelled words, double words, numbers embedded in words, and certain types of capitalization errors and typos. You can use the Speller to scan a single word, a page, a document, or selected text from your current document.

Before learning the functions of the Speller in detail, you should know a few things about what it can and cannot do. The Speller works by comparing words in your document against its own dictionary of about 115,000 words. If it can't find a word in its dictionary, it offers suggestions on correct spelling, providing a list of alternatives from which to choose. Even though the Speller can do this, keep in mind that it's still up to you to choose the correct word.

The English language has nearly half a million words, with new ones being added almost daily. Even more words exist when you count last names, names of businesses, technical terms used in certain professions, and other proper nouns that don't appear in dictionaries. You can add these words, such as your last name, your hometown, and other correctly spelled but uncommon words, to a *supplemental dictionary*. The Speller will then check for words there as well as in its own dictionary.

Keep in mind that the Speller does not check context. Even though you may have spelled a word correctly, it may not be the word you intended to type. Common mistakes like typing *the* instead of *they* or *he* instead of *the* are not caught by the Speller, because *the* and *he* are not incorrectly spelled words— they're just the wrong words for the occasion. Until a contextual speller comes along, it's up to you to spot these kinds of errors. (Grammar checkers can catch some mistakes like these.)

Likewise, the Speller cannot check grammar. Hence, it will not catch homonym mistakes. Common foul-ups include using *it's* instead of *its* or switching *their, there,* and *they're.*

The Speller will also check for some mistakes in the use of upper- and lowercase letters. If only the first two letters of a word are capitalized (for example, *THere*), or if the first letter is lowercase and the second letter is uppercase (such as *yOur*), WordPerfect will point out the irregular use of case. I'll discuss this topic in more detail later in the chapter.

NOTE *You can add proper nouns and technical terms to the Speller's supplemental dictionary, as described a little later in the chapter.*

NOTE *A **homonym** is one of two or more words pronounced alike but different in meaning or spelling.*

USING THE SPELLER
TO CORRECT MISSPELLINGS

TO START THE SPELLER,

choose Tools ➤ Speller or press Ctrl+F1.

To use the Speller, follow these steps:

1. If you don't want to check the entire document, move the insertion point to the location where you want to start checking your spelling. Optionally, you can select a block of text to check by using the normal text-selection techniques.

2. Choose **T**ools ➤ **S**peller, or press Ctrl+F1. The Speller window (Figure 10.1) appears.

3. Notice the Chec**k** pop-up list box in the Speller window, which indicates how much of the document the Speller will check. You can change this setting by moving the mouse pointer to the button, holding down the left mouse button, highlighting another option, and then releasing the mouse button. Or, press Alt+K and use the ↑ and ↓ keys to scroll to an option, as summarized below:

Word	Checks only the spelling of the word at the insertion point
Document	Checks the spelling of the entire document
To **E**nd of Document	Checks the spelling from the insertion point to the end of the document
Page	Checks the spelling of the current page only
To E**n**d of Page	Checks the spelling of the page from the insertion point to the end of the page
Selected **T**ext	Checks the spelling of a block of selected text (you must select the text where you want to check spelling before you start the Speller)
To End of **S**election	Checks the spelling of the selected text from the insertion point to the end of the selected text

4. Choose **S**tart.

5. When the Speller finds a "suspect" word, it usually presents options for replacing the word and places the first suggested replacement in the **W**ord text box. For example, in Figure 10.2 the Speller has found the misspelled word *truely,* listed some suggested replacements, and placed the word *truly* in the Word box.

6. Depending on the type of error, you can choose any one of the buttons that now appear in the Speller window to determine how to handle the current word:

If none of these options corrects the problem, you can edit the word in the Word box, then choose Replace.

Suggest	Displays suggested replacement words (the Speller does this automatically if the Suggestions check box is chosen)
Add	Adds the current word to the supplemental dictionary, so it's never considered a misspelling again (for example, you might want to add your own name to the supplemental dictionary so it's not considered a misspelling)
Replace	Replaces the word in your document with the word in the Word box (as a shortcut, double click the word in the Word box)
Skip Once	Ignores the misspelling, this time only
Skip Always	Ignores the misspelling here and throughout the rest of the document

7. When the Speller has finished its job, it displays the message "Spell Check Completed" in a message box. Choose OK or press ↵.

8. If you want to remove the Speller window, choose **C**lose.

In the sections that follow, I'll describe individual features and options in more detail.

EDITING WITH THE SPELLER

When the Speller locates a suspect word, it either places that word in the Word text box in the Speller window, or, if it can find homonyms for that word in its dictionary, it displays a list of suggested words and places the first word from the list of suggestions in the Word box.

Suggested homonyms are displayed automatically only if the Suggestions check box in the Speller window is marked, *and* if it can locate homonyms in its dictionary. If the option is turned off, you can still display suggestions for the current word by choosing Suggest in the window. (You

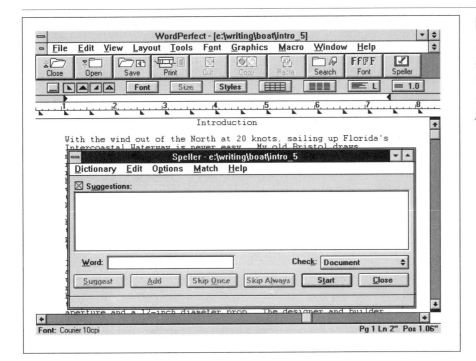

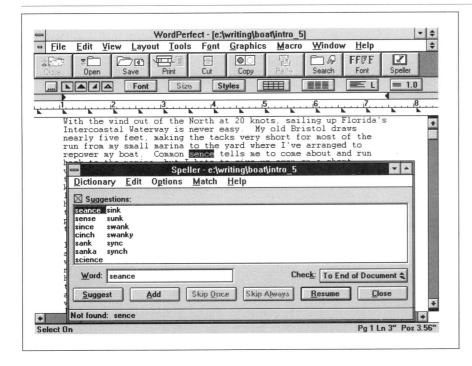

FIGURE 10.1:
The Speller window appears at the bottom of the screen after you choose Tools ➤ Spell or press Ctrl+F1.

FIGURE 10.2:
The Speller has found a word likely to be misspelled.

can also click on any word in the list of homonyms, then click Suggest, to see homonyms for that word.)

You can also edit the word in the Word box directly, using the usual text-editing keys (←, →, Backspace, Delete, and so forth). This is handy when the misspelling is actually caused by inadvertently combining words, such as typing *onceagain* rather than *once again*. When you've corrected the word, just choose Replace to put the correction into your document.

As I'll discuss in the following sections, the Speller does more than look for misspelled words. It also looks for embedded numbers, irregular use of case, and double words. If you prefer, you can disable any one of these options by choosing it from the Options menu and turning it off.

You can use Edit ➤ Undo in the Speller window to undo the most recent change to a word.

Checking Words with Numbers

The Speller stops at words that have numbers embedded in them, like *Shift+F1* or a part number like *SKN047-112*. It treats these as it does any other misspelling and presents suggestions for correct spelling. If you want the Speller to ignore embedded numbers, turn off the option by choosing Options ➤ Words with Numbers in Speller window. Then you can choose Skip Once or Skip Always to proceed.

Checking Irregular Case

While scanning your document, the Speller also checks for irregular use of upper- and lowercase letters in the first three characters of words. This feature can help you find common typos that result from the following:

◆ Holding the Shift key down a bit too long, causing the first two letters to be capitalized (as in *THe*)

◆ Pressing the Shift key a little too late, causing the second letter to be capitalized (as in *tHe*)

◆ Pressing the Shift key inadvertently (as in *thE*)

WordPerfect can find and correct five types of capitalization errors, summarized below, where *U* indicates uppercase and *l* indicates lowercase:

◆ UUl is changed to Ull (e.g., *THis* becomes *This*).

◆ lUl is changed to Ull (e.g., *tHis* becomes *This*).

◆ lUU is changed to UUU (e.g., *tHIS* becomes *THIS*).

◆ llU is changed to lll (e.g., *thIs* becomes *this*).

◆ lU is changed to Ul in two-letter words (e.g., *iS* becomes *Is*).

The capitalization of the entire word is based on the first three characters only. For example, the variations of *apple* shown below would be replaced as follows:

WORD	REPLACEMENT
aPple	Apple (matches lUl pattern)
apPle	apple (matches llU pattern)
APple	Apple (matches UUl pattern)
APPLE	APPLE (no change)

Once WordPerfect locates an irregular use of case, it presents the message box shown in Figure 10.3.

If you choose Continue, the word is ignored. If you choose Replace, Word-Perfect corrects the word. If you choose Disable Checking, case checking is disabled for the current word and the remainder of the spelling check.

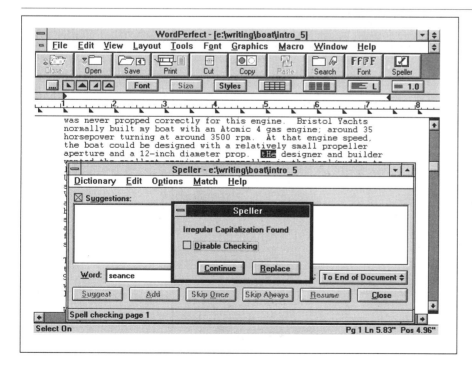

FIGURE 10.3:

The Speller after finding irregular use of upper- and lowercase letters

Optionally, you can turn off case checking for future sessions with the Speller, by choosing Options ➤ Irregular Capitalization.

CHECKING DOUBLE WORDS

The Speller also points out double (or duplicate) words, such as *the the,* while scanning your document. When it encounters a double word, it highlights the second word and presents the dialog box shown in Figure 10.4.

If you choose Continue, the double word is ignored and both words are left in the document. If you choose Delete 2nd, WordPerfect deletes the second word. To stop checking for double words, choose Disable Checking by placing an *X* in the check box.

Optionally, if you want the Speller to ignore double words in future sessions as well, turn off the option by choosing Options ➤ Duplicate Words.

CLOSING THE SPELLER

You can temporarily disable the Speller at any time by clicking anywhere in your document. The Speller window remains on the screen, but you can edit text normally. To resume spell checking, just choose Start in the Speller window.

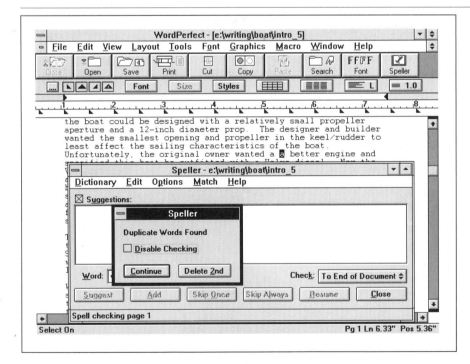

FIGURE 10.4:

The Speller after finding double words

Optionally, to close the Speller window, choose **C**lose.

USING THE SPELLER TO LOOK UP A WORD

You can use the Speller to look up a word even when you're not using Word-Perfect for Windows, as described later in this chapter.

You can also use the Speller like an electronic dictionary, to look up the spelling of a word *before* you type it. To do so, follow these steps:

1. Choose **T**ools ➤ **S**peller, or press Ctrl+F1.

2. Type a word or word pattern in the **W**ord text box and choose **S**uggest. The Speller will display words similar in pronunciation or construction to that word (including the word itself, if the Speller can find it in the dictionary).

For example, suppose you want to use the word *quick* but forget how it is spelled. You can type the following word pattern in the Word text box and choose Suggest:

kwik

The Speller displays homonyms (if any), as shown in Figure 10.5.

USING WILDCARDS WITH SUGGEST

When specifying a word to look up, you can use the ? and * wildcards to stand for letters you're not sure about. These wildcards are used to replace a single letter or group of letters within a word. The Speller will then scan the dictionary and look for any words that match the letters and wildcards you've specified.

The ? wildcard stands for a single character in a word. For example, if you specify *?ing,* the Speller will display all four-letter words in its dictionary that end in *-ing,* as shown in Figure 10.6.

Word-Perfect Corp. offers a product called "Rhymer," which is specifically designed to find rhyming words.

To use wildcards, you can enter them from the keyboard, or use the Match menu and choose either 1 Character or Multiple Characters.

The * wildcard stands for a group of any number of letters (from no letters to all the letters in the word). For example, specifying **ing* displays all words (of any length) that end in *-ing.* This can be a real boon to poets yearning for the perfect rhyme.

The * wildcard can appear anywhere in a word. And you can use both ? and * together to create a specific search, for example,

i?p*

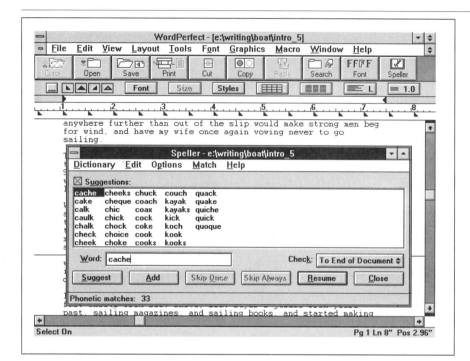

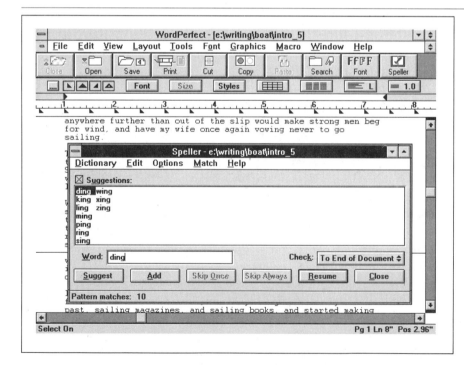

This combination will find any word that starts with *i,* has a *p* in its third position, and ends with any combination of characters. Figure 10.7 shows the results.

When the correctly spelled word appears in the list, click on it once to copy it to the Word box. Then you can choose Edit ➤ Select All, then Edit ➤ Copy to copy that word to the Windows Clipboard. Next, move the insertion point to where you want to copy that word in your document, then choose Edit ➤ Paste from the WordPerfect menu bar (*not* the Speller menu bar). As described later in this chapter, you can paste the word into any Windows application's document window.

SPECIFYING ANOTHER LANGUAGE

By default, your main and supplemental dictionaries will be in United States English. You can purchase other dictionaries from WordPerfect Corporation separately and use those dictionaries when checking your spelling.

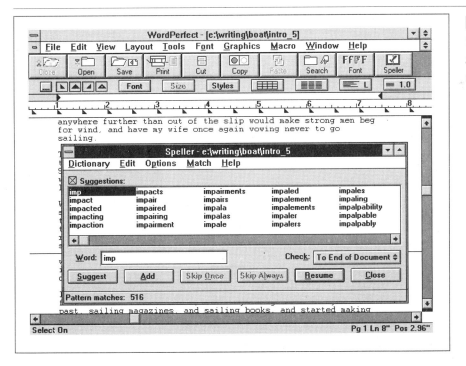

FIGURE 10.7:

The results of the Suggest command trying to match i?p*

If you choose a language for which you have not installed an optional dictionary, you'll see the error message "Dictionary not found or bad format." Use Select Dictionary to choose another dictionary, or Skip Language to proceed, using the current dictionary.

If you've purchased and installed other dictionaries, you can choose which dictionary to use to check any section of your document by following these steps:

1. Move the insertion point to where you want to use a different language dictionary (e.g., at the top of the document if you want to use a foreign-language dictionary for the entire document).

2. Choose **T**ools ➤ **L**anguage from the WordPerfect menu bar.

3. Choose the language you want to use from the insertion point forward, either by double-clicking on it or by highlighting it and pressing ↵.

WordPerfect inserts a [Lang:] code at the insertion point and, when checking your spelling, automatically switches to the appropriate dictionary. You can place multiple [Lang:] codes throughout your document to use multiple dictionaries.

SPECIFYING ANOTHER DICTIONARY

By default, the Speller uses its own main dictionary to check words. This dictionary is stored in the shared programs directory (typically C:\WPC); in the United States it is named WP{WP}US.LEX. If you've added any words of your own while spell-checking a document, those words are stored in a file named WP{WP}US.SUP, in the same directory as the main dictionary. WordPerfect uses both dictionaries when spell-checking a document.

You can choose a different dictionary by using the Dictionary menu on the Speller's menu bar. Choose either Main or Supplementary, and enter a valid path and file name for the main or supplemental dictionary you want to use. The sections that follow discuss dictionaries in more detail.

REFINING THE SPELLER DICTIONARIES

If you create your own main dictionary, its file name must follow the general pattern WP{WP}xx.LEX.

You can determine, and optionally change, the directory location of a dictionary by choosing File ➤ Preferences ➤ Location of Files ➤ Thesaurus/-Spell/Hyphenation. If you change the location, you must move the dictionary files to that new location.

There's rarely a need to tamper with either the main or supplemental dictionary directly, because WordPerfect automatically handles both quite efficiently. However, if you accidentally added a misspelled word to the supplemental dictionary, or you want to create a unique supplemental dictionary of specialized terms, such as technical, legal, or medical terms that you use frequently in your work, use the Speller Utility.

The Speller Utility is a separate program that comes with your Word-Perfect package, but it is accessed directly from DOS or the Windows Program Manager (it is the same as the 5.1 Speller Utility). It's stored on disk with the file name SPELL.EXE, usually in the same directory where the other Word-Perfect Corporation shared programs are installed (typically C:\WPC) during the installation procedure. If you cannot find the SPELL.EXE file on your hard disk, you may need to perform a custom installation and install the Shared Utilities files, as discussed in Appendix A.

RUNNING THE SPELLER UTILITY

To run the Speller Utility, use the Windows Program Manager:

1. If the Windows Program Manager is obscured by some other Windows application, go to the Task List (press Ctrl+Esc) and choose Program Manager.

2. Choose **File** ➤ **R**un from the Program Manager window.

3. Type

spell.exe

If you have an earlier version of WordPerfect installed on your computer (c:\wpc\spell.exe) specify the shared programs path.

4. Choose OK or press ↵.

The Speller Utility menu appears, as shown in Figure 10.8.

Some options on the Speller Utility menu are available for both main and supplemental dictionaries (options 0, 1, 2, 3, 7, and 8) and others for the main dictionary only (options 4, 5, 6, 9, and A). In addition, option B is used only with supplemental dictionaries, and option C requires a main dictionary, an algorithmic dictionary, and a supplemental dictionary. The following sections describe how to use these various options.

NOTE
NOTE
Optional algorithmic dictionaries are also available from WordPerfect Corp. in some languages; they generally offer more suggested spellings for a word.

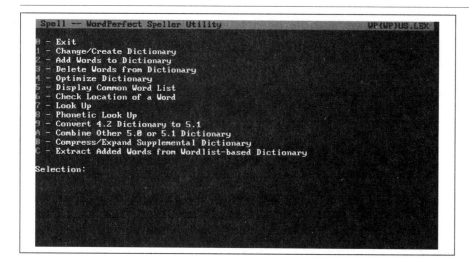

CHOOSING A DICTIONARY TO WORK WITH

The first step in using the Speller Utility is to choose the dictionary you want to work with by choosing option 1 – Change/Create Dictionary. You see three options:

0 – Cancel – do not change dictionary
1 – Change/Create main dictionary
2 – Change/Create supplemental dictionary

Choosing option 1 presents the screen shown in Figure 10.9. Choosing option 2 presents a similar screen, except that it shows the name of the supplemental dictionary instead of the main dictionary. The name of the default main dictionary (e.g., WP{WP}US.LEX) or supplemental dictionary (e.g., WP{WP}US.SUP) is displayed, and you can press ↵ to use that dictionary. Optionally, you can enter a new dictionary name, including the path, if the dictionary is not in the current directory, then press ↵.

If the dictionary name you enter does not exist, you'll be asked whether it should be created. Choose No if you simply misspelled the dictionary name, or choose Yes if you do want to create a new dictionary.

ADDING WORDS TO THE DICTIONARIES

When you choose 2 – Add Words to Dictionary from the Speller Utility menu in Figure 10.8, you'll see the options shown in Figure 10.10. As the menu indicates, you can enter words by typing them at the keyboard or by reading them from a file (discussed in a moment).

You can add words to the common word list or the main word list. The common word list contains frequently used words, like *the, that,* and so forth. When checking your spelling, the Speller first checks the common word list in the main dictionary. If the word is not on that list, it checks the main list. If the word still can't be found, the Speller checks the supplemental dictionary. This allows the Speller to run at top speed, since the common word list is considerably smaller than the main list. To view the common word list in the main dictionary, choose option 5 – Display Common Word List. Choose OK or press ↵ to exit the list.

To keep the Speller running at top speed, avoid adding infrequently used words to the common word list.

Only the main dictionary is divided into common and main word lists. If you are currently working with a supplemental dictionary, options 1 and 2 (Add to common word list) are not functional.

Because the automatic hyphenation feature (Chapter 11) uses the same main dictionary as the Speller, you should include hyphens when adding words to the main dictionary. (The hyphens you add to words here are really just *hyphenation indicators,* which WordPerfect will use only to hyphenate the word, if necessary, when you activate automatic hyphenation.) For example, if you want to add the word *pipelining* (a computer term) to the current main dictionary, you can enter it as

pipe-lining

You can include as many hyphens as you wish. If you don't include any hyphens, the automatic hyphenator will not hyphenate the word.

Pressing ↵ after typing a word ends your entry, but if you accidentally press ↵ instead of the spacebar, you can just choose the Add Words option again and pick up where you left off.

Adding Words from the Keyboard

If you choose one of the options marked *(from keyboard),* you can type in the words you wish to add to the specified dictionary, separating them with spaces. Remember to include hyphens.

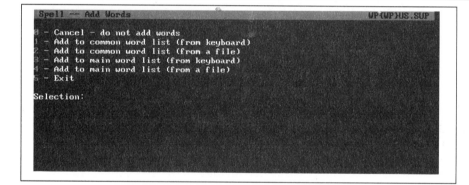

FIGURE 10.9:

The screen for choosing a dictionary to work with

```
Spell -- Change Dictionary                              WP{WP}US.LEX
0 - Cancel - do not change dictionary
1 - Change/Create main dictionary
2 - Change/Create supplemental dictionary

Selection: 1

You may now safely exchange diskettes in any drive.


Name of dictionary to use: WP{WP}US.LEX
```

FIGURE 10.10:

The options for adding words to the current dictionary

```
Spell -- Add Words                                      WP{WP}US.SUP
0 - Cancel - do not add words
1 - Add to common word list (from keyboard)
2 - Add to common word list (from a file)
3 - Add to main word list (from keyboard)
4 - Add to main word list (from a file)
5 - Exit

Selection:
```

When you're finished specifying the words you want to add, choose option 5. This will update the current dictionary. Be forewarned that updating the main dictionary can take twenty minutes or more. If you change your mind about adding the words, or you don't have twenty minutes to spare, you can press 0 to cancel your additions and return immediately to the Speller Utility menu.

When you've finished adding words, you can choose 0 – Exit to leave the Speller Utility and return to the Program Manager window.

Adding Words from a File

A quick way to add many words to a dictionary is to first create a list of the words you want to add. You do this in WordPerfect, not the Speller Utility. (If you happen to be in the Speller Utility, exit by choosing option 0 until you get back to the Program Manger window, then click anywhere in the Word-Perfect document window to hide the Program Manager. (If WordPerfect isn't already running, run it as usual from the Program Manager.)

You can type your word list in any WordPerfect document window. When typing your list, include hyphens and separate each word with a hard return (by pressing ↵). Figure 10.11 shows an example.

Before saving your word list, you might want to use the Speller to check the spelling. Any words that the Speller does not catch as misspelled words are already in the dictionary; therefore, you should remove those words from the list to avoid replacing them in the dictionary (and to save yourself the trouble of hyphenating them). Also, because adding these words to the

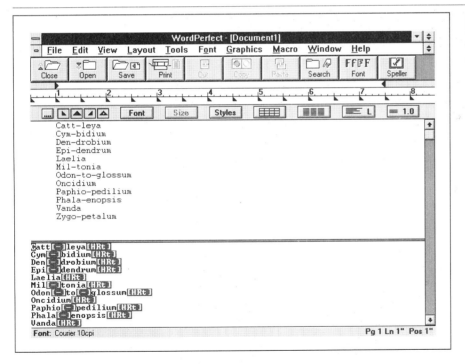

FIGURE 10.11:

A list of words to be added to a dictionary

dictionary will be faster if the words are in alphabetical order, you might want to *line sort* the entire list first, as discussed in Chapter 17.

Finally, save the entire list and exit WordPerfect by choosing File ➤ Exit (Alt+F4). For simplicity, you can save your list on the same drive and in the same directory where the dictionary files are stored. For example, enter the name of the file as C:\WPC\MYLIST.WP when prompted for a file name.

When you've left WordPerfect, you should be back to the Program Manager.

1. Choose **File** ➤ **R**un from the Program Manager.

2. Run the Speller Utility as described earlier.

3. Choose the dictionary where words will be added by using option 1.

4. Choose option 2 – Add Words to Dictionary, and choose one of the *(from a file)* options.

5. Enter the name of the file (including the directory if it's not the same as the current directory) containing the words you want to add, and press ↵.

6. Be sure to choose option 5 – Exit to actually add the words to the dictionary. You can then use option 7 – Look Up to look up any words to verify the addition if you wish.

7. When you're finished, choose option 0 – Exit to leave the Speller Utility and return to the Program Manager window.

WHY BOTHER WITH ALL OF THIS?

You may be thinking that everything I've discussed so far is an awfully complicated way to go about adding words to the dictionary. After all, simply choosing Add when you're spell-checking a document does all this for you automatically. You are absolutely correct in your thinking.

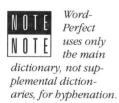
Word-Perfect uses only the main dictionary, not supplemental dictionaries, for hyphenation.

But one slight advantage of manually adding words to the main dictionary in this manner is that you can add hyphens to the dictionary used by the automatic hyphenator. Another advantage is that you can create specialized supplemental dictionaries that you use with some documents but not with others. This might come in handy if you work with highly technical manuscripts, because a smaller, specialized supplemental dictionary will be slightly faster than a larger, more general one, particularly on a slow computer.

Unlike the main dictionary, file names of supplemental dictionaries need not follow the WP{WP}xx.SUP pattern—you can use any valid DOS file name. Just be sure to store the names in the same directory that contains your other supplemental dictionaries.

To create a specialized supplemental dictionary, start by creating and saving your list of specialized terms in WordPerfect, as discussed earlier in "Adding Words from a File." Then exit WordPerfect, go to the Windows Program Manager, and run the Speller Utility.

In the Speller Utility, choose option 1 – Change/Create Dictionary on the main Utility menu. Then choose option 2 – Change/Create Supplemental Dictionary to create a new supplemental dictionary with a unique name in the same directory where the other dictionary files are stored (e.g., C:\WPC\MYDICT.SUP). Finally, choose option 2 – Add Words to Dictionary on the Utility menu to add the words from your word list file to this new dictionary, and exit the Speller Utility.

In the future, when you want WordPerfect to use this new supplemental dictionary, first choose Tools ➤ Speller from the WordPerfect menus. Then choose Dictionary ➤ Supplementary from the Speller window and enter the name of the specialized dictionary. Then proceed with your spell checking. WordPerfect will use the specified supplemental dictionary while spell-checking the current document. (You can use only one main dictionary and one supplemental dictionary when spell-checking a document.)

DELETING WORDS FROM A DICTIONARY

Remember, words added to the Speller dictionary with the Add option in Word-Perfect are added to the current supplemental dictionary, not the main dictionary.

If you accidentally add a misspelled word to one of the Speller dictionaries, you'll probably want to delete it so that the Speller catches the misspelling in the future. You can do so by choosing 3 – Delete Words from Dictionary from the Speller Utility menu. WordPerfect presents options for deleting words from either the common word list (available for the main dictionary only) or the main word list (available for both main and supplemental dictionaries). You can specify the words either by typing them directly from the keyboard or by entering the name of a file that contains the words to be deleted.

The Delete Words options work exactly the same as the Add Words options explained above, except that the specified words will be deleted rather than added. Press 5 – Exit after deleting a word or words (or 0 to cancel the deletion). Then you have to wait for the updating process again, which can take twenty minutes or more. Again, if you are deleting words from a list in a file, the process will be faster if the words are in alphabetical order; therefore, you might want to line sort the entire list first, as discussed in Chapter 17.

COUNTING WORDS

The Count feature is a useful tool for writers who are paid by the word, people who write to spec (i.e., who write just enough text to fit within a particular space), and students who need to write essays of a particular length. Follow these steps to count words in the entire document or a selected passage of text:

1. If you want to count words in only a portion of your document, select that text.

2. Choose **Tools** ➤ **W**ord Count.

WordPerfect counts the words and displays the result in the small dialog box shown below. Choose OK or press ↵ to return to your document.

Count always moves the insertion point to the end of the document. To return to your previous position, use Go To (press Ctrl+G and choose Last position).

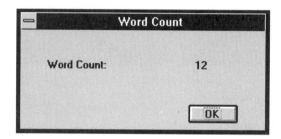

WordPerfect counts the following as part of a word:

◆ a–z

◆ A–Z

◆ International alphabetical characters

◆ Apostrophe (')

◆ Hard hyphen (Home hyphen)

The numerical digits 0–9 are also valid characters; however, WordPerfect does not count "words" that consist entirely of numbers (e.g., *999* is not a word). Therefore, the Speller will count five words in the following:

Please call (800) 555-0102 for an appointment.

USING THE THESAURUS

TO USE THE THESAURUS,

position the insertion point on the word you want to check, and choose Tools ➤ Thesaurus or press Alt+F1.

WordPerfect's Thesaurus helps you out when you are at a loss for words. It can help you find a more precise or expressive synonym for a word, such as *enormous* instead of just *big*. It can also help you find an antonym. For example, when you need a word that means the opposite of *arrogant,* but just can't quite think of the right word, you can look up *arrogant* and discover antonyms like *polite* and *humble.*

Choosing the best word can add spice to your writing. For example, suppose you're writing about a mountain-climbing adventure and write the sentence *We climbed the big hill.* With the help of the Thesaurus, you can find more exciting words, changing that rather dull sentence to something a bit more dramatic, such as *We scaled the towering peak.*

To use the Thesaurus, follow these steps:

1. Place the insertion point on the word for which you want a synonym or an antonym.

You can scroll though suggested words with the scroll bars, and move and resize the Thesaurus window as necessary.

2. Choose **T**ools ➤ **T**hesaurus, or press Alt+F1. Suggested synonyms and antonyms are displayed, as shown in Figure 10.12.

3. If you see a good replacement word in the list, you can click it once, then choose **R**eplace to replace the existing word with the highlighted word. If you decide not to replace the word, choose **C**lose to return to the document without making any changes.

There are several techniques you can use while in the Thesaurus window to look up additional synonyms and antonyms, as discussed in the sections that follow.

LOOKING UP MORE SYNONYMS AND ANTONYMS

After the Thesaurus window displays suggested words, you can look up additional synonyms and antonyms. You'll notice that the Thesaurus window is divided into three columns. Each column can contain a group of synonyms and antonyms. The columns can also contain uses of the word as an adjective (*a*), a noun (*n*), or a verb (*v*). If the word has any antonyms, that group will be marked by *(ant)* at the bottom of the column.

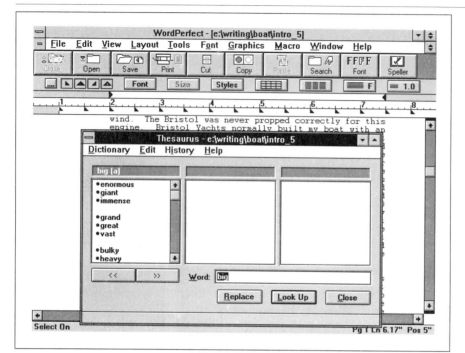

A bullet next to a word indicates a *headword,* a word for which the Thesaurus has a synonym list. (The Thesaurus contains about 10,000 headwords.) If you double-click on a headword, synonyms and antonyms for that word will be listed in their own column to the right, and a pointing-hand icon indicates the headword from the current column. For example, Figure 10.13 shows the screen after double-clicking on the word *vast*.

You can use the columns to search for refined meanings of a word, by double-clicking on any word in any column, until you find exactly the word you want. You can scroll left and right through the columns by clicking the << and >> buttons, or by pressing the → and ← keys (after moving to the columns with the or Shift+Tab, if necessary). When you find the word you want, highlight it in its column (by clicking on it once or by using the ↑ and ↓ keys), then choose Replace.

USING THE THESAURUS TO LOOK UP A WORD

You can also use the Thesaurus to find the word before you type it. Just run the Thesaurus as you normally would, type the word that you want to look up in the Word box in the Thesuarus window, and choose Look Up. Now you can use the Thesaurus columns, as usual, to find additional synonyms and antonyms. When you find the word you want, highlight it and choose Replace.

REVIEWING THE HISTORY

The History menu lets you view the last words you've looked up with the Thesaurus. If you choose a word from the History menu, that word becomes the new headword. This lets you "back up" after making a series of headword choices to start over from an earlier headword choice.

CHOOSING A THESAURUS DICTIONARY

The default Thesaurus dictionary is named WP{WP}US.THS on the Word-Perfect Corp. shared programs directory (\WPC). Like the Speller, you can purchase optional foreign langurage Thesaurus dictionaries from WordPerfect. When you install one of these dictionaries, it automatically becomes the default dictionary that the Thesaurus uses. If you want to use some other installed dictionary, choose Dictionary ➤ Change Dictionary from the Thesaurus window, then specify the dictionary you want to use.

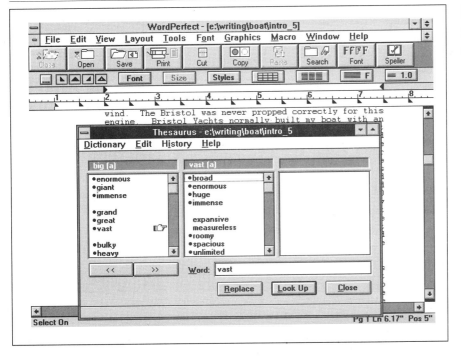

FIGURE 10.13:

The synonyms for the word "vast"

USING SPELLER AND THESAURUS
WITH OTHER WINDOWS PRODUCTS

Both the Speller and Thesaurus are stand-alone Windows applications stored in the WordPerfect Corporation shared programs directory (typically C:\WPC). You can use the Look Up feature of either of them any time you are in Windows, even if WordPerfect for Windows isn't running at the moment. Follow these steps:

1. Go to the Windows Program Manager, and open the WordPerfect group window.

2. Double-click either the Speller or Thesaurus icon, depending on which you want to run.

3. Use the techniques described earlier to look up and choose a word in either the Speller or Thesaurus, until the word you want is in that window's Word box.

 You can only use the Look Up feature when using the Speller outside of Word-Perfect; you can't spell-check an entire document or spreadsheet.

4. Choose **Edit ➤ S**elect All.

5. Choose **Edit ➤ C**ut (Shift+Del) to move, or **Edit ➤ C**opy (Ctrl+Ins) to copy that word to the Windows Clipboard.

6. Go to whatever application you want to copy the pasted word to, and position the insertion point where you want to place the pasted word within a document window (or spreadsheet, or whatever).

7. Choose **P**aste from that application's **E**dit menu.

You can close the Thesaurus or Speller window whenever you're ready by choosing the Close.

In the next chapter, you'll learn about how to use WordPerfect's automatic hyphenation feature.

CHAPTER 11

Hyphenating Text

ust as WordPerfect can use a dictionary to check your spelling, it can also use a dictionary to hyphenate words. The main purpose of hyphenation is to tighten loose lines that contain too much white space. For example, the first paragraph in Figure 11.1 has a very loose line because of a lengthy word. The figure shows how much tighter that same paragraph looks with a hyphen added.

There are two ways to hyphenate words with WordPerfect: You can insert your own hyphens or let WordPerfect do it for you. I'll discuss both ways in the sections that follow.

HYPHENATING TEXT AUTOMATICALLY

TO ACTIVATE AUTOMATIC HYPHENATION,
position the insertion point where you want to start hyphenating and choose Layout ➤ Line ➤ Hyphenation, or press Shift+F9 E. Mark the Hyphenation On check box to activate automatic hyphenation.

Very long words like supercalifragilisticexpialidocious, of Mary Poppins fame, cause very loose lines (too much white space) if left unhyphenated, particularly when squeezed into tight margins.

Very long words like supercalifragilisticexpialidocious, of Mary Poppins fame, cause very loose lines (too much white space) if left unhyphenated, particularly when squeezed into tight margins.

FIGURE 11.1:
A paragraph with and without hyphenation

Unlike the Speller and Thesaurus, automatic hyphenation is a formatting feature that is activated at the current insertion point. That is, only text below the current insertion point will be hyphenated after you activate automatic hyphenation. Therefore, if you want to use hyphenation throughout your entire document, you must position the insertion point at the top of the document before turning on automatic hyphenation.

TURNING ON AUTOMATIC HYPHENATION

NOTE *To move before the codes at the beginning of the document, press Ctrl+Home+Home.*

To activate automatic hyphenation, follow these steps:

1. Move the insertion point to the location where you want to start using automatic hyphenation or to the beginning of the document (press Ctrl+Home).

2. Choose **L**ayout ➤ **Line** ➤ Hyph**e**nation, or press Shift+F9 E. You see this dialog box:

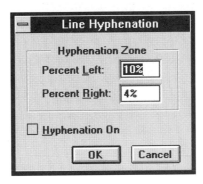

3. Mark the **H**yphenation On check box.

4. Choose OK or press ↵ to return to the document window.

As you type new text, or move the insertion point through existing text below the insertion point, WordPerfect checks for long words at the end of lines. When it encounters a line where the spacing could be improved by hyphenation, one of two things will occur:

◆ WordPerfect will hyphenate the word without asking for your help.

◆ In some circumstances (discussed later), WordPerfect will not be certain how to hyphenate the word; you'll hear a beep and be asked to choose a position for the hyphen.

 You might want to buy one of those handy little books containing lists of words that are divided and spelled correctly. Proper word division can be tricky.

WordPerfect uses the Speller dictionary to hyphenate words. If the word that needs to be hyphenated is in the dictionary, WordPerfect will hyphenate according to the dictionary. If WordPerfect cannot find the word, then it will either leave the word unhyphenated or ask for your help in hyphenating the word.

For example, if you type *supercalifragilisticexpialidocious* near the end of a line, WordPerfect won't find that word in its dictionary (because it's not a bona fide word). You'll hear a beep and see the Position Hyphen dialog box at the bottom of your screen:

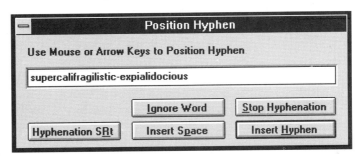

At this point, you have four options:

◆ To insert the hyphen where WordPerfect suggests (between the letters *c* and *e* in this example), press ⏎, or choose Insert **H**yphen. You can also choose Hyphenation S**R**t to insert a soft return or Insert S**p**ace to separate the word with a space.

◆ If the suggested hyphenation point is not acceptable, use the mouse or the ← or → key to reposition the hyphen, and then press ⏎ or choose Insert **H**yphen. You can only move the insertion point to a location that falls within the hyphenation zone.

◆ If you prefer that the word not be hyphenated at all, press Escape or choose **I**gnore Word. Ignore Word wraps the entire word to the next line and places the [Hyph Ign Word] code in front of the word; you will not be prompted for hyphenation again, even if you change the text.

◆ If you want to turn hyphenation off, you can choose **S**top Hyphenation. (This is useful when you are scrolling through a document or spell-checking, and do not *want* to be interrupted by hyphenation prompts.)

CHANGING AN AUTOMATIC HYPHEN

Let's suppose WordPerfect automatically hyphenates a word in your document. Then, while scrolling through the document, you find that you don't like the way WordPerfect hyphenated the word. If automatic hyphenation is still turned on, you can follow these steps to change the position of the hyphen:

1. Move the insertion point to the hyphen that WordPerfect placed in the word (at the end of the line).

2. Press the Delete key.

3. You'll hear a beep, and the Position Hyphen dialog box will appear.

Your choices are now the same as before: Use the mouse or the ← and → keys to move the hyphen to where you want it to break the word, then press ⏎, or select one of the other hyphenation options. Or, if you prefer that Word-Perfect not hyphenate the word, press the Escape key instead.

TURNING OFF AUTOMATIC HYPHENATION

TO DEACTIVATE AUTOMATIC HYPHENATION,

position the insertion point where you want to stop hyphenating, and choose Layout ➤ Line ➤ Hyphenation or press Shift+F9 E.

You can use Search and Replace (Chapter 9) to help locate and remove [Hyph On] codes.

When you turn on automatic hyphenation, WordPerfect inserts a [Hyph On] code at the current insertion point. All text beneath that position is subject to automatic hyphenation, either to the end of the document or to the place where WordPerfect finds a [Hyph Off] code.

Therefore, you have two choices for turning off automatic hyphenation:

◆ Remove the [Hyph On] code in Reveal Codes.

◆ Insert a [Hyph Off] code where you want to end automatic hyphenation, by positioning the insertion point and choosing **L**ayout ➤ Line ➤ Hyph**e**nation (or pressing Shift+F9 E), and unchecking the **H**yphenation On check box.

The first method deactivates automatic hyphenation below the insertion point but does not remove existing hyphens. However, as you add and change text, WordPerfect will no longer hyphenate words.

The second method keeps automatic hyphenation active above the insertion point but turns it off for text below. Use this method when you want WordPerfect to hyphenate some sections of your text but not others. You can have as many [Hyph On] and [Hyph Off] codes in your document as you please, and you can place any amount of text—from a few lines to many pages—between a [Hyph On] and [Hyph Off] code.

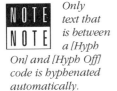

Only text that is between a [Hyph On] and [Hyph Off] code is hyphenated automatically.

HYPHENATING TEXT MANUALLY

TO ADD A NORMAL HYPHEN TO YOUR TEXT,

just type the hyphen.

You can hyphenate words without the aid of WordPerfect at any time. However, an understanding of several characters—hyphen characters, soft hyphens, and dashes—is helpful.

HYPHEN CHARACTERS

A *hyphen character* is really a normal hyphen, which you use to divide compound words, like *thirty-three,* and compound names, like *Livingston-Gladstone.* It is used to break a word at the end of a line only when it's convenient to do so.

Because the hyphen character is really just a normal hyphen, no special techniques are required to type it. For example, to type *Livingston-Gladstone,* you type *Livingston,* then type the hyphen, and then type *Gladstone,* just as on a typewriter. In Reveal Codes, however, the hyphen character appears between square brackets, like this: [–].

Another method of inserting a hyphen is by using the Hyphenation Codes section in the Insert Special Codes dialog box.

> *You can use Layout ➤ Line ➤ Special Codes to insert any of the hyphen characters discussed in this chapter.*

1. Use the mouse or ← and → keys to position the cursor where you want the hyphen.

2. Choose **Layout ➤ Line ➤ Special Codes.** You'll see the Insert Special Codes dialog box, shown in Figure 11.2.

3. Choose **Hyphen** [–], and choose **Insert** or press ↵.

SOFT HYPHENS

When you use automatic hyphenation, WordPerfect inserts *soft hyphens* in hyphenated words. They are called soft hyphens because they disappear

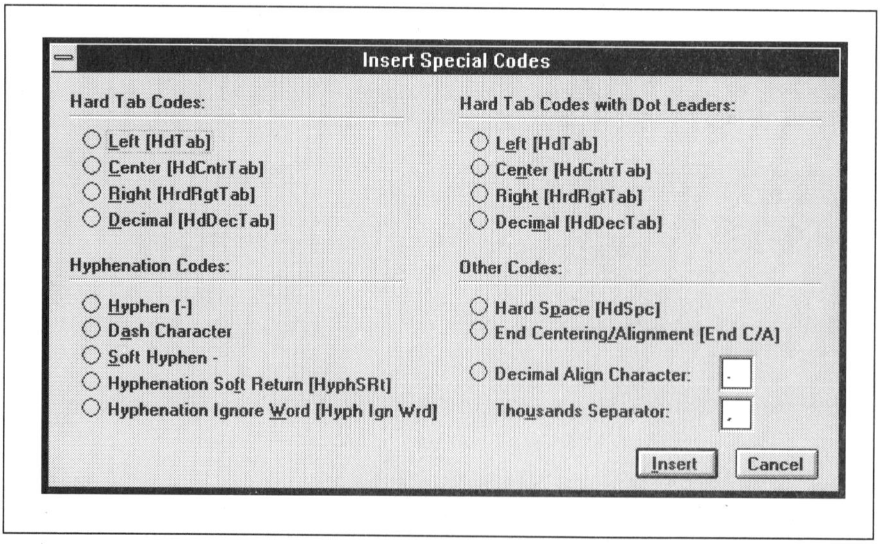

FIGURE 11.2:

The Insert Special Codes dialog box

automatically when they are no longer needed. For example, if the word *instructions* is too long to fit at the end of a line, WordPerfect inserts a soft hyphen in the word, breaking it over two lines. If later editing changes shorten the line enough to display *instructions* entirely on the line without hyphenating it, WordPerfect simply removes the soft hyphen.

You can insert a soft hyphen yourself to indicate where you want the word to be hyphenated, should it become necessary to do so. Follow these steps:

1. Make sure you are in Insert mode (if "Typeover" appears in the lower-left corner of the screen, press the Insert key).

2. Position the insertion point where you want to insert a soft hyphen in the word.

3. Choose **Layout** ➤ **Line** ➤ Special Codes ➤**S**oft Hyphen, or press Ctrl+Shift+ -. Note that the hyphen appears *only* in Reveal Codes.

Optionally, you can use the mouse or ← and → keys to move the cursor to the spot where you want the soft hyphen, and then choose Layout ➤ Line ➤ Special Codes. Choose Soft Hyphen and click on Insert or press ↵.

If WordPerfect can use the soft hyphen to better format the line, it will do so. If WordPerfect can't use the soft hyphen now, it will keep it in the word for possible use later. In Reveal Codes, you'll see the soft hyphen displayed as a highlighted (or bright) hyphen.

Dashes

Dashes are treated like any other normal character in automatic hyphenation.

A *dash* is a character that is sometimes used as a punctuation mark to connect two sentences. To type the dash, press Ctrl+− (hold down Ctrl and type the hyphen). In Reveal Codes, the dash appears as −, but is not shaded like other hyphenation codes and is not used in automatic hyphenation.

Breaking Words without Hyphens

An en dash (the width of an "n") is special-character 4,33. An em dash (the width of an "m") is special-character 4,34.

It's also possible to break words at the ends of lines without inserting hyphens. This is handy when you want to use a character other than a hyphen to break long words, such as a slash (/), an en dash, or an em dash. For example, if you create your own compound word, such as *Cattleya/Cymbidium/ Dendrobium,* and that word comes at the end of a line, you might want to have WordPerfect break it onto two lines at a slash, without inserting a hyphen, as was done in this paragraph.

The character used to tell WordPerfect where to break a word at the end of a line without hyphenating is a *hyphenation soft return*. This character is invisible in the document window and printed document, but it appears as [HyphSRt] in Reveal Codes.

Suppose you type a word like *Cattleya/Cymbidium/Dendrobium* in your document while automatic hyphenation is turned on. Then, WordPerfect inserts a hyphen, placing *Cattleya/-* on the first line and *Cymbidium/Dendrobium* on the next line. To delete the hyphen and break the words at the slash, follow these steps:

1. Move the insertion point to the hyphen.

2. Press the Delete key to delete the hyphen.

3. The Position Hyphen dialog box appears. Position the cursor where you want to hyphenate the word and select Hyphenation S**R**t.

DELETABLE SOFT RETURNS

There is another, rather odd, code that WordPerfect sometimes uses to break long words, called the *deletable soft return*. WordPerfect inserts this code automatically when you type long words into very narrow columns when automatic hyphenation is turned off. It is invisible in the document window, but appears as [DSRt] in Reveal Codes.

 *Multi-column layouts are covered in Chapter 20.*

This code tells WordPerfect to split the word without hyphenating it. You never type this code yourself and really don't need to be concerned with it until you start working with very narrow columns of text.

Table 11.1 summarizes the various characters that you can use to handle breaks at the ends of lines and the keystrokes to type each character (you can also select a character by using Layout ➤ Line ➤ Special Codes). The table also lists how each type of hyphen appears in Reveal Codes.

WHAT TO DO WHEN A WORD REFUSES TO BE HYPHENATED

IF A LONG WORD REFUSES TO BE HYPHENATED, check for and remove the [Hyph Ign Wrd] code in front of that word in Reveal Codes.

If you find that a word you expected to be hyphenated isn't, it may be that

HYPHEN	DESCRIPTION	KEYSTROKE	CODE
Hyphen character	Permanent hyphen that may be used to break two words at the end of a line	–	[–]
Soft hyphen	Temporary hyphen used to break a word when necessary (the kind used in automatic hyphenation)	Ctrl+Shift+–	– (highlighted)
Dash	A hard hyphen, never separated at the end of a line	Ctrl+–	–
Hyphenation soft return	Breaks words at a certain place without showing a hyphen	None	[HyphSRt]
Ignore Word	Wraps the entire word to the next line and prevents future hyphenation	None	[Hyph Ign Wrd]

TABLE 11.1:

A Summary of Hyphens and Dashes

New words that you add to the Speller dictionary without hyphen indicators may not be hyphenated—more on this later.

the word is marked for no hyphenation. This occurs when you select Ignore Word in response to WordPerfect's request to position the hyphen in a word that needs to be hyphenated.

If you are certain that a word needs to be hyphenated, follow these steps:

1. Move the insertion point to the first character in the word that refuses to be hyphenated.

2. In Reveal Codes, check to see whether the word is preceded by or contains the [Hyph Ign Wrd] code.

3. Move the highlight to the [Hyph Ign Wrd] code by using the mouse or arrow keys.

4. Press the Delete key.

5. At this point, WordPerfect may beep and display the Position Hyphen dialog box. Position the hyphen by using the mouse or the ← and → keys, and select the type of hyphenation you need.

You will not be able to hyphenate one-syllable words, like "big," "small," "the," and so on.

PREVENTING A WORD
FROM BEING HYPHENATED

If WordPerfect's automatic hyphenation hyphenates a word, and you decide that you don't want to hyphenate that particular word, follow these steps to prevent it:

1. Use the mouse or ← and → keys to position the insertion point at the word you don't want hyphenated.

2. Choose **L**ayout ➤ **L**ine ➤ Special C**o**des.

3. Choose Hyphenation Ignore **W**ord, then choose **I**nsert or press ↵.

In Reveal Codes, you'll see that the word begins with the [Hyph Ign Wrd] code. If you later change your mind and decide that you do want to hyphenate the word after all, remove the [Hyph Ign Wrd] code from the front of the word.

REFINING AUTOMATIC HYPHENATION

TO CUSTOMIZE SOME FEATURES OF HYPHENATION,

choose File ➤ Preferences ➤ Environment.

You'll find the features for customizing hyphenation in the Environment Settings dialog box that appears after you select File ➤ Preferences ➤ Environment (shown in Figure 11.3). In most cases, WordPerfect's automatic hyphenation will be sufficient for your needs, but there are several ways to refine and customize the automatic hyphenation techniques. These are optional, so if you are doing well with what you've learned so far, feel free to skip the rest of this chapter.

CHOOSING A HYPHENATION DICTIONARY

When automatic hyphenation is on and WordPerfect decides to hyphenate a word, it looks into either an internal or external hyphenation dictionary. The internal dictionary is built into WordPerfect and is always available. The external dictionary is much larger than the internal one and is stored on your hard disk.

The external dictionary provides many more hyphenation possibilities than the internal dictionary and will also prompt you less often during automatic

FIGURE 11.3:

*The Environment
Settings dialog box*

Environment Settings

Settings
- ☒ Auto Code Placement
- ☐ Confirm on Code Deletion
- ☒ Fast Save
- ☒ Allow Undo
- ☒ Format Retrieved Documents for Default Printer

Ruler
- ☐ Tabs Snap to Ruler Grid
- ☒ Show Ruler Guides
- ☐ Ruler Buttons on Top
- ☐ Automatic Ruler Display

Beep On
- ☐ Error
- ☒ Hyphenation
- ☐ Search Failure

Prompt for Hyphenation
- ○ Never
- ◉ When Required
- ○ Always

Menu
- ☒ Display Shortcut Keys
- ☐ Display Last Open Filenames

Hyphenation
- ◉ External
- ○ Internal

OK Cancel

hyphenation. If you've installed WordPerfect according to the usual procedure, you'll probably want to use the external dictionary. If your hard disk is
short of space, or you don't want to store the large hyphenation files on your
hard disk, you might prefer to use the smaller, internal dictionary.

You can choose either dictionary by following these steps:

1. Choose **File ➤ Preferences.**

2. Choose **Environment.** You'll see the Environment Settings dialog box.

3. Choose the E**x**ternal button in the Hyphenation area if you want to use
the external dictionary, or choose **I**nternal if you want to use the internal dictionary.

4. Choose OK or press ↵.

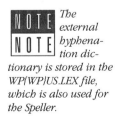

*The
external
hyphena-
tion dic-
tionary is stored in the
WP\WP\US.LEX file,
which is also used for
the Speller.*

Your choice will affect the current WordPerfect session, as well as all future
sessions. If, at some time in the future, you want to use a different dictionary,

just repeat the steps above.

If you want to designate a different directory for your hyphenation dictionary, choose File ➤ Preferences ➤ Location of Files, and enter a new directory name in the Main text box in the Thesaurus/Speller/Hyphenation area of the dialog box.

CHOOSING THE FREQUENCY OF HYPHENATION PROMPTS

During automatic hyphenation, WordPerfect usually asks you to position the hyphen only when it cannot find the current word in one of its dictionaries. This is the most convenient way to use automatic hyphenation, because WordPerfect will usually be able to hyphenate long words without your help.

There are actually three different settings to choose from for determining when WordPerfect asks you for help in positioning a hyphen:

Never: WordPerfect never prompts you to position the hyphen and always hyphenates according to the current hyphenation dictionary. If a word that needs to be hyphenated is not in the dictionary, it will be wrapped to the next line without hyphenation.

When Required: This is the normal setting; WordPerfect asks for help in positioning the insertion point only when it cannot find that word in the current dictionary.

Always: WordPerfect stops and asks you for help in positioning the insertion point every time it finds a word that needs to be hyphenated (this can be pretty tedious but gives you practice using the feature).

To choose one of the options listed above, follow these steps:

1. Choose **File** ➤ **Pre**ferences.

2. Choose **E**nvironment. You'll see the Environment Settings dialog box.

3. In the Prompt for Hyphenation area, choose the **N**ever, **W**hen Required (the usual technique), or **A**lways button to select the frequency.

4. Choose OK or press ↵ to return to your document.

Your choice will affect automatic hyphenation in the current document and all future documents as well (until you repeat the steps above and choose a different option).

DISABLING THE HYPHENATION BEEP

Normally, WordPerfect beeps when it needs help with hyphenating a word. If you would prefer that it not beep, follow these steps:

1. Choose **F**ile ➤ Pr**e**ferences ➤ **E**nvironment to bring up the Environment Settings dialog box.

2. In the Beep On area, uncheck the **H**yphenation checkbox to deactivate beeping.

3. Choose OK or press ⏎ to return to your document.

Beeping will be deactivated for the current session and all future sessions, until you recheck the Hyphenation box.

USING HYPHENATION ZONES

TO CHANGE THE HYPHENATION ZONES,

choose Layout ➤ Line ➤ Hyphenation (or press Shift+F9 E) and either decrease the zones (for more hyphens and tighter text) or increase them (for fewer hyphens and looser text).

When you use automatic hyphenation, WordPerfect decides whether or not to break a word at the end of a line by using *hyphenation zones.* You can think of a hyphenation zone as the place on a standard typewriter where the bell sounds to indicate that you are nearing the end of a line as you type. Of course, WordPerfect doesn't sound a bell because it hyphenates automatically.

WordPerfect's hyphenation zones are not visible on your screen. Word-Perfect uses two zones, one on each side of the right margin, to control hyphenation. Figure 11.4 shows how these zones would look if they were visible on your screen.

WordPerfect uses the following rules to decide whether or not to hyphenate a word (when automatic hyphenation is on, or when you insert your own hyphen or soft hyphen):

◆ If the last word on a line starts before the left edge of or within the hyphenation zone and extends past the right edge of the hyphenation zone, it will be hyphenated.

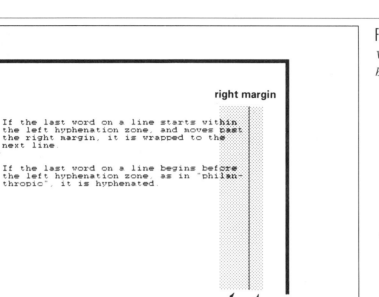

◆ If the last word on a line starts before the left edge of or within the hyphenation zone and is narrower than the zone, it will be wrapped to the next line without hyphenation.

Figure 11.4 is only for illustration. If you type the paragraphs shown, they will not necessarily be wrapped or hyphenated the way they are in the figure.

The sample paragraphs in Figure 11.4 illustrate this. At the end of the first line in the first paragraph, there is not enough room for the word *the* before the right margin. But the word is narrower than the hyphenation zones, so it is wrapped to the next line. In the second paragraph, the long word *philanthropic* is hyphenated, because it begins before the left hyphenation zone and would extend past the right hyphenation zone if it weren't hyphenated.

CHANGING THE HYPHENATION ZONES

The hyphenation zones are measured as percentages of the line length. This allows the hyphenation zone to adjust to the width of the line and simplifies matters when you start developing multicolumn documents with narrow columns of text.

By default, WordPerfect uses a left hyphenation zone of 10 percent and a right hyphenation zone of 4 percent. Hence, when you are printing on standard 8.5" × 11" paper, with 1-inch margins at the left and right and a standard print size of 10 characters to the inch, the length of each line is 6.5 inches. Therefore, a left hyphenation zone of 10 percent is 0.65 inches long, and a right hyphenation zone of 4 percent is about 0.26 inches long.

These preselected hyphenation zones provide a sort of happy medium between how tight the text is in justified paragraphs (or how much space is at the end of ragged-right lines) and the amount of hyphenation required. But you can change the sizes of the hyphenation zones to tighten the text further or loosen it a bit.

Basically, it works like this: Smaller hyphenation zones produce tighter text, but you'll pay the price of having to hyphenate more words. Larger hyphenation zones require less hyphenation but produce looser text.

The decision on whether to use wide or narrow hyphenation zones is entirely up to you. You can leave them as preset by WordPerfect or change them. If you decide to change them, remember that, like all formatting codes, new hyphenation measurements affect only text that is to the right of and below the insertion point.

To change the hyphenation zones, follow these steps:

> *When Word-Perfect prompts you to hyphenate a word and lets you move the hyphen by using the mouse or ← and →, the distance you're allowed to move it is equal to the width of the hyphenation zones.*

1. Move the insertion point to the location where you want new hyphenation zones to take effect (e.g., to the top of the document if you want the entire document to use the new hyphenation zones).

2. Choose **L**ayout ➤ **L**ine ➤ Hyph**e**nation (or press Shift+F9 E).

3. Type in new settings (in percentages) for either or both zones.

4. Choose OK or press ↵ to return to the document window.

If help with automatic or manual hyphenation is turned on (as described above), any new text that you type will trigger hyphen help, using the new hyphenation zones. If you scroll through existing text beneath the insertion point, WordPerfect will adjust the existing text to comply with the new hyphenation zone settings.

REMOVING NEW HYPHENATION ZONE SETTINGS

If you alter the hyphenation zone settings in your document and then change your mind and want to use the preset hyphenation zones, you'll need to remove the [HZone:] code from your document in Reveal Codes. If you then scroll through existing text beneath the current insertion point, WordPerfect will readjust the hyphenation to the original settings, again prompting you (when necessary) to help with any revised hyphenation (assuming that you've activated manual or automatic hyphenation help).

In the next chapter, you'll learn how to keep better track of your files and also how to search for missing ones. As you'll see, you can use these file management techniques to move, copy, rename, and delete files, as well as to create and change directories.

CHAPTER 12

Managing Your Files

As you know, WordPerfect stores your saved documents in files on-disk. As you create and save documents, your collection of files can become quite large. Managing that collection of files can be a job in itself. For example, you might need to delete old files to make room for new ones. Or you might need to look for a file that you know you saved, but whose name you have forgotten.

These kinds of jobs fall into the category of file management, which is what this chapter is all about. You'll find the various File Management options on the File menu.

You should already be familiar with basic DOS terminology; the terms *file, drive,* and *directory* are summarized below for quick review:

 If you are not already ready familiar with basic DOS concepts, you might want to refer to your DOS manual or "The ABC's of DOS 5," by Alan Miller, SYBEX, 1991.

Drive: short for *disk drive*, where all files are stored. The first floppy drive is named *A:*, the second (if any) is named *B:*. Hard drives are named *C:*, *D:*, and so forth. A disk drive is like a file cabinet.

Directory: (also called a subdirectory) a portion of a drive where numerous files are stored. For example, your WordPerfect for Windows program, and its various related files, may be stored in C:\WPWIN (the directory named WPWIN on hard-drive C). A directory is like a single drawer within a file cabinet.

File: a single document or single program. File names can be up to eight characters long and optionally can be followed by a period (dot) and an extension up to three characters long. A file is like a single manila folder in a file drawer.

Often, the drive and directory locations of a file are referred to as the *path*, since they tell the computer the route to take to find a particular file. For example, the path and file name C:\WPWIN\MYFILES\HANDOUT.WP tells the computer, "Go to drive C:, then to the directory named WPWIN, then to the directory below named MYFILES, and there you can locate a file named HANDOUT.WP."

HAND-OUT.WP is spoken as "handout dot wp."

SAVING DOCUMENTS

As discussed in chapters 1 and 2, it's important to remember that while you are creating or editing a document, your work is stored in RAM (random access memory) only. If you turn off the power, or a power failure turns it off for you, your current work will be lost. That's because your work is not "permanent" until you save a copy to the disk. You can save your work at any time by choosing File ➤ Save or by pressing the Save key (Shift+F3) and responding to the prompts that appear. In the sections that follow, I'll look at some additional options and techniques you can use while saving files.

ABOUT DRIVES, DIRECTORIES, AND FILE NAMES

The first time you save a file, you will see the Save As dialog box, shown in Figure 12.1. You have the full range of flexibility that Windows offers at this point to determine the name and location of your file.

Here's how it works:

*You can also choose a path to store the file on by double-clicking any drive or directory name (enclosed in brackets) in the Directories list. Double-click **parent directory** (..) if you want to move up a directory level.*

◆ If you enter only the file name (e.g., MYDOC.WP) in the Save As text box, the file is stored on the default drive and in the default directory for WordPerfect documents (which, in turn, are determined by the Location of Files options, covered in Chapter 13). This directory is the current directory and appears after Current Dir in the dialog box.

◆ If you enter a subdirectory name and file name (e.g., WPFILES\MY-DOC.WP), the file is stored in the named subdirectory of the current directory, with the file name you provided (assuming that subdirectory exists). For example, if the current directory is C:\WPWIN, and there is also a C:\WPWIN\WPFILES directory, the sample name will work. If there is no WPFILES directory beneath the current directory, the entry is rejected with the error message: "Invalid filename specified in WPFILE\MYDOC.WP."

◆ If you enter a complete drive and path, such as C:\WPWIN\WP-FILES\MYDOC.WP, the file is saved to that drive and directory only if they already exist. If C:\WPWIN\WPFILES (in this example) does not exist, WordPerfect returns the error message "Invalid filename specified in C:\WPWIN\WPFILE\MYDOC.WP."

When you press ↵ or click the Save button, the file will be saved and the Save As dialog box will disappear. Clicking Cancel or pressing Escape will close the dialog box and the file will not be saved. Once you save a file, WordPerfect remembers its name and location. The file's path will appear at the top of the document window while you are editing it. The next time you work with the file, you can save it by choosing File ➤ Save or by pressing Shift+F3. WordPerfect will save it with the same name and in the same location; the dialog box will not appear.

If you want to change the file's name or location, you must choose File ➤ Save As or press F3. This will display the Save As dialog box and allow you to save the file under a different name. You can save multiple drafts of the same document simply by changing the file name slightly with each save (e.g., DRAFT1.WP, DRAFT2.WP, DRAFT3.WP, and so forth).

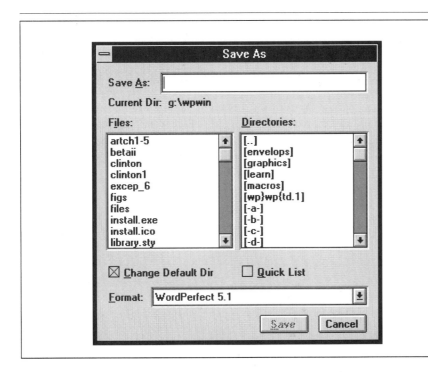

FIGURE 12.1:
The Save As dialog box

SAVING FILES IN DIFFERENT FORMATS

WordPerfect, by default, saves files in its own WordPerfect for Windows format. Sometimes you might want to save them in a different format, such as Word for Windows format, or WordStar format, or as a DOS text file, so that it can be edited with a different word processor. To do this, simply click the down arrow in the Format box in the Save As dialog box (or press Alt+F), and select the desired format from the pop-up list:

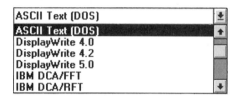

Once WordPerfect has saved or opened a document that is in a different format, all later saves will be made in the same format, until changed in the Save As dialog box. This means that if a Word for Windows document is opened, all saves will be made in Word for Windows format, *not* WordPerfect format. (See Chapter 25 for more information on DOS text files and interacting with other programs.)

CHANGING THE CURRENT DIRECTORY

When Change Default Dir is checked, WordPerfect remembers the current directory for all later file operations.

Rather than specify the entire path for the file, you can change the current directory by browsing through the Directories list box. The Files list box contains all the files currently in the directory. When Quick List is not checked, the directory list contains all the subdirectories underneath the current directory, the parent directory (listed as [..]), and all available drives. By clicking on a directory, the selected directory will be added to the path typed in the Save As text box, just as if you typed it yourself. By double-clicking on a directory, the selected directory becomes the current directory.

QUICK LISTS

Word-Perfect will remember your Quick List, even in different sessions of Word-Perfect.

WordPerfect also allows you to define a list of directories you frequently use for opening and saving files, called your Quick List. You can attach descriptive names to the directories for easy access and quick recognition. By checking Quick List in the Save As dialog box, the dialog box will grow, as shown in Figure 12.2, with the Quick List list replacing the directory list.

For example, if all your personal tax records for 1991 are stored in the directory C:\WPWIN\PERSONAL\TAX\YEAR91, you can assign the description *TAX 1991* to the path and add it to the Quick List. Now you don't have to remember long and complex directory paths to where your files are stored.

When you double-click on a name in the Quick List, the current directory will automatically change to the corresponding path. In the example above, if you double-click on *Tax 1991,* the current directory will automatically change to C:\WPWIN\PERSONAL\TAX\YEAR91.

To add, edit, or delete entries, click the Edit Quick List button in the Save As dialog box. More information on editing the Quick List can be found later in this chapter, in the section called "Using the File Manager."

TIMED AND ORIGINAL BACKUPS

As added protection against power outages and other mishaps, you can have WordPerfect automatically save your work at timed intervals. You can set the interval with the WordPerfect Preferences feature, covered in Chapter 13. You may also want to look into original document backup in that chapter, which lets you store both a new and a previously saved copy of a file on disk.

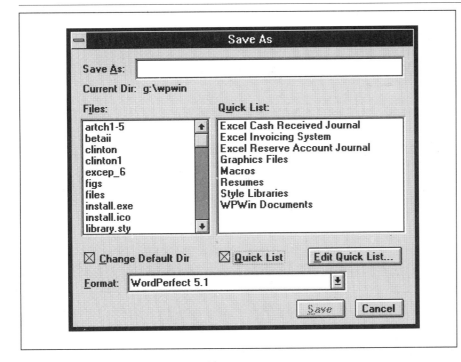

FIGURE 12.2:

The Save As dialog box, with Quick List checked

PASSWORD-PROTECTING FILES

> **TO ADD, CHANGE, OR DELETE A PASSWORD FOR A DOCUMENT,**
>
> choose File ➤ Password, then choose Set to add or change a password, or Remove to remove a password. Then save the file.

If you share a computer with others, and you want to prevent them from viewing, printing, or modifying a document, you can assign it a password of up to 23 characters. Only people who know the password will be able to gain access to the document.

Use the same password in all your documents to avoid confusion later.

There's one catch, though: If you forget the password, even *you* won't be able to access the document. So once you think up a password, write it down and store it in a safe place. Then follow these steps to use the password to "lock" your document:

1. Choose **F**ile ➤ Pass**w**ord. You'll see this dialog box:

2. In the Type Password for Document text box, type the password (each character will appear as a *), then choose **S**et or press ↵.

3. In the Re-Type Password to Confirm text box, type the password again (just to be sure you typed it correctly the first time), and choose **S**et or press ↵.

If you type the same password both times, WordPerfect will accept it. Otherwise, you'll have to start over at step 2. When you've successfully typed your password, you'll be returned to the document window.

Now you must save the file in the usual manner, with File ➤ Close (Ctrl+F4), File ➤ Exit (Alt+F4), File ➤ Save (Shift+F3), or File ➤ Save As (F3).

In the future, whenever you open that document, you'll first see this dialog box:

In the Enter Password text box, you must type the correct password (each character will appear as a *), and then press ↵. If you type the wrong password, you'll see the error message "File is password protected" and will need to start over and try to open the file again.

If you decide to change the password in the future, open the document and choose File ➤ Password. At the Password dialog box, follow the same steps outlined above for creating a password. Optionally, if you prefer to delete the password at that point so that anyone can open it, choose Remove in the same dialog box. Always remember to resave the document after changing or deleting the password.

Incidentally, password-protecting a file does not prevent other users from *deleting* that file. For that kind of protection, you should always keep an extra copy of your document on a floppy disk, in a safe place. Or, use the WordPerfect File Manager Change Attributes command or the DOS ATTRIB command, which offer techniques for protecting and hiding files. (Refer to your Windows manual or *Mastering Windows 3.0,* by Robert Cowart, SYBEX, 1990.)

NOTE **NOTE** *You must know the password before you can change or delete it, because you first must be able to open the document!*

OPENING DOCUMENTS

As you learned in Chapter 2, you can open a document in a new window by choosing File ➤ Open (F4) or retrieve a document into the current window by choosing File ➤ Retrieve. In either case, you will be asked to enter the name of the document you want to work with. If the file name you enter cannot be found, you'll see the error message "File not found." There are three possible reasons for this:

TIP *Word-Perfect for Windows and Word-Perfect 5.1 use the same file format, so no conversion is necessary when retrieving version 5.1 documents.*

◆ You misspelled the file name or forgot to add the extension (e.g., MYDOC instead of MYDOC.WP).

◆ You spelled the file name correctly, but the file is not in the current drive\directory or disk. Use the Directories list or Quick List to change the current directory, as described earlier in this chapter, or choose File ➤ File Manager to view and optionally change the current drive and directory, as discussed later in this chapter.

◆ You (or somebody else) deleted the file you're looking for.

Browsing through the Files list or using the File Manager feature, discussed later in this chapter, can help you determine which of the above is the problem.

COMBINING DOCUMENTS

If you already have a document on the screen, you can combine the on-screen document with another one by choosing File ➤ Retrieve. This inserts the retrieved file in the current document at the current insertion-point position. For example, if your insertion point is at the beginning of the on-screen document when you retrieve another document, the entire retrieved document will be placed at the beginning, before the existing text. Likewise, if your insertion point is in the middle of the on-screen document when you retrieve another document, you'll end up with the first part of your original document, all of the retrieved document, then the remainder of the original document.

When you attempt to retrieve a document into the current document, you will be prompted "Insert file into current document?" If you choose Yes or press ↵, the document you are retrieving will be retrieved and combined with the existing document at the current insertion-point position. If you choose No or press Escape, the file will not be retrieved, and you will be returned to the document window.

OPENING PASSWORD-PROTECTED FILES

If the file you are opening has been saved with a password, you'll see the File Password Protected dialog box. In the Enter Password text box, you must type the correct password (each character will appear as a *), and then press ↵. If you type the wrong password, you'll see the error message: "File is locked" and will need to start over and try to open the file again.

OPENING EARLIER VERSIONS AND NON-WORDPERFECT DOCUMENTS

If you open or retrieve a document that was created and saved with an earlier version of WordPerfect (such as 4.2 or 5.0) or another word processor (such as

Word for Windows or WordStar), WordPerfect displays the following dialog box:

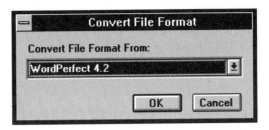

After Word-Perfect retrieves a file that is in a non-WordPerfect format, saves of that file will be in the same non-WordPerfect format.

WordPerfect will attempt to determine which file format the file was originally saved in and will display the format name in the pop-up list (click on the underlined down arrow). If the format is correct, choose OK or press ↵ to retrieve the document. Otherwise, scroll through the pop-up list and select the format which matches the file type. If WordPerfect does not recognize the format of the file, it will display "Unknown Format" in the pop-up list.

ORGANIZING YOUR FILES WITH DOCUMENT SUMMARIES

TO ADD A DOCUMENT SUMMARY TO THE CURRENT DOCUMENT,

choose Layout ➤ Document ➤ Summary, then fill in whatever fields you want. Choose OK or press ↵.

The file name assigned to a document when you save it is limited to the eight-character name, followed by the optional dot (.) and three-character extension. This really limits how descriptive the file name can be.

The Document Name and Document Type options are the most useful, because as you'll see later, they're readily visible when you browse through files with the File Manager.

One way to work around this restriction is to add a *summary* to your document. That way, if you lose track of which files are which, you can just view your document summaries along with the file names (you'll see how later in this chapter).

To create a document summary for a particular document, you must first open that document. Then follow these steps:

1. Choose **L**ayout ➤ **D**ocument ➤ **S**ummary (or press Ctrl+Shift+F9 and ↵). The Document Summary dialog box appears.

2. Choose any field you want (details provided below).

3. Type whatever you want for that field. Figure 12.3 shows a sample completed document summary.

4. Choose **OK** or press ↵ to return to editing your document.

The document summary is saved the next time you save the document.

USING EXTRACT TO BUILD DOCUMENT SUMMARIES

Once you're at the Document Summary screen, you can use the Extract button as a shortcut to retrieve information from the document itself or to repeat information from a previous document summary in the same editing session. When you click this button, you'll be prompted "Extract Document Summary Fields?" Choosing Yes fills in a few of the fields, as summarized in the next section.

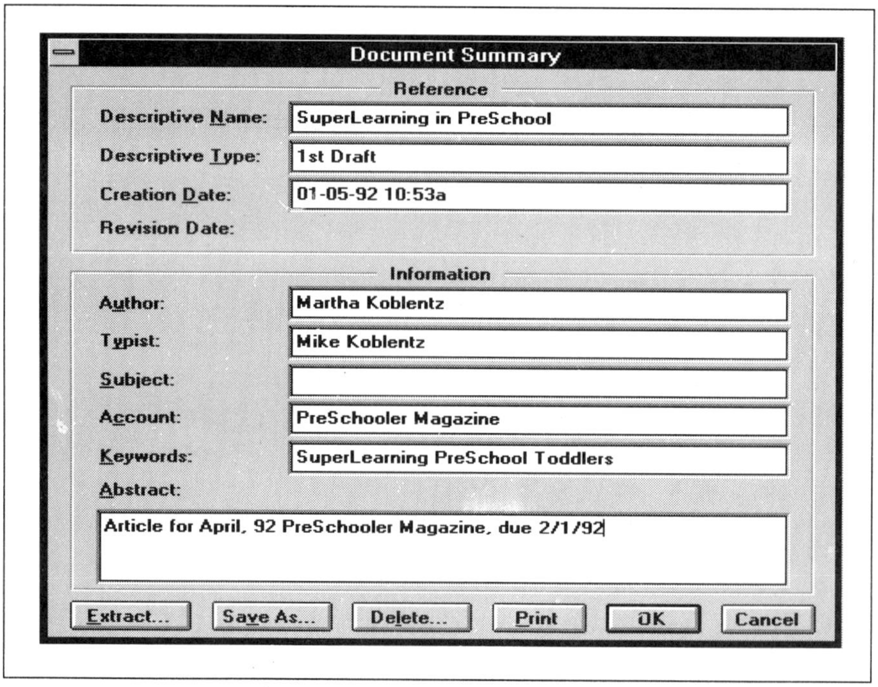

FIGURE 12.3:

A sample completed document summary

DOCUMENT SUMMARY CATEGORIES

Here is a brief description of each category that appears in the Document Summary dialog box:

NOTE *The creation and revision dates and times are based on the system clock, which you can set with the DATE and TIME commands in DOS or with the Date/Time option in the Windows Control Panel.*

Descriptive **N**ame	This option lets you add a longer name, up to 68 characters long, to override the eight-character file-name limit of DOS. You can search through these longer names by using the WordPerfect File Manager (discussed later).
Descriptive **T**ype	The document type can be 20 characters long, can contain whatever text or numbers you wish (e.g., *DRAFT, FINAL, TYPE-47*), and can also appear in the File Manager.
Creation **D**ate	This is the date and time the summary was created. It remains constant unless you choose this option and change the date or time.
Revision Date	This is the date and time the document was last changed and saved. You cannot change this entry.
Author	You can enter an author's name (up to 60 characters) for this entry. If you choose **E**xtract, the author entry from the previous document summary (if any) is entered.
T**y**pist	You can enter a typist's name (up to 60 characters) for this entry. Like the Author entry, if you choose **E**xtract, the typist entry from the previous document summary (if any) is entered .
Subject	Type a subject of your choosing. If your document contains the abbreviation *RE:*, with text to the right of these letters, choosing **E**xtract copies the first 39 characters to the right of RE: to the document summary.
Account	Type an account name of your choosing, if it will help you identify the document.

Keywords	Enter a list of any keywords (separated by spaces) that might later help you locate the document or a group of documents on the same subject. For example, you could later isolate all documents having the keyword *Saturn* when looking for documents on that topic.
Abstract	The abstract can contain up to 780 characters that summarize the contents of the document. Choosing **E**xtract copies the first 400 characters of the document to the document summary.

The document summary can also help you find a file later. For example, if you forget the file name of a document, you can look for it by document name, type, or keywords. You'll learn how a bit later in this chapter.

DELETING DOCUMENT SUMMARIES

If you want to delete a document summary (but not the file itself), choose Delete while in the Document Summary dialog box. Choose Yes when prompted "Delete Document Summary?"

PRINTING DOCUMENT SUMMARIES

If you want to print the document summary along with the rest of the document, follow these steps:

1. With the document on your screen, choose **F**ile ➤ **P**rint.

2. When the Print dialog box appears, choose the **M**ultiple Pages option button; if the document is not on your screen, choose the **D**ocument on Disk button.

3. Choose **P**rint.

4. When the Multiple Pages or Document on Disk dialog box appears, check the Document Summary box.

5. Choose **P**rint.

 *You can also view, print, and save document summaries with the WordPerfect File Manager.*

If you want to print a quick copy of the contents of the document summary while the Document Summary dialog box is visible, just choose Print.

If you want to save a copy of the document summary while the Document Summary dialog box is visible (perhaps to print it later), choose Save As, type a file name, and press ↵. Be aware that the file name you enter will contain *only* the document summary (stored as a regular document) and will not contain any text of the document whose summary you are saving. Therefore, be sure to use a unique file name if you decide to save only a copy of the document summary to disk.

CUSTOMIZING DOCUMENT SUMMARIES

Chapter 13 covers some ways in which you can customize document summaries, such as making the Document Summary dialog box appear automatically when you save a document, changing the characters used to retrieve a subject from RE:, and more.

ALL ABOUT THE WORDPERFECT FILE MANAGER

> **TO GET TO THE FILE MANAGER,**
>
> choose File ➤ File Manager.

You can also manage your files on the fly, as discussed at the end of this chapter.

The WordPerfect for Windows File Manager is a powerful application that lets you easily search through drives and directories for files. It also has options for managing those files, including copying, deleting, opening, viewing, and searching for files. All these features can make it much easier to manage your WordPerfect documents and other files as well.

To access the File Manager from WordPerfect,

◆ Choose **File** ➤ **F**ile Manager.

An example of the File Manager screen is shown in Figure 12.4.

ABOUT THE FILE MANAGER WINDOW

The File Manager window is a standard Windows application and is divided into four parts:

◆ The menu bar, at the top of the screen

◆ The Button Bar, which may be located at any edge of the screen.

◆ The File Manager workspace, in the middle of the screen

◆ The status bar, at the bottom of the screen

The most important part of the File Manager is the File Manager workspace. Here, directories can be listed and browsed, files can be viewed and printed, and searches and many other operations can be performed. There are four different types of File Manager windows that can appear in the File Manager workspace (each of which will be discussed at length in the following sections):

The File Manager also has its own help system (press F1 or Shift+F1), and Button Bar that you can view or change with the usual View ▶ Button Bar options described in Chapter 3.

◆ A *File List* window, which contains a list of files in a given directory, with their sizes and creation dates and times, (similar to the DIR command in DOS)

◆ A *Navigator* window, which lists only file names but allows much easier browsing through directories and files

◆ A *File Viewer* window, which displays the contents of the currently selected file in either a File List window or a Navigator window

◆ A *Quick List* window, which contains the current Quick List settings

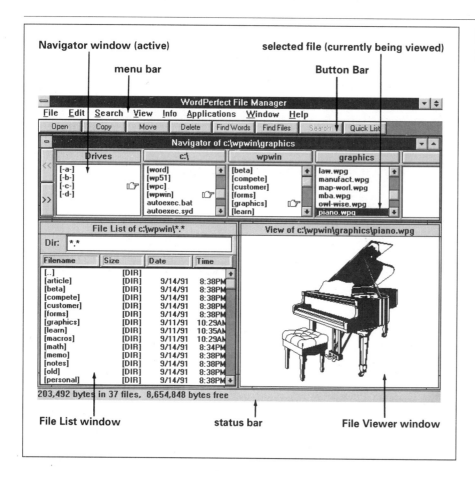

FIGURE 12.4:

The File Manager

You can manipulate the windows like all other windows, including minimizing them, maximizing them, resizing them or moving them. In addition, by choosing View ➤ Layouts, you can select predefined arrangements of windows. If you want to create your own custom layout, choose View ➤ Layouts ➤ Setup.

NAVIGATOR AND FILE LIST WINDOWS

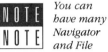

You can have many Navigator and File List windows visible at the same time.

Of the four types of File Manager windows, Navigator windows and File List windows are the most important. From these windows you can do most file operations, including viewing, retrieving documents into WordPerfect, copying, moving, and searching. Becoming familiar with these windows and how to manipulate them is the key to working efficiently in the File Manager.

Using the Navigator Window

One of the windows that appears in the File Manager is the Navigator window. If there is no Navigator window visible, choose View ➤ Navigator (or press Ctrl+N). See Figure 12.5 for a sample Navigator window.

The Navigator window lets you browse through drives and directories to view file names. The leftmost list box shows all the drives. Double-clicking a drive takes you to the root (uppermost) directory of that drive, and a pointing hand (shown at left) indicates the currently selected drive. All directories on that drive are listed in the next column, enclosed in square brackets.

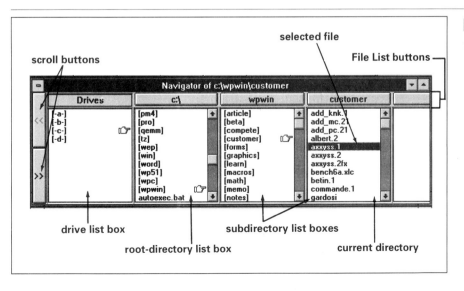

FIGURE 12.5:

The Navigator window

If you double-click any directory in the second column, the names of the subdirectories below that directory, if any, are enclosed in brackets in the next column over. If you want to go down yet another directory, just double-click the directory's name. You can do so as many times as necessary to get to whatever directory level you wish.

The name of the directory being viewed in each list box appears on a button at the top of the list box. Clicking this button brings up a File List window for the given directory.

As you go deeper in directory levels, more columns are added to the Navigator window. You can use the arrow buttons (marked << and >>) at the left of the dialog box, or the ← and → keys, to scroll across columns as needed.

Each column (except for the Drives column), also lists the names of files on the current directory. Unlike directory names, file names are not enclosed in brackets. Clicking any file name, in any Navigator column, displays the contents of the file in the View window (described under "Searching the File Viewer Window" later).

Using the File List Window

The File List window shows the contents of a single directory. If there is no File List window visible, choose View ➤ File List (or press Ctrl+L) or click the buttons on top of any Navigator column. See Figure 12.6 for a sample File List window.

A File List window can display the name and other useful items of information for each file, including:

A byte is equal to one character—the word "cat" uses three bytes.

◆ Size in bytes

◆ Creation date

◆ Creation time

◆ DOS file attributes

◆ Full path to the file

◆ Descriptive name, extracted from the file's document summary

◆ Descriptive type, also taken from its document summary

File and subdirectory names appear in the file list with subdirectories first, indicated by square brackets, followed by the names of all the files. Usually the file list shows the contents of an entire directory, with files and subdirectories listed in alphabetical order. The first item (unless you are viewing the root directory) is listed as [..], which refers to the parent directory.

The top of the File List window indicates which directory is currently being viewed. The Dir text box allows you to type another path name or file specifier to be viewed in the File List window. For example, typing ***.EXE** and pressing ↵ will display only those files in the current directory that end in .EXE.

Below the Dir text box are the column headings. Normally only the file name, file size, date, and time are displayed; however, changing and adding new columns headings can be done very easily. (This is discussed later in the section "Customizing the File List Window.")

You can change the subdirectory that is displayed by performing one of the following actions:

◆ Double-click on the subdirectory you want to change to.

◆ Choose **F**ile ➤ Chan**g**e Directory (or press Ctrl+G).

◆ Enter the new directory in the Dir text box.

Like the Navigator, if you click on a file, it will be selected, and its contents will appear in the View window.

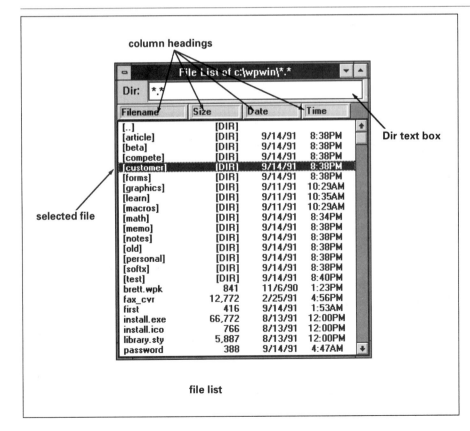

column headings

selected file

Dir text box

file list

FIGURE 12.6:

The File List window

Customizing the File List Window

The File Manager also allows you to customize File List windows. You can view only a portion of the files in a subdirectory or change the order in which the files appear. You can also add or delete columns in the file list or change their order. File lists also appear as the result of name or text searches, so they may display a mixture of files from different subdirectories—changing their order can be useful.

By default, all files are displayed in File List windows in alphabetical order. You can change the order by choosing View ➤ Options. The dialog box shown in Figure 12.7 appears.

Choosing among the Sort List By options decides the column by which the files are listed. Possible options are as follows:

NOTE NOTE *Changing the view options only applies to the current File List window.*

Full **P**ath	Sorts the files by full path name—for example, \WPWIN\LETTERS\ZZZZ.WP comes before \WPWIN\MEMOS\AAAA.LET.
Filename	Sorts the files by short file name
File E**x**tension	Orders the files by their three-character extension
File **S**ize	Smaller files appear before larger files

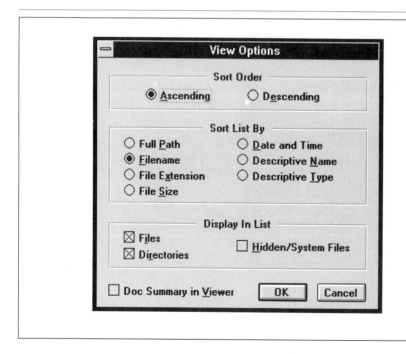

FIGURE 12.7:
The View Options dialog box

Date and Time	Files modified most recently appear last
Descriptive **N**ame	Orders files by the Descriptive Name field in their document summaries
Descriptive **T**ype	Orders files by the Descriptive Type field in their document summaries

Choosing Ascending or Descending for Sort Order chooses whether the list is displayed in forward or reverse order. Thus, if sorting by date and time, you could choose Descending to have the most recently edited files listed first.

You can also choose whether to view only files by unchecking Directories, view only directories by unchecking Files, or both by leaving both checked. Checking Hidden/System files chooses whether you want to see files with the hidden and system attributes. For more information on these attributes, consult your DOS manual.

You can also add, resize, reorder, or delete any of the columns displayed.

ACTION	PROCEDURE
Add a column	Click and hold your mouse in the empty portion of the column heading row. A pop-up menu will appear. Select the column you want to add from the menu.
Resize a column	Move the mouse pointer to the edge of a column heading. When the pointer changes to a double arrow, drag the edge to make the column heading smaller or larger.
Reorder columns	Drag the column heading left or right to a new position.
Delete a column	Drag the column heading out of the File List window.

CLOSING THE FILE LIST

You can close the File List window as you would any other; just double-click its Control-menu box, or press Alt+− and choose Close (or press Ctrl+F4).

FILE VIEWER WINDOW

The File Viewer (or simply Viewer) window allows you to quickly and easily view a file's contents, including the document summary, before taking action on it—for example, printing or opening it. A sample File Viewer window is shown in Figure 12.8.

Follow these steps to view a file:

*Only one
File Viewer
window
can be
visible at a time.*

1. Select the file whose contents you want to view in either a Navigator or File List window. You can do this by simply clicking on the file name.

2. If there is no File Viewer window visible, choose **View ➤ Viewer** (or press Ctrl+V).

3. You can scroll through the document by using the scroll bars.

Using the File Viewer does not open the document, but instead shows the contents. Note that for WordPerfect files, this is a single-spaced, text-only peek at a file's contents. The File Viewer window can view files in any of the following formats:

◆ WordPerfect 5.1 for Windows

◆ WordPerfect 5.1 for DOS

◆ WordPerfect 5.0

◆ WordPerfect 4.2

◆ ASCII (DOS text)

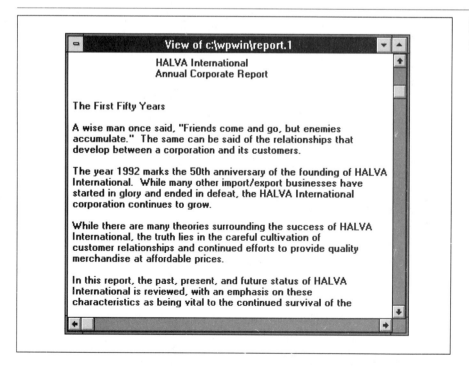

FIGURE 12.8:

The File Viewer window

◆ WordPerfect Graphics (.WPG)

◆ Windows 3.0 Bitmaps (.BMP)

◆ .TIF

◆ .EPS

QUICK LIST WINDOW

To make the Quick List window visible,

◆ Choose **View ➤ Q**uick List or press Ctrl+Q.

The purpose of the Quick List is discussed in the section on saving files, earlier in this chapter. A sample Quick List window is shown in Figure 12.9.

The Quick List window shows all directories currently in the Quick List. By double-clicking on any line, a File List window for that directory is automatically created. You can easily edit or create new Quick List entries by choosing View ➤ Edit Quick List. You will then see the dialog box shown in Figure 12.10.

The dialog box contains a list of the current Quick List names. Underneath the list is the directory of the current Quick List. By choosing Add, you can add a new entry to the Quick List. You will be prompted for the directory name and a descriptive name of the directory. For example, you might type C:\WPWIN\LETTERS\NEWS as the directory name and *Letters to the Editor* as the descriptive name. By choosing Edit in the dialog box, you can change the descriptive name *or* the directory name. By choosing Delete, you can delete

The Quick List is always saved and remains the same for all WordPerfect programs.

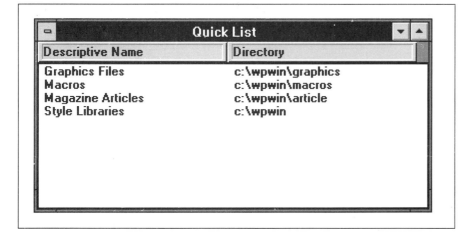

FIGURE 12.9:

The Quick List window

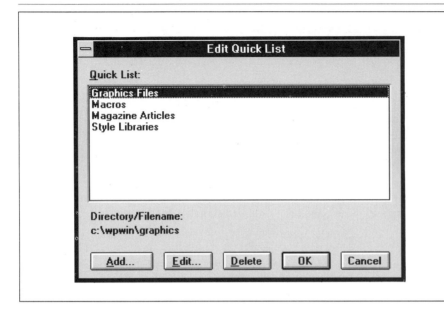

entries from the Quick List. Choose OK when you are finished editing the Quick List.

PRINTING THE CONTENTS OF A WINDOW

You can print the contents of a Navigator, File List, or Quick List window by choosing File ➤ Print Window. You will be given the option of printing the entire contents of the window or just the selected files.

USING THE FILE MANAGER

SELECTING FILES OR GROUPS OF FILES

For added convenience, the File Manager lets you mark a single file or group of files and manipulate them all at the same time. You select a file or group of files in either a Navigator window or a File List window. You can select or un-select files in a window as follows:

◆ To select a single file, click on it.

◆ To select all the files in a window, choose **E**dit ➤ **S**elect All (Ctrl+S).

If you continue to hold the mouse button down and drag the pointer to another Navigator or File List window, those files will be moved to that window automatically.

◆ To select a group of files, click on the first file in the group and drag the mouse pointer to the last file in the group.

◆ To unselect all the files in a window, choose **E**dit ➤ **U**nselect (Ctrl+U).

There are some special features available when selecting files with the mouse. If you hold down the Shift key while selecting a single file or group of files, the new files you selected, the files you selected previously, and all those in between will be selected. If you hold down the Ctrl key while selecting a single file or group of files, the new selection will be added to the previous selection.

Once you've marked a group of files, you can open, delete, move, rename, print, or copy them all in a single step, as discussed in the sections that follow.

OPENING DOCUMENTS FROM THE FILE MANAGER

Double-clicking on a file also opens it.

To use the File Manager to open files, select the file or group of files (up to three at a time) in either a File List or Navigator window. Do this in the normal way, by just clicking on each file's name. Then choose File ➤ Open or press ↵. If the selected file is a WordPerfect file, it will be loaded into WordPerfect. If the selected file is not a WordPerfect file but is *associated* with another application, the File Manager will load the file into that application (see "Associating Files with Applications" later in this chapter).

You can also retrieve a file into the document you are editing in WordPerfect. First select the file and then choose File ➤ Retrieve. WordPerfect prompts "Insert file into current document?" If you choose Yes, the file will be brought into the current document at the insertion point.

VIEWING A FILE'S DOCUMENT SUMMARY

If a WordPerfect file doesn't have a document summary, all the fields will be empty. All other documents, including ASCII text and graphic files, will not show the fields at the top.

If the document you are viewing in the File Viewer window has a document summary, you can easily view the summary. First choose View ➤ Options and check Doc Summary in Viewer. This will change the Viewer window as shown in Figure 12.11.

Notice that at the top of the File Viewer window, the Descriptive Name and Descriptive Type are now visible, with the rest of the text below. This information is extracted from the document summary. By clicking on the Summary button, the document text disappears and is replaced by the rest of the document summary, as shown in Figure 12.12. Clicking the Text button removes the document summary and restores the document text.

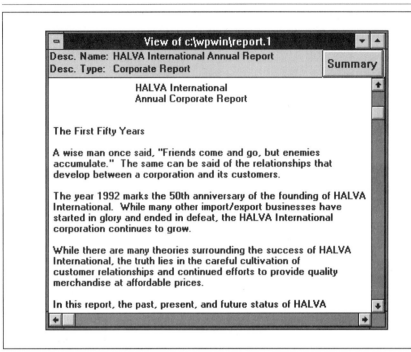

FIGURE 12.11:

A File Viewer window with summary (text visible)

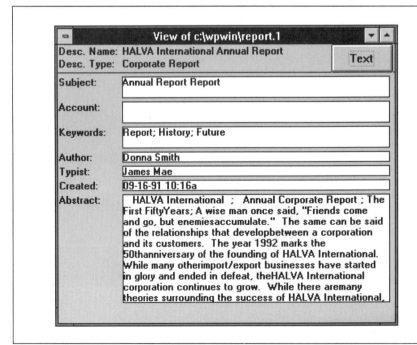

FIGURE 12.12:

A File Viewer window with summary (summary visible)

DELETING FILES

Once you delete a file, you cannot simply undelete it. You'll need to use the UNDELETE command in DOS 5 or some other undelete program to undelete an accidentally deleted file. But you must do so before saving any new files.

If a directory is cluttered with outdated drafts or other files you don't need anymore, using the File Manager is a great way to clean house. To delete a file from the disk, follow these steps:

1. In a File List or Navigator window, select the name of the file(s) you want to delete.

2. Choose **File** ➤ **Delete**. (You can also click the Delete button, press Ctrl+D, or press the Delete key).

3. If you've selected only a single file to delete, you'll be prompted for permission to delete the file. Choose **Delete** or press ↵ to delete the file, click Cancel or press Esc to abort the deletion.

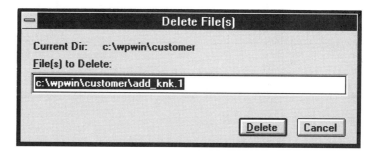

You can skip the delete confirmation dialog by choosing File ➤ Preferences ➤ Environment and un-checking Confirm File Delete Operations.

4. If you've selected a group of files, you'll see the following dialog box shown in Figure 12.13. The files that you have selected for deletion will appear in the dialog box. By choosing Delete **A**ll (or pressing ↵), all the files will be deleted. If you want to delete only some files, choose **D**elete for each file you want to delete and **S**kip for each file you want to keep. To chose not to delete any files, choose Cancel or press Esc.

MOVING OR RENAMING FILES

You can move or rename files selected in a Navigator or File List window by following these steps:

1. Select the name of the file(s) you want to delete.

2. Choose **File** ➤ **M**ove/Rename (Ctrl+R), or if you've selected files with the mouse, drag the files to another File List or Navigator window. The mouse pointer will change to the icon shown at left. (This procedure is called "drag and drop.")

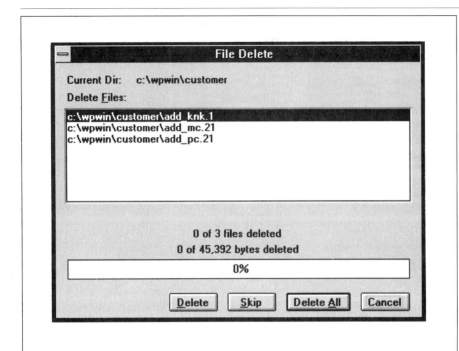

FIGURE 12.13:

The File Delete dialog box

 *If you've dragged the file to another File List or Navigator window, the directory of that window will appear in the **T**o text box.*

 If you've selected a group of files, you must move them to another drive or directory. You cannot move them to the same directory.

If you've selected only one file to be moved or renamed, you will see the Move/Rename File dialog box. In the To text box, type the new name for the file or type the directory you want to move the file to. You can use the button to the right to quickly choose the directory. Choose Move or press ↵ to move the file, or choose Cancel or press Esc to cancel the move.

If you've selected a group of files to be moved, you will see the Move/Rename files dialog box shown in Figure 12.14. In the To text box, type the new directory for the files. By choosing Move All (or pressing ↵), all the files will be moved to the chosen directory. If you want to move only certain files, choose Move for each file to move and Skip for each file you want to keep in the current directory. To not move any files, choose Cancel or press Esc.

Sometimes you might move files to a directory where there are already files with the same name. For example, you might move the file ADR_LIST.WP from C:\WPWIN to C:\WPWIN\OLD, and there might already be a file called ADR_LIST.WP in C:\WPWIN\OLD. With Replace Files with Same Name checked, the File Manager assumes that you want to replace it with a new copy. Because Confirm Replace is also checked, the File Manager automatically prompts "Replace C:\WPWIN\OLD\ADR_LIST.WP?" if the file already exists, just to make sure.

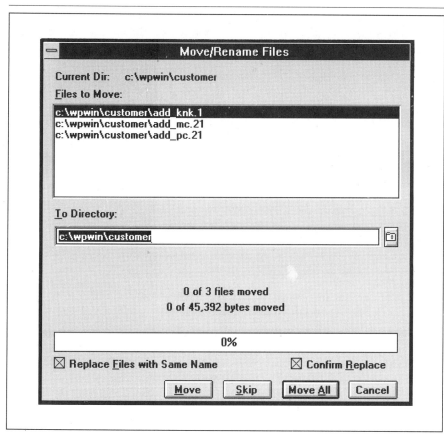

FIGURE 12.14:

The Move/Rename Files dialog box

You can uncheck Confirm Replace to tell the File Manager not to prompt you to replace files. You can also uncheck Replace Files with Same Name if you want to be sure that you never overwrite old files. The defaults for these check boxes can be changed by choosing File ➤ Preferences ➤ Environment (see the section on "Changing the File Manager Environment" in this chapter).

COPYING FILES

By using the Copy feature of the File Manager, you can make a duplicate of a selected file or group of files (with different names), copying them to another location on the disk or to another disk. Unlike moving a file, the original file remains in place when you use Copy; otherwise, the steps are nearly identical.

Follow these steps to copy the highlighted file:

1. In a File List or Navigator window, select the name of the file(s) you want to copy.

2. Choose **File ➤** Copy (or press Ctrl+C). (If you've made the selection with the mouse, you can hold down the Ctrl key and drag the files from this window to another File List or Navigator window.)

3. You'll be prompted with similar dialog boxes to confirm your copy, similar to Move/Rename. Select the destination the same way as for a Move/Rename operation.

 *If you mark a group of files, you must copy them to another drive or directory name, not to a file name.*

You can use the steps above to copy any set of files from your hard disk to any formatted disk in one of your floppy drives. It's a good idea to do so just in case you accidentally erase the copies from your hard disk or your hard disk crashes; that way, you'll still have the copies to work with.

If you want to copy files *from* a floppy disk to your hard disk, do the following:

1. Choose **View ➤** Navigator (or press Ctrl+N) to bring up a new Navigator window.

2. Double-click on [-a-] in the first list box to bring up a directory of drive A in the second file list.

3. Select the files you want to copy to your hard disk with the mouse.

4. Choose **File ➤** Copy (Ctrl+C) and specify **C:\WPWIN** (or whatever destination you choose) as the place to copy these files to.

CHANGING FILE ATTRIBUTES

You can use the File Manager to change the file attributes for any file. There are four different attributes that files can have:

♦ *Read-only attribute.* If a file has this attribute, it can only be read; it cannot be deleted or written to.

♦ *Archive attribute.* This attribute is set for any files that have been modified since they were last backed up. Many backup programs use this attribute.

♦ *Hidden attribute.* Setting this attribute makes a file invisible to most directory list.

♦ *System attribute.* This is a special attribute used by system programs. You probably won't need to worry about this one.

You can change the attributes for a single file or group of files by first selecting the file(s) in a File List or Navigator window, then choosing **File ➤** Change Attributes (Ctrl+A). You can then set or reset the attributes for each file.

PRINTING A DOCUMENT FROM THE FILE MANAGER

You can choose any document file or group of files to print from the File Manager screen. This operation is similar to choosing the Document on Disk option button in the Print dialog box, but you have the advantage of seeing all the file names at once and selecting the ones you want to print. The basic procedure is the following:

1. In a File List or Navigator window, select the name of each file you want to print.

2. Choose **File ➤ P**rint, or press Ctrl+P.

3. The File Manager will automatically load the files into the right application (usually WordPerfect) and print them. WordPerfect will print the document using whatever fonts in the current printer match the fonts selected in the document (but it will *not* change the font choices within the document).

Remember, you can select any file in the File Manager, but the File Manager can only print the files for which it understands the format (see "Associating Files with Applications" later in this chapter).

CREATING A NEW DIRECTORY

 If a Navigator or File List window is active, the File Manager assumes that you want to create a directory beneath the currently displayed one; otherwise, the current directory is used.

To create a new directory in the File Manager,

◆ choose **File ➤ C**reate Directory, press Ctrl+T, or press Insert.

You'll see this dialog box:

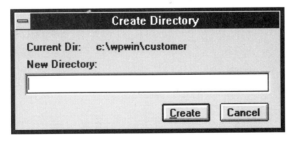

In the New Directory text box, type the name of the directory you want to create. Then choose Create or press ↵.

RUNNING APPLICATIONS FROM THE FILE MANAGER

If you've selected an application program (a program with a .COM or an .EXE extension) in a File List or Navigator window, you can run it by choosing File ➤ Run. The application will be started automatically, with the File Manager left running in the background. If you run the same file often from the File Manager, you can add it to the Applications Menu by choosing Applications ➤ Assign to Menu.

SEARCHING THE CONTENTS OF FILES

If you forget the name of a file but remember something about its name or contents (such as the addressee of a business letter), you can have Word-Perfect search the contents of documents for a specific word or phrase. This narrows down the file list considerably, and if your search is specific enough, it may pinpoint the exact file you're looking for.

To narrow the list in this way, choose from the Search menu in the File Manager. Each option is summarized below:

Find **W**ords	Searches for specific words in a set of files
Find **F**iles	Searches for files by name only
Advanced Find (Ctrl+F2)	Searches with a detailed range of criteria, including specific words, specific file names, and particular dates (it can even be set to search particular parts of the document summary)
Search Active Window (F2)	Searches for specific words in a File Viewer for a File List window
Search **N**ext (Shift+F2)	Searches for the next occurrence of text that was specified by a Search Active Window command
Search **P**revious (Alt+F2)	Searches for the previous occurrence of text that was specified by a Search Active Window command

Searching for Particular Files

NOTE *If you are searching an entire drive, you only need to make sure that the active Navigator or File List window displays any directory on that drive.*

If you've forgotten where you stored a certain file or only remember a portion of its name, you can use the File Manager's Find File feature to help you find it. The File Manager can search by name or portion of name, and can search a single directory, multiple directories, or even a whole drive. To activate the Find File feature, follow these steps:

1. Make sure that the active Navigator or File List window displays the directory to search (or the directory whose subdirectories you want to search).

2. Choose **S**earch ➤ Find **F**iles. You will see the following dialog box:

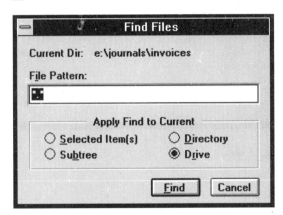

Find Files

Current Dir: e:\journals\invoices

F**i**le Pattern:

Apply Find to Current

○ **S**elected Item(s)   ○ **D**irectory
○ Su**b**tree   ◉ D**r**ive

[**F**ind]   [**C**ancel]

3. In the F**i**le Pattern text box, type the name or partial name of the file you want to search for. You can use standard DOS file-name wildcards, so to search for all files with the .DOC extension, you would type *.DOC.

4. If you are searching this directory and all subdirectories, check S**u**btree. If you are searching an entire drive, check D**r**ive.

5. Choose **F**ind or press ↵.

NOTE *If the File Manager is unable to find the words in the files specified, it displays "No files were found which meet the specified search criteria."*

The File Manager will begin searching files that match the pattern that you specified. When the search is complete, the File Manager will display a new File List window, titled "Search results of …," which contains files that matched your file pattern. You can perform all actions in this window that you can in any other File List window, including opening, printing, deleting, moving, and copying files.

Searching for Words in Files

To search the contents of files for particular words, follow these steps:

1. Make sure that the active Navigator or File List window displays the directory that contains the files you want to search.

2. Choose **S**earch ➤ Find **W**ords in the File Manager. You'll see the following dialog box:

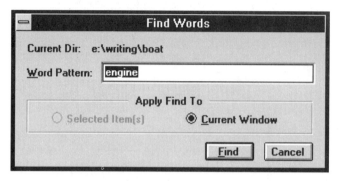

3. In the **W**ord Pattern text box, type the text (up to 39 characters) you want to search for.

4. If you want to search all the files listed in the window, leave the option button **C**urrent Window chosen. If you want to search only files selected in the Navigator or File List window, choose **S**elected Items.

5. Choose **F**ind or press ↵.

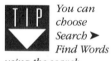
You can choose Search ➤ Find Words using the search results, perhaps with more specific word patterns, to narrow the list even further.

The File Manager will begin searching files for the words that you specified. When the search is complete, the File Manager will display a new File List window titled "Search results of ...," which contains files that have the words specified.

Entering the Word Pattern

When entering your word pattern, you can type letters in uppercase, lowercase, or any mixture of the two—all are treated the same. So, for example, typing *PRIMordial* is the same as typing *Primordial* or *primordial*. If your search text consists of only one word, just type it in at the "Word Pattern" text box and press ↵. To search for multiple words, you must enclose them in quotation marks; for example,

"Cream of Primordial Soup"

The ? and * wildcards can help you find various word combinations. As in DOS, the ? represents a single character or letter in a word, and the * represents multiple letters. So if in the Word Pattern text box you enter

T?P*

The resulting window will show you only files containing words starting with *T,* with any second character, with *P* as the third letter, and ending in any combination of characters. This includes words such as *tap, type,* and *topographical.* The names of all documents that contain any of these words will be displayed in a "Search Results" File List window after the search is over.

You can also impose more complex, specific conditions on your search from the Word pattern text box. These conditions are determined by the following *logical operators:*

OPERATOR	SYMBOL
AND	; (or space)
OR	, (comma)
NOT	- (hyphen)

For example, to locate documents containing both the words *computer* and *debt,* you can specify either of the following word patterns:

computer;debt

or

computer debt

Similarly, to find documents with both *computer* and *more productive,* you can use

computer "more productive"

or

computer;"more productive"

To find documents that contain either *New York* or *New Jersey,* you can use

"New York","New Jersey"

And to find documents that contain *New York,* but not *New Jersey,* you can use

"New York"-"New Jersey"

If you need to find documents containing a hyphen (-), place the phrase containing the hyphen in quotation marks, as in "two-bit."

Advanced File Searches

The Find Words and Find Files search options are well suited to simple searches. However, you need the Advanced Find option if you want to do more detailed searches, which might combine Find Words and Find Files searches or involve the document summary or specific document creation dates. When you choose Search ➤ Advanced Find (or press Ctrl+F2), you will see the dialog box in Figure 12.15.

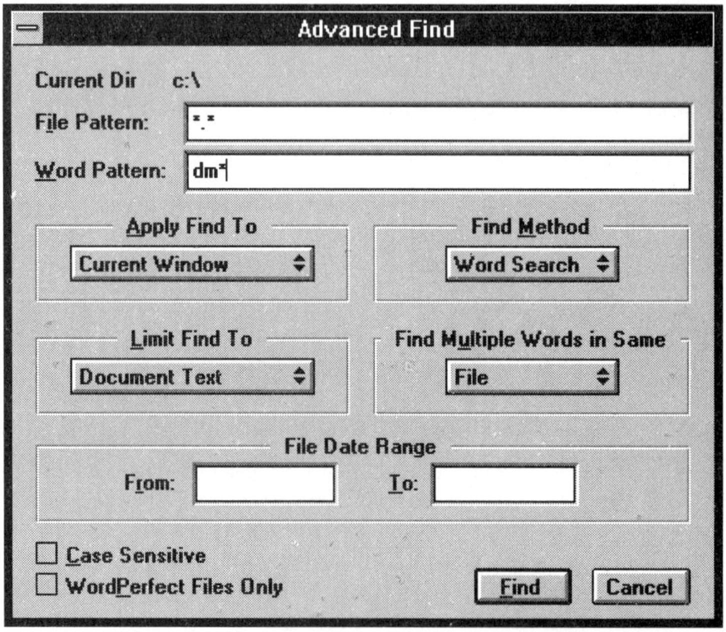

FIGURE 12.15:
The Advanced Find dialog box

The available options and search criteria and their meanings are listed below:

File Pattern	This is the same as **S**earch ➤ Find **F**iles. Use standard DOS file-name wildcards.
Word Pattern	This is the same as **S**earch ➤ Find **W**ords. Use the same criteria as discussed in "Entering a Word Pattern."
Apply Find To	This pop-up list allows you to narrow your search to particular parts of the drive. You can choose to search the selected items, the contents of the current window, the current directory, the current directory and all its subdirectories, or the entire drive.
Find **M**ethod	Choose either **W**ord Search or **S**tring Search. In a string search, a word pattern can be part of a larger word. For example, the pattern *doc* would match *indoctrinate* in a string search, but not in a word search.
Limit Find To	This specifies the portion of the document in which text is searched for. Document Te**x**t means the entire document. You can speed up the search by specifying **F**irst Page, which limits the search to the first page of each document. Document **S**ummary limits the search to the whole document summary. You can even limit the search to particular fields of the document summary, such as the Abstract or Keyword field.
Find Multiple Words in Same	If you've specified more than one word in the **W**ord Pattern text box, you can make sure that the words lie in the same file, page, section, paragraph, sentence, or line.
File Date Range	You can limit the search to files that were created after a certain date (by entering a date in the F**r**om field), before a certain date (by entering a date in the **T**o field), or between two dates (by entering dates in both fields).
Case Sensitive	Checking this box makes searches sensitive to the case of the word pattern. A case-sensitive search means that searching for *Europe* will match only *Europe* and not *EUROPE* or *europe*.

WordPerfect Files Only	Checking this box limits searches to only WordPerfect files. This can save a lot of time if you have a mixture of WordPerfect files and other files in a directory.

Using the criteria listed above is ideal for speeding up searches and limiting them to specific details. For example, limiting the search to the document summary or first page is much faster than searching an entire document.

To begin the search, choose Find or press ↵ when all criteria have been entered. As when you use the Find Words and Find Files options, a "Find Results" File List window will be created that contains all the files that match your search criteria. You can use this file list to continue your search for files, or perform any other File Manager action.

Searching the File Viewer Window

Searching a File Viewer window lets you search for text in a long document, without having to load the document into WordPerfect. To start the search, follow these steps:

1. In a File List or Navigator window, choose on the file you want to search.

2. Click on the File Viewer window to make it active. If there is no File Viewer window, choose **V**iew ➤**V**iewer (or press Ctrl+V).

3. Choose **S**earch ➤ **S**earch Active Window (F2) and the following dialog box will appear:

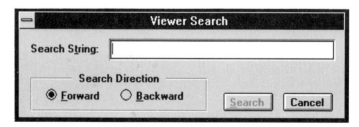

4. Type the text you want to search for.

5. If you want to search backward from a previous search, choose **B**ackward.

6. Choose **S**earch or press ↵ to begin the search.

If the search is successful, the matching pattern is made visible and selected in the File Viewer window. If there is no match, the File Manager reports "Search String not found."

You can easily repeat your last search by choosing Search ➤ Search Next (Shift+F2). You can repeat your search backward by choosing Search ➤ Search Previous (Alt+F2).

Searching the File List Window

The File Manager can also search the contents of a File List window. It only searches for an exact string within the file list. To use wildcards or search subdirectories, use Find Files or Advanced Find. To search a file list, follow the same steps as for searching a File Viewer window, outlined in the previous section.

GETTING INFORMATION ABOUT YOUR SYSTEM

The File Manager Info pull-down menu allows you to find information about various parts of your system.

OPTION	INFORMATION
System Information	Displays information about DOS version, number of drives, CPU type, and parallel printer and serial ports
Windows Info	Displays Windows-specific information, including screen type, mouse used, memory available, and Windows operating mode
Printer Info	Displays information on installed printers and what ports they are attached to
Disk Info	Displays the name and type (fixed, floppy, or network) of each disk installed; also displays drive size and available space

Disk Info is especially useful, because it can tell you whether you have enough space on a floppy disk to copy files onto it.

If you want a printed report of all the information on this menu, choose Info ➤ Print Info Report. This allows you to send a report on system information to either the printer or a separate text file.

ASSOCIATING FILES WITH APPLICATIONS

The File Manager automatically makes associations between applications and files. It knows what file types are created by different applications. That's why when you open, retrieve, or print a WordPerfect file, the File Manager knows to load the document into WordPerfect. You can also assign your own associations so that, for example, when you open an Excel spreadsheet, the document is automatically loaded into Microsoft Excel. There are two types of assocations:

◆ *Primary associations.* First, the File Manager looks at the contents of the file to determine which application is associated with it. WordPerfect automatically does this with WordPerfect and other word processor files.

◆ *Secondary Association.* Next, the File Manager looks at the file's extension to determine which application is associated with it. For example, if you open a .bmp file (Windows Bitmap), the File Manager runs the Windows Paintbrush application.

Application associations make using the File Manager much easier and more transparent. You don't have to specify the application to run every time you open or print a file.

The File Manager already has many application associations built in, but it is easy to change existing associations or add new ones. To do so, choose File ➤ Preferences ➤ Associate, and the dialog box shown in Figure 12.16 will appear:

If a file does not have an associated application, the File Manager won't understand how to open, retrieve, or print it.

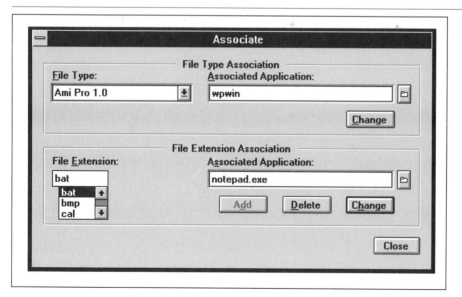

FIGURE 12.16:

The Associate dialog box

For a primary association, you change which application is run for file formats that the File Manager already knows. To change an associated application, follow these steps:

1. Choose the file type from the **F**ile Type pop-up list.

2. Type a new application name in the **A**ssociated Application text box to the right. You can click the Directory icon to browse for the application.

3. Choose **C**hange to change the primary assocation.

A secondary association associates file extensions with an application. You can either change an existing file extension or add a new one. To change or add a secondary association, do the following:

1. To change an association, choose the file extension from the File **E**xtension pop-up list. To add a new association, type the new file extension in the File **E**xtension text box.

2. Type a new application name in the **A**ssociated Application text box to the right. You can also browse for the application by clicking on the Directory icon.

3. Choose C**h**ange to change the secondary association.

Once you are finished making modifications to associations, choose Close.

GAINING QUICK ACCESS TO APPLICATIONS

The Applications menu in the File Manager gives quick access to WordPerfect applications, including

◆ WordPerfect

◆ WordPerfect Speller

◆ WordPerfect Thesaurus

◆ WordPerfect Macro Facility

To run one of these applications, just choose it from the Applications menu.

You can also add your own applications to the Applications menu. To do so, choose Applications ➤ Assign to Menu. You will then see the dialog box shown in Figure 12.17.

You can do any of the following:

ACTION	PROCEDURE
Add an application	Type a new Descriptive **N**ame (which will appear on the **A**pplications menu and on the Command **L**ine to run the application). Then choose **A**dd to add it to the application list.
Delete an application	Select the application to delete and choose **D**elete. Choose **Y**es when asked whether you really want to delete it.
Change an application	Select the application to change and make changes to the Descriptive **N**ame and Command **L**ine. Then choose **C**hange.

When you are finished making changes to the Application menu, choose OK. If you don't want to save the changes you just made, choose Cancel.

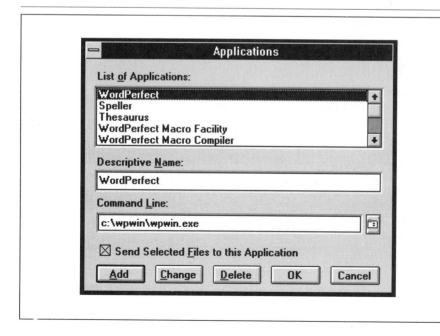

FIGURE 12.17:
The Application dialog box

CHANGING THE FILE MANAGER ENVIRONMENT

The File Manager can be customized to suit personal taste or to increase productivity. Like WordPerfect itself, the File Manager has its own Button Bar. To add or remove the Button Bar, choose View ➤ Button Bar. Just like in WordPerfect, the File Manager's Button Bar can be completely customized. Just choose View ➤ Button Bar Setup (for more information on customizing the Button Bar, refer to Chapter 3).

Preferences specific to the File Manager can be selected by choosing File ➤ Preferences ➤ Environment. You will see the Environment dialog box shown in Figure 12.18.

The Environment settings and their meanings are as follows:

Not confirming file delete operations can easily lead to accidental erasure of files on the disk.

SETTING	MEANING
Confirm **F**ile Copy/Move Operations	The File Manager will prompt you to confirm any file move or copy operations.
Confirm File **D**elete Operations	The File Manager will ask you for confirmation before deleting any file.
Replace Files with Same **N**ame	The File Manager will allow move operations to overwrite other files.

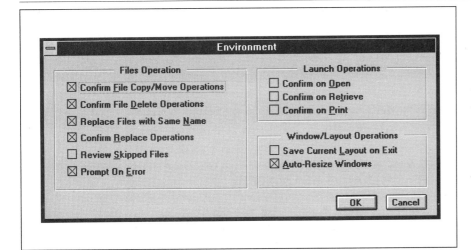

FIGURE 12.18:
The Environment dialog box allows you to change the default settings of the File Manager.

SETTING	MEANING
Confirm **R**eplace Operations	If you check this option and Replace Files with Same **N**ame, the File Manager will prompt you before overwriting files during file moves.
Review **S**kipped Files	If you move, copy, or delete multiple files, and you choose to skip certain files, you will be allowed another chance to perform the operation.
Prompt on **E**rror	The File Manager will display a dialog box every time an error occurs.
Confirm on **O**pen	All open operations must be confirmed.
Confirm on Re**t**rieve	All retrieve operations must be confirmed.
Confirm on **P**rint	All print operations must be confirmed.
Save Current **L**ayout on Exit	The current arrangement of windows will be retained every time you run the File Manager.
Auto-Resize Windows	When the File Manager is resized, windows will grow or shrink to accommodate the change.

You can also change the fonts which are used for any and all windows on the screen. By choosing View ➤ Font (or pressing F9), you can change the fonts for the current window, all windows of a certain type, or *all* windows. This can be useful if you want to see more information in a window (particularly a File Viewer window), or you want to distinguish windows of different types at a glance.

CLOSING THE FILE MANAGER

When you finished using the File Manager, just choose File ➤ Exit from its menu bar (or press Alt+F4). Any windows you open within the File Manager will be closed, and you'll be returned to WordPerfect.

USING THE FILE MANAGER
AS A WINDOWS STANDALONE APPLICATION

File Manager

The File Manager is a completely stand-alone application; it doesn't have to be run at the same time as WordPerfect. It can be launched from the Windows Program Manager by double-clicking on its icon, shown at left, which is in the WordPerfect group window.

MANAGING FILES ON THE FLY

As an alternative to using the File Manager to manage files, you can use options that are readily available in the Open File and Retrieve File dialog boxes. These are handy for managing files on the fly. Follow these steps:

1. Choose either **File ➤ O**pen or **File ➤ R**etrieve to get to the appropriate dialog box.

2. Optionally, choose a drive or directory from the Directories list or Quick List by double-clicking.

3. Optionally, highlight the name of any file in the Files list (by using the arrow keys or clicking once) that you want to copy, move, rename, or delete.

4. For a quick look at the contents of the currently selected file, choose **V**iew. You can repeat steps 2 and 3, as necessary, to view the contents of another file if you wish, until you find the file you want.

5. Open the Op**t**ions pop-up list, and choose one of the options.

6. A dialog box for the option you've chosen will appear. Fill in the dialog box and save your choices as described in the sections that follow.

DELETING FILES

Once you delete a file or group of files, the only way to recover them is to use an un- delete program.

If you chose Delete in step 5, the name of the selected file (if any) appears in the Delete File dialog box. You can type in a new file name, if you wish, replacing the current one. You can also use the DOS wildcard characters ? and * to identify a group of files. Then choose Delete to delete the file(s), or choose Cancel if you change your mind.

COPYING FILES

If you chose Copy in step 5, you'll be taken to the Copy File dialog box. If you chose a file from the Files list, its name appears in both the From and To text boxes. Modify the drive\directory\filename entry in the To text box to indicate the destination for the copied file. Or, fill in both the From and To text boxes to indicate the file you want to copy and its destination. (Be aware, however, that wildcards are not supported by this feature.) Choose Copy to copy the file, or choose Cancel to leave the dialog box without copying the file.

MOVING AND RENAMING FILES

If you chose Move/Rename in step 5, you'll be taken to the Move/Rename dialog box. The name of the currently selected file (if any) appears in the From and To text boxes. If you want to move the file, change the drive\directory portion of the name in the To text box. If you want to rename the file, just change the file name. Choose Move to move the file, or choose Cancel if you change your mind.

You can change both the To and From text boxes to move or rename any single file, not just the selected file. You cannot, however, use wildcards to move or rename a group of files.

FINDING FILES

If you chose Find in step 5, you'll be taken to the Find dialog box, where you can search for a file based on its name or its contents. The names of the current drive and directory appear near the top of the dialog box.

Searching by File Name

To find a file based on its file name, choose Find Files and enter a name or pattern of file names to search for. You can use the standard DOS wildcard characters: ? for any single character or * for any group of characters. For ex- ample, specifying *.WP lists all files that have the extension .WP.

You can also use the option buttons to determine where you want to search:

Directory	Searches the current directory only
Subtree	Searches the current directory and all subdirectories beneath the current directory
D**r**ive	Searches all the directories on the current drive

Choose Find to begin the search.

Searching by Contents

To search for a file based on a word or phrase within the file, choose Find Words. Enter a word or word pattern to indicate the words or phrase to search for. You can also opt to search the current directory, subdirectories, or entire drive. Finally, you can also choose whether to search WordPerfect files (documents) only, or through all files, using the check box. Choose Find when you are ready to begin the search.

Using the Search Results

Regardless of whether you search by file name or contents, the Search Results list box will display the names of all files that match your search criteria. You can then scroll through the list with the arrow keys or scroll bar.

You can then highlight any file name and choose View to view its contents, or choose Options to move, copy, rename, or delete the file. Or, choose Open or Retrieve to open the file for editing.

This chapter has shown you the many ways to manage files stored on-disk. As you've seen, your options are nearly limitless, and you will do much of your basic file management with the File Manager.

Chapter 13 covers some optional techniques that let you customize many elements of the WordPerfect package to suit your own tastes and work habits.

CHAPTER 13

Customizing WordPerfect

This chapter describes WordPerfect's many *customization* features. With these features, you are free to make changes to almost any aspect of WordPerfect, tailoring it to your tastes, work habits, and office requirements.

Everything in this chapter is optional, and your eventual use of it, if at all, is entirely up to you. You might just want to glance through the chapter at first to see what customization options are available. Then, should you decide to customize a feature, you can return to this chapter to see how to do so.

USING THE PREFERENCES OPTIONS

TO GET TO THE MENUS FOR CUSTOMIZING WORDPERFECT,

choose File ➤ Preferences.

WordPerfect's customization features are on the Preferences submenu, which is on the File pull-down menu (choose File ➤ Preferences, or press Ctrl+ Shift+F1). Each option leads to a dialog box that, in turn, lets you customize certain features of WordPerfect, as discussed in the sections that follow.

Any changes you make to WordPerfect by using the Preferences menu will take effect as soon as you return to the current document window. Furthermore, your changes will affect not only the current WordPerfect session but all future sessions as well. Of course, no setting change is irreversible; you can always go back and make a different choice or restore the original setting.

Moreover, for many features, you can temporarily override the Preferences options, for just the current document or the current WordPerfect session. For example, you can alter the initial settings for the printer (described later) to handle the majority of situations, then use the Print options (accessed by choosing File ➤ Print or pressing F5) to change the settings for just the current document. This way, you can have your cake and eat it too.

ORGANIZING YOUR FILES

TO CHANGE THE DEFAULT LOCATIONS OF VARIOUS TYPES OF WORDPERFECT FILES,

choose File ➤ Preferences ➤ Location of Files.

As you may know, DOS lets you divide your hard disk into separate drives, directories, and subdirectories. In a sense, each directory on a drive is its own file cabinet and contains its own set of files. Storing files in separate directories helps keep information organized and prevents individual directories from becoming cluttered with too many file names.

With the Location of Files options, you can specify a directory location for each of several categories of WordPerfect files so that WordPerfect always knows where to store files as they are created and where to look for them when they are needed.

To display and work with the Location of Files options, follow these steps:

1. Choose File ➤ Preferences.

2. Choose Location of Files. The Location of Files dialog box appears, shown in Figure 13.1. Note that WordPerfect inserted C:\WPWIN (or the name of your own WordPerfect directory) as the location for most files when you installed the program.

3. Choose the category of files whose directory location you want to set.

Actually, the Styles Filename text box expects you to enter a file name, but all other entries must be directory locations.

4. Type the drive or directory location for that category of files, using proper DOS conventions (e.g., C:\WPWIN\DOCS), then press ↵. (For best results, include both the drive letter and directory name.)

5. Optionally, you can choose Directory in the Styles area (see Chapter 14) and type a directory name for style files. Then you can type a default style file name (or complete path name, including the file name). The file specified in the Filename text box is automatically retrieved as the default style when you create a new document.

6. Choose another category of files and enter its location, or choose OK (or press ↵) to return to the current document window.

When you can't remember the exact name of a directory, choose the file-folder icon at the right of any directory text box to display the Select Directory dialog box (see Figure 13.2). In this dialog box, you can quickly locate the names of all the directories on your hard-disk drive.

Location of Files

Backup Files:	
Documents:	
Graphics Files:	c:\wpwin\graphics
Printer Files:	c:\wpc
Spr**e**adsheets:	

Macros/Keyboards/Button Bars

Fi**l**es:	c:\wpwin\macros

Styles

D**i**rectory:	c:\wpwin
Filename:	c:\wpwin\library.sty

Thesaurus/Speller/Hyphenation

Main:	c:\wpc
Supplementary:	c:\wpc

☒ Update **Q**uick List with Changes   OK   Cancel

FIGURE 13.1:

The Location of Files dialog box

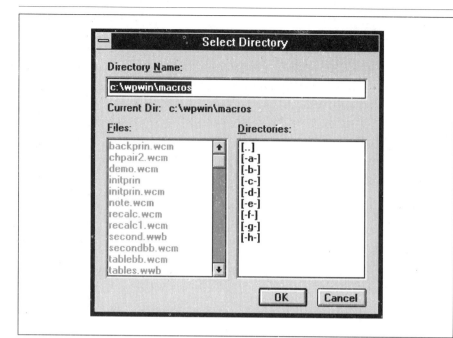

If you specify a nonexistent directory in the Location of Files dialog box, WordPerfect will offer to create that directory for you when you attempt to leave the dialog box. You can choose OK to create the directory or Cancel to specify a different directory. You can also use the WordPerfect File Manager (File ➤ File Manager), described in Chapter 12, or the Windows File Manager to create a new directory.

Also, once you choose a new location for a certain type of file, such as documents, be sure to move all your existing files of that type to the new location. You can choose File ➤ Move/Rename (or press Ctrl+R) in the File Manager window.

MAXIMIZING COMPUTER SPEED

The fewer the number of files stored in directories listed in the PATH statement, the faster overall system performance will be.

If you are responsible for configuring systems, you should keep in mind that if the WordPerfect for Windows directory (typically C:\WPWIN) is in the PATH statement in the AUTOEXEC.BAT file, DOS must search every file in that directory before searching other directories listed after it. For example, suppose your AUTOEXEC.BAT file contains this command:

```
PATH C:\WPWIN;C:\DOS;E:\WINDOWS;D:\123
```

If the WordPerfect for Windows directory contains hundreds, or thousands, of files, access to programs in the DOS, Windows, and 1-2-3 directories will be slowed dramatically.

To regain some speed, either move the C:\WPWIN directory to the end of the PATH statement or store only the WordPerfect program files in the C:\WPWIN directory, and use the Location of Files option to choose other directories for storing WordPerfect documents, macros, keyboard files, Button Bars, and so forth.

BACKING UP YOUR FILES AUTOMATICALLY

By now you should understand the importance of saving your work regularly with File ➤ Save (Shift+F3), File ➤ Save As (F3), or Close (Ctrl+F4). This practice will minimize your loss of work in case of a power failure or other mishap that shuts down your computer without giving you a chance to exit Word-Perfect normally. WordPerfect offers two additional safety valves, which you can adjust by choosing File ➤ Preferences ➤ Backup and making changes in the Backup dialog box:

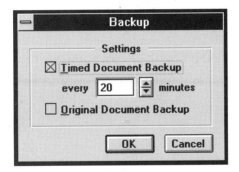

TIMED DOCUMENT BACKUP

By default, WordPerfect backs up your document automatically every 30 minutes, using the file name WP{WP}.BKn, where n is a number from 1 to 9 (.BK1 is a backup for the Document1 window, .BK2 is a backup for the Docu-ment2 window, and so on). You may open up to nine document windows at once, and each opened document window has its own backup file. These backup files are automatically deleted when you exit WordPerfect normally, but remain on-disk if a power failure or static electricity ends your WordPerfect work session unexpectedly. They are also saved if a computer problem forces you to reboot without exiting WordPerfect properly.

Always save your work and exit Word-Perfect properly after ending a session. Use the timed backups only to recover from emergencies.

Uncheck the Timed Document Backup option in the Backup dialog box if you decide you don't want automatic timed backups (though there's very little benefit to canceling them—you just eliminate the slight interruption caused when WordPerfect performs the backup, and you save a little disk space). If you have checked this option, you can enter a different backup interval, in minutes. Since automatic backups cause only the slightest inconvenience, you may want to make them more frequent—perhaps every 10 minutes.

If you've switched off Timed Document Backup and decide you want to reinstate it, mark the check box, and, if necessary, change the displayed backup interval.

When you start WordPerfect, it checks for the existence of the backup files and, if it finds any, displays the Timed Backup dialog box and this message:

Document1 Backup file exists.

If you get this message, you either failed to exit WordPerfect properly the last time you used it or a power outage terminated WordPerfect before you could exit properly. Hence, the backup files from the previous WordPerfect session are still stored on the disk.

If you want to save the backup file, so you can later open it, choose Rename, type any file name, then press ↵. After renaming the files, you can open them normally and resume your work. If you choose Delete, the backup file will be deleted. (The timed backup files are stored in the backup directory specified in the Backup Files text box in the Location of Files dialog box or in the same directory as WPWIN.EXE [typically C:\WPWIN] if no directory is specified.)

If you want to open a timed backup file for some reason, choose the Open command in the Timed Backup dialog box. Or you can choose File ➤ Move/Rename in the File Manager window to rename the backup file, and then open it as you would any other file.

A network timed-backup file is named WPxxx).BKn, where n is a number from 1 to 9, and xxx is the user's ID.

ORIGINAL DOCUMENT BACKUP

The Original Document Backup option in the Backup dialog box saves a backup copy of any document replaced by any of these Save commands:

◆ File ➤ **S**ave (Shift+F3) or File ➤ Save **A**s (F3), to save and continue

◆ File ➤ **C**lose (Ctrl+F4), to save and close an open file window

◆ File ➤ E**x**it (Alt+F4), to save and exit

The backup copy will be stored in the same directory with your document file and will have the same file name as the document being replaced, but with the extension .BK!. For example, if you're replacing a file named MEMO.WP, the backup file will be named MEMO.BK!.

If you use one of the Save commands to replace a document and then realize you still need the original version, you can open the .BK! file in the current document window the same way you open any document (choose File ➤ Open or press F4) and resave it under any name.

When you are finished making changes in the Backup dialog box, choose OK (or press ↵) to return to the current document window.

CHANGING ENVIRONMENT SETTINGS

TO CHANGE THE WORDPERFECT ENVIRONMENT DEFAULTS,

choose File ➤ Preferences ➤ Environment.

Choose File ➤ Preferences Environment to change the status of certain background operations. You will see the Environment Settings dialog box, shown in Figure 13.3. These are really miscellaneous settings, so I will discuss them separately in the sections that follow.

CONTROLLING MISCELLANEOUS SETTINGS

Customizing mouse settings is covered at the end of this chapter.

The Settings area in the Environment Settings dialog box contains options for controlling five miscellaneous WordPerfect features. Among other things, you can determine how WordPerfect formats, saves, and retrieves your documents by using the following options:

Auto Code Placement: By default, this option is turned on when you first load WordPerfect. This allows WordPerfect to automatically move certain formatting codes—such as margin, font, and justification codes—to the beginning of a paragraph or a page in the event you insert them in the middle of a paragraph or page.

Confirm on Code Deletion: This option (disabled by default) causes WordPerfect to prompt you when you are attempting to delete a formatting code from the current document. When you are editing a document in full-screen mode (without the benefit of Reveal Codes), you may want to choose this option.

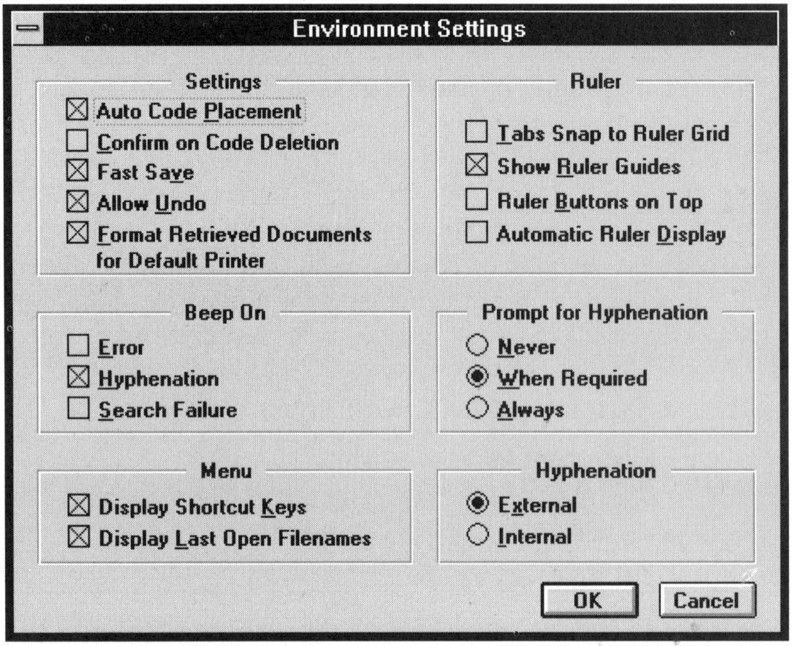

FIGURE 13.3:

*The Environment
Settings dialog box*

Fast Save: When turned on (the default), this option saves your documents a little faster by not reformatting them for printing. The amount of time saved is slight. Printing a fast-saved document from disk takes a little longer, because WordPerfect must format the document before sending it to the printer.

Allow Undo: This option enables the Undo feature. Once you activate this option, you can select Edit ➤ Undo to reverse the most recent formatting and editing changes made in the current document.

Format Retrieved Documents for Default Printer: This option updates documents that were originally formatted for printing on other printers. When this option is on, WordPerfect reformats all such documents for the current printer (the printer listed in the Select Printer dialog box when you choose File ➤ Select Printer). Occasionally, reformatted documents appear slightly different because WordPerfect cannot match the original fonts and attributes to those available with the current printer.

Once you've made final decisions about the miscellaneous environment settings, choose OK (or press ↵) to return to the current document window.

CONTROLLING THE WARNING BEEPS

By default, the only time WordPerfect beeps at you is when the Hyphenation feature is active and it needs you to place a hyphen in a word. Using the Beep On options in the Environment Settings dialog box, you can deactivate this warning beep or set others.

You can mark any of these check boxes for warning beeps:

Error: WordPerfect beeps whenever it encounters an error.

Hyphenation: WordPerfect beeps to notify you that it needs help positioning the hyphen in a word.

Search Failure: WordPerfect beeps when a search operation does not locate the search string.

Choose OK (or press ↵) to return to the current document window from the Environment Settings dialog box. Your new settings take effect immediately.

CONTROLLING THE MENU DISPLAY

In the Environment Settings dialog box, the Menu area offers two options for controlling the appearance of the pull-down menus:

Display Shortcut Keys: Switched on by default, this option displays the shortcut keys in the right margin of a pull-down menu.

Display Last Open Filenames: Switched on by default, this option displays on the bottom of the File menu the names of the last four documents you had open.

 *Word-Perfect updates file-name references in the bottom of the File menu only when changes to the file (or to its directory path) are made from within Word-Perfect.*

To retrieve a document whose name appears at the bottom of the File menu, choose the file name as if it were a menu command. If WordPerfect is unable to locate the file, you'll see the message "Can't open/retrieve file." This error message will occur if you change a Last Open Filename name or modify its directory path outside of the WordPerfect environment.

Choose OK (or press ↵) to return to the current document window from the Environment Settings dialog box. Your new settings take effect immediately.

CONTROLLING THE RULER DISPLAY

The Ruler options in the Environment Settings dialog box control how the ruler is operated and displayed in a document window:

Tabs Snap to Ruler Grid: Switched on by default, this option causes all tabs to snap to invisible gridlines in the current document. Gridlines appear every $\frac{1}{16}$ of an inch and are useful for aligning text and objects in the current document.

Show Ruler Guides: Switched on by default, this option displays a dotted vertical line extended from a tab or margin marker that you are dragging. This allows for more accurate alignment of markers in the current document.

Ruler Buttons on Top: Check this option to display the ruler buttons at the top of the ruler instead of the bottom.

Automatic Ruler Display: Check this option to have WordPerfect automatically display the ruler each time you open a document.

Choose OK (or press ↵) to return to the current document window from the Environment Settings dialog box. Your new settings take effect immediately.

RESETTING THE HYPHENATION PROMPT OPTION

Hyphena-tion is dis-cussed in Chapter 11.

The options in the Prompt for Hyphenation area of the Environment Settings dialog box tell WordPerfect when you would like to be prompted when it needs help hyphenating a word:

Never: WordPerfect hyphenates words without prompting you.

When Required: WordPerfect prompts you to choose from among two or more hyphenation alternatives (the default).

Always: WordPerfect always prompts you to choose the hyphenation style.

WordPerfect makes hyphenation decisions based on the rules in the currently selected hyphenation dictionary. (See the next section for more information about hyphenation dictionaries.) When you've made your choice, choose OK (or press ↵) to return to the current document window.

CHANGING THE HYPHENATION RULES

Removing the .LEX file disables the Speller.

When the automatic hyphenation feature is active, WordPerfect normally bases its hyphenation decisions on the contents of two dictionaries: an internal dictionary that is built into WordPerfect and an external dictionary that is stored in a file called WP{WP}US.LEX. The external dictionary is much larger and offers more choices than the internal dictionary. However, if you don't have room for the dictionary file on your hard disk, you can still use hyphenation capabilities by switching to the internal rules.

Whatever your decision, choose the appropriate option in the Hyphenation area of the Environment Settings dialog box, which has the following options:

External: tells WordPerfect to hyphenate words based on the hyphenation file (dictionary) described above (the default at start-up). This setting offers a much larger set of hyphenation choices and alternatives.

Internal: tells WordPerfect to hyphenate words based on a set of general rules concerning syllabication in English. This setting conserves hard-disk space.

The Internal option, while helpful, will produce some errors and therefore is not as efficient as the .LEX file. If you've been working with the internal rules but have reinstalled the .LEX file, choose External in the Hyphenation area to activate the more reliable hyphenation system. When you've made your choice, choose OK (or press ↵) to return to the current document window.

MODIFYING THE SCREEN DISPLAY

TO CUSTOMIZE THE SCREEN DISPLAY,

choose File ➤ Preferences ➤ Display.

Choose File ➤ Preferences ➤ Display to bring up the Display Settings dialog box, shown in Figure 13.4, which allows you to adjust the document window, the scroll bars, the hard-return character, and the units of measure. Although you can use this dialog box just to spruce up the screen—especially if you have a color monitor—some of the options can make your work a little easier or can display your document so that it more closely resembles the printed version.

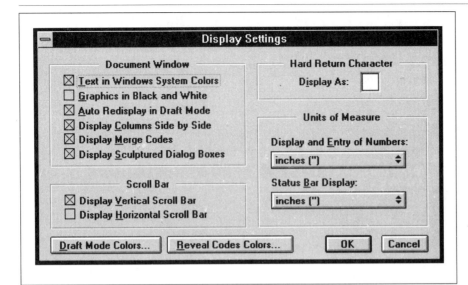

CUSTOMIZING THE DOCUMENT WINDOW

The Document Window area in the Display Settings dialog box contains six miscellaneous options that affect the display in the current document window.

> NOTE *Some of the options for customizing the document window affect only specific features, such as merges or multicolumn layouts.*

Text in Windows System Colors: Switched on by default, this option turns over control of the color of text to the Windows Control Panel. Uncheck this option if you want WordPerfect to control text color.

Graphics in Black and White: Choose this option to display graphics in black and white inside the document window and Print Preview window.

Auto Redisplay in Draft Mode: By default, WordPerfect reformats text immediately after you press a movement key when making an editing change from draft mode. Uncheck this box if you do not want automatic reformatting to take place. This can be useful when working with narrow columns (where frequent screen reformatting can be distracting), because it prevents WordPerfect from reformatting your paragraphs with every insertion-point movement as you edit. (When you are in draft mode and the Auto Redisplay in Draft Mode option is unchecked, you can press the Redisplay key [Ctrl+F3] to reformat text. Otherwise, WordPerfect will reformat the text as soon as you use the insertion point to scroll through the text.)

Display Columns Side by Side: Switched on by default, this option displays columns side by side rather than on separate pages. This speeds up scrolling somewhat and makes editing easier in multi-column layouts. Uncheck this option to display columns on separate pages (see Chapter 20).

Display Merge Codes: This option determines whether WordPerfect displays merge codes on the screen. Uncheck this option to suppress the display of merge codes.

Display Sculptured Dialog Boxes: Switched on by default, this option displays sculpted dialog boxes, rather than the plain-line dialog boxes displayed by Windows.

DISPLAYING SCROLL BARS

To maximize the size of the work area in a document window, remove the Button Bar and the display of both scroll bars.

WordPerfect allows you to control the display of scroll bars in the current document window. The horizontal and vertical scroll bars make it easy to move around a document—just click on the arrow or drag the scroll box in the direction you want to move. Because WordPerfect also offers keystroke alternatives for navigating a document window, you may prefer to remove the display of scroll bars in order to increase the size of the work area in the current document window.

There are two options for controlling the display of scroll bars:

Display Vertical Scroll Bar: Switched on by default, this option displays the vertical scroll bar at the right edge of the current document window.

Display Horizontal Scroll Bar: Choose this option when you want to display the horizontal scroll bar at the bottom of the current document window.

DISPLAYING A CUSTOM HARD-RETURN CHARACTER

Type any character or any WordPerfect character (Ctrl+W) in the Display As text box to have that character represent each hard return in the current document window; WordPerfect will display the character on-screen, but it will never be printed. Press the spacebar as the hard-return character if you decide you no longer want hard returns displayed as characters.

CHANGING THE DEFAULT UNIT OF MEASUREMENT

WordPerfect is preset to display measurements in inches, such as those on the status bar. It assumes that your measurement entries, such as those for new margin settings, are in inches as well. If you'd rather work with another unit of measure, you can simply tell WordPerfect your preferred unit; all affected displays will be changed immediately, and WordPerfect will expect the measurements you enter from then on to be in the specified unit.

To change the default unit of measurement, choose an option from the Units of Measure area in the Display Settings dialog box. Though you'll most likely want to change the default unit across the board, WordPerfect lets you choose the unit of measurement for two components separately:

> **Display and Entry of Numbers:** controls the display and entry of numbers in WordPerfect dialog boxes.

> **Status Bar Display:** controls the display of numbers and measurements on the status bar, in the Ln (line) and Pos (Position) entries.

When you choose either Display and Entry of Numbers or Status Bar Display, a pop-up list with five measurement options appears:

"   Inches, displayed with the inch symbol

i   Inches, displayed with the letter *i*

c   Centimeters

p   Points (a typesetting unit in which 72 points equals 1 inch)

w $\frac{1}{1200}$ of an inch

Remember to set the same unit for both Status Bar Display and Display and Entry of Numbers if you want a consistent measurement and display system for all your work. Choose OK (or press ↵) to return to the current document window from the Environment Settings dialog box. Your new settings take effect immediately.

If you ever need to enter a measurement in a unit that's not your current default, you don't need to change the default unit. Instead, you can type the measurement followed by the symbol representing the unit you want to use (see the table above).

For example, if you are preparing a document for typesetting and need to set the left and right margins to 90 points, but you are working with inches in WordPerfect, you can choose Layout ➤ Margins (or press Ctrl+F8), then set both the left and right margins to *90p*. WordPerfect automatically converts your entries to 1.25 inches.

CHANGING DRAFT MODE AND REVEAL CODES COLORS

In its normal display mode, WordPerfect shows text appearance and size attributes on-screen much as they will appear in a printed document. When you are working in draft mode or in Reveal Codes, however, WordPerfect does not show many of these attributes on the screen. For instance, boldface, underline, and custom font styles do not appear as they would in a printed document. Thus, to remind yourself of where these attributes appear in your document, you must review codes in Reveal Codes, check the Print Preview window, or print the document.

Text appearance is covered in Chapter 5.

Choosing Draft Mode Colors from the Display Settings dialog box gives you an opportunity to change this sometimes inconvenient state of affairs. It brings up the dialog box shown in Figure 13.5. The Draft Mode Colors dialog box lets you define the foreground and background colors used to signify specific appearance and size attributes of text in a document, as well as set one or more of three properties—Highlighted Text, Bold/Underline, and Combinations—for the display of any text attribute. Remember, these settings apply only when you are viewing a document in draft mode. Setting color attributes in this dialog box in no way alters the appearance of a document in normal display mode, and it does not affect the final printed look of a document.

To change a setting, use the mouse or arrow keys to move to the display property you want to set for a given attribute, and choose the item. For example, to have strikeout appear in the current document window as purple text with a white background, choose the Strikeout attribute in the Appearance area, then click the purple color box in the Foreground Palette and the white color box in the Background Palette.

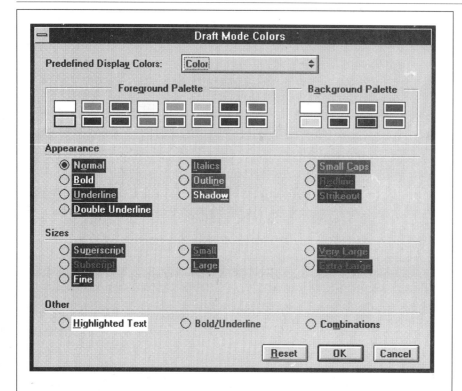

To select one of the predefined color display settings so that you don't have to choose color combinations for each and every attribute, choose Predefined Display Settings. WordPerfect displays a pop-up list containing the following seven options:

◆ Color

◆ Monochrome

◆ Blue on White

◆ LCD Display

◆ LCD Display - No intensity

◆ Plasma Display

◆ Custom

Choose the Reset option to restore the original color scheme that was in effect when you opened the Draft Mode Colors dialog box. Choose OK (or press ↵ twice) to return to the current document window. If you've reset the display for attributes that happen to be in the text on your draft mode screen, you'll notice that your new settings have already taken effect.

Choosing Reveal Codes Colors from the Display Settings dialog box gives you an opportunity to change the color attributes of the codes displayed in Reveal Codes. You'll see this dialog box:

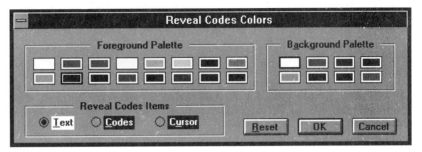

The Reveal Codes Colors dialog box lets you define the foreground and background colors used to display text, codes, and the highlight in Reveal Codes. These settings apply only when you are viewing a document in draft mode. Setting color attributes in this dialog box in no way alters the appearance of a document in normal display mode, and it does not affect the final printed look of a document.

To change a setting, use the mouse or arrow keys to move to the display property you want to set for a given attribute, and choose the item. For example, to have codes appear in Reveal Codes as blue text with a cyan background, choose the Text attribute in the Reveal Codes Items area, then click the blue color box in the Foreground Palette and the cyan color box in the Background Palette.

Choose OK (or press ↵ twice) to return to the current document window from the Reveal Codes Colors dialog box. If you've reset the display for attributes that happen to be in the text in Reveal Codes, you'll notice that your new settings have already taken effect.

CHANGING THE PRINTER DEFAULTS

You can change the default settings that WordPerfect uses to print your documents. Follow these steps:

1. Choose **F**ile ➤ **Pr**eferences ➤ **P**rint.

2. Make your choices from the Print Settings dialog box, shown in Figure 13.6.

3. After making your choices, choose OK (or press ↵) to return to the current document window.

Changing any of the options in the Print Settings dialog box makes them defaults for future documents, rather than just the current document.

The options in the Multiple Copies and Document Settings areas are described in Chapter 8. The Redline Method options are described in Chapter 5, as are the Size Attribute Ratio options, which let you customize how Word-Perfect defines the various size options in relation to the current font.

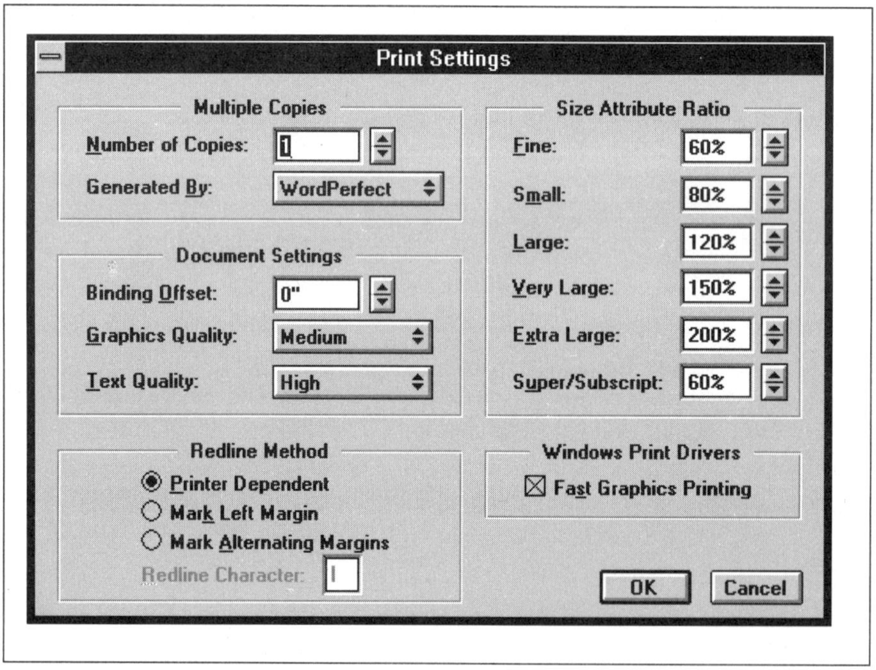

FIGURE 13.6:
The Print Settings dialog box

The remaining area has a single option: Fast Graphics Printing. Although this option has no effect on printing text or printing with WordPerfect printer drivers, it can speed up the printing of graphics when switched on (the default setting). If for some reason you experience problems printing graphics when this option is on, return to the Print Settings dialog box and uncheck it.

FORMATTING DOCUMENTS FOR THE DEFAULT PRINTER

The Format Retrieved Documents for Default Printer option in the Environment Settings dialog box affects WordPerfect's retrieval of documents that use paper sizes and fonts for a printer other than the currently selected one. If you check this box, the current printer remains selected, and fonts and paper sizes in the incoming document are modified to best match those available in the current printer. If you uncheck this box, WordPerfect automatically chooses whatever printer was used to create the current document (if it's available) and leaves fonts and paper sizes unchanged.

SELECTING A KEYBOARD

Choosing the Keyboard option on the Preferences menu lets you select the keyboard layout you want to use with WordPerfect. You can also use this option to create new, or edit existing, keyboard layouts (see Chapter 27 for information on this topic). Once the Keyboard option is selected, you'll see the dialog box:

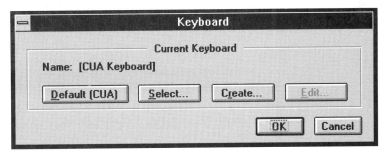

The name of the current keyboard appears after Name in the WordPerfect Keyboard dialog box. The default keyboard layout used by WordPerfect for Windows is called the Common User Access (CUA) layout. The CUA layout is the standard, internal keyboard layout that is used with most Windows applications. Having a standard keyboard layout option for all Windows applications makes it easy to learn how to use the various "for Windows" software programs, because each program assigns the same keys to Help, Cancel, Escape, Exit, and so on.

 If you reassign your keyboard, make a mental note of these changes whenever you read this book or use WordPerfect's online help.

Most Windows programs use the F1 key for Help and the Escape key for Cancel. By default, WordPerfect for Windows follows this CUA standard, but it also lets you switch to a non-CUA keyboard layout if you wish. To load a noninternal keyboard layout file, follow these steps:

1. Choose **F**ile ➤ P**r**eferences ➤ **K**eyboard.

2. Choose **S**elect in the Keyboard dialog box.

3. In the Select Keyboard File dialog box, highlight the name of the keyboard file.

4. Choose **S**elect (or press ↵) to load the highlighted keyboard file.

WordPerfect for Windows arrives with a keyboard layout file for the WordPerfect 5.1 for DOS keyboard. If after selecting this keyboard you want to switch back, choose Default in the WordPerfect Keyboard dialog box, and WordPerfect will recall the internal definition for the CUA keyboard layout.

CHANGING THE INITIAL CODE DEFAULTS

WordPerfect has chosen the most common document format as the default for each document you create: All documents, unless you specify otherwise, are single-spaced and left-justified, with 1-inch margins on all four sides.

But defaults are simply suggested values that WordPerfect uses if you do not request some other option. If you find that the margins, spacing, or justification need changing in nearly every document you create, it may be easier to change the default settings. For example, if you use full justification in most documents, you can change the default justification to Full. In the future, all documents will be fully justified automatically (unless, of course, you change the justification for a specific document with Layout ➤ Justification).

To change a default initial code setting, follow these steps:

1. Choose **F**ile ➤ P**r**eferences.

2. Choose **I**nitial Codes. WordPerfect displays a document window, with Reveal Codes showing and Default Initial Codes in the title bar.

3. Choose the normal menu options or press the shortcut keys to insert the formatting codes you want to have in effect for every document.

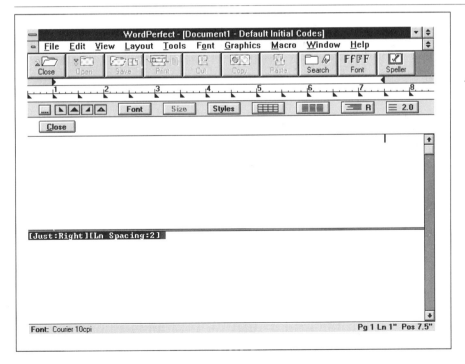

NOTE *Not all formatting options can be defined in Initial Codes, and any text you type will be ignored. If a particular option seems to be ignored, try placing it at the top of the document rather than in Initial Codes.*

For example, to change from left justification to full justification, choose Layout ➤ Justification ➤ Left (or press Ctrl+L). Figure 13.7 shows an Initial Codes window with double spacing and right justification set as the new defaults. When you've finished entering the new defaults, choose Close to return to a full-screen document window.

Your new settings will affect only documents that you create in the future. They will not change the format of the document currently in the document window or of previously saved documents that you open for editing.

Moreover, the codes you enter in this window are automatically stored as the initial codes in every new document you create. For example, even when you first start WordPerfect and are in a blank document, choosing Layout ➤ Document ➤ Initial Codes (Ctrl+Shift+F9 C) displays the default codes. You can delete any of these codes for the current document only, or choose Close to leave them unchanged.

Remember that the formatting codes in the document are saved as part of the document. Hence, they will be in effect even if you open the document on a computer with different default settings.

FIGURE 13.7:

The Initial Codes window, with new format defaults set

[Just:Right][Ln Spacing:2]

Font: Courier 10cpi   Pg 1 Ln 1" Pos 7.5"

Keep in mind that any settings in Document Initial Codes (Chapter 7) for the current document (only) take precedence over the settings in Initial Codes. In turn, the format settings at specific locations in a document override both Initial Codes and Document Initial Codes.

AUTOMATING THE DOCUMENT SUMMARY

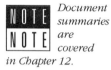

Document summaries are covered in Chapter 12.

If creating a document summary is something you do regularly when you create a document—or if you'd like it to be—you can make life a little easier by having WordPerfect prompt you to create one and by specifying defaults for some of the entries in the Document Summary Preferences dialog box. Choose File ➤ Preferences ➤ Document Summary. You'll see this dialog box:

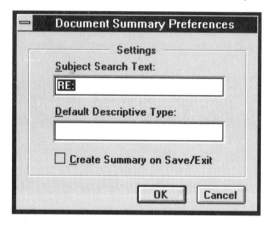

Here are your choices:

Subject Search Text: lets you change the preselected characters WordPerfect uses to search on the first page of the document for the document summary's suggested Subject entry. The default is *RE:*, which means that WordPerfect searches for *RE:* in the document and pulls the word or phrase immediately following it into the Subject entry. Type up to 39 characters and press ↵.

Default Descriptive Type: sets the default for Document Type in the document summary for all future documents. Type up to 20 characters and press ↵. The first three characters will also be suggested as the file-name extension when you name the file (for example, the Document Type *Letter* will make .LET the default extension).

Create Summary on Save/Exit: causes WordPerfect to prompt you to create a document summary when saving a document that doesn't already have one.

Choose OK (or press ↵) to return to the current document window when you've finished automating your document summaries. You will notice your new settings at work the next time you create a document summary or save a new document (depending on the settings you've made).

CHANGING THE DEFAULT DATE FORMAT

By choosing Date Format from the Preferences menu, you can control the default date and time format used with the Date Codes and Time Codes options (introduced in Chapter 3). Initially, the default format is [Month][Day #], [Year ####](e.g., *October 1, 1992*). When you choose this option, you'll see the Date/Time Preferences dialog box:

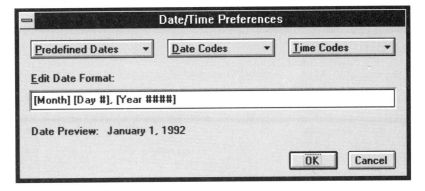

Designing date formats is discussed in Chapter 3.

Choose Date Codes to specify only the date code portion of the date/time preferences. There are 12 style codes available. Choose Time Codes to specify only the time code portion of the date/time preferences. There are 10 style codes available.

Choose Edit Date Format to modify the current date format. The new format becomes the default format for all future Date Text or Date Code entries. (You can override this default for any current WordPerfect session by choosing Tools ➤ Date ➤ Define.)

If you want to use a predefined date format, choose Predefined Dates and select one of the six date formats from the pop-up list:

March 5, 1992

Mar 5, 1992

5 March 1992

Thursday, Mar 5, 1992

Thursday, 5 March, 1992

3/5/92

REDEFINING THE DELIMITERS FOR MERGE FILES

Merges are covered in Chapter 16, DOS text files in Chapter 25.

If you are planning to merge data stored in DOS text files into a WordPerfect document, WordPerfect needs to know how to recognize the beginning and end of each field and record. By default, WordPerfect assumes that fields are separated by commas and that each record ends with a carriage return (↵). Choosing Merge from the Preferences menu lets you redefine these characters to reflect the structure of the text file.

When you choose Merge, you'll see this dialog box:

Merge Preferences

Field Delimiters

Begin: [   ] ◄

End: [,   ] ◄

Record Delimiters

Begin: [   ] ◄

End: [[CR]   ] ◄

[**OK**]   [**Cancel**]

Choose the options in Field Delimiters to redefine the characters that begin and end fields. Choose the options in Record Delimiters to redefine the characters that begin and end records.

CHANGING THE
TABLE OF AUTHORITIES DEFAULTS

The Table of Authorities feature is discussed in Chapter 23.

If you often use WordPerfect's Table of Authorities feature and must reset the format every time to follow the conventions of your law firm, you can reset certain formats permanently by choosing File ➤ Preferences ➤ Table of Authorities. This command displays the TOA Preferences dialog box:

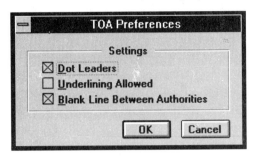

The authorities that you define via the Preferences menu remain in effect for future WordPerfect sessions, whereas those defined from the Tools Define menu remain in effect only for the current session (until you exit WordPerfect). See Chapter 23 for more information on this topic.

SETTING THE DEFAULT EQUATION STYLE

If you are using WordPerfect's Equations feature (Chapter 21), you can choose Equations from the Preferences menu to change some settings that affect how you set up your equations and how WordPerfect prints them. The options in the Equation Preferences dialog box are described in Chapter 21.

CUSTOMIZING THE MOUSE

You can make your mouse more comfortable to use by adjusting the mouse defaults. Also, if you change mouse types, you must tell Windows what kind of mouse you're using and where it is attached to your computer.

Before you can use some mice, you must run a *device driver,* often named MOUSE.COM. Typically, you must change your computer's CONFIG.SYS or AUTOEXEC.BAT file. See your mouse documentation for further information.

Here are the steps for customizing mouse operation:

1. Press Ctrl+Esc to display the Windows Task List.

2. Choose Program Manager to display the Program Manager group window.

3. Choose the Control Panel icon.

4. In the Control Panel window, choose the Mouse icon. The Mouse dialog box appears:

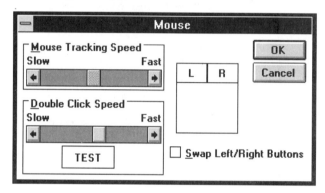

5. Make your choices as summarized below, then choose OK (or press ↵) to return to the Program Manager window.

6. Press Ctrl+Esc again to display the Windows Task List.

7. Choose WordPerfect to return to the current document window.

Here are the choices you can make:

Mouse Tracking Speed: lets you change the speed at which the I beam travels across a document window; drag the scroll box from Slow to Fast.

Double Click Speed: lets you increase or decrease the amount of time that defines a double click; drag the scroll box from Slow to Fast. Click on TEST to test the double-click speed setting.

Swap Left/Right Buttons: reverses the functions of the left and right mouse buttons.

This concludes Part 3 of this book. In the next part, you'll start to learn about additional tools that can save you time and effort by automating portions of your work.

PART FOUR

Automating Your Work

! n this part you'll learn about two important features of Word-Perfect that both simplify your work and help automate portions of it. The first tool, Styles, lets you predefine the appearance of certain elements of your documents. Not only does this feature save you time and ensure consistency, it also lets you easily redesign an entire document with just a few keystrokes. The second tool, Macros, lets you automate complex tasks, reducing them to just a couple of keystrokes.

CHAPTER 14

Using Styles to Simplify Your Work

f you look at just about any document that's longer than a page or two, particularly a professionally published document, you'll notice that it consists of certain design elements, or *styles*. For example, as you flip though this book, you'll see that every chapter contains a chapter title, chapter-opening text (like this paragraph), several main section headings (called A heads), subsection headings (B heads), sub-subsection headings (C heads), margin notes, body text, and more.

HANDS-ON

LESSON 6

For a hands-on lesson in creating and using styles, see Lesson 6 in Part 9.

The fonts used to print these elements are used consistently throughout the book. For example, all the margin notes are printed in the same small size and typeface. This consistent use of design makes it easier for the reader to scan the material and find needed information.

WHAT IS A STYLE?

You'll learn to create documents like the one in Figure 14.1 in Part 6.

Virtually any size of document can benefit from consistent use of styles. For example, Figure 14.1 shows a sample newsletter that uses three basic design elements (styles) to print each article: a headline (or article title), a byline (the author's name), and body text (which ends with a small graphic to indicate the end of each article).

The WordPerfect Styles feature lets you predefine the appearance and format of various elements of your document. For example, you could create these three styles before creating the newsletter in Figure 14.1:

◆   Headline (style of each article title)

◆   Byline (style for printing the author name)

◆   Body (style for the article text and closing graphic)

When you're about to type the headline, byline, or article text, you simply press a few keys to activate the appropriate style, rather than press all the keys required to choose the font and change the print size or print attribute. This saves you a lot of time and guarantees that the elements are used consistently throughout the document.

Chapter 5 discusses fonts and special characters, which you'll probably want to use when creating styles.

But the real advantage of styles is this: If you change your mind about the appearance of a style, you only need to change the style once—you need not change it repeatedly throughout the document. Suppose you decide to change the font of all the headings for the newsletter in Figure 14.1. With styles already set up, you only need to change the font in the Headline style one time, not repeatedly throughout the document. All the headlines in the document are instantly converted to the new style.

Figure 14.2 shows this idea in action. It's exactly the same newsletter as the one in Figure 14.1, but the font of the Headline style has been changed from Times to Univers. Now all the headlines are printed in the new font, and because a style was used to format each headline, all the headlines were changed in a matter of seconds simply by changing the style.

Needless to say, if your document has several dozen, or several hundred, headings in it, you can save yourself from a great deal of boring, repetitive

FIGURE 14.1:

A sample newsletter with three consistently used styles: Headline, Byline, and Body

The Vacationer

Vol. 1 No. 1   Travel fun for everyone   January 1991

Celebrate with us ← headline
by Jill Evans ← byline

In honor of our newsletter's maiden voyage, we'd like to invite you to an Open House at 7:00pm on January 11, 1991, at our offices. Please dress casually or come in your most fashionable travel togs. **body**

Tropical travel ← headline
by Elizabeth Olson ← byline

Travel to tropical islands is on the increase. Just look at the graph showing our clients' recent tropical trips and you'll see how dramatic the numbers really are. There's a good reason for these increases -- tropical vacations are great fun, especially when the wind and snow are swirling at your doorstep! **body**

Newsletter debut ← headline
by Joan Smith ← byline

We're pleased to bring this first issue of our newsletter, *The Vacationer*, to our many loyal customers. The newsletter was inspired by your ideas and questions. You've asked us where to find the best travel fares, where to go for the person who has been everywhere, what to eat and how to eat it when visiting faraway countries. We've responded by creating this newsletter. **body**

Here we'll bring you the latest news about great deals on vacations in exotic corners of our planet, fun places for inexpensive weekend getaways, and out-of-the-way spots you might never have thought to ask us about. We'll include handy vacation planning tips and introduce you to exciting foods, puzzling customs, and important laws you'll encounter during sojourns to foreign lands. So relax, enjoy, and travel with us as we bring you a new issue every quarter of the year...

Inside...

The Vacationer

Vol. 1 No. 1   Travel fun for everyone   January 1991

Newsletter debut
by Joan Smith

We're pleased to bring this first issue of our newsletter, *The Vacationer*, to our many loyal customers. The newsletter was inspired by your ideas and questions. You've asked us where to find the best travel fares, where to go for the person who has been everywhere, what to eat and how to eat it when visiting faraway countries. We've responded by creating this newsletter.

Here we'll bring you the latest news about great deals on vacations in exotic corners of our planet, fun places for inexpensive weekend getaways, and out-of-the-way spots you might never have thought to ask us about. We'll include handy vacation planning tips and introduce you to exciting foods, puzzling customs, and important laws you'll encounter during sojourns to foreign lands. So relax, enjoy, and travel with us as we bring you a new issue every quarter of the year... ✿

Celebrate with us
by Jill Evans

In honor of our newsletter's maiden voyage, we'd like to invite you to an Open House at 7:00pm on January 11, 1991, at our offices. Please dress casually or come in your most fashionable travel togs. ✿

Tropical travel
by Elizabeth Olson

Travel to tropical islands is on the increase. Just look at the graph showing our clients' recent tropical trips and you'll see how dramatic the numbers really are. There's a good reason for these increases -- tropical vacations are great fun, especially when the wind and snow are swirling at your doorstep! ✿

Inside...

FIGURE 14.2:

The newsletter after changing the Headline style

With the aid of the Master Document feature, you can easily change a style throughout many separate documents at once. Be sure to read Part 7 if you work with large documents.

work. This is especially true when you remember the many limitations of the Search and Replace feature for locating and changing fonts, paired codes, and other specific formatting codes.

After you've worked up a nice set of styles for a document, you can save those styles and reuse them in other documents, without re-creating them from scratch. This can be very handy for creating a monthly newsletter or a monthly report to management, or if you need to create a large book, report, or dissertation consisting of several sections or chapters that must follow specific formatting guidelines.

Styles are easy to create, easy to use, and easy to change. So even if your particular documents only use a handful of simple styles, like boldface, italics, and extra-large size, you'll probably find it worthwhile to use styles. You'll find the Styles features conveniently located both on the Layout menu (at the bottom) and on the ruler's Style button (shown later in this chapter).

PAIRED, OPEN, AND OUTLINE STYLES

Before learning how to work with styles in WordPerfect, you need to get a bit of terminology under your belt. There are three types of styles: *paired, open,* and *outline.*

♦ A paired style is used to switch a specific format on and off; for example, to format a heading or a table caption. It behaves like the paired codes of "regular" print attributes, such as the [Bold On] and [Bold Off] codes that activate and deactivate boldface for the words between the codes.

♦ An open style is switched on once and applies indefinitely, except where explicitly overridden by another style or specific formatting codes. This kind of style acts like any other single code, such as [Ln Spacing:], affecting all text below the position of the code (up to the next overriding code, if any).

♦ An outline style is used only with the Outline feature to apply styles to outlines. This specialized category of style is covered in Chapter 22.

CREATING A NEW STYLE

> **TO CREATE A NEW STYLE,**
>
> choose Layout ➤ Styles (or press Alt+F8) to display the Styles dialog box. Choose Create to create a new style and the Style Properties dialog box will open. Enter a style Name and optionally a Description, choose a Type, and optionally choose Enter Key Inserts to specify a role for the ↵ key to play. Then choose OK or press ↵ and enter your formatting codes. Choose Close to close the Styles dialog box.

NOTE *Since an open style generally affects all text below the insertion point, a single document generally uses only one open style, though it may use several paired styles.*

To create a style, you first must consider whether it should be a paired style, which is used for headings and small blocks of text, or an open style, which affects the entire document. Then you must think about what features you want it to activate, such as a particular font or appearance, or a formatting code. A style can also contain text, which is typed automatically as soon as you activate the style.

To create a style, follow these steps:

1. Choose **L**ayout ➤ **S**tyles, or press Alt+F8. This displays the list of available styles, as shown in the Styles dialog box (your list will probably be different):

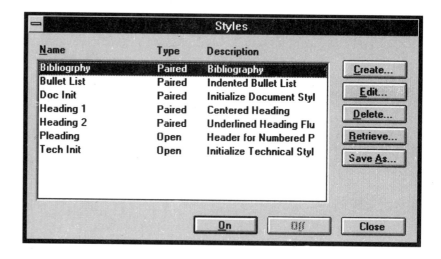

Name	**T**ype	**D**escription
Bibliogrphy	Paired	Bibliography
Bullet List	Paired	Indented Bullet List
Doc Init	Paired	Initialize Document Styl
Heading 1	Paired	Centered Heading
Heading 2	Paired	Underlined Heading Flu
Pleading	Open	Header for Numbered P
Tech Init	Open	Initialize Technical Styl

Styles

Create... **E**dit... **D**elete... **R**etrieve... Save **A**s...

On Off Close

2. Choose **C**reate, which takes you to the Style Properties dialog box, for defining a style:

3. The insertion point will be positioned in the **N**ame text box. Type a descriptive name of your choosing, up to 20 characters long (including blank spaces if you want them).

4. Optionally, type a description of this style in the Description box, up to 55 characters long, which will be displayed along with the list of available styles (see the Description column in the Styles dialog box).

5. If you want to create an open style, choose **T**ype, and then choose **O**pen from the pop-up list. Otherwise, leave this option unchanged to create a paired style.

6. Choose OK or press ↵ to display the Style Editor screen. If you are creating a paired style, you will see the screen below. If you are creating an open style, there is no comment box.

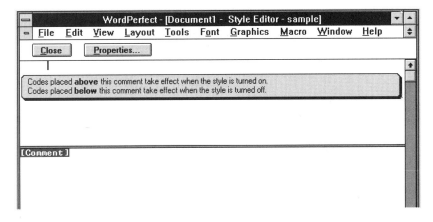

7. Use the pull-down menus or shortcut keys to choose formatting features for the style. The hidden code for each format you choose appears in Reveal Codes, at the bottom of the screen. You can also type any text that you want the style to insert for you automatically.

If you are creating an open style, skip steps 8–10.

8. If you are creating a paired style and want it to end by doing something more than simply terminating the codes it uses, press End to move the insertion point beneath the comment box.

9. Again, use the menus or shortcut keys to choose formatting features, fonts, etc., or type the text that you want the style to insert for you. (Any codes above the comment box are automatically deactivated when you leave the style, so it's not necessary to turn off codes that are activated above the comment. The only exceptions are Page Format codes, which are chosen from the **L**ayout ➤ **P**age dialog box, which are not deactivated.)

10. If you are defining a paired style, you can alter the function of the ↵ key (as described below) by choosing **P**roperties, which will open the Style Properties dialog box.

11. Choose **C**lose or press ↵ after defining your formatting codes and text, to return to the list of available styles in the Styles dialog box.

Your newly created style will be added to the list of available styles and will be saved for future use (in the current document only) when you save the document. In a moment, I'll talk about ways to use the style to make it accessible to multiple documents. First, though, I'll discuss the Enter Key Inserts option, which is used to change the role of the ↵ key.

Defining the Enter Key for Paired Styles

If you are creating a paired style, you might want to think about how you want the ↵ key to behave while the insertion point is within the paired style. Your options are the following:

Hard Return   The ↵ key works normally, inserting a hard-return code [HRt]. Use this option for paired codes that will be used to format text that's more than a single paragraph long or will contain hard returns. When using the style later, you must press → to move the insertion point past the [Style Off] code to end the style.

Style O**ff**   When using the style later, the ↵ key terminates the
                                 style and activates any features defined in the [Style
                                 Off] code. This is best used with styles that define
                                 headings and other short lines of text that do not
                                 contain hard returns.

Style **O**ff/On   The ↵ key turns off the style, activating the codes
                                 in the [Style Off] code, and then immediately
                                 reactivates the style. This is useful with a style that
                                 types a list or formats a series of paragraphs. When
                                 using the style later, you must press → to move the
                                 insertion point past the [Style Off] code to end the
                                 style.

CREATING A STYLE FROM EXISTING CODES

TO COPY EXISTING CODES INTO A STYLE,

select and copy the codes in Reveal Codes, then choose
Layout ➤ Styles (or press Alt+F8) to display the Styles dialog
box. Enter a name and any other options you want for the
new style. Choose Create and paste the codes automatically.
Choose Close to return to the Styles dialog box.

If you've already formatted some text in a document (without using styles) and
now want to use those formatting codes as a general style, you can easily do
so. This is handy when you want to repeat the codes elsewhere in the same
document or save them for use in other documents. Follow these steps:

1. Position the insertion point near the codes you want to save as a style.

2. Open Reveal Codes by choosing **View** ➤ Reveal **C**odes or by pressing
   Alt+F3, so you can see the codes accurately.

3. Position the highlight on the first code to be used in the style.

4. Instead of using your mouse, press F8 to start the selection and → until
   you have moved the insertion point to the immediate right of the last
   code you want to select (so the highlight in Reveal Codes is *after* the
   last code you want to copy).

5. Choose **E**dit ➤ **C**opy (or press Ctrl+Ins) to copy the selection to the
   Clipboard.

6. Choose **L**ayout ➤ **S**tyles or press (Alt+F8) to display the Styles dialog box.

7. Choose **C**reate to create a new style. In the Style Properties dialog box, enter the style name, a description, the type, and the enter-key profile (if applicable). Then Choose OK or press ↵.

8. Choose **E**dit ➤ **P**aste (Shift+Ins) to paste the selection from the Clipboard. The lower window will show that the codes you selected are now in the style.

9. Choose **C**lose to return to the Styles dialog box.

In the Styles dialog box, you can also choose Edit to further refine the codes in your new style, or add text to it. Once you've finished defining your new style, choose Close to return to the document window, then use the style normally, as discussed in the following sections.

USING STYLES

> **TO USE AN EXISTING STYLE,**
>
> **position the insertion point where you're about to start typing new text, or select existing text with your mouse. Click the Styles button on the ruler, or choose Layout ➤ Styles. Then choose the name of the style you want to activate.**

Once you've created a style, using it is no different from using any other WordPerfect feature: You can activate the style before you start typing new text, or you can select existing text and then turn on the style.

ACTIVATING A STYLE FROM THE RULER

Styles
Bibliogrphy
body
Doc Init
Pleading
Tech Init

As a shortcut to going through the menus to activate a style, you can use the Styles button, shown at left, from the ruler. To turn on the ruler, choose View ➤ Ruler from the pull-down menus (or press Alt+Shift+F3). (Remember to use the ruler buttons, you must have a mouse.) The sections that follow describe how to use styles from the Styles button and the Layout ➤ Styles pull-down menu.

ACTIVATING A STYLE BEFORE YOU TYPE

You can activate a style before typing the text you want formatted. Just start in the document window and follow these steps:

1. Position the insertion point where you're about to type text that uses the style.

2. Choose a style from the Styles button on the ruler, or choose **L**ayout ➤ **S**tyles (or press Alt+F8).

3. If you didn't use the ruler, choose the style you want to use from the Style list box, and then choose **O**n or press ↵.

4. Type your text. If you've activated an open style, skip the next step, since open styles can't be deactivated (you normally won't want to deactivate an open style anyway).

5. When you want to resume typing "unstyled" text, press → once to move the insertion point beyond the [Style Off] code, or choose **L**ayout ➤ **S**tyles (Alt+F8) and choose O**ff**. Alternatively, if you set the role of the Enter key to Off or Off/On, you can just press ↵ to move past the [Style Off] code and resume typing normal text.

NOTE *If you want to turn off an open style, you must choose a different open style that cancels the codes in the style, or insert the equivalent codes in the document window in the normal manner.*

ACTIVATING A STYLE FOR EXISTING TEXT

If you've already typed some text, you can reformat it later with an existing style. Just follow these steps, starting in the document window:

1. If you're activating an open style, move the insertion point just before the text that should be formatted with the new style, or to the beginning of the document if you want to format all the text. If you're activating a paired style, select the text that you want to format.

2. Choose a style from the Styles button on the ruler, or choose **L**ayout ➤ **S**tyles (or press Alt+F8) and move the highlight bar to the style you want to use. Choose **O**n or press ↵ to activate the style.

After activating a style, you are returned to your document, and the codes and text from your style are in effect.

HIDDEN CODES FOR STYLES

Whenever you format text with a paired style, WordPerfect inserts [Style On] codes where you activate the feature and [Style Off] codes where you deactivate it. The name of the style is included in the code. For example, Figure 14.3 shows a portion of the sample newsletter from Figure 14.2 in both the document and Reveal Codes portions of the screen. As you can see, the title "Newsletter debut" is formatted with a style named *Headline,* the line "by Joan Smith" is formatted with a style named *By line,* and the text of the article is formatted with a style named *Body.*

When you move the highlight directly onto a [Style On] or [Style Off] code, the code expands, and you can see the actual formatting codes within the style, including any codes that were automatically determined by Word-Perfect in the [Style Off] code when you first created the style.

Open styles are activated with an [Open Style] code, which includes the name of the style. There is no closing code for an open style, since an open style is designed to format all text below the code.

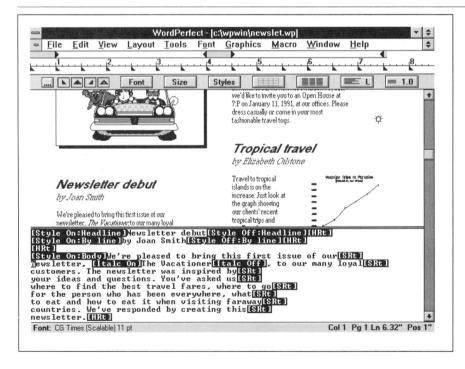

FIGURE 14.3:

[Style On] and [Style Off] codes in Reveal Codes

CHANGING A STYLE

TO ALTER AN EXISTING STYLE,

choose Layout ➤ Styles (Alt+F8), highlight the name of the style you want to alter, and choose Edit.

NOTE *You can edit the codes in WordPerfect's prepackaged styles the same way you edit a style you created yourself.*

If you decide that a style is not doing exactly what you want, you can edit the style by using the same basic techniques you used to create it. Follow these steps:

1. Choose **Layout ➤ S**tyles, or press Alt+F8.

2. Highlight the name of the style you want to change.

3. Choose **E**dit. The Style Editor for the chosen style appears—it's the same screen you worked with when you created the style.

4. You can make any adjustments to the codes on this screen, and you can verify the exact positions of the codes in Reveal Codes. If you're editing a paired style, remember that actions to be performed when the style is activated go before the [Comment] code, and actions to be performed when the style is deactivated go after the [Comment] code.

5. Optionally, choose **P**roperties to change the style's name, type, and description, and the function of the ↵ key, using techniques you learned for creating a style. Then choose OK to close the dialog box.

6. When you are finished with the Styles Editor screen, choose **C**lose twice or press ↵ twice to return to the document window.

If the style has been used anywhere in the current document, the text affected by it will be reformatted automatically to reflect the changes you have made.

REMOVING A STYLE FROM TEXT

If you apply the wrong style to part of your document, or if you decide that one section doesn't require special formatting after all, you can delete the style without going to the Styles dialog box and without affecting the use of the same style elsewhere in the document. To do so, simply open Reveal Codes, move the insertion point to the [Style On] or [Open Style] code that's activating the style you want to deactivate, and then press Delete to delete the code.

For a paired style, both the [Style On] code and the [Style Off] code are deleted automatically, regardless of which one was highlighted when you pressed Delete. Note that any text that was part of the style itself (*not* text you typed between the two style codes) is deleted along with the style's formats.

SAMPLE STYLES AS FOOD FOR THOUGHT

LESSON 6

See Lesson 6 in Part 9 for a hands-on example of creating and using similar styles.

Take a look at some sample styles now, referring back to Figure 14.2, to give you some food for thought when creating your own styles. Each style in this section was created using the general steps described at the outset of this chapter, and each can be used either before typing text or after selecting existing text.

EXAMPLES OF PAIRED STYLES

A paired style is used to format a short passage of text, for example, to define the fonts and text appearances of titles, headings, margin notes, footnotes, lists, and other elements of text that are used consistently throughout a document. Using paired styles is also a good means of storing frequently used special symbols, such as bullets or "graphic" quotation marks. In short, a paired style can be used for any element in a document that has a beginning and an end. Sample paired styles are discussed in the following sections.

A Paired Style to Format Headlines

Figure 14.4 shows a paired style named *Headline* that was used to format the headlines (article titles) in the sample newsletter in Figure 14.2.

Here's how each code was inserted, along with a description of what each code does:

[Cndl EOP:4][HRt]: This code was inserted in the style by choosing Layout ➤ **P**age ➤ Conditional **E**nd of Page, and choosing 4 lines. The conditional end of page keeps the article title, byline, and first line of text together (preventing them from being split across two pages or two columns).

NOTE
NOTE

Conditional End of Page is covered in Chapter 7.

[Font:Univers Bold Italic (Scalable) 16pt]: This code was inserted by choosing Font ➤ **F**ont and choosing the font and point size for printing article titles.

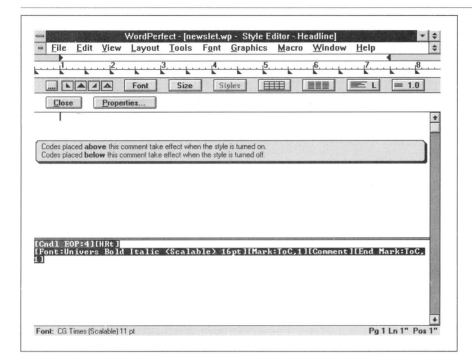

FIGURE 14.4:

*A sample paired style
to format article titles
in the newsletter in
Figure 14.2*

[Mark:ToC,1][End Mark:ToC,1]: This code pair is entirely optional
and was entered by selecting the [Comment] code (place the insertion
point to the left of the Comment code in Reveal Codes, and press
Shift+→ once to highlight the code), then choosing **T**ools ➤ Mar**k**
Text ➤ Table of **C**ontents, and entering *1* as the Table of Contents
level. This makes it easy to automatically generate a table of contents
when the newsletter is finished. (See Chapter 23 for additional
information.)

Normally, you do not need to bother with inserting closing codes in paired
styles. Exceptions to this rule include the Table of Contents, List, and Block
Protect features. For these features, you first must move the highlight to the
[Comment] code in the style, then press Shift+→ before choosing the feature.

After creating the style, choose Properties to set the Enter Key Inserts option to either Hard Return or Style Off, depending on whether you want to be
able to turn off the style by pressing → or ↵.

A Paired Style to Format Bylines

NOTE *Both the Byline and Body Text styles in these examples use the default font for the overall document or the font specified just above the first article title. They could, however, contain their own [Font] code to specify any font you wish.*

The paired style for formatting bylines is shown in Figure 14.5, again on the Style Editor.

This simple style uses two formatting features:

[Large On]: This code was entered by choosing Font ➤ Size ➤ Large (Ctrl+S L) to format the byline using the same typeface as body text, but slightly larger.

[Italc On]: This code was entered by choosing Font ➤ Italic (**Ctrl+I**) to display the byline in italic style.

Note that, even though [Large On] and [Italc On] are paired codes, it's not necessary to place the closing codes (e.g., [Large Off] and [Italc Off]) to the right of [Comment], since paired codes are placed there automatically. Again, after entering the codes, choose Properties to choose either Hard Return or Style Off as the role of the Enter key, depending on whether you'd prefer to end the style by pressing → or ↵.

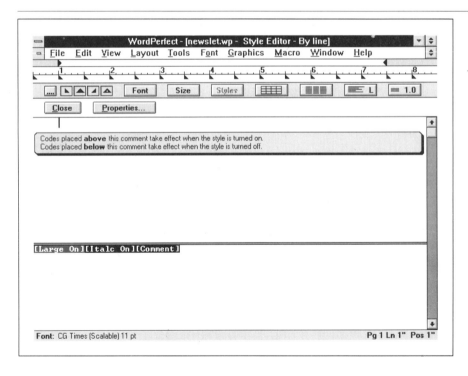

FIGURE 14.5:

A sample style for formatting bylines

A Paired Style to Format Body Text

The style for formatting the body text in each article is shown in Figure 14.6. This style has no codes in front of the [Comment] code and the following codes to the right of the [Comment] code:

[Flsh Rgt]: This code, entered by choosing **Layout** ➤ **Line** ➤ **Flush Right** (or pressing Alt+F7), moves the insertion point to the right margin (or right edge of the column).

[*:5,6]: This code, entered by pressing Ctrl+W and typing *5,6* to display the WordPerfect Character dialog box and choosing Insert **and** Close, is the WordPerfect special character for the little sunshine graphic used at the end of each article.

After entering the codes for this particular style, you'll want to choose Properties, to be sure the Enter Key Inserts option is set to Hard Return so that ↵ behaves normally and does not turn off the style. This prevents the ↵ entered between multiple paragraphs typed in this style from turning off the style.

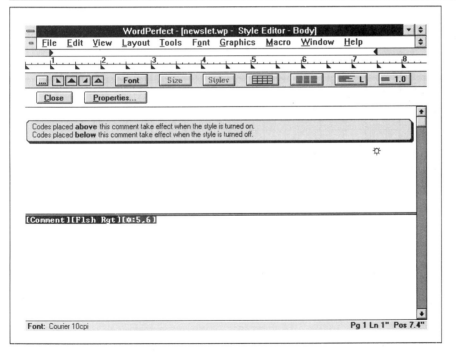

FIGURE 14.6:

A paired style to format body text

If you try out any of these open styles, remember that some of the features they use (such as Top/Bottom margin) are best viewed on the Print Preview screen or on the printed copy of the document.

EXAMPLES OF OPEN STYLES

An open style is generally used to set the format of an entire document, such as margins, paper size and type, columns, and so forth. For example, you can use an open style to predefine a commonly used combination of paper size, margins, and spacing. That way, when you need to create a document with that particular paper format, you simply need to choose the appropriate style rather than bother to choose all the formatting codes.

With some ingenuity and experience, you can also create advanced styles that use more sophisticated WordPerfect features. In all these examples, keep in mind that you could place the same codes at the top of any document, without using a style, and come up with the same results. But ease of use is the clear advantage gained by placing the codes in a style. You can easily activate the style in each new document you create, rather than go through the steps required to enter each code independently.

An Open Style to Format a Brochure

Figure 14.7 shows an example of a style that prints text sideways on the page and divides it into three columns, making it easy to create a three-fold brochure.

Here is an explanation of the various codes placed in the style:

[Paper Sz/Typ:11" × 8.5", Standard]: This code was inserted by choosing options from the **Layout** ➤ **Page** ➤ Paper **S**ize dialog box to choose landscape (sideways) printing.

[T/B Mar:0.5",0.5"][L/R Mar:0.5",0.5"]: These codes were inserted by choosing options from the **Layout** ➤ **Margins** dialog box to set the top, bottom, left, and right margins to $\frac{1}{2}$ inch.

[Just:Left]: This code was inserted by choosing **Layout** ➤ **J**ustification ➤ **L**eft (Ctrl+L).

[Col Def:Newspaper…][Col On]: These codes were inserted by choosing **Layout** ➤ **C**olumns and defining three columns across the page (see Chapter 20).

[VLine:Column 1…][VLine:Column 2…]: These codes were inserted by choosing **G**raphics ➤ **L**ine ➤ **V**ertical (Ctrl+Shift+F11) and positioning the line between columns.

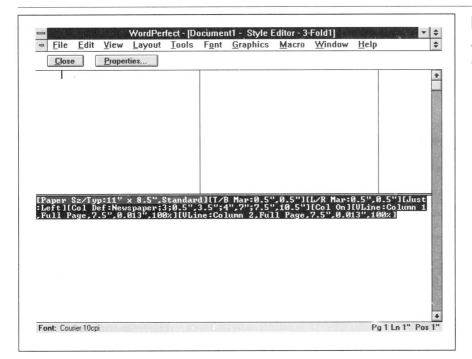

An open style for typing a brochure

See Chapter 20 for more information on creating multicolumn documents.

Figure 14.8 shows how the style, when used alone and viewed on the Print Preview screen, prints lines between columns on a sheet of paper. Figure 14.9 shows an example in which the style was used to format a three-fold brochure, complete with text and graphics.

An Open Style to Print a Letterhead

If you have a laser (or other high-quality printer), you can design and develop your own letterhead with WordPerfect, then place it in a style. When you need to type on letterhead paper, just choose the letterhead style and type your letter. Then insert a plain sheet of paper in the printer, and print your document. You'll see that both your letterhead and the letter will be printed for you. Figure 14.10 shows a sample letterhead that was created by choosing a letterhead style and printing the document on plain paper.

The letterhead is an open style and hence contains no [Comment] code.

Figure 14.11 shows the Style Editor screen for the open style used to create the letterhead.

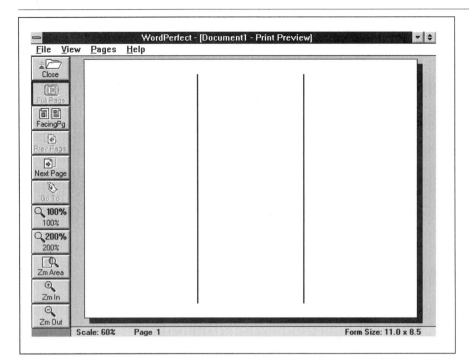

FIGURE 14.8:

An example of an open style used to format a blank page into three columns

---

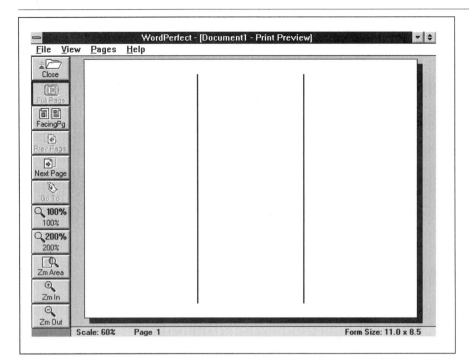

FIGURE 14.9:

The open style used in Figure 14.8, as the basic format for typing a three-fold brochure

Charters	Hot Air Balloons Paddle Boats Helicopters	*Seasonal*		
		Spring	MARCH Run for Fun Heart Builders	
Cultural Events	Paramount Square Fifth Opera Stage Scott Balk Center Symphonic Arts Jackson Center Center for the Arts Bates Assembly		APRIL Jenson County Golf Tournament Governor's Cup Sailing MAY County Trail Run 10K for Health	
Entertainment	Laffs on Us Jamison Theater Cross Center Auditorium Five Theater for Art Public Dance	*Summer*	JUNE Quarterhorse Racing City Marathon JULY Fiesta Riverfest	
Museums & Galleries	Orl Southwest Gallery Geoffrey Gallery Santa Fe Style Dillman Museum Art in Sound		AUGUST Symphony Outdoor Series	
		Fall	SEPTEMBER Riverfront School Festival OCTOBER Pumpkin Pick City Hall Masquerade	
		Winter	DECEMBER Capital Christmas Santa's Visit New Year's Gala	

CALENDAR OF EVENTS

Weekend Activities for Visitors

City of Metropolis
Chamber of Commerce
345 Main Street
Metropolis, AZ 12345
(999) 555-3452

A sample letterhead created and printed with WordPerfect

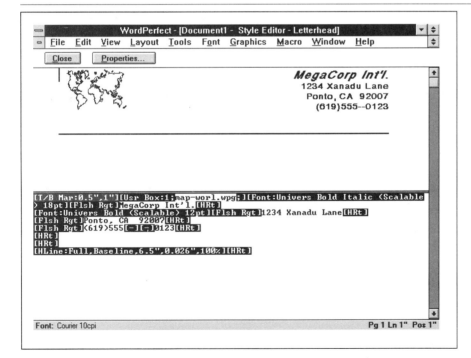

FIGURE 14.11:

An open style for printing a sample letterhead

Here's how each code in the letterhead style works:

[T/B Mar:0.5",1"]: This code was entered by choosing **L**ayout ➤ **M**argins (Ctrl+F8) and setting the top margin to 0.5 inch.

[Usr Box:1;map-world.wpg.WPG;]: This code was entered by choosing **G**raphics ➤ **U**ser Box ➤ **C**reate; it contains the WordPerfect world-map image with a width of 1.5 inches, page-anchored to the top-left corner of the page **W**rap Text Around Box was set to No.

[Font…]: These codes were entered by choosing F**o**nt ➤ **F**ont (F9).

[Flsh Rgt]: These codes were entered by choosing **L**ayout ➤ **L**ine ➤ **F**lush Right (Alt+F7).

[HLine:…]: The horizontal line was entered by choosing **G**raphics ➤ **L**ine ➤ **H**orizontal (Ctrl+F11), with a thickness of 0.026 inch. A blank line ([HRt]) separates the two lines.

A REPEATING STYLE TO TYPE A LIST

A *repeating* style is just a paired style with the Enter option set to Off/On. Figure 14.12 shows an example of a style that helps you type a bulleted list

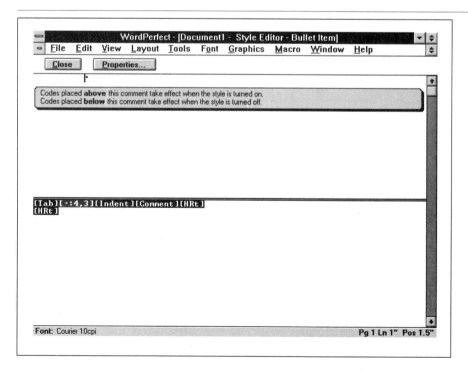

FIGURE 14.12:

A style to format a bulleted list

without manually typing the special bullet codes, indents, and extra space between list entries.

Here is a list of the codes that were entered in the style and what they do:

[Tab]: This code was entered by pressing Tab; it indents the bullet one tab stop.

[•:4,3]: This code was entered by pressing **Ctrl+W**, typing *4,3* and pressing ↵.

[Indent]: This code was entered by pressing Indent (F7); it indents the text to the right of the bullet.

[HRt][HRt]: These codes were entered by moving the insertion point to the right of the [Comment] code, then pressing ↵ twice; they insert a blank line between each item in the bulleted list.

After entering the codes for this style, choose Properties and change the Enter Key Inserts option to Style Off/On. Choose OK or Close, and then On to go back to the document windows with the style turned on. When activated, the style types the bullet and indent for the first item automatically. You type the text for the bulleted list, and press ↵. A blank line, the bullet, and the indent for the next item in the list appear automatically. Repeat this until you've typed each item in the bulleted list (do not press ↵ after typing the last item in the list). Then press → to move the insertion point past the [Style Off] code, and resume typing normal text.

SAVING A SET OF STYLES

TO USE A STYLE IN MORE THAN ONE DOCUMENT,

you must first save the style in a library by choosing Layout ➤ Styles ➤ Save As.

When you create a style or several styles, then save the overall document, the styles are saved with that document and can only be used in that document. However, you can build a collection of "generic" styles for use in several documents by saving your styles in a separate *style library,* which will be available to all documents.

For example, if you print a monthly newsletter, you can create a collection of styles called NEWSLET.STY for formatting the newsletter. If you also happen to be working on a book, you can create another style library named BOOK.STY that contains styles relevant to the book.

When you first install WordPerfect, it automatically displays its own sample style library, named LIBRARY.STY. This library contains seven sample styles, described a little later in the chapter. To create and save your own style library, follow these steps:

N O T E
N O T E
When working with two or more open documents, each can have its own separate style library.

1. From the document window, choose **L**ayout ➤ **S**tyles or press Alt+F8. (A quicker way to display the Styles dialog box is to double-click the Styles button on the ruler.)

2. Optionally, delete any styles that you do not want to save in the current library (such as some of the examples provided by WordPerfect), by highlighting the name of the unwanted style and choosing **D**elete (described in more detail later).

3. Choose Save **A**s. WordPerfect displays the Save Styles dialog box, shown in Figure 14.13. Type the name you want to give the new style library. (You don't have to enter the .STY suffix to the library name; WordPerfect will do that for you.) Use the Files and Directories list boxes to view and change directories.

WordPerfect saves the styles in the current listing as a file and leaves you at the Styles dialog box with the same styles available. Be sure to save or replace a style library whenever you add, change, or delete any styles within that library; otherwise, the saved library will no longer match the library in the current document.

If you want to *replace* a style library, you must use the same name as the existing style-library file.

RETRIEVING A STYLE LIBRARY

TO USE A STYLE IN THE CURRENT DOCUMENT THAT YOU'VE PREVIOUSLY SAVED IN A STYLE LIBRARY,

choose Layout ➤ Styles ➤ Retrieve, and enter the file name of the library containing the style or styles you want to use.

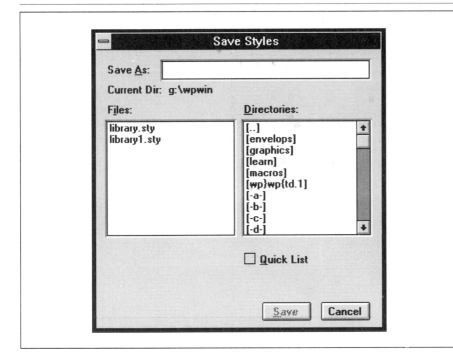

*The Save Styles
dialog box*

When you're in a new document, and you want to use the styles you've pre-viously saved in a library, follow these steps:

Double-click the Styles button in the ruler to display the dialog box quickly.

1. Starting in the document window, choose **L**ayout ➤ **S**tyles or press Alt+F8 to display the Styles dialog box and view the current style library.

2. Optionally, delete any styles from the current library that you do not want to use in the current document, by moving the highlight to the name of any unwanted style and choosing **D**elete.

3. Choose **R**etrieve. WordPerfect displays the Retrieve Styles dialog box, shown in Figure 14.14.

4. The Files list box shows all styles in the default styles subdirectory. Double-click on the style library you want to retrieve, or use the Files and Directories list boxes to view and change directories, and choose **R**etrieve or press ↵ to retrieve the style library.

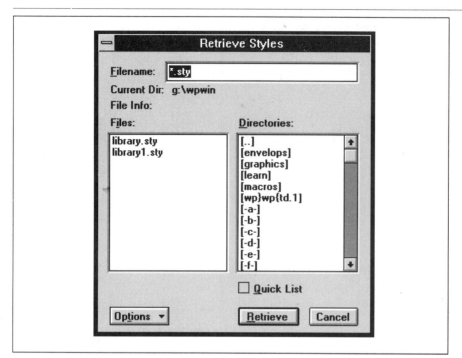

FIGURE 14.14:

The Retrieve Styles dialog box

5. If any of the styles in the current style library has the same name as a style in the library you are retrieving, WordPerfect will prompt

Style(s) already exist. Replace?

6. If you want to replace the current styles with the incoming styles, choose **Y**es. Otherwise, choose **N**o to avoid replacing any existing styles (this way, the unique styles will be combined with the existing styles, but the existing styles won't be changed).

The styles in the retrieved file will appear in your Styles dialog box, along with any that were already listed. The listing is alphabetized automatically. If you save the current document, all the styles in it are saved along with it. If you save this new, larger library with the same name as the original library, you will overwrite the old library with the new one (if in doubt, save it with a new name).

Because styles in a retrieved style library are *combined* with existing styles, you can easily use styles from several separate libraries in any single document.

DELETING A STYLE FROM A LIBRARY

If a particular style library contains a style that you don't really want, you can easily delete the style. Follow these steps:

1. Choose **L**ayout ➤ **S**tyles or press Alt+F8, or double-click the Styles ruler button to display the Styles dialog box.

2. Move the highlight to the name of the style that you want to delete.

3. Choose **D**elete. You'll see this dialog box:

Choose one of the options summarized below:

Leave Format Codes: deletes the style from the Styles dialog box and all style codes with the deleted style name from the document. Any hidden codes that were contained in the style remain in the current document, replacing the [Style On], [Style Off], and [Open Style] codes that were deleted.

Delete Format Codes: deletes the style from the Styles dialog box and all style codes with the name of the style you're deleting from the document. This option also deletes all hidden codes associated with the style in the document.

If you want to build a new style library from scratch, first delete all the styles in the current library by choosing the Delete Definition Only option.

Delete Definition Only: deletes the style from the dialog box of style names, but has no effect on the document itself. You can use this option to help you determine which styles are actually used in your document. To do this, delete the name of every style in the list of available styles, and then return to the document window and scroll through the entire document. WordPerfect will automatically recreate the list of styles, using only the names of styles actually used in the current document.

The style is deleted from the list of available styles immediately. Don't forget to save the library again (using Layout ➤ Styles ➤ Save As or Alt+F8) if you want to update the copy of the library on disk as well as the copy in the current document.

TIPS FOR USING STYLES

Learning to use styles effectively is largely a matter of recognizing when you will be using a format repeatedly throughout a document or several documents, and having the foresight to predefine that format as a style to save time and effort. The sections that follow contain some tips that will help you as you gain experience and learn to use styles to your advantage.

MANAGING YOUR STYLE LIBRARIES

If you work on lots of different kinds of documents and need to create numerous style libraries, there are several things you can do to keep your libraries organized:

◆ Assign the same file-name extension, such as *.STY,* to all style libraries, so you can easily recognize them by name. If you don't add the extension, WordPerfect will automatically assign .STY.

◆ Store all your style libraries in the same directory. You can choose **F**iles ➤ **Pr**eferences ➤ **L**ocation of Files to specify a directory. Be sure to move any existing libraries to that directory if you change the location.

◆ Create a library of general-purpose styles, and make this the default library that appears automatically when you first run WordPerfect. After you create, name, and save this library, make it the default one by choosing **F**ile ➤ **Pr**eferences ➤ **L**ocation of Files and specifying its name in the **F**ilename text box.

◆ Type the date of the most recent revision to a style as part of the style's description. Because styles are stored with individual documents, as well as in style libraries, it's often difficult to keep track of the most recent version of a style that's been modified.

SEARCHING FOR STYLES

When using the Search and Replace feature (Chapter 9), you can search for the generic style codes, such as [Style On], [Style Off], and [Open Style]. But you cannot search for a specific, named style.

GRAPHIC IMAGES IN STYLES

If you include a graphic image in a style, you must specify Graphic on Disk as the graphic type. Consequently, you can only print that document on a computer that also has a copy of the graphic image (that image must be stored on the same drive and in the same directory that was specified when you created the graphic). If you transmit or mail a floppy disk with a copy of a document that contains a style with a graphic image, remember also to include a copy of the graphic file. For more information, see Chapter 19.

NESTING STYLES

You can nest styles while using them, but you cannot use a style as part of another style while creating or editing a style's codes.

Nesting is a technique where you use one paired code or paired style as part of another. You may have already used nesting if you applied both bold and underline to some text before you typed it. If you nest paired styles, the result is the same as nesting any other paired style: The formats are combined (provided that one does not cancel the other). For example, if Style ABC formats text for boldface, and Style XYZ formats text for italics, then the codes and text

[Style On:ABC][Style On:XYZ]Hello[Style Off:ABC][Style Off:XYZ]

print the word *Hello* in boldface and italics.

STYLES VS. MACROS

A *macro* records keystrokes and menu selections and plays them back just as they were recorded. If you want the editing convenience of styles, along with the keystroke convenience of macros, create the style first, then create a macro to activate the style.

OVERCOMING STYLE LIMITATIONS

Not all codes work with or can be used in styles. Such codes are simply ignored when you try to enter them in a style. For example, you cannot place [Col On] and [Col Off] codes in a style to manage columns.

One way around this is to create a macro that inserts the codes that the style cannot and activates the style so that you still get the best of both worlds—the keystroke savings of macros with the editing ease of styles.

Another way to overcome style limitations is to place the code you want in the document, via the regular document window, then move or copy the code into a style. This works well for many codes that you would normally access by choosing Tools ➤ Define. While you're on the Style Editor screen, the Define option is dimmed on the Tools menu, so it is unavailable.

EXPLORING WORDPERFECT'S SAMPLE STYLES

As mentioned earlier, WordPerfect comes with seven sample styles for you to explore. If you haven't already changed the default style library, you can view the style names by choosing Layout ➤ Style or pressing Alt+F8. Figure 14.15 shows them listed in the Styles dialog box.

To view the codes within any style, simply choose Layout ➤ Styles (or press Alt+F8), highlight the name of the style, and choose Edit. After looking at the codes, choose Close to return to the Styles dialog box. Descriptions of each style follow:

Bibliogrphy: hangs (outdents) the first line of a paragraph and ends each paragraph with two hard returns. To try this style, activate the

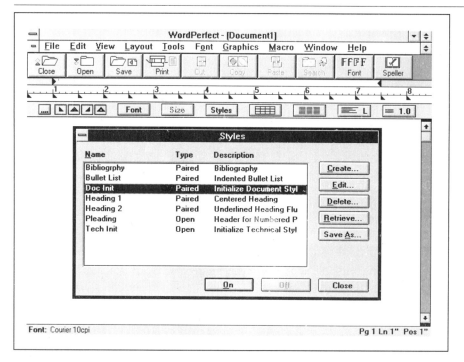

FIGURE 14.15:

A list of the sample styles that come with WordPerfect

style, and type several brief paragraphs (slightly wider than the screen), pressing ↵ after typing each one. Press → to move out of the style.

Bullet List: similar to the bulleted list examples presented earlier in this chapter, lets you type each item in a bulleted list, automatically adding each bullet and formating text.

Doc Init: automatically puts in the codes needed to generate a table of contents from [Mark:Toc] codes within the document, when placed near the top of the document. This style also turns on automatic paragraph numbering and outlining (used in conjunction with the Document outline style, discussed in Chapter 22).

Heading 1: centers a short line of text and prints in Very large size with boldface, with one blank line beneath.

Heading 2: displays and underlines a short line in Large size.

Pleading: places line numbers and a graphic line in the left margin. Activate this style near the top of an empty document window, and switch to Print Preview to view the result.

Tech Init: defines the numbering style for a technical outline and turns on automatic outlining (used in conjunction with the Technical Outline style, discussed in Chapter 22).

In this chapter you've learned about the Styles feature, which can make some of your bigger projects more manageable, lend consistency to the appearance of your documents, and save you considerable time.

In the next chapter, you'll learn about another timesaving feature: Macros.

CHAPTER 15

Saving Time with Macros

Macros help you automate some of the more mundane, repetitive word processing tasks by letting you record all the necessary keystrokes to perform those tasks, then "play back" those keystrokes at any time with just a few keypresses.

HANDS-ON
· · · · · · · · · · · · ·
LESSON 8

To create some macros that can simplify your work right now, see Lesson 8 in Part 9.

Though the term "macro" sounds somewhat mysterious, macros are easy to use and have something for everyone. If you know how to perform a task in WordPerfect, you can probably just as easily create a macro to perform it for you more quickly and easily in the future. Anytime you find yourself typing the same text or choosing the same series of menu options over and over, remember that you can just record those keystrokes in a macro, and play them back as often as you wish with just a couple of keypresses.

WHAT IS A MACRO?

Macro is the opposite of micro (small). In a sense, a macro is a "large keystroke," because a single macro keystroke can perform many keystrokes. For example, if you have to type your company name many times, in many documents, you might want to record those keystrokes in a macro.

When referring to macros, the terms "run," "invoke," and "execute" all mean the same thing: to play back the keystrokes recorded within the macro.

In the future, whenever you need to type your company name, you don't need to type it over again. Instead, just run the macro and let it do the typing. Once you create a macro, you can reuse it as many times as you wish. Options for creating (recording) a macro, as well as for playing back (running) a macro, are both found on the Macro pull-down menu or by pressing the shortcut key Macro Record (Ctrl+F10) or Macro Play (Alt+F10), as described below.

CREATING A MACRO

TO RECORD KEYSTROKES IN A MACRO,

choose Macro ➤ Record, or press Ctrl+F10. Enter a name and optional description for the macro, then press ↵ to begin. You can access commands from any menu (using either the mouse or the keyboard), and you can type text into the document. However, during macro recording, you cannot use the mouse to select text. When you are finished recording, choose Macro ➤ Stop or press Ctrl+Shift+F10.

Creating a macro is easy; just follow these steps:

1. Choose **Macro ➤ R**ecord, or press Ctrl+F10. You'll see the dialog box shown in Figure 15.1.

2. In the Record Macro dialog box, enter a name from one to eight characters in length (no spaces or punctuation) in the **F**ilename text box. WordPerfect uses the default file-extension .WCM for macros, so you don't need to include an extension.

3. Optionally, you can provide a long description (up to 69 characters), as well as a multiline abstract. The long description will appear in the Description field in the WordPerfect File Manager (discussed in Chapter 12). And, when using the File Manager, you can use text you've included in the description and abstract when searching for files. Both the long description and abstract also appear in the Document Summary window (**L**ayout ➤ **D**ocument ➤ **S**ummary).

4. When you're finished entering the name, description, and abstract, choose **R**ecord or press ↵.

5. If a macro with the name you've entered already exists, you'll be asked whether you want to replace it. Choose **Y**es or **N**o.

You can switch to other Windows applications while recording macro keystrokes, but only those activities you perform in WordPerfect are recorded. For example, if you start a macro then switch to Windows Paintbrush, macro recording will be suspended until you return to WordPerfect.

The drive\directory where macros are stored is defined in the Location of Files dialog box, described under "Organizing Your Macros" later in this chapter.

6. WordPerfect always tells you it is recording a macro by displaying "Recording Macro" in the status bar. Type whatever keystrokes you want to record, including any menu choices and shortcut keypresses.

7. When you've finished recording, choose **M**acro ➤ **S**top, or press Ctrl+Shift+F10.

Before I talk about how to run your macro, I'll discuss some of the options you'll come across while creating the macro.

NAMING A MACRO

Macros are identified by file names. These names follow standard DOS conventions; that is, the name must be from one to eight characters in length and cannot include punctuation marks. WordPerfect automatically adds a .WCM extension to the character file name you provide (if you don't provide one yourself.) This extension identifies the file as a macro. When playing back macros, only files with the .WCM extension are initially displayed in the Play Macro dialog box.

You can give your macros any extension you want. However, you'll need to provide the full file name—a one- to eight-character name plus the

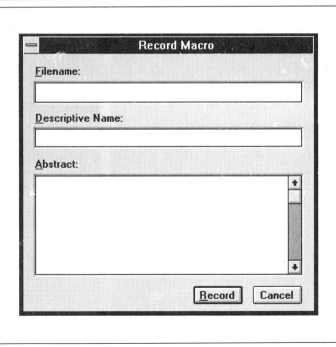

FIGURE 15.1:
The Record Macro dialog box

extension—when playing it back. Macros with the standard .WCM extension can be played back by typing just the name in the Play Macro dialog box.

If you are familiar with WordPerfect for DOS, be aware that WordPerfect for Windows only accepts full file names for macros; you do not have the option of recording an Alt+*letter* macro. An Alt+*letter* macro in DOS is played by pressing the Alt key in combination with a letter key (A–Z). In the Windows environment, Alt+*letter* combinations are reserved for choosing menu items.

In WordPerfect for DOS, Alt+*letter* macros provide a convenient means of playing back commonly used macros, because you don't have to type a complete file name to identify the specific macro you want to run. However, WordPerfect for Windows regains some of that lost functionality by letting you "assign" macros to any of the following shortcuts:

◆ Macro menu—choose the macro from a list on the Macro menu.

◆ Button Bar—click on a button to run the macro.

◆ Shortcut key—identify a particular key combination (like Ctrl+Shift+A) to play a particular macro (covered in Chapter 27).

DESCRIBING A MACRO

See Chapter 12 for more information on the File Manager and document summaries.

The Descriptive Name text box in the Record Macro dialog box lets you type a brief description of the macro. You can enter a phrase or sentence up to 69 characters long describing your macro (for example, "Quick Save," "Mark page and copy," or "Change italic to underline"). Similarly, the Abstract text box lets you provide a detailed discussion of the macro and can be handy if you need to explain how the macro should be used, or if you forget its purpose after not using it for a long time.

The macro description is shown in the WordPerfect File Manager, as well as in the Document Summary dialog box.

RECORDING ACTIONS

Recording a WordPerfect macro isn't that different from recording a nephew's birthday with your camcorder. With the camcorder, press Record, then point the camera to where the action is. Press the Stop button when you're tired of all the cake thrown at you. Once recorded, you can go back and view the action. If you don't like what you see, you can record over the tape again (erasing what was there before), or edit out the bad parts.

When WordPerfect is recording a macro (the "Recording Macro" message is displayed in the status bar), it monitors the activity of the keyboard and mouse. Just about everything you do is stored in the macro file as you do it.

◆   Macros record all text you type into the document, as well as all editing and insertion-point movement keys (like ↵, ↓, and Backspace).

◆   Macros record nearly all commands you access with the mouse or the keyboard. The exceptions are commands like Macro Play and Macro Record, which don't apply when you are already recording a macro.

Although you're free to select text in the document window, you can only do so by using the keyboard, not the mouse. In fact, when the I beam is in the document, it turns into a "circle-and-slash," indicating that all mouse activity within the boundaries of text is prohibited.

Unlike the macro-recording techniques used in some Windows programs, WordPerfect records the *event,* not the specific keys you press or the commands you choose. This is an important point. During macro recording, you can use the mouse to hunt through menus and dialog boxes, but unless you specify some action (like change the margins or select a new paper/page size), the macro will not record anything.

While you are recording keystrokes, don't forget that they are also being played out in your document window and are therefore affecting your document now. (Be sure to have a backup of your document available, just in case you make a mistake when recording your macro.)

When you've finished recording your keystrokes, choose Macro ➤ Stop or press Ctrl+Shift+F10. WordPerfect stops recording keystrokes and saves the macro. The "Recording Macro" message disappears, and everything returns to normal. You can play back your macro right now or at any time in the future (discussed later in "Running a Macro").

CANCELING RECORDING

If you start recording a series of actions—whether they are keystrokes or command selections—then make a mistake and want to start all over, you can't press Cancel (Esc or Shift+Esc), as this keystroke would just be recorded like any other. Instead, you have to stop recording keystrokes and start over from scratch: Choose Macro ➤ Stop or press Ctrl+Shift+F10. Restart recording, as described in "Replacing an Existing Macro" later in this chapter.

RUNNING A MACRO

TO RUN (PLAY BACK) A MACRO,

choose Macro ➤ Play, or press Alt+F10, type the macro name, and press ↵.

You can also attach macros to the pull-down menus and Button Bar, and play them back simply by clicking on them, as described later in this chapter.

Running a macro is even easier than creating one:

1. If the macro will be working on a particular section of text (such as italicizing a word), position the insertion point where you want the macro to start taking action.

2. Choose **M**acro ➤ **P**lay, or press Alt+F10. You'll see the dialog box shown in Figure 15.2.

3. In the Filename text box, type the name you assigned to the macro when you created it, and press ↵ (or double-click the file name).

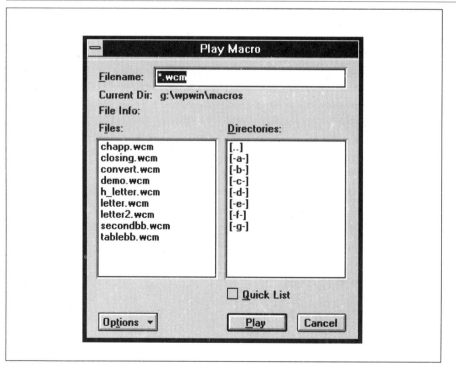

The Play Macro dialog box

WordPerfect replays all the keys you recorded when you defined the macro, then returns you to the document window. What you'll see in the document window are the *results* of the keys being played back, not the actual keystrokes.

STOPPING A RUNNING MACRO

The "Please Wait" message appears in the lower-left corner of the screen while a macro is running.

If you start a macro and want to stop it dead in its tracks (perhaps because you've run the wrong macro or didn't properly position the insertion point before running it), press Cancel (Esc or Shift+Esc). This will leave you at whatever point the macro was when you canceled it—maybe in the document window, or maybe at a dialog box or prompt. Since the macro probably will play back some keystrokes before you cancel it, you might want to take a quick look in your document window to see what changes have been made and make any necessary corrections.

You may want to try creating some macros on your own now. As mentioned earlier, if you want to get some hands-on experience in (as well as some suggestions for) creating and using some practical macros, refer to Lesson 8 in Part 9. Macros are one area where a little experience is very enlightening.

REPLACING AN EXISTING MACRO

Remember that macros are very literal—they record your keystrokes exactly. For example, suppose that while recording keystrokes you mistype a word, backspace over the mistake to correct it, then continue recording keystrokes. When you play back that macro, it too will misspell the same word, backspace over the mistake, and type the correction.

This is harmless, but you may get tired of seeing the macro make and correct the same mistake over and over again. There are two possible ways to fix this problem: Replace the faulty macro by starting over and re-creating it from scratch, or edit the macro to remove the mistake.

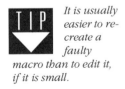

It is usually easier to re-create a faulty macro than to edit it, if it is small.

The first method is generally the easiest for small macros. Follow the same basic steps you used to create the first macro:

1. Choose **Macro ➤ Record**, or press Ctrl+F10.

2. In the Filename text box, type the name of the macro you want to replace, and press ↵. Enter the same name you originally assigned to the macro.

3. A dialog box appears that asks whether you want to replace the existing macro. Choose **Y**es; you want to replace the original with a new macro. (Once you choose Yes, there's no turning back. The old macro file will be erased forever, and even the unerase utilities in PC Tools and DOS 5 will not be able to recover it.)

The macro you create completely replaces the previous macro.

As an alternative to replacing an existing macro, you can edit the macro as you would any normal WordPerfect file, to make changes and corrections. Macro-editing techniques are described later in this chapter.

ATTACHING MACROS TO THE MACRO PULL-DOWN MENU

Macros you use regularly can be attached to the Macro pull-down menu. That way, you don't have to go through the steps of using the Macro Play command and entering a file name. The Macro pull-down menu accepts up to nine macro entries, and you can add and delete entries at any time.

To attach a macro to the Macro pull-down menu, follow these steps:

1. Choose **M**acro ➤ **A**ssign to Menu. The Assign Macro to Menu dialog box appears, as shown in Figure 15.3.

2. Choose **I**nsert to add a new macro entry to the menu.

3. In the Macro Name text box, type the file name of the macro you want to add to the menu, and press Tab.

4. In the Menu Text text box, type the text for the Macro menu (up to 30 characters). Press ↵.

5. Repeat steps 2–4 for each additional macro you want to attach to the Macro menu.

6. When you are finished attaching macros, choose **OK** to return to the document window.

If you want to select a macro that's in another directory of your hard drive, be sure to add the full path name, such as C:\MYMACRO\MACNAME.WCM (the .WCM extension is optional).

To run a macro that has been attached to the Macro menu, merely pull down the menu (use the mouse or press Alt+M), then choose the macro you want.

The Macro menu lists the macros in the order you attached them and appends identification numbers to each one. You can use these numbers to run a macro with the keyboard only. You may find this method faster and easier than reaching for the mouse each time you want to run a macro.

To run any macro attached to the Macro menu,

1. Press Alt+M to highlight the Macro menu.

2. Press a number from 1 to 9 (each number corresponds to the macro you want to invoke).

REMOVING A MACRO FROM THE MENU

To remove a macro from the Macro pull-down menu, follow these steps:

1. Choose **M**acro ➤ **A**ssign to Menu.

2. Select the macro you want to remove.

3. Choose **D**elete.

4. Repeat steps 2 and 3 for any other macro you want to remove from the Macro menu.

5. When you are finished, choose OK to return to the document window.

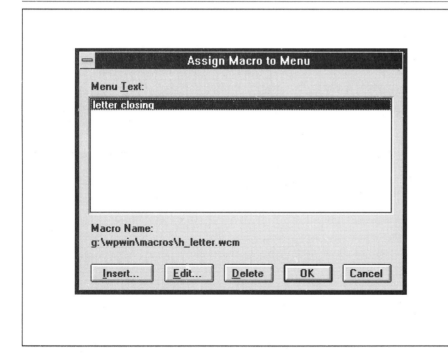

FIGURE 15.3:

The Assign Macro to Menu dialog box

EDITING A MACRO ENTRY

To change a macro item on the Macro menu, follow these steps:

1. Choose **M**acro ➤ **A**ssign to Menu.

2. Select the macro you want to edit.

3. Choose **E**dit.

4. Change the name of the macro in the Macro Name text box, if desired, then press Tab.

5. Change the text of the macro item in the Menu Text text box, if desired, then press ↵.

6. Repeat steps 2–5 for any other macro items you want to edit.

7. When you are finished, choose OK to return to the document window.

ASSIGNING MACROS TO THE BUTTON BAR

Button Bars are the true time-savers in WordPerfect for Windows. You are not limited to creating only buttons for menu commands. Any macro you record can be assigned to a button: Click the button with the mouse (buttons cannot be activated with the keyboard) and the macro runs. You can freely mix buttons for menu commands with buttons for macros. A macro button is shown with a small audiocassette icon and the macro file name underneath.

 *Techniques for creating, saving, and using Button Bars are covered in Chapter 3.*

If you've created several Button Bars, be sure to bring the one to which you want to assign the macro to the screen (View ➤ Button Bar Setup ➤ Select). Or, if you want to create a new Button Bar, use View ➤ Button Bar ➤ New to start from scratch. Then follow these steps to assign a macro to the current Button Bar:

1. Choose **V**iew ➤ Button Bar **S**etup ➤ **E**dit.

2. Choose **A**ssign Macro to Button.

3. In the list box that appears, select the macro you want to use.

4. Choose **A**ssign.

5. Repeat steps 2–4 for each additional button you want to add.

6. Choose OK when you're finished.

WordPerfect automatically saves the new Button Bar settings for you. You can always remove a button you no longer need, or move it around if its position in the bar doesn't suit you. Techniques for moving and deleting buttons are covered in Chapter 3.

ASSIGNING MACROS TO SHORTCUT KEYS

You can also assign macros to selected shortcut keys: Use File ➤ Preferences ➤ Keyboard. Chapter 27 discusses this topic in detail.

ORGANIZING YOUR MACROS

By now you know that all macros are stored on disk as files. This makes it easy for you to run any existing macro, regardless of the document you happen to be working on at the moment.

When recording and playing back a macro, you can temporarily override the default location for macro files by typing the complete drive\directory\file name (e.g., C:\WPWIN\MY-STUFF\MYMACRO) when prompted for a macro name.

You can choose where to store macro files by choosing the Location of Files option (File ➤ Preferences ➤ Location of Files; go into the Macros/Keyboards/Button Bars area). To prevent cluttering the C:\WPWIN directory, you might want to store all your macros (and keyboard files, discussed in Chapter 27) in a separate directory, such as C:\WPWIN\MACROS. In fact, the WordPerfect for Windows installation program will automatically create this directory structure for you (unless you chose to provide your own directory names).

If you change the location of your keyboard or macro files, remember that you should immediately move all those files (i.e., *.WCM and *.WWK) to the new directory. You can use the WordPerfect File Manager (File ➤ File Manager) to do so. Note that WordPerfect places the Button Bar files (these have a .WWP extension) with the keyboard/macro files as well.

WHAT'S INSIDE A MACRO?

When you record keystrokes in a macro, WordPerfect actually divides your recorded keystrokes into two types of actions: *keystrokes* and *tokens* (also sometimes referred to as *functions* or *product commands*).

If you type text, such as your name and address, WordPerfect stores exactly those keystrokes in the macro and plays them back when you run the macro. However, if you enter keystrokes that invoke a menu command, WordPerfect simply records the token for that command rather than the keystrokes or mouse movements. For example, if you choose Layout ➤ Styles, or press

Alt+F8, to get to the Styles dialog box, WordPerfect doesn't record these exact keystrokes or mouse steps. Instead, it converts them to the token *StylesDlg()*, which simply tells the macro to "get to the Styles dialog box" when it's played back. This helps WordPerfect to produce smaller, faster-running macros. The concept of tokens can be a difficult one to understand, but if you plan on spending much time with macros, especially writing and editing them, it's a concept you'll want to master.

A token is a reference to some complete action within WordPerfect. With the exception of text that you type in the document window, WordPerfect macros don't care what keys you press or how you move the mouse; it's the final action that matters. For example, while recording a macro, you can scan through the various pull-down menus, and as long as you don't choose a command, the macro won't store anything. However, the moment you choose a command, it is stored as a token in the macro, a reference to the command you used.

A third type of element found in macros is a *programming command*, but these are not added during recording. They are only found in macros that were edited or written from scratch. Programming commands direct the macro during playback, giving it some intelligence. For instance, you can program a macro to perform certain steps if one condition is met and an entirely different set if another condition is met.

As you'll see in a moment, you can change any of the elements of a macro directly from a WordPerfect document window.

OPENING A MACRO

Macros are standard WordPerfect documents, so you can open them like any other kind of document.

If you're not sure you have found the right macro, highlight it in the Files list box, then choose View. A View window will appear, showing you the contents of the file. You can scroll through the file, but you cannot edit it.

1. Choose **File ➤ O**pen, or press F4. The Open File dialog box appears.

2. Locate the macro you want to edit. It is more than likely that your macros are stored in a different directory than your regular Word-Perfect text documents. If you know the directory used to store your macros, type it in the Filename text box, followed by *.WCM (such as \WPWIN\MACROS*.WCM). Or, use the Directories list box to navigate the directories of your hard drive until you find the file you want.

3. Choose **O**pen to open the macro file.

ANATOMY OF A MACRO

Figure 15.4 shows a macro that was created by using the Macro Record function. At first glance, the macro looks rather odd, with its unique formatting and unusual commands, but the basic anatomy is rather simple:

◆ All macros start with an application identification, in this case, Application (WP.WPWP;Default; "WPWPUS.WCD"). You should not alter this, or the macro may not run.

◆ Text you typed into the document window during macro recording appears within a Type command. The text is displayed inside parentheses and double quote marks. If you want to add more text or edit existing text, be watchful that you follow the same pattern. The macro will not run if you leave off a quote mark or a parenthesis.

◆ Editing keys (like ↵, Ins, and so forth) appear as tokens and are followed by a set of parentheses. See Chapter 26 for a list of some of the more common editing-key tokens you are likely to encounter. You can always add these to your own macros, but you should be sure that they are spelled correctly and that the parentheses follow.

◆ Similarly, menu commands are also shown as tokens, but some commands include *arguments*. An argument is an additional piece of information that WordPerfect uses to determine how the command is to be carried out. For instance, there are two possible settings (or *states*) for bold: on and off. Therefore, the command for bold appears as FontBold(State:On!) or FontBold(State:Off!).

The exclamation point used in the argument for the command token looks rather strange, but it has a purpose. It helps WordPerfect differentiate an argument from a macro variable. You can learn more about variables and other advanced macro programming topics in Chapter 26.

EDITING TEXT IN A MACRO

Inserting and deleting text in a macro is the same as editing text in a document window. For example, Figure 15.5 shows a macro in the document window that types a name and address.

Suppose you want to change the address from 1234 Oak Tree Lane to 6789 Oak Tree Lane. This is a simple job: Just move the insertion point to the *1* in *1234*, press Delete four times to delete *1234*, then type *6789* to insert this new text. Figure 15.6 shows the completed change.

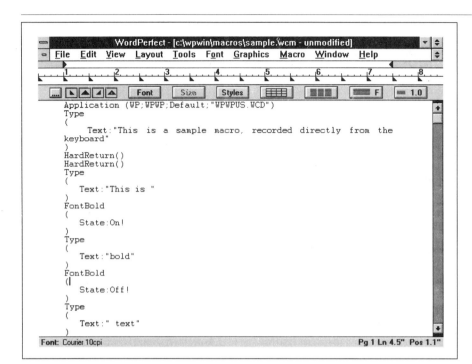

FIGURE 15.4:

A sample macro

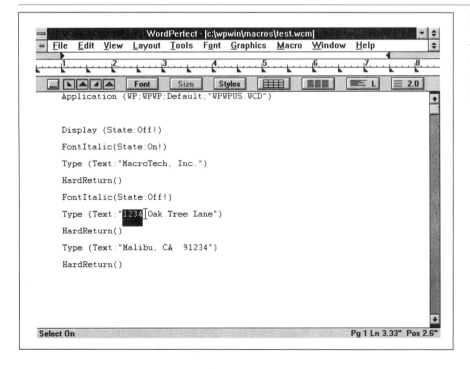

FIGURE 15.5:

A sample name-and-address macro in the document window

When you are finished editing your macro, you can save your changes by choosing File ➤ Save or pressing Shift+F3. Before running your macro, you may want to open a blank document screen or close the saved macro document.

COMPILING MACROS

Though you write macros by typing text into a standard WordPerfect document, WordPerfect is not able to read the text files directly and decipher what you want the macro to do. Before executing any commands, WordPerfect compiles the macro—a process in which the commands are converted to a form more readily understandable by the computer. The compiled version of the macro is stored in the hidden prefix of the file (which also includes style, printer, and document summary information). That way, the one macro file contains both the version of the macro readable by you and the version readable by WordPerfect.

If the macro has never been played before, it is not yet compiled. Word-Perfect senses this and takes a few moments to compile it. That's why the first time you use a macro, there is a slight delay, but subsequent times the macro plays almost immediately. If you edit the macro and save your changes, the

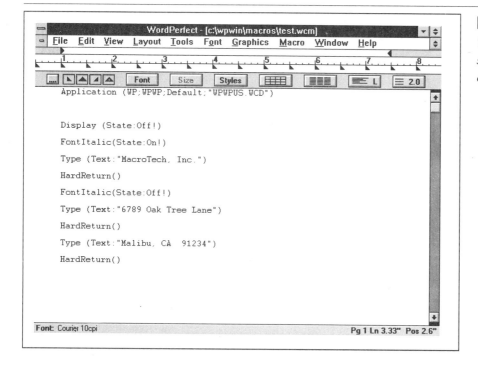

FIGURE 15.6:

The address in the sample macro has been changed.

compilation is no longer current, so WordPerfect again compiles the macro the next time it runs.

The Macro Facility program included with WordPerfect (with the file name MFWIN.EXE) allows you to compile a macro without executing it. It is the program WordPerfect uses to record and play back macros, and is always running in the background if you've used the Macro feature. In addition, the Macro Facility lets you convert WordPerfect 5.0 or 5.1 DOS macros to the format used by WordPerfect for Windows. (See "Converting Macros from Word-Perfect 5.0 and 5.1," later in this chapter.)

The easiest way to get to the Macro Facility program is simply to run any macro while in WordPerfect to preload the program. Then follow these steps:

Even if you haven't run any Word-Perfect macros in the current session, you can get to the Macro Facility through the Windows Program Manager (use File ➤ Run and the program name MFWIN.EXE).

1. After running any macro, press Ctrl+Esc to bring up the Task List, then choose the WordPerfect Macro Facility option (by double-clicking it or highlighting it and pressing ↵).

2. In the Macro Facility program, choose **Macro** ➤ Compile Macro.

3. Find the .WCM macro you want to compile and highlight it (change the current directory if necessary). Press ↵ to start compiling.

If you've written or edited a macro, there is a chance it contains errors that will prevent it from operating properly. During compilation, the Macro Facility program flags errors that must be corrected in order for the macro to run properly. The Macro Facility will display an error box, like that shown in Figure 15.7, when an error occurs. WordPerfect lists the type of error and the line in the macro file where it occurs. Depending on the complexity of the macro, the error may in fact be located elsewhere. You'll have to do some sleuthing to get your macro working properly. This same error box is shown when you run macros in WordPerfect.

SOME MORE ADVANCED MACROS

Here are some additional tips and some advanced techniques that will help you create more powerful macros.

RUNNING MACROS AUTOMATICALLY

You can have WordPerfect run a macro automatically as soon as you start the program. Such a macro can be designed to reset some of WordPerfect's default format settings to your preferences—a handy macro if you share your computer and can't make your preferences permanent. Actually, Windows provides you

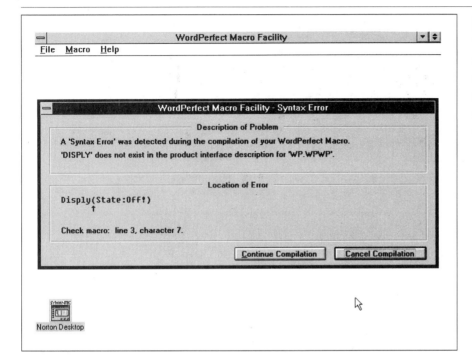

FIGURE 15.7:

WordPerfect displays an error box when an error occurs while it is trying to compile a macro. The macro must be edited to correct the mistake.

with several options for playing back an automatic macro:

◆ When you choose File ➤ Run from the Windows Program Manager menu

◆ Every time you double-click the WordPerfect application icon

◆ Only when you start up Windows on your computer (typically once a day)

Running a Macro with File ➤ Run

See your Windows manual, book, or on-line help for more information on starting applications.

To run a macro when you start WordPerfect by using File ➤ Run in the Program Manager, you must add the /M-*macroname* start-up switch after the WP command, where *macroname* is the name of the macro you want to run. For example, to start WordPerfect and run a macro named *MyPrefs,* follow these steps:

1. Choose **F**ile ➤ **R**un from the Windows Program Manager menu.

2. Type **C:\WPWIN\WPWIN.EXE /M-MyPrefs** in the Command Line text box. The Run dialog box screen will look like this:

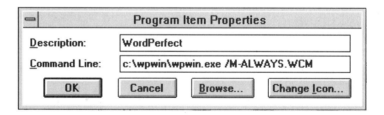

3. Choose OK or press ↵ to start WordPerfect.

Auto-executing a Macro Every Time You Start WordPerfect

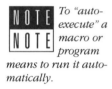 *To "auto-execute" a macro or program means to run it automatically.*

If you want a particular macro to be played back every time you start Word-Perfect by double-clicking its icon in Windows, you can edit the properties of the WordPerfect icon and add the /M-macroname command as an optional parameter. For example, if you want your computer to run a macro named ALWAYS.WCM every time you start WordPerfect, follow these steps:

1. Locate the WordPerfect for Windows icon in the Windows Program Manager and select it.

2. Choose **F**ile ➤ **P**roperties.

3. In the Command Line text box, skip past the name of the program, type a space, and add **/M-ALWAYS.WCM**. After completing this step, the Program Item Properties dialog box will look like this:

Program Item Properties
Description: WordPerfect
Command Line: c:\wpwin\wpwin.exe /M-ALWAYS.WCM
OK Cancel **B**rowse... Change **I**con...

4. Choose OK or press ↵.

In the future, when you double-click the WordPerfect icon, WordPerfect will play the ALWAYS.WCM macro as it starts up.

Auto-executing a Macro at Start-up Only

Be careful never to save a DOS batch file in WordPerfect format; you must save it as DOS text.

Windows, and any Windows program, can be started by using the following syntax at the command line:

WIN *ProgramName*

In place of *ProgramName,* type the name of the program you want to run, in this case, **WPWIN**. So, to start Windows and run WordPerfect at the same time, type the following at the DOS command line:

WIN WPWIN

If you want to run WordPerfect and a macro just once when you first start Windows on your computer, you can include the instructions to do so on the DOS command line. Because this entails more keystrokes, you may want to automate the process by creating a small *batch file* (if you already start Windows using a batch file, you can add the instructions for starting WordPerfect and a macro to it; however, for this discussion I'll assume you don't already use a batch file to start Windows).

To start Windows and WordPerfect, and automatically run a macro when WordPerfect finishes loading, create a batch file that contains the following line:

WIN WPWIN */m-macroname*

In place of *macroname,* type the name of the macro you want to run. The .WCM extension is optional.

If you're an experienced Windows user, you know you can start any application by including it in the RUN= statement of the WIN.INI file. So why go through this route when Windows lets you automatically run applications anyway? The RUN= statement doesn't expect you to add any optional command-line switches such as */m-macroname* . If you include the switch to run a macro, Windows will interpret it as another application, and you'll get an error message.

To create the batch file, type the line in a new WordPerfect document. Then follow these steps:

1. Choose File ➤ **S**ave (or press Shift+F3).

2. Access the **F**ormat list, and scroll through it until you find ASCII Text (DOS). Choose this entry so that it is displayed on the very top line of the Format list.

3. Change the directory to \WPWIN in the Save **A**s text box if this directory is not already the current directory.

4. Type **WPW.BAT** and press ↵.

The next time you want to start Windows and WordPerfect, type **WPW** at the DOS prompt. DOS will run the WPW.BAT batch file you created, automatically starting Windows, loading WordPerfect, and running the macro you specified. Note that when started this way, the Windows Program Manager is loaded as an icon, instead of opening into one or more windows. To access the Program Manager, double-click its icon.

If you'd like to start WordPerfect and run different macros at different times, create additional batch files and give them unique names. Be sure there are no batch files with the same name anywhere else on your disk. Also, make sure there are no .COM or .EXE program files with the same file name. Otherwise, DOS will execute these before it finds your batch file (for example, don't name a batch file WPWIN.BAT, because DOS will find WPWIN.EXE first and attempt to run it instead).

If DOS can't find your batch file, it could be because it was not saved in a directory that is listed in the PATH= statement of your AUTOEXEC.BAT file. You should either include the directory in the PATH= statement (refer to your DOS manual for details) or place the batch file in a directory that is listed in the PATH= statement.

COMBINING MACROS

Sometimes it's handy to be able to combine two or more macros into one. WordPerfect lets you combine macros so that when you run one, another is executed automatically. The process of combining macros requires you to edit at least one of them.

Say, for example, you have created two macros, called FIRST.WCM and SECOND.WCM, using the procedures outlined in "Creating a Macro." The macro programming command that actually links the two macros together is *CHAIN*. Using the CHAIN command is relatively simple: Merely add it to the end of the first macro, and indicate the name of the macro you want to run (the second macro). Follow these steps:

1. Close the temporary document used to record the two macros by choosing **F**ile ➤ **C**lose or pressing Ctrl+F4. Choose **N**o—you don't want to save the changes.

2. Choose **F**ile ➤ **O**pen, and locate the first macro in your MACROS directory.

3. Select the first macro and choose **O**pen.

4. Position the insertion point at the end of the document. Press ↵ to be sure that you're starting a new line, and type

CHAIN ("second macroname")

where macroname is the name of the second macro. Don't forget the double quotemarks or the parentheses. Your macro should look like the one in Figure 15.8.

5. Save the macro by choosing **F**ile ➤ **S**ave or pressing Shift+F3.

6. Close the macro document by choosing **F**ile ➤ **C**lose or pressing Ctrl+F4.

NESTING MACROS

The previous section showed how to combine macros by chaining. There's another method available in WordPerfect called *nesting*. To understand the difference between chaining and nesting, consider this example: Suppose you have two macros, named *Macro1* and *Macro2*. Suppose Macro2 is chained to Macro1. When you run Macro1, it completes all the actions in its job. It then passes control to Macro2. Finally, Macro2 does its own job, and all macro playback stops. (You're returned to the document window.)

Now suppose Macro2 is nested in Macro1. When you run Macro1, it does just a portion of its job. Before it finishes, it passes control to Macro2, which runs in its entirety. When Macro2 finishes, it passes control back to Macro1, which picks up where it left off. Figure 15.8 illustrates these differences.

The technique for creating a macro that nests another macro is basically the same as for chaining another macro, except you use the Run command instead. Repeat the steps outlined in "Combining Macros" above, but use the RUN("macroname") command instead of CHAIN.

MAKING A MACRO PAUSE FOR AN ENTRY

As you know, once you start a macro it plays back *all* its keystrokes very quickly. However, you might want a macro that pauses for an entry. For example, you could create a macro that types your company name and address, but pauses to allow you to type in a specific department name.

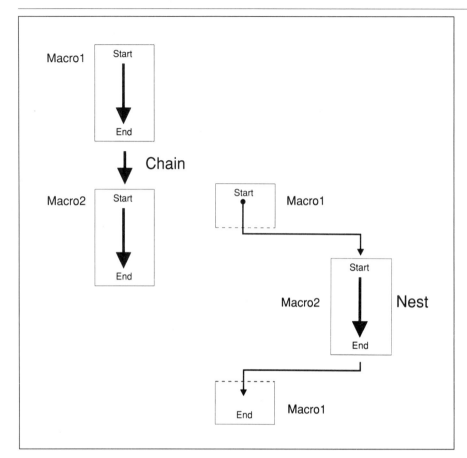

FIGURE 15.8:

How two sample macros named Macro1 and Macro2 are played back when chained and when nested

Pausing a macro requires that you edit it to include a PauseKey(0) command. This command temporarily stops the macro, letting you type text or choose commands. You press ↵ to reactivate the macro. For best results, you should limit macro pausing to text entry only.

To make a macro pause, follow these steps:

1. Record the macro in the usual manner. Mentally note where the pauses are to be inserted, or—if possible—insert a unique character to mark the spot (the tilde, ~, is a good choice).

2. Open the macro so that you can edit it in a document window.

3. Locate those portions of the macro where you want it to pause. If you've used a special character (like a tilde) to identify the pause points, use the Search feature of WordPerfect to find the marks.

4. On a separate line, type **PauseKey(0).** Spell it exactly as shown here (capitalization does not matter), and include the parentheses and the numeral 0.

5. Save and close the file.

You can now run the program to test the pause commands. Edit the macro if it doesn't work properly the first time. Figures 15.9 and 15.10 show a macro before and after the PauseKey(0) commands were added.

RUNNING A MACRO SEVERAL TIMES

There are more sophisticated ways to control how many times a macro is played back, using the advanced macro commands WHILE, FOR, and ON, discussed in Chapter 26.

Suppose you create a macro that performs a single job, such as changing italic text to underlined text or recalculating all the formulas in a single table. Later, you decide you want to run that macro many times in a document so that it changes all the italics to underlines or recalculates all the tables in a document.

One way way to make a macro run repeatedly is to chain it to itself by placing the CHAIN("*macroname*") command at the end of the macro, where *macroname* is the name of the macro. For example, if the name of the macro you want to use is called *Mymacro,* add **CHAIN("Mymacro")** as the last

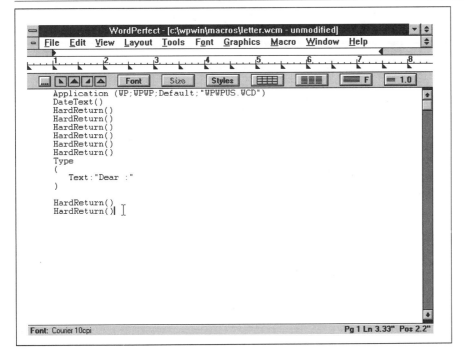

FIGURE 15.9:

A sample macro that addresses a letter before pause commands have been added

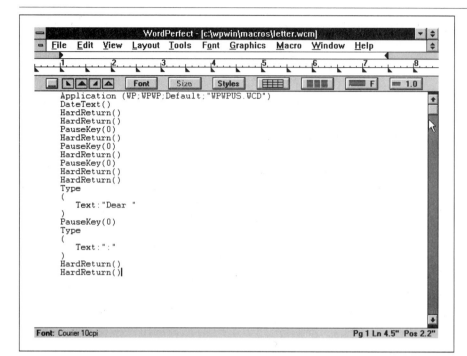

The sample macro with PauseKey(0) commands inserted

command in a macro. WordPerfect will automatically restart the same macro over and over again. You can stop it from repeating by pressing Esc to cancel it.

CONVERTING MACROS FROM WORDPERFECT 5.0 AND 5.1

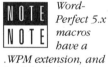

Word-Perfect 5.x macros have a .WPM extension, and by default, WordPerfect for Windows macros have a .WCM extension.

WordPerfect for Windows cannot run macros that were originally created for WordPerfect for DOS. To use these macros, you'll need to convert them by using the WordPerfect for Windows conversion program, MFWIN.EXE (referred to as *Macro Facility*). This program is installed automatically on your hard disk when you install the WordPerfect Utility programs, which are normally stored in the \WPC directory.

To use the macro conversion program, follow these steps:

1. Go to the Windows Program Manager and locate the Macro Facility icon. Double-click it to start the Macro Facility program. If you can't locate the icon, start it with the Program Manager Run command (choose **File ➤ R**un, type **MFWIN.EXE**, and press ↵).

If you're currently in WordPerfect and you've been using macros, the Macro Facility program is already loaded and ready to go. You can merely switch to it by using the Windows Task List: Press Ctrl+Esc, highlight WordPerfect Macro Facility, and press ↵.

2. In the Macro Facility program, choose **Macro** ➤ Con**v**ert.

3. Find the .WPM macro you want to convert and highlight it (change the current directory if necessary). Press ↵ to start conversion.

Macro Facility will convert the macro, creating a new one with the same name and in the same directory, but with a .WCM file extension. The original macro is left untouched.

Although Macro Facility can convert most simple WordPerfect 5.0 and 5.1 macros, it is not capable of converting most macros that make moderate or heavy use of programming commands. After converting a macro, you should always review it first. Most keystroke commands should be converted without much trouble. For example, a WordPerfect 5.1 macro containing keystroke commands to turn on italics and set justification to Full would be converted as follows:

WORDPERFECT 5.1 MACRO	WORDPERFECT FOR WINDOWS MACRO
{Font}ai	Italics{State:On!)
{Format}ljf	JustifyFull()

A few keystroke commands will not be converted, specifically those that have no counterparts in WordPerfect for Windows (such as {Shell}). Additionally, many of the WordPerfect for DOS programming commands are not converted. Commands that cannot be directly converted are shown with a // comment. You'll have to edit these commands manually to conform to the WordPerfect for Windows macro language.

To adequately convert complex macros for use with WordPerfect for Windows, you should obtain a copy of the *WordPerfect for Windows Macro Manual,* available directly from WordPerfect Corporation. This book contains all the commands available under WordPerfect for Windows.

This chapter has taken you from the basics of recording and playing back basic macros to some of the more advanced macro techniques. Be sure to try Lesson 8 in Part 9 if you need help getting started on creating your own macros.

In Part 5, you'll learn how to use a variety of tools that will make your office work easier, including mail merge and WordPerfect's Sort and Math features.

NOTE **NOTE** *If you are using a macro created in WordPerfect 4.2, you must use the MACRO-CNV.EXE program to convert it to WordPerfect 5.0/5.1 format before you can use Macro Facility.*

PART FIVE

Office Tools

In this part you'll learn about specialized features of Word-Perfect that are particularly useful in a business setting. The Merge feature lets you merge data and text; it is particularly useful for mass-producing form letters, mailing labels, envelopes, and fill-in forms. The Sort and Select features can be used with merges to better control mass mailings; they are also handy for managing just about any type of document that requires you to organize some or all of the text alphabetically or numerically. WordPerfect's Math feature, which you use in conjunction with the Tables feature, performs basic math calculations with numbers.

CHAPTER 16

Form Letters, Mailing Labels, and Other Merges

HANDS-ON
....
LESSON 9

For a hands-on lesson in using the Merge feature, see Lesson 9 in Part 9.

f you ever send mass mailings, you will surely appreciate WordPerfect's Merge feature. With it you can create a list of names and addresses, type up a single letter, and then have WordPerfect automatically print personalized copies of that letter to everyone on the list, along with envelopes or mailing labels. Once you create your basic list of names and addresses, you can use it over and over again as often as you need, without ever retyping a single name or address.

As you'll see, the Merge feature is useful for more than just mass mailings. It can be used to fill in blank forms, create invoices and packing slips, created sorted, alphabetized lists, and much more. You'll find all the merge options on the Tools ➤ Merge pull-down menu.

MERGE TERMINOLOGY

Merging uses two files, the *primary merge file* and the *secondary merge file*. The primary file can be a form letter, a mailing label, an envelope, an invoice, a packing slip, a fill-in form, or any other kind of document. The secondary file is a list that contains the data (variable information) to be printed on each copy of the document. Figure 16.1 shows an example of a primary merge file.

The primary file contains fixed information, which does not change from letter to letter. For example, in Figure 16.1, the letterhead, date, and all the text of the letter will be the same on every printed copy of the letter. The variable information will be inserted in the primary merge file wherever you have placed commands enclosed in braces, like this:

{FIELD}First Name~ {FIELD}Last Name~

The secondary merge file contains variable information, which changes from letter to letter. Figure 16.2 shows a secondary merge file that contains a list of *field names* (e.g., First Name, Last Name, Address) and actual names and addresses.

If your signature has been scanned and stored on disk, you can have it printed automatically on each merged document.

When you merge the primary and secondary files, WordPerfect automatically replaces the {FIELD} commands in the primary file with data from the secondary file, producing a third document with information from both files. Figure 16.3 shows the results of merging the primary and secondary merge files displayed in figures 16.2 and 16.3. WordPerfect produces a copy of the letter for each person in the secondary merge file.

Two terms you need to know if you are going to work with secondary merge files are *field* and *record,* which come from the realm of database management. In databases, data is organized into columns (fields) and rows (records), as the example in Figure 16.4 shows.

As you can see in the figure, a field is a column of similar information. For example, the third field in Figure 16.4 contains addresses. A record is all the information (that is, all the fields) for one item in the list. In Figure 16.4, the first record consists of all of the data for Frank Fleinder.

PLANNING A MERGE

Before you start creating your own merge files, you should ask yourself the following questions:

◆ What information is fixed and therefore belongs in the primary merge file?

Acme Furniture
P.O. Box 1234
Los Angeles, CA 91234

August 11, 1991

{FIELD}First Name~ {FIELD}Last Name~
{FIELD}Address~
{FIELD}City~, {FIELD}State~ {FIELD}Zip~

Dear {FIELD}Salutation~:

Just a quick note to remind you that our annual clearance sale is happening next weekend at the Los Angeles Civic Center.

As usual, prices will be slashed below *our* production costs, so don't miss this important event.

Hope to see you there!

Best Regards:

Jason Klemmer
Vice President

FIGURE 16.1:

An example of a primary merge file

◆ What information varies and therefore belongs in the secondary merge file?

One way to get started is "to pre-write" a finished document. Then, circle the information that will vary from one document to the next, and give each circled item a unique name. For example, Figure 16.5 shows a form letter with variable information circled, and a brief name jotted down next to each item.

```
{FIELD NAMES}
     First Name~
     Last Name~
     Address~
     City~
     State~
     Zip~
     Salutation~~
{END RECORD}
================================================================
Frank{END FIELD}
Fleinder{END FIELD}
123 Oak St.{END FIELD}
Glendora{END FIELD}
KS{END FIELD}
54321{END FIELD}
Frank{END FIELD}
{END RECORD}
================================================================
Nita{END FIELD}
Bonita{END FIELD}
P.O. Box 5432{END FIELD}
Glendora{END FIELD}
KS{END FIELD}
54320{END FIELD}
Miss Bonita{END FIELD}
{END RECORD}
================================================================
Jane{END FIELD}
Tarzana{END FIELD}
555 Apple St.{END FIELD}
Jackson{END FIELD}
KS{END FIELD}
54300{END FIELD}
Jane{END FIELD}
{END RECORD}
================================================================
```

FIGURE 16.2:

A secondary merge file with field names and actual names and addresses

When creating your list of field names, keep in mind that each field must have a unique name. For example, you cannot have two separate fields with the name *Date*. You can, however, have a field named *Date 1* and a field named *Date 2*.

Use brief, descriptive names of no more than a word or two in length. So perhaps rather than having two fields named *Date 1* and *Date 2,* use the names *Date Hired* and *Date Discharged,* or some other, more descriptive names. This will make it easier for you to keep track of what each field actually contains.

Also, be sure to include enough fields to cover every possible situation. For instance, if you are creating a secondary merge file for mass mailings, do you need to include a job title with some names and addresses? Do you need two address lines for some? If you think you'll need only a job title or second-line address in *some* cases, you still must include these in your list of field

Results of merging the files shown in figures 16.1 and 16.2

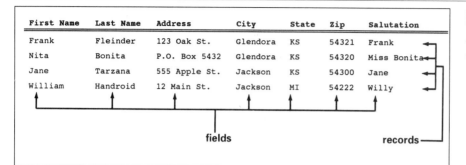

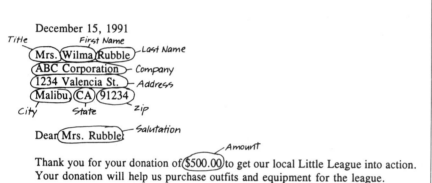

names, because every record in a secondary merge file must have exactly the
same number of fields.

Also, try to break the information down into discrete, independent fields.
There's no advantage to combining different types of information into a single

field. So even though you typically print city, state, and zip code information in the format

Albuquerque, NM 76543

you should store this information as three separate fields in your secondary merge file, like this:

City	State	Zip
Albuquerque	NM	76543

As you'll see later, this gives you the greatest flexibility in managing the information in the future. For example, if you later decide to sort this information into zip code order for bulk mailing, or to print letters, labels, or envelopes for people in a certain city or state only, you can easily do so, because the city, state, and zip codes are each in their own fields.

Don't worry about the comma between the city and state, or the spacing between the city, state, and zip code fields. That comma is a fixed format that won't vary from letter to letter (or label to label, or envelope to envelope), so it can be handled in the primary merge file. All you want to store in the secondary file is the pure, unformatted ("raw") data that varies from one document to the next.

Finally, think of the long-range possibilities of your merge file. Suppose you're creating a list of names and addresses. Perhaps you'd like to send birthday cards to these people once a year. If so, include a field for their birth dates (perhaps named simply *Birthday*) so that you can easily isolate those people with birth dates in the current month, and then print envelopes and birthday greetings for these people. When you've decided on your fields, jot them down on a piece of paper.

TIP *When designing your secondary merge file, include data that may be useful in future projects. You can then use any of the fields in your primary merge files.*

CREATING A SECONDARY MERGE FILE

Once you've determined the individual fields that you'll need, you can create your secondary merge file. First, you'll enter the field names, then enter the record information. Finally, you'll save your file.

As with earlier versions of WordPerfect, it's not absolutely necessary to create a list of field names in a secondary merge file, but it makes your work easier in the long run. If you omit the list, each field will be numbered sequentially, starting with 1.

ENTERING FIELD NAMES

To enter your field names, follow these steps:

1. Start at a blank WordPerfect document window.

2. Choose **T**ools ➤ **M**erge ➤ Merge **C**odes (or press Ctrl+F12 C) to display the merge commands.

3. Move the highlight to the {FIELD NAMES}name1~...nameN~~ option in the Insert Merge Codes dialog box:

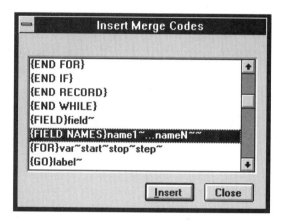

4. Choose **I**nsert or press ↵ to choose that option. (You can also double-click on the option.)

5. The Merge Field Name(s) dialog box shown, below, appears. Type a field name from your handwritten list in the box. Do *not* press ↵!

6. Choose **A**dd to add the field to the list of field names. (The order of fields in a secondary merge file is not important, but for your own convenience, you should list them in whatever order seems most natural for typing them in—for example, Address, City, State, Zip is more common than State, Address, Zip, City.) Continue typing in field names and adding to the list until you have listed all field names. Choose OK or press ↵ and then choose Close when you're finished.

The dialog box disappears, and your field names are displayed across the top of the screen, starting with a {FIELD NAMES} command. A hard page break appears beneath the list.

If your list of names is wider than the screen, some of them may be scrolled off the right edge of the screen. If so, you can move the insertion point to the start of any field name, and press ↵ to start the name on a separate line. You can also press Tab (but not the spacebar or any other key) to indent each field name if you wish. When you're finished, make sure that each of the following is true:

Merge commands in braces must be entered by using the menus; you cannot simply type a merge command, like {FIELD NAMES}, at your keyboard.

◆ The list of field names begins with a {FIELD NAMES} command (which appears as [Mrg:FIELD NAMES] in Reveal Codes).

◆ Each field name is followed by a tilde (~).

◆ The last field name is followed by two tildes (~~).

◆ The entire list is followed by an {END RECORD} command and a hard page break (which appear as [Mrg:END RECORD][HPg] in Reveal Codes).

Figure 16.6 shows an example where the field names have been entered on the screen, following the steps described earlier. WordPerfect has automatically word-wrapped the Last Name field at the blank space between *Last* and *Name,* but in some cases, it may scroll the field names off the right edge of the screen.

Figure 16.7 shows the field names from Figure 16.6 after the ↵ and Tab keys have been used to reformat the field name list. This format is not required but makes it much easier to see each field name at a glance, which will come in handy later.

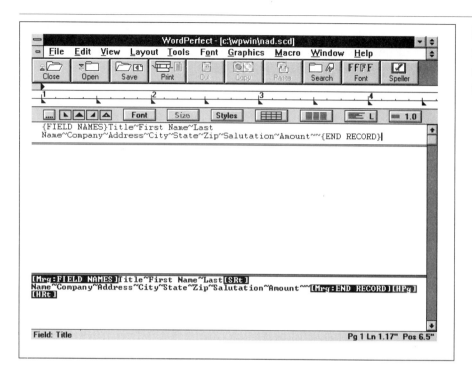

FIGURE 16.6:

The field names initially entered in a secondary merge file

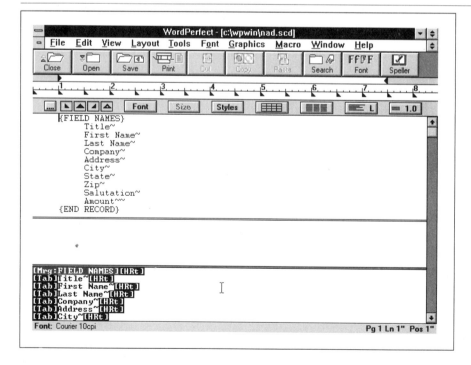

FIGURE 16.7:

The field name list from Figure 16.6 reformatted to make it easier to view the field names

FILLING IN SECONDARY MERGE RECORDS

After entering the field names, you can start typing your secondary merge data. Remember these three important points:

◆ You must choose **T**ools ➤ **M**erge ➤ **E**nd Field, or press Alt+↵, after typing the contents of a single field (the document window displays {END FIELD} at the end of the field).

◆ You must choose **T**ools ➤ **M**erge ➤ End **R**ecord, or press Alt+Shift+↵, after typing the last field to mark the end of the record.

◆ Don't forget that each record must contain the same number of fields, even if this means leaving a field empty. If there is no information for a given field, press Alt+↵ to leave it blank. The field will then contain only an {END FIELD} command.

Let's take it from the top, step by step, to add records to a new (or existing) secondary merge file:

1. If the secondary merge file is not currently in your document window, open it.

2. Move the insertion point to the bottom of the secondary merge file (press Ctrl+End). Note that the left side of the status bar indicates which field you need to type.

You can enter several lines or paragraphs as the value for a single field. Keep in mind that pressing ↵ places a [HRt] code in your document; it doesn't end the field.

3. Type in the field data (i.e., the information to be stored in that field). If there is no information for this field, don't type anything, but *do* proceed to the next step. The field value can be a single line of text, many lines, or several paragraphs.

4. Choose **T**ools ➤ **M**erge ➤ **E**nd Field, or press Alt+↵, even if you left this field blank in the preceding step. The {END FIELD} command appears to the right of your entry (or in the otherwise blank field), the insertion point moves down a line, and the name of the next field appears in the status bar, as shown in Figure 16.8.

5. Repeat steps 3 and 4 for every field in the record.

6. After you type in the last field for the record and press Alt+↵ to end that field, the insertion point waits on the next line (as usual), but the status bar shows a field number rather than a field name (for example, "Field: 11"). Choose **T**ools ➤ **M**erge ➤ End **R**ecord, or press Alt+Shift+↵, to indicate that you've finished typing this record.

At this point, an {END RECORD} command followed by a hard page break (double underline) appears on the screen, and the insertion point moves down to the next row. WordPerfect waits for you to type the first field of the next record in the secondary merge file, as shown in the example in Figure 16.9.

At this point, you can repeat the basic steps above to type in as many records as you wish. Figure 16.10 shows a second record added to the sample secondary merge file shown in Figure 16.9.

Notice in Figure 16.10 that the Company field for the second record is blank, containing only an {END FIELD} command. Why is it so important to leave the field blank when there is no information for that field? Simply because WordPerfect knows nothing about the information in each field—it can't tell a name from an address, or a zip code, or a bologna sandwich. Hence, if you type the wrong information in a field, WordPerfect won't know the difference.

For example, suppose you completely omit the Company field by forgetting to place an {END FIELD} command in it:

Mr.{END FIELD}
Dustin{END FIELD}

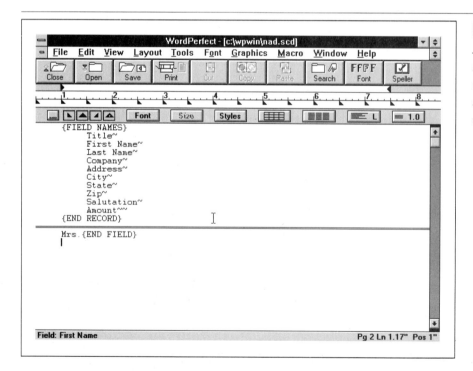

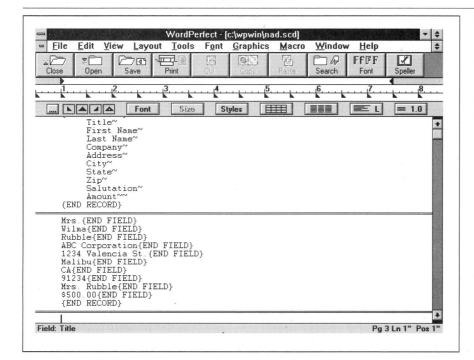

FIGURE 16.9:

One complete record is entered on the screen. The insertion point waits for the first field of the next record.

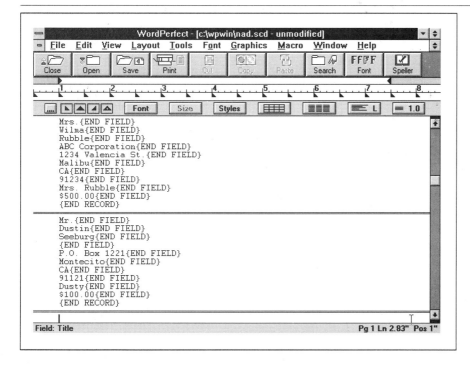

FIGURE 16.10:

A second record has been added to the secondary merge file. Notice the blank Company field above the address.

Seeburg, III{END FIELD}
P.O. Box 1221{END FIELD}
Montecito{END FIELD}
CA{END FIELD}
91121{END FIELD}
Dusty{END FIELD}
$100.00{END FIELD}
{END RECORD}

WordPerfect will accept your entry, and at first glance it will seem correct. However, when you perform the merge later, the top of the letter will come out looking something like this:

Mr. Dustin Seeburg, III
P.O. Box 1221
Montecito
CA, 91121 Dusty

Dear $100.00:

Why? Because in the secondary merge file you've placed the address where the company belongs, the city where the address belongs, the state where the city belongs, and so forth. You can see the problem quite clearly by moving the insertion point through each field in the secondary file and noting the field name shown in the status bar. For example, if you place your insertion point in the field entered above as *$100.00,* you'll see the field name Salutation (not Amount) displayed in the status bar.

In short, you must make sure that you correctly type each item of information in its correct place in the secondary merge file. If there is no entry for a particular field, you must choose Tools ➤ Merge ➤ End Field or press Alt+↵ to mark the end of the field, so WordPerfect knows that the field has been intentionally left blank.

SAVING YOUR SECONDARY MERGE FILE

After creating your secondary merge file, save it as you would any other document. You may want to use a file-name extension, such as *.SCD,* that will make it easy for you to recognize this as a secondary merge file in the future. For example, you could save the sample file above as NAD.SCD; NAD is a common abbreviation (in computer circles) for "name and address," and SCD is short for "secondary."

CREATING A PRIMARY MERGE FILE

> ### TO CREATE A PRIMARY MERGE FILE,
>
> **type the fixed text as you normally would, but where you want to incorporate text from the secondary merge file, choose Tools ➤ Merge ➤ Field to insert a {FIELD} command, followed by the name (or number) of the field you want to insert and a tilde (~).**

A primary merge file can use any combination of fields, in any order, from a secondary merge file, and can use any single field more than once.

Creating a primary merge file is much like creating any other document in WordPerfect: You start at a clear document window and type and edit as necessary. The only difference is that, wherever you want to merge variable text from your secondary merge file, you need to insert a command that tells WordPerfect exactly where to place that text. Here's the complete procedure:

1. Start at a clear document window (if the secondary merge file is still on the screen, save it and clear the screen).

2. Type your primary merge file as you would any other document. However, wherever you want to use text from the secondary merge file, position the insertion point where you want that text to appear.

3. Choose **T**ools ➤ **M**erge or press Ctrl+F12.

4. Choose **F**ield. You'll see the Insert Merge Code dialog box:

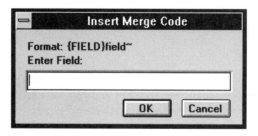

When typing the field name for the primary merge file, be sure to spell it exactly as you did in the secondary merge file. If you type it incorrectly, the field will be ignored during the merge.

5. Type the name of the field that you want to place at the insertion point, and press ↵. The command {FIELD} followed by the field name and a tilde appears. If you created the secondary file without using the {FIELD NAMES} command, your fields will be numbered sequentially, starting with 1; if so, type a field number instead of a name.

6. Repeat steps 2–5 for whatever fields you want to place in the current primary merge file.

7. When you've finished creating the primary merge file, save it and clear the screen, as you would for any other document.

When inserting codes in your primary merge file, be sure to include any necessary blank spaces and punctuation marks, just as though you were typing the actual information. For example, if your secondary merge file contains the fields City, State, and Zip, and you place these commands in your primary merge file as

{FIELD}City~{FIELD}State~{FIELD}Zip~

they will be printed as

EncinitasCA92024

However, if you place the commands in your primary merge file as

{FIELD}City~,   {FIELD}State~ {FIELD}Zip~

they will be printed as

Encinitas, CA 92024

Figure 16.11 shows a sample primary merge file for the secondary merge file presented earlier in this chapter.

PERFORMING THE MERGE

TO MERGE YOUR PRIMARY AND SECONDARY MERGE FILES,

be sure to save each one, get to a blank document window, then choose Tools ➤ Merge ➤ Merge. Enter the name of the primary and secondary merge files in the appropriate text boxes, and press ↵.

After you've created and saved your primary and secondary merge files, you're ready to merge them. Follow these steps:

1. Start from a blank document window.

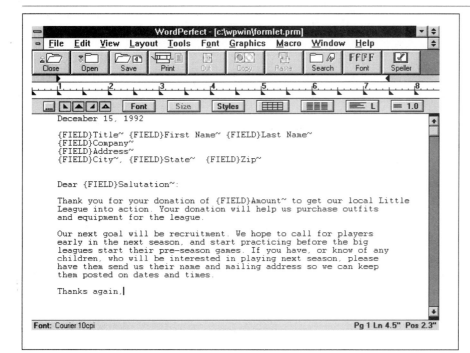

FIGURE 16.11:

A sample primary merge file

2. Choose **T**ools ➤ **M**erge or press Ctrl+F12, and choose **M**erge. You'll see the Merge dialog box:

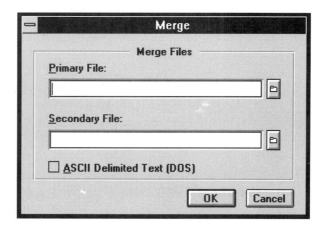

3. In the Primary File text box, type the name of the primary file, including the extension (for example, **FORMLET.PRM**).

If you can't remember the name of the primary file or the secondary file, you can click on the file-folder icon to display a list of files on disk.

You can also view the results on-screen by choosing File ➤ Print Preview (or pressing Shift+F5). This is especially handy when you're experimenting with merges and want to view the results without wasting paper.

4. In the Secondary File text box, type the name of the secondary file, including the extension (for example, **NAD.SCD**).

5. Choose OK or press ↵ to start the merge.

6. Wait for the "Merging" message to disappear from the status bar.

The merge combines both documents into one new merge document in your document window, with the insertion point positioned at the end of the document. You can press Ctrl+Home to move to the top of the document, then scroll through the document with the usual movement keys, including Page Up, Alt+Page Up, Page Down, and Alt+Page Down. To print the results, choose File ➤ Print ➤ Print (or press F5 P).

After the merge, your original primary and secondary merge files are still on the disk, so you can reuse either in the future, if need be. In fact, there really is no reason to save the results of the merge on your screen, because once you've printed the merged documents, the job is finished.

If you happen to notice an error in the merged document, you're better off clearing the document from the document window, correcting the primary or secondary file, saving the corrected file, and then repeating the merge. This way, you can clean up the problem at its source, so it won't pop up again the next time you perform the merge.

If the error is only in the variable information for one record (a misspelled name or address, for example), you needn't reprint the entire merged file. Just make your corrections to the secondary merge file and repeat the merge as described above. Then move the insertion point to the page you want to reprint and choose File ➤ Print ➤ Current Page ➤ Print (or press F5 C P). See Chapter 8 for more information on printing selected pages of a document.

You can use ASCII delimited text files when merging. For more information on ASCII delimited text files, see Chapter 25. This is useful if you are importing a list from a spreadsheet or database. With minor revisions, these files can be used in WordPerfect. To use an ASCII delimited text file for a merge, mark the ASCII Delimited Text (DOS) check box in the Merge dialog box.

PRINTING ENVELOPES AND LABELS

TO MERGE TEXT TO ENVELOPES OR MAILING LABELS,

insert the appropriate paper size in the Document Initial Codes area of the primary merge file. Arrange the {FIELD} commands

in the primary merge file to print a single envelope or label.
Save that file and merge it with the secondary merge file.

You can create any number of primary merge files for a single secondary merge file. Hence, you can use the same secondary merge file repeatedly to print a monthly newsletter, form letters, fliers, lists, envelopes, and labels.

You can use any size of paper with your primary merge file—even form letters or mailing labels. Just be sure to place the appropriate paper size for the primary merge file in the Document Initial Codes area (so it's not repeated on each merged document). If you've installed WordPerfect for use with multiple printers, be sure to choose the appropriate printer before defining a primary merge file for envelopes or labels, so you can find or create the correct paper size. Follow these steps:

1. In a blank document window or at the top of an existing document, choose **L**ayout ➤ **D**ocument ➤ Initial **C**odes, or press (Ctrl+Shift+F9 C).

2. Choose **L**ayout ➤ **P**age ➤ Paper **S**ize (Alt+F9 S).

3. Move the highlight to the paper size you want to print on (see Chapter 7 if you need to create a paper size), and choose Select to select it.

4. Choose **C**lose to return to the document window.

5. Create and save your primary merge file, as described earlier in "Creating a Primary Merge File."

6. Perform the merge and print the resulting document, as described in "Performing the Merge."

Techniques for formatting individual envelopes and letters will also work for primary merge files. The Print Preview screen can also help you define your format.

As an example, Figure 16.12 shows a primary merge file for printing envelopes, which is very similar to the envelope format shown in Chapter 7. Figure 16.13 shows a primary merge file for printing labels. You can see the basic formatting codes in Reveal Codes. Note, however, that the [Paper Sz/Typ] code is not visible in Reveal Codes, simply because that code was placed in the Document Initial Codes area for each document, to prevent it from being repeated throughout the final merge document.

Refining Label Alignment

If you use a merge file to print labels, and your labels are not properly aligned, here are a few tips that may help you align them.

If the name and address are printed too high on each label, edit the primary merge file for printing labels, and press ↵ to move all the {FIELD} commands down one or more lines (or, if you are using tractor-fed labels, align the first label to be printed a little higher above the print head).

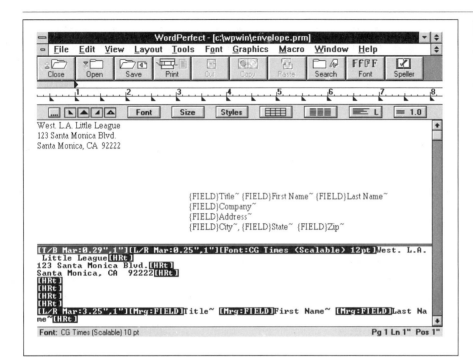

FIGURE 16.12:

A sample primary merge file for printing envelopes

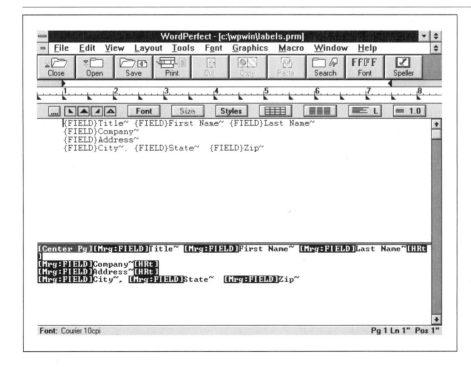

FIGURE 16.13:

A sample primary merge file for printing labels

If the name and address are printed too far to the left, edit the primary merge file, and use the Tab key (and tab stops) to move each row of {FIELD} commands a little to the right (or, if you are using tractor-fed labels, position the labels a little farther to the left before printing).

Because labels are much more expensive than paper, you may want to use plain paper while initially trying to align your label text correctly. After printing, align the sheet of paper directly over the blank labels and hold both sheets together up to a light, so you can see how the text lines up with the label outlines.

If the first label prints correctly, but the labels that follow are out of alignment, the label size or paper size definition is incorrect. Choose Layout ➤ Page ➤ Paper Size (Alt+F9 S), and move the highlight to the paper type definition for printing labels. Then do one of the following:

Word-Perfect may make adjustments to your label entries to accommodate the printer. Or, it may reject an "impossible" label size, such as when the labels could not possibly fit on the label sheet.

◆ Choose **E**dit and choose **L**abels. Under Label Size, type in a larger or smaller height, depending on whether you need to increase or decrease the height of each printed label. Press ↵ until you get back to the document window.

◆ Choose **E**dit and choose **L**abels. Under Distance Between Labels, increase or decrease the space as necessary.

When printing labels other than for mailing (for example, disk labels or ID labels), you may want to center text on each label. To center text horizontally on each label, place a [Just:Center] code at the top of the primary merge file (choose Layout ➤ Justification ➤ Center or press Ctrl+J before merging the file). To center text vertically on each label, place a [Center Pg] code at the top of the primary merge file (choose Layout ➤ Page ➤ Center Page or press Alt+F9 C) before merging the files.

After changing your primary merge file or label paper size, be sure to save your primary merge file, and remerge the primary and secondary files, before attempting to print the labels again.

REFINING YOUR MERGES

One problem almost invariably arises when you merge documents: Empty fields in the secondary merge file appear as blank lines or blank spaces in the primary merge file. For example, the address for a person who does not have a company affiliation in the secondary file will come out with a blank line above it (where the company is normally printed):

Mr. Dustin Seeburg, III

P.O. 1221
Montecito, CA 91121

Another problem is that there may be an extra blank space in front of names that do not have an entry in the Title field (this is caused by the blank space normally used to separate the title from the first name):

  Alicia Ramirez
311 Valley Parkway
Escondido, CA 92001

Fortunately, both these problems are quite easy to solve.

ELIMINATING BLANK LINES

TO PREVENT AN EMPTY FIELD IN A SECONDARY FILE FROM PRODUCING A BLANK LINE IN THE FINISHED DOCUMENT,

insert a question mark (?) at the end of the field name (but before the tilde,~) in the primary merge file.

To prevent a blank field from becoming a blank line in your finished document, add a question mark (?) to the {FIELD} command in the primary merge file (not the secondary file), just before the closing tilde (~). The question mark tells WordPerfect to print nothing, rather than a blank line, if the field is empty.

For example, to prevent the blank line caused by the empty Company field in the Dustin Seeburg example, bring the primary merge file back to the document window, and add a question mark to the Company field, just in front of the tilde that ends the field name:

You can type the question mark right at the keyboard; you don't need to use a merge command or the menus.

{FIELD}Company?~

Save the primary merge file, and then merge the primary and secondary files again. This time, records with blank Company fields will print properly:

Mr. Dustin Seeburg
P.O. 1221
Montecito, CA 91121

HANDLING BLANK FIELDS

If you're using several fields across a single line in a merged document, and one of those fields is empty, the blank space used to separate the fields is still printed, causing extra blank spaces in your final merged document, as shown in the Alicia Ramirez example.

A potentially more embarrassing problem with blank fields occurs when they are required, but omitted by accident. For example, if the Salutation field is inadvertently left blank in a record, or several records, the salutation in the letter may come out looking like this:

Dear   :

WordPerfect offers two merge commands for handling blank fields,

{IF BLANK}*field~print this*{END IF}

{IF NOT BLANK}*field~print this*{END IF}

where *field* is the name of the field you want to test as blank (or not blank), and *print this* is whatever you want to insert in the merged document (including any spaces and hard returns), based on whether or not the field is blank. For example, consider this line:

{IF NOT BLANK}Title~{FIELD}Title~   {END IF}

This sequence of commands says, "If the Title field is not blank, print the Title field, followed by a blank space." Of course, this also prevents either the title or the blank space from being printed if the title is blank.

You can add an {ELSE} command to the {IF...} statements to choose an alternative course of action should the field prove to be blank, or not blank. You must structure the commands this way:

{IF BLANK}*field~print this*{ELSE}*print this*{END IF}
{IF NOT BLANK}*field~print this*{ELSE}*print this*{END IF}

For example, the command line below prints the word *Dear,* and then decides, "If the Salutation field is blank, print the words *Valued Customer;* otherwise, print the contents of the Salutation field." Then it prints the colon:

Dear {IF BLANK}*Salutation~ Valued Customer*{ELSE}{FIELD}Salutation~{END IF}:

The word *Dear* and the colon at the end are always printed, regardless of whether or not the Salutation field is blank, because both are outside the {IF} and {END IF} commands.

To use the {IF}, {END IF}, and optional {ELSE} commands in your primary merge file, follow these steps:

1. Position the insertion point where you want to insert an {IF} command in your document.

2. Choose **T**ools ➤ **M**erge ➤ Merge **C**odes (or press Ctrl+F12 C).

3. In the Insert Merge Codes dialog box, use the mouse or arrow keys to highlight the specific command (either {IF BLANK}field~ or {IF NOT BLANK}field~). Choose Insert or press ↵ to choose the command.

4. In the Insert Merge Code dialog box, type the name of the field that you want to test, then choose OK or press ↵.

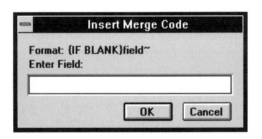

5. Type whatever you want to appear when the {IF} condition proves true. If you want a field inserted, choose **T**ools ➤ **M**erge ➤ **F**ield (Ctrl+F12 F), type the field name (or number), and choose OK or press ↵. Remember, fields, text, spaces, and hard returns that you enter here will be included in the merged document *only* if the {IF} condition proves true.

6. If you are using the {IF} command to prevent extra blank spaces only (as in the Title example earlier in this section), skip to step 8. If, on the other hand, you want WordPerfect to print something specific when the {IF} condition proves *false* (as in the Valued Customer example), choose **T**ools ➤ **M**erge ➤ Merge **C**odes (or press Ctrl+F12 C).

Each {IF} BLANK} and {IF NOT BLANK} command must have one, and only one, {END IF} command associated with it. The {ELSE} command in between is optional.

Move the highlight to {ELSE} and choose **I**nsert or press ↵. Choose **C**lose to close the Insert Merge Codes dialog box.

7. Type whatever you want to appear when the {IF} condition proves *false*. As in step 5, if you want a field inserted, choose **T**ools ➤ **M**erge ➤ **F**ield (or press Ctrl+F12 F), type the field name (or number), and choose OK or press ↵. Remember, fields, text, spaces, and hard returns that you enter here will be included in the merged document *only* if the {IF} condition proves false.

8. Choose **T**ools ➤ **M**erge ➤ Merge **C**odes (or press Ctrl+F12 C). Insert the {END IF} command, and close the Insert Merge Codes dialog box.

The {END IF} command marks the end of the "if" decision. Any fields, text, blank spaces, or hard returns to the right of the {END IF} command are part of the general primary file and will be included in the resulting merge regardless of whether the {IF} condition proves true or false.

Figure 16.14 shows a more refined version of the primary merge file commands used in previous merges. The question mark next to the Company field prevents empty Company fields from being printed as blank lines, and {IF} commands control potentially blank titles and salutations.

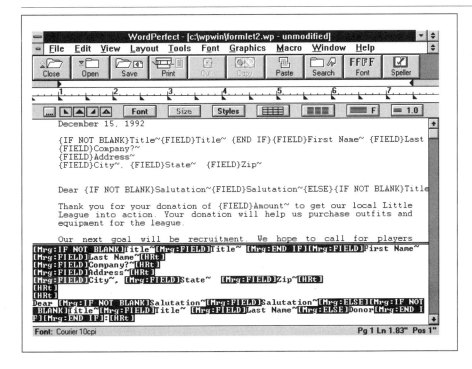

FIGURE 16.14:

A more refined primary merge file, capable of handling empty fields

These more complex merge commands use a pair of *nested* {IF} statements to determine the best way to print the salutation. The logic of the decision goes like this:

IF the salutation isn't blank

    Print the salutation

ELSE (the salutation is blank)

    IF the title isn't blank

        Print the title and last name

    ELSE (both salutation and title are blank)

        Print the word "Donor"

    END IF (title is not blank)

END IF (salutation is not blank)

The line scrolls past the right edge of the document window, but you can see the commands in Reveal Codes (where each command starts with *Mrg:* and is enclosed in brackets rather than braces).

Figure 16.15 shows two sample records from a secondary merge file that might cause some problems with a basic primary merge file. The first sample record has an empty Company field and an empty Salutation field. The second example has empty Title, First Name, Last Name, and Salutation fields. (The empty fields are easy to spot because each one has just an {END FIELD} command on a line by itself, without any additional text.)

The merge commands in Figure 16.14, however, could handle these two records quite easily, presenting each one in this format when the merge is complete:

Mr. Wallace Wilcox
P.O. Box 999 L.A., CA 91234

Dear Mr. Wilcox:

MegaCorp
Box 3311
L.A., CA 90023

Dear Donor:

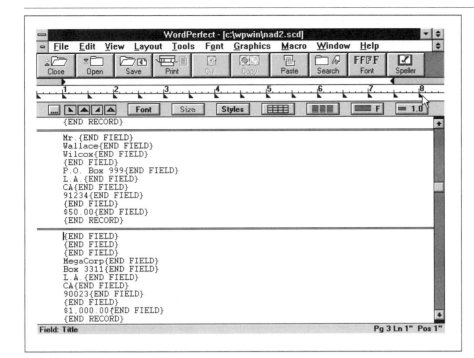

You can use many additional commands to further refine your Word-Perfect merges, as will be discussed later in this chapter. Before I talk about these, however, let's return our attention to the secondary merge file.

MANAGING YOUR
SECONDARY MERGE FILE

You can use the Search feature to search through a large secondary merge file to locate a specific record.

Chances are that you will use your secondary file many times in the future. And as situations change, you'll need to add new records, change them, and delete them. For the most part, you'll use the standard WordPerfect editing techniques to do so. But in this section, I'll discuss techniques that pertain specifically to secondary merge files.

ADDING OR CHANGING RECORDS
IN A SECONDARY MERGE FILE

To add new records to a secondary merge file, use the sequence of steps listed in "Filling In Secondary Merge Records" earlier in this chapter. You can also

You need not be concerned about the alphabetical order of names in your secondary merge file because you can sort the names anytime (see Chapter 17).

change the information in the secondary merge file by using the same editing keys and techniques you use in the regular document window. Just be sure to keep an eye on the current field name, shown in the status bar in the lower-left corner of the screen, to make sure you put the right information in the right field (for instance, you don't want to put a zip code in a city field).

If you simply forget to leave a field blank when typing in information, you can insert a new (blank) field in a record by moving the insertion point to wherever the blank field should appear and choosing Tools ➤ Merge ➤ End Field or pressing Alt+↵. Then you can scroll the insertion point through the fields and check the prompt in the status bar to make sure the correct information is in each field.

If you want to delete an entire record, be sure to delete all the text and codes from the first character of the record to the [HPg] code that ends the record. Alternatively, you can use the Select feature (Chapter 17) to limit your merges to certain types of records in your secondary merge file. This feature isolates certain types of records (for example, all New York residents or all orders for a particular part number) and makes it unnecessary to delete records from your secondary merge file.

ADDING OR DELETING A FIELD

Remember to save the entire file after making any changes to your secondary merge file.

Any field in a secondary merge file can contain a hard return. So, in a pinch, you can split the contents of a single field into two rows of text by pressing ↵ after typing the first line. For example, Figure 16.16 shows a record with the job title *Vice President,* as well as the name *WaterSport, Inc.,* in the Company field of a secondary merge file.

But as mentioned earlier, if you want to manage your secondary merge file by using the sorting and selection techniques described in Chapter 17, break the information into several fields, and use the fields consistently in each record.

If you've already created your secondary merge file and added some records, then later decide to add a field to the overall structure, you should first add the field name to the {FIELD NAMES} section of the secondary file. Be sure to start the field name after a tilde (~), and add a new tilde after typing your new field name. For example, Figure 16.17 shows the field name Job Title added to the list of field names shown in Figure 16.18.

Be sure to update every record in the secondary merge file to match the new list of field names. You can then use the new field name in any primary merge files.

Next, save the entire secondary merge file and clear the screen, then open the secondary merge file. As you scroll down through existing fields, the new field name will appear in the status bar of the screen when the insertion point is positioned on it. Choose Tools ➤ Merge ➤ End Field or press Alt+↵ to insert a blank field at the new position, or type an entry, and then press Alt+↵.

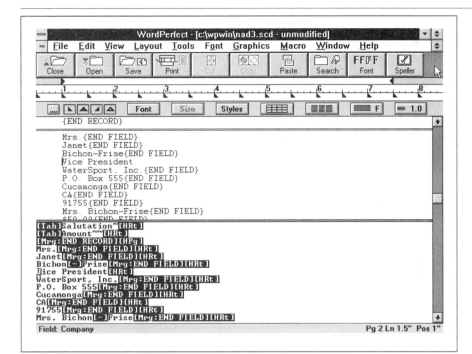

FIGURE 16.16:
A field that uses a hard return to split text into two lines within a secondary merge file

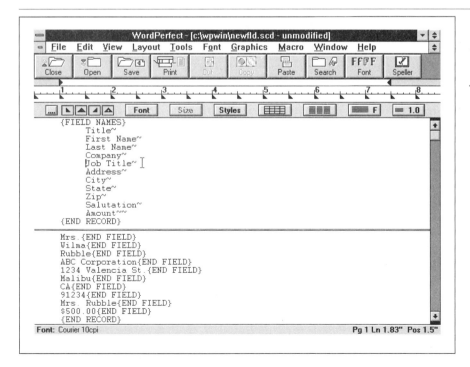

FIGURE 16.17:
A Job Title field has been added to the list of field names

Anytime you change the field names between the {FIELD NAMES} and {END RECORD} commands at the top of a secondary merge file, you must save, then open, the file before the changes will take effect.

Figure 16.18 shows a blank Job Title field properly inserted in Wilma Rubble's record (after the new Job Title field was inserted in the list of field names and the secondary file was saved and then opened again).

You can use the same basic technique to delete a field from a secondary merge file: Move the insertion point to the field name you want to delete (between the {FIELD NAMES} and the {END RECORD} commands), then delete the entire field name, the tilde (~), and the [HRt] code (if there is one). Save the entire secondary merge file, clear the screen, and then open the secondary merge file. As you scroll through existing text in the records, the status bar shows which field the insertion point is in. Press Ctrl+Delete, then Delete, to delete the field contents and the [HRt] code that follows the field entry.

MORE MERGE OPERATIONS

So far you've seen how to perform merges and have been introduced to several merge commands. For the remainder of this chapter, I'll present some additional types of merges and introduce some more merge commands.

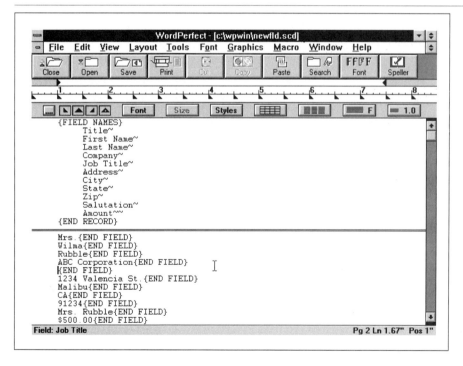

FIGURE 16.18:

A blank field inserted in the first record to match the new list of field names

MERGING STRAIGHT TO THE PRINTER

If your secondary merge file is very large, you may not be able to complete a merge in your computer's memory. As an alternative, you can tell WordPerfect to send the results of each merge directly to the printer instead of the document window. Simply bring the primary merge file to the document window, move the insertion point to the bottom of the primary merge file (press Ctrl+End), and then choose Tools ➤ Merge ➤ Merge Codes (or press Ctrl+F12 C). Highlight the {PRINT} command, choose OK or press ↵, and then select Close. This places a {PRINT} command at the bottom of the merge file.

Now you can save the primary merge file and perform the merge. Word-Perfect prints each completed document as it is merged.

CREATING LISTS FROM MERGE FILES

The sample primary merge file uses {IF} and {ENDIF} commands to omit the Last Name, Title, and First Name fields when the Last Name field is empty and to omit the company when the Company field is empty.

Normally, when you perform a merge, information from each record in the secondary merge file is printed on a separate page, which is ideal for printing form letters, envelopes, and labels (the latter because WordPerfect treats each label as a page). In some cases, however, this separation into pages may not be desirable, such as when you want to print a list or directory from your secondary merge file. For instance, Figure 16.19 shows a sample directory assembled from a secondary merge file of names and addresses.

Figure 16.20 shows the primary merge file used to print the directory, in both the Edit and Reveal Codes. The {PAGE OFF} command at the bottom of the primary merge file prevents each name and address from being printed on a separate page. Each blank line (i.e., [HRt] code) above the {PAGE OFF} command becomes one blank line between each printed record in the merged document.

MegaCorp, Box 3311, L.A., CA 90023

Seeburg, III, Mr. Dustin, P.O. Box 1221,
   Montecito, CA 91121

Rubble, Mrs. Wilma, ABC Corporation, 1234
   Valencia St., Malibu, CA 91234

Wilcox, Mr. Wallace, P.O. Box 999, L.A., CA
   91234

FIGURE 16.19:

A sample directory printed from a secondary merge file

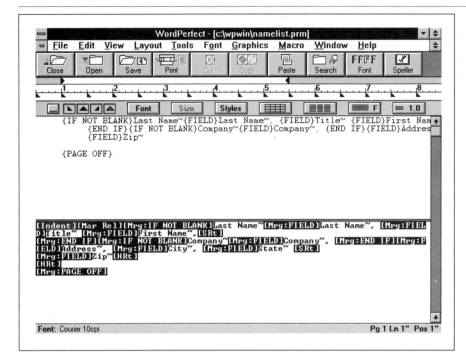

FIGURE 16.20:

The primary merge file uses a {PAGE OFF} command to prevent page breaks when printing the directory shown in Figure 16.19.

ADDING TEXT ON THE FLY

It's not necessary to store all the information for a merge in the secondary merge file. You can type in some or all of the fields for a merged document as the merge is taking place. This may come in handy if you need to add some variable text for a particular form letter that you'll be printing only once, and therefore don't want to bother changing the secondary merge file.

Let's suppose you have a secondary merge file of company personnel, most of whom have submitted potential passwords for the company computer. You need to send a final password to each person, but don't want to add the password to the secondary merge file. You could set up the primary merge file as shown in Figure 16.21. The name, address, and so forth will come from the primary merge file, but the password will be typed in as the merge takes place, because of this command:

{INPUT}Enter user's password ~

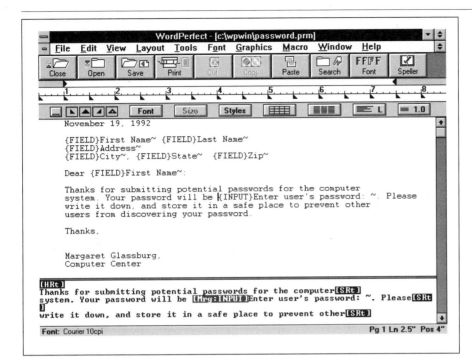

FIGURE 16.21:
A primary merge file containing an {INPUT} command that asks for an entry from the keyboard during the merge

To insert an {INPUT} command in your primary merge file, position the insertion point, then choose Tools ➤ Merge (or press Ctrl+F12) and choose Input. Type the message you want displayed during the merge, then choose OK or press ↵.

Once you start merging the files, the {INPUT} command will display its prompt, as shown below for this example:

Enter user's password

At that point you can type the individual's password, then press Alt+↵ to complete the merge. You'll be prompted to enter a user password for each record in the secondary merge file.

During the merge, your first tendency might be to press ↵ after typing the password (or whatever text you're being prompted for), but you should resist this urge and press Alt+↵ instead; otherwise, you'll add an extra blank line to the merged text, and WordPerfect will continue waiting until you press

You might want to include the phrase "then press Alt+Enter" in your message prompt as a reminder to the user to press Alt+↵ after typing text.

Alt+↵. Of course, if you actually want to add a blank line, or even several paragraphs, you can easily do so just by typing text as usual. When entering your input text, you can even use bold, underline, the movement keys, and any other WordPerfect features (including Tables and Graphics).

FILLING IN A BOILERPLATE FORM

The {TEXT} and {VARIABLE} commands provide another way to insert text from the keyboard in a primary merge file. These commands are particularly handy for merges that you perform only occasionally and that reuse the same information in several places. For example, Figure 16.22 shows a "boilerplate will" that will print the husband's name, wife's name, and wife's maiden name in several places throughout the document.

The {TEXT} commands display a message to the user (e.g., "Type husband's name") and then place whatever the user types—up to 129 characters—in a variable (e.g., *HusbandName*). The {VARIABLE} commands insert the contents of a variable (e.g., *HusbandName*) at that place in the text. Because all the fields in this primary merge file come from {VARIABLE} commands (which get their data from {TEXT} commands), you don't even need a secondary merge file.

```
{TEXT}HusbandName~Type husband's name (all caps), then press
Enter: ~{TEXT}WifeName~Type wife's name (all caps), then press
Enter: ~{TEXT}MaidenName~Type wife's maiden name, then press
Enter: ~          LAST WILL AND TESTAMENT
                         OF
              {VARIABLE}HusbandName~

         I, {VARIABLE}HusbandName~, a resident of Oxford County,
State of New Jersey, declare that this is my Will.
         FIRST:  I hereby revoke all wills and codicils that I
have previously made.
         SECOND:  I declare that I am married to
{VARIABLE}WifeName~, formerly known as {VARIABLE}MaidenName~, and
all references in this Will to "my wife" are to her.
         THIRD:  I hereby confirm to my wife her interest in our
community property.
         FOURTH:  I give all the residue of my estate to my
wife, {VARIABLE}WifeName~, if she survives me for sixty (60)
days.
         FIFTH:  I nominate and appoint my wife,
{VARIABLE}WifeName~, as my executor of this Will to serve without
bond.
         The term "my executor" as used in this Will shall
include any personal representative of my estate.  The executor
may administer my estate under the Independent Administration of
Estates Act.
         I subscribe my name to this Will this 31st day of July,
of 1991, at Oxford, New Jersey.
```

FIGURE 16.22:

A "boilerplate will" that merges text from the keyboard

FILLING IN PREPRINTED FORMS

You can also use the Merge feature to fill in preprinted forms. Preprinted forms can be anything from job applications to a series of tractor-fed payroll checks—the size and shape of the form doesn't really matter, as long as your printer can handle the required paper size.

To print on preprinted forms, you first need to determine the exact location of each blank field on the form. Start with a clear document window and a copy of the preprinted form in hand, and follow these steps:

1. If the preprinted form is not the standard 8½" × 11" size, choose **Layout ➤ Page ➤ Paper Size** (or press Alt+F9 S) to choose (or first create, then choose) the appropriate paper size.

2. Change the top, bottom, left, and right margins, if necessary, to match the form's margins.

3. Make sure the insertion point is in the upper-left corner of the document window (Ctrl+Home) and note the Ln and Pos measurements in the status bar.

4. Type a character (such as *X*).

To prevent waste, use photocopies of the preprinted form, rather than originals, when first trying to align text on the form.

5. Insert a copy of the preprinted form in the printer. If you are using a dot-matrix or other tractor-fed printer, insert the form in a manner that will be easy to repeat in the future (because you'll need to insert future blank forms in exactly the same way to align the text properly).

6. Print the current document.

7. Using a ruler, measure the distance from the upper-left corner of the page to the base of the *X* on your preprinted form. (If this measurement is not the same as what the Ln and Pos indicators showed in step 3, you'll need to make some adjustments.)

8. Measure the distance, from the upper-left corner of the page, of every blank that needs to be filled in on the form, and write each measurement on the form, as shown in Figure 16.23. (See below for making any necessary adjustments.)

If the measurement in step 7 was different from the measurement in step 3, you'll need to adjust your measurements accordingly. For example, if the document window shows the insertion point at Ln 1" and Pos 1" in step 3, but the *X* actually appears at .5" and .5" in step 7, the page is ½ inch higher and ½ inch to the left of what the document window shows. You will need to

Saturnine Lending Corporation
"Our rates are out of this world."

NOTICE OF RIGHT TO CANCEL

IDENTIFICATION OF LOAN TRANSACTION

Customer	Amount	Security
Ln 2.82", Pos 1.1"		Ln 2.82", Pos 5.7"
Ln 3.15", Pos 1.1"		Ln 3.15", Pos 5.7"
Ln 3.46", Pos 1.1"	Ln 3.46", Pos 3.5"	Ln 3.46", Pos 5.7"

YOUR RIGHT TO CANCEL

We have agreed to establish an open-end credit account for you, and you have agreed to give us the security interest in your home as security for the account. You have a legal right under federal law to cancel the account, without cost, within three business days after the latest of the following events:

      (1) the opening date of your account which is _Ln 4.85", Pos 5.2"_ ; or
      (2) the date you received your Truth-in-Lending disclosures; or
      (3) the date you received this notice of your right to cancel the account.

If you cancel the account, the security interest in your home is also canceled. Within 20 days of receiving your notice, we must take the necessary steps to reflect the fact that the security interest in your home has been canceled. We must return to you any money or property you have given to us or to anyone else in connection with this account.

You may keep any money or property we have given you until we have done the things mentioned above, but you must then offer to return the money or property. If it is impractical or unfair for you to return the property, you must offer its reasonable value. You may offer to return the property at your home or at the location of the property. Money must be returned to the address below. If we do not take possession of the money or property within 20 calendar days of your offer, you may keep it without further obligation.

HOW TO CANCEL

If you decide to cancel this account, do so by notifying us in writing at _Ln 7.55", Pos 5.2"_
Ln 7.80", Pos 1.1"

You may use any written statement that is signed and dated by you and states intention to cancel, or you may use this notice by dating and signing below. Keep one copy of this notice no matter how you notify us because it contains important information about your rights.

If you cancel by mail or telegram, you must send the notice no later than midnight of _Ln 8.55", Pos 6.0"_ (or midnight of the third business day following the latest of the three events listed above).

I WISH TO CANCEL

Customer's Signature	Date

compensate by adding ½ inch to all your measurements. What you do next depends on whether you prefer to print multiple preprinted forms from a secondary merge file or fill in and print one form at a time.

Filling In Multiple Preprinted Forms

If you want to merge data from a secondary merge file to multiple preprinted forms, you'll need to set up a secondary merge file with the appropriate fields defined. Figure 16.24 shows a sample record in a secondary merge file, with field names at the top, which can be used to fill in the blanks on the form shown in Figure 16.23.

Next, create a primary merge file with the {FIELD} commands to print data at specific locations on the page. Be sure to use the proper page size and margins, as determined in the first two steps above. You can use the Advance feature to ensure that the text in each field appears just where you want it, by following these steps:

> **NOTE NOTE** *The Advance feature is covered in more detail in Chapter 20.*

1. Choose **Layout** ➤ **Ad**vance, choose To **Li**ne in the Advance dialog box. Type a vertical (line) measurement in the Advance text box for where you want an item of text to appear, and then choose OK or press ↵. (This corresponds to the Ln measurements you jotted down earlier.)

2. Go through the same steps and enter a horizontal measurement for where you want the same item of text to appear, and press ↵. (This corresponds to the Pos measurements you jotted down earlier.)

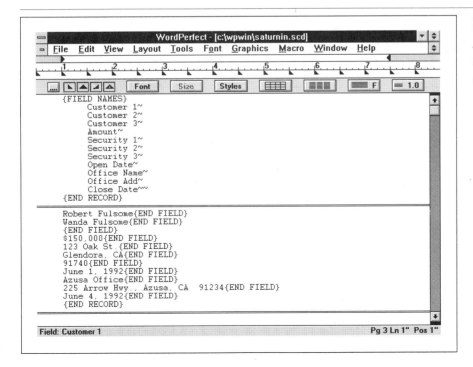

FIGURE 16.24:

A secondary merge file that can be used to fill in a form

3. Choose **Tools** ➤ **Merge** ➤ **Field** (or press Ctrl+F12 F). Then type the name (or number) of the field that you want to position at the location defined in the preceding two steps, and press ↵.

4. Repeat steps 1–3 for each field that needs to be filled in on the form.

5. When you're finished, save the entire document.

At this point, your document is a primary merge file that merges text from a secondary merge file to the exact locations required to fill in the form. Figure 16.25 shows how that primary merge file might look in the document window and Reveal Codes. (In Figure 16.25, you can't see the Advance code that advances text to Ln 8.55" and Pos 6" for the Close Date field, but it's really there.)

To actually print on the preprinted forms, first merge the primary and secondary merge files in the usual manner. Then load the blank forms in the printer, and print the entire merged document. If you made all your measurements accurately and loaded the blank forms in the printer correctly, your text should be aligned properly on the form, as shown in Figure 16.26.

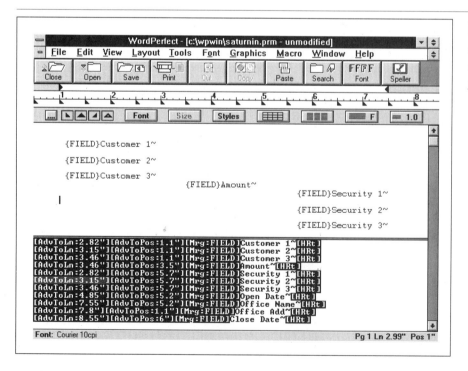

FIGURE 16.25:

A primary merge file for merging text to a preprinted form

Saturnine Lending Corporation
"Our rates are out of this world."

NOTICE OF RIGHT TO CANCEL

IDENTIFICATION OF LOAN TRANSACTION

Customer	Amount	Security
Robert Fulsome		123 Oak St.
Wanda Fulsome		Glendora, CA
	$150,000	91740

YOUR RIGHT TO CANCEL

We have agreed to establish an open-end credit account for you, and you have agreed to give us the security interest in your home as security for the account. You have a legal right under federal law to cancel the account, without cost, within three business days after the latest of the following events:

(1) the opening date of your account which is __June 1, 1991__ ; or
(2) the date you received your Truth-in-Lending disclosures; or
(3) the date you received this notice of your right to cancel the account.

If you cancel the account, the security interest in your home is also canceled. Within 20 days of receiving your notice, we must take the necessary steps to reflect the fact that the security interest in your home has been canceled. We must return to you any money or property you have given to us or to anyone else in connection with this account.

You may keep any money or property we have given you until we have done the things mentioned above, but you must then offer to return the money or property. If it is impractical or unfair for you to return the property, you must offer its reasonable value. You may offer to return the property at your home or at the location of the property. Money must be returned to the address below. If we do not take possession of the money or property within 20 calendar days of your offer, you may keep it without further obligation.

HOW TO CANCEL

If you decide to cancel this account, do so by notifying us in writing at __Azusa Office__
__225 Arrow Hwy., Azusa, CA 91234__

You may use any written statement that is signed and dated by you and states intention to cancel, or you may use this notice by dating and signing below. Keep one copy of this notice no matter how you notify us because it contains important information about your rights.

If you cancel by mail or telegram, you must send the notice no later than midnight of __June 4, 1991__ (or midnight of the third business day following the latest of the three events listed above).

I WISH TO CANCEL

Customer's Signature	Date

FIGURE 16.26:

Data from a secondary merge file merged to a fill-in form

Filling In a Single Preprinted Form

If you only need to fill in one blank form at a time, you may not want to bother

Check out Chapter 3 if you want to learn more about creating document comments.

with merge files. You can place Advance codes (as in the preceding example) to position the insertion point exactly where you want text to be printed on the form. Next to each pair of Advance codes, place a comment (choose Tools ➤ Comment ➤ Create) that describes the text to be typed on the form. Press ↵ after typing each comment.

Repeat this basic procedure for each blank on the fill-in form. Figure 16.27 shows an example that advances the insertion point to each blank on the sample form shown earlier in Figure 16.23. Note the comments in the document window and the Advance codes in Reveal Codes.

Figure 16.28 shows text for the same fill-in form. Here, the text to be printed on the form is typed below each comment (though in your document window, you'll need to scroll to view all the comments in this lengthy document). Once you've typed the text to be printed on the fill-in form, you can print the entire document on your preprinted form. Since document comments are never printed, only the typed text will be printed on the form, producing a neatly filled-in form, just like the example shown in Figure 16.26.

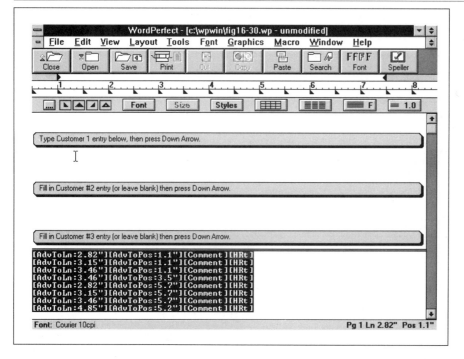

FIGURE 16.27:

A document to fill in a single fill-in form without merging

OTHER ADVANCED MERGE COMMANDS

Word-Perfect offers still more merge options and techniques, as described in Chapter 26.

If you want to merge data to documents that involve math, use the math capabilities of the Tables feature, discussed in Chapter 18. If you want to use data from other programs, such as a database management system or a spreadsheet program, for your merges, refer to Chapter 25.

In the next chapter, you'll learn how to sort lists and how to choose data from lists, including secondary merge files. These techniques will add a lot of power to your merging capabilities.

FIGURE 16.28:

Text to be printed on the fill-in form is typed between the document comments.

> Type Customer #1 entry below, then press Down Arrow.

Robert Fulsome

> Type Customer #2 entry (or leave blank) then press Down Arrow.

Wanda Fulsome

> Type Customer #3 entry (or leave blank) then press Down Arrow.

> Type in the Amount below, then press Down Arrow.

$150,000

> Type Security address line 1 below, then press Down Arrow.

123 Oak St.

> Type Security address line 2 below, then press Down Arrow.

Glendora, CA

> Type Security address line 3 below, then press Down Arrow.

91740

> Enter account Opening Date below, then press Down Arrow.

June 1, 1991

> Type Branch Office, then press Down Arrow.

Azusa Office

> Type complete Branch address below, then press Down arrow.

225 Arrow Hwy., Azusa, CA 91234

> Type Closing Date below, then press Down Arrow.

June 4, 1991

CHAPTER 17

Sorting and Selecting Records

! f you work with lists, tables, or secondary merge files, chances are you often need to sort and select text from those lists. By *sort,* I mean to put the items into some kind of order, such as alphabetical order, or zip code order for bulk mailing. By *select,* I mean to "pull out" certain items from the list. For example, when using a secondary merge file, you might need to pull out New York residents only or customers with past-due accounts to send a mailing to only those customers. This chapter describes both how to sort and select records from any kind of document.

SORTING TERMINOLOGY

Like merging, sorting borrows some terms from the field of database management, which offers, among other things, comprehensive sorting and selecting capabilities.

RECORDS AND FIELDS

The terms "tab and indent codes" in this chapter refer to all codes that align text on, or between, tab stops and margins, including [Tab], [Indent], [Center], [Flsh Rgt], [Dec Tab], and others described in Chapter 4.

Before you can properly sort your text, you need to understand the concepts of *records* and *fields*. WordPerfect sorts your text based on fields within each record. Generally, records are separated by one or more returns ([HRt] or [SRt] codes). Fields are separated by tab and indent codes. But the exact definitions of these terms depend on how the text being sorted is organized in the first place.

In a *line sort,* a record is any line of text that ends with a single hard return ([HRt]) or soft return ([SRt]). Each *field* is separated by a single tab or indent code. For example, Figure 17.1 shows some text organized into rows and columns in a document and Reveal Codes portions of the screen and illustrates how you define records and fields for sorting purposes.

In a *paragraph sort,* each record is separated by two or more hard-return ([HRt]) codes. Any given record in a paragraph might contain several lines of text, each line ending with a single hard return or soft return. Furthermore, any given line within the paragraph might be separated into fields, where each field is separated by a tab or an indent code. Figure 17.2 shows an example of some paragraphs separated by two hard returns and illustrates how the terms *record, line,* and *field* are defined in a paragraph sort. Only the top line

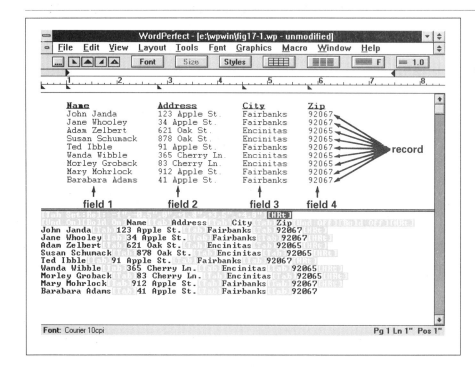

FIGURE 17.1:

Records and fields for performing a line sort; records are separated by single hard returns.

of each record includes indent codes in this example ([Center] and [Flsh Rgt], visible in Reveal Codes), so only that line in each record is divided into fields.

Merge sorts are used for sorting secondary merge files (Chapter 16). Here, the terms *record* and *field* mean the same as they do in merges. Each field ends with an {END FIELD} command, and each record ends with an {END RECORD} command, as shown in Figure 17.3. The fields in this example aren't divided into lines, because no field contains a hard- or soft-return code (the hard return at the end of each field is not part of the text within the field). WordPerfect does allow you to sort secondary merge files whose fields consist of multiple lines.

Figure 17.4 doesn't show any entries with multiple lines, but you can certainly use them in your own tables.

In *table sorts,* a record is simply a row. A line is any single line of text that ends with a hard or soft return within the row. The term *field* is not used when sorting tables. Instead, each record (row) is separated into cells, each cell being a column of text. That is, the leftmost column is cell 1, the next column is cell 2, and so forth, as shown in Figure 17.4.

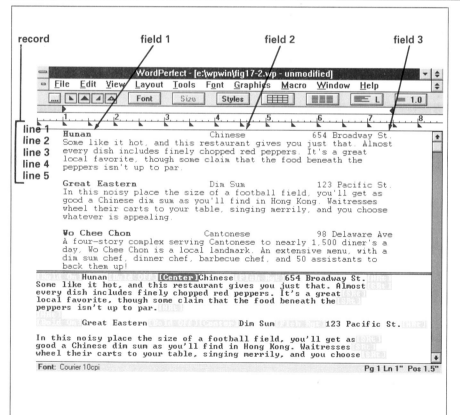

FIGURE 17.2:

Records, lines, and fields for a paragraph sort, where records are separated by two hard returns

WORDS

As you'll see later, words can also be separated by forward slashes (/) or dashes. This is handy for sorting dates.

Often, you need to define exactly which word in a field (or table cell) you want to use for sorting. A *word* is any text that's preceded by a blank space, rather than a tab or an indent. For example, take a look at this list of names:

Martha Mellor

Andy Bowers

Bonnie Zeepers

Wanda Carneros

If you sort these names on the first word, the names are displayed in this order:

Andy Bowers

Bonnie Zeepers

Martha Mellor

Wanda Carneros

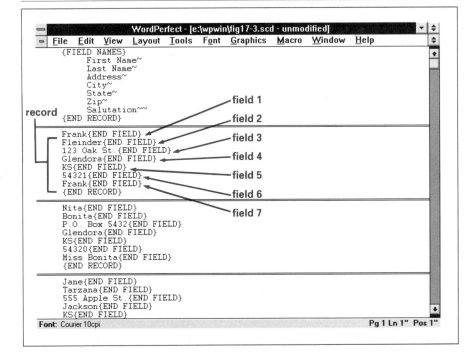

FIGURE 17.3:

A secondary merge file, with records and fields defined for sorting purposes

Notice how the names are sorted by each person's first name. If you want these names alphabetized by each person's last name, you sort on the second word (that is, the text after the first blank space). Sorting on the second word displays the names alphabetized by each person's last name, like this:

Andy Bowers

Wanda Carneros

Martha Mellor

Bonnie Zeepers

NOTE *You can also count backward by line when doing a table or merge sort. For example, line number −1 would be the last line.*

When identifying a word to sort on within a field or line, you can "count backward" from the end of the field or line. For example, word number −1 is the last word in the line or field. So, to sort the list of names above into proper last-name order, you could also identify the sort key (see the next section) as word −1 in the name field. This technique of counting backward is especially helpful if some names have middle initials and some don't (in this case, if you sort by word 2 instead of word −1, some names will end up sorted by middle initial, and others will be sorted by last name).

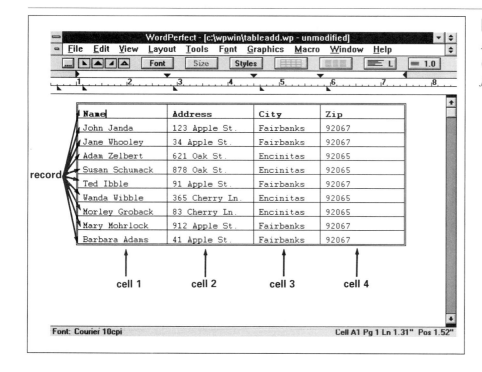

FIGURE 17.4:
A table, with records (rows) and cells defined for a table sort

THE SORT KEY

The *sort key* is the most important element of the sorting process, because it defines how the sort should take place. For example, when sorting information in a list of names and addresses into zip code order for bulk mailing, the sort key is the zip code. When sorting names and addresses into alphabetical order by name, the last name must be defined as the key. You identify a sort key by its exact line, field (or cell), and word position in each record. That's why it's important to understand what each of these terms means with respect to the text you want to sort. I'll provide exact steps for performing the sort and more examples of sort keys later in this chapter.

THE SORT TYPE

When defining a sort key, you can also define a key type, from one of these two options:

Alphanumeric	Use this option to sort text, combined text and numbers (e.g., part numbers like 123-ZY-KLM), or numbers of equal length (e.g., five-digit zip codes).
Numeric	Use this option to sort numbers that vary in length, such as quantities (e.g., 1, 999, 1,000) and currency amounts (e.g., $1.00, $1,000.00, $123.43).

SORTS WITHIN SORTS

WordPerfect lets you define up to nine sort keys for a single sort operation. If you define more than one key for a sort, the additional keys act as "tiebreakers" when the previous key or keys are identical. You can use multiple keys to produce a "sort within a sort." This is useful both for sorting large amounts of text and for grouping information.

The white pages of the phone book may be the most common example of a sort within a sort, where entries are sorted by each person's last name; within each identical last name, the names are sorted by each person's first name (e.g., *Smith, Ann* comes before *Smith, Millie*, which comes before *Smith, Zeke*).

As another example, here's a small list of eight records with four fields each—Department, Last Name, First Name, and Extension—in random order:

DEPARTMENT	LAST NAME	FIRST NAME	EXTENSION
Accounting	Smith	Zeke	2312
Marketing	Leeland	Lee	5434
Accounting	Smith	Michelle	7434
Marketing	Boorish	Babs	8433
Accounting	Smith	Adrian	5423
Marketing	Argosy	Steve	8323
Accounting	Adams	Wanda	8434
Accounting	Zastrow	Ernie	8434

Here's the same list after sorting the records by field 1, the department. Notice how within each department, employee names are in random order:

DEPARTMENT	LAST NAME	FIRST NAME	EXTENSION
Accounting	Adams	Wanda	8434
Accounting	Smith	Zeke	2312
Accounting	Smith	Adrian	5423
Accounting	Zastrow	Ernie	8434
Accounting	Smith	Michelle	7434
Marketing	Leeland	Lee	5434
Marketing	Argosy	Steve	8323
Marketing	Boorish	Babs	8433

NOTE
NOTE
This example also shows how sorting can be used as a means of grouping. In this case, employee names are grouped according to department.

Here's the same list sorted with two sort keys: the Department field and the Last Name field. The departments are listed in alphabetical order, and within each department, employee names are sorted by last name:

DEPARTMENT	LAST NAME	FIRST NAME	EXTENSION
Accounting	Adams	Wanda	8434
Accounting	Smith	Adrian	5423

DEPARTMENT	LAST NAME	FIRST NAME	EXTENSION
Accounting	Smith	Zeke	2312
Accounting	Smith	Michelle	7434
Accounting	Zastrow	Ernie	8434
Marketing	Boorish	Babs	8433
Marketing	Argosy	Steve	8323
Marketing	Leeland	Lee	5434

In yet another example, three sort keys are used to sort the rows: the Department field, Last Name field, and First Name field. This list is almost identical to the preceding list, except that the Smiths are in alphabetical order by first name, because First Name was defined as the third sort key.

DEPARTMENT	LAST NAME	FIRST NAME	EXTENSION
Accounting	Adams	Wanda	8434
Accounting	Smith	Adrian	5423
Accounting	Smith	Michelle	7434
Accounting	Smith	Zeke	2312
Accounting	Zastrow	Ernie	8434
Marketing	Argosy	Steve	8323
Marketing	Boorish	Babs	8433
Marketing	Leeland	Lee	5434

In general, the larger your list, the more likely you'll want to use more sort keys to organize it. In the example above, it's easy to see all the Smiths in the Accounting department, so it's not crucial that they be in alphabetical order by first name. But if there were dozens of Smiths in Accounting, it would be much easier to find a particular one if they were listed alphabetically by first name.

THE SORT ORDER

The *sort order* is the direction of the sort. You can choose either *ascending* order (from A to Z, or smallest number to largest), or *descending* order (from Z to A, or largest number to smallest).

PERFORMING A SORT OPERATION

The Sort option is on the Tools pull-down menu. The general procedure for sorting text in a document is as follows:

Don't confuse selecting records with selecting text.

1. To play it safe, save a copy of your document by choosing **File ➤ S**ave or pressing Shift+F3, so you can easily recover from a mistake.

2. If you do *not* want to sort all the text in the document, select the text that you do want to sort. If you want to sort a table, place your insertion point anywhere within the table, or select the table rows you want to sort.

3. Choose **T**ools **➤ S**ort, or press Ctrl+Shift+F12. You'll see the dialog box shown in Figure 17.5

4. Choose **L**ine, **P**aragraph, **M**erge Record, or **T**able Row, depending on which type of record you want to sort (this is a very important step!).

If the insertion point is within a table when you start a sort operation, WordPerfect automatically defines the sort as a table sort.

5. Choose **A**scending, **D**escending, or **N**o Sort (used with record selection), depending on the sort order that you want to use.

6. Define up to nine sort keys in the Key Definitions area, as described in the next section.

7. Choose OK or press ↵ to perform the sort.

It may take a few seconds or minutes (depending on the amount of text you want to sort) for WordPerfect to complete the job. If your sort results are not what you expected, you can abandon the current version of the document (choose **File ➤ C**lose **➤ N**o, or press Ctrl+F4 N), and open the previous version (choose **File ➤ O**pen or press F4), provided you saved it before sorting.

DEFINING SORT KEYS

The Key Definitions area of the Sort dialog box lets you define up to nine sort keys. The line sort example in the dialog box shown in Figure 17.5 shows several headings for each sort key:

Key: identifies which key number you are defining.

Type: lets you indicate whether the sort is to be alphanumeric or numeric.

Field: lets you define the field number for this key.

Word: lets you define the word number for this key.

For merge, paragraph, and table sorts, you'll also see a heading for *Line* (lets you define the line number for this key). Note that table sorts display the heading *Cell* in place of *Field* to let you define a cell (column) number for the key.

You'll see many examples of sort keys throughout this chapter, but before looking at these, let's go over the procedure for defining a sort key. Follow these steps:

1. In the Key Definitions area of the Sort dialog box, you can do any of the following:

- ◆ Insert a new key by choosing the Insert Key button.
- ◆ Choose any existing key by clicking on it or by pressing Tab or Shift+Tab to move through keys.
- ◆ Delete the currently selected key (the one with > next to it) by choosing the Delete Key button.

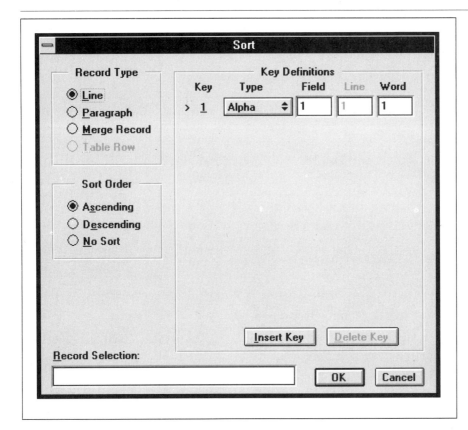

FIGURE 17.5:

The Sort dialog box

2. To change the key type from Alpha to Numeric, move the mouse pointer to the key's Type button, hold down the left mouse button, highlight the key type you want, and then release the mouse button. Or, use Tab and Shift+Tab to choose the button, then use ↑ and ↓ to choose a key type.

3. Change any key definition option (i.e., Field, Line, or Word) by typing over it.

When all your keys are defined, choose OK or press ↵ to perform the sort and return to the document window.

SORTING LINES

> **TO SORT LINES OF TEXT,**
>
> Select the text you want to sort, choose Tools ➤ Sort ➤ Line, define your sort keys and order, and choose OK.

If you need to get another look at the document window to scroll around, choose Cancel and use the mouse to scroll. Choose Tools ➤ Sort when you're ready to return to the Sort dialog box.

Use the Line option in the Sort dialog box when your text is in a simple list format and each line is broken by a single hard return ([HRt] code), as in Figure 17.1. Remember to select the lines that you want to sort, and after choosing Tools ➤ Sort ➤ Line (or pressing Ctrl+Shift+F12 L), define your sort keys.

Figure 17.6 shows a list of records with the sort keys set up to sort the list by each person's last name. In this example, each person's last name is the second word in the first field (that is, the first field in each row is a name, the first word in each name is the person's first name, and the second word is the last name). Therefore, you want to set up the sort key as shown in the figure, and below:

Key	Type	Field	Line	Word
1	Alpha	1		2

Figure 17.7 shows the same list of names and addresses with sort keys defined to sort records into zip code order, and then by address within each zip code. Notice that the first sort key is, of course, the zip code field (field 4). The second sort key is the street name (the second word in the Address field). The third sort key is the street number (the first "word" in the address field, sorted as a number). After you choose OK, records will be in order by zip code and by address within each zip code area (as shown by the sorted results in the figure).

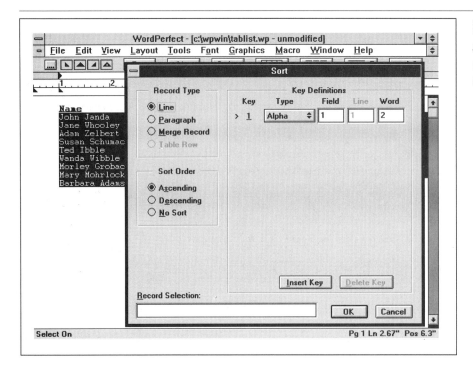

FIGURE 17.6:
Sort keys defined to sort names and addresses by last name

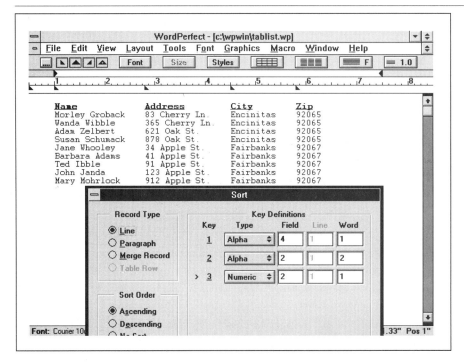

FIGURE 17.7:
Sort keys set up to sort records into street-address order within each zip code

SORTING PARAGRAPHS

> ### ▌ TO SORT PARAGRAPHS,
>
> **select the text you want to sort, choose Tools ➤ Sort ➤ Paragraph, define the sort Keys and Order, then choose OK.**

N O T E
N O T E

To sort by zip code, use an alphanumeric type for the key so that extended and foreign zip codes will be sorted properly.

If you want to sort a series of paragraphs, first select the paragraphs (unless you want to sort every paragraph in the document). Before defining your sort keys, remember to choose Paragraph in the Sort dialog box so that you can properly identify the sort key or keys. Notice in the upper-left corner of the dialog box in Figure 17.8 that the sort type is Paragraph, which lets you identify each sort key by Type, Line, Field, and Word.

Figure 17.8 shows the paragraph sort with the zip code in each field identified as the sort key. In the figure, you can see that the only sort key is line 3, field 1, word −1. That's because the city, state, and zip code are on the third line of each record. There is only one field on that line because the city, state, and zip code are separated by blank spaces, not tabs. The zip code is the last "word" on each line, hence its position is identified as word −1.

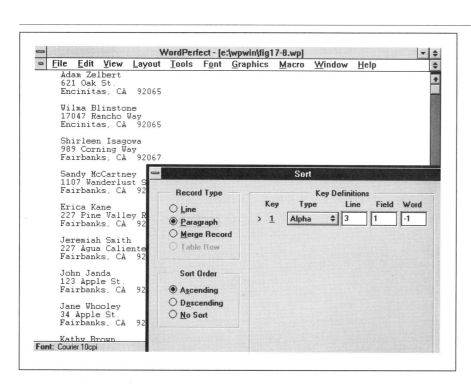

FIGURE 17.8:

A paragraph sort to list names and addresses in zip-code order

Another example of a paragraph sort is presented in Figure 17.9, where each bibliography entry is separated by two hard returns. This is a tricky one, because the first line of each paragraph is outdented one tab stop with a combination of [Indent] and [Mar Rel] codes (i.e., with a hanging paragraph format, as discussed in Chapter 4).

The tab and indent codes define new fields.

Take a look at the defined sort key. Line 1 is chosen because the author name is on the first line of each record. But even though each author's name appears to be at the beginning of the line, the sort key must be defined as field 3 in this example because the [Indent] and [Mar Rel] codes at the start of each paragraph are treated as tab and indent codes. Therefore, WordPerfect assumes that field 1 is to the left of the [Indent] code and that field 2 is to the left of the [Mar Rel] code (even though there is no text in either place), so field 3 starts at the right of the [Mar Rel] code. Hence, each author's last name is actually in field 3, and this list will be sorted correctly only if the sort key is defined accordingly.

SORTING A SECONDARY MERGE FILE

TO SORT A SECONDARY MERGE FILE,

choose Tools ➤ Sort ➤ Merge Record, define the sort keys and order, and then choose OK.

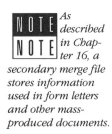

As described in Chapter 16, a secondary merge file stores information used in form letters and other mass-produced documents.

To sort a secondary merge file, just bring it to a document window and remember to choose Merge Record from the Sort dialog box, so you can properly define your sort keys. Remember that the [HRt] code at the end of each field is *not* included when defining a line to sort by; you only need to specify the line number for a sort key if a particular field contains more than one line of text.

Figure 17.10 shows a secondary merge file with the sort key defined to sort the records into zip code order (perhaps for a bulk mailing). Field 6 identifies the sixth field from the top of each record (in this example, the name *Frank* is in the first field). The field is not divided into additional lines or words, so both the Line and Word options are set to 1.

If you want to sort the secondary merge file into name order, like the telephone directory (that is, by last name and by first name within identical last names), you define sort keys 1 and 2 as below:

Key	Type	Field	Line	Word
1	alpha	2	1	1
2	alpha	1	1	1

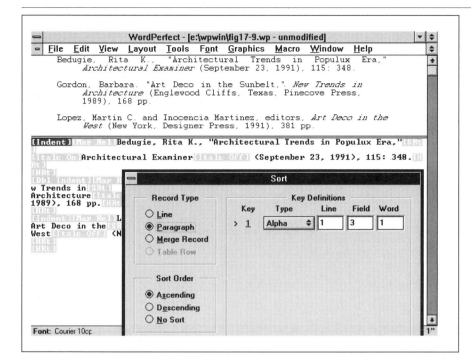

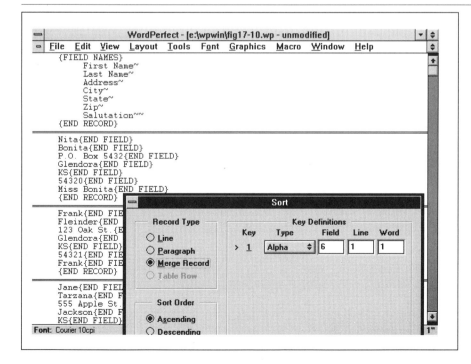

This sets up each person's last name as the main sort key and each person's first name as the tiebreaker within each identical last name.

SORTING A TABLE

▌ TO SORT A TABLE,

select the rows that you want to sort, choose Tools ➤ Sort, define the sort keys and order, and then choose OK.

Before sorting text in a table, be sure to do the following:

1. Move the insertion point anywhere into the table.

2. Save the entire document by choosing **F**ile ➤ **S**ave or pressing Shift+F3.

3. Use your mouse to select the rows you want to sort.

The last step is particularly important because, as with line and paragraph sorting, if you don't select any rows, all the rows in the table will be sorted. Generally, you don't want to sort column titles, table titles, totals, or other information at the bottom of the table. In Figure 17.11, the table title, column titles, and totals have been excluded from the sort operation.

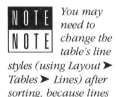 *You may need to change the table's line styles (using Layout ➤ Tables ➤ Lines) after sorting, because lines are sorted with their rows.*

Also, you should avoid including rows with more, or fewer, cells than other rows in the sort. For example, if the sort included the row of joined cells at the top of the table shown in Figure 17.11, that row's position after sorting would be quite unpredictable.

After you've selected the rows you want to sort, you can then proceed with the sort as described earlier in this chapter. You don't need to choose a sort type, because WordPerfect automatically sets the option to Table Row when the insertion point is within a table.

Figure 17.12 shows the sort key used to sort the rows of the table in Figure 17.11 in descending order from the greatest increase to the greatest decrease. Note that the Sort Order is Descending, and the Record Type is Table Row, as shown in the dialog box. The sort key is Numeric and is in the fourth column of the table.

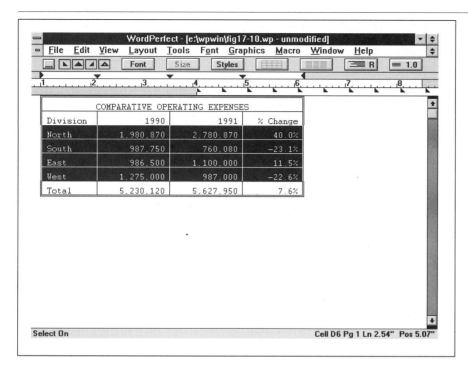

FIGURE 17.11:

The rows to be sorted in the table are selected before starting the sort operation.

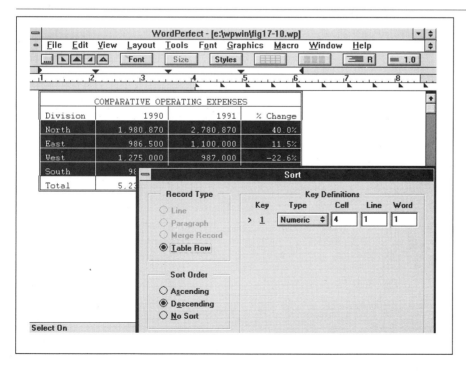

FIGURE 17.12:

A sort key set up to sort a table in descending order from greatest increase to greatest decrease (column 4)

TROUBLESHOOTING SORTS

If your sorted text does not come out in the order you expected, then typically one of four things is wrong:

◆ You defined the wrong text as the sort key, so the sort order appears to be random.

◆ You did not choose the correct sort type (i.e., Line, Paragraph, or Merge).

◆ The fields don't correspond to one another's position in the records.

◆ You forgot to choose OK after correctly defining the sort keys.

The first mistake is the most common, particularly when sorting lines or paragraphs. When you are sorting lines or paragraphs, it's important to realize that *every* tab or indent defines a new field. Thus, if the first column of text is indented, then it will be in field 2, the next field will be field 3, and so forth. This situation, where the first visible column isn't actually the first field, was described earlier in the example of sorting a bibliography and is shown in Figure 17.13.

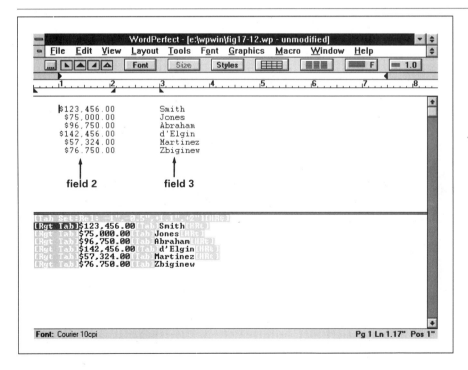

FIGURE 17.13:

Every tab or indent code counts as a field, even the first one, as in this example, where the dollar amounts are in field 2 and the names are in field 3.

If you did not define your tab stops before typing columns, your sort may also go awry, because the fields are not positioned the same way in each record. For example, in the first of two records shown below, the address is in field 3 because it's preceded by two [Tab] codes. But in the second record, the address is in field 4 because it's preceded by three [Tab] codes (field 3 contains nothing in that record).

John Jones[Tab]	ABC Corporation[Tab]	123 Apple St.
Nancy Wilcox[Tab]	XYZ Co.[Tab][Tab]	345 Oak St.

Redefining tab stops is covered in Chapter 4.

To fix this problem, you must first redefine the tab stops so that only one [Tab] code is required to separate each column of text. Then remove any extra [Tab] codes so that text aligns properly in each column. When that's finished, you can define your sort key or keys and perform the sort.

Some text is impossible to sort, simply because it is not arranged in any kind of field-and-record order. For example, you could not possibly sort the bibliography shown earlier in Figure 17.9 in title, publisher, or date order, because these items are not in consistent, identifiable positions within each record.

TRICKY NAME SORTS

A common, though solvable, sort problem occurs when names are stored in a single field without a specific word to latch onto for sorting, like this:

Mr. A.H. Smith

Mr. and Mrs. George C. Lott

Windham Earl III

Winston Fitzgerald Jr.

Word-Perfect counts only normal spaces, forward slashes, and dash characters.

There's no hope of counting words from the front to identify each person's last name, and a −1 will incorrectly identify the *III* and the *Jr.* as the last name in two of these records. There is a solution, however.

When counting words, WordPerfect does not count hard spaces. If you always remember to use a hard space (by choosing Layout ➤ Line ➤ Special Codes or pressing Ctrl+spacebar) to separate the III and the Jr. from the last name in every record, you can use word −1 as the sort key in this field, and the names will be alphabetized properly.

SORTING DATES

You type a dash by pressing Ctrl + –, or choosing Layout ➤ Line ➤ Special Codes ➤ Dash Character.

If you type dates in the format *mm/dd/yy* (e.g., *12/31/91*), or *mm-dd-yy* (e.g., *12-31-91*) by using dashes, you can sort records in date order. The slashes or dashes are treated as spaces and therefore can be used to divide each date into words representing month, day, and year. When defining the sort key, define the year as the first sort key (in word –1), the month as the second key (in word 1), the day as the third key (in word 2), and the type of each key as Numeric. Figure 17.14 shows an example where the dates are in the second column of a table (cell 2), and all three fields are defined for proper sorting by date. After OK is chosen in this example, the records will be listed in earliest to latest date order.

SELECTING RECORDS

TO SELECT RECORDS,

select your text and define your sort keys. If the text you want to select is not already a sort key, define it as one. Define your selection criterion in the Record Selection text box, and then choose OK.

When you're maintaining a list, such as a mailing list, you often need to isolate certain items in it. For example, you may want to send a special holiday catalog to customers who have spent above a certain amount in the last year, or tell customers living in one state about a new insurance discount available to them. WordPerfect's record selection feature lets you pick out the records you need from your larger list, and optionally, sort them in the process.

To select records, follow these steps:

1. Perform steps 1–6 described in "Performing a Sort Operation" earlier in this chapter to select the text you want to sort and define the sort keys.

2. If the text you want to use to identify records for selection is not already defined as a sort key, identify that text as a sort key (it doesn't have to be the first key; any valid key will do).

3. Define your selection criterion in the Record Selection text box, as described in the sections that follow. Use the normal typing keys to enter your criterion. If you make a mistake when typing your

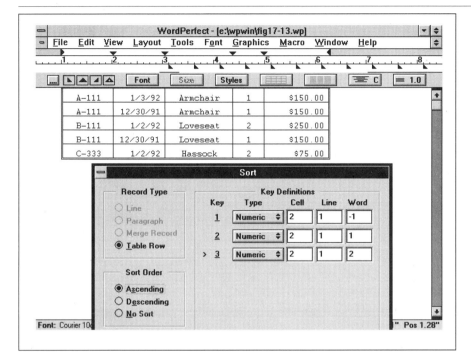

Sort keys set up to sort records in a table by date

criterion, or you need to make some changes, you can use the mouse or the usual movement and editing keys to move through the line and make corrections. To delete the criterion entirely, move to the end of the line and press the Backspace key.

4. Choose OK to sort and select records.

In short, selecting records is virtually identical to sorting them, except that you must define your selection criterion before choosing OK.

DEFINING A SELECTION CRITERION

The *selection criterion* comprises the conditions a record must meet to remain in the output of the selection operation. A selection criterion has three elements:

◆ Key number

◆ Selection operators

◆ Search values

Be sure to read the next section, "Warning! Word-Perfect Deletes When It Selects." It contains valuable advice on preventing the accidental deletion of records.

The *key number* is the number of the key as you've defined it in the Sort dialog box. As you know, you can define up to nine keys, numbered 1 to 9. When typed as part of a selection criterion, the first key is *key1*, the second is *key2*, and so on.

The *selection operators* define the type of relationship that you are seeking. The available operators are listed below:

=	Equals
<>	Does not equal
>	Is greater than
<	Is less than
>=	Is greater than or equal to
<=	Is less than or equal to

The *search values* define what you are looking for or comparing to. For example, suppose you want to limit your mailing to California residents. First, you define the state field in a secondary merge file as the second sort key (key2). Then, because you want to pull out only those records with CA in that field, the selection criterion is

key2=CA

which in English says, "Delete all records *except* those with CA in the second sort key" (which you've previously defined as the state field in your secondary merge file). The resulting merge file can then be used to print letters and labels for California residents only.

Two special operators allow you to combine expressions in search criteria:

+	OR
*	AND

When combining expressions, you must use all three elements—key numbers, selection operators, and search values— on both sides of the * (AND) and + (OR) operators. For example, suppose you want to print letters and labels only for people in certain zip code areas, such as 92000 to 92999 (which covers most of the cities in San Diego County). If you define the zip code as your first sort key (key1), your selection criterion is

key1>=92000*key1<=92999

which in English says, "Isolate records with zip codes that are greater than or equal to 92000, and are also less than or equal to 92999." Table 17.1 offers examples of other search criteria and a quick summary for future reference.

One of the most common mistakes people make when combining expressions in selection criteria is to forget to use all three elements on both sides of the * (AND) and + (OR) operators. For example, if you enter the selection criterion

key1>=92000*<=92999

you might think that WordPerfect would be smart enough to read this as "zip codes that are greater than or equal to 92000 and less than 92999." But neither WordPerfect nor your computer is smart enough to make this inference. Instead, your entry is interpreted as "zip codes that are greater than or equal to 92000 and who-knows-what is less than or equal to 92999."

The same holds true for the + (OR) operator. For example, suppose you want to send letters to people in the states of Georgia, Alabama, and Florida, and have already defined the state field as sort-key number 1 (key1). Now you need a selection criterion that deletes all records *except* those with GA, AL, or FL in the state field, like this:

key1=GA+key1=AL+key1=FL

If you incorrectly enter the selection criterion as

key1=GA+AL+FL

or

key1=GA+=AL+= FL

WordPerfect will reject the criterion and display the "Incorrect format" message.

If you enter a faulty search criterion, as in this example, WordPerfect will display the message "Incorrect format" when you try to exit the Sort dialog box.

SYMBOL	FUNCTION	EXAMPLE	MEANING
=	Equal to	key1=45	Selects all records for which key 1 is equal to 45
<>	Not equal to	key1<>45	Selects all records for which key 1 is not equal to 45
>	Greater than	key1>45	Selects all records for which key 1 is greater than 45
<	Less than	key1<45	Selects all records for which key 1 is less than 45
>=	Greater than or equal to	key1>=45	Selects all records for which key 1 is greater than or equal to 45
<=	Less than or equal to	key1<=45	Selects all records for which key 1 is less than or equal to 45
*	AND	key1=45*key2=M	Selects all records for which key 1 is equal to 45 and key 2 is equal to M
+	OR	key1=45+key2=M	Selects all records for which key 1 is equal to 45 or key 2 is equal to M
g	Global	keyg=45	Selects all records with the value 45 in any key

TABLE 17.1:

Selection Operators

It's also very important not to confuse the AND (*) and OR (+) operators, because they don't always relate directly to how you might represent criteria in English. Consider the example of mailings to residents of Georgia, Alabama, and Florida. You might think that this selection criterion will do the trick:

key1=GA*key1=AL*key1=FL

In English, this says, "Delete records except those that have GA in the state field, and AL in the state field, and FL in the state field." WordPerfect, however, interprets this as meaning something like "records that have *GA AL FL* in the state field." But a single record could not possibly have all three states in its state field, so the results of the selection are no records at all!

Understanding this difference between AND and OR is crucial to creating valid selection criteria. Remember that WordPerfect performs a selection by comparing every record, individually, with the selection criterion. That is, when WordPerfect performs your selection with a criterion such as

key1=GA+key1=AL+key1=FL

it looks at one record at a time and asks, "Does this record have GA, *or* AL, *or* FL in the state field?" If WordPerfect can answer *Yes* to this question, it does not delete the record.

On the other hand, when WordPerfect sees a selection criterion like

key1=GA*key1=AL*key1=FL

it asks, "Does this record have GA, AL, *and* FL in the state field?" WordPerfect is bound to come up with the answer *No* for each record it compares to this selection criterion, because it's impossible for any single record (i.e., one person's home address) to contain three different states.

If you're not accustomed to using computers to select items from a list (or records from a merge file), your mind may be reeling with all this business of "and" and "or." But a little practice and experience will surely help you to get things right.

When defining your selection criterion, it's important to keep in mind that you are not asking a question in English. Instead you are setting up a screen, or filter, through which some records will pass and some will not. That is, Word-Perfect will compare each record, one at a time, with your selection criterion. If *all* the expressions joined by the AND operator (*) in your selection criterion can be answered with Yes for a single record, that record is retained. If *any* of the expressions joined by the OR (+) operator in your selection criterion can be answered with Yes for a single record, that record is retained.

You and I know what the sentence "Send letters to everyone in Georgia, Alabama, *and* Florida" means. However, your computer can't understand plain English like this. You must set up your selection criterion specifically to say, "Keep only those records that have GA in the state field, *or* AL in the state field, *or* FL in the state field." And the only way to do this (assuming that the first sort key represents the state field) is with the selection criterion

key1=GA+key1=AL+key1=FL

WARNING! WORDPERFECT DELETES WHEN IT SELECTS

When you make a selection, it's important to understand that WordPerfect actually deletes records that do not match the selection criterion. Therefore, you should always send the results of a selection to a separate file so that you do not accidentally delete some records from your existing list (some people refer to this as the "master list").

For example, suppose you create a secondary merge file named NAMELIST.WP, with 500 names and addresses. If you then do a selection operation on that file to isolate, say, Nebraska residents, WordPerfect will delete all the records except those for the Nebraska residents. If you then save the results of the selection with the original name, NAMELIST.WP, you will permanently lose every record except those for Nebraska residents in your NAMELIST.WP file—they cannot be recovered! You have to retype the records for residents of all the other states—not a pleasant task.

If you are going to be sorting and selecting often, I recommend that you save two copies of your list or secondary merge file, one with all the records and one that will be used to hold only the results of the most recent selection operation. You might want to name this results file *SELECTED.WP.*

Always use the original secondary merge file to add and edit data. Then use the SELECTED.WP file only to store the results of selections. This will prevent confusion about which file is which by avoiding the creation of dozens of files that are simply the results of selections (which can gobble up your valuable disk space).

REFINING YOUR SELECTION CRITERIA WITH PARENTHESES

If your selection criterion starts becoming rather complicated, you must be careful about how you combine AND and OR operators. For example, suppose your secondary merge file contains (among others) a field for the state where each person lives and a field for each person's credit limit. You then decide to write a form letter to all the people in Georgia and only those in Florida whose credit limits are $500 or greater, informing them that you've raised their credit limits by $1000 (perhaps because the value of their real estate has gone up).

 *Word-Perfect evaluates your selection criterion from left to right unless you use parentheses to change the order.*

If you want to isolate records from your secondary merge file to address only your intended customers, you must create a selection criterion that combines *and* logic and *or* logic. That is, you must isolate all people who live in Georgia and only those in Florida who have credit limits of $500 or more.

If you're not careful, you may end up creating an ambiguous selection criterion while trying to isolate these customers. For example, assuming that you've already defined the first sort key (key1) as the state field, and the second sort key (key2) as the credit-limit field, you might compose your selection criterion as

key1=GA+key1=FL*key2>=$500

But WordPerfect will interpret this as, "Select records that have GA or FL in the state field; from that list, select records where the credit limit is greater than or equal to $500." The result includes those people in both Georgia and Florida whose credit limits are $500 or greater (but since you want to include *everyone* in Georgia, regardless of their present credit limit, this interpretation doesn't accomplish your intended goal).

To avoid potential confusion with such a complicated selection criterion, you can use parentheses to refine the meaning and control how WordPerfect interprets your criterion. For example, the criterion

key1=GA+(key1=FL*key2>=$500)

says that, to avoid being deleted, a record must have GA in the state field (so all Georgians will be selected), *or* it must have FL in the state field *and* have a value that's greater than or equal to $500 in the credit-limit field. This resolves the ambiguity and ensures that *all* Georgians (with any credit limit at all) and *only* those Floridians with credit limits of $500 or more will remain after the selection operation is finished.

GLOBAL SELECTIONS

You can use the *keyg* key name to search *all* the sort keys for a specific value. For example, suppose you create a secondary merge file that includes both a business address and a home address for each individual. If you want to mail to everyone who has either a home or business address in New York, define both the home and business state fields as sort keys. Then specify *keyg=NY* as the selection criterion. This will delete all records except those with NY in either the home or business state field.

SELECTING RECORDS WITHOUT SORTING

You can select records from a file without sorting them. You still need to define your sort keys so that you can refer to them in your selection criterion, then specify your criterion. However, before you choose the OK option, choose the No Sort option from the Sort Order selections in the Sort dialog box. The resulting output will contain only the selected records, but not in sorted order. This can speed things up a bit when you're performing selections from very large files.

EXAMPLES OF RECORD SELECTIONS

Figure 17.15 illustrates a sort key set up to sort a list of names and addresses in alphabetical order by last name, as shown earlier in Figure 17.6. In this example, however, only those records with *Schumack* as the last name (key1=Schumack) will be retained.

As you can see, the first sort key (key1) is defined as the second word in the first field. The selection criterion, which you can see in the Record Selection text box in the lower portion of the dialog box, is

key1=Schumack

After OK is chosen, only records that have Schumack as the last name will remain in the document.

Figure 17.16 shows another example, which sorts records in zip code order. In this example, however, the following selection criterion has been added:

key1=92067

This will select records in only the 92067 zip code area.

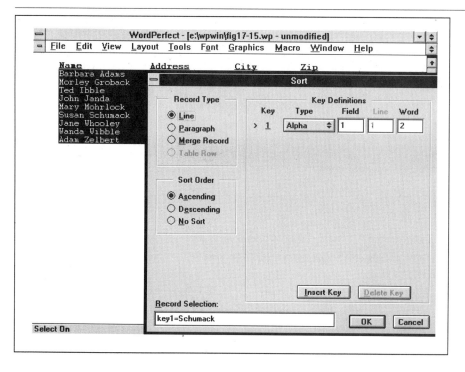

FIGURE 17.15:

Records with Schumack as the last name will be selected

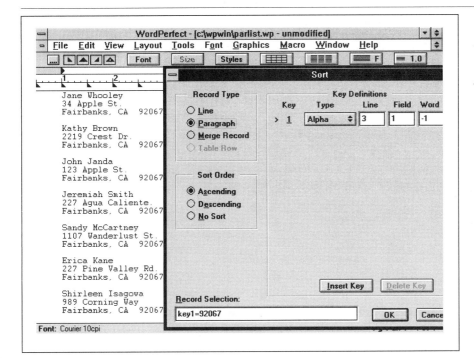

Figure 17.17 shows a sample secondary merge file, with the city (field 4) defined as the first sort key and the state (field 5) defined as the second sort key. The selection criterion is

key1=Layton*key2=KS

After OK is chosen, the secondary merge file will contain only names and addresses for residents of Layton, Kansas.

In the next chapter, you'll learn another handy technique for the office: performing math calculations within a table. As you'll see, this technique can also be convenient for certain types of merges.

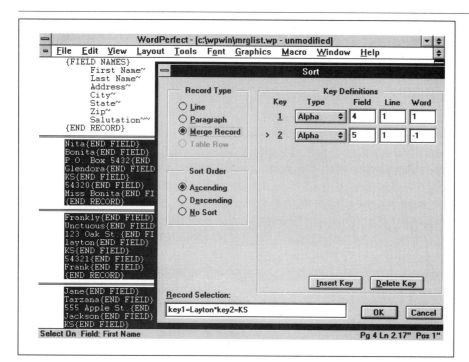

FIGURE 17.17:

*A sort-and-select
operation designed to
isolate residents of
Layton, Kansas*

CHAPTER 18

Perfect Math

his chapter discusses WordPerfect's Math feature, which is handy for typing invoices, financial statements, and other documents that require some basic business computations. You use the Tables feature, introduced in Chapter 6, to do math.

If you prefer to use a spreadsheet program like Microsoft Excel or Plan-Perfect for math, you will be glad to know that you can still use your spreadsheet program for all your math needs, and then import a spreadsheet into a WordPerfect document for printing. This topic is covered in Chapter 25.

For now, I'll review some of the basics of the WordPerfect Tables feature so that I can talk about using it for math. You'll find all of the Tables features, including Math, on the Layout ➤ Tables pull-down menu.

TABLES AND MATH

As described in Chapter 6, every cell in a table has an *address,* which identifies its position in the table. The first (leftmost) column is *A,* the next column is *B,* and so forth. The rows are numbered from top to bottom, starting with *1.*

The place where a column and row meet is called a *cell,* and each cell is identified by its column and row coordinates. The cell in the upper-left corner is A1 (column A, row 1), the cell to the right of that is B1, the cell to the right of that is C1, and so on. The cell beneath A1 is A2, the next cell down is A3, and so on.

You can always tell which cell the insertion point is in by looking at the status bar, near the bottom of the screen. For example, Figure 18.1 shows a table with the insertion point in cell C4. The figure also identifies each cell in the table.

USING MATH FORMULAS

Pressing either the hyphen key or the gray −key on your numeric keypad are valid ways of entering a leading minus sign.

Within a table, you can perform calculations by creating math *formulas.* The numbers can contain decimal points, commas to separate thousands, and leading dollar signs ($). For example, *1000, 1,000.00,* and *$1,000.00* are all valid ways of expressing the number one thousand. A negative number can be expressed with a leading minus sign or enclosed in parentheses. To express a negative value of one thousand, you can enter −1000, −1000.00, −1,000.00, −$1,000.00, $−1,000.00, or ($1,000.00).

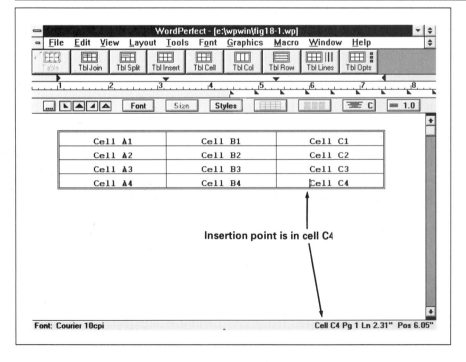

FIGURE 18.1:

Cell addresses in a table

You can use any combination of the following arithmetic operators in your formulas:

( )	Parentheses (used for grouping)
+	Addition
– (hyphen)	Subtraction or negative number
/	Division
*	Multiplication

You have to recalcu-late the en-tire table before WordPerfect will display the correct results of formulas, as discussed a little later in this chapter.

A formula can contain numbers, cell addresses, or both. For example, the for-mula *2 * 100* displays *200* in its cell. If cell A1 contains *25,* cell A2 contains *10,* and cell A3 contains the formula *A1 * A2,* then cell A3 displays *250* (the result of multiplying 10 and 25). If cell A1 contains *$100.00,* and cell A2 con-tains the formula *1.065 * A1,* then cell A2 actually displays *106.50* (a handy formula for adding a 6.5 percent sales tax to the number in another cell).

If a formula contains two or more operators, they are calculated from left to right. For example, the result of the formula *1 + 5 * 10* is *60.* However, you can designate any part of the formula to be calculated first by enclosing it in parentheses. Therefore the result of *1 + (5 * 10)* is *51,* because the paren-theses indicate that the multiplication takes place first.

If you want to enter a number that involves a complex fraction into a cell and do not know the decimal equivalent of the fraction offhand, enter the number as a formula instead. For example, to enter the number *17 $15/16$* (seventeen and fifteen-sixteenths) into a cell, create a formula that calculates 17 + (15 / 16) in that cell. The cell will then display the correct decimal equivalent of the number.

You can *nest* up to seven pairs of parentheses in a formula. This allows you to perform complex calculations within a table. For example, if cell A1 contains the cost of an item, A2 the salvage value of that item, A3 the useful life in years, and A4 the current year, then the formula

A1 – A2 * (A3 – A4 + 1) / (A3 * (A3 + 1) / 2)

calculates the current depreciation using the sum-of-the-years-digits method.

As I'll discuss later in this chapter, your table can also include special math functions to calculate subtotals, totals, and a grand total. These are indi-cated by a +, =, or * character (respectively) and are chosen from dialog box options, not typed directly into a cell. Figure 18.2 shows a table designed for printing invoices. This figure shows math formulas (e.g., *C2 * D2*) used in cells in the rightmost column.

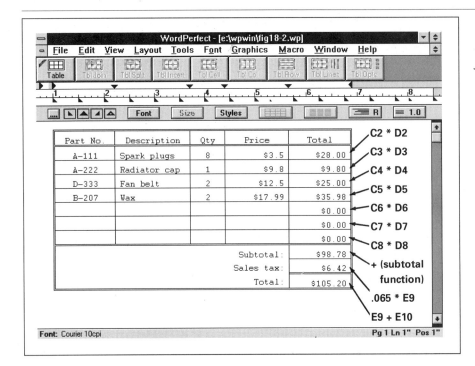

You might not need to type each formula into a cell. If the formulas follow the same pattern, as in Figure 18.2, where each cell calculates the quantity times the unit price, you can just enter one formula in the topmost cell, and then copy it to the cells below. You'll learn how to copy formulas later in this chapter.

ENTERING FORMULAS

TO ENTER A FORMULA IN A TABLE CELL,

move the insertion point into the cell where you want to place the formula. Choose Layout ➤ Tables ➤ Formula, type your formula, and choose OK or press ↵.

To determine the address of a cell that you want to use in a calculation, move the insertion point to that cell and check the status bar.

Once you create a table, you can enter a formula in any cell. Follow these steps:

1. Move the insertion point to the cell where you want to put the formula.

2. Choose **L**ayout ➤ **T**ables, or press Ctrl+F9.

3. Choose **F**ormula. You'll see this dialog box:

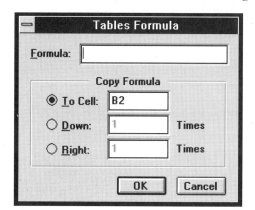

CAUTION *When typing a formula, do not include blank spaces. WordPerfect considers them to be illegal characters, and will reject your formula.*

4. Type in your formula.

5. Choose OK or press ↵ to return to the document window.

The results of the calculation appear on the screen immediately, and the formula itself appears in the status bar, preceded by an equal sign (=).

RECALCULATING FORMULAS

TO UPDATE THE RESULTS OF ALL THE FORMULAS IN A TABLE,

move the insertion point into the table. Then choose Layout ➤ Tables ➤ Calculate.

NOTE NOTE *Unlike a spreadsheet program, Word-Perfect does not automatically recalculate the results of formulas when you change a number in a table.*

If you change a number in a cell that is used in a calculation, WordPerfect will not recalculate the result of the formula automatically. To recalculate the entire table, follow these steps:

1. Move the insertion point anywhere into the table.

2. Choose **L**ayout ➤ **T**ables, or press Ctrl+F9.

3. Choose Ca**l**culate.

All the formulas in the table will be recalculated.

CONTROLLING THE DECIMAL ACCURACY OF FORMULAS

To control the decimal accuracy of formulas in a table, you can format the columns where the numbers will be stored. Follow these steps:

1. Move the highlight to the column you want to format, or use your mouse to select as many columns as you want to format.

2. Choose **L**ayout ➤ **T**ables, or press Ctrl+F9.

3. Choose Col**u**mn ➤ Di**g**its, and type the number of decimal places (from 0 to 15) you want displayed in each number. For example, enter *2* if you will be displaying dollar amounts.

4. Choose OK or press ↵ to return to the document window.

If the table already contains some formulas, choose Layout ➤ Tables ➤ Calculate to recalculate their values and adjust the decimal accuracy.

CHANGING OR DELETING FORMULAS

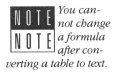 *You cannot change a formula after converting a table to text.*

If the results of a calculation are incorrect, even after you have recalculated the entire table, chances are the formula itself is incorrect. Similarly, if you add or delete table rows and columns, or you move or sort the contents of cells in the table, you may need to adjust your formulas accordingly. Follow these steps:

1. Move the insertion point into the cell containing the formula that you want to change.

2. Choose **L**ayout ➤ **T**ables, or press Ctrl+F9.

3. Choose **F**ormula.

4. Use the editing keys to make changes, or type an entirely new formula from scratch. To delete a formula, just press Delete until the formula is removed. You may also need to delete any numbers remaining in the cell, and then recalculate the results.

5. Choose OK or press ↵ to return to the document window.

6. Choose **L**ayout ➤ **T**ables ➤ **C**alculate, or press Ctrl+F9 A, if you want to recalculate all the formulas in the table.

COPYING FORMULAS

TO COPY A FORMULA,

move the highlight to the cell containing the formula that you want to copy. Choose Layout ➤ Tables ➤ Formula.

If several cells perform similar calculations, you can enter the first formula and then copy it to cells in adjoining rows or columns. Like most spreadsheet programs, WordPerfect will automatically adjust the copied formulas to reflect the pattern of the original formulas. For example, if you copy a formula that adds cells A1 and B1 (A1 + B1) to the next row down, the copied formula will automatically be adjusted to add cells A2 and B2 (A2 + B2).

To copy a formula, follow these steps:

1. Position the insertion point in the cell containing the formula you want to copy.

2. Choose **L**ayout ➤ **T**ables, or press Ctrl+F9.

3. Choose **F**ormula. The Tables Formula dialog box reappears, showing the formula in the current cell and three options for copying that formula:

◆ To copy the formula to a specific cell, choose **T**o Cell, and type in the cell address where you want the formula copied to (the destination cell). This option does not adjust the formula to the current cell; it makes an exact copy of the current formula.

◆ To copy the formula to several cells beneath the current cell, choose **D**own, and type the number of times to copy the formula.

◆ To copy the formula to several cells to the right, choose **R**ight, and type the number of times to copy the formula.

4. Choose OK or press ↵ to return to the document window.

Remember to recalculate the table after copying your formulas.

If you copied down or to the right, the cell addresses of the copied formulas are altered to retain the pattern of the original formula. For example, in Figure 18.2, the formula in cell E2 was entered as C2 * D2, and it correctly calculated the quantity (8) times the unit price ($3.5) for that row to come up with the total ($28.00). That formula was then copied down six rows to produce the other formulas (C3 * D3, C4 * D4, C5 * D5, and so forth), each of which correctly calculates the quantity times the price for its row.

CALCULATING SUBTOTALS, TOTALS, AND GRAND TOTALS

> **TO CALCULATE A SUBTOTAL, TOTAL, OR GRAND TOTAL IN A CELL,**
>
> position the highlight on the cell in which you want to display the calculation. Choose Layout ➤ Tables ➤ Formula, followed by one of the math functions: + (subtotal), = (total), or * (grand total).

You can also include in your tables special math functions to calculate subtotals, totals, and grand totals. However, you do not enter these functions directly from the keyboard. Instead, you must choose them from the Formula dialog box, as outlined below:

The total function displays 0 if there are no subtotals above it, and the grand-total function displays 0 if there are no totals above it. If you simply want to sum a column of numbers, use the subtotal function.

+	Subtotal (sums the numbers above)
=	Total (sums the subtotals above, up to the preceding total)
*	Grand total (sums the totals above)

To include a subtotal, total, or grand-total calculation in a table, follow these steps:

1. Position the insertion point in the cell where you want to use the subtotal, total, or grand-total function.

2. Choose **L**ayout ➤ **T**ables, or press Ctrl+F9.

3. Choose **F**ormula.

   ◆ To calculate a subtotal, type +.

   ◆ To calculate a total, type =.

   ◆ To calculate a grand total, type *.

4. Choose OK or press ↵.

Be aware that any numeric column headings, such as *1992,* will be added along with other numbers in the column. To exclude a number from a totals calculation, move the insertion point to the cell containing the number you want to exclude. Then, choose Layout ➤ Tables ➤ Cell, and change the cell's attributes to Ignore Cell When Calculating. Choose OK to leave the dialog box, then use Layout ➤ Tables ➤ Calculate to recalculate the entire table.

Remember to recalculate your table after putting in (or removing) subtotal, total, and grand-total functions.

Figure 18.3 shows a sample table that uses the subtotal, total, and grand-total functions. The figure also illustrates how you can use the Math feature in a table to create common financial statements, and then remove and change table lines (see Chapter 6) to give the document a more traditional appearance.

DELETING A TOTALS OPERATOR

To delete a total, subtotal, or grand-total operator, move the insertion point to the cell that contains that operator and choose Layout ➤ Tables ➤ Formula. Press Backspace to delete the operator, then press ↵. The previous total, if any, will remain in the cell, though you can delete that number with the usual text-editing keys if you wish.

INCLUDING DOLLAR SIGNS

To use a currency symbol other than $, use the WordPerfect character key (Ctrl+W), discussed in Chapter 5.

If you want to insert a leading dollar sign ($) in a cell that shows the results of a calculation (or just a regular cell containing a number), follow these steps:

1. Move the insertion point to the first character of the cell that contains the formula and displays its results, or to the first character of the cell containing the number.

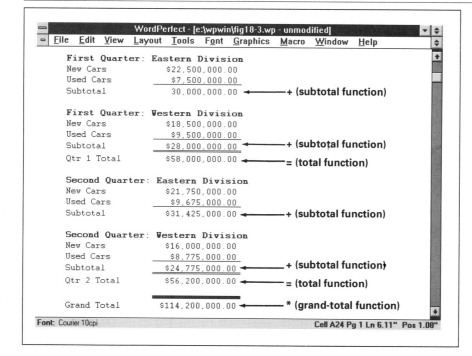

FIGURE 18.3:

The subtotal, total, and grand-total functions

2. Type the dollar sign ($).

DISPLAYING NEGATIVE RESULTS IN PARENTHESES

Normally, WordPerfect displays negative results of calculations with leading minus signs. If you prefer to display negative results in parentheses, follow these steps:

1. Move the insertion point into the table.

2. Choose **L**ayout ➤ **T**ables, or press Ctrl+F9.

3. Choose **O**ptions. You'll see the dialog box shown in Figure 18.4.

4. Choose **P**arentheses to display all negative calculation results in parentheses.

5. Choose OK or press ↵ to return to the document window.

6. If your table already contains formulas, choose **L**ayout ➤ **T**ables ➤ Calculate (Ctrl+F9 A) to recalculate all the formulas and display negative results in parentheses.

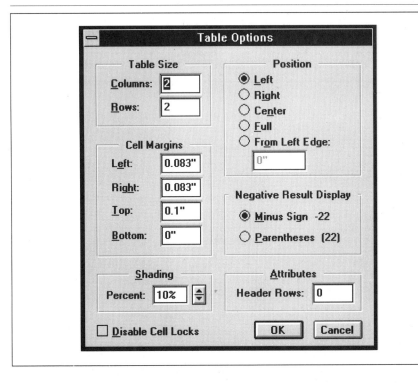

FIGURE 18.4:
The Table Options dialog box

Keep in mind that this option does not automatically put parentheses around numbers originally entered with a leading minus sign (or vice versa); it only affects the display of negative calculation *results*. So, for instance, if you want the number *−247.50* displayed with parentheses, (247.50), you must delete the leading minus sign (in the document window) and place parentheses around the number.

KEEPING NUMBERS ALIGNED

When displaying negative values in parentheses, you'll probably want to align all the numbers so that the decimal points line up. Move the insertion point to the column containing the numbers you want to align, and choose Layout ➤ Tables or press Ctrl+F9. If you want to align several columns, select them with your mouse.

Choose Layout ➤ Tables ➤ Column ➤ and change the Justification to Decimal Align. If necessary, you can then choose Column Width to widen the column to accommodate the parentheses surrounding negative numbers.

To correctly decimal-align negative numbers displayed in parentheses, you will probably need to increase the Digits setting of that column by choosing Layout ➤ Tables ➤ Column ➤ Digits (see Chapter 6).

NEGATING A TOTAL

You can precede any formula with a minus sign (you can use the hyphen key or the minus sign on the numeric keypad) to convert its value to a negative number. This is handy in situations where you want to display income and expenses as positive values, but prefer to calculate the sum of expenses as a negative value and then use that calculation in subtotals, totals, grand totals, or other formulas.

For example, if cells B3, B4, and B5 contain expenses expressed as positive values, then the formula *−(B3 + B4 + B5)* in cell C6 displays their sum as a negative value. Subtotal, total, and grand-total functions in column C, and any other formulas using cell C6, also treat that cell as a negative value.

You can also negate the results of a subtotal, total, or grand-total function in the same way. Go through the usual dialog box options to put the +, =, or * function in its cell. Then, move the insertion point to the cell containing the function, and type a hyphen. When you recalculate the table, you'll see the result displayed as a negative number.

Figure 18.5 shows two examples of using negative numbers to manage income and expenses figures. In both examples, the numbers and calculation results are the same, but they're expressed somewhat differently with respect to positive and negative numbers.

Sales		5,980,000.00
Cost of Goods Sold		
Inventory (6/1/90)	1,550,000.00	
Purchases	4,550,000.00	
Inventory (7/1/90)	-3,000,000.00	
Total		-3,100,000.00
Gross Profit on Sales		2,880,000.00
Operating Expenses		
Salaries	1,159,200.00	
Phone	25,000.00	
Mail	57,500.00	
Utilities	47,500.00	
Office Supplies	15,500.00	
Total Expenses		-1,304,700.00
Net Profit		1,575,300.00

=(B4 + B5 + B6)

C1 + C7

−(B11 + B12 + B13 + B14 + B15)

C1 + C7 + C16

Sales		5,980,000.00
Cost of Goods Sold		
Inventory (6/1/90)	1,550,000.00	
Purchases	4,550,000.00	
Inventory (7/1/90)	3,000,000.00	
Total		3,100,000.00
Gross Profit on Sales		2,880,000.00
Operating Expenses		
Salaries	1,159,200.00	
Phone	25,000.00	
Mail	57,500.00	
Utilities	47,500.00	
Office Supplies	15,500.00	
Total Expenses		1,304,700.00
Net Profit		1,575,300.00

B4 + B5 + B6

C1 − C7

B1 + B12 + B13 + B14 + B15

C1 − C7 − C16

In the first example, the ending Inventory (7/1/92) and formulas for Total Cost of Goods Sold and Total Operating Expenses are expressed as negative numbers, with the formulas for Gross Profit on Sales and Net Profit adjusted accordingly (the figure shows the formulas used). In the second example, the ending Inventory (7/1/92) and formulas for Total Cost of Goods Sold and Total Operating Expenses are expressed as positive numbers, with the formulas for Gross Profit on Sales and Net Profit adjusted accordingly.

LOCKING FORMULA CELLS

You can lock any cell in a table to protect it from change or erasure. This is particularly handy in tables that you want to use repeatedly for performing calculations. You can lock the cells containing formulas, fill in the numbers to be calculated, print the table, and then simply erase all the cells in the table when you want to enter a new set of numbers. Only the unlocked cells will actually be erased.

Because the formulas are locked, you don't have to worry about accidentally erasing them. Therefore, you can reuse the same table repeatedly. This technique is ideal for multiple invoices, packing slips, and similar forms.

To lock a cell or group of cells, follow these steps:

1. Move the insertion point to the cell or the corner of a group of cells that you want to lock. If you want to lock several cells, drag your mouse to select them.

2. Choose **L**ayout ➤ **T**ables, or press Ctrl+F9.

3. Choose **C**ell.

4. Choose **L**ock under Cell Attributes to turn the option on.

5. Click OK or press ↵ to leave the dialog box.

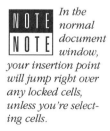

In the normal document window, your insertion point will jump right over any locked cells, unless you're selecting cells.

If the cell contains a formula, it will still be recalculated when you recalculate the table. Also, you can import data from spreadsheets into locked cells.

To unlock a cell or cells, repeat the steps above but turn off the Lock option in the last step.

PREVENTING RECALCULATION

As previously mentioned under "Calculating Subtotals, Totals, and Grand Totals," you can use Ignore Cell When Calculating to exclude cells from calculating operations.

Normally, every formula in a table is recalculated when you recalculate the table. If, for whatever reason, you do not want a particular formula to be recalculated, you can instruct WordPerfect to prevent recalculation of that cell. To do so, move the insertion point into the cell containing the formula that you do not want recalculated. Choose Layout ➤ Table or press Ctrl+F9, then choose Cell ➤ Ignore Cell When Calculating from the dialog box.

Be forewarned, however, that any other cell using that changed cell's address in a formula will display only ?? (double question mark) the next time you recalculate. That's because you cannot refer to the cell in a formula.

The ?? result occurs only if a referenced cell containing a formula is marked to be ignored, not if the referenced cell contains a number.

If you end up with ?? in a formula, make sure that none of the cells referenced by that formula are marked to be ignored. You can tell whether a cell will be ignored by moving the insertion point to the cell and checking the status bar in the document window. If quotation marks appear in front of the cell's address, it will be ignored (for example, *Cell A1* would be calculated, and *Cell "A2"* would not). To turn off the Ignore Cell option, move the highlight to the cell, then choose Layout ➤ Tables ➤ Cell ➤ Ignore Cell.

MERGING TO TABLES

You can merge data from a secondary merge file into a table that contains {FIELD} commands. (This is the same technique discussed in Chapter 16.) The primary file contains {FIELD} commands that indicate which field goes where. Figure 18.6 shows an example where 18 fields have been placed in a primary merge file that resembles an invoice (the form was made small to fit on one screen).

If you decimal-align columns that have {FIELD} commands in them, the commands may move partially out of the cell or be partially obscured in the document window, but the merge will still be successful.

You create the primary merge file in the normal way, using Tools ➤ Merge ➤ Field (Ctrl+F12 F) to enter each {FIELD} command. Some columns may expand to accommodate the {FIELD} command. Use the Print Preview screen rather than the document window to see the actual width of each column in your table.

The rightmost column of the table in Figure 18.6 contains the formulas required to perform calculations. The insertion point is in cell E2, which contains the formula C2 * D2, to calculate the hours times the rate. (You can see the formula in the lower-left corner of the screen.) The cell in the bottom-right corner of the table contains the subtotal function, + (not visible on the screen),

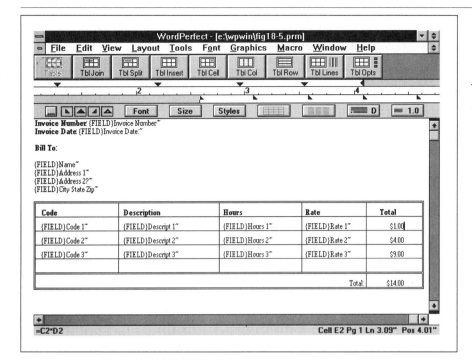

FIGURE 18.6:

*A primary merge file
with merge fields and
formulas*

to calculate the total. Currently, the first three results are incorrect because the data from the secondary merge file has not been merged with this file yet.

Figure 18.7 shows a secondary merge file for this example. You can see the field names and one sample record (though, of course, this file could have enough data to print dozens of invoices).

After merging the primary and secondary files, you can scroll through the results in your document window. Figure 18.8 shows an example, where the first record from the sample secondary merge file has been merged with the primary file.

There's one catch, though. As you can see in Figure 18.8, the figures for the Total column do not reflect the actual numbers in the table. All of the tables involved in the merge need to be recalculated before printing. Needless to say, you wouldn't want to recalculate the tables one at a time, so you can create a macro to make this job easier, which starts at the top of the document, locates each table in the document, and recalculates it.

Because you have to recalculate tables after a merge, you cannot merge straight to the printer when there's math involved.

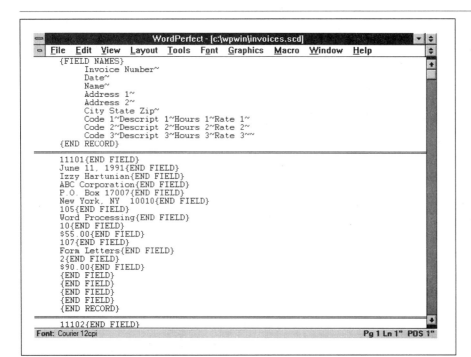

FIGURE 18.7:

*A secondary merge file
with invoice data*

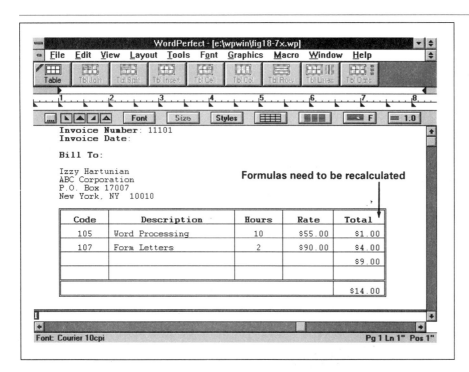

FIGURE 18.8:

*The files merged but not
yet calculated*

Figure 18.9 shows just such a macro. To create it, you'll need to know about macros and how to edit them (Chapter 15), and a little bit about the advanced macro commands (Chapter 26). Once it's created, you can use the macro in any document containing multiple tables (whether or not that document is the result of a merge) to recalculate all the tables.

Starting in the next chapter, you'll learn about integrating text and graphics in your WordPerfect documents, the foundation of desktop publishing.

```
Application (WP;WPWP;Default;"WPWPUS.WCD")

//*** Recalc.wcm
//*** Recalculates all the tables in a document.

Display (STATE:On!) //This command is optional.

//*** Move to top of document.
PosDocVeryTop()

//*** When search for a [Tbl Def] code fails, we're done.
OnNotFound (AllDone@)

//*** Main loop of the macro.
Label (NextTable@)

SearchText
(
   SearchString:"";
   SearchDirection:Forward!;
   SearchScope:Extended!
)
TableCalculate()
PosLineDown()
Go (NextTable@)

//*** No more tables, so end macro.
Label (AllDone@)
Quit
```

FIGURE 18.9:

A macro that recalculates every table in a document

PART SIX

Desktop Publishing

! n this part you'll build upon the basic desktop publishing skills you've acquired in previous chapters and learn to create truly dazzling documents. You'll learn how to position and size graphic images, and to combine graphics and text. Then you'll learn to create more advanced documents that use newspaper and parallel columns. Finally, you'll learn how to type equations, which is handy for producing mathematical or scientific literature.

CHAPTER 19

Using Graphics in Your Documents

HANDS-ON
....
LESSON 7

For a hands-on lesson in using graphic boxes, see Lesson 7 in Part 9.

t's an old cliché but certainly true: A picture is worth a thousand words. Pictures are not only informative, they are also appealing to the eye, and they can be used to make any document more attractive and more readable. For example, take a look at the "plain-text" document in Figure 19.1. Then take a look at the same document in Figure 19.2 with some graphics and fonts called into play. Granted, both documents say the same thing; but which one would *you* be more inclined to read?

In this chapter, you'll learn about some techniques for adding graphics to your own documents. This will let you move from the realm of word processing into more advanced document generation and desktop publishing.

```
          Another BRIGHT IDEA from BulbCo

             A Lightbulb Guaranteed
               to Last a Lifetime

Your life or the bulb's (we're betting on the bulb, by the way).
That's right, with BulbCo's new Perennial Lightbulb, you and your
descendants will never again need to replace another lightbulb.
Sure, these babies cost almost $300 apiece, and we don't recommend
juggling with them, but think of the savings!

             They Pay for Themselves in
               Just Ten Years (Or So)

Waitaminit! you're thinking now, these lightbulbs we're talking
about here cost a fortune!  Well, sure they do, at first.  You can
get a lightbulb from one of the other guys for just over one-
hundredth of the cost but just think, in six months to two years
(see chart, above), you'll be browsing through the hardware store
looking for another replacement.  Add it up for yourself,  in
twenty,  twenty-five,  fifty years ...tops... our award-winning
Perennial bulbs will have paid for themselves.

             Breakage Insurance Available

So,  what's in it for BulbCo,  you may wonder.  Well, first, we
should point out that we're going to do land-office business with
this product.  Planned obsolescence?  Pfuui!  Give us a good, solid
(unbeatable,  that is) product and just let us sell 'em one at a
time.  Of course, however, you are going to want to protect your
investment.  We'll guarantee these lightbulbs for a lifetime, yours
or theirs, as we've asserted, but we'll only guarantee that they'll
continue operating as long as they remain intact.  If that sounds
to you like that might be a big if, you're right.  You drop one of
our Perennials on the linoleum and you've dropped about three
hundred dollars and smashed them into shards all over your kitchen
floor.  Give one of our Perennials to baby to use as a rattle.
Shake, shake, shake, and there goes the filament.  We build 'em
sturdy, but, face it, they're lightbulbs.

                   Easy Terms

So what are we going to do for you?  Glad you asked.  We'll insure
every single one of your lightbulbs for a small premium, ranging
from $.50 a year for the 30-watt model to a still-negligible $1.97
a year for our superpowerful 250-watt bulbs.  See the table to the
left for details.
```

UNDERSTANDING GRAPHICS BOXES

Using graphics is basically a matter of positioning a *graphics box* in the text, then filling the box. WordPerfect offers five different types of graphics boxes: Figure box, Text box, Table box, User box, and Equation box. Each type of box has an initial border style, shading, and caption position, and each has its own independent, automatic numbering system to help you manage and reference boxes from within your text.

Another *BRIGHT IDEA* from B*ulb*C*o*

A Lightbulb Guaranteed to Last a Lifetime

Your life or the bulb's (we're betting on the bulb, by the way). That's right, with BulbCo's new Perennial Lightbulb you and your descendants will never again need to replace another lightbulb. Sure, these babies cost almost $300 apiece, and we don't recommend juggling with them, but think of the savings!

They Pay for Themselves in Just Ten Years (Or So)

Waitaminit! you're thinking now, these lightbulbs we're talking about here cost a

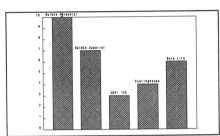

The Perennial outlasts even our old favorite, the Superior, and makes mincemeat of the competition. (The chart only shows ten years projected, but the Perennial will, of course, last forever.)

fortune! Well, sure they do, at first. You can get a lightbulb from one of the other guys for just over one-hundredth of the cost but just think, in six months to two years (see chart, above), you'll be browsing through the hardware store looking for another replacement. Add it up for yourself, in twenty, twenty-five, fifty years …tops… our award-winning Perennial bulbs will have paid for themselves.

Breakage Insurance Available

So, what's in it for BulbCo, you may wonder. Well, first, we should point out that we're going to do land-office business with this product. Planned obsolescence? Pfuui! Give us a good, solid (unbeatable, that is) product and just let us sell 'em one at a time. Of course, however, you are going to want to protect your investment. We'll guarantee these lightbulbs for a lifetime, yours or theirs, as we've asserted, but we'll only guarantee that they'll continue operating **as long as they remain intact.** If that sounds to you like that might be a big if, you're right. You drop one of our Perennials on the linoleum and you've dropped about three hundred dollars and smashed them into shards all over your kitchen floor. Give one of our Perennials to baby to use as a rattle. Shake, shake, shake, and there goes the filament. We build 'em sturdy, but, face it, they're lightbulbs.

Insurance Rates

Model	Premium	Deductible
30 watt	$.50	$25
75 watt	$.75	$35
100 watt	$.99	$50
150 watt	$1.49	$70
250 watt	$1.97	$99

Easy Terms

So what are we going to do for you? Glad you asked. We'll insure every single one of your lightbulbs for a small premium, ranging from $.50 a year for the 30-watt model to a still-negligible $1.97 a year for our superpowerful 250-watt bulbs. See the table to the left for details.

By default, Equation boxes are borderless, like User boxes, and have no shading (see Chapter 21).

Figure 19.3 shows examples of empty graphics boxes with their default borders, shading, and caption positions. As you'll find out later in this chapter, you can easily change the border style, shading, or caption position of any box, or all the boxes of a given type (e.g., all the Figure boxes).

The automatic numbering feature is especially helpful for saving you time and trouble. For example, you could put all your document figures in Figure boxes, and let WordPerfect number them automatically (e.g., Figure 1.1, Figure 1.2, and so forth). In the same document, you could place all your tables in Table boxes, and let WordPerfect number them separately and automatically

FIGURE 19.3:

Examples of empty Figure, Table, Text, and User boxes with their default borders, shading, and caption positions

Empty Table Box: Thick lines at top and bottom, caption above.

Empty Figure Box: Single line border on all sides, caption below.

Empty Text Box: Thick lines at top and bottom, shaded, caption below.

Empty User Box: No border lines or shading, caption below.

A single document can have any combination of up to 999 boxes, with a maximum of 100 boxes per page. However, your computer's memory may impose additional limitations.

(e.g., Table 1.1, Table 1.2, and so forth). Whenever you insert, move, and delete tables and figures, WordPerfect will renumber them for you. What's more, WordPerfect can also automatically generate figure lists and table lists from these figures and tables, using the List option in Automatic Referencing, as described in Chapter 23.

As mentioned earlier, each box type initially has its own unique border style. For example, in Figure 19.2, the ribbon in the upper-right corner of the document is in a User box (no border). The bar graph is in a Figure box (full, single-line border), and the table in the lower-left corner is in a Table box (thick lines at the top and bottom and no lines on the sides).

WHAT CAN GO IN A BOX?

Every box you create is initially empty. But you can fill any empty box with a graphic figure, a table, text, or an equation, as described below.

GRAPHIC IMAGES

If you have an earlier version of Word-Perfect, or Draw-Perfect, you can also use any .WPG files from those packages.

Graphic images come from files stored outside of your document, which you can read into a box. Your WordPerfect package comes with 36 WordPerfect graphics files, which you can see in Figure 19.4. Each of these files has the file-name extension .WPG (for *WordPerfect graphic*). If you have installed WordPerfect properly, these are stored on your hard disk in a separate Word-Perfect graphics directory (typically C:\WPWIN\GRAPHICS).

You can also create your own graphics, using spreadsheet and graphics programs, screen-capture programs, and scanners. See the section titled "Sources of Graphics" near the end of this chapter for additional information.

TABLES

You can display a table in your document with or without the aid of a box. Either way, you still use the Tables feature to create and edit the table. However, there are a few advantages to placing tables in boxes:

◆   If the table is in a Table box, you can wrap text around it (like the table in the lower-left corner of Figure 19.2).

◆   If the table is in a box and is small enough to fit on one page, Word-Perfect will never split the table across two pages.

◆   You can display two or more tables side by side if the tables are in boxes.

AUTO.WPG

BEACH-1.WPG

BIKE.WPG

BIRTHDAY.WPG

BKGRND-2.WPG

BLUERIBN.WPG

BOOKWORM.WPG

BORD-2.WPG

CHECKMAR.WPG

COMPUTR.WPG

DAISIES.WPG

DEGREE.WPG

DESK-W.WPG

DRAMA.WPG

DUCKLING.WPG

FATPENCL.WPG

GOLF-DGN.WPG

GUITAR-2.WPG

HARVEST.WPG

JET-2.WPG

LAW.WPG

MANUFACT.WPG

MAP-WORL.WPG

MBA.WPG

OWL-WISE.WPG

PIANO.WPG

QUIET.WPG

SAIL-BT.WPG

STAND.WPG

SUNDIAL.WPG

TAXI.WPG

TBEAR.WPG

VACATION.WPG

WAITER.WPG

WALL-CLK.WPG

WPWIN.WPG

FIGURE 19.4:
WordPerfect graphic images (continued)

♦ If you caption and number each table (e.g., Table I.1, Table I.2, and so forth), WordPerfect can handle all the numbering automatically, letting you add, delete, and move Table boxes without having to readjust all the numbers manually.

♦ You can automatically generate a list of tables for your completed document if all the tables are in Table boxes (see Chapter 23).

TEXT

A box can also contain text, using whatever fonts and features your printer offers for printing text. Text boxes are commonly used to display quotations or catchy phrases from a document.

EQUATIONS

A box can contain an equation that you create using the WordPerfect Equation Editor. For information on the Equation Editor, refer to Chapter 21.

A BOX IS JUST A BOX

Remember that the only reason WordPerfect offers different types of boxes is to simplify the automatic numbering of boxes and to provide a border style and shading for boxes within a particular category. WordPerfect categorizes boxes as Figure, Table, Text, User, and Equation simply because many documents use these types of boxes. This means that any box, regardless of its type, can contain a graphic figure, a table, text, or an equation. For example, you can use Figure boxes for business graphs, graphic images, photos, diagrams, and so forth; Table boxes for tables; Text boxes for sidebars, quotes, catchy phrases, and other text that's set off from the main body text; Equation boxes for mathematical and scientific equations; and User boxes for additional graphics that don't fit into any of the other categories.

CREATING A GRAPHICS BOX

TO CREATE A GRAPHICS BOX,

pull down the Graphics menu, choose a graphics box type, and then choose Create. For Table boxes and User boxes, choose an editor. Fill in the box with a graphic, text, or an equation, then choose File ➤ Close or click the Close button.

Sometimes you will know precisely which graphic you want to use in a box, where you want to position the box, and exactly what measurements you want to use for the height and width of the box. Other times, you may have absolutely no idea about these things; you'll just want to let your imagination run free and experiment by trying out different pictures, adjusting the size of boxes interactively, and moving boxes around with your mouse until the screen looks just right. WordPerfect lets you work in whatever way is most comfortable: You can specify all the details precisely, you can use your mouse to size and position graphics boxes, or you can use a combination of these techniques until the screen shows exactly what you want.

The general steps for creating any box are summarized below:

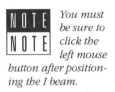

You must be sure to click the left mouse button after positioning the I beam.

1. Position the insertion point at the character, paragraph, or page to which you want to attach the box (discussed in more detail in "Anchoring a Box").

2. Pull down the **G**raphics menu.

3. Choose a box type from the options offered (**F**igure, Text **B**ox, **E**quation, **T**able Box, or **U**ser Box).

4. Choose **C**reate. The next step depends on what kind of box you create.

   ◆ If you create a Figure box, you'll see the Figure Editor window, shown in Figure 19.5.

◆ If you create a Text box, you'll see the Text Box Editor window shown in Figure 19.6.

◆ If you create an Equation box, you'll see the Equation Editor window (see Chapter 21).

◆ If you create a Table box or User box, you'll see the dialog box shown below. Choose an editor and press ↲ or click OK.

Word-Perfect graphic images all have the file name extension .WPG, and are usually stored in the \WPWIN\GRAPHICS directory (named Graphics Files in the Quick List).

5. To retrieve an existing file into the box, choose **File ➤ R**etrieve from the graphics box editor menu. Type the directory and full file name of the file you want to retrieve, or choose a file name from the file list or Quick List (Chapter 12), then press ↲. Alternatively, if you're using the Text Box Editor, you can type in the text or create a table in the usual way. See "Filling a Box" later in this chapter for more information.

6. If you want to fine-tune your graphics box now, choose **File ➤ B**ox Position from the menu, or click the Fig Pos button in the Figure Editor, or click the Box **P**osition button in the Text Box Editor. Choose any options you want from the Box Position and Size dialog box, shown in Figure 19.7, then press ↲ or click OK. These options let you control the box type, how the box is anchored to the page, the vertical and horizontal position of the box, the size of the box, and whether you want to wrap text around the box.

7. Choose **File ➤ C**lose or click the Close button to return to the document window.

You can just estimate the position and size of a box or not bother to set the position or size at all when first defining it, because you can easily make adjustments later.

When you return to the document window, WordPerfect adjusts existing text on the screen to accommodate your new graphic; your graphics box will appear on-screen much as it will be printed.

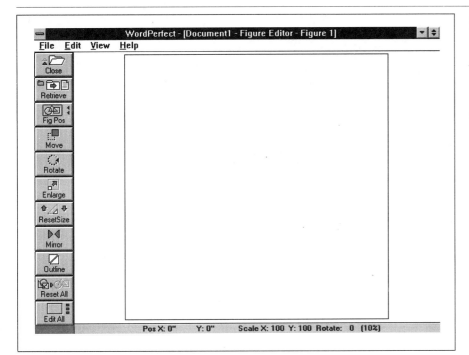

FIGURE 19.5:

Use the Figure Editor to fill your graphics box with a graphic image, change the box position and size, and adjust the contents of the box in different ways.

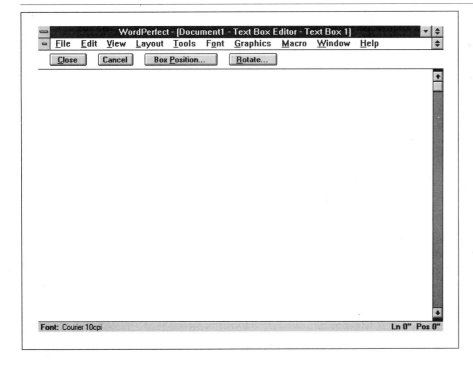

FIGURE 19.6:

Use the Text Box Editor to fill your graphics box with text and tables, to change the box position and size, and to rotate the text or table.

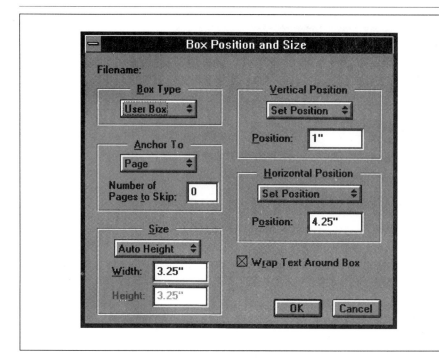

FIGURE 19.7:

The Box Position and Size dialog box

Using your mouse, you can easily move or resize the box right in the document window:

1. Move the I beam to any spot on the box (the I beam changes to a mouse pointer when it's on the box).

2. Click the left mouse button. The I beam changes to a four-headed "Move" icon, and a dotted frame with handles surrounds the box.

◆ To move the graphic box, hold down the left mouse button and drag the frame border to its new location. Then release the mouse button.

◆ To resize the box, move the mouse pointer onto any one of the sizing handles on the frame (the mouse pointer becomes a two-headed arrow). Hold down the left mouse button and drag the sizing handle until the frame becomes whatever size you want the graphic to be. Then release the mouse button.

3. When you're satisfied with the size and position of the graphic box, just move the I beam to where you want to resume typing text and click the left mouse button. The box frame returns to normal, and the insertion point appears in text.

These basic procedures will let you create, size, and position boxes throughout your document. We'll describe these, and other procedures, for controlling the exact appearance of your graphic boxes in detail throughout this chapter. But first, let's look at a couple of handy shortcuts for creating a graphic box.

SHORTCUTS FOR CREATING FIGURE AND TEXT BOXES

If you create many Figure or Text boxes, you will quickly grow to appreciate these two shortcuts:

◆   To create a Figure box: Choose Graphics ➤ Figure ➤ Retrieve, or press F11. Type the directory and full file name of the file you want to retrieve, or choose a file name from the file list or Quick List, and then press ↵. WordPerfect will create the Figure box and return you to the document window.

◆   To create a Text box: Press Alt+F11. This opens the Text Box Editor window, where you can either retrieve a file or type in your text or table. Click the Close button when you're ready to return to the document window.

UNDERSTANDING GRAPHICS BOX ANCHORING

The procedure described in the preceding section will let you place a graphic image just about anywhere in your document. If you do not change the box position settings when you first create your graphics box, the graphic will be *anchored,* or attached, to the current page if you are using the Figure or Text Box Editor, or to the current paragraph if you are using the Equation Editor.

To gain complete control over graphics boxes, you need to understand the three basic types of anchoring:

Paragraph anchoring: A paragraph-anchored box floats with its paragraph as you add and delete surrounding text. You use such a box when the text refers to "this figure" or "the figure at the left," or when you want to make sure that "Figure X.X" stays near the first reference to Figure X.X in a paragraph. The graphics box code is placed at the beginning of the paragraph.

Page anchoring: A page-anchored box is anchored to a particular spot on the page and never moves, no matter what happens to the text around it. Use this option when you want to position a graphic image or text at a specific place, such as in the lower-right corner or center of the page. You can also use a page anchor to position a box so that is spans one or more columns (see Chapter 20).

Character anchoring: A character-anchored box is anchored to whatever character appears to the left of the box. You use it for small in-line graphics and graphics boxes in page headers, footers, footnotes, and endnotes. The graphics box code is placed at the insertion point.

Multi-column layouts are covered in the next chapter.

Figure 19.8 shows a few examples of different kinds of boxes and explains how they are anchored. The figure uses a multicolumn layout, but the basic anchoring principles work with single-column layouts as well.

CHANGING A GRAPHICS BOX

> **TO CHANGE AN EXISTING BOX,**
>
> **position the mouse pointer on the box, click the right mouse button, and choose Edit Caption, Edit Box, or Position. Or double-click the box you want to change to go directly to the Figure, Text Box, or Equation Editor.**

If you are not happy with the size, location, box type, anchoring, or contents of a box, or you want to add a caption, you can change a graphics box by using any of the methods described in the following sections.

USING THE MOUSE TO CHANGE A GRAPHICS BOX

As you know, you can easily size or position a graphic box with your mouse. You can also use the mouse to get to the graphic box editors and dialog boxes.

Sometimes the pop-up menu includes a Select Box or Unselect Box option, as described in "Positioning a Box" later in this chapter.

1. Starting from the document window, position the mouse pointer on the graphic you want to change—the status bar in the lower-left corner of the document window will display the box type, box number, and the prompt "Use RIGHT Button for Graphics Menu," as shown in Figure 19.9.

2. Click the right mouse button. You will see a pop-up menu similar to the one shown in Figure 19.10.

FIGURE 19.8:

Examples of anchored boxes

Examples of Anchoring Boxes

CHECK BOX

We start with a small graphic image that is anchored to this paragraph (the box's hidden code is just before the first character of this paragraph).

The box is sized small, and the text of the paragraph wraps around it.

DIPLOMA

Another case for anchoring a figure to a paragraph is when you want a figure to closely follow its callout in text.

For example, Figure 1 shows a diploma. To keep that figure near, but below, it's anchored to the top of the next paragraph. Its Horizontal Position is Full (the width of the column).

Figure 1.

Because the box is as wide as this column, no text wraps around the side of it.

TEXT BOX

The text box in the center of the page is anchored to the page. Its hidden code is at the top of the page. All text wraps around it. Page anchoring is the only way to create boxes that cross columns.

TABLE BOX

The Table box in the lower right corner of the page is

WordPerfect has lots of tools for aligning graphic boxes in columns

also anchored to the page (bottom right corner). Page anchoring was required here because we needed the table to be wider than one column.

FOOTER

The pencil symbol at the lower left corner of the page is actually in a footer. It's character-anchored, because that's the

only anchor type allowed in headers and footers.

IN-LINE GRAPHIC

Next we have a small graphic airplane in the text. The airplane graphic is in a character anchored User Box, and is sized small enough to fit on a line of text.

Small character-anchored graphics like that can be used as icons in text, margins, or in margin notes -- or perhaps for amusing pictures in children's books.

COLUMNS & LINES

The columns in this example are newspaper columns with a distance of .4" between them. Chapter 20 discusses multi-column layouts in detail.

The lines are all graphic lines with the Graphics ▶ Line menu options (see Chapter 5).

The table below shows the Column (horizontal) and Vertical position, as the length, of each vertical line.

Line	1st	2nd	3rd	4th
Column	1	2	1	2
Vertical	1.51	1.51	6.35	6.35
Length	2.83	2.83	3.45	2.08

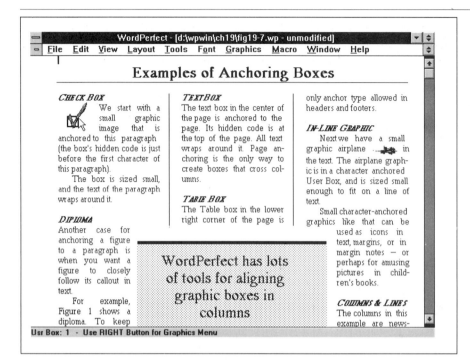

FIGURE 19.9:
When the mouse pointer is positioned over a graphic in the document window, it changes to an arrow (near the check-mark graphic in this example), and the status bar shows the box type, box number, and a prompt.

◆ Choose Edit **C**aption if you want to add a new caption or change an existing caption.

◆ Choose **E**dit Figure Box, **E**dit Text Box, or **E**dit Equation Box to switch to the appropriate editor for your graphics box. The pop-up menu shows whichever editor option is appropriate for the graphics box you are changing. For example, if you change a box created with the Text Box Editor, the option will be **E**dit Text Box.

◆ Choose **P**osition to display the Box Position and Size dialog box. Use this dialog box to change settings for the box type, anchoring, size, vertical position, horizontal position, and to determine whether text wraps around the box. As an alternative to using the dialog box, you can use your mouse to change the position and size of a box, as described later under "Positioning a Box with the Mouse."

3. Make your changes and refine your graphics box as described in the following sections.

4. When you're finished, click the Close or OK button as appropriate.

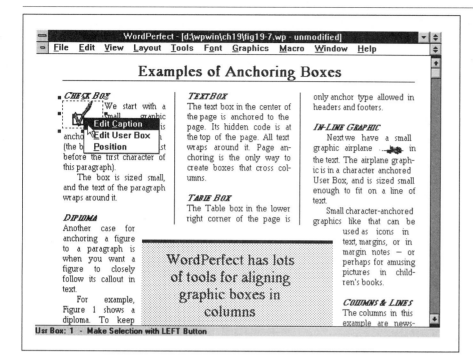

FIGURE 19.10:

A pop-up menu is displayed after you position the I beam on a graphic and click the right mouse button.

HANDY SHORTCUTS FOR CHANGING A BOX

WordPerfect for Windows offers some handy shortcuts for going directly to the appropriate graphics box editor and for opening the Box Position and Size dialog box. Follow these steps:

1. Scroll through your document until you see the graphics box you want to change.

2. Position the I beam over the graphic you want to change. The I beam will usually change to a arrow. (If it does not, click the right mouse button and choose **S**elect Box from the pop-up menu.)

3. Take one of the following shortcut steps.

◆ Double-click the graphics box to go directly to the Figure, Text Box, or Equation Editor. Or click the left mouse button once and press Shift+F11 to go to the Figure Editor or Alt+Shift+F11 to go to the Text Box Editor.

◆ Hold down the Shift key and double-click the graphics box to open the Box Position and Size dialog box.

CHANGING A BOX
BY ENTERING ITS BOX NUMBER

When you create a new graphics box, WordPerfect assigns it a sequential box number. For example, the first Figure box you create is Figure box 1, the second one is Figure box 2, and so on. Each type of box—Figure, Table, Text, User, and Equation—is numbered in separate lists; for example, a document with both a Figure and a Table box will have a Figure box 1 and a Table box 1.

In addition to using the mouse procedures described in the previous sections, you can choose a box to edit by referring to its box number. The box number is always displayed in the lower-left corner of the document window when you move the mouse pointer over the box, and in the title bar of the graphics box editor.

Follow these steps to change a box by specifying its box number:

If you click on the box you want to edit before pulling down the Graphics menu, you won't be prompted for a box number and can skip step 4.

1. Pull down the **G**raphics menu.

2. Choose the type of box that you want to change.

3. Choose **E**dit, **P**osition, or **Ca**ption, as appropriate. A dialog box prompts you for the number of the box you want to change. Initially, the dialog box shows the next higher number or the number of the next box below the insertion point.

4. Type the number of the box you want to change, then press ↵ or click OK.

5. Change your graphics box as needed.

6. When you're finished making changes, click the Close or OK button to return to the document window.

CHANGING A BOX'S ANCHOR TYPE

As I mentioned earlier, graphics boxes can be anchored in three ways: to a paragraph, to a page, or to a character. Initially, any box you create with the Figure Editor or Text Box Editor is anchored to the current page, and any box you create with the Equation Editor is anchored to the current paragraph. You change the anchor type of a box by choosing the Anchor To option from the Box Position and Size dialog box.

To change the anchor type of a box, follow these steps.

1. Use any of the methods described above to open the Box Position and Size dialog box. For example, hold down the Shift key and double-click the box you want to change.

2. Open the pop-up list under the **A**nchor To option and choose **Pa**ragraph, **Pa**ge, or **C**haracter.

3. If you choose **Pa**ge, you can change the setting for **N**umber of Pages to Skip. Leave the setting at zero if you want the graphics box to appear on the current page. Type *1* to print the box on the next page, type *2* to print the box two pages from the current page, and so on.

4. Press ↵ or click OK.

FILLING A BOX

As you've seen, the graphics box editors have many uses, including positioning and sizing a box, as well as filling the box with a graphic, a table, or text. In this section, I'll describe the options for filling a box in a more detail.

FILLING A BOX WITH A GRAPHIC IMAGE

You use the Figure Editor to place a graphic image stored on disk in a graphics box. Follow these steps:

1. Open the Figure Editor by using any of the techniques described earlier. The quickest way is to double-click the graphics box you want to edit.

2. Choose **F**ile ➤ **R**etrieve, or click the Retrieve button on the Button Bar. The Retrive Figure dialog box, shown in Figure 19.11, appears.

3. If you want to view each graphics file as you scroll through the list of choices, click the **V**iew button.

4. Choose a graphics file from the dialog box, or type in the complete name (including the three-letter extension) of the file that you want to pull into the box.

5. Click the **R**etrieve button in the dialog box or press ↵.

6. Choose **F**ile ➤ **C**lose, or click the Close button on the Button Bar.

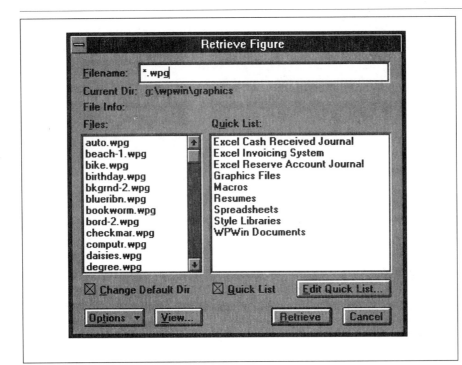

Word-Perfect expects to find graphic images in the place defined under Location of Files in Preferences (Chapter 13), but you can use the Quick List (Chapter 12) to temporarily override this location.

When you use the procedures above to choose a graphic from a disk file (including the .WPG graphics files that came with your WordPerfect package), WordPerfect looks for the graphic and displays it on your screen. If the file is not on the disk drive and in the directory where WordPerfect expects to find graphic images, you must specify the complete location of the file. For example, to import a Lotus 1-2-3 graph file named MYGRAPH.PIC that is stored in the directory named *123* on drive C, you have to enter the complete name C:\123\MYGRAPH.PIC. Once you import a file into a box, its name is listed on the status bar in the lower-left corner of the Figure Editor.

Note that when you pull a graphic figure into a box, WordPerfect adjusts the size of the graphic so that it fits into the box. You can change the size of the graphics box itself, and to some extent, you can also change the appearance of a graphic image that has been imported into a box. You can use the buttons on the Button Bar or the Edit options on the Figure Editor menu (described in "Editing a Graphic Image" later in this chapter).

FILLING A BOX WITH TEXT OR A TABLE

You use the Text Box Editor to place text or tables in a graphics box. You can type any text and WordPerfect codes or retrieve a document (no longer than one page) into the box. Follow these steps:

1. Open the Text Box Editor by using any of the techniques described earlier.

2. If you want to create the box's contents now, just type whatever text, or create any table, that you want to place in the box. Then skip to step 5.

3. If you want to pull in existing text or a table, choose **File ➤ R**etrieve. The Retrieve File dialog box appears. Type the directory and full file name, or highlight a file name with your mouse. After choosing the file name, click the **R**etrieve button in the dialog box or press ↵.

4. The screen displays

   Insert file into current document?

   Click **Y**es or press ↵ if you are sure you want to add the contents of the new file to the box.

5. Edit the text and tables in your box just as you would in the normal document window. You can choose fonts and use centering, right alignment, or the Advance feature (Chapter 20)—just about any normal editing option from the Layout, Tools, and Font menus—to control the appearance of your text or table. Any choices you make will affect only the contents of the box, not the text outside the box. Just remember that your text cannot exceed a page.

6. When you're finished, choose **File ➤ C**lose, or click the Close button near the top of the window.

 *To move existing text or a table into a box, select the text or table in the document window, and then choose Edit ➤ Cut or press Shift+Del. Next, create or edit the graphics box (using the Text Box Editor), and then choose Edit ➤ Paste from the Text Box Editor menu or press Shift+Ins.*

In step 3, you can import text or a table. For example, if you use the Tables feature to create and save a table in a document named TABLE1.WP, you can use File ➤ Retrieve to pull a copy of the table stored in TABLE1.WP into the box. If you pull text or a table into a box that is not large enough to hold that text or table, WordPerfect does not adjust the size of the box. The table may extend beyond the right edge of the box; with excess text, only as much text as can fit in the box is displayed. If this occurs, change the size of the box, as described in "Sizing a Box," later in this chapter.

Rotating Text in a Box

While using the Text Box Editor, you can choose to rotate the text in the box by 0 (None), 90, 180, or 270 degrees, respectively. Follow these steps:

1. Open the Text Box Editor, using any of the techniques described earlier.

2. Click the **R**otate button near the top of the Text Box Editor window. You'll see this dialog box:

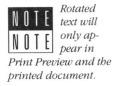 *Rotated text will only appear in Print Preview and the printed document.*

3. Click the button next to the amount of rotation you want.

4. Press ↵ or click OK to return to the Text Box Editor window.

5. Choose **F**ile ➤ **C**lose or click the **C**lose button to return to the document window.

When you return to the document window, the box will be rotated by the amount you specified, and will also be resized, if necessary, to hold the rotated text. Figure 19.12 shows examples of Text boxes rotated by using each of the options.

Note, however, that the amount of rotation is limited by your printer (check your printer manual for information). Many printers can print at only 0-degree rotation (normal, right-side-up). Many laser printers can print at only 0-degree and 90-degree rotation. PostScript and HP LaserJet III printers can usually print at all degrees of rotation.

The "Too Much Text" Error Message

If you add more to a Text, Table, or User box than the page size can handle, WordPerfect will immediately display a soft page break (a horizontal line) at the place where you've typed beyond the boundaries. If this happens, you

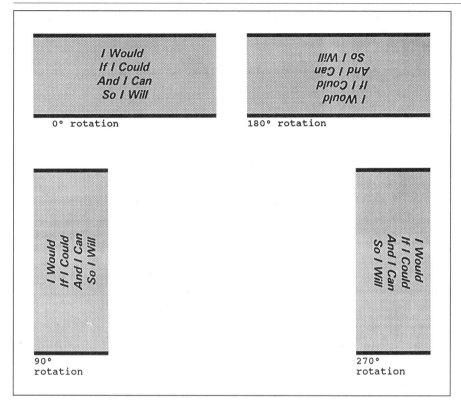

Examples of rotated
Text boxes

should use the Backspace key, or select some text and press Del, to erase text until the page break disappears. Otherwise, when you try to close the editing window, you'll see the message

Too much text

and you won't be able to leave the Text Box Editor. If you see this message, press ↵ or click OK. If you want to keep all the text, you can enlarge the box by using the Box Position button in the Text Box Editor window. If the "Too much text" message remains when you try to close the Text Box Editor, or you don't need the extra text, delete enough text to get rid of the page break.

To avoid the "Too much text" message, size the box before you put text or a table in it.

CHANGING THE CONTENTS OF A BOX

Suppose you place a graphic image or file in a box and then decide to use a different image or file instead. It's easy to replace the contents of any box that contains a file with the contents of a new file:

To delete all the existing text and tables from a graphics box created with the Text Box Editor, open the editor as usual, select all the existing text, press Del, and then retrieve the file containing the new text, or type your new text.

1. Open the Figure or Text Box Editor.

2. Choose **R**etrieve from the editor's **F**ile pull-down menu.

3. Type in the complete name of the new file that you want to display in the box and press ↵ (or use the dialog box to help you locate a file), as described earlier.

4. If you are using the Figure Editor to retrieve a file, you'll immediately see the new graphic on the screen. If you are using the Text Box Editor to retrieve a file, you'll be asked whether you want to insert the file into the current document. Click **Y**es or press ↵ if you are sure you want to add the contents of the new file to the box.

CREATING EMPTY BOXES

If you are not yet ready to fill a box, but you know what type of information the box will contain, you can just create the box after choosing the appropriate graphics box editor (Text, Figure, or Equation) without retrieving a file or typing in any text. This sets up the default size, border types, shading, anchor type, and numbering for the type of information that will eventually be in the box, which can help you correctly place boxes that are still empty.

WRAPPING TEXT AROUND A BOX

The Wrap Text Around Box option in the Box Position and Size dialog box controls how the text adjacent to the box is printed. If you place an *X* in this check box, text outside of the box wraps around the box (as in all the boxes shown in Figure 19.8). This box is automatically checked when you create any graphics box. If you uncheck this box, text outside the box writes over it.

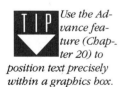

Use the Advance feature (Chapter 20) to position text precisely within a graphics box.

In most cases, you probably don't want neighboring text to write over a graphic image. The one exception to this, however, is when you want to combine text and a graphic within a graphics box. The only way to get both text and graphics into the same box is to uncheck the Wrap Text Around Box check box. Then you can position any text so that it's printed "on top of" the box.

If you want to include text in a graphic *and* wrap text around that box, you need to use two graphics boxes. Create the box that contains the graphic image, and remove the *X* from the Wrap Text Around Box check box. Then, create a second box (typically a borderless User box) at the same position as the first box, and place the text within that second box. Put an *X* in the Wrap

Text Around Box option for this second box, and position it in the same place and make it the same size as the first box. The text will then wrap around this second box.

Figure 19.13 shows some examples of combined text and graphics. The text in this figure also explains how each example was created.

SELECTING A GRAPHICS BOX WITH THE MOUSE

When graphics boxes over-lap, you may be unable to select the "hidden" boxes with your mouse.

In addition to changing the look of your graphics box, you may also want to move it around on the screen, delete it, copy it, or change its size. One of the easiest ways to accomplish these and other tasks is to first select the box by using your mouse, then take some action.

1. Position the I beam in the box you want to work with. Keep an eye on the status bar, which will display the box type, box number, and the prompt "Use RIGHT Button for Graphics Menu" when the I beam is positioned in a graphics box. The I beam will usually change to an arrow.

To unselect a graphics box, click outside it.

2. When the I beam changes to an arrow, click the left mouse button; if it doesn't change to an arrow, click the right mouse button and choose **S**elect Box from the pop-up menu. A dashed selection box with sizing handles surrounds the graphics box, and the I beam changes to a four-headed arrow when the box is selected, as shown in Figure 19.14.

POSITIONING A BOX

▌ **TO POSITION A GRAPHICS BOX,**

select the box, hold down the left mouse button while dragging the box to its new position, and then release the mouse button.

Whereas anchoring a box defines what the box is fixed to, *positioning* the box defines the box's position with respect to the anchor point. WordPerfect offers you two convenient ways to position a graphics box: You can use your mouse to position the box visually, or you can use the Box Position and Size dialog box for more precise control over vertical and horizontal positioning. The following sections explain how to use each of these methods.

Here the DESK-W.WPG graphic is in a Figure box, with Wrap Text Around Box unchecked. Normally this causes a paragraph of text (like this one) to write over the box. But a User box the same size as the Figure box, with Wrap Text Around Box checked, is printed at exactly the same position. This text is wrapping around that User box. The writing on the wall is in the User box.

On a PostScript printer, the Shadow text appearance is opaque white. In this example, similar to the one above, the BOOKWORM.WPG graphic is in a Figure box with Wrap Text Around Box unchecked. The shadow text is in a User box, at the same position, and the same size, as the Figure box, with Wrap Text checked. This explanatory text wraps around the User box.

This could be a full-page sign with the margins set to about 0.25 inch around the page. A User box, containing the BORDER-2.WPG graphic, is anchored to the page, with vertical and horizontal positions set to Full Page and Margin, Full and Wrap Text Around Box unchecked. The words Wet Paint are centered horizontally and vertically on the page (on the regular Edit window).

FIGURE 19.13:

Examples of combining text with graphics

POSITIONING A BOX WITH THE MOUSE

If you want immediate feedback about how your document will look when you move a graphics box, use your mouse to move it. As you move the box around the document window, the text will automatically adjust to accommodate the new position of the box, and you'll instantly see how your document will look with the box in a new position.

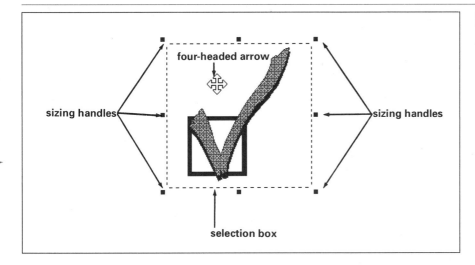

FIGURE 19.14:

A selected graphics box

You can use the markings on the ruler to help you position the graphic more accurately when moving the box to the left or right on the screen.

Be careful not to drag the sizing handles or you will change the size of the box instead of moving it (see "Sizing a Box" later in this chapter).

In addition to providing visual feedback, the mouse method offers another advantage: You can use it to move a graphic out of the way if it is covering up another graphic that you want to change. After changing the second graphic, you can then move the first graphic back to its original position.

Follow these steps to move the graphics box with your mouse:

1. Select the box as described earlier.

2. Hold down the left mouse button and drag the graphic to its new position. As you drag the graphics box up, down, left, right, and diagonally, the surrounding outline of the box moves in the direction that you drag.

3. Release the left mouse button. The graphic will appear in its new position. You can then move the graphic again, or click anywhere in the document window to deselect it.

VERTICALLY POSITIONING A BOX MORE PRECISELY

You can precisely control the vertical position of a box, using the Box Position and Size dialog box. The options available depend on whether you've anchored the box to a paragraph, page, or character. Follow these general steps:

1. Move the mouse pointer to the box, click the right mouse button, then open the Box Position and Size dialog box by choosing Box **P**osition.

2. For boxes anchored to a page or character, choose an option from the **V**ertical Position pop-up list. Page options are **F**ull Page, **T**op, **C**enter, **B**ottom, and **S**et Position. Character options are **T**op, **C**enter, **B**ottom, and **B**aseline. These options are described in more detail in the sections that follow.

3. If you chose **S**et Position in step 2, or the box is anchored to a paragraph, type a position measurement in the Vertical Position text box.

4. Press ↵ or click OK.

Vertically Positioning a Paragraph-Anchored Box

The vertical position you specify for a paragraph-anchored box in step 3 is an offset measurement from the top of the paragraph. If you set the position at 0", the top of the box will be even with the top of the first line of the paragraph. Any measurement you enter other than zero will move the box down with respect to the top of the paragraph, placing the outside border space of the box at that vertical position, as in the example shown in Figure 19.15.

Getting the vertical measurement just right can be tricky for two reasons:

◆ Text always wraps around the outside border space defined for the box (by means of the Outside Border Spacing options, described later).

◆ WordPerfect always adds 2 points of leading to the top of proportionally spaced fonts, but no leading to monospaced fonts.

Therefore, to center the box on the right in Figure 19.15 relative to the text surrounding it, the outside border space for the box was set at the top and

> **NOTE** *Word-Perfect never splits a graphics box across two pages. If there isn't enough room to print the entire box on the current page, Word-Perfect automatically bumps it to the next page.*

In this example, I anchored the figure to this paragraph, with a vertical position of 0", so the top of the box is aligned with the top of the paragraph. To reduce extra blank space at the bottom of the box, I set the Outside Border Spacing at the bottom of the box (via Options) to 0".

In this example, I set the vertical position of the box to 29p, which causes the box to be placed a little lower in the paragraph. I also set the Outside Border Spacing at the top and bottom of the box to 0" to reduce extraneous white space surrounding the box (picky picky!).

FIGURE 19.15:

Examples of vertically positioning a paragraph-anchored box

bottom to 0 inches. The vertical position of the box was set to 29p (29 points): 28 points to compensate for two 12-point lines of text, each with 2 points of additional leading, and one additional point based on a visual inspection after printing, which indicated that the box was a little too close to the line of text above it.

Vertically Positioning a Page-Anchored Box

The vertical-positioning options available for page-anchored boxes are shown below:

Full Page	The box will fill the entire page.
Top	The top of the box will line up with the top margin of the page (below the page header, if any).
Center	The box will be centered between the top and bottom margins of the page.
Bottom	The bottom of the box will line up with the bottom margin of the page (above the page footer, if any).
Set Position	This lets you place the box at an exact distance from the top of the page (not from the top margin).

Vertically Positioning a Character-Anchored Box

The vertical-positioning options available for character-anchored boxes are shown below:

Top	The top of the box will be aligned with the top of the character.
Center	The box will be centered next to the character—the most commonly used option for aligning small in-line graphics.
Bottom	The bottom of the box will be aligned with the bottom (baseline) of the character.
Baseline	The baseline of the text or equation within the box will line up with the baseline of the text. This option is generally used to align in-line equations with their surrounding text.

Be aware that aligning a box with a character causes the space allotted to the line to be as tall as the box, in much the same way that placing a single large character within a line of text causes the entire line to be as tall as that one character.

To maintain an equal line height among lines of text that do and do not contain boxes, you must either adjust the height of the box so that it does not change the line height (by using the Size option in the Box Position and Size dialog box) or set a fixed line height for the entire paragraph that matches the line height of the box (by choosing Layout ➤ Line ➤ Height or by pressing Shift+F9 H).

HORIZONTALLY POSITIONING A BOX MORE PRECISELY

The Horizontal Position option in the Box Position and Size dialog box lets you specify the horizontal position of the box relative to its anchor point. Again, the options available to you depend on how you've chosen to anchor the box.

To horizontally position a box, follow these steps:

1. If you haven't already done so, open the Box Position and Size dialog box.

2. For boxes anchored to a page or paragraph, choose an option from the **H**orizontal Position pop-up list. (The horizontal position of a character-anchored box is determined solely by the position of the character it's anchored to, so this option is not available or needed for character-anchored boxes.)

3. If you chose **S**et Position for a page-anchored box in step 2, type a position measurement in the Position text box beneath the **H**orizontal Position option as described below. If you chose one of the column options for a page-anchored box in step 2, type in a column number or range of columns, as explained in "Horizontal Positioning in a Multicolumn Layout" below.

4. Press ↵ or click OK.

Horizontally Positioning a Paragraph-Anchored Box

If the box is anchored to a paragraph, you'll see these options in the Horizontal Position pop-up list:

Margin, **L**eft   The box will be aligned at the left side of the paragraph.

Margin, **R**ight	The box will be aligned at the right side of the paragraph.
Margin, **C**enter	The box will be in the center of the paragraph, but only text to the left of the box will wrap around it.
Margin, **F**ull	The box will be placed above the paragraph it's anchored to and will span the width between the page's left and right margins.

Horizontally Positioning a Page-Anchored Box

If the box is anchored to the page, you'll see these options for setting the horizontal position with respect to the margins:

Margin, **L**eft	The left edge of the box will be aligned with the left margin.
Margin, **R**ight	The right edge of the box will be aligned with the right margin.
Margin, **C**enter	The box will be centered between the left and right margins.
Margin, **F**ull	The box will be expanded to fill all the space between the left and right margins.
Set Position	This lets you place the box at an exact distance from the left edge of the page (not the distance from the left margin). For example, if the left margin is 1 inch, and you enter a measurement of 1.5 inch, the outside border space of the figure will be one-half inch from the left margin.

Horizontal Positioning in a Multicolumn Layout

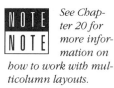

See Chapter 20 for more information on how to work with multicolumn layouts.

If your document uses a multicolumn layout (as in a newsletter) and your graphics box is anchored to the page, you can choose one of the Column options from the Horizontal Position pop-up list to align the graphics box with respect to the page's columns.

Follow these steps:

1.   Open the Box Position and Size dialog box.

2.   Choose one of the Column options from the **H**orizontal Position pop-up list.

3.   Type a column number or range in the **C**olumns box. You can type in a single column number (such as *1* or *2*) or a range of columns (such as *1–2* or *2–4*) if you want the box to be wider than a single column.

4.   Press ↵ or click OK.

The following options are available on the Horizontal Position pop-up list:

Column, L**e**ft   The box will be aligned with the left edge of the column (or the left edge of the leftmost column if you specify two or more columns in step 3).

Column, R**i**ght   The box will be aligned with the right edge of the column (or the right edge of the rightmost column if you specify two or more columns in step 3).

Column, Ce**n**ter   The box will be centered in the column you specified (or centered between the columns if you specify two or more columns in step 3).

Column, F**u**ll   The box will be as wide as the column (or as wide as several columns if you specify two or more columns in step 3).

DELETING A BOX

If you decide that you no longer need a graphics box, you can easily delete it:

1.   Select the graphics box, usually by clicking on it, as described earlier.

2.   Press the Delete or Backspace key.

If you accidentally delete a box and realize your mistake immediately, choose Edit ➤ Undo (Alt+Backspace) to restore the box. Or, if you discover the mistake a little later, choose Edit ➤ Undelete and restore the box just as you would any deleted text.

COPYING A BOX

One handy trick with graphics boxes is to set up a box, and then copy it somewhere else. After making the copy, you can change the new box as needed, perhaps inserting a different graphics file into the box or changing the text inside the box. When you make the copy, the new box will retain as many of the attributes (type, size, position, and so on) of the original box as possible.

The steps for copying a box are almost the same as for copying text:

If you want to move the box instead, choose Edit ➤ Cut or press Shift+Del in step 2.

1. Select the box.

2. Choose **E**dit ➤ **C**opy, or press Ctrl+Insert.

3. Position the insertion point wherever you want the copied box to appear.

4. Choose **E**dit ➤ **P**aste, or press Shift+Insert.

SIZING A BOX

WordPerfect offers you two convenient ways to size a graphics box: You can use your mouse to size the box visually, or you can use the Box Position and Size dialog box. Sizing with the mouse offers a good visual technique to get the graphics box "in the ballpark," and using the dialog box lets you enter exact measurements. The following sections explain how to use each of these methods.

SIZING A BOX WITH THE MOUSE

Sizing a box with the mouse involves some of the selecting and dragging techniques you learned earlier, but with a few twists involving the *sizing handles* that appear around the selected box. Follow these steps:

Use the markings on the ruler to narrow or widen your graphics box more accurately.

1. Select the graphics box whose size you want to change, as described earlier. A border and handles appear around the graphic, and the I beam changes to a four-headed arrow.

2. Move the I beam to one of the handles. The I beam will change to a two-headed arrow:

   ◆ If you point to the middle handle on the left or right side of the box, you see a two-headed horizontal arrow.

   ◆ If you point to the middle handle on the top or bottom edge of the box, you see a two-headed vertical arrow.

◆ If you point to any of the corner handles, you see a two-headed diagonal arrow.

3. Hold down the left mouse button and drag in the direction of the arrow: Drag one of the middle arrows to move only the side you drag; drag one of the corner arrows to move the two adjoining sides at the same time. The dashed outline of the box will move in the direction you drag.

4. When the outline is the size you want, release the left mouse button and the graphic will readjust to fit inside the box.

5. Click anywhere in the document window (outside the graphics box) to deselect the box.

SIZING A BOX MORE PRECISELY

NOTE
NOTE

When you retrieve a scanned image, WordPerfect automatically scales it to fit in the box. Choosing Auto Both restores the original dimensions and resolution of the scanned image.

The Size option in the Box Position and Size dialog box lets you precisely control the size of the box. When chosen, it provides these options:

Auto Both	WordPerfect calculates both the width and height automatically. If the box contains a graphic, the box is sized to fit the original dimensions and resolution of the graphic. If the box contains text or a table, the box is sized to fit snugly around its contents.
Auto **W**idth	Lets you enter the height (in inches). WordPerfect will calculate the width to retain the box shape.
Auto **H**eight	Lets you enter the width of the box (in inches). WordPerfect will calculate the height to retain the box shape.
Set Both	Lets you enter both the width and height (in inches).

CHANGING THE TYPE OF A BOX

Let's suppose that you create a particular type of box, such as a Text box, then later decide to change it to a Table box. You can do this very easily from the Box Position and Size dialog box. Follow these steps:

1. Open the Box Position and Size dialog box. The current box type appears below the **B**ox Type option.

2. Choose a box type from the **B**ox Type pop-up list. Your choices are **F**igure, **T**able Box, Text **B**ox, **U**ser Box, and **E**quation.

3. Press ↵ or click OK to return to the document window.

When you return to the document window, you'll see that the box borders and shading have changed to match those of the box type you've switched to. For instance, if you convert a Figure box to a Text box, your borders change from a single line all the way around to a thick line above and below the box. The caption numbers (if any) also change to reflect the proper sequence of numbers for the various types of boxes in the document.

Although you can change the type of a box, you cannot switch to a different graphics box editor after creating the box. For example, if you create a box with the Figure Editor, you cannot edit it with the Text Box Editor. To use a different editor, you must delete the existing box, and then create a new one using the appropriate editor.

CAPTIONING A BOX

You can add a caption to any box. Follow these steps:

1. Select the box with your mouse.

2. Click the right mouse button.

3. Choose Edit **C**aption from the pop-up menu.

You'll be taken to the Caption Editor, shown in Figure 19.16, for typing the caption. You can use all the general editing techniques, most menu options (including fonts, sizes, and appearances), the ruler, and Reveal Codes to help you create your caption. By default, the [Box Num] hidden code, which defines the style of caption numbers, appears at the beginning of your entry.

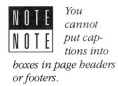
You cannot put captions into boxes in page headers or footers.

Type your caption, up to a maximum of 256 characters in length, to the right of the [Box Num] code. Optionally, you can delete the [Box Num] code by using the Backspace or Delete key. If you inadvertently delete the [Box Num] code and want to reinsert it, click the Box Number button. When you're finished typing your caption, choose File ➤ Close or click the Close button to return to the document window.

You can change the appearance and numbering style for caption numbers and adjust the caption's position relative to the box, as described later under "Changing the Appearance of All Boxes of a Given Type."

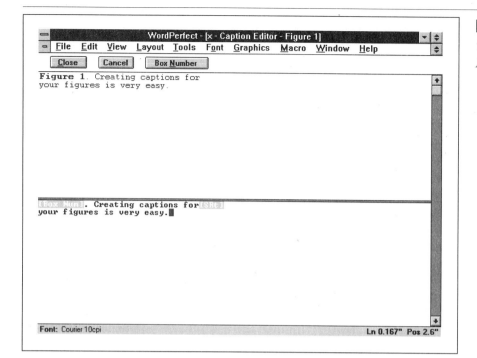

FIGURE 19.16:

The Caption Editor, with Reveal Codes open

EDITING A GRAPHIC IMAGE

TO CHANGE THE SCALE, ANGLE, POSITION, LOCATION, OR SIZE OF A GRAPHIC IMAGE FOR ANY BOX CREATED WITH THE FIGURE EDITOR,

open the Figure Editor, and choose options from the File and Edit menus or choose buttons on the Button Bar.

If the box you are editing contains a graphic image, you can use the Figure Editor to change the appearance of the graphic. First, you need to follow the general steps listed earlier for changing a graphic by opening the Figure Editor window.

For example, you could use any of the following steps to edit Figure 1 in your document:

◆ Place the I beam over Figure 1 and double-click the left mouse button.

◆ Place the I beam over Figure 1, click the right mouse button, and choose **E**dit Figure Box.

◆   Choose **G**raphics ➤ **F**igure ➤ **E**dit from the pull-down menus in the document window, type **1** and press ↵.

◆   Click on Figure 1 and choose **G**raphics ➤ **F**igure ➤ **E**dit from the pull-down menus (or press Shift+F11).

The menu options and buttons that you can use to manipulate the image appear near the top of the window and in the Button Bar, respectively (see Figure 19.17). These options and buttons let you adjust the graphic interactively or by specified amounts.

The status bar at the bottom of the window displays the following information:

◆   Graphic file name

◆   Horizontal position (Pos X) and vertical (Pos Y) position, in inches, within the graphics box, as compared with the original

◆   Scale, where Scale X is the width and Scale Y is the height, in percent, of the graphic figure as compared with the original (for example, *Scale X: 150* means the graphic on-screen is 50 percent larger than the original graphic stored on-disk)

FIGURE 19.17:
The wise-owl graphic (OWL-WISE.WPG) in the Figure Editor window

◆ Rotation (in degrees) of the figure

◆ Percentage, in parentheses, by which certain keys, buttons, or menu options adjust the graphic

Feel free to experiment—you can always return the image to its original form simply by clicking the Reset All button or choosing Edit ➤ Reset All.

The window surrounding the graphic image on the screen is actually the frame of the box being used to display the graphic within your document. Most of the graphic-editing options control the appearance of the graphic image *within* the box, but do not change the size and shape of the box itself. The only exceptions are the Fig Pos button on the Button Bar and the Box Position option on the File menu, both of which have the same effect: They open up the Box Position and Size dialog box.

Before discussing each option in detail, I'll summarize the Figure Editor buttons and their equivalent menu options:

 If you need more control over graphic images than Word-Perfect provides, you should consider using a graphics package, such as DrawPerfect.

 You can change or reposition the Figure Editor Button Bar as you would any other Button Bar, using options on the View menu (Chapter 3).

BUTTON	ACTION	MENU EQUIVALENT
Close	Closes the Figure Editor and returns you to the document window	**File** ➤ **C**lose
Retrieve	Retrieves a graphic stored on-disk	**File** ➤ **R**etrieve
Fig Pos	Opens the Box Position and Size dialog box	**File** ➤ Box **P**osition
Move	Moves the image within the frame	**Edit** ➤ **M**ove
Rotate	Rotates the image within the frame	**Edit** ➤ **R**otate
Enlarge	Selects a portion of the graphic and enlarges it to fill the frame	**Edit** ➤ **S**cale ➤ **E**nlarge Area
ResetSize	Returns the figure to the scale and position it had when you retrieved it into the document	**Edit** ➤ **S**cale ➤ **R**eset Size
Mirror	Flips the figure on its vertical axis so that it is displayed from right to left instead of left to right	**Edit** ➤ **M**irror

BUTTON	ACTION	MENU EQUIVALENT
Outline	Displays the figure as a line drawing; all colors in the figure become white, but black portions remain black	**E**dit ➤ **O**utline
Reset All	Undoes all settings made in the Figure Editor and redisplays the figure as it appeared when you retrieved it	**E**dit ➤ Reset **A**ll
Edit All	Lets you move, scale, and rotate the figure in specific amounts, and apply the appearance options (mirror image, outline, invert, and black and white) to your figure	**E**dit ➤ **E**dit All

Moving a Graphic within Its Box

You can also move the graphic by a precise amount (see "Editing an Image by Precise Amounts" later in the chapter).

You can move a graphic by a preset percentage, or interactively, using your mouse. To move the graphic by the percentage shown in parentheses in the Figure Editor status bar, press the ↑, ↓, →, and ← keys. The graphic will move in the direction of the arrow key you press, and the X and Y Pos indicators in the status bar will show the position with respect to the original. For example, Figure 19.18 shows the OWL-WISE.WPG graphic, which was originally centered in its box, after pressing ← a few times.

You can also move the graphic within the frame by dragging the image with your mouse. Follow these steps:

1. Click the Move button or choose **E**dit ➤ Mo**v**e.

2. Hold down the left mouse button. The I beam will change to a four-headed arrow.

3. Drag the four-headed arrow in the direction you want to move the graphic. As you drag, the X and Y Pos indicators in the status bar show the position with respect to the original graphic. Moving the graphic to the left changes the X position by a negative amount; moving it to the right changes the X position by a positive amount. Likewise, moving the graphic down changes the Y position by a negative amount; moving it up changes the Y position by a positive amount.

The owl graphic has been moved to the left within its frame.

4. When you are finished moving the graphic image, release the mouse button, then click the Move button or choose **Edit** ➤ Move again.

If you move a portion of the image outside of the box, that portion will not be printed. Note that moving part of the image outside the box creates an equal amount of white space within the box on the other end, which you may not want.

ROTATING A GRAPHIC WITHIN ITS BOX

You can also rotate the graphic by a precise amount (see "Editing an Image by Precise Amounts").

You can rotate a graphic by a preset percentage, or interactively, using your mouse. To rotate the graphic by the percentage shown in the status bar, press the Ctrl+← key (rotates the image counterclockwise) and Ctrl+➤ key (rotates the image clockwise).

To use your mouse to rotate a figure, follow these steps:

1. Click the Rotate button or choose **Edit** ➤ **R**otate. A rotation angle, like the one in Figure 19.19, appears on the figure and the I beam changes to an arrow.

FIGURE 19.19:

The rotation angle in the Figure Editor window

2. Rotate the figure, using the rotation angle—the status bar changes to indicate the degrees of rotation clockwise or counterclockwise.

◆ Drag the top, left, or right axis clockwise or counterclockwise to rotate the figure any number of degrees.

◆ Position the arrow anywhere in the figure and click to rotate the figure so that the right end of the axis points to where you clicked.

◆ Click the top axis to rotate the figure counterclockwise 90 degrees.

◆ Click the left axis to rotate the figure counterclockwise 180 degrees.

3. When you're finished, click the Rotate button again or choose **E**dit ➤ **R**otate.

Figure 19.20 shows the owl after rotating the graphic a full 180 degrees.

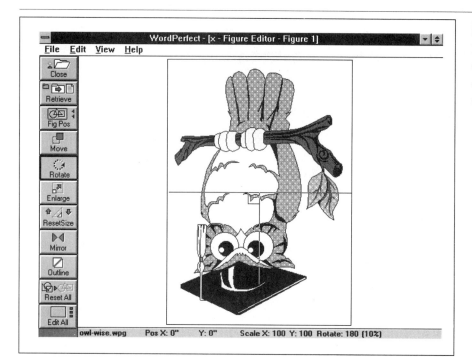

The owl graphic is rotated 180 degrees by clicking the left axis of the rotation angle.

SCALING A GRAPHIC WITHIN ITS BOX

You can scale a graphic by a preset percentage, or interactively, using your mouse. You can also select any portion of the figure and zoom in on it.

Enlarging or Reducing the Graphic by a Percentage

You can also scale the graphic by a precise amount (see "Editing an Image by Precise Amounts").

You can change the 10% increment setting by pressing the Insert key.

Initially, the graphic appears at 100 percent of its original size, as indicated by the X and Y scale in the status bar (see Figure 19.18). To enlarge a graphic by the percentage shown in parentheses in the status bar, choose Edit ➤ Scale ➤ Enlarge % or press Ctrl+↑. To reduce the graphic by that percentage, choose Edit ➤ Scale ➤ Reduce % or press Ctrl+↓. The image will grow by the same amount in both the X (width) and Y (length) dimensions each time you press Ctrl+↑ and shrink by the same amount in both the X and Y directions each time you press Ctrl+↓.

Figure 19.21 shows the owl graphic enlarged by four presses of Ctrl+↑ to 140 percent of it original size (the graphic scale increases by 10 percent each time the key is pressed, as indicated by the 10% setting in the status bar).

The graphic scaled to a larger size by choosing Edit ➤ Scale ➤ Enlarge % or pressing Ctrl+↑

Scaling an image larger is an excellent way to take unnecessary background out of an image and highlight the parts you really want the reader to notice. (It's often very helpful with figures imported from scanners.)

Zooming in on Part of the Image

Suppose you want to zoom in on the leaves in the owl image shown in Figure 19.17, or you want to show just one room in a complicated floor plan. The Enlarge feature is perfect for the job because it lets you select any rectangular portion of the figure and then zoom in on it. Follow these steps:

1. Click the Enlarge button in the Figure Editor Button Bar, or choose **E**dit ➤ **S**cale ➤ **E**nlarge Area.

2. Move the I beam to any position where you want to start selecting a portion of the figure. The I beam will change to a arrow, and dashed cross hairs will indicate the top-left corner of the selection area.

3. Hold down the left mouse button and drag the outline box around the area you want to select, as shown in Figure 19.22.

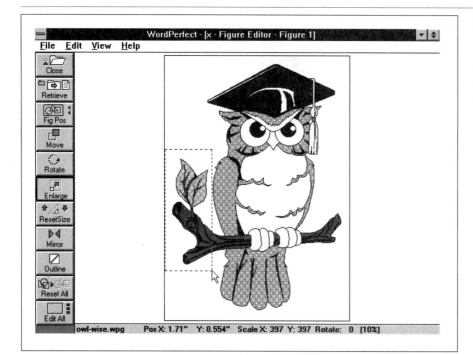

The selection box helps you select the part of a graphic you want to zoom in on.

4. Release the left mouse button. The selected portion of the image will now fill the graphics box. You can enlarge the area again by repeating steps 2–4. (Click the Reset Size button on the Button Bar or choose **E**dit ➤ **S**cale ➤ **R**eset Size to restore the figure to its original size.)

5. When you're finished, click the Enlarge button again or choose **E**dit ➤ **S**cale ➤ **E**nlarge Area.

Figure 19.23 shows the Figure Editor window after zooming in on the leaf and part of the branch of the owl graphic.

CONTROLLING THE DEGREE OF CHANGE

The Insert key adjusts the percentage of change shown in parentheses in the status bar of the Figure Editor. This percentage determines the amount of change when you use keys, buttons, and Edit menu options to move, scale, and rotate a graphic in the Figure Editor.

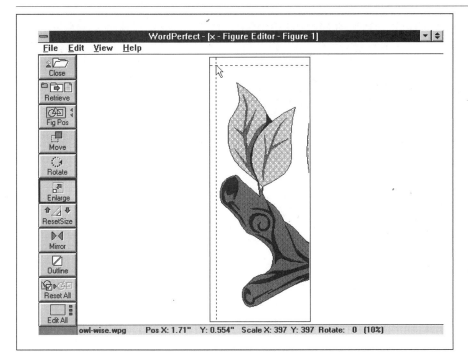

FIGURE 19.23:

*The Figure Editor
window after using
Enlarge to zoom in on a
portion of the owl image*

*You can al-
ways over-
ride the per-
centage
setting by using the
Edit All feature, as ex-
plained later in "Edit-
ing an Image by
Precise Amounts."*

Each press of the Insert key switches the percentage among 25, 10, 5,
and 1. Choose a smaller percentage if you want to make more precise changes.
Choose a larger percentage if you want to work with broad increments. This
feature is very helpful when you are trying to fine-tune a graphic to fit just
right in its box.

CREATING A MIRROR IMAGE

You can click the Mirror button on the Button Bar or choose Mirror from the
Edit menu if you want to display the mirror image of a graphic. Choosing this
option reverses the image as though you were viewing it in a mirror. Figure 19.24 shows examples of the WordPerfect BIKE.WPG and DESK-W.WPG
graphics (on the left) and their mirror images (on the right).

To restore a mirror image to its normal form, click the Mirror button
again, or choose Mirror from the Edit menu.

FIGURE 19.24:

Examples of normal and mirror-image graphics

INVERTING AN IMAGE

The actual appearance of a color image depends on the kind of monitor and printer you have.

To invert (or reverse) a graphic and treat it like a photographic negative, choose Edit ➤ Invert. This converts black to white and white to black (like the negative of a black-and-white photograph) and displays the complementary color of each dot (pixel) in a color image. For example, red changes to turquoise, blue changes to yellow, and yellow changes to blue.

You can restore your graphic to its normal appearance by choosing Edit ➤ Invert or clicking Reset All again.

OUTLINING AN IMAGE

If you prefer to display an image as a line drawing, without color or shading, click the Outline button on the Button Bar, or choose Outline from the Edit menu. On a color image, all colors become white, but any black portions remain black. This option can give your output a crisper appearance, especially when you use a low-resolution printer, like a dot-matrix printer, which cannot produce fine shading in a graphic.

DISPLAYING IMAGES IN BLACK AND WHITE

You can change the display of a color graphic to black and white on a color screen by choosing the Edit ➤ Black and White. Be aware that switching a graphic to black and white—regardless of whether or not your printer can print in color—may affect the printout, because colors print as shades of gray on noncolor printers.

The example in Figure 19.25 shows the BOOKWORM.WPG graphic printed in its normal "color" form (top left), with outline on (top right), in black and white (bottom left), and in black and white with invert (bottom right).

UNDOING YOUR CHANGES

If you're not happy with the changes you've made in the Figure Editor, you can undo them in several ways. For example, the appearance features—mirror, invert,

Color

Black and white

Outline

Black and white with invert

FIGURE 19.25:

A color graphic printed in "color" (top left), outline (top right), black and white (bottom left) and black and white with invert (bottom right)

outline, and black and white—are *toggle options* that you can turn on or off. You choose an option once to turn it on, and choose it again to turn it off.

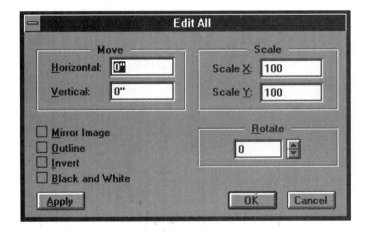

You can also undo several changes at once by using the Reset Size and Reset All options. Click the Reset Size button or choose Edit ➤ Scale ➤ Reset Size to return the figure to the scale and position it had when you retrieved it into the document. If you prefer to undo *all* changes—including position, rotation, scaling, and appearances—click the Reset All button or choose Edit ➤ Reset All. Your figure will be redisplayed exactly as it was when you retrieved it. You can also selectively undo (or make) changes using the Edit All option, discussed next.

The Mirror, Invert, Outline, and Black and White options on the Edit menu have a check mark next to them if they are turned on.

EDITING AN IMAGE BY PRECISE AMOUNTS

The Edit All dialog box (shown below) lets you move, scale and rotate a figure in specific amounts and lets you apply appearance options to your figure all at once. To open this dialog box in the Figure Editor, click the Edit All button or choose Edit ➤ Edit All.

You can change any or all of the options shown in the box, as explained in the following sections. If you want to see the changes you've made so far, without leaving the dialog box, click the Apply button. (Before clicking the Apply button, you may want to drag the dialog box to a corner of the window to see more of the figure.) When you're finished, press ↵ or click OK to return to the Figure Editor window and display the figure with all the changes.

Moving by a Precise Amount

You can override the current unit of measure by entering a different unit, such as 2p for two points.

The Move option in the Edit All dialog box lets you move a graphic image within the box by a precise horizontal and vertical amount. Type in the Horizontal distance and Vertical distance to move in inches (unless you've changed the Units of Measure setting in Preferences). Positive numbers move the graphic right or up from its original position; negative numbers move it left or down from its original position.

Scaling by a Precise Amount

You can use the Scale option to scale a graphic border to fill the entire page after setting the vertical position to Full Page and the horizontal position to Margin, Full.

The Scale option in the Edit All dialog box lets you scale a graphic by a precise amount. Enter the percentage by which to scale the x-axis and y-axis, where *100* equals 100 percent (the original scaling factor), *50* equals 50 percent (half the original size), *200* equals 200 percent (twice the original size), and so forth. Scaling the x-axis makes the image narrower or wider than the original image; scaling the y-axis makes the image taller or shorter than the original.

You can individually scale both the x-axis and the y-axis, and you can scale each axis by a different amount. For example, Figure 19.26 shows the owl graphic with *250* as the X scale and *100* as the Y scale.

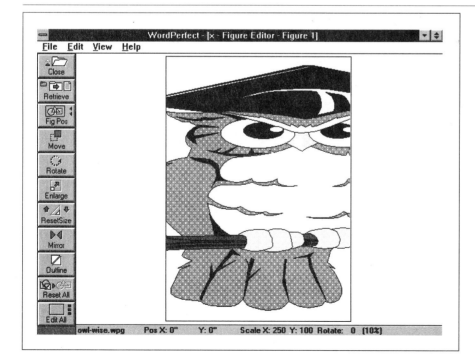

FIGURE 19.26:

The owl graphic scaled at 250 percent of its width and at its original height

Remember, if your scaling gets out of hand and you want to go back to the original scaling factor, you can simply click the Reset Size button or choose Edit ➤ Scale ➤ Reset Size.

Rotating by a Precise Amount

The Rotate option in the Edit All dialog box lets you rotate a graphics box a precise number of degrees. Enter the number of degrees (1–360) you want to rotate the image (for example, type *180* to flip the image upside down). You can also click the arrows next to the Rotate box to increase or decrease the rotation in 15-degree increments. This option rotates the graphic from its original position, not from any rotation amount you have previously specified.

SAVING A GRAPHIC IMAGE

The File menu in the Figure Editor includes two options for saving graphic images, although neither option preserves changes you make in the editor. The first option, Save As, lets you save a figure in WordPerfect graphics format. The second option, Graphic on Disk, is helpful for conserving disk space.

Saving a Graphic in WordPerfect Format

As you will learn later in this chapter, WordPerfect's Figure Editor can read many types of graphic files, created by many different graphics programs, into your document. In most cases, you simply retrieve the file (using File ➤ Retrieve or the Retrieve button in the Figure Editor), and WordPerfect automatically converts the file to WordPerfect graphics format (.WPG). This conversion must take place before WordPerfect can display or print the graphic and can take some time.

You can speed up the process and prevent WordPerfect from having to convert the file in the future by saving it in WordPerfect graphics format. Follow these steps:

1. Click the Figure Editor's Retrieve button or choose **File** ➤ **R**etrieve to retrieve the graphic you want to use.

2. Choose **File** ➤ Save **A**s.

The graphic will be saved in its unedited version.

3. Type a file name for the figure in the Save As text box and press ↵. If the file already exists, you'll be asked whether you want to replace it. Choose **Y**es to replace it or **N**o to enter a different file name.

4. Press ↵ or click the **S**ave button to return to the Figure Editor.

The file name you specify in step 3 will contain the original graphic image, except it will be in WordPerfect format. In the future, you can retrieve the WordPerfect file into your graphics box instead of the non-WordPerfect file.

Conserving Disk Space

You can use the Graphic on Disk option in the Figure Editor to tell Word-Perfect not to make an imported graphic file part of the document but to read the file from disk whenever it's needed for viewing or printing. Because documents containing imported graphics can be very large, setting this option to read the file from disk can be useful for conserving your hard-disk space, especially if you use the same image in a document multiple times. You also need this option when using a graphics box containing an image in a style.

With this option set, WordPerfect will not permanently copy the graphic into the document. When you print the document, WordPerfect will look for the graphics file first in your default graphics directory, then in your default document directory (both specified in Location of Files, as explained in Chapter 13). It then places the graphic in a temporary file, which is deleted after printing is complete.

To use this feature, follow these steps for each graphics file to be read from disk:

1. Click Figure Editor's Retrieve button or choose **File ➤ R**etrieve to retrieve the graphic you want to use.

2. Choose **F**ile **➤ G**raphic on Disk.

3. Type a file name for the figure in the Save **A**s text box and press ⏎. If the file already exists, you'll be asked whether you want to replace it. Choose **Y**es to replace it or **N**o to enter a different file name.

4. Press ⏎ or click the Save button to return to the Figure Editor window.

 *The graphic will be saved in its unedited version.*

The next time you retrieve this graphic into a graphics box, it will be read from the disk rather than incorporated into your document. The only disadvantage of the Graphic on Disk option is that if you copy the document to another computer that does not have the referenced graphic on its own disk, or you delete or rename the graphic, you will not be able to view or print the graphic image. When printing the document with another computer, you can play it safe by copying both the graphics file and your document.

HIDDEN CODES FOR GRAPHICS BOXES

Like most WordPerfect features, graphic boxes are controlled by hidden codes in your document. When you attach a box to a paragraph, the code is placed before the first character in the paragraph. The code starts with the type of box—Fig Box, Text Box, Tbl Box, Usr Box, or Equ Box—followed by a colon, the box number, and a semicolon.

If the contents of the box came from a file, the file name follows the first semicolon. If the box has a caption, the [Box Num] code (which displays the box number next to the caption) and the caption follow. For example, the code below is for Figure box No. 1, which contains the OWL-WISE.WPG graphic image with a caption.

[Fig Box:1;OWL-WISE.WPG;[Box Num]: This is a Figure box]

Because WordPerfect uses hidden codes to manage figures, you can use Reveal Codes to help you move, delete, and edit figures in a document, although it's usually easier to use the mouse techniques described earlier in this chapter.

CHANGING THE APPEARANCE OF ALL BOXES OF A GIVEN TYPE

TO CHANGE THE BORDER, CAPTION, OR NUMBERING STYLE, OR THE SPACING OF ALL BOXES OF A GIVEN TYPE,

position the insertion point before the code for the first box that you want to change. Choose Graphics from the menu bar. Choose the type of box you want to change, and then choose Options.

Up to this point, I've focused on ways to refine the appearance of an individual box in a document. But WordPerfect also lets you change the appearance of *all* boxes of a given type in one fell swoop. For example, you can change the appearance of all Figure boxes or all Table boxes.

Such choices do not affect the contents of any individual box. Rather, they alter the general appearance of that box style, such as the border style, the numbering style, the caption style, the spacing between boxes and text, and other features associated with a particular type of box.

 *You can change the appearance of Figure, Text, Table, User, and Equation boxes at any time, before or after creating the boxes.*

If you are satisfied with the general appearance of all the types of boxes in a document, there's no need for you to change any of the default values. But as you gain experience, you may want an extra level of refinement. Follow these steps:

1. Position the insertion point before the code for the first box of the type whose style you want to set. If you haven't created any boxes yet, put the insertion point at the top of the document or somewhere before the spot where you expect to place the first box.

2. Pull down the **G**raphics menu.

3. Choose the type of box you'll be working with: **F**igure, Text **B**ox, **E**quation, **T**able Box, or **U**ser Box.

4. Choose **O**ptions. The Options dialog box for the selected box type appears. A dialog box for changing Figure options is shown in Figure 19.27. (All the Options dialog boxes are the same, except for their title bars.)

Figure Options

Border Styles

Left:	Single
Right:	Single
Top:	Single
Bottom:	Single

Border Spacing

	Outside	Inside
Left:	0.167"	0"
Right:	0.167"	0"
Top:	0.167"	0"
Bottom:	0.167"	0"

Gray Shading

Percent: 0%

Minimum Offset from Paragraph

0"

Caption Numbering

First level: Numbers
Second level: Off
Style: [Bold On]Figure 1[Bold Off]

Caption Position

Below, Outside

OK   Cancel

FIGURE 19.27:

The Figure Options dialog box

5. Set the options as discussed in the sections that follow.

6. Press ↵ or click OK to return to the document window.

Whenever you access an Options menu, WordPerfect puts a hidden code—[Fig Opt], [Tbl Opt], [Txt Opt], [Usr Opt], or [Equ Opt]—in your document at the insertion point. The settings represented by that code affect all boxes of the given type that follow the code's position in the document.

The following sections describe the various items in the Options dialog box.

SETTING BORDER STYLE

The border style is the type of line used to frame the box. You can change the border style for the left, right, top, and bottom lines. To choose a style from the Options dialog box, open the pop-up list under the Border Styles option for the type of line you want to change. Then choose one of the following line styles: None, Single, Double, Dashed, Dotted, Thick, or Extra Thick. Figure 19.28 shows examples of each style of line.

You can also draw a border around text by placing that text in a single-cell table (Chapter 6).

Choose one of these styles or a combination of styles for your border. The first option, None, lets you hide the border on some or all sides of the box. By choosing different styles for each of the four sides of the box, you can create drop shadows like the one around the lawyer's shingle in Figure 19.28. Single lines were used for the top and left borders, and extra thick lines were used for the right and bottom borders.

An easy way to create a coupon like the one in Figure 19.28 is to use a single-cell table (Chapter 6) with the Layout ➤ Tables ➤ Lines ➤ Outside set to Dashed for the outermost border. The text, lines, and check boxes (Zapf Dingbat graphics in this example) are placed right in the cell. The sunburst graphic behind "Free Offer!" is in a borderless User box, also within the cell, with Wrap Text Around Box turned off.

SETTING OUTSIDE BORDER SPACING

You can set two kinds of Border Spacing options: Outside and Inside. The Outside option sets the amount of space between the left, right, top, and bottom borders and the text outside your box, as Figure 19.29 shows. The default width is usually acceptable, but can easily be changed for special requirements. Making sure there is enough white space around your graphics boxes is important to the layout of a document and makes it easier to read.

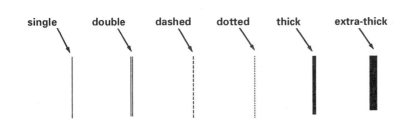

FIGURE 19.28:

The available border styles and some examples using these styles

James T. Wadsworth, Esq.

Attorney at Law

Free Offer!

Send completed coupon to:
Groovy Juice, Inc.
P.O. Box 1234
Valencia, CA 91234
(123)555-0986

❏ *Yes, rush my free sample today.*
❏ *Yuk, no thanks, I hate that stuff.*

Name:_____

Address: _____

City, State, Zip: _____

Daytime phone: (___)___-_____
(Used only if problems with order)

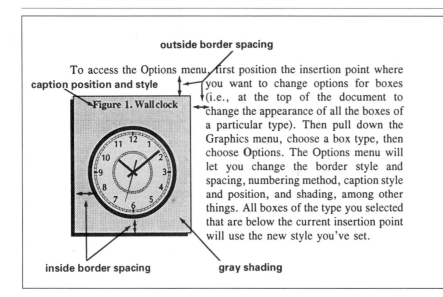

FIGURE 19.29:

*You can add extra
white space to the
outside and inside
borders of the graphic,
as shown here.*

Because WordPerfect generally reserves space under the box for the caption, you may find the white space under boxes without captions to be too wide; set the outside border space at the bottom of the figure to 0" to close it up.

SETTING INSIDE BORDER SPACING

The Inside Border Spacing options prevent the text or graphic within the box from being printed right against the border. Choose the exact amount of space that should remain blank inside the left, right, top, and bottom borders, or accept the default: either 0.167 inches (12 points) or 0 inches, depending on the box type.

SHADING THE BOX BACKGROUND

The Gray Shading option controls the background on which the box contents are printed. WordPerfect lets you print with gray backgrounds of various intensities; the higher the percentage you choose, the darker the background. Only Text boxes are shaded by default, but you can set gray shading for any type of box by using the Gray Shading box options.

SETTING MINIMUM OFFSET FROM PARAGRAPH

You can use Block Protect to keep the paragraph with the graphics box (see Chapter 7).

The Minimum Offset from Paragraph option limits how much a paragraph-anchored box can move up in a paragraph before being bumped to the next page. Normally, WordPerfect honors the Vertical Position setting in the Box Position and Size dialog box. But when a graphics box would otherwise be split by a page break, WordPerfect tries to keep the box on the same page by moving it up in the paragraph until the box fits on the page or its top border is flush with the first line of the paragraph (a minimum offset of 0 inches). If the box still won't fit on the page, it is bumped to the next page. If you prefer not to have the graphics box moved up as far as the first line of the paragraph, you can set a minimum amount for the box offset.

For example, let's suppose you anchor a rather large box to a paragraph near the bottom of a page. If the vertical position of the box is set to 1 inch (below the top of the paragraph), and the Minimum Offset from Paragraph setting is 0.5 inch, WordPerfect will move up the box only $1/2$ inch into the paragraph (instead of as much as 1 inch) before bumping the box to the next page.

NUMBERING THE BOXES

The Options dialog box includes two Caption Numbering options: First level and Second level. The First level option controls the numbering of the boxes. *Level* is an organizational term that refers to the numbering of graphics by sub-section. For example, a two-level system of figure numbering is used in this book. *Figure 19.1* is the first figure in the nineteenth chapter; *19* is the first level, and *1* is the second level.

To choose a first-level caption-numbering method, open the First-level pop-up list under the Caption Numbering option. Then choose one of the following methods from the list: Off, Numbers, Letters, or Roman Numerals. The option you choose here will be the first level used to number all captions for the particular box type.

You use the Second level option to create multilevel numbering for graphics boxes. For example, if you specify Roman Numerals for the first level and choose Letters for the second level, the boxes you create will be numbered *I-a, I-b, I-c,* and so on. You choose Second-level caption numbering from a pop-up list that offers the same options as First-level numbering. Keep in mind that the second level will not appear in the captions unless you refer to it in the Caption Numbering Style setting (discussed next).

CHOOSING A CAPTION NUMBER STYLE

This option controls the format of the caption number. To add a caption to an individual box, move the mouse pointer over the graphics box, click the right mouse button, and choose Edit Caption.

The Caption Numbering Style can include only as many characters and formatting codes as fit in the Style text box.

The Caption Numbering Style option lets you tell WordPerfect how to print the caption number and related text, such as the word *Figure,* in boxes that have captions. Your caption number style can include text, formatting codes, and numbering levels (these are inserted in the [Box Num] code, which automatically appears in captions when you add a caption to your graphics box). You switch on formatting features by clicking the little button (marked with a triangle) to the right of the Style option and choosing Bold, Italics, Underline, or Small Caps from the pop-up list that appears. For example, to italicize the word *Figure* and the First level number of Figure box captions, follow these steps:

1. Open the Options dialog box for a Figure box as described earlier.
2. Select all the existing text in the Style text box.
3. Press the Delete or Backspace key to remove the existing text.
4. Open the pop-up list next to the Style option, then choose Italics from the list. (To add another formatting style, just repeat this step and choose a different style, such as Bold.)
5. Position the insertion point between the [Italc On] and [Italc Off] codes.
6. Type *Figure 1*.

The Caption Numbering Style is important to the printed numbering of boxes. The default style for each box type, although varying from box type to box type, always includes the number *1,* representing the first numbering level. If you want to print the second numbering level, you must include the number *2* in the Caption Number Style entry. For example, the entry

[Bold On]Figure 1[Bold Off]

will print captions using only the First level number (or letter), even if you switched on a second level with the Second level option for Caption Numbering. Your captions will print like this: **Figure 1**, **Figure 2**, **Figure 3**, and so on. (See "Choosing a Font for Captions" later in this chapter for information on choosing a font for all captions.)

The following entry for Caption Number Style will produce two-level caption numbers like the ones used in this book:

[Bold On]Figure 1.2[Bold Off]

Use the numbers 1 and 2 when defining Caption Number Style, even if you chose letters or Roman numerals for the numbering methods.

Your captions will print like this: **Figure 19.1**, **Figure 19.2**, **Figure 19.3**, and so on.

POSITIONING THE CAPTION

With Equation boxes, you can place the caption above or below the borders, or to the left or right of the box (inside the box borders).

The Caption Position option places the caption in one of four places around and in the box. The choices are

◆ Below Box, Outside of Border

◆ Above Box, Outside of Border

◆ Below Box, Inside of Border

◆ Above Box, Inside of Border

A WARNING ABOUT BOX OPTION CODES

As mentioned before, whenever you make choices from the Options dialog box, WordPerfect inserts a hidden [Opt] code at the insertion point, which affects all boxes of that type from the code position forward—or until the next [Opt] code of the same box type, if any. Therefore, if an old [Opt] code follows a newer one, the old code takes precedence over the new one. To avoid confusion and prevent code clutter, make a habit of deleting any old [Opt] codes at the insertion point.

One shortcut might be worth mentioning at this point. Let's suppose you have set some Figure box options and are satisfied with most, but not all, of the settings. You can move your insertion point just to the right of the existing [Fig Opt] code (most easily done after opening Reveal Codes), and then choose the Figure box options as usual. Since your insertion point is to the right of an older [Fig Opt] code, WordPerfect will remember all the existing settings, and you can just change the few settings that need fine-tuning. After making your changes, delete the old code to prevent clutter.

CHOOSING A FONT FOR CAPTIONS

You can choose a font for all the captions of a given box type (e.g., all Figure boxes or all Table boxes) by preceding the options code for the box type with a font choice for the captions and following the code with a font for the normal text. For example, the following codes define the font for Figure box captions as Courier 10-cpi (Bold) and the font for normal text as Courier 12-cpi:

[Font:Courier 10cpi (Bold)][Fig Opt][Font:Courier 12cpi]

To set a different font for your captions, follow these steps for each box type you use in your document:

 *Chapter 5 covers how to choose fonts.*

1. Choose Font ➤ Font (or press F9), choose the font and size you want, then press ↵.

2. Choose **G**raphics from the menu bar, choose a box type, and then choose **O**ptions.

3. Change the options, if you wish, and then press ↵ or click OK to create the [Opt] code.

4. Move the insertion point past the [Opt] code, and choose the font you want to use for the normal text of the document.

Be aware that, in addition to setting the font for the caption, these steps also set the font for boxes created with the Text Box Editor. But this should be no problem, because you can change the font for whatever you type inside the text box: Open the Text Box Editor, move the insertion point to the beginning of the text, and change the font in the usual way. Then click the Close button.

RENUMBERING BOXES

TO RENUMBER ALL THE BOXES IN A DOCUMENT,

move the insertion point above the box where you want to start the new numbering. Choose Graphics from the menu bar. Choose the box type, then New Number. Type the new box number and press ↵.

Let's say your document is divided into several chapters, and you're numbering the figures within each chapter using a two-level system. Perhaps the first number is the chapter number, and the second number is the number of the figure within that chapter. WordPerfect cannot recognize the start of a new chapter and update the numbering automatically; you must tell it where to update the numbering. Follow these steps to adjust your First level box numbers:

1. Position the insertion point before the first box to be renumbered, but *after* the preceding box. WordPerfect renumbers the boxes from the insertion point forward.

2. Pull down the **G**raphics menu.

3. Choose the type of box you want to renumber: **F**igure, Text **B**ox, **E**quation, **T**able Box, or **U**ser Box.

4. Choose **N**ew Number. WordPerfect displays a dialog box prompting you for the number of the next box of the selected type.

5. Type the number, and press ↵ or click OK. WordPerfect inserts a hidden code at the insertion point, indicating the new number you just specified.

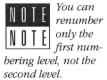

You can renumber only the first numbering level, not the second level.

This will automatically renumber the boxes in the document window and will adjust all caption numbers for the type of box you specified. For example, to restart figure numbering at the beginning of Chapter 2, just enter *2* in step 5. WordPerfect knows to restart the second numbering level, if one is set, and to renumber correctly all remaining boxes or all boxes up to the next New Number code.

CHOOSING A PRINT QUALITY FOR GRAPHICS

If your printer does not have enough memory to print text and graphics, you can print just the text, then reload the same pages and print just the graphics (see Chapter 8).

If your printer can print graphics, it may also be able to print them with various levels of quality. You can even prevent graphics from being printed. Basically, the higher quality of printing you use, the longer it takes to print the graphics. So you might want to omit graphics or use draft quality to print the initial rough drafts of your document. When you are ready for the final draft, you can switch to medium or high quality.

Here are the general steps for choosing the graphics quality for your printout:

1. From the document window, choose **F**ile ➤ **P**rint, or press F5.

2. Open the **G**raphics Quality pop-up list under the Document Settings option.

3. Choose one of these options: **H**igh, **M**edium, **D**raft, or Do **N**ot Print.

You can then use the Full Document or Current Page option to print the document.

LINKING A REFERENCE TO ITS BOX

Automatic numbering of boxes is a great convenience. If you currently have figures numbered 1.1 to 1.20 in a document, and then add a new figure above Figure 1.2, WordPerfect automatically renumbers all the figures below the new one; the captions show the new, correct figure numbers. But any text references to those figures (for example, a phrase that says "see Figure 1.6") will not be updated to match the new figure numbers, unless you use automatic cross-referencing, as discussed in Chapter 23.

PLACING BOXES IN TABLES

You can place a box in any single table cell: Move the insertion point into the cell where you want the graphics box to appear, then just go through the normal steps of creating a box. Here are some general tips to make the procedure easier and to help ensure that the table cell is nicely filled with the graphic image:

◆ Set the outside border spacing for User boxes to 0 for all four borders, so each box best fills the cell. To do so, move the insertion point just before the [Table Def] code that defines the table (open Reveal Codes to see the code), then choose **G**raphics ➤ **U**ser Box ➤ **O**ptions and set the Outside Border Spacing options.

◆ Define every box that you place within a cell as a User box, so the frame surrounding each table cell becomes the frame surrounding each graphics box.

◆ While defining a box in a table cell, anchor it to a paragraph. Also, to best fill the box, set the horizontal position to Margin, Full.

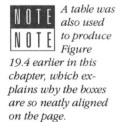 *A table was also used to produce Figure 19.4 earlier in this chapter, which explains why the boxes are so neatly aligned on the page.*

Of course, these guidelines are just general. You may want to experiment with boxes in table cells to create your own unique effects. Figure 19.30 shows an example of a storyboard, where these guidelines were used to place graphics boxes in table cells. Each graphic figure is in a borderless User box within a table cell, and the text beneath each graphic is in the cell immediately below. The lines in the table were then removed or modified to give the desired appearance.

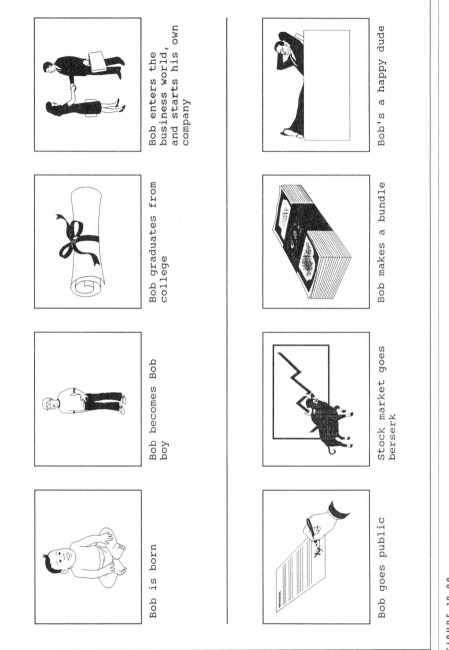

FIGURE 19.30:

A storyboard created by placing graphic images in User boxes within a table

STORING GRAPHICS FILES

See Chapter 13 for more information

about the Preferences options for customizing WordPerfect. See Chapter 12 for information on using the Quick List.

The WordPerfect installation program normally stores all WordPerfect graphic images in a separate directory, usually C:\WPWIN\GRAPHICS, and automatically sets the location of files to that directory. You can create a separate directory for your own graphic files, using DOS, Windows, or the WordPerfect File Manager, then have WordPerfect automatically search your new directory, by choosing File ➤ Preferences ➤ Location of Files ➤ Graphics Files or including that directory in your Quick List. If you do this, be sure to move any existing .WPG files to that directory, again using the File Manager.

SOURCES OF GRAPHICS

Any image can be digitized and stored as a file on your computer. To display most digitized images in a WordPerfect document, you simply choose the image and WordPerfect displays it. If your file format is unsupported, however, you need to convert it to a WordPerfect graphic (.WPG file), using the GRAPHCNV program. Figure 19.31 shows just a few examples of graphic images, described in the sections that follow.

Another source of graphics is screen captures, where you "capture" the image displayed on your screen in a graphics file. These graphics are useful when you're writing about a computer program and want to show the reader something that appears on the screen. Figure 19.32 shows examples of captured screens, which are also discussed below.

CLIP ART AND SCANNED IMAGES

Don't assume all clip art is free

of copyright—you cannot use copyrighted art without permission.

Clip-art images are small pieces of art often used to jazz up newsletters and other documents. Thousands of ready-to-use clip-art images are available, as a trip to your local computer store will confirm. Most clip art is free of copyright restrictions, so you can just purchase it for a onetime fee, then use it freely in your work without paying a royalty to the artist.

You can make your own clip art by scanning a printed image of the art (as long as you have permission). If you don't have a scanner, typically you can have a commercial printing house or desktop publishing bureau scan the image for you. You can even scan your signature, your company logo, or photographs, then place them in graphics boxes in your WordPerfect documents or primary merge files.

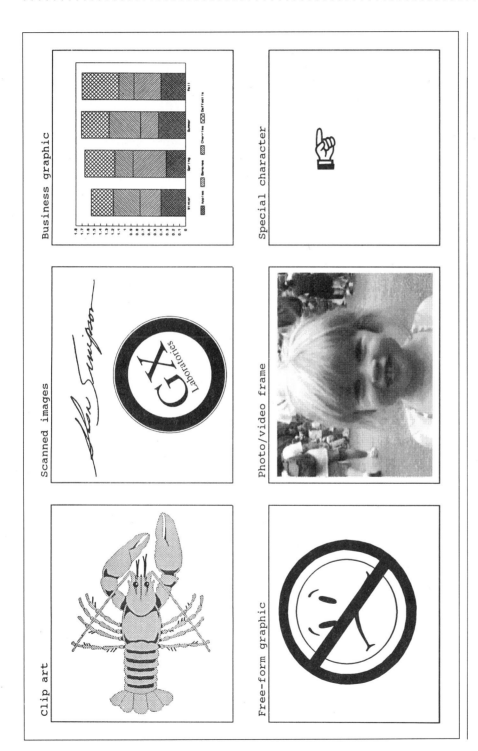

FIGURE 19.31:

Examples of graphic images

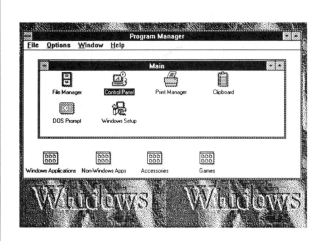

Captured Windows Screen

Capture Graphics Screen

Captured Text Screen

FIGURE 19.32:

Examples of captured screens

Scanned images are generally stored as TIFF (Tagged Image File Format) files, with the .TIF extension. You can use the GRAPHCNV program (see "Importing Graphic Images" later in this chapter) or the Save As option on the File menu in the Figure Editor to convert these to .WPG files.

BUSINESS AND FREE-FORM GRAPHICS

Most spreadsheet programs let you display data in bar graphs, pie charts, and other business graphic formats. Most graphics programs let you create free-form graphics, as well as business graphs. Specialized graphics programs are also available for scientific, engineering, and other types of graphics.

Virtually any image created by any program can be read into a Word-Perfect graphics box by using the Retrieve button or the Retrieve option on the File menu in the Figure Editor. You just need to specify the directory location and complete file name of the graphic you are importing (e.g., C:\123\MYGRAPH.PIC to import a Lotus 1-2-3 business graph that's stored in the 123 directory of drive C).

In some cases, you may prefer to use the techniques described below to capture a graph that's on the screen. Or, you may need to convert the graphic image to a .WPG file (see "Importing Graphic Images").

Dynamic Data Exchange: Linking Data Automatically

If you use Windows applications that support DDE (Dynamic Data Exchange), you can link text or graphics data from those applications to your WordPerfect document, and you can update the information automatically, whenever it changes in the applications. For example, suppose your accounting department updates a Microsoft Excel profit-and-loss spreadsheet every month. You want to print a WordPerfect report for the company's managers that includes the numbers from the spreadsheet—automatically updated—and some accompanying text. You link the spreadsheet to your WordPerfect document just once, and from then on, your document will include up-to-the-minute numbers whenever you print it (assuming the accounting department is on the ball). See Chapter 25 for more information on using DDE.

CAPTURED WINDOWS SCREENS

If Word-Perfect is already running, you can just press Ctrl+Esc and double-click Program Manager to get to its window.

It's easy to capture screens from Windows 3 or any Windows 3 application, including WordPerfect for Windows. Follow these steps:

1. Run Windows in the usual manner (if you don't have a color printer, you might want to use the Control Panel in the Main window to switch Colors to the Monochrome color scheme).

2. Start WordPerfect for Windows.

3. Do whatever is necessary to get to the screen you want to capture. For example, switch to the Paintbrush application if you want to capture one of its screens.

Refer to your Windows 3 manual for details on switching between applications and capturing Windows screens.

4. To capture the entire screen, press Print Screen, or, to capture only the active window, press Alt+Print Screen. Optionally, use that application's selection techniques to select any portion of the screen, then choose **E**dit ➤ **C**opy to copy the selection. The screen, window, or selected area is copied to the Windows Clipboard.

5. Return to WordPerfect and position the insertion point to where you want the captured graphic to appear.

6. Choose **E**dit ➤ **P**aste or press Shift+Insert to import the captured screen (see "Importing Graphic Images" for additional information).

You must be running Windows in 386 enhanced mode to use the Alt+Print Screen feature.

WordPerfect automatically creates a Figure box containing your captured screen. From here, you can move or size the box, add a caption, use the Figure Editor, and otherwise treat your captured screen as you would any other box created with the Figure Editor.

If you need more control over the appearance of the captured screen or the format in which it's saved, try using a third-party Windows screen-capture utility, such as Tiffany Plus from Anderson Consulting and Software or Collage Plus from Inner Media.

CAPTURED TEXT SCREENS

Applications that aren't designed for the Windows environment are called non-Windows applications. These non-Windows applications typically have simple text-based screens, although the screens may be displayed in color and look quite attractive. Capturing a text screen and pasting it into your Word-Perfect for Windows document is just as easy as capturing a graphics screen.

Follow these steps:

1. Starting from within WordPerfect for Windows, switch to the Windows Program Manager (press Ctrl+Esc and double-click the Program Manager option).

2. Run your non-Windows application (typically by going through the Non-Windows Applications group icon).

3. Do whatever is necessary in the non-Windows application to display the screen you want to capture. (You can capture either a "pure text" screen, or a DOS "graphics screen," such as the DOS 5 Shell or Lotus 1-2-3 "Graph View" screen.)

4. To capture the entire screen, press Print Screen. Then skip to step 10.

5. If you want to capture only a portion of the screen, press Alt+spacebar to reduce the application to a window.

6. Choose **E**dit ➤ **M**ark from the Control menu. (You may see a warning about the application being suspended. Just click OK or press ↵.)

7. Drag your mouse over the portion of the screen you want to capture.

8. Open the Control menu (by pressing Alt+spacebar or clicking the Control-menu box in the current application), and choose **E**dit ➤ **C**opy.

9. To return the non-Windows application to full-screen mode, open the Control menu again, choose **S**ettings ➤ **F**ull Screen, and then choose OK.

10. To conserve memory, you can now exit the non-Windows application, using whatever method you always use within that application to exit. You'll be returned to the Windows Program Manager.

11. Return to WordPerfect either by clicking anywhere in its window or by pressing Ctrl+Esc and choosing WordPerfect from the Task List.

12. Position the insertion point where you want the text to appear.

13. Choose **E**dit ➤ **P**aste or press Shift+Insert to import the captured text screen.

WordPerfect inserts the text of the captured screen at the insertion point in the document window. From here, you can edit the text as if you had typed it at the keyboard. Be aware that the text might not look as nice in the document window as it did on the non-Windows application screen, so you may need to reformat it by changing margins, replacing spaces with tabs, deleting extra text, choosing a different font, and so on.

PHOTOS AND VIDEOTAPE IMAGES

To include photographs in your documents, first have the photo scanned to produce a TIFF file, which you can then import into a graphics box. You can also capture still images from TV, video games, or videotapes if you have a video digitizer card and appropriate software. See your computer dealer for more information.

If you want to retouch a photo or video image to improve its appearance before printing it, you need a program that can edit gray-scale Images, such as Gray F/X from Xerox, available at any computer store.

SPECIAL CHARACTERS

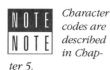

Character codes are described in Chapter 5.

For added spice, you can use any of more than one thousand special characters that WordPerfect offers as graphics, particularly if your printer can print these characters in large sizes. If you have a PostScript printer, or the Zapf Dingbats font on some other printer, you also can use the special characters shown in Figure 19.33. Just choose Font ➤ Font (or press F9), then choose the Dingbats font and a point size. When you're ready to insert the character, choose Font ➤ WP Characters or press Ctrl+W, type the code shown in the chart, and press ↵.

IMPORTING GRAPHIC IMAGES

Many different formats are used to store graphic images in files on a disk. Although WordPerfect directly supports only the WordPerfect Graphics (.WPG) format, you can typically import files from any of these popular graphic formats:

◆ AutoCAD (.DXF)

◆ Computer Graphics Metafiles (.CGM)

◆ Dr. Halo (.DHP)

◆ GEM (.IMG)

◆ Hewlett-Packard plotter files (HPGL)

◆ Lotus (.PIC)

◆ Macintosh Paint (PNTG)

◆ PC Paint and PC Paint Plus (PPIC)

◆ PC Paintbrush and Publisher's Paintbrush (.PCX)

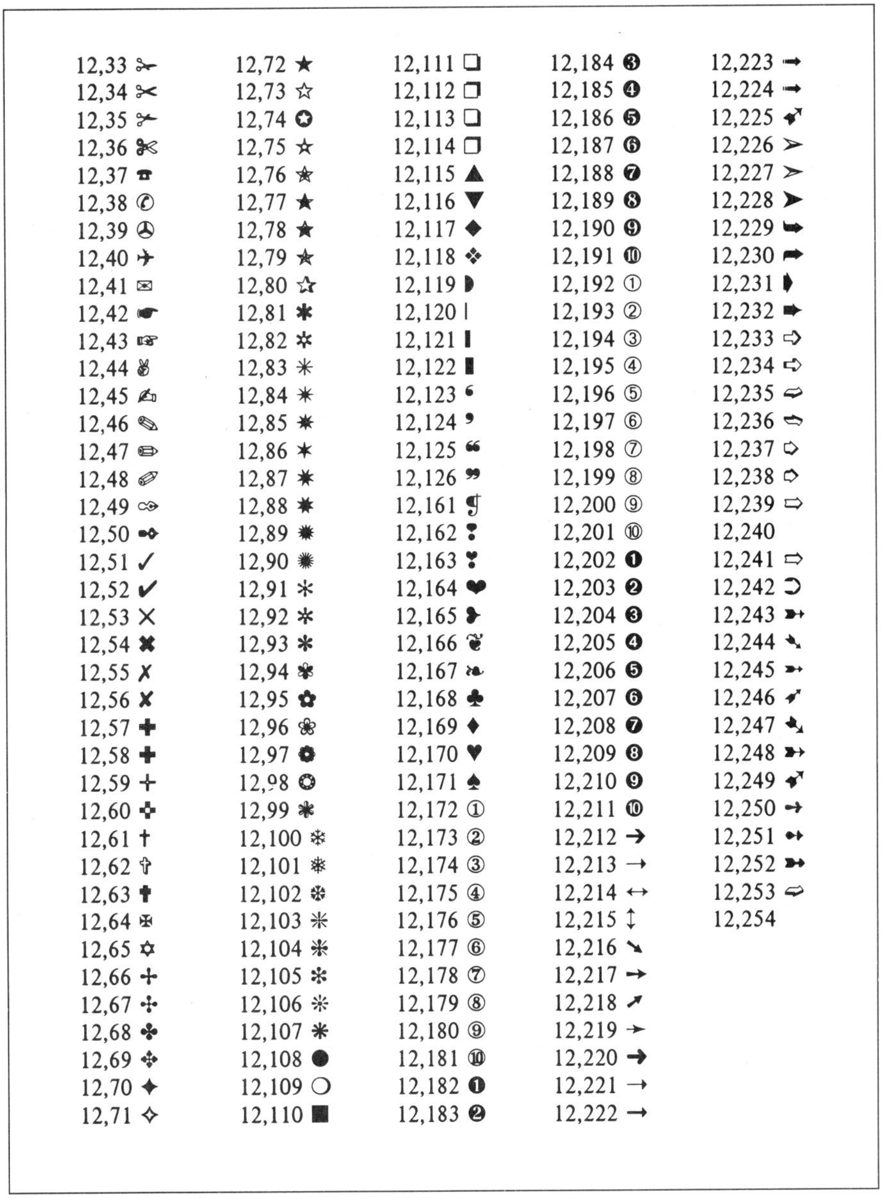

FIGURE 19.33:

The Zapf Dingbats special characters

12,33 ✂	12,72 ★	12,111 ❏	12,184 ❸	12,223 ➡
12,34 ✂	12,73 ☆	12,112 ❐	12,185 ❹	12,224 ➡
12,35 ✂	12,74 ✇	12,113 ❑	12,186 ❺	12,225 ➴
12,36 ✄	12,75 ★	12,114 ❒	12,187 ❻	12,226 ➢
12,37 ☎	12,76 ✶	12,115 ▲	12,188 ❼	12,227 ➢
12,38 ✆	12,77 ★	12,116 ▼	12,189 ❽	12,228 ➤
12,39 ✈	12,78 ✷	12,117 ◆	12,190 ❾	12,229 ➥
12,40 ✈	12,79 ✸	12,118 ❖	12,191 ❿	12,230 ➦
12,41 ✉	12,80 ☆	12,119 ◗	12,192 ①	12,231 ➧
12,42 ☛	12,81 ✹	12,120 ❘	12,193 ②	12,232 ➨
12,43 ☞	12,82 ✺	12,121 ❙	12,194 ③	12,233 ⇨
12,44 ✌	12,83 ✳	12,122 ❚	12,195 ④	12,234 ⇨
12,45 ✍	12,84 ✳	12,123 ❛	12,196 ⑤	12,235 ⇦
12,46 ✎	12,85 ✳	12,124 ❜	12,197 ⑥	12,236 ➩
12,47 ✏	12,86 ✳	12,125 ❝	12,198 ⑦	12,237 ⇨
12,48 ✐	12,87 ✳	12,126 ❞	12,199 ⑧	12,238 ⇨
12,49 ✑	12,88 ✴	12,161 ❡	12,200 ⑨	12,239 ⇨
12,50 ✒	12,89 ✵	12,162 ❢	12,201 ⑩	12,240
12,51 ✓	12,90 ✶	12,163 ❣	12,202 ❶	12,241 ⇨
12,52 ✔	12,91 ✳	12,164 ❤	12,203 ❷	12,242 ⊃
12,53 ✕	12,92 ✳	12,165 ❥	12,204 ❸	12,243 ➺
12,54 ✖	12,93 ✳	12,166 ❦	12,205 ❹	12,244 ➘
12,55 ✗	12,94 ✳	12,167 ❧	12,206 ❺	12,245 ➻
12,56 ✘	12,95 ✿	12,168 ♣	12,207 ❻	12,246 ➷
12,57 ✚	12,96 ❀	12,169 ♦	12,208 ❼	12,247 ➚
12,58 ✚	12,97 ❁	12,170 ♥	12,209 ❽	12,248 ➹
12,59 ✛	12,98 ❂	12,171 ♠	12,210 ❾	12,249 ➹
12,60 ✜	12,99 ✳	12,172 ①	12,211 ❿	12,250 ➙
12,61 ✝	12,100 ❅	12,173 ②	12,212 →	12,251 ↔
12,62 ✞	12,101 ❆	12,174 ③	12,213 →	12,252 ➳
12,63 ✟	12,102 ❇	12,175 ④	12,214 ↔	12,253 ➼
12,64 ✠	12,103 ❈	12,176 ⑤	12,215 ↕	12,254
12,65 ✡	12,104 ❉	12,177 ⑥	12,216 ➘	
12,66 ✢	12,105 ❊	12,178 ⑦	12,217 →	
12,67 ✣	12,106 ❋	12,179 ⑧	12,218 ➹	
12,68 ✤	12,107 ✳	12,180 ⑨	12,219 →	
12,69 ✥	12,108 ●	12,181 ⑩	12,220 →	
12,70 ✦	12,109 ○	12,182 ❶	12,221 →	
12,71 ✧	12,110 ■	12,183 ❷	12,222 →	

◆ PostScript and Encapsulated PostScript (.EPS)

◆ Tagged Image File Format (.TIF)

◆ Windows (2.*x*) Paint (.MSP)

◆ Windows (3.*x*) and OS/2 Presentation Manager Bitmap (.BMP)

◆ Windows Metafile Format (.WMF)

◆ WordPerfect and DrawPerfect Graphics (.WPG)

In most cases, just entering the proper directory location and full name of the graphic file you want to import into the Figure Editor is sufficient. For example, if you choose Retrieve from the Figure Editor's File menu, and enter **d:\windows\myart.pcx** as the name of the file to import, WordPerfect will know that the file is in .PCX format and convert it to .WPG format as the importing takes place.

Some conversions are a little more difficult. If WordPerfect reports that it cannot convert a file, or you want to convert a group of graphics files to .WPG format so that WordPerfect can use them directly, try using the GRAPHCNV program that comes with WordPerfect.

To use GRAPHCNV, follow these steps:

For more information on GRAPHCNV, enter ***graphcnv /b*** *at the DOS command prompt.*

1. Switch to the Program Manager.

2. Choose **File ➤ R**un to open the Run dialog box.

3. Type the directory and file name for the GRAPHCNV program, then press ↵ or click OK. Typically, this will be **c:\wpwin\graphcnv** if you installed the WordPerfect utility programs on drive C.

4. Type the full path name of the input file or files to be converted and press ↵. For example, if you want to convert all the .DXF (AutoCAD) files in your D:\WINDOWS directory, type **d:\windows*.dxf** as the input file name.

5. Type the full path name of the converted file or files you want to create. For example, if you want to convert the files above to .WPG files stored in your C:\WPWIN\GRAPHICS directory, type **c:\wpwin\graphics*.wpg** as the output file name.

Now you should be able to import the converted .WPG files into your graphics boxes by using Retrieve on the Figure Editor's File menu in WordPerfect.

Once you've mastered these techniques for adding graphics to your documents, you can move further into the realm of desktop publishing by learning more about columns and page layout, discussed in the next chapter.

CHAPTER 20

FEATURING

Creating Newspaper-Style
Columns

Creating Parallel Columns

Combining Columns, Lines,
and Graphics

Using WordPerfect's Typesetting
Features

Desktop Publishing Examples

Working with Columns and Typesetting Features

**A**lthough graphics can enhance any document, a truly polished, publication-quality finished product requires some additional touches. Using multiple columns is one way to make a document more inviting and even easier to read (which is one reason that newspapers use them).

Beyond using columns, there are other elements of your document's layout that you can make changes to, such as the amount of space between lines, the spacing between letters, and the exact positioning of text. This chapter covers these more advanced desktop publishing features, which you can use to gain accurate control over the appearance of your text.

CREATING NEWSPAPER-STYLE COLUMNS

TO CREATE NEWSPAPER-STYLE COLUMNS,

move the insertion point to where you want the columns to begin, or select the text you want placed in columns. Choose View ➤ Ruler to display the ruler. Choose the desired number of columns (2–5) from the Columns button.

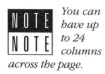

Newspaper columns (also called *snaking* columns) organize your text like the text in a newspaper: Text runs down the leftmost column to the bottom of the page, wraps to the top of the next column, continues to the bottom of the page, and then wraps either to the next column or, if there are only two columns, to the leftmost column on the next page. Figure 20.1 shows an example of a newsletter, where the text snakes through three columns.

WordPerfect automatically takes care of all the business of wrapping, even as you add, change, and delete text.

DEFINING NEWSPAPER COLUMNS

The first step in using newspaper-style columns is to define how you want the columns to look: How many columns do you want across the page? How much space do you want between the columns (often called *gutter space*)? The Columns button on the ruler provides the easiest way to create up to five evenly-spaced columns. If you prefer to define column measurements more precisely, or you need to define more than five newspaper columns, you use the Define Columns dialog box instead. Regardless of the method you use to create the columns, WordPerfect will automatically activate the columns for you and will reformat any existing text to fit in the new columns.

Defining Newspaper Columns with the Ruler

Follow these steps to define up to five evenly-spaced newspaper columns, using the ruler:

1. If necessary, display the ruler by choosing **View** ➤ **R**uler or pressing Alt+Shift+F3.

2. Position the insertion point above (or at) the paragraph where you want to start arranging text into columns, either before or after you've typed the text. Alternatively, you can select the text you want to arrange into columns.

3. Move the insertion point to the Columns button (shown at left), then click and hold down the left mouse button to open the menu of column options shown in Figure 20.2.

4. Choose any of these options from the menu: 2 Columns, 3 Columns, 4 Columns, or 5 Columns.

5. Release the mouse button.

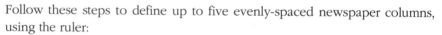

The Vacationer

Vol. 1 No. 1	Travel fun for everyone	January 1992

Newsletter debut
by Joan Smith

We're pleased to bring this first issue of our newsletter, *The Vacationer*, to our many loyal customers. The newsletter was inspired by your ideas and questions. You've asked us about where to find the best travel fares, where to go for the person who has been everywhere, what to eat and how to eat it when visiting faraway countries. We've responded by creating this newsletter.

Here we'll bring you the latest news about great deals on vacations in exotic corners of our planet, fun places for inexpensive weekend getaways, and out-of-the-way spots you might never have thought to ask us about. We'll include handy vacation planning tips and introduce you to exciting foods, puzzling customs, and important laws you'll encounter during sojourns to foreign lands. So relax, enjoy, and travel with us as we bring you a new issue every season.   ✿

Celebrate with us
by Jill Evans

In honor of our newsletter's maiden voyage, we'd like to invite you to an Open House at 7:00pm on January 11, 1991, at our offices. Please dress casually or come in your most fashionable travel togs.   ✿

Tropical travel
by Elizabeth Olson

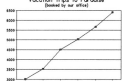

Travel to tropical islands is on the increase. Just look at the graph showing our

Inside...

FIGURE 20.1:

A newsletter with text in three newspaper-style columns

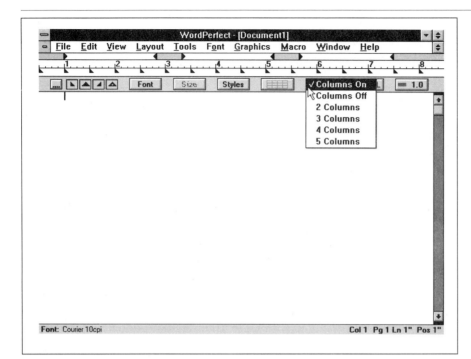

FIGURE 20.2:

To define up to five evenly-spaced newspaper columns, open the menu from the Columns button on the ruler, then choose one of the options.

If you don't want to activate the columns just yet, you can delete the [Col On] code now, then activate the columns later (as described in "Activating Newspaper Columns").

When you complete the steps above, WordPerfect will automatically format any text below the insertion point into the number of columns you chose, or if you selected the text first, it will rearrange only the selected text without affecting any text below it.

These steps insert two codes at the insertion point: a [Col Def:] code defines the number of columns and the column margins, and a [Col On] code activates the columns. These codes might look something like this in Reveal Codes (depending on your choices):

[Col Def:Newspaper;2;1",4";4.5",7.5"][Col On]

If you selected text before defining the columns, WordPerfect also inserts a [Col Off] code after the selected text to deactivate the column definition.

Once these codes are in place, you can activate or deactivate columns anyplace below (or to the right of) the [Col Def:] code (see the section "Deactivating Newspaper Columns" later in this chapter).

Defining Newspaper Columns with the Dialog Box

Although the Columns button on the ruler can be very handy for defining a few evenly-spaced newspaper columns, it won't be of much help when you need to define more than five columns, when you need to assign precise measurements for left and right column margins, or when you want to define parallel columns (as described later in this chapter). For these jobs, you must use the Define Columns dialog box. Follow these steps:

1. Position the insertion point above (or at) the paragraph where you want to start arranging text into columns, either before or after you've typed the text. Alternatively, you can select the text you want to arrange into columns.

2. Choose **Layout ➤ Columns ➤ Define** (or press Alt+Shift+F9 D), or double-click the Columns button on the Ruler. The Define Columns dialog box appears, shown in Figure 20.3.

3. If **Newspaper** is not already chosen for Type, choose it.

4. Enter the number of columns you want across each page in the Number of Columns text box.

5. By default, WordPerfect allows ½ inch of empty space between each column. If you want more or less space, enter a measurement (e.g., .25 or ¼ for ¼ inch, or 24p for 24 points) in the Distance Between Columns text box.

6. By default, WordPerfect makes each column the same width. These widths are listed in the Margins portion of the dialog box, with the left and right margin settings appearing to the right of the column numbers to which they apply. If you want to manually set the width of a margin, enter the margin positions in the Left and Right text boxes next to the column you want to change.

7. By default, WordPerfect automatically activates the columns at the insertion point. If you prefer not to activate the columns right now, mark the Columns **On** check box to remove the *X*.

8. When you're finished defining the columns, press ↵ or choose OK.

Column margin measurements are from the left edge of the page. Therefore, if the margins for the first column are 1" and 2.5", that column starts at the 1" left margin and is 1.5" wide. If the margins for the second column are 2.75" and 5.75", that leaves 0.25" between the first and second column, and the second column is 3" wide.

As when creating columns with the ruler, these steps insert a [Col Def:] code to define the column and a [Col On] code to activate the column (assuming you left columns turned on in step 7). If you selected text before defining the

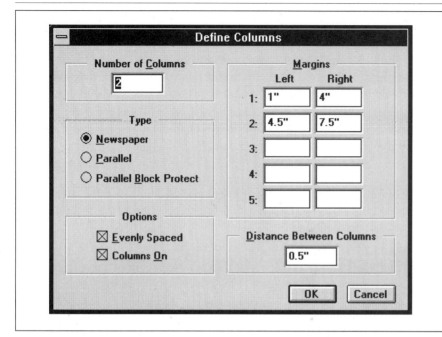

columns, WordPerfect also inserts a [Col Off] code after the selected text to deactivate the column definition. You can activate or deactivate columns anyplace below (or to the right of) the [Col Def:] code (see the next section).

TYPING AND EDITING IN NEWSPAPER COLUMNS

Typing and editing within columns is quite easy, although many experienced WordPerfect users prefer to type and edit all their text before putting it in columns. Whether you create your columns ahead of time or after you've typed in the text, it helps to know that WordPerfect treats each column as though it were a page.

For example, when you are typing along and reach the end of a column, the insertion point automatically moves to the top of the next column (just as typing off the end of a page automatically takes you to the top of the next page). If you insert a hard page break (by pressing Ctrl+↵) in a column, the insertion point is automatically positioned at the top of the next column. This is useful when you want to force text, such as an article title, to start at the top of a new column.

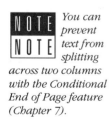
You can prevent text from splitting across two columns with the Conditional End of Page feature (Chapter 7).

Moving from Column to Column

Editing text in columns is quite easy: First you move the insertion point, then you type or edit the text as usual. To move the insertion point with your mouse, simply move the I beam to the mistake, and click the left button to place the insertion point there.

The Go To feature provides several options for moving the insertion point within a column and from one column to another. Follow these steps:

You can move left or right across columns by pressing Alt+→ or Alt+←.

1. Position the insertion point within a column.

2. Choose **Edit** ➤ **G**o To or press Ctrl+G. You will see the Go To dialog box.

3. Choose one of the following **P**osition options from the pop-up list (see the Go To dialog box below):

Top of Column: moves the insertion point to the top of the current column (same as pressing Alt+Home).

Bottom of Column: moves the insertion point to the bottom of the current column (same as pressing Alt+End).

Previous Column: moves the insertion point one column to the left (same as pressing Alt+←).

Next Column: moves the insertion point one column to the right (same as pressing Alt+→).

First Column: moves the insertion point to the first column.

Last Column: moves the insertion point to the last column.

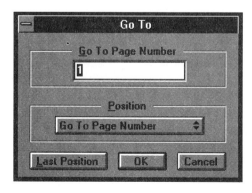

4. Press ↵ or choose OK.

Here are some additional tips for controlling the insertion point when editing text in a multicolumn layout:

Only text and graphics between the [Col On] and [Col Off] codes are formatted as columns.

◆ When adding new text at the end of the last column, make sure the insertion point is above and to the left of the [Col Off] code (if there is one) so that the new text is also in the column format.

◆ If you need to do a lot of editing and want to get rid of the columns, just delete the [Col On] code at the top of the text. Then do all your editing, go back to the top of the text (just to the right of the [Col Def] code), and reactivate the columns (described later). Optionally, just turn off side-by-side column display, as discussed below.

As an alternative to deactivating columns, you can just turn off the side-by-side display of the columns. This lets you edit the text within the columns, and see where one column ends and another begins, without the confusion of having multiple columns across the document window. Follow these steps:

1. With the insertion point anywhere in any document, choose **F**ile ➤ P**r**eferences ➤ **D**isplay. The Display Settings dialog box appears.

2. Choose the check box next to the Display **C**olumns Side by Side option in the dialog box to remove the *X*.

3. Choose OK or press ↵ to return to the document window.

In this format, each column is on a separate page in the document, and you can use Go To or the combination keys to move within columns or from column to column. (Of course, on the Print Preview screen and printed copy, the columns will still be side by side.) The side-by-side display will remain turned off until you deselect the Display Columns Side by Side check box.

DEACTIVATING NEWSPAPER COLUMNS

If you want to deactivate the columns so that text below the insertion point spans the page again, follow these simple steps:

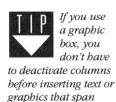

If you use a graphic box, you don't have to deactivate columns before inserting text or graphics that span two or more columns.

1. Position the insertion point where you want to deactivate the columns.

2. Choose **L**ayout ➤ **C**olumns ➤ Columns O**ff** (or press Alt+Shift+F9 F), or display the ruler and choose Columns Off from the Columns button pop-up list. (You can also deactivate columns by opening the Define Columns dialog box and choosing the Columns On check box to remove the *X*.)

WordPerfect inserts a [Col Off] code at the insertion point, and text below the insertion point ignores the previous column definitions. You can reactivate columns at any point below in the document or define a different set of columns if you wish, as described next.

ACTIVATING NEWSPAPER COLUMNS

By default, WordPerfect activates the columns with a [Col On] code as soon as you finish defining them. At times, however, you may want to deactivate columns, and then reactivate them later in your document. As long as you have defined the columns at least once in your document, you need not define them again unless you want to define additional columns with different settings. Once the columns are defined, you can turn them on at any time by following these steps:

1. Move the insertion point to the location where you want to activate the columns (the insertion point must be to the right of or below the [Col Def:] code), or select the text you want to format in columns.

2. Choose **Layout ➤ Columns ➤ On** (or press Alt+Shift+F9 O) from the pull-down menus, or display the ruler and choose Columns On from the Columns button pop-up list.

 Narrow margins often make text look too loose, particularly when text is fully justified. You can use WordPerfect's hyphenation feature (Chapter 11) to tighten the text.

A [Col On] code is inserted in your document at the insertion point. Any text to the right of and below the code is formatted into columns, in both the document window and on the Print Preview screen, unless you selected text first (in which case WordPerfect also inserts a [Col Off] code after the selected text to deactivate the column definition and reformats the selected text only). A look at Reveal Codes will show a [Col On] code where you activated the columns. You'll also notice that the Col indicator in the document window status bar shows the column number of the current location of the insertion point.

CREATING PARALLEL COLUMNS

TO CREATE PARALLEL COLUMNS,

move the insertion point to where you want the columns to begin, or select the text you want placed into columns. Follow the same steps as for creating newspaper-style columns by using the Define Columns dialog box, except choose Parallel or Parallel with Block Protect.

Parallel columns are similar to newspaper columns except that text does not "snake" from one column to the next. When text reaches the end of a column, it simply moves to the top of the same column on the next page.

WordPerfect offers two types of parallel columns:

Parallel Columns: Text in one column stays aligned with text in the next column, but text in any given column can be broken across two or more pages. This is useful for scripts and text with margin notes.

Parallel Columns with Block Protect: Same as Parallel Columns, but text in any given column does not break across pages, as with tables. Hence, if the page can't hold all the text in a column, all columns are bumped to the next page. This is useful for trip itineraries and schedules.

Figure 20.21, near the end of this chapter, shows an example of parallel columns (without Block Protect), where the main text of the document is in the right column, and a margin note and graphic are in the left margin. As text is added or deleted in the right margin, the margin note to the left will stay with the paragraph to its right.

Parallel columns with Block Protect are often used to type large, multiple-page tables. In general, using the Tables feature is easier, but it can slow down processing dramatically when the table spans several pages. So if you need to type a lengthy document formatted like a table, and you want to make sure text across each column stays aligned, you should probably use the Parallel Columns with Block Protect feature to format your text.

DEFINING AND ACTIVATING PARALLEL COLUMNS

You cannot create parallel columns by opening the ruler and ● choosing options from the Columns button. You can, however, double-click the button to open the Define Columns dialog box.

Unlike newspaper columns, parallel columns are not very simple or convenient if they're activated *after* you've typed your text. So it's a good idea to define and activate your parallel columns before typing the text that goes into the columns. The basic procedure is practically identical to that for defining and activating newspaper columns with the Define Columns dialog box:

1. Move the insertion point to where you want to begin the parallel columns.

2. Choose **Layout ➤ Columns ➤ Define** (or press Alt+Shift+F9 D). The Define Columns dialog box, shown earlier in this chapter, appears.

3. Choose either **Parallel** or Parallel **Block** Protect in the Type area of the dialog box.

4. Specify the number of columns, the distance between columns, and optionally the column margins, using the same techniques described in "Defining Newspaper Columns with the Dialog Box" earlier in this chapter.

5. If you want to activate the parallel columns now, leave the Columns **O**n check box marked. If you don't want to activate the columns now, choose the check box to remove the *X*.

6. Press ↵ or choose OK to return to the document screen.

As with newspaper columns, if you do not activate the columns immediately after defining them, you can activate them later by moving the insertion point to the top of the text (to the right of or below the [Col Def:] code) and choosing **L**ayout ➤ **C**olumns ➤ **O**n (or pressing Alt+Shift+F9 O), or by opening the ruler and choosing Columns On from the Columns button pop-up list.

TYPING AND EDITING IN PARALLEL COLUMNS

As with newspaper columns, WordPerfect treats each parallel column as a page. Therefore, to type in parallel columns, type the text in the current column, and press Ctrl+↵ to move to the next column. Each time you press Ctrl+↵, the insertion point moves to the next column (or back to the previous column if there is no column to the right).

Pressing Ctrl+↵ in parallel columns usually inserts a hard page break code ([HPg]) at the insertion point and moves the insertion point to the next column. However, if there is no column to the right of the current column when you press Ctrl+↵, WordPerfect inserts [Col Off] and [Col On] codes, which move the insertion point back to the first (leftmost) column.

If you defined Parallel Columns with Block Protect, the text in the first column begins with a [Block Pro:On] code, and the text in the last column ends with a [Block Pro:Off] code. These codes prevent the text across the columns from being split across two pages.

If you need to leave a column blank, either permanently or temporarily (because you don't yet know what to enter), you should still press Ctrl+↵ to move the insertion point to the "blank" column, and then move on to the next entry by pressing Ctrl+↵ again.

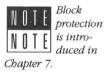

Block protection is introduced in Chapter 7.

When editing, you move the insertion point just as you do in newspaper columns:

◆ Move the I beam and click the left mouse button to move the insertion point to that position.

◆ To move within and across columns, choose **E**dit ➤ **G**o To (or press Ctrl+G), then choose one of the Position options: **T**op of Column, **B**ottom of Column, **P**revious Column, **N**ext Column, **F**irst Column, or **L**ast Column, depending on which direction you want to move. Then press ↵ or choose OK.

◆ As an alternative to using Go To, press a key combination to move within and across columns: Alt+Home (top of current column), Alt+End (bottom of current column), Alt+← (left one column), or Alt+→ (right one column).

If you discover that a section of text is in the wrong column while typing or editing, you can easily correct the problem by managing the codes (with Reveal Codes open), as summarized below:

◆ To move text one column to the left, delete the [HPg] code at the top of the text.

◆ To move text one column to the right, move the insertion point to the spot where you want to divide the text and press Ctrl+↵.

◆ To move text from the first (leftmost) column to the last (rightmost) column, first delete the [Col On] code that appears just before the text you want to move. Then press ← until you have highlighted the [Col Off] code that appears at the end of the last column. Delete that code and remove any extra [HRt] codes that you do not want. (If you defined Parallel Columns with Block Protect, you can also delete the [Block Pro:On] and [Block Pro:Off] codes.) This is handy if you accidentally press Ctrl+↵ in the last column and then type text in the first column that really belonged with the text in the last column.

DEACTIVATING PARALLEL COLUMNS

You deactivate parallel columns the same way you deactivate newspaper columns: Position the insertion point where you want the columns to end, and choose Layout ➤ Columns ➤ Off (or press Alt+Shift+F9 F) or open the ruler and choose Columns Off from the Columns button pop-up menu. From the insertion point down, you can resume typing with the normal margins or define a new set of columns. This lets you combine regular text with text that's formatted into parallel columns.

For example, Figure 20.4 shows text in two parallel columns after a [Col Def:] code and [Col On] code. The final [Col Off] code after the word *almonds* deactivates the columns, and text typed beneath that code is in paragraph format.

CHANGING THE COLUMN DEFINITIONS

NOTE NOTE
Only text and graphics between the [Col On] and [Col Off] codes are formatted as columns.

After defining newspaper or parallel columns, you may decide that you would rather have more or fewer columns, or you might want to adjust the margin settings for one or more columns. As with so many features, WordPerfect offers more than one way to skin the proverbial cat, and you can choose whichever method seems most convenient. For example, you can use the ruler to redefine the number of newspaper columns or to adjust the newspaper and parallel column margins visually. You can also use the Define Columns dialog box to make more precise changes, just as you did when creating the columns.

As mentioned earlier in this chapter, working with columns is much easier if you leave the Auto Code Placement feature turned on. This is especially true when you use the ruler to change columns, but also applies to changes you make with the Define Columns dialog box. For example, if you turn

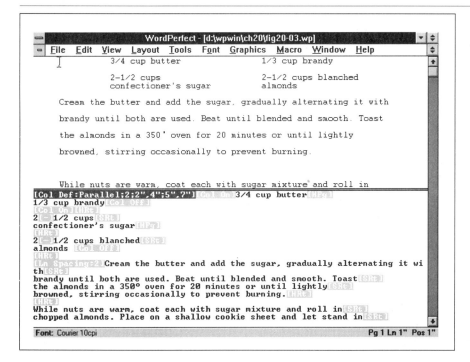

FIGURE 20.4:

An example of parallel columns and regular text combined

Auto Code Placement off, WordPerfect inserts a new [Col Def:] code *each time* you move a column margin, which can place a lot of unnecessary and potentially confusing codes in your document. Preventing these extra codes in the first place, by leaving Auto Code Placement on, is much easier than trying to delete all the extraneous codes later. The discussion below assumes that Auto Code Placement is on.

USING THE RULER TO ADJUST COLUMN WIDTHS

To use the ruler to adjust the width of newspaper or parallel columns, follow these steps:

1. If necessary, open Reveal Codes by choosing **V**iew ➤ Reveal **C**odes (Alt+F3).

2. If necessary, display the ruler by choosing **V**iew ➤ **R**uler or pressing Alt+Shift+F3.

3. Position the insertion point to the right of the [Col On] code for the column or columns you want to change.

4. Drag the left margin marker to adjust the left margin or the right margin marker to adjust the right margin of the column, as needed. As you drag the marker, broken vertical lines extend below the marker to help you adjust your column more accurately, as shown in Figure 20.5.

5. Release the mouse button when the column is the width you want.

6. Repeat steps 4 and 5 to adjust the current column again, or repeat steps 3, 4, and 5 as needed to adjust another column.

 When the insertion point is properly positioned in a column, you will see gray areas and marker triangles at the top of the ruler. The gray areas show the empty space between the columns; the triangles mark the left and right margins of each column.

When you release the mouse button in step 5, the text on-screen will be reformatted automatically and WordPerfect will change the [Col Def:] code to reflect the changes you made. If you change your mind *immediately* about a column adjustment, just choose Edit ➤ Undo, or press Alt+Backspace, and the column will return to its previous setting.

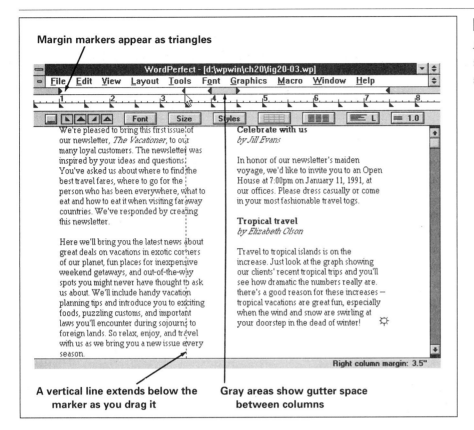

Margin markers appear as triangles

A vertical line extends below the marker as you drag it

Gray areas show gutter space between columns

FIGURE 20.5:
Drag the margin markers to narrow or widen your columns.

USING THE RULER TO CHANGE THE NUMBER OF COLUMNS

If you have defined newspaper-style columns, you can use the ruler to change the number of columns. Follow these steps:

1. If necessary, open Reveal Codes by choosing **View** ➤ Reveal **C**odes (Alt+F3).

2. If necessary, display the ruler by choosing **View** ➤ **R**uler or pressing Alt+Shift+F3.

3. Position the insertion point to the right of the [Col Def:] code for the columns you want to change.

4. Choose the number of columns you want from the Columns button pop-up list, as described earlier in this chapter.

> **NOTE** *This technique is useful only for newspaper-style columns and when you want to change the format to use up to five columns.*

The text will be reformatted to the number of columns you chose and the old [Col Def:] code will change to reflect the new settings. You can choose Edit ➤ Undo or press Alt+Backspace if you change your mind about the new settings.

USING THE DIALOG BOX TO CHANGE COLUMN DEFINITIONS

You can change any column setting, including the column type, by using the Define Columns dialog box. The steps are nearly the same as when creating columns:

1. If necessary, open Reveal Codes by choosing **View** ➤ Reveal **C**odes (Alt+F3).

2. Position the insertion point to the right of the [Col Def:] code for the columns you want to change.

3. Open the Define Columns dialog box by choosing **L**ayout ➤ **C**olumns ➤ **D**efine (Alt+Shift+F9 D) or by double-clicking the Columns button on the Ruler.

4. Change the settings in the dialog box, as described earlier.

5. When you are finished, press ↵ or choose OK.

The text will be reformatted automatically. You can change your mind about these new settings by choosing **E**dit ➤ Undo or pressing Alt+Backspace.

DELETING COLUMNS

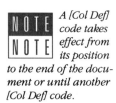

A [Col Def] code takes effect from its position to the end of the document or until another [Col Def] code.

Deleting columns is merely a matter of deleting the codes that define or activate them. This is more permanent than just deactivating the columns, because it returns all text between the [Col On] and [Col Off] codes to its normal margin-to-margin formatting.

To delete columns, open Reveal Codes, and then position the insertion point on the code you want to delete. You can delete just the [Col On] code that activates the columns, or you can delete the [Col Def] code that defines the columns.

In either case, the column formatting is removed, and text again extends from margin to margin. However, deleting only the [Col On] code allows you to reactivate columns later and has no effect on other [Col On] codes in your document. Deleting a [Col Def] code is more extreme, because it not only deletes the column definitions you set up but also deletes every [Col On] code up to the next [Col Def] code. As a result, you may end up deleting more columns than you bargained for.

THE EFFECT OF COLUMNS ON MARGINS

Once you've defined and activated newspaper or parallel columns, the position of the insertion point in relation to the [Col On] and [Col Off] codes affects formatting options in a variety of ways:

◆ When the insertion point is not between a [Col On] and a [Col Off] code, the terms *page* and *margin* have their usual meanings.

◆ When the insertion point is between a [Col On] and a [Col Off] code, the left and right margins are *always* the left and right margins of the current column (not the left and right margins of the page), and each column is essentially a "page."

Consider two examples of the latter point. If you are typing within a column and press Shift+F7 to center text or Alt+F7 to right-justify text, the text is centered or right-justified within the column, *not* the page margins. And if you add a ¼-inch tab stop just beneath a [Col On] code by using **Layout ➤ Line ➤ T**ab Set or the ruler, that tab stop is available at the left side of each column, not only at the left of each page.

USING COLUMNS WITH GRAPHIC BOXES AND LINES

Without a doubt, the snazziest desktop-published documents often use a combination of columns, graphic boxes, and lines. These documents also can be the most intimidating, since it's hard to imagine how to create such things. But if you remember the two basic points described in the preceding section, even combining graphics, lines, and columns can be fairly simple.

NOTE NOTE *See Chapter 19 for reminders on how to anchor and position graphic boxes.*

If you want a graphic box to always appear near specific text in a column, anchor the box to a paragraph or character in the column. When you define the horizontal position of the box, you can choose *Margin, Full* to make the box as wide as the column (not the page margins), *Margin, Right* to place the box against the right edge of the column (not the right edge of the page), *Margin, Left* to place the box against the left edge of the column, and *Margin, Center* to center the box within the column.

If you want the text in the columns to flow around the graphic box, or if you want the graphic box to be wider than a single column, you must anchor the box to the page. Ideally, you'll first want to position the insertion point at the top of the document (above [Col Def], [Col On], and all text). Then you can define the box's horizontal position in relation to the page margins or a column or range of columns.

Graphic lines (introduced in Chapter 5) follow the same basic rules as graphic boxes and formatting features in columns. For example, if you define a horizontal graphic line while the insertion point is within a column and set the line's horizontal position to Full, the line will be as wide as the column.

When defining the horizontal position of a vertical graphic line, you're given the option to place it between columns. If you do so, WordPerfect automatically centers the line to the right of the column you choose (splitting columns with lines is commonly used in newsletters and magazines).

Chapter 4 explains how to set left and right margins.

A few words of caution are now in order: If you are using graphics boxes or lines with columns, you should be certain to set the left margin of the *first* column to match the current left margin setting of the document. You should also set the right margin of the *last* column to match the current right margin setting of the document. Otherwise, you may have problems when placing the graphics.

USING WORDPERFECT'S TYPESETTING FEATURES

Whether or not your desktop-published document uses columns, WordPerfect offers quite a few features that give you more precise control over your page layout and the positioning and appearance of text. These "typesetting" features (as they are sometimes called) are discussed in the following sections.

CONTROLLING THE EXACT POSITION OF TEXT

TO POSITION TEXT PRECISELY ON THE PAGE,

move the insertion point to the text you want to position or to the place where you're about to type. Choose Layout ➤ Advance. Choose a direction to move the text, then type the distance to move it.

I discuss the Advance feature in terms of inches, but you can use any unit of measure allowed by WordPerfect (see Chapter 13).

WordPerfect's Advance feature lets you position text exactly on the page, relative to the insertion point on the screen. This can be helpful when you need to print at an exact position on a preprinted form or when you need to combine text and graphics. To use the Advance feature, follow these steps:

1. Move the insertion point to the start of the text that you want repositioned on the page (or where you are about to type the text).

2. Choose **Layout** ➤ **Advance**. You will see the Advance dialog box:

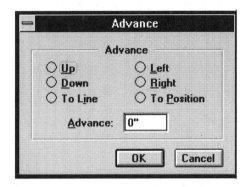

3. Choose the direction in which you want to move the text:

Up	Moves the text up without changing its horizontal position
Down	Moves the text down without changing its horizontal position
To **L**ine	Moves the text to a specific line on the page, measured in inches from the top edge of the page
Left	Moves the text to the left on the same line
Right	Moves the text to the right on the same line
To **P**osition	Moves the text to an exact horizontal position, measured from the left edge of the page

4. Enter the distance you want to move the text, in inches (e.g., *2.5* for 2½ inches) or in points (e.g., *2p* for 2 points).

5. Press ↵ or choose OK to return to your document.

Print Preview displays advanced text most accurately.

You can repeat these steps as needed, for example, to move text both up and to the right, or to an exact vertical and horizontal position on the page. These steps place a hidden [Adv] code in the document, which affects the document window, as well as the printed document and the Print Preview windows. For example, if you advance the print 2.5 inches to the right, WordPerfect places the hidden code [AdvRgt:2.5"] in the document, and the text is displayed in its new position. Whenever the insertion point is to the right of the advanced text, the Ln and Pos indicators in the lower-right corner of the screen indicate the actual position of the insertion point in relation to the printed page. (You can control the position of letters within a word by using manual kerning, discussed later.)

It's important to keep in mind that Advance codes are additive. That is, if you advance text 2 inches to the right, then change your mind and advance it 2.5 inches to the right, the result is a 4.5-inch advancement to the right if you don't delete the original [Adv] code.

Resuming Normal Printing

If you want to advance only a portion of text, you'll need to use Advance a second time to determine where the text that follows will be printed. If you moved the insertion point up, down, left, or right slightly, you can get back on track by moving the insertion point in the opposite direction by the same amount. For example, if you use Advance to move text up by 0.02 inches, then type the text to be moved up, you must use Advance to move text down by 0.02 inches to resume printing at the baseline.

You may want to resume printing exactly where you left off before you advanced a certain chunk of text. The easiest way to do this is to position the insertion point one character to the left of the [Adv] codes. Then, check the Ln and Pos indicators to determine position of the insertion point (jot these down). Next, move the insertion point to the start of the text that should be printed at the original insertion-point position (past the text that's already been advanced). Finally, use the Line and Position options on the Advance menu to position the text according to the Ln and Pos measurements.

CONTROLLING LETTER, WORD, AND LINE SPACING

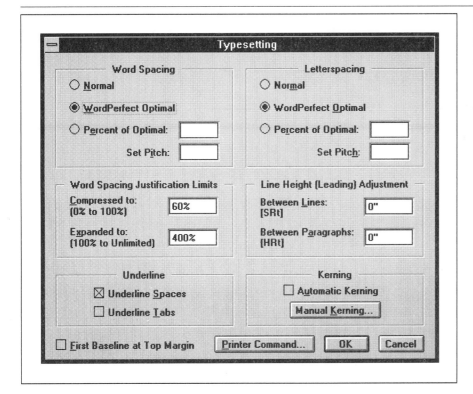

If your printer does not support a feature that the typesetting options offer, it ignores any settings you change.

Some printers allow precise control over the placement and spacing of text, and WordPerfect offers several typesetting options to support that control. To use the options, follow these steps:

1. Move the insertion point to where you want the feature to start in your document.

2. Choose **L**ayout ➤ Typesetting. The Typesetting dialog box appears (see Figure 20.6).

3. Choose an option and enter your settings.

4. When you're finished, press ↵ or choose OK to return to the document window.

FIGURE 20.6:

The Typsetting dialog box

The options available in the Typesetting dialog box are described in the sections that follow.

Using Automatic Kerning

Kerning is a technique used to reduce the amount of white space between certain combinations of letters by "tucking" smaller letters under larger ones. For example, look carefully at the word *Tools* on the first two lines of Figure 20.7. The top example is not kerned, and the bottom example is kerned so that the letter *o* is slightly tucked under the letter *T.* Similarly, the second sentence beginning with the word *Wonderful* is somewhat tighter because of kerning.

WordPerfect offers two kinds of kerning: automatic kerning and manual kerning (described in the next section). To activate automatic kerning, follow the general steps for using the typesetting options, and mark the check box next to Automatic Kerning. Automatic kerning does not affect the appearance of text in the document window, but it is visible on the Print Preview screen and the printed document.

If you want to turn off automatic kerning at some other place in your document, position the insertion point, go to the Typesetting dialog box, and remove the *X* from the Automatic Kerning check box. WordPerfect inserts a hidden [Kern:On] code where you activate kerning and a [Kern:Off] code where you deactivate it.

Your Word-Perfect package includes a file named KERN.TST in the \WPC subdirectory that lets you print a kerning table for your printer and base font.

Using Manual Kerning

You can use manual kerning whether or not automatic kerning is in effect.

If automatic kerning doesn't make a dramatic enough difference in the spacing between two letters, or you want to create some unusual effects with large text or headlines, you can use manual kerning. For example, in Figure 20.7, I used automatic kerning to move the letters closer together in the second example of *Tools.* But if I wanted to tuck the letter *o* even closer to the *T* (or farther away for that matter), I would need to use manual kerning.

In reality, manual kerning is just a special use of the Advance feature, but it's more convenient because you can make your adjustments interactively on the screen. Like Advance, manual kerning inserts an [AdvLft:] or [AdvRgt:]

into your document. Follow these steps:

1. Starting from the document window, position the insertion point between the letters you want to adjust. For instance, to move the *o* closer to the *T* in the example in Figure 20.7, you would place the insertion point to the right of the *T*.

_____**Kerning**

Tools
Tools

Wonderful Available Radar, VA: Unkerned
Wonderful Available Radar, VA: Kerned

_____**Word and Letter Spacing**
Optimal Word and Letter Spacing
2 0 0 %   o f   O p t i m a l
75% of Optimal

_____**Word Spacing Justification Limits**
This line demonstrates the word spacing justification limits (normal)

This line demonstrates the word spacing justification limits (100%)

E   V   E   N   L   Y

_____**Baseline**
The baseline is the invisible line that text is printed on. Line height is the distance between two baselines, and includes any leading between the top of tall letters and the next baseline above.

FIGURE 20.7:

Examples of WordPerfect typesetting options

2. Choose **L**ayout ➤ Typesetting.

3. Choose Manual **K**erning in the Kerning section of the Typesetting dialog box. You'll see the Manual Kerning dialog box:

Notice the vertical line that appears in the small Preview window, just to the left of the letter you'll be moving.

4. If you want to temporarily change the units of measure, open the pop-up list below the **U**nits option, and choose **I**nches, **C**entimeters, **P**oints, or **1**200ths.

5. In the **A**mount box, type the exact amount you want to move the letter. Typing a positive number moves the letter to the right; typing a negative number moves it to the left. Alternatively, you can click the upward-pointing triangle to increase the measurement, or click the downward-pointing triangle to decrease it. When you click, the Preview window changes to reflect the new amount.

6. Press ↵ or choose OK to return to the Typesetting dialog box.

7. Press ↵ or choose OK to return to the document window.

When you return to the document window, WordPerfect inserts an [AdvLft:] or [AdvRgt:] code, and the text will reflect the changes you made. If you want to kern the two letters again, simply repeat the steps above.

Setting Word and Letter Spacing

Word and letter spac-ing affect the spacing of text regardless of how it's justified.

The options listed under Word Spacing and Letterspacing in the Typesetting dialog box let you control the spacing between words and letters on some printers:

Normal	Uses the spacing the printer manufacturer considers best
WordPerfect Optimal	Uses the spacing that WordPerfect considers best (this is the default and may be the same as Normal)
Percent of Optimal	Lets you modify the Optimal setting by increasing or decreasing the spacing between letters and words as a percentage (for example, entering *110* increases spacing by 10 percent, and entering *90* decreases spacing by 10 percent)
Set Pitch	Lets you enter your own pitch (in characters per inch) for spacing

Figure 20.7 shows examples of word and letter spacing at optimal, 200 percent of optimal (the spacing is double its normal amount), and 75 percent of op-timal (the spacing is three-fourths its normal amount). If you choose Set Pitch, you can enter word or letter spacing as a characters-per-inch measurement. Your entry is automatically converted to a percentage of optimal. For example, if the Optimal setting is 10 characters per inch, and you set the pitch to 12 characters per inch, your choice is converted to 84 percent of optimal ($^{10}/12$ is about 0.84).

Setting Word-Spacing Justification Limits

The jus-tification settings are percent-ages of the current Word Spacing and Let-terspacing settings.

You can also adjust the compression and expansion used for printing fully justified paragraphs by choosing options listed under Word Spacing Justification Limits in the Typesetting dialog box. Normally, WordPerfect allows for 60 percent com-pression and 400 percent expansion of spacing between letters and words when printing fully justified text. The percentage is a percentage of an existing space. In lines that require expansion to be fully justified, WordPerfect first expands the spacing between words. When the limit for spacing between words is reached, WordPerfect then starts adjusting the spacing between characters.

The first paragraph starting with "This line demonstrates" in Figure 20.7 shows an example of the default spacing justification. The paragraph beneath it shows an example of 100 percent compression and expansion. Because WordPerfect can only expand the space between words to 100 percent (rather than 400 percent), it must also expand the space between letters; thus, the space between words is reduced, and the space between letters is increased.

Use the *Compressed to* option to enter a maximum compression limit in the range 0 to 100 (percent), and use the *Expanded to:* option to enter an expansion limit in the range 100 percent to unlimited (0). WordPerfect inserts a hidden [Just Lim:] code at the current insertion point.

If you want to space a few characters evenly across a line, like the word *EVENLY* in Figure 20.7, it's not necessary to change the word/letter spacing or word justification. Instead, try this trick:

1. Make sure the justification is set to Full (choose **L**ayout ➤ **J**ustification ➤ **F**ull, or press Ctrl+F) and Reveal Codes is open.

2. Type the word or words that you want to spread across the line.

3. Press the spacebar once to insert a blank space.

4. Repeatedly insert hard spaces (by pressing Ctrl+spacebar— they appear as [HdSpc] in Reveal Codes) until WordPerfect inserts a soft return [SRt] after the word or words you typed.

When you switch to the Print Preview screen, you'll see that the text is spaced evenly across the line.

Placing Baselines

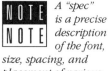

A "spec" is a precise description of the font, size, spacing, and placement of various text elements on a page.

The *baseline* is the invisible line on which each letter rests (see the bottom of Figure 20.7 for an illustration). If you need to control the exact position of each baseline on a page to match some publishing specs, you should first lock in the position of the first baseline on the page. Otherwise, if you increase the size of text printed at the first baseline, WordPerfect will move that baseline (and all the baselines beneath it) to avoid pushing the text up into the top margin.

If you mark the First Baseline at Top Margin check box, WordPerfect will print the first line of text inside the top margin, and the first baseline on the page will not move if you change the size of the print on that line. Consequently, all baselines below the first line will also remain fixed. This option is especially useful for publications that have facing pages or multiple columns, where you want text to line up evenly across the pages or columns.

To use this feature, follow these steps:

1. Set the top margin by choosing **L**ayout ➤ **M**argins (Ctrl+F8).

2. Choose **L**ayout ➤ Typesetting, mark the check box next to **F**irst Baseline at Top Margin, and press ↵ or choose OK.

3. Set a fixed line height by choosing **Layout ➤ Line ➤ Height** (Shift+F9 H), choosing **Fixed**, and pressing ⏎.

Once you've completed these steps, the baselines on the page will be spaced at exactly the intervals you specified for fixed line height, regardless of the fonts used on any line. (See "Setting the Line Height" later in this chapter for more information on baselines and line height.)

Adjusting Leading

The term "leading" comes from earlier typesetting days, when line spacing was inserted with strips of lead.

Leading (pronounced "ledding") is a typesetting term that refers to the vertical spacing of lines (the distance between two baselines). The Line Height (Leading) Adjustment options on the Typesetting dialog box let you change both the *primary* leading and *secondary* leading. (Primary leading is the spacing between lines in a paragraph; secondary leading is the spacing between paragraphs.) The Between Lines option controls the vertical spacing between lines within paragraphs; that is, lines that are separated by soft returns ([SRt] codes). The Between Paragraphs option controls the vertical spacing of lines between paragraphs; that is, lines that are separated by hard returns ([HRt] codes), which are entered whenever you press ⏎. Figure 20.8 shows examples of leading used to control the spacing between lines within paragraphs and between paragraph titles and the paragraphs themselves.

You can enter a leading adjustment in inches or fractions (e.g., ¹⁄72) or in points (e.g., *1p* for 1 point). You can also use negative numbers to reduce leading (e.g., *−1p* to remove a point of leading).

When you change the leading, WordPerfect inserts a hidden [Line Height Adj:] code at the insertion point. All text below the code up to the next [Line Height Adj:] code (if any) uses the leading measurements defined in the code. The text in the document window will not look any different, but you can see the change on the Print Preview screen and the printed document.

The Line Height (Leading) Adjustment options are very useful for expanding or contracting text to fill out a page. If the text is running a little short (that is, it doesn't quite reach the bottom of the page), you can increase the leading to increase the spacing between lines and better fill the space. If the text is running a little long (a couple of lines extend to the next page), you can decrease the leading a little to move some text back from the next page.

FIGURE 20.8:

Examples of leading

Leading Adjustment

WordPerfect adds two points of leading to proportionally spaced fonts, no leading to monospaced fonts. Here is the default leading with a proportionally spaced font.

Leading Between Lines [SRt]

In this example we've added 4 points (4p) of primary leading (between lines), so the lines in this paragraph are spaced wider.

Leading Between Paragraphs [HRt]

In this example we've added 8 points (8p) of secondary leading (between paragraphs), so the gap between this paragraph's title and this text is widened.

Using Alien Printer Commands

You cannot use the Printer Command option if you have chosen a Windows printer driver.

In the unlikely event that your printer offers some feature that WordPerfect can't access, you can use the Printer Command option in the Typesetting dialog box to send a code directly to the printer and activate that feature.

When defining the code to send to the printer, you must express command codes that are less than 32 or greater than 126 in angle brackets (<>). For example, if your printer requires the code Escape-E to activate a feature, that code must be expressed as <027>E (the ASCII code for the Escape character is 27). You can create a file of the codes to send to the printer by an ASCII text editor. (To determine the code required to activate a feature on your printer, refer to the printer's documentation.)

To insert a printer command code, move the insertion point to the place in your document where you want the special code to be sent to the printer, then go to the Typesetting dialog box and choose Printer Command. You'll see the dialog box:

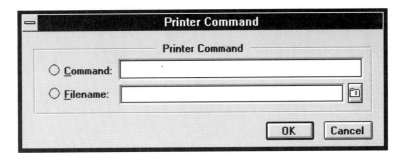

If you want to type the printer code directly, choose Command, type the printer code in the text box, and press ↵. If you've already stored the printer code in a file, choose Filename, type the name of the file, and press ↵. You can click the button to the right of the Filename text box to open up a dialog box that lets you search for and choose the file name you want.

If you view the document in Reveal Codes, you'll see that WordPerfect has inserted a [Ptr Cmnd:] code at the current insertion point. If you change your mind about sending this code to your printer, you can delete it.

SETTING THE LINE HEIGHT

You'll need to choose the Line Height option if you marked the First Baseline at Top Margin check box in the Typesetting dialog box.

Normally, WordPerfect automatically determines the height of a line by the height of the largest character on that line. You, in turn, can add or delete a little space between lines by changing the leading. You can also change the line height directly by turning off the automatic line height feature and entering a fixed line height. This gives you greater control over the spacing of lines and can be handy when you want to print on preprinted forms that also use fixed line heights, or when you need to control line spacing for publication specs.

To change the line height method to Fixed, follow these steps:

1. Move the insertion point to where you want the new line height to take effect (above or to the left of the lines).

2. Choose Layout ➤ Line ➤ Height (or press Shift+F9 H). You'll see this dialog box:

You cannot change the line height on printers that can only print six lines to the inch.

3. Choose **F**ixed.

4. Enter a height in inches or in points followed by a lowercase *p*.

5. Press ⏎ or choose OK to return to your document.

WordPerfect inserts a hidden [Ln Height:] code in the document at the insertion point, which affects all text to the end of the document or to the next [Ln Height:] code. (You can delete this code in Reveal Codes if you change your mind about the line height you've chosen.)

If you want to resume automatic line height later in the document, position the insertion point and repeat the steps above, but choose Auto rather than Fixed in the third step, and skip the fourth step.

If you need very precise line-height measurements, remember that line height is the measurement from one baseline to the next and is not based solely on the height of the tallest letter in that font. The line height also includes any leading that's built into the font.

WordPerfect does not add any leading to monospaced fonts; any extra leading is generally built in by the manufacturer of the font. Thus, if you are using a 10-point monospaced font from a manufacturer that has not added any leading, the line height for that font is 10 points.

For proportionally spaced fonts, WordPerfect adds two points of leading, in addition to any leading that the manufacturer adds. Thus, if you are using a 10-point proportionally spaced font from a manufacturer that has not added any leading, WordPerfect still adds two points of leading to the font, making the actual line height 12 points.

SOME DESKTOP PUBLISHING EXAMPLES

NOTE NOTE *Many of the features presented here are printer-specific, so when you print the finished example, it may not look exactly like the one you see in the figure.*

WordPerfect offers many advanced features to precisely control the appearance of your text and graphics, but it's not always easy to envision productive and creative ways of using these features without some examples to follow. In the sections that follow, I'll present some examples and a graphic presentation of the exact keystrokes used to create each example. You may want to try duplicating the examples by following the keystroke figure for each document at your computer. As you do so, keep an eye on the screen, and check the Print Preview screen every once in a while to monitor your progress and get an understanding of how each series of commands progresses toward the finished document.

When following the keystroke figures, keep in mind that some elements of the examples may not be available to you; these are presented in square brackets, as in [Times Roman 14pt]. In such cases, you may need to substitute a font or graphic image that is available to you if you want to continue following along.

TEXT WRAPPED AROUND A GRAPHIC

Figure 20.9 shows an example of text combined with a graphic with the aid of the Advance feature. Figure 20.10 shows the exact keystrokes used to create the example. This example uses two graphic boxes to accomplish the goal: The graphic image is in a box that has Wrap Text set to No, and the large text is in a User box that's printed right over the graphic (its Wrap Text option is set to Yes to make text in the outside paragraph wrap around the second, borderless box).

DROP CAPS

Figure 20.11 shows an example of a *drop cap,* where the first letter of a paragraph is large and dropped down. (Figure 20.12 shows the exact keystrokes used.) To create this, you put the large letter in a graphic User box at the start of the paragraph. But because WordPerfect allows room for a caption in a graphic box, you may have trouble getting the spacing around the box just right.

To deal with the extra-space problem in this example, Wrap Text was turned off around the User box where the letter *S* is stored. Then a smaller User box was created in the same position as the first one, and Wrap Text was left on so that the outside text wraps tighter around the drop cap.

In this example, the border is in a Figure box that has Wrap Text Around Box turned off. The text (Welcome) is in a User box. Both boxes are the same size and in the same position.

The User box prints over the Figure box because the Figure box's Wrap Text Around Box option is turned off. But the Wrap Text Around Box option is turned on for the User box, so text wraps around the User box.

Make sure that the hidden code for the box that wraps text comes after the code for the box that doesn't wrap the text.

FIGURE 20.10:

The keystrokes used to create the example shown in Figure 20.9

Graphics ▸ Figure ▸ Create ▸ File ▸ Retrieve ▸ BORD-2.WPG⏎
File ▸ Box Position ▸ Wrap Text Around Box⏎ File ▸ Close
Graphics ▸ User Box ▸ Create⏎
Font ▸ Font ▸ [Univers Bold 36pt] **⏎**
Layout ▸ Advance ▸ Down ▸ Advance ▸ 1.0⏎
Layout ▸ Advance ▸ To Position ▸ Advance ▸ 0.54⏎Welcome
Box Position ▸ Size ▸ Set Both ▸ Width ▸ 3.25 ▸ Height ▸ 2.35⏎
File ▸ Close

In this example, the border is in a Figure box that has Wrap Text Around Box turned off. The text (Welcome) is in a User box. Both boxes are the same size and in the same position.⏎
⏎
The User box prints over the Figure box because the Figure box's Wrap Text Around Box option is turned off. But the Wrap Text Around Box option is turned on for the User box, so text wraps around the User box.⏎
⏎
Make sure that the hidden code for the box that wraps text comes after the code for the box that doesn't wrap the text.

For a similar effect, create just one User box to hold the letter *S,* and leave Wrap Text turned on. Then place a User-box options code before the User box, reducing the outside border space on the right and on the bottom (to 0.12 inches and 0.05 inches, respectively, for this example).

S ometimes work itself can be a form of work avoidance. Recently, while writing a chapter that absolutely had to be done by 3:00, I suddenly had the urge to vacuum my closet. While waving the vacuum nozzle around without paying attention, I (or rather, the vacuum cleaner) sucked some ties off my tie rack. They came out of the hose looking like little silk prunes. So now there was another job to do--iron some ties.

FIGURE 20.11:

An example of drop-cap text

Graphics ▸ User Box ▸ Create⏎Font ▸ Font ▸ [Times Bold 72pt]⏎
S
Box Position ▸ Horizontal Position ▸ Margin, Left ▸ Wrap Text Around Box ▸
Size ▸ Set Both ▸ Width ▸ .55 ▸ Height ▸ .8⏎ File ▸ Close
Graphics ▸ User Box ▸ Create⏎
Box Position ▸ Horizontal Position ▸ Margin, Left
Size ▸ Set Both ▸ Width ▸ .5 ▸ Height ▸ .65⏎ File ▸ Close
Font ▸ Font ▸ [Times 14pt]⏎
ometimes work itself can be a form of work avoidance. Recently, while writing a chapter that absolutely had to be done by 3:00, I suddenly had the urge to vacuum my closet. While waving the vacuum nozzle around without paying attention, I (or rather, the vacuum cleaner) sucked some ties off my tie rack. They came out of the hose looking like little silk prunes. So now there was another job to do--iron some ties.

FIGURE 20.12:

The keystrokes used to create the drop cap shown in Figure 20.11

WHITE TEXT ON A BLACK BACKGROUND

If your printer can print white or shades of gray, you can print white text or a black background. Just create a graphic box with the gray shading set at 100 percent of black, and within that box, set the print color to white and type your text. Figure 20.13 shows an example, with the keystrokes used to create the example listed below it.

Reversed -- White on Black

Graphics ▸ User Box ▸ Options ▸ Gray Shading ▸ `100`↵
Graphics ▸ User Box ▸ Create↵
Box Position ▸ Horizontal Position ▸ Margin, Full ▸
Size ▸ Set Both ▸ Width ▸ `6.5` ▸ Height ▸ `.7`↵
↵
Font ▸ Font `[Univers Bold Italic 32pt]`↵
Font ▸ Color ▸ Predefined Colors ▸ White↵
Layout ▸ Line ▸ Center
`Reversed -- White on Black`
File ▸ Close

FIGURE 20.13:

White text on a black background, and the keystrokes used to create the example

RAISED OR FLOATING TEXT

Raised or floating text can add real drama, dimension, and depth to headlines and newsletter nameplates. With this special shadowing effect, the text seems to float off the page. If your printer can handle colors or shades of gray, you can create floating text by printing the text once in gray (or another color, such as red), advancing the printer up and to the left, then printing the text again in black. Figure 20.14 shows an example, with the keystrokes used to create the example listed below it.

WordPerfect

↵
Layout ▸ Justification ▸ Center
Font ▸ Font `[Times Bold Italic 72pt]`↵
Font ▸ Color ▸ Predefined Colors ▸ Red↵`WordPerfect`
Layout ▸ Advance ▸ Up ▸ Advance ▸ .052↵
Layout ▸ Advance ▸ Left ▸ Advance ▸ 5.2↵
Font ▸ Color ▸ Predefined Colors ▸ Black↵`WordPerfect`

FIGURE 20.14:

Floating or raised text, and the keystrokes used to create the example

NEWSLETTER

Newsletters are one of the most common applications of WordPerfect's desktop publishing features and generally use some combination of fonts, columns, graphic images, and graphic lines. Figure 20.1 at the start of this chapter shows one example. Figure 20.15 shows the keystrokes used to create the basic layout for that newsletter.

Styles are covered in Chapter 14.

When creating documents of this complexity on your own, you'll probably want to use styles for the main elements, such as article titles, bylines, and body text. This makes it easy to globally change the appearance of each element throughout a document.

TWO-FOLD MAILER

Figure 20.16 shows an empty two-fold mailer format, and Figure 20.17 shows the keystrokes used to create it. Figure 20.18 completes the sequence by showing an example of the basic layout put to use. Essentially, this is a three-column newspaper-style format, so once the basic layout is complete, you just press ↵ a few times, then type the text for the brochure ("Do you know the true value…"), changing the fonts as desired. When you're ready to format the text and graphics on the opposite flap of the brochure, you press Ctrl+↵ twice to move to the last column.

```
Graphics ▸ Text Box ▸ Create ▸ Box Position ▸
Horizontal Position ▸ Margin, Full ▸
Size ▸ Set Both ▸ Width ▸ 6.5 ▸ Height ▸ 2.24 ↵
Font ▸ Font [Nameplate font (62pt) and The Vacationer (Flush
Right)]
File ▸ Close

Graphics ▸ Text Box ▸ Create ▸ Box Position ▸ Vertical Position ▸ Bottom ▸
Horizontal Position ▸ Margin, Right ▸
Size ▸ Set Both ▸ Width ▸ 4.12 ▸ Height ▸ 2.12 ↵
Font ▸ Font ▸ [Font and Inside...]
File ▸ Close

Font ▸ Font ▸ [Univers 14pt] ↵
Vol. Shift + F7           Centered Alt + F7              Date
Graphics ▸ Line ▸ Horizontal ↵ ↵ ↵

Layout ▸ Columns ▸ Define ▸ 3 ▸ Distance Between Columns ▸ .35 ↵
```

FIGURE 20.15:

The keystrokes used to create the basic layout of the newsletter shown in Figure 20.1

Your Return
Address Goes
Here

FIGURE 20.16:
A basic two-fold mailer layout

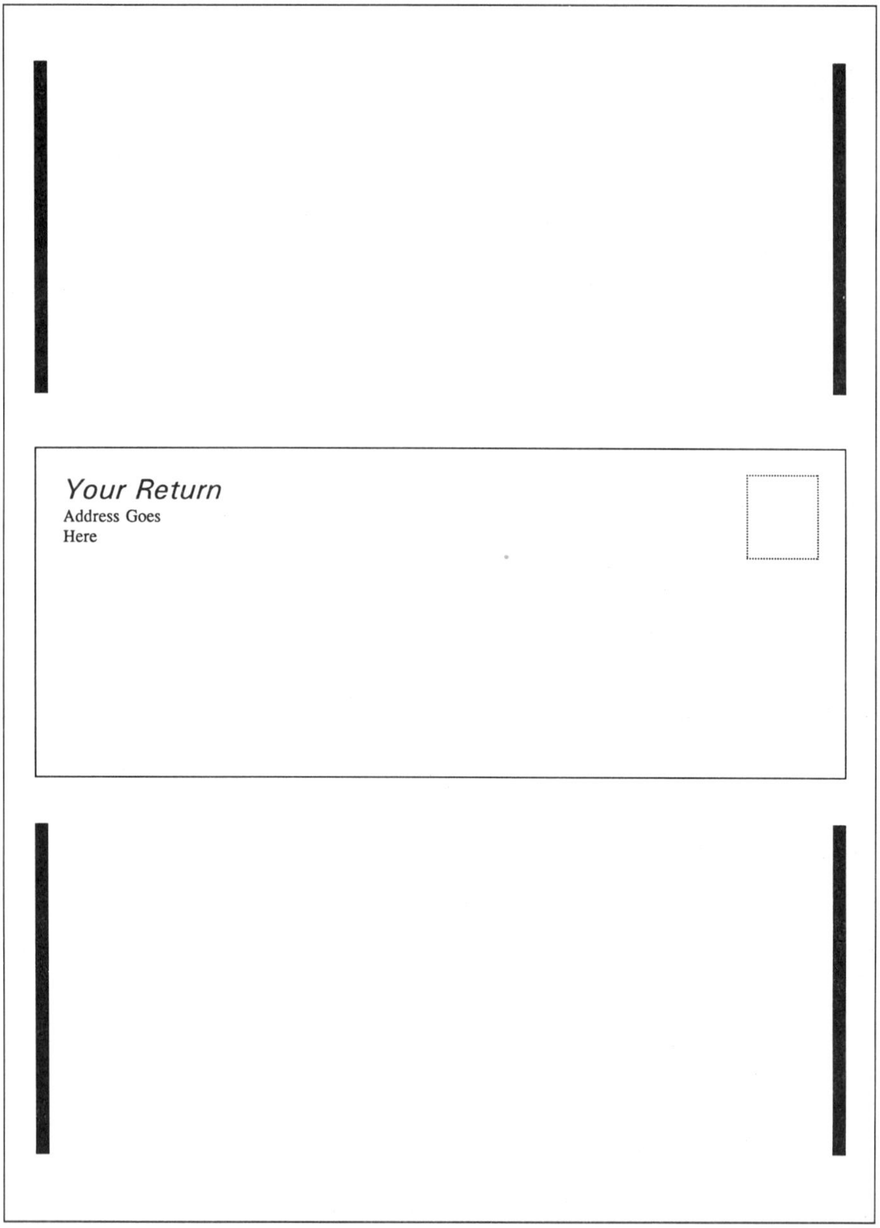

FIGURE 20.17:

The keystrokes used to create the layout in Figure 20.16

```
Layout ▸ Page ▸ Paper Size ▸ [Standard - Rotated font]⏎
Layout ▸ Margins ▸ .3 [Tab] .3 [Tab] .3 [Tab] .3⏎
Layout ▸ Columns ▸ Define ▸ 3⏎

Graphics ▸ Line ▸ Horizontal ▸ Vertical Position ▸ Specify ▸ Position ▸ 0.3 ▸
Thickness ▸ 0.13⏎

Graphics ▸ Line ▸ Horizontal ▸ Vertical Position ▸ Specify ▸ Position ▸ 8.07 ▸
Thickness ▸ 0.13⏎

Graphics ▸ Line ▸ Horizontal ▸ Horizontal Position ▸ Specify ▸ Position ▸ 7.5 ▸
Vertical Position ▸ Specify ▸ Position ▸ 0.3 ▸ Length ▸ 3.13 ▸
Thickness ▸ 0.13⏎

Graphics ▸ Line ▸ Horizontal ▸ Horizontal Position ▸ Specify ▸ Position ▸ 7.5 ▸
Vertical Position ▸ Specify ▸ Position ▸ 8.07 ▸ Length ▸ 3.13 ▸
Thickness ▸ 0.13⏎

Graphics ▸ User Box ▸ Create⏎ Box Position ▸ Vertical Position ▸ Top ▸
Horizontal Position ▸ Column, Left ▸ Columns ▸ 2 ▸ Wrap Text Around Box ▸
Size ▸ Set Both ▸ Width ▸ 1.05 ▸ Height ▸ 1.1⏎
Font ▸ Font ▸ [Courier 12cpi]⏎⏎⏎
Layout ▸ Tables ▸ Create ▸ 1⏎
Layout ▸ Tables ▸ Lines ▸ Outside ▸ Dotted⏎
Layout ▸ Tables ▸ Options ▸ Right⏎⏎⏎⏎
[Open Ruler (Alt+Shift+F3) and adjust right cell margin until
"Right margin" in status line indicates a width of about 0.8]
File ▸ Close

Graphics ▸ Figure ▸ Options ▸ Left ▸ .3 [Tab] .3 [Tab] .3 [Tab] .3⏎

Graphics ▸ Text Box ▸ Create ▸
Font ▸ Font ▸ [font for return address]⏎
[type return address]
Rotate ▸ Rotate 90⏎
Box Position ▸ Box Type ▸ Figure ▸ Vertical Position ▸
Full Page ▸ Horizontal Position ▸ Column, Full ▸ Columns ▸ 2⏎ File ▸ Close
```

FLIER

The sample flier in Figure 20.19 was printed on a PostScript printer and uses graphic images from the DrawPerfect package. Obviously, not everyone has this much printer power or the need to create documents quite so complex. But in case you're interested in giving it a whirl, Figure 20.20 shows the keystrokes used to create this example.

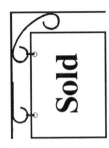

Apgar Realty

Sold

Serving Cuesta Verde Since 1991

Apgar Realty
P.O. Box 1234
Cuesta Verde, CA 92067

Do you know the true value of your home?

Few people realize the value of their home in today's market. If you'd like to find out the current market value of your home, just call Apgar Realty for a free appraisal. One of our qualified professionals will gladly stop by to appraise your property. And it won't cost you a penny.

Of course, should you decide to sell your home now, and cash in on some of that wonderful equity, we can help you do that as well.

Just think of what you could do with all that cash. You could buy fancy cars, jewelry, yachts, or just take an ocean cruise around the world. Or if you're more frugal than that, you could buy another house exactly like the one you're in now (don't forget, yours isn't the *only* house on the block that's gone up in value).

For more information on what Apgar Realty can do for you today, just look inside this wonderful brochure. Trust us, you'll be glad you did.

FIGURE 20.18:
An example of the two-fold mailer layout put to use

FIGURE 20.19:

A sample flier, printed with a PostScript printer

Layout ▸ Page ▸ Paper Size ▸ [Standard - Rotated font]⏎
Layout ▸ Margins ▸ .3 [Tab] .3 [Tab] .3 [Tab] .3⏎
Layout ▸ Page ▸ Center Page
Layout ▸ Justification ▸ Center

Graphics ▸ User Box ▸ Create ▸ Figure Editor⏎
File ▸ Retrieve ▸ [Border Graphic]⏎ File ▸ Box Position ▸ Vertical Position ▸
Full Page ▸ Horizontal Position ▸ Margin, Full ▸ Wrap Text Around Box⏎ File ▸ Close

Graphics ▸ User Box ▸ Create ▸ Figure Editor⏎
File ▸ Retrieve ▸ [Dog Graphic]⏎ File ▸ Box Position ▸ Position ▸ 2.45 ▸
Position ▸ 1 ▸ Width ▸ 3 ▸ Wrap Text Around Box⏎ File ▸ Close

Graphics ▸ User Box ▸ Create ▸ Figure Editor⏎
File ▸ Retrieve ▸ [Dog Graphic]⏎ File ▸ Box Position ▸ Position ▸ 2.45 ▸
Position ▸ 7 ▸ Width ▸ 3 ▸ Wrap Text Around Box⏎ Edit ▸ Mirror
File ▸ Close

Font ▸ Font ▸ [ITC Bookman Demi 36pt] ▸ Outline ▸ Shadow⏎
So How's About a Donation?→ → ⏎ ⏎
Font ▸ Color ▸ Red ▸ 90 ▸ Green ▸ 90 ▸ Blue ▸ 90⏎
Font ▸ Font ▸ [ITC Zapf Dingbats 36pt]⏎
Font ▸ WP Characters ▸ 12,113⏎
Font ▸ Font ▸ [Palatino Italic 36pt]⏎ $10.00⏎
Font ▸ Color ▸ Red ▸ 70 ▸ Green ▸ 70 ▸ Blue ▸ 70⏎
Font ▸ Font ▸ [ITC Zapf Dingbats 36pt]⏎
Font ▸ WP Characters ▸ 12,113⏎
Font ▸ Font ▸ [Palatino Italic 36pt]⏎ $49.99⏎
Font ▸ Color ▸ Predefined Colors ▸ Gray ⏎
Font ▸ Font ▸ [ITC Zapf Dingbats 36pt]⏎
Font ▸ WP Characters ▸ 12,113⏎
Font ▸ Font ▸ [Palatino Italic 36pt]⏎ $74.99⏎
Font ▸ Color ▸ Predefined Colors ▸ Black⏎
Font ▸ Font ▸ [ITC Zapf Dingbats 36pt]⏎
Font ▸ WP Characters ▸ 12,113⏎
Font ▸ Font ▸ [Palatino Italic 36pt]⏎ $99.99⏎ ⏎
Font ▸ Font ▸ [ITC Bookman Light 18pt]⏎
for the Font ▸ Font ▸ [ITC Zapf Dingbats 30pt]⏎
Layout ▸ Advance ▸ Down ▸ Advance ▸ 0.05⏎
Font ▸ Font ▸ Outline⏎ Font ▸ WP Characters ▸ 12,100⏎
Font ▸ Font ▸ [ITC Bookman Demi 30pt]⏎
Layout ▸ Advance ▸ Up ▸ Advance ▸ .02⏎
Font ▸ Font ▸ Shadow⏎ Save the Snowflake →
Layout ▸ Advance ▸ Down ▸ Advance ▸ .02⏎
Font ▸ Font ▸ [ITC Zapf Dingbats 30pt] ⏎
Font ▸ WP Characters ▸ 12,100⏎
Font ▸ Font ▸ [ITC Bookman Light 18pt]⏎
Layout ▸ Advance ▸ Up ▸ Advance ▸ 0.05⏎ society⏎ ⏎
Font ▸ Font ▸ [Palatino 22pt]⏎
P.O. Box 1234⏎
Corn Flake, CA 91234

MARGIN NOTE

Styles and macros are covered in detail in Part 4.

For added convenience, you can assign the macro to the Button Bar or Macro menu.

Figure 20.21 shows a small passage of text with a margin note in the left margin, which illustrates a practical application of the Parallel Columns feature. Using this complicated format for a long document can grow tiresome, so I created a style and macro to simplify things. Figure 20.22 shows the keystrokes used to type the example *after* creating the style and macro discussed in a moment.

After creating the style and macro, it is easy to type a margin note with the wise-owl graphic next to it: You need only choose Macro ➤ Play (or press Alt+F10), double-click the name of the macro (for example, NOTE.WCM), then type the text of the note and press ↵. The macro handles all the tedious tasks of creating the note: It switches to the left column, creates the owl graphic, waits for you to type the text of the note, then switches back to the right column.

Creating the Style

Figure 20.23 shows the paired style used to set up the margin note, with Enter Key Inserts set to Style Off.

The codes within the style are summarized below:

[Line Height Adj:–00014",0"]: This code, entered via Layout ➤ Typesetting ➤ Line Height (Leading) Adjustment, reduces the leading of text within the margin note slightly for a tighter text appearance.

This small passage illustrates a practical application of parallel columns: notes in the left margin. It also demonstrates a way to combine two of WordPerfect's more advanced features to simplify your work, Styles and Macros.

This is a margin note, created with a macro, but formatted with a style.

In this example, parallel columns were defined and activated at the top of the document. Then a style was created, named Tip, to format the margin notes and put in the graphic. Then a macro was created, named note, so that a margin note could be typed at any time simply by pressing Alt+F10, double-clicking note.wcm, typing the note, and pressing Enter.

This combination of features makes it easy to type even a seemingly complex document like this one. Furthermore, you can create styles for other kinds of margin notes, such as Notes and Warnings, as well as icons.

FIGURE 20.21:

Sample text from a document with a margin note and graphic

```
Layout ▶ Columns ▶ Define ▶ Parallel ▶
Margins ▶ 1 [Tab] 2.5 [Tab] 2.75 [Tab] 7.5 [⏎]
Font ▶ Font ▶ [Times 12pt][⏎]
[Ctrl]–[⏎]
```
                    This small passage illustrates a practical
                    application of parallel columns: notes in the
                    left margin. It also demonstrates a way to
                    combine two of WordPerfect's more advanced
                    features to simplify your work, Styles and
                    Macros.
                    [⏎]
                    [⏎]
This is a   Macro ▶ Play ▶ note[⏎] In this example,
margin note,   parallel columns were defined and activated at
created with a   the top of the document. Then a style was
macro, but   created, named Tip, to format the margin notes
formatted with   and put in the graphic. Then a macro was
a style.[⏎]   created, named note, so that a margin note
                    could be typed at any time simply by pressing
                    Alt+F10, double-clicking note.wcm, typing the
                    note, and pressing Enter.
                    [⏎]
                    [⏎]
                    This combination of features makes it easy to
                    type even a seemingly complex document like
                    this one. Furthermore, you can create styles
                    for other kinds of margin notes, such as Notes
                    and Warnings, as well as icons.

FIGURE 20.22:

The keystrokes used to create Figure 20.21 after creating the style and NOTE.WCM macro

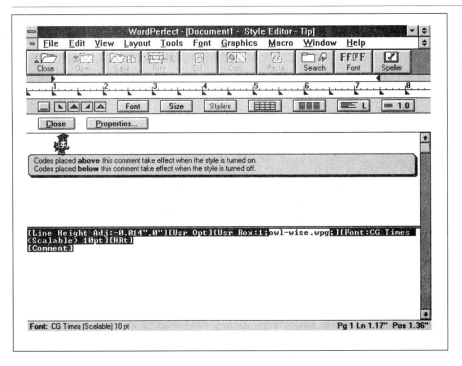

FIGURE 20.23:

A sample style to format margin notes with a graphic and 10-point font

[Usr Opt]: This code, entered via Graphics ➤ User Box ➤ Options, sets the inside border space for User boxes to 0" on all sides, so text wraps close to the graphic image.

User Box:1;owl-wise.wpg]: This code entered via Graphics ➤ User Box ➤ Create, displays the owl graphic in the margin note. The box is anchored to the paragraph, with a horizontal position of Left Margin, a width of 0.36", and a height of 0.45".

[Font…]: This code, entered via the Font ➤ Font options, defines the font of text in the note as Times 10-point.

[HRt]: This code, entered by simply pressing ↵, inserts a blank line to align the start of the text near the center of the graphic.

The [Comment] code is the code that WordPerfect always inserts in a paired style.

Creating the Macro

Figure 20.24 shows the macro that you can create to further simplify using the style. (I actually recorded the keystrokes for this macro, then later edited the macro to insert the PauseKey(0) command and comments.)

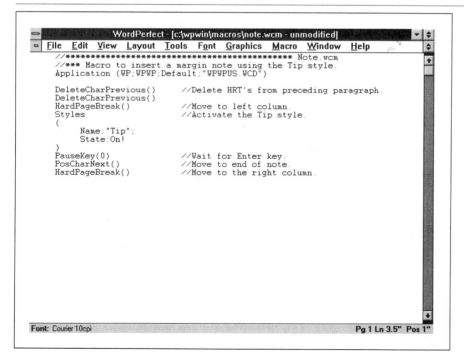

FIGURE 20.24:

A sample macro to simplify the use of the Tip style for inserting margin notes

```
WordPerfect - [c:\wpwin\macros\note.wcm - unmodified]
File  Edit  View  Layout  Tools  Font  Graphics  Macro  Window  Help
//*********************************************** Note.wcm
//*** Macro to insert a margin note using the Tip style.
Application (WP;WPWP;Default;"WPWPUS.WCD")

DeleteCharPrevious()      //Delete HRT's from preceding paragraph.
DeleteCharPrevious()
HardPageBreak()           //Move to left column.
Styles                    //Activate the Tip style.
(
     Name:"Tip";
     State:On!
)
PauseKey(0)               //Wait for Enter key.
PosCharNext()             //Move to end of note.
HardPageBreak()           //Move to the right column.




Font: Courier 10cpi                                    Pg 1 Ln 3.5" Pos 1"
```

Here's how the commands in this macro work:

DeleteCharPrevious( ): This macro assumes that each paragraph in the main text is separated by two hard returns. The two DeleteChar-Previous commands near the top of the macro delete the two hard returns between two paragraphs, in preparation for moving to the left column.

HardPageBreak( ): moves the insertion point into the left column.

Styles(Name:"Tip";State:On!): turns on the Tip style described in the previous section.

PauseKey(0): pauses the macro, giving you time to type the text of the margin note. When you press ↵ after typing the text of the note, macro execution resumes at the next line.

PosCharNext( ): moves the insertion point past the hard return that ends the margin note.

HardPageBreak( ): moves the insertion point back over to the right column, where you can resume typing normal text.

Using the Macro and Style

To use the macro and style correctly, you must first define two parallel columns, and load the Tip style described earlier, in the current document. Press Ctrl+↵ to move to the rightmost column, and start typing "regular" body text in the right column. Separate each paragraph of body text with two hard returns (by pressing ↵ twice).

To use the macro, position the insertion point at the first character of an existing paragraph, or press ↵ twice to end the previous paragraph so that the insertion point is placed where you're about to type a new paragraph.

Run the Note macro with the Macro ➤ Play options, and type the text of the note. Then press ↵. The margin note appears in the left column, and the insertion point appears in the right column, where you can resume typing normal text.

At any time, you can reformat all the margin notes, or change the graphic in each note, simply by changing the Tip style. You could also create similar styles and macros to insert other types of margin notes, such as Cautions or Notes, each with its own graphic, like the margin notes used throughout this book.

With the help of Chapter 19 and this chapter, you've mastered some new techniques for working with text, lines, graphics, and multiple columns—key ingredients for producing publication-quality documents. In the next chapter,

I'll look at a somewhat specialized task in desktop publishing: creating equations. If your work involves mathematical, scientific, or engineering publications, you're sure to appreciate WordPerfect's Equation Editor.

CHAPTER 21

Adding Equations to Your Documents

or mathematicians, scientists, and the people who type their documents, WordPerfect offers the Equations feature. This feature lets you type complex mathematical equations into a document and print them using all the special symbols and typesetting standards. Note, however, that the Equations feature does not *solve* the equations for you; it just lets you *edit* them. The Equation option on the Graphics pull-down menu contains everything you need to produce professional-looking equations. Figure 21.1 shows a sample equation typed with Word-Perfect.

WordPerfect follows standard rules of typesetting when printing equations:

◆ The equation is centered horizontally and vertically on its own line.

◆ Variables are printed in italics.

The equation below demonstrates some of the capabilities of WordPerfect's equation editor. You can find a similar equation in the WordPerfect PRINTER.TST file to see how it looks in the equation editor.

$$\int_0^\infty x^{n-1} e^{-x} dx = \int_0^1 \left(\log \frac{1}{x} \right) dx = \frac{1}{n} \prod_{m=1}^\infty \frac{\left(1 + \frac{1}{m} \right)}{1 + \frac{n}{m}} = \Gamma(n) , \ n > 0$$

Equations follow typesetting standards; they are centered on their own lines, and variable names are printed in italics. However, you can change those standards, and put an equation anywhere you wish, even right in your text.

◆ Numbers and mathematical functions are printed in a roman (non-italicized) font.

As you'll learn later, you can change any of these defaults.

CREATING EQUATIONS

▌ TO CREATE AN EQUATION,

move the insertion point to where you want to place the equation, then choose Graphics ➤ Equation ➤ Create.

You can use View ➤ Button Bar Setup in the Equation Editor to change the appearance and the position of the Button Bar, and to add your own buttons.

You can place equations in any of the five types of graphic boxes discussed in Chapter 19, although for this purpose, it's often simplest to stick with using Equation boxes. WordPerfect offers a special *Equation Editor* for creating, editing, and previewing your equations. To add an equation to a document and access the Equation Editor, follow these steps:

1. If you've already typed some or all of the text in the document, move the insertion point to the line where you want to place the equation.

2. Choose **G**raphics ➤ **E**quation ➤ **C**reate. You'll be taken to the Equation Editor.

Figure 21.2 shows the Equation Editor, after a sample equation has been typed and zoomed. It's divided into three major sections, as shown in the figure: the display pane in the bottom-right portion shows the equation graphically (much as it will be printed); the editing pane in the upper-right portion is used to type in and edit the equation; and the equation palette on the left contains commands, symbols, and functions you can insert in the equation instead of, or in addition to, typing them from the keyboard. There's also a Button Bar, which displays equation-related command shortcuts, and a status bar at the bottom of the screen.

TYPING EQUATIONS

Typing and editing an equation in the editing pane is much like typing and editing any other text in WordPerfect, with some differences. For the most part, you can type symbols and special operators either from the keyboard or from the various equation palettes, as described a little later.

While the insertion point is in the editing pane, you can use the usual editing techniques to modify the equation. For example, you can use your

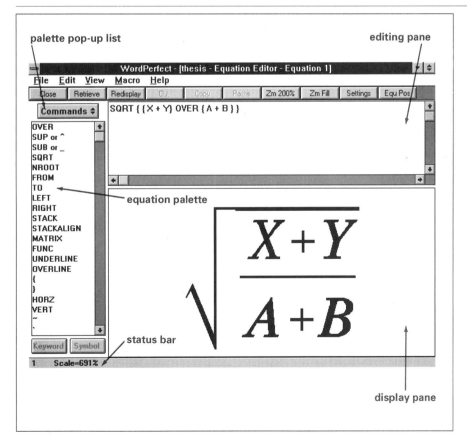

mouse and the ← and → keys to position the insertion point. You can also use the Backspace and Delete keys to delete characters, and the Insert key to switch between Insert and Typeover modes.

When you're ready to see a graphical representation of what you've typed so far, you can choose View ➤ Redisplay, and then look at the display pane.

 *You can also click the Redisplay button in the Button Bar to refresh the display pane.*

When you are satisfied with the looks of the equation, choose File ➤ Close or press Ctrl+F4 to save it in the document. If you decide that you don't want the equation in the document, choose File ➤ Cancel.

The Role of Braces

When you're entering equations in WordPerfect, you should type them as they might be spoken aloud and use braces ({ }) to group items together. For example, the expression shown in Figure 21.2 could be expressed verbally as "the square root of $X + Y$ over $A + B$." This expression is expressed in the Equation Editor as

SQRT {{X+Y} OVER {A+B}}

Because everything to the right of the SQRT command must be under the radical, this entire portion of the expression is enclosed in braces. And, because the entire $X + Y$ portion should be placed over the entire $A + B$ portion, each of these is also contained in its own braces. Figure 21.3 shows more examples illustrating the important role played by braces.

 The same error message may be displayed if your equation uses equation commands improperly, even though the braces are correct.

It's important that the braces in an equation make sense. For example, if you have more open braces than closing braces, or vice versa, the Equation Editor will not be able to make sense of the grouping. Hence, when you choose View ➤ Redisplay to view such an equation, you'll see the message "<<ERROR: Incorrect syntax>>" displayed in the status bar, and the display pane will remain blank.

Entering Blanks and New Lines

Blanks entered with the spacebar are used to separate equation commands, but these blank spaces are *not* part of the final equation. If you want to include a blank space in an equation, type a tilde (~) where you want the blank space to appear.

You can also insert a thin space (a quarter space) by using the backward accent character (`). (It's on the same key as the tilde on most keyboards.) Use one accent to add a quarter space, two accents to add a half space, and so

SQRT X+Y OVER A+B	$\sqrt{X}+\dfrac{Y}{A}+B$
SQRT {X+Y} OVER A+B	$\dfrac{\sqrt{X+Y}}{A}+B$
SQRT X+Y OVER {A+B}	$\sqrt{X}+\dfrac{Y}{A+B}$
SQRT X+{Y OVER A}+B	$\sqrt{X}+\dfrac{Y}{A}+B$
SQRT {X+Y OVER A+B}	$\sqrt{X+\dfrac{Y}{A}+B}$
SQRT {{X+Y} OVER {A+B}}	$\sqrt{\dfrac{X+Y}{A+B}}$

FIGURE 21.3:

The use of braces in equations

forth. The tilde and accent appear only in the editing pane, never in the printed document.

Pressing ↵ while editing an equation moves the insertion point to the next line, as in a normal document window. However, this does not insert a line break in the actual equation (it just gives you more room to type the equation and makes the editing pane easier to read). To stack items in an equation, you need to use the STACK, STACKALIGN, MATRIX, #, or similar commands described later.

Typing Numbers, Variables, and Operators

> **NOTE NOTE** *When typing a real number containing a decimal point or negative sign, you must surround the number in braces.*

You will need to type numbers and variables (such as x, y, a, and b) directly from the keyboard. And because the following operators and symbols aren't on the equation palette, you'll also need to type them directly from the keyboard:

+ − * / = < > ! ? .¦ @ " , ;

In addition, you can type commands like SQRT and OVER directly from the keyboard, in either upper- or lowercase letters, provided that you know the exact command to use. Similarly, you can type special symbols by choosing Edit ➤ WP Characters or pressing Ctrl+W. When you are first learning to use the Equation Editor, however, you'll probably prefer to choose most commands and symbols from the equation palette.

USING THE EQUATION PALETTE

You can choose commands or special symbols from the equation palette anytime you are in the Equation Editor by following these steps:

```
✓ Commands
   Large
   Symbols
   Greek
   Arrows
   Sets
   Other
   Functions
```

1. With the insertion point in the editing pane, move the insertion point to the location where you want to place an item from a palette.

2. Click in the equation palette or choose a group from the palette pop-up list, shown at left. The button for the pop-up list has the name of the current palette on it. (You can also press Shift+F6 to move to the equation palette.)

3. Scroll through the displayed palette with the mouse until you find the one you want and click on it. You can also use the cursor keys to scroll through the palette.

4. Click the Keyword button or press ↵ to choose the item. (You could also click the Symbol button or press Ctrl+↵, as described below).

5. To view the equation, choose **View** ➤ **R**edisplay or click the Redisplay button.

Figure 21.4 shows examples of equations created with the Equation Editor. Keywords in the examples that don't come directly from the Commands palette (described in the next section) were chosen from other palettes. For example, ALPHA, OMEGA, and THETA were chosen from the Greek palette; SUM and INT were chosen from the Large palette; INF and THEREFORE were chosen from the Symbols palette.

Numbers, letters, and operators (such as those in $m + n = 0$) were typed in directly from the keyboard. The techniques used were the same as those described earlier for Figure 21.2.

The ways in which you can combine equation commands and symbols are nearly endless. When you are first learning, it may take some trial-and-error to get everything just right. You should build your equation gradually,

Examples of equation commands and symbols

ALIGNC 10 OVER 100000	$\dfrac{10}{100000}$
ALIGNL 10 OVER 100000	$\dfrac{10}{100000}$
ALIGNR 10 OVER 100000	$\dfrac{10}{100000}$
BINOM ALPHA OMEGA	$\begin{pmatrix} A \\ \Omega \end{pmatrix}$
BINOMSM ALPHA OMEGA	$\left(\begin{smallmatrix} A \\ \Omega \end{smallmatrix}\right)$
BOLD THETA	$\boldsymbol{\theta}$
SUM FROM {x=0} TO INF	$\displaystyle\sum_{x=0}^{\infty}$
FUNC {no~italics}	no italics
ITAL cosine	*cosine*
123 HORZ 100 45	123 45
LEFT ({1^x} OVER m RIGHT)	$\left(\dfrac{1^x}{m}\right)$
MATRIX {MATFORM {ALIGNL & ALIGNR} 1&2 # 10&20 # 100&200}	1 2 10 20 100 200
LEFT DLINE MATRIX {a & b & c # x & y & z} RIGHT DLINE	$\left\|\begin{matrix} a & b & c \\ x & y & z \end{matrix}\right\|$
NROOT 3 {-{x OVER y}}	$\sqrt[3]{-\dfrac{x}{y}}$
tan ''THETA'='{sin''THETA} OVER {cos''THETA}	$\tan\theta = \dfrac{\sin\theta}{\cos\theta}$

OVERLINE {n != 0}	$\overline{n \neq 0}$
1 OVER {x OVERSM {y+1}}	$\dfrac{1}{\frac{x}{y-1}}$
STACK {m+n=0 # m PHANTOM {+n}=2}	$\begin{aligned} m+n &= 0 \\ m\ \ \ &= 2 \end{aligned}$
LEFT. {X^1} OVER {Y_2} RIGHT LINE	$\left. \dfrac{X^1}{Y_2} \right|$
SQRT {a^2 + b^2}''=c	$\sqrt{a^2+b^2} = c$
STACK {x+y # a+b # m+n}	$\begin{aligned} x+y \\ a+b \\ m+n \end{aligned}$
STACK {ALIGNR x+y # a+b+c # ALIGNL m+n}	$\begin{aligned} y+z \\ a+b+c \\ m+n \end{aligned}$
STACKALIGN {a&<=b-c # x-y&>=z}	$\begin{aligned} a &\leq b-c \\ x-y &\geq z \end{aligned}$
x SUB 1 (or x_1)	x_1
x SUP 1 (or x^1)	x^1
x SUB y SUP 1 (or x_y^1)	x_y^1
INT SUB 0 SUP INF	$\displaystyle\int_0^\infty$
UNDERLINE THEREFORE	$\underline{\therefore}$
A VERT 100 B VERT 100 C	$\begin{aligned} C \\ B \\ A \end{aligned}$
THEREFORE ~\THEREFORE	$\therefore\ \ THEREFORE$

FIGURE 21.4:

Examples of equation commands and symbols (continued)

choosing View ➤ Redisplay (or clicking Redisplay) often to see how things are progressing. That way, you can correct mistakes and refine your equation as you type it.

The sections that follow describe the various palettes. As you read these sections, be sure to refer back to Figure 21.4 for examples of how to type these commands and what they look like when printed or when displayed in the display pane.

The Commands Palette

Remember that any command or character from the Commands palette, such as { }, can be typed in the editing pane directly or chosen from the equation palette.

The Commands palette (the default) offers commands that are used to organize and position values in an equation and to draw some special characters, such as the radical (SQRT) sign. As you scroll through the palette, the status bar displays the purpose of the command and shows an example of its usage.

As you saw in figures 21.2 and 21.3 earlier, the way you group expressions with braces has a major effect on how the equation appears. See Table 21.1 for complete descriptions of the equation commands. The italicized word *variable* refers to either a single character or a group of characters enclosed in braces. (See Figure 21.4 for printed examples of these commands.)

The Other Palettes

You can also double-click on the symbol you want to use. This method is the same as selecting a command or symbol and clicking Keyword or pressing ⏎.

The other palettes in the Equation Editor offer a visual means of choosing special symbols. There are eight palettes in all (counting the Commands palette). You can select them from the palette pop-up list.

You can choose a symbol from one of these palettes by clicking on the symbol you want to select and then clicking the Keyword button (or pressing ⏎) or clicking the Symbol button (or pressing Ctrl+⏎). Clicking Keyword or pressing ⏎ copies the *keyword* for the symbol into the editing pane. For example, pressing ⏎ when the Greek letter Θ is highlighted copies the word *theta*. Clicking Symbol or pressing Ctrl+⏎ copies the actual symbol for theta to the editing pane.

Note that regardless of whether you use Keyword or Symbol, the display pane and the printed copy of your document always display the actual symbol. The only exception is if you type a backslash (\), type a keyword, such as *theta,* and then press ⏎. In this case, your equation will contain *theta,* which will be spelled out rather than displayed as the Greek letter.

COMMAND	DESCRIPTION
ALIGNC	Center-aligns a variable over a line or in a matrix
ALIGNL	Left-aligns a variable over a line or in a matrix
ALIGNR	Right-aligns a variable over a line or in a matrix
BINOM	Creates a binomial construction from two variables that follow
BINOMSM	Creates a binomial construction from two variables that follow, but in the next smaller font (printer- and font-dependent)
BOLD	Boldfaces the *variable,* symbol, or function that follows
FROM	Provides beginning and ending limits for a symbol, and must be used in conjunction with the TO command
FUNC	Treats a variable name as a mathematical function so that it will not be printed in italics
HORZ	Specifies a distance to move horizontally, in increments that are a percentage of the current font size (for example, *HORZ 100* moves the cursor 12 points to the right if you're using a 12-point font; *HORZ – 100* moves the cursor 12 points to the left for a 12-point font)
ITAL	Italicizes a *variable,* symbol, or function
LEFT	Defines a delimiter that will expand to the size of the subgroup it encloses; if LEFT is used in an equation, RIGHT must also be used, but you don't have to use identical (or matched) left and right delimiter symbols
MATFORM	Used with MATRIX to align *variables,* where ALIGNC, ALIGNL, and ALIGNR specify the alignment (& separates columns and # separates rows)
MATRIX	Creates a matrix of *variables,* where & separates columns and # separates rows (think of & as meaning "and" and # as meaning "over," e.g., x & y # a & b means "x and y over a and b")
NROOT	Creates the *n*th root sign over a *variable,* such as NROOT 3 {x+y} (the cube root of $x + y$)
OVER	Creates a fraction by placing one variable over a second variable
OVERLINE	Places a line over a variable

COMMAND	DESCRIPTION
OVERSM	Same as OVER, but reduces the entire construction to the next smaller available font (printer- and font-dependent)
PHANTOM	Occupies the same space as the variable that follows, but displays only blank space; useful for lining up stacked equations
RIGHT	Used in conjunction with LEFT to display the right delimiter (*see* LEFT)
SQRT	Places a square-root radical over a variable
STACK	Stacks equations; # is used to start a new line for variables that appear on separate rows
STACKALIGN	Stacks variables on specified characters; & precedes the character used for alignment in each row, and # separates the rows
SUB *or* _	Changes into a subscript the variable to its right
SUP *or* ^	Changes into a superscript the variable to its right
TO	Used in conjunction with FROM to set starting and ending limits for a symbol
UNDERLINE	Places a bar under the variable
VERT	Like HORZ, but moves the cursor vertically in increments that are a percentage of the current point size
{ *and* }	Delineates a group
~	Inserts a full space
`	Inserts a quarter space
&	Used with the MATRIX and MATFORM commands to delineate columns; used with STACKALIGN to indicate the alignment character
#	Used with MATRIX, STACK, and STACKALIGN to delineate rows
.	Used with LEFT and RIGHT to display an invisible delimiter
\	Prints a command literally; for example, *THETA* alone displays the Greek letter theta (Θ), but *THETA* displays the word *THETA*

TABLE 21.1:

Equation Commands (continued)

The other palettes are summarized below:

Large	Offers many symbols that can be sized as small or large, and delimiters that can be sized with the LEFT and RIGHT commands
Symbols	Contains a set of miscellaneous symbols used in math and logic
Greek	Contains uppercase and lowercase Greek letters
Arrows	Contains arrows, circles, triangles, and squares
Sets	Contains set symbols (though the union and intersection symbol are on the Large palette)
Other	Provides diacritical marks and ellipses that are attached to the variable that precedes them
Functions	Contains such functions as *cos* and *sin,* which the Equation Editor recognizes as mathematical functions and does not print in italics

USING THE DISPLAY PANE

The display pane in the Equation Editor lets you preview how the equation will look when printed. The pane is updated when you choose View ➤ Redisplay or click the Redisplay button.

By using the View menu, you can easily change the magnification of the equation. This allows you to inspect certain portions of complex equations to make sure they look right. The available options are the following:

◆   1**00% lets you view the equations in the same size as it will be printed.

◆   2**00% lets you view the equation at twice its printed size (this is the default display size).

◆   Zoom **In** increases the magnification by 50 percent.

◆   Zoom **Out** decreases the magnification by 50 percent.

◆   Zoom **Area** lets you use the mouse to zoom in on a specific area of the equation in the display pane. After you choose this option, click your mouse in one corner of the rectangular area you want to magnify and drag the mouse diagonally to the other corner. The area selected will be shown in the display pane.

NOTE **NOTE** *Keep in mind that nothing you do in the display pane affects the printed equation; this pane is provided solely for checking your work as you build your equation.*

♦ Zoom **F**ill magnifies the equation so that it fills the entire display pane. This way you can see the entire equation in as large a size as possible.

The current magnification for the equation is shown on the status bar.

EQUATION NUMBERING

The automatic numbering of Equation boxes is the same as the automatic numbering of other boxes, as explained in Chapter 19.

Every equation is automatically numbered in the order it appears in the document. If you add a new equation above others that are already in the document, WordPerfect automatically assigns that Equation box its correct number in the sequence and renumbers all boxes beneath it accordingly.

To determine the number of an Equation box, just position the mouse pointer on top of the box, and the equation number will be displayed in the status bar. You can also use Reveal Codes to determine the box number. The equation is identified as a hidden code that begins with *Equ Box,* followed by the equation number.

CHANGING AN EQUATION

If you don't select an equation, and choose Graphics ➤ Equation ➤ Edit, you will be prompted for the equation number.

To change an equation, you must first click on its box in the document to select it. Then choose Graphics ➤ Equation ➤ Edit to bring up the Equation Editor. Alternatively, you can double-click on the Equation box to edit it.

With the Equation Editor, make all your changes to the equation. When you are finished, choose File ➤ Close (Ctrl+F4) and your modifications will be saved. If you don't want to save your changes, choose File ➤ Cancel, and choose Yes when prompted "Close Equation without saving changes?"

DELETING OR MOVING AN EQUATION

The method for deleting and moving equations is exactly the same as that for deleting and moving all other graphic boxes, as explained in Chapter 19.

CONTROLLING THE SIZE OF PRINTED EQUATIONS

The size and style of characters used for printing an equation are controlled by two factors: the current font and whether or not the equation is printed graphically, with the current font being the most important factor. By default, WordPerfect will print all equations using whatever font is in effect for the rest of the document.

If you want a particular equation to be printed in a different size, follow these steps:

1. Begin editing the equation in the Equation Editor (as described earlier in this chapter).

2. Choose **F**ile ➤ **S**ettings. You will see the following dialog box:

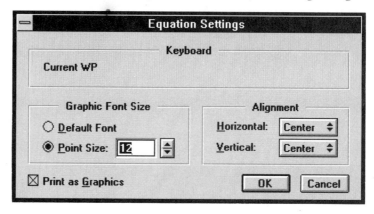

3. By default, **D**efault Font is checked, meaning equations will be the same size as the printed text. Choose **P**oint Size and enter the desired point size in the text box.

4. Choose OK or press ↵ when you're finished.

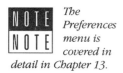
The Preferences menu is covered in detail in Chapter 13.

If you want to print all the equations in a document in the same special size, you don't need to change the size for each equation in the document. Instead, choose File ➤ Preferences ➤ Equations. You will see an Equation Preferences dialog box, which is identical to the one shown above except for the title. Just change the Point Size as described above.

You can also change the equation to a different typeface and font size. To do this, you must change the font just before the hidden [Equ Box:] code for that equation. Then, change the font back to the font used for printing text after the code.

When choosing a typeface for equations, it's best to use Helvetica, Times Roman, or Courier, because these are the three that WordPerfect can best emulate graphically.

For example, suppose you want a particular equation to be printed in 18-point size and text to be printed in 10-point size. The sequence of hidden codes in Reveal Codes might be:

[Font:Helvetica 18pt][Equ Box:1;;][Font:Times Roman 10pt]

If you want to print all the equations in a document in the same special font (one that's different from the font used for the rest of the document), you don't need to change the font for each [Equ Box:] code. Instead, you can insert an equation options code at the top of the document. Follow these steps:

1. Move the insertion point to the top of the document (to the left of the first [Equ Box:] code).

2. Choose **Graphics ➤ E**quation ➤ **O**ptions. You'll see the Equation Options dialog box, shown in Figure 21.5, which controls the appearance of the Equation boxes.

3. Change any of the options if you wish. Choose OK or press ⏎ to return to the document.

This procedure inserts a hidden [Equ Opt] code in the document at the current insertion point.

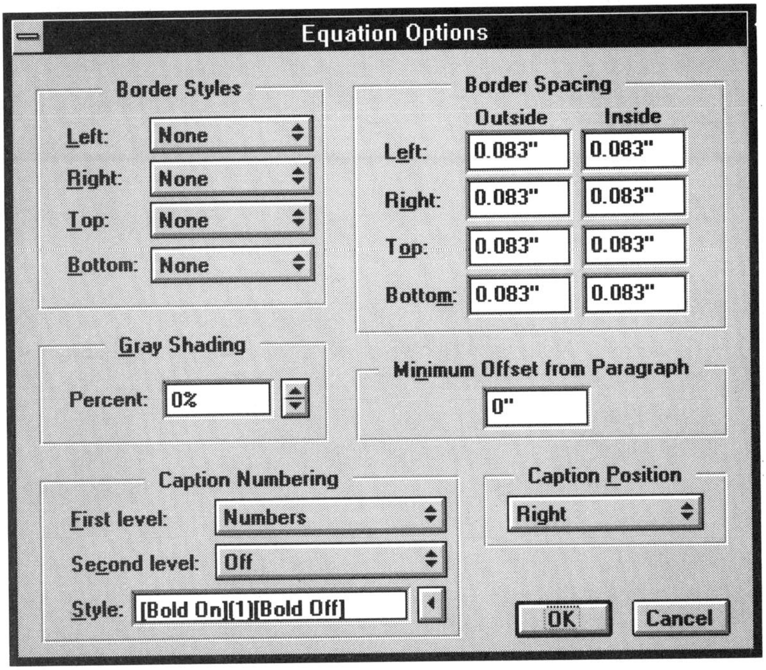

FIGURE 21.5:

The Equation Options dialog box

You can now move to the left of the [Equ Opt] code and set the font for printing equations, and then move to the right of the code and set the font for printing text, as below:

[Font:Helvetica 18pt][Equ Opt][Font Times:Roman 10pt]

Unless you make another font change elsewhere, all equations will be printed in the 18-point size, and all text will be printed in the 10-point size.

CONTROLLING GRAPHICS PRINTING AND ALIGNMENT

By default, WordPerfect prints all equations graphically, "drawing" each character rather than choosing it from the current font. This may make your equations look a little different from the rest of text (which in most cases is probably acceptable). WordPerfect also centers your equation horizontally and vertically in an "invisible" box.

You can control the quality of graphically printed equation characters by setting the Graphics Quality option in the Print dialog box (see Chapter 8).

You can change either or both of these defaults for individual equations or for all the equations in the document. To change these settings for a single equation, begin editing the equation in the Equation Editor (as described earlier in this chapter). Choose File ➤ Settings. You will see the dialog box shown in the previous section.

To print equations using characters from the current font, uncheck Print as Graphics. WordPerfect will then print characters graphically only if they cannot be found in the current font. To print the entire equation graphically, leave Print as Graphics checked. Note that setting the point size has no effect if the Print as Graphics option is set to No.

Normally, equations are centered both vertically and horizontally in their boxes. The Horizontal and Vertical pop-up lists allow you to change these settings. For Horizontal Alignment, you can choose Left (align at the left edge of the box), Center (center horizontally within the box), or Right (align at the right edge of the box). For Vertical Alignment, you can choose Top (align at the top edge of the box), Center (center vertically within the box), or Bottom (align at the bottom edge of the box).

To change the equation settings for the whole document, choose File ➤ Preferences ➤ Equations. You will see a dialog box similar to the one for a single equation, except changing the settings in this dialog box will affect the whole document. The dialog box also has a Select button for choosing a keyboard. WordPerfect comes with a keyboard named *EQUATION* that lets you enter equations and special symbols without using the palettes. See Chapter 27 for additional information about alternative keyboards.

After making your choices from the dialog box, you can choose OK or press ↵ to return to the document window or the Equation Editor (whichever you started from).

USING THE SAME EQUATION IN MULTIPLE DOCUMENTS

Saving an equation does not save the entire document. If you want to keep the equation and the current document, save the document normally when you exit Word-Perfect.

If you want to use the same equation in multiple documents, you can save a text version of the equation in its own file. You first must be in the Equation Editor with the equation you want to save displayed on the screen. Then choose File ➤ Save As (F3), type in a file name for the equation, and press ↵. (Save your equation with the .EQN extension. When you attempt to retrieve an equation, WordPerfect first looks for files with this extension.)

In the future, you can retrieve a copy of the equation into any blank (or partially filled) Equation Editor editing pane. To do so, leave the insertion point in the editing pane, and choose File ➤ Retrieve. Specify the same path, file name, and extension that you specified when saving the equation, and choose Retrieve or press ↵. A copy of the equation will be brought into the Equation Editor.

POSITIONING EQUATIONS

Chapter 19 provides detailed information about working with boxes. Using the techniques described there, you can present equations in a variety of formats, some of which are shown in Figure 21.6.

Keep in mind that an equation can be placed in any type of box. For example, if you want to present an equation as a figure (like the top example in Figure 21.6), follow these steps:

1. Choose **Graphics** ➤ **Equation** ➤ **Create**.

2. In the Equation Editor, choose **File** ➤ Box **P**osition. You should see the Box Position and Size dialog box.

3. Choose **B**ox Type and select **F**igure on the pop-up list.

This chapter concludes my discussion of desktop publishing techniques. Part 7 of this book introduces you to some of the features that will make your work with large documents a lot easier, including automatic outlining and numbering, the subject of the next chapter.

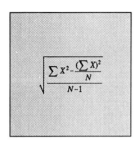

You can put equations into any type of box and adjust the appearance of the box using techniques described in Chapter 19. This equation is in a shaded Figure box. To put an equation into a box, first create an equation, then under the Box Position and Size dialog in the Equation Editor, change the Box type to Figure. Then, when you select Edit, you'll be taken to the Equation editor to create or change your equation.

The base font determines the size of the characters in the equation. We changed the base font to 18 point to the left of the hidden code that displays the equation above. Then we changed the base font back to Courier 10 pitch before typing these paragraphs.

An equation can be placed in a line, like $\cos\theta = \sqrt{1-\sin^2\theta}$, by anchoring its box to a character. In this example, the equation is in a User box that's anchored to the comma following the equation, and has a vertical position of Baseline. You may also need to increase the line height so that all lines are equally spaced.

In the example below, the equation is in a centered, auto-sized User box. The box itself is in a table cell.

PROD FROM {x=1} TO INF	$\prod\limits_{x-1}^{\infty}$

PART SEVEN

Managing the Big Jobs

This part covers WordPerfect's powerful automatic referencing features, which help you to automatically create outlines, tables of contents, indexes, tables of authorities, figure lists, table lists, and cross-references. You'll also learn about the Master Document feature, which lets you divide large files into smaller, more manageable files and use all the general automatic reference features across multiple documents. These features will be particularly valuable to you if you develop larger documents, like books, dissertations, or corporate reports.

CHAPTER

Automatic Numbering and Outlining

Automatic numbering is a powerful and versatile tool that you can use for any type of task requiring sequential numbers, including numbered lists and section numbers. The advantage of using automatic, as opposed to manual, numbering is that if you add, change, or delete a numbered item, all the other numbered items are updated instantly to reflect the change.

For many people, this one feature alone is worth the price of the Word-Perfect product, and as you'll see, is also quite easy to use. You'll find the automatic outlining and paragraph numbering features on the Tools ➤ Outline pull-down menu.

AUTOMATIC PARAGRAPH NUMBERING

If you need to number items in a list or sections in a document, you can use the *paragraph-numbering* feature. You can use a simple, single-level numbering scheme, like a numbered list (1, 2, 3, 4, 5, and so on), or a hierarchical scheme with up to eight levels (1, 1.1, 1.1.1, 1.1.1.1, and so on).

Because there are so many ways to number items in documents, Word-Perfect offers many different numbering schemes, as well as the ability to create your own scheme. The basic procedure is simple: Move the insertion point to where you want to begin using automatic numbering, define your numbering scheme, and then use the scheme.

If you number items or sections in your document, then change your mind about your numbering scheme, you can easily switch to a different scheme without retyping. And you can use as many different numbering schemes as you wish throughout a document.

DEFINING YOUR NUMBERING SCHEME

TO DEFINE A NUMBERING SCHEME FOR AUTOMATIC NUMBERING,

choose Tools ➤ Outline ➤ Define (or press Alt+Shift+F5). Then choose a predefined format from the pop-up list, or create your own, user-defined scheme. Then choose OK or press ↵.

A numbering scheme is simply a way of numbering items. Figure 22.1 shows two examples: a simple list, with one level of indentation, and a more complex numbering scheme, with three levels of indentation, used in a contract.

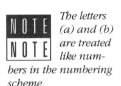

The letters (a) and (b) are treated like numbers in the numbering scheme.

If your numbering scheme requires several levels, like the second example shown in Figure 22.1, the automatic number that appears in your document is determined by how far the insertion point is indented when you insert the automatic number. For example, in Figure 22.1, the numbers *1* and *2* are not indented; the numbers *2.1, 2.2,* and *2.3* are each indented one tab stop; *(a)* and *(b)* are each indented two tab stops.

As a convenience, WordPerfect offers four predefined numbering schemes, named Paragraph, Outline, Legal, and Bullets. If none of these schemes meets your needs, you can easily create your own, "user-defined" numbering scheme. (Keep in mind that you can define a numbering scheme for a document you've already typed.)

To choose your numbering scheme, follow these steps:

1. Move the insertion point to where you want to start using automatic numbering.

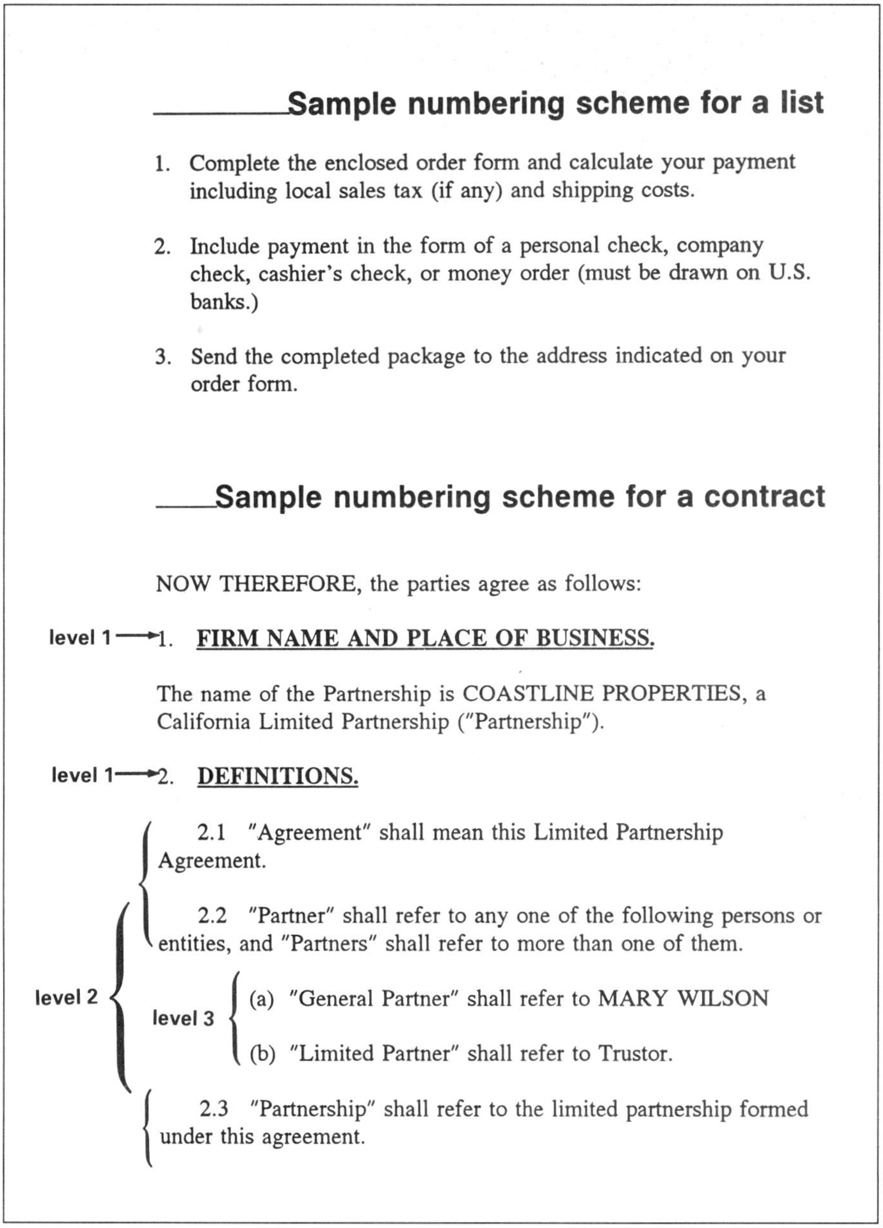

_____Sample numbering scheme for a list

1. Complete the enclosed order form and calculate your payment including local sales tax (if any) and shipping costs.

2. Include payment in the form of a personal check, company check, cashier's check, or money order (must be drawn on U.S. banks.)

3. Send the completed package to the address indicated on your order form.

_____Sample numbering scheme for a contract

NOW THEREFORE, the parties agree as follows:

level 1 ⟶ 1. **FIRM NAME AND PLACE OF BUSINESS.**

The name of the Partnership is COASTLINE PROPERTIES, a California Limited Partnership ("Partnership").

level 1 ⟶ 2. **DEFINITIONS.**

2.1 "Agreement" shall mean this Limited Partnership Agreement.

2.2 "Partner" shall refer to any one of the following persons or entities, and "Partners" shall refer to more than one of them.

level 2 {   level 3 {
(a) "General Partner" shall refer to MARY WILSON

(b) "Limited Partner" shall refer to Trustor.

2.3 "Partnership" shall refer to the limited partnership formed under this agreement.

FIGURE 22.1:

Two examples of numbering schemes: The first is a simple one-level list, and the second uses three levels.

2. Choose **T**ools ➤ **O**utline ➤ **D**efine, or press Alt+Shift+F5. You'll see the Define Paragraph Numbering dialog box, shown in Figure 22.2.

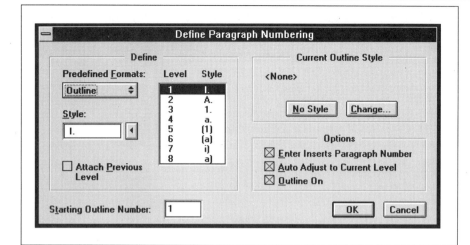

The Define Paragraph Numbering dialog box

3. Use the ↑ and ↓ keys to scroll though predefined format options, or use your mouse to choose an option from the Predefined **F**ormats pop-up list. Your options are **P**aragraph, **O**utline, **L**egal, **B**ullets, and **U**ser-Defined.

4. Choose OK or press ↵ to return to the document window.

WordPerfect inserts a [Par Num Def:] code at the insertion point, and any automatic numbers that you insert below that point will adhere to the numbering scheme you've chosen. (When Auto Code Placement is on, the [Par Num Def:] code is automatically positioned at the beginning of the current paragraph.)

INSERTING AUTOMATIC NUMBERS

TO INSERT AN AUTOMATIC NUMBER,

choose Tools ➤ Outline ➤ Paragraph Number (or press Alt+F5). Leave the Numbering Level option set to Auto to have the numbering level based on the indent, or choose Manual and type a level number. Choose Insert or press ↵.

Once you've defined your numbering scheme, it's easy to insert the automatic numbers:

1. Position the insertion point where you want to insert a number. If you want to indent, press Tab, Indent (F7), or Double Indent (Ctrl+Shift+F7) as necessary.

2. Choose **T**ools ➤ **O**utline ➤ **P**aragraph Number, or press Alt+F5. You'll see this dialog box:

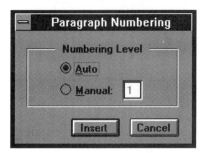

3. If you want WordPerfect to automatically determine the numbering level based on how far the insertion point is currently indented, leave the Numbering Level option set to Auto. If you want to choose the level yourself, choose **M**anual. Then type a level number in the text box. (For example, if you are using the Legal scheme and enter **2** as the level, the number will be in the format "X.X" regardless of how far the insertion point is indented, because "X.X" is the format of level-2 numbers in the Legal scheme.)

4. Choose OK or press ↵ to return to the document window.

WordPerfect inserts a [Par Num:] code at the insertion point, which appears as the appropriate number in the document window. You can then type any text, or press the spacebar, Tab, Indent (F7), or Double Indent (Ctrl+Shift+F7) to indent before typing additional text.

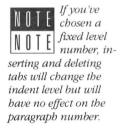
If you've chosen a fixed level number, inserting and deleting tabs will change the indent level but will have no effect on the paragraph number.

If you're using automatic numbering, you can easily change the level number and indentation of your paragraph after you've typed it. Just turn on Reveal Codes, move the insertion point to highlight the [Par Num:Auto] code, then press Tab to insert a [Tab] code and indent a level, or press Backspace to delete a [Tab] code and outdent a level. Each time you press Tab, you'll indent and move down one level; each time you delete a tab, you'll outdent and move up one level.

To save time and keystrokes, you can create a style or macro that inserts an automatic number and any tab, indent, or margin-release codes associated with it.

If the wrong automatic number appears on your screen, keep in mind that the number is determined by three factors: 1) the currently defined numbering scheme, 2) how far the insertion point is indented with tab or indent codes, and 3) whether you let WordPerfect determine the level or enter the level yourself. If necessary, you can use Reveal Codes to delete the [Par Num:] code, and then change your numbering scheme or tab settings on the ruler and try again.

Note also that if you insert or delete an automatic number, or change the paragraph-numbering scheme, WordPerfect will immediately adjust automatic numbers below the insertion point.

CREATING YOUR OWN NUMBERING SCHEME

TO DEFINE YOUR OWN NUMBERING SCHEME,

choose Tools ➤ Outline ➤ Define (or press Alt-Shift+F5). Choose User-Defined from the Predefined Formats pop-up list, and define the format of each automatic number at each indent level. Choose OK or press ⏎ to return to the document window.

If none of WordPerfect's predefined numbering schemes fits the bill for you, you can create your own by following these steps:

1. Position the insertion point where you want to start your numbering scheme. (Use Reveal Codes to remove any previous [Par Num Def:] codes so they don't cancel your new definition.)

2. Choose **T**ools ➤ **O**utline ➤ **D**efine (or press Alt+Shift+F5) to get to the Define Paragraph Numbering dialog box.

3. Choose **U**ser-Defined from the Predefined **F**ormats pop-up list.

4. Use the **S**tyle and Attach **P**revious Level options to define the format of up to eight levels of automatic numbers in the Level/Style list. (These two options are described in the sections that follow.)

5. Choose OK or press ⏎ to return to the document window.

WordPerfect inserts a [Par Num Def:] code at the current insertion point, and any [Par Num:] codes beneath the insertion point adhere to the defined numbering scheme. The sections that follow describe your options for defining the format of numbers at each numbering level.

Choosing a Number Style

You can choose any level number, 1 through 8, in the list under the Level/Style headings, either by clicking the level once with your mouse or by using the ↓ and ↑ keys to highlight any level (after tabbing over to the list). As you scroll through the levels, the style of the number at the current level appears in the text box under the Style option.

To change the appearance of the number at the current level, choose a style from the Style pop-up list (see Figure 22.3). Each option is described below:

1	Digits (1, 2, 3, 4)
A	Uppercase letters (A, B, C, D)
a	Lowercase letters (a, b, c, d)
I	Uppercase Roman numerals (I, II, III, IV)
i	Lowercase Roman numerals (i, ii, iii, iv)
X	Uppercase Roman (digits if attached) (I, II, III, IV if not attached to previous level; 1, 2, 3, 4 if attached to previous level)
x	Lowercase Roman (digits if attached) (i, ii, iii, iv if not attached to previous level; 1, 2, 3, 4 if attached to previous level)

Remember that the symbols above are just examples, not the actual letters or numbers that appear in your document, except in the case of other characters (bullets or punctuation marks) not listed as symbols.

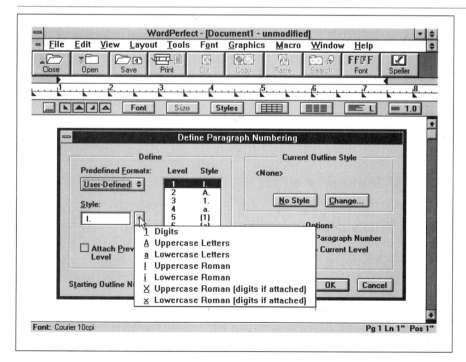

FIGURE 22.3:

The number formats available for User-Defined numbering schemes. The current format, if any, is shown in the Style text box, as well as in the Level/Style list.

If you want actual characters in your numbering scheme, type them into the Style text box directly. For example, if you define the numbering style for the first level as *1.,* where *1* is the Digits symbol and the period is typed directly, the first-level numbers appear as *1., 2., 3., 4.,* and so on.

You can also insert any special character in the Style text box. While the insertion point is in the box, press Ctrl+W to bring up the WordPerfect Characters window. Choose any character set, and any character, then choose Insert and Close to insert the character and close the window.

The Bullets format uses a variety of special characters to print a different bullet at each level of indentation.

Attaching to the Previous Level

When defining the format for each numbering level, mark the Attach Previous Level check box (an asterisk appears next to that level number in the Level/Style list). This lets you determine whether or not to attach the current level number to the previous one. For example, if you define the level-1 number format as *1* and the level-2 format as *.1,* and set the Attach Previous Level option for the level-2 number to Yes, the automatic numbers appear in this format:

```
9
        9.1
        9.2
        9.3
```

If, however, the Attach Previous Level option for the level-2 number is set to No, the automatic numbers appear in this format:

```
9
        .1
        .2
        .3
```

OPTIONS FOR THE ENTIRE NUMBERING SCHEME

The Level/Style list, Style text box, and Attach Previous Level check box described in the preceding sections let you define the format of numbers at each level of indentation in the numbering scheme. The check boxes in the Options area of the Define Paragraph Numbering dialog box, described below, let you choose options for the overall numbering scheme.

Enter Inserts Paragraph Number This option determines whether pressing ↵ automatically inserts the next automatic number when you are using your numbering scheme in Outline mode, as described in "Automatic Outlining" later in this chapter. If this option is turned off, you must choose Tools ➤ Outline ➤ Paragraph Number (or press Alt+F5) to enter automatic numbers, even when you are in Outline mode.

Auto Adjust to Current Level This option determines whether pressing ↵ causes the next line to be at the same level as the current line. When this option is turned on (the default), pressing ↵ in Outline mode creates a new *sister* topic—a topic at the same level as the one just completed—and you must press Shift+Tab to remove a level of indentation or Tab to add one. When this option is turned off, WordPerfect automatically brings the insertion point back to the leftmost level of the outline whenever you press ↵.

Outline On If this option is selected, activating the current numbering scheme automatically turns on Outline mode, by inserting an [Outline On] code next to the [Par Num Def:] code. If this option is not selected, activating the numbering scheme does not automatically activate Outline mode.

Determining the Starting Outline Number

The Starting Outline Number option in the Define Paragraph Numbering dialog box lets you determine the starting automatic number. By default, this is *1,* which is interpreted according to the style of the first level (e.g., *1* for digits, *I* for uppercase Roman numerals, *A* for uppercase letters, and so on).

In some cases, you may want the numbering to start with some other number. For example, if the current document is actually Part 3 of a large document (or a master document, covered in Chapter 24), you might want to number the sections as *3.1, 3.1.1, 3.2,* and so forth. Your starting number in that case would be *3,* not *1.*

You can change the starting number scheme at the start of the document or anywhere within the document.

When entering the starting number, be sure to use a number. For example, even if your level-1 "numbers" are A), B), C), and so forth, and you want to start numbering at C), enter **3** as your starting number. WordPerfect will automatically convert that to C) when you use the numbering scheme.

Regardless of whether you use a predefined numbering scheme, or define you own numbering scheme, you can use the automatic outlining feature to instruct WordPerfect to insert numbers for you.

AUTOMATIC OUTLINING

▎**TO TURN ON AUTOMATIC OUTLINING,**

choose Tools ➤ Outline ➤ Outline On.

As we all learned in school, an outline is a great way to get started with any large document. But developing an outline is usually a trial-and-error effort. You start with a basic list, add topics and subtopics, and then add, delete, change, and move topics.

Developing and refining an outline manually is often a messy job, involving lots of erasing, cutting, pasting, and rewriting, simply because the outline changes as you refine your thoughts. But WordPerfect's Outline feature lets you easily change and even reorganize your outline to match your latest whim and, as you may have guessed, automatically renumbers every item as you make changes.

USING AUTOMATIC OUTLINING

NOTE *If you don't choose a numbering scheme before turning on Outline mode, WordPerfect will automatically use the predefined Outline numbering scheme.*

In a nutshell, WordPerfect's Outline mode is just a minor variation of automatic paragraph numbering. When you are not in Outline mode, you must position the insertion point and choose Tools ➤ Outline ➤ Paragraph Number (Alt+F5) to insert a new automatic number. But in Outline mode, just pressing ↵ automatically inserts the next automatic number for you, which can save a lot of keystrokes. Outline mode also lets you move, copy, or delete entire chunks of outline text without losing the numbering sequence.

To use automatic outlining, follow these steps:

1. Move the insertion point to where you want to start typing your outline.

2. Choose **T**ools ➤ **O**utline ➤ Outline **O**n. The word "Outline" appears in the lower-left corner of your screen as a reminder that Outline mode is turned on, and WordPerfect inserts an [Outline On] code at the insertion point.

3. Press ↵ to insert the first outline number automatically.

4. Press the spacebar, Tab, or other indent key, then type the text of the outline item.

5. Press ↵ to move to the next item; WordPerfect inserts the next number

Steps 5 and 6 are true only if the Enter Inserts Paragraph Number and Auto Adjust to Current Level options in the Define Paragraph Numbering dialog box are on for the current numbering scheme.

at the current outline level. You can press ↵ more than once if you want to add blank lines between items and move the outline number down. If you want to insert a new line of text without adding another outline number, press Shift+↵. (To delete an automatic number, press Backspace, or use Reveal Codes to delete its [Par Num:] code.)

6. If you want to *demote* (indent a level), press Tab once for each level. If you want to *promote* (outdent a level), press Shift+Tab once for each level.

7. Repeat steps 4–6 as many times as you wish.

8. When you are ready to start working with normal, unnumbered paragraph text, deactivate Outline mode by choosing **T**ools ➤ **O**utline ➤ Outline O**ff**. (If there's a leftover outline number above the insertion point, use Reveal Codes to delete its [Par Num:] code.)

When you turn off Outline, WordPerfect inserts an [Outline Off] code at the insertion point. Anytime the insertion point is between the [Outline On] and [Outline Off] codes, automatic outlining is available. Hence, there is no need to reactivate the Outline feature should you decide to add to your outline later; just move the insertion point anywhere within the existing outline.

MODIFYING YOUR OUTLINE

The Outline scheme is WordPerfect's default numbering scheme.

Because an outline is just a specialized mode of paragraph numbering, modifying it is as easy as modifying any automatic number. For example, to change the numbering scheme of your outline, move the insertion point to the top of the outline (*before* the [Outline On] code). Delete the existing [Par Num Def:] code (if any), then choose Tools ➤ Outline ➤ Define, and choose your predefined format or define your own numbering scheme as explained earlier in this chapter.

To indent or outdent an item, open Reveal Codes and insert or delete [Tab] codes until the item is at the level you want. To insert an item, move the insertion point to the end of the item above the line where you want to insert the new item, and press ↵.

You can use Alt+→, Alt+←, Alt+↑, and Alt+↓ to move through an outline. You can use all the usual deletion techniques to delete any text, as well as [Par Num:Auto] codes that display the item number. However, if you want to delete entire line items or groups of line items, you'll find the Delete Family option, described next, much easier and more convenient.

MOVING, COPYING, AND DELETING OUTLINE FAMILIES

An outline consists of groups of related topics. Each topic is placed on a line by itself. Ideas related to the main topic are placed one level below the topic as subtopics, or *daughters,* of the main topic. Topics at the same organizational level are called *sisters.* A topic and all its subtopics make up a *family,* as illustrated in Figure 22.4.

OUTLINE

sister topics, both daughters to
topic A. above

I. Prologue
    A. Introduction of Child Secret-Keeping
        1. Overview of Topic Area
        2. Purpose of the Study
    B. Hypotheses

family

II. Assessment of Secret-Keeping
    A. Literature Review
        1. Research Findings
        2. Family Background Factors
    B. Family Systems Theory
    C. Theory of Conditions
    D. Theory About Secrecy

III. Patterns of Secrecy
    A. Method
        1. Description of Subjects
        2. Protection of Subjects
    B. Design Considerations

IV. Description of Research
    A. Secret-Keeping Behavior
    B. Description of Procedure
    C. Examples of Secret-Keeping
    D. Design and Data Analysis

V. Results
    A. Tests of the Hypotheses
    B. Summary of Results

VI. BIBLIOGRAPHY

VII. APPENDICES

FIGURE 22.4:
A sample outline showing the definitions of sister, daughter, and family

WordPerfect provides a few special options for manipulating entire families of topics in an outline: Move Family, Copy Family, and Delete Family. To use one of these options, follow these steps:

1. Position the insertion point at the beginning of the line of the topmost topic of the family you want to move, copy, or delete.

2. Choose **T**ools ➤ **O**utline.

3. Choose **M**ove Family, **C**opy Family, or **D**elete Family. The entire family is highlighted. You can now choose to do one of the following:

◆ Press → to indent the family or ← to outdent it (within one level of the preceding family).

◆ If you chose Move Family or Copy Family, use the ↑ and ↓ keys to position the highlighted family within the outline. As you move through the outline, the highlighted family will also move and its numbering levels will be adjusted accordingly. Press ↵ to complete the move or copy operation.

◆ If you chose Delete Family, you'll see a message box asking for verification. Choose either **Y**es to delete the highlighted family or **N**o if you change your mind.

As you gain experience with the outline feature, you'll undoubtedly find that the options for manipulating outline families boost your productivity in creating and refining your outlines.

USING OUTLINE STYLES

NOTE
NOTE
A user-defined numbering scheme lets you define the general numbering scheme (e.g., digits, Roman numerals, etc.); an outline style lets you define the actual appearance of numbers and text at each level.

Chapter 14 discusses WordPerfect styles, which are a great tool for using design elements easily and consistently throughout a document. The general techniques for creating and using paired and open styles are discussed in detail there.

Outline styles, discussed in this chapter, are unique in that you can assign formatting codes and other attributes to each numbering level within an outline. For example, you could assign boldface and underline to all the level-1 topics (as in the sample contract scheme shown earlier in Figure 22.1), another format to level-2 topics, and so forth, for up to eight levels.

Later, when you type the outline with the outline style activated, all the formatting will be done for you automatically as you type. And, as with regular styles, if you change your mind about the appearance of a certain level (for example, you might decide not to underline the level-1 topics), you need only go back and change the style once, instead of having to go back and reformat every level-1 topic in your outline individually.

CREATING OUTLINE STYLES

You can create and assign styles by using the Define Paragraph Numbering dialog box, the same dialog box used to define other aspects of numbering schemes. Follow these steps:

1. Choose **T**ools ➤ **O**utline ➤ **D**efine (or press Alt+Shift+F5). You'll see the Define Paragraph Numbering dialog box.

2. Choose **C**hange. You'll see the Outline Styles dialog box, shown in Figure 22.5.

3. Choose **C**reate to go to the Edit Outline Style dialog box, shown in Figure 22.6.

4. Type a name for the style in the Name text box. The name can contain up to 17 characters and include blank spaces.

5. Optionally, enter a brief description of the style up to 54 characters in the Description text box.

6. In the Define Outline Style area, move the highlight to the level for which you want to define the style.

7. From the **S**tyle Type pop-up list, choose either Paired or Open. (In most cases, you'll want to choose Paired so that the style codes for the current level do not affect other levels).

8. Choose **E**dit. This takes you to the screen for entering formatting codes. You can use the pull-down menus, shortcut keys, or Button Bar to choose formatting codes defining the appearance of text at this outline level (see the next section, "Codes for Outline Levels").

9. When you've finished defining the style. Choose **C**lose to return to the Edit Outline Style dialog box.

10. From the Enter **K**ey pop-up list, choose the role played by the ↵ key after you type the text for the level. Your choices are:

The Enter Key option is available only for paired outline styles.

Hard Return	Inserts a normal hard return without turning off the style. In Outline mode, you must press → and then ↵ to insert another paragraph numbere.
Style O**ff**	Turns off the style. In Outline mode, you must press ↵ again to insert another paragraph number.

Style **Off/On**   Turns the style off and then on so that you can insert the next numbered item. If you want to insert a blank line between items, include one or more hard returns below the [Comment] code.

11. Repeat steps 6–10 for each level for which you want to define a style.

12. Choose OK to return to the Outline Styles dialog box. Choose **C**lose to return to the Define Paragraph Numbering dialog box. Choose OK to return to the document window.

CODES FOR OUTLINE LEVELS

In Figure 22.1, at the start of this chapter, the style for level-1 topics in the second example is Bold and Underlined.

When defining the style of the number and text at a given outline level, you'll see the same dialog box used for defining regular styles, except that the [Par Num:] code is inserted automatically to display the paragraph number. For example, you'll see [Par Num:1] when defining level 1, [Par Num:2] when defining level 2, and so on. If you want to use an automatic paragraph number instead of a manual paragraph number, you must delete the existing [Par Num:] code, then insert a [Par Num:Auto] code by choosing Tools ➤ Outline ➤ Paragraph Number (Alt+F5), and then Auto (by leaving the Numbering Level option set to Auto).

You can also use any formatting codes that you'd use with other kinds of styles, including fonts, print attributes (bold, underline, and so forth), print

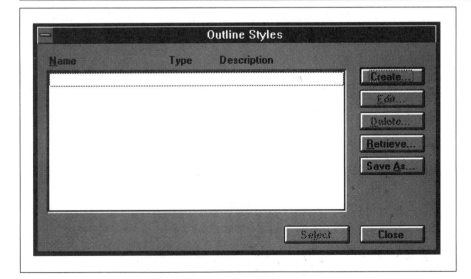

FIGURE 22.5:
The Outline Styles dialog box

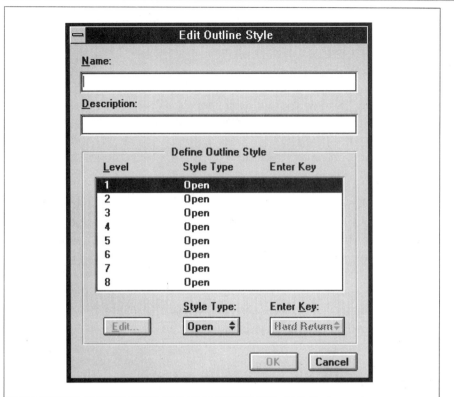

FIGURE 22.6:

The Edit Outline Style dialog box

sizes, tab and indent codes, and graphics. Place your formatting codes either before or after the [Par Num:] code to determine whether the paragraph number itself or just the text that follows the number will be formatted. If you are using a paired style to define the current outline level, codes above the [Comment] code are turned on when the style is activated, and codes below the [Comment] code are turned off when the style is deactivated.

Figure 22.7 shows an example of a style definition for a single paragraph level. Here's the role played by each code:

[HdDecTab]   This decimal-aligns the automatic paragraph number at the next tab stop (entered by pressing Alt+Shift+F7).

<table>
<tr><td>

NOTE
NOTE

</td><td>

Because the [Bold On] and [Und On] codes follow the [Par Num:] code, only the text next to the number, not the number itself, will be bold and underlined. [Bold Off] and [Und Off] are not necessary, because this is a paired style.

</td></tr>
</table>

[Par Num:] — Inserted for you when defining an outline style, this code displays the automatic number in your document.

[Indent] — This code indents the insertion point to the next tab stop (entered by pressing F7).

[Bold On][Und On] — These codes boldface and underline the text to the right of the automatic number at this level (entered by pressing Ctrl+B and Ctrl+I)

[Comment] — This code separates the codes activated when the style is turned on from codes that are activated when the style is turned off. The [Comment] code appears automatically when defining a paired style.

[HRt][HRt] — These codes insert two hard returns after the text at this level when you later put this style to use (entered by pressing ↵ twice after pressing End to move the insertion point past the [Comment] code).

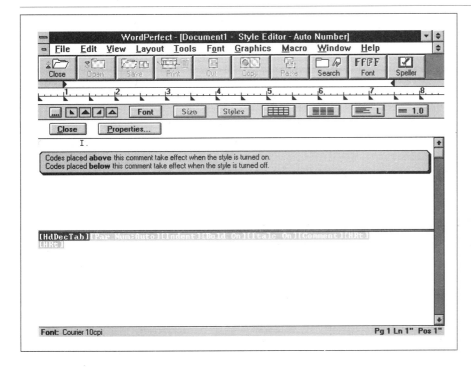

FIGURE 22.7:

Sample style codes for a single outline level. The [Par Num] code is inserted automatically. All the other formatting codes were inserted using the menus.

ACTIVATING OUTLINE STYLES

TO ACTIVATE AN OUTLINE STYLE,

choose Tools ➤ Outline ➤ Define (or press Alt+Shift+F5).
Choose Change. Highlight the outline style you want, and
choose Select. Choose OK to return to the document window.

When you want to use an outline style to format an automatic outline, follow these steps:

1. In the document window, move the insertion point to where you want to use the outline style.

2. Choose **T**ools ➤ **O**utline ➤ **D**efine (or press Alt+Shift+F5). You'll see the Define Paragraph Numbering dialog box.

3. Choose **C**hange in the Current Outline Style area. This brings you to the dialog box of existing outline styles.

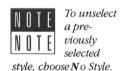 *To unselect a previously selected style, choose* **N** *o Style.*

4. Move the highlight to the name of the outline style you want to activate, and then choose Se**l**ect. You will be returned to the Define Paragraph Numbering dialog box, and the name of the outline style you just chose will be listed in the Current Outline Style area.

5. Choose OK to return to the document window.

At this point, WordPerfect inserts a [Par Num Def:] code in your document at the insertion point, with the name of the outline style after the colon. This code acts like the [Par Num Def:] code for any of the predefined numbering schemes described earlier (Paragraph, Legal, Bullets, etc). That is, if Outline mode is on (or you turn it on), you can press ↵ to start inserting numbers automatically. If you do not turn on Outline mode, you can still use the styles by inserting paragraph numbers with the Tools ➤ Outline ➤ Paragraph Number.

MANIPULATING OUTLINE STYLES

See Chapter 14 for reminders on how to manage style libraries.

Outline styles are saved with the document and can be stored in libraries, just like other styles. In fact, a style library can contain regular styles as well as open styles. However, the names of the outline styles appear only in the Outline Styles dialog box.

You can manipulate your outline styles from the Outline Styles dialog box the same way you manipulate ordinary styles from the Styles dialog box. The same options (Create, Edit, Delete, Retrieve, and Save As) are available for managing style libraries and modifying existing styles.

SAMPLE OUTLINE STYLES

The sample style library, LIBRARY.STY, that comes with your WordPerfect package includes these three sample outline styles:

Document: Each level sets the style of a section heading in a document and includes codes for automatically generating a table of contents. For example, level 1 is large type and might be a main heading, level 2 is underlined, level 3 is boldface, and so forth. (Activate the Doc Init style from the Styles dialog box first; then use the Document outline style.)

Right Par: This style right-aligns automatic numbers at the current tab stop; this is useful for typing general numbered lists.

Technical: Like Document, this includes table-of-contents codes, but has different spacing and formatting styles at each level. Activate the Tech Init style from the Styles dialog box first, then activate the Technical outline style to try it out.

You might want to explore these styles on your own to learn more about outline styles. Start with an empty document window, choose Layout ➤ Styles, and use the Retrieve button to retrieve the sample LIBRARY.STY file. If you see the message "Style(s) already exist. Replace?" choose Yes.

If you want to try the Document or Technical outline style, you must first choose either Doc Init or Tech Init from the Styles dialog box, and turn it on. Then use Tools ➤ Outline ➤ Define to pick the current outline style.

After working your way back to the document window, you may want to turn on Reveal Codes, so you can see the various codes that have been inserted in your document. Then experiment with ↵, Tab, Shift+Tab, and just basic typing to try out each style.

To review a given outline style, you can choose Tools ➤ Outline ➤ Define ➤ Change, and style you want to look into. Then choose Edit to view the type (paired or open) and the function of the Enter key for each level within the style. You can also highlight any level and choose Edit to view the formatting codes for that level.

NUMBERING LINES

> ### TO TURN ON AUTOMATIC LINE NUMBERING,
>
> choose Layout ➤ Line ➤ Numbering, choose a Line Numbering option, then choose OK.

NOTE NOTE *The vertical line separating the line numbers from the text in Figure 22.8 is a graphic line, discussed a little later in this section.*

WordPerfect can number each line in your document or just certain sections, formats that are commonly used in the legal profession. The numbers are generally printed in the left margin of the document, as in the example shown in Figure 22.8. As you'll see, however, you can print the numbers anywhere on the page.

Line numbering is a completely separate feature from automatic and outline numbering. You cannot devise your own numbering schemes or use multiple levels. In fact, line numbering is activated as a formatting option from the Layout menu rather than from the Tools menu.

ADDING LINE NUMBERS

To add line numbers to a document automatically, follow these steps:

1. Position the insertion point where you want the line numbering to start.

2. Choose **L**ayout ➤ **L**ine ➤ **N**umbering (or press Shift+F9 N). The Line Numbering dialog box appears:

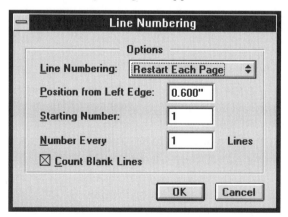

3. Open the **L**ine Numbering pop-up list, and choose **R**estart Each Page (so that line numbers begin with *1* on each page) or **C**ontinuous (so that lines are numbered continuously from page to page).

FIGURE 22.8:

A sample document with line numbers in the left margin and a graphic line separating the numbers from the text

```
 1   STEVEN C. SMITH
 2   53505 Orange Avenue
 3   Los Angeles, CA  90025
 4
 5   Telephone:  (123) 435-1200
 6
 7
 8   STEVEN C. SMITH, Complainant
 9
10
11
12
13                 UNITED STATES OF AMERICA
14
15                      BEFORE THE
16
17        COMMODITY FUTURES TRADING COMMISSION
18
19
20
21   In the Matter of the Reparations   )   CFTC DOCKET NO. 90-S205
22   Proceeding Between:                 )
23                                       )   COMPLAINANT'S APPEAL
24   STEVEN C. SMITH                     )   INFORMAL DOCUMENT
25                                       )
26        Complainant,                   )
27                                       )
28   and                                 )
29                                       )
30   LEVER BROTHERS, INC.                )
31   and JOHN JONES                      )
32                                       )
33        Respondents.                   )
34        _____
35
36
37                    INTRODUCTION
38   My Work Priority Policy - A prerequisite to other outside
39   involvement activities.  My work requires that I have no outside
40   interruption of any kind, except in an emergency.
41      As an introduction to any discussion of my undertaking with
42   others, including financial investments that could disturb me at my
43   work, except for emergencies, that the above policy be carefully

                             -1-
```

4. Choose any other options you want, as explained in the sections that follow.

5. Choose OK or press ↵ to return to your document.

WordPerfect inserts a hidden [Ln Num:On] code at the insertion point, marking the spot in the document where line numbering will start. The following sections explain the options available in the Line Numbering dialog box.

 Line numbers appear only on the printed document and on the Print Preview screen, and only on lines that contain text or a hard return.

Position from Left Edge This option sets the position of the line number from the left edge of the page, inside the margin. Be careful not to set the line numbers between the page margins. For example, if you have a 1-inch left margin, your entry should be some number that's less than *1*. Otherwise, the line numbers will be printed on top of your text.

Starting Number This option lets you set a new starting number for the lines. Normally, line numbering starts at *1* whenever you activate it. You might need this option if you stop line numbering in the middle of a document and then want to pick it up again later, using numbers relative to the previous numbering rather than starting over again from *1*.

Number Every This option sets the increment for the *printed* line number. When set to *1,* every line number is printed. When set to *2,* only every other line number is printed. This option does not affect how the line numbers are calculated, only how often WordPerfect actually prints the numbers.

Count Blank Lines This option determines whether blank lines created by multiple hard returns will be counted in the numbering. Uncheck this box if you want to number lines only that contain text. Note that lines left blank by your line-spacing setting are never numbered.

Footnotes and endnotes are included in line numbering, but page headers and footers are not. To ensure that new codes and text do not affect line numbering, you may want to place the line-numbering code in the Document Initial Codes area.

FONTS FOR LINE NUMBERS

The line numbers are printed using the font in effect at the position of the [Ln Num:On] code. To change the font of the numbers, open Reveal Codes and place your [Font:] code just to the left of the [Ln Num:On] code. Then move the insertion point to the right of the [Ln Num:On] code, and choose the font you want to use in the rest of the document. When Auto Code Placement is on, the [Ln Num:On] code is placed automatically at the beginning of the current paragraph.

TURNING OFF LINE NUMBERING

To turn off line numbering, follow these steps:

1. Position the insertion point where you want the numbering to stop.

2. Choose **L**ayout ➤ **L**ine ➤ **N**umbering (or press Shift+F9 N)

3. Open the **L**ine Numbering pop-up list, and choose **O**ff.

4. Choose OK or press ↵

WordPerfect inserts a [Ln Num:Off] code at the insertion point; lines beneath that code will not numbered.

ADDING A SEPARATOR LINE

 You can print graphic lines only if you have a printer that can print graphics.

If you want to add a line that separates the line numbers from the text, as in Figure 22.8, and you want that line to appear on every page, place a vertical graphic line in a header that's printed on every page. Follow these steps:

1. Move the insertion point to the top of the document (or to the top of the page where you want the header to begin).

2. Choose **L**ayout ➤ **P**age (or press Alt+F9).

3. Choose **H**eaders, and then either Header **A** or Header **B**.

4. Choose where you want headers to be printed (e.g., Every **P**age to print the header on every page).

5. Choose **C**reate to get to the screen for defining the header.

6. Choose **G**raphics ➤ **L**ine ➤ **V**ertical (or press Ctrl+Shift+F11).

7. Define the line from the options shown in the dialog box (Figure 22.8 uses these default options: Thickness = 0.013"; Gray Shading = 100%; Vertical Position = Full Page; Horizontal Position = Left Margin.)

8. Choose OK to leave the dialog box.

9. Choose **C**lose to leave the header editing screen and return to the document window.

You'll need to switch to the Print Preview screen or print a page to see the vertical line.

In the next chapter, I'll look at automatic referencing, a tool that helps you create tables of contents, indexes, figure lists, table lists, footnotes, and endnotes, and also lets you update them automatically as you make changes to your document.

CHAPTER 23

Automatic Referencing

Many documents require referencing with footnotes and endnotes, tables of contents, indexes, figure and table lists, cross-referencing, and more. As you'll see in this chapter, WordPerfect can simplify the creation and management of all these items and, in true WordPerfect style, can automatically update them as you add, change, and delete text in your document.

ADDING FOOTNOTES AND ENDNOTES

Many scholarly, scientific, and technical documents use footnotes and endnotes to reference additional reading material or to provide parenthetical or related information that is not essential to the flow of the text. Footnotes are typed at the bottom of the page, and endnotes are generally typed at the end of the document.

Figure 23.1 shows an example of a page printed with two footnotes at the bottom. These footnotes refer to the superscripted numbers 1 and 2 in the text. Figure 23.2 shows an example of endnotes used as a bibliography at the end of a document.

Only two of Archimedes' works on mechanics have been handed down to us. These are titled *On the Equilibrium of Planes or Centers of Gravity of Plane Figures* and *On Floating Bodies*. Both were published in 1543 by Nicolo Tartaglia, and Italian mathematician. In the *Equilibrium*, Archimedes dealt with the lever which, along with the wedge, roller, pulley, and inclined plane, belonged to the simple machines of his time. Archimedes used the concept of the center of gravity, or barycenter, throughout his discussion of the lever, but never explicitly defined this notion.[1]

Great progress in the theory of equilibria followed Archimedes' time. In 1717 Johann Bernoulli proposed the principle of virtual work[2] as the fundamental law of statics. The law states that

> *in equilibrium, no work is needed to achieve an infinitesimal displacement of a given mechanical system.*

The rule captures both stable and unstable configurations. That is, imagine a steel ball that is free to roll on a landscape with depressions and elevations. If the ball is at the top of a hill, it lies in unstable equilibrium. In the center of a

---

[1] There have been many speculations about why Archimedes never defined the center of gravity. Most scholars believe that the concept had already been defined elsewhere, either by Archimedes or earlier scientists, in a work that has since been lost.

[2] This principle was stated in a letter by Bernoulli to the French physicist Pierre Varignon (1654-1722), written January 26, 1717. It was first published in Varignon's *Nouvelle Mécanique*, vol 2, p. 174, in 1725.

NOTES

1. Cf. Bernard Williams, "Tertullian's Paradox" in Antony Flew and Alasdair MacIntyre, eds., *New Essays in Philosophical Theology* (London: Macmillan, 1963), esp. pp 203-205.

2. From a contradiction *anything* follows, see Copi, *Symbolic Logic* (New York: Macmillan, 1954), or any other introductory text in logic.

3. For more remarks on this topic see Ronald Hepburn, *Christianity and Paradox* (London: Watts, 1966), Chs. 9 and 10; and Paul Tillich, *Systematic Theology* (London: Nisbet, 1955) Vol. 1 pp. 231-243.

4. These are ways set forth in the *Summa Theologica*, I q.2, a.3. (Cf. Text Number 3 in the Texts Without Comment at the end of the volume.) We propose to restate the same arguments, however divesting them of all examples borrowed from ancient physics and formulating them in a language appropriate to modern times.

5. In *De Aeternitate Mundi* (written in 1270-71) St. Thomas made room in advance for the speculations of modern mathematics on infinite multitude.

FIGURE 23.2:
An example of WordPerfect endnotes

If you've ever had to use a standard typewriter to type a document with footnotes, you know what an unpleasant task this can be. As you might expect, this process is much easier with WordPerfect, because you just type the note right at its reference point in the document, and WordPerfect automatically places it at the bottom of the page or at the end of the document. You can easily add and delete notes without having to worry about renumbering them, since WordPerfect handles this automatically. If you add, change, or delete text later, WordPerfect will properly reposition the note, if necessary, the next time you print the document.

TYPING FOOTNOTES AND ENDNOTES

TO TYPE A FOOTNOTE OR AN ENDNOTE,

position the insertion point where you want the note number to appear in the text, choose Layout ➤ Footnote *or* Endnote ➤ Create. Press the spacebar, Tab, or the Indent key (F7), then type the text of your note. Choose Close when you're finished.

Other than their positions when printed, footnotes and endnotes are virtually the same in Word-Perfect, so I'll just refer to both as "notes" and indicate differences where appropriate.

If you press ↵ accidentally after typing a footnote, WordPerfect will print an extra blank line beneath your note—just press Backspace to delete the hard return.

All notes consist of two elements: a superscripted number that appears in the text to alert the reader to the note and the note itself. WordPerfect numbers notes automatically; you need not type a number. Typing either kind of note is a simple procedure:

1. Move the insertion point to where you want the superscripted note number to appear in the text (usually at the end of a sentence, after the period).

2. Choose **L**ayout, then choose either **F**ootnote or **E**ndnote, depending on where you want the note positioned.

3. Choose **C**reate. You'll see the screen in Figure 23.3. You will see the note number at the top, and the *Footnote* or *Endnote* in the title bar.

4. Depending on how you want to space or indent the text following the note number, you can press the spacebar, Tab, or Indent (F7), then type the text of your note. You can use all the usual editing and formatting features of WordPerfect, including fonts, print attributes, graphics, special characters, Reveal Codes, the Speller, and the Thesaurus, just as you would in the normal document window.

5. When you've typed the entire footnote, choose **C**lose.

You'll be returned to the document window. WordPerfect inserts a [Footnote] or [Endnote] code at the insertion point. This code actually contains the text of the note, and some of the text is visible when you move the insertion point to the hidden code in Reveal Codes. (The text of an endnote or footnote is never visible in the document window.) When you print the document or preview it on the Print Preview screen, WordPerfect will put the note in the appropriate place.

EDITING NOTES

TO EDIT AN EXISTING FOOTNOTE OR ENDNOTE,

move the insertion point to the start of the page containing the faulty note. Choose Layout ➤ Footnote *or* Endnote ➤ Edit, type the number of the note you want to edit, and press ↵.

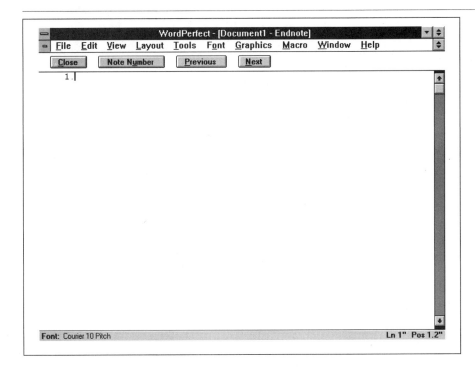

FIGURE 23.3:

The Footnote/Endnote Screen

You can use the Search feature (Chapter 9) to look for notes in a large document.

If you make an error in the text of a note, you can easily go back and fix it. Follow these steps:

1. If you have chosen to start note numbering with *1* on each page, move the insertion point to the start of the page containing the faulty note. If you're using consecutive note numbering, the insertion point can be anywhere in the document.

2. Choose **L**ayout, then choose either **F**ootnote or **E**ndnote, depending on which kind of note you need to change.

3. Choose **E**dit. You'll see the Edit Footnote dialog box.

4. Type the number of the note you want to edit, and choose OK or press ↵.

5. The note-editing screen looks exactly like the Create screen. Use the normal WordPerfect editing techniques to edit your note. Use these buttons to help you edit your note:

A single note can contain up to 65,000 bytes, which is basically the same as 65,000 characters.

Note **N**umber	Inserts a note number on the screen
Previous	Displays the previous note

Next	Displays the next note

6. Choose **C**lose when finished.

MOVING AND DELETING NOTES

You can move the superscripted number that refers to a note from one place in your document to another simply by moving the [Footnote] or [Endnote] code for that note. Briefly, the technique is the following: open Reveal Codes, place the insertion point on the note number you want to move, press Delete, move the insertion point to the new position for the note number, choose Edit ➤ Undelete or press Alt+Shift+Backspace, then choose Restore. WordPerfect will automatically renumber all the notes (as necessary) as you scroll through the document and will print them in their proper places the next time you print the document.

If you inadvertently type regular text inside of your footnote or endnote (or vice versa), you can use Cut and Paste to move that text. For example, if you need to move some text out of your footnote into your document, go to the editing screen for that footnote, select the text that needs to be moved, then choose Edit ➤ Cut or press Shift+Delete. Next, choose Close to leave the editing screen, position the insertion point wherever you want to move the text, and choose Edit ➤ Paste or press Shift+Insert to paste the text into your document.

To delete a footnote or an endnote, use Reveal Codes to locate its [Footnote] or [Endnote] code, and delete the code. WordPerfect will renumber all the other notes as you scroll through the document.

RENUMBERING NOTES

As an alternative to remarking the note starting numbers in multiple files, you can use Master Document (Chapter 24) to number notes consecutively in multiple documents.

Normally, the first note in a document is numbered *1,* and any others are numbered consecutively. You can change the starting number at any place in your document. This might be handy if, say, your document is divided into several files, and you need the numbering in one file to pick up where the numbering in another file left off.

To set a new note starting number, follow these steps:

1. Move the insertion point to wherever you want to restart the numbering sequence (before the code for the first note that you want to renumber).

2. Choose **L**ayout, and then choose either **F**ootnote or **E**ndnote, depending on which kind of note you want to renumber.

3. Choose **N**ew Number. You'll see the Footnote Number dialog box:

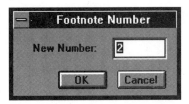

4. Type the new starting number, and choose OK or press ↵.

WordPerfect inserts a hidden [New Ftn Num:*n*] or [New End Num:*n*] code, where *n* indicates the new starting number, at the insertion point. All notes below that hidden code will be renumbered starting at the new number when you scroll through the document.

CHANGING THE APPEARANCE OF FOOTNOTES

By default, footnotes are printed in the format shown in Figure 23.1, near the start of this chapter. However, you can change the appearance of footnotes in several ways, by means of the Footnote Options dialog box. Here's the general procedure:

If you previously changed the footnote options, delete the old [Ftn Opt] code to prevent conflicting codes.

1. Move the insertion point to where you want to define the new footnote appearance (e.g., to the top of the document if you want to redefine the appearance of all the footnotes in the document).

2. Choose **L**ayout ➤ **F**ootnote ➤ **O**ptions. You'll see the Footnote Options dialog box, shown in Figure 23.4.

3. Choose the options for the appearances you want, as described in the following sections.

4. Choose OK or press ↵ to return to the document window.

WordPerfect inserts a [Ftn Opt] code at the insertion point, and all footnotes below this code will adhere to the choices you made in step 3. You can check the notes on the Print Preview screen or by printing the document.

Changing the Footnote-Marking Style

As you know, WordPerfect normally uses numbers to mark notes. But you can use letters (like *A, B,* and *C*) or special characters (like *, †, and ‡) to mark footnotes instead. To change the appearance of the numbering marker in both the text and the notes, choose Numbering Method in the Numbering area of the

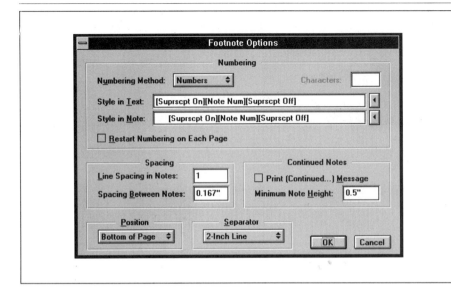

FIGURE 23.4:

The Footnote Options dialog box

Footnote Options dialog box. You can choose one of the following options from the pop-up list:

Numbers	Each note is numbered, starting with *1*.
Letters	Each note is lettered, starting with *A*.
Characters	Each note is marked by the character or characters you specify.

The Characters option merits some explanation. You can choose a single character, such as the asterisk (*), to mark notes. The first note will be marked with one asterisk, the second note with two asterisks, the third with three asterisks, and so on. When the character has been repeated 15 times, WordPerfect starts over with one character.

You can use the Characters text box in the Footnote Options dialog box to select the character you want:

1. Choose **C**haracters.

2. Press Ctrl+W to access the WordPerfect Characters dialog box.

3. Choose the set of characters you want from the Set pop-up list.

4. Choose the character you want.

5. Choose Insert **a**nd Close. The selected character will appear in the Characters box.

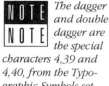

The dagger and double dagger are the special characters 4,39 and 4,40, from the Typographic Symbols set. For more information about special characters, see Chapter 5.

You can specify up to five characters, each separated by a single blank space. For example, if you specify the three characters

      *   †   ‡

the first note will be marked with an asterisk, the second with a dagger, and the third with a double dagger (note the blank space between each one). A fourth note will be marked with two asterisks, a fifth by two daggers, and so forth, up to 15 repetitions.

You can delete any existing blank spaces or codes with the Delete key. You can insert codes by placing the insertion point at the appropriate position, and either typing the characters or using the WordPerfect Characters dialog box (Ctrl+W). If you want extra space before or after your note number, press the spacebar, not Tab or Indent (F7). Keep in mind that the position of the note number with respect to the text or any formatting codes will be the same as the position of the [Note Num] code.

When using special characters instead of note numbers in a document with many notes, it's best to restart note marking on each page in order to prevent lengthy strings of character note markers. This way, your note markers will be "recycled" on each page, starting again with the first special character.

Changing the Appearance of Footnote Numbers

By default, the numbers that identify footnotes in text are superscript. Within the note itself, the number is superscript and indented. However, you can change the appearance of these numbers with the Style in Text and Style in Note options in the Numbering area of the Footnote Options dialog box.

The default or current option is shown, as in the example below:

[Suprscpt On][Note Num][Suprscpt Off]

where [Suprscpt On] and [Suprscpt Off] are the starting and ending codes for the superscript appearance, and [Note Num] is the code that calculates and prints the note number. If you accidentally delete the [Note Num] code while changing the appearance of the note number, press Alt+Shift+Backspace to undelete the code.

Restarting Numbering on Each Page

Normally, WordPerfect numbers footnotes consecutively throughout the document. As an alternative, you can have WordPerfect assign the number *1* (or the first special character in your list) to the first footnote on each page. Mark the Restart Numbering on Each Page check box in the Footnote Options dialog box.

Changing the Spacing of Footnotes

By default, WordPerfect prints one blank line between each footnote at the bottom of the page and single-spaces the text within each footnote. Enter a new value in the Line Spacing in Notes text box in the Spacing area of the Footnote Options dialog box to change the spacing within notes (e.g., *1* for single spacing, *1.5* for one-and-a-half spacing, and *2* for double spacing).

 *If you press ⏎ after typing a footnote a blank line is printed beneath the footnote and will be added to the measurement you enter for this option.*

After choosing Spacing Between Notes, you can enter a measurement for spacing between footnotes, either in inches (such as *0.167,* the default) or in points, followed by a *p* (for example, *12p,* which is automatically converted to 0.167 inches if Units of Measure is set to inches).

Keeping Footnotes Together

Footnotes are usually brief, but some documents require longer ones. If you have a lengthy footnote that spreads across two or more pages, you can have WordPerfect automatically print "(Continued...)" below the part of the footnote that is continued on the next page and above the part that is continued from the previous page. To do so, mark the Print (Continued...) Message check box in the Footnote Options dialog box. Only lengthy footnotes that cross pages will be affected by this change.

By default, WordPerfect will print about ½ inch of a lengthy footnote at the bottom of each page, and then "spill" the rest of the note in ½-inch increments onto the pages that follow. To change this, type a new measurement in the Minimum Note Height text box of the Footnote Options dialog box. For example, if you want each page to display up to 1 inch of text from a lengthy footnote, type *1.*

Positioning Footnotes

You can place footnotes immediately following the text on a page that is not completely filled, rather than at the bottom of the page. This method is sometimes used in books to keep the footnotes close to the text on the last page of a chapter, which may be only partly filled with text. If you need to use this feature in your own work, choose **A**fter Text from the Position pop-up list in the Footnote Options dialog box. Otherwise, leave this option set to Bottom of Page (the default).

Separating Footnotes from Text

As you saw in Figure 23.1 early in this chapter, WordPerfect automatically uses a 2-inch horizontal line to separate text from footnotes. To change this format, choose Separator from the Footnote Options dialog box, then one of these options from the pop-up list: No Line, 2-Inch Line, or Margin to Margin.

If you choose No Line, WordPerfect does not draw a line separating the text from the footnotes. If you choose Margin to Margin, WordPerfect draws a horizontal line from the left margin to the right margin.

CHANGING THE APPEARANCE OF ENDNOTES

If your document uses endnotes, you can refine them by using many of the techniques described previously in "Changing the Appearance of Footnotes." Even though you use a different dialog box, the techniques are generally the same. However, whereas WordPerfect uses [Ftn Opt] as the hidden code to mark the starting position for footnote appearance changes, it uses [End Opt] for endnote appearance changes.

To change the appearance of all the endnotes in your document, follow these steps:

1. Move the insertion point to the top of the document.

2. Choose **L**ayout ➤ **E**ndnote ➤ **O**ptions. You'll see the Endnote Options dialog box, shown in Figure 23.5.

3. Choose the options for the appearance and numbering you want to use for the endnotes.

4. Choose OK or press ↵ to return to the document window.

WordPerfect inserts an [End Opt] code at the insertion point, and all endnotes beneath that code adhere to the format and numbering choices you made in step 3.

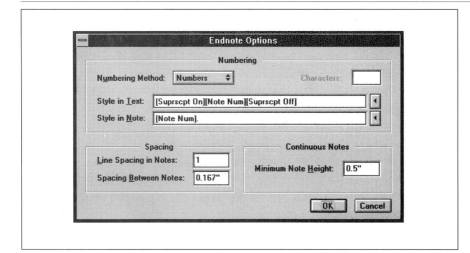

FIGURE 23.5:

The Endnote Options dialog box

DETERMINING WHERE ENDNOTES WILL APPEAR

WordPerfect endnotes are automatically numbered and placed at the end of a document. But if you have combined several sections or chapters in a single file, you may want to place endnotes closer to their source; for example, at the end of each section or chapter. To change the location of the endnotes, follow these steps:

Delete any old [End Opt] codes before changing the endnote options to prevent multiple codes from canceling each other out.

1. Move the insertion point to where you want the endnotes to appear. (To ensure that endnotes start on a new page, you can choose **L**ayout ➤ **P**age ➤ **P**age Break or press Ctrl+↵ to insert a hard page break.)

2. Choose **L**ayout ➤ **E**ndnote ➤ **P**lacement. You'll see this dialog box:

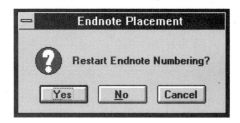

3. Choose **Yes** if you want to renumber any remaining endnotes, starting with *1*. Choose **No** to continue numbering any remaining endnotes consecutively from where the preceding note left off. A box containing this message appears in your document window:

Endnote Placement
It is not known how much space endnotes will occupy here.
Generate to determine.

The techniques for generating reference lists, including endnotes, are covered in more detail later in this chapter.

WordPerfect is telling you that until it actually has to print the endnotes, it will not know how much space is needed to print them. You can complete the following steps to have WordPerfect insert the endnotes in your document now:

1. Choose **Tools** ➤ **G**enerate (or press Alt+F12). You will see a dialog box indicating that any existing tables, lists, and indexes will be updated.

2. Choose **Yes**.

At this point you can move the insertion point to wherever you placed the endnotes. You'll see a box containing the message

Endnote Placement

indicating where the endnotes will be printed. WordPerfect places a hard page break below the boxed message. Any text you type above that page break will be printed on the same page as the endnotes. Any text you type below that page break will be printed on a new page, after the last endnote. If you switch to the Print Preview screen with the insertion point on the endnotes page, you'll see the actual endnotes.

To title all your endnote pages, you can place a page header at the end of your document with the appropriate title. Or, if you have changed the endnote placement, put the page header between the [HPg] code that ends the body text and the [Endnote Placement] code.

CHOOSING A FONT FOR NOTES

By default, footnotes and endnotes are printed in the same font as the rest of the text, or using whatever font is in effect at the location of the [Ftn Opt] or [End Opt] code. This means that you can set a font for all notes by moving the insertion point to the left of a [Ftn Opt] or an [End Opt] code and choosing a font for the notes, then moving the insertion point to the right of the options code and choosing a font for the regular body text. For example, in the following code sequence, all the footnotes will be printed in Times Roman Italic 10-point; regular body text will be printed in Times Roman 12-point:

[Font:Times Roman Italic 10pt][Ftn Opt][Font:Times Roman 12pt]

Of course, any font choice within the text of a note will override the font choice specified here.

If you want to insert a [Ftn Opt] or an [End Opt] code at the insertion point without changing the default settings, just choose Layout ➤ Footnote ➤ Options or Layout ➤ Endnote ➤ Options, and choose OK or press ↵ without making choices from the dialog box.

USING AUTOMATIC REFERENCE LISTS

TO MARK AND GENERATE LISTS AND CROSS-REFERENCES,

select the items to be referenced, choose Tools ➤ Mark Text, and choose an option. Move the insertion point to where you want the generated list to appear, choose Tools ➤ Define, and choose an option. Choose Tools ➤ Generate ➤ Yes to generate the lists or cross-references.

NOTE *The Master Document feature (Chapter 24) lets you generate reference lists from multiple documents stored in separate files.*

A *reference list* is a list of items in a document and the page numbers on which they appear. With WordPerfect you can *mark* items to be placed in a reference list and define the location and format of the list. Then, before printing the document, you can instruct WordPerfect to *generate* the final list, complete with the proper page-number references. You can regenerate your reference list at any time to reflect changes in page numbers resulting from changes made to your document.

WordPerfect documents can have four types of reference lists:

◆ Index

◆ General list (useful for lists of figures and tables)

◆ Table of contents

◆ Table of authorities (a legal-style bibliography)

The general steps for creating each kind of list are basically the same:

◆ Mark all the items in the document that belong in the list, by choosing **T**ools ➤ Mar**k** Text (or pressing F12).

◆ Define the list (i.e., specify its format and position in the document), by choosing **T**ools ➤ **D**efine (or pressing Shift+F12).

◆ Adjust the page numbers if necessary.

◆ Generate the list.

You can do any of these steps at any time, so you can create your lists as you write your document or after your document is complete. And of course, you can make any additions, deletions, and changes to your document, and have Word-Perfect automatically update all the lists to reflect your changes. I'll discuss the specific steps for marking items and defining each type of list in the sections that follow.

MARKING TABLE-OF-CONTENTS ENTRIES

If you want to mark titles, headings, or any other text for inclusion in a table of contents (TOC), follow these steps:

1. Select the text that you want to include in the TOC, as in the example shown in Figure 23.6.

2. Choose **T**ools ➤ Mar**k** Text ➤ Table of **C**ontents (or press F12 C). You'll see the Mark Table of Contents dialog box:

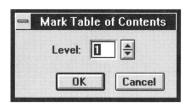

3. Click on the up or down arrow keys at the right-hand side of the box or use the arrow keys on the keyboard to choose the level of indenta-tion, or enter the level of indentation (1–5) in the text box, where *1* is the leftmost level.

4. Choose OK or press ↵.

WordPerfect surrounds the selected text with [Mark:TOC] and [End Mark:TOC] codes.

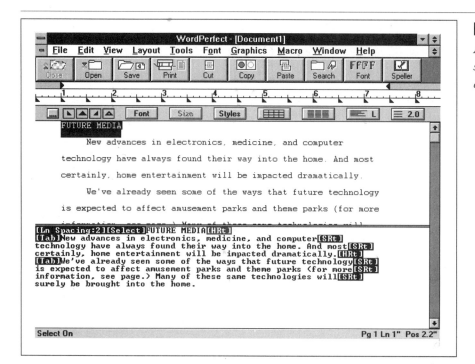

FIGURE 23.6:

*A sample heading
selected for inclusion in
a table of contents*

Defining a Table of Contents

After marking all (or some) TOC entries, you can define the position and format of the TOC by following these steps:

1. Move the insertion point to the start of your document (or wherever you want to place the table of contents).

2. Create a page break (press Ctrl+↵) to put the TOC on its own page.

3. To ensure proper page numbering, move the insertion point to the top of the first numbered page (i.e., page number 1 after the title page, TOC, figure lists, and any other front matter). Then choose **L**ayout ➤ **P**age ➤ **N**umbering ➤ **N**ew Page Number (or press Alt+F9 N N) and assign page number 1 to that page. Choose OK or press ↵ to return to the document window.

4. Move the insertion point back to the page where you want to print the TOC (on or above the [HPg] code you inserted in step 2).

5. Choose **T**ools ➤ De**f**ine ➤ Table of **C**ontents. You'll see the Table of Contents Definition dialog box, shown in Figure 23.7.

*You can
use also
number
the front
matter pages with
Roman numerals,
as described in
Chapter 7.*

6. Choose whatever options you need to specify the format of each level within your TOC (described next in "Formatting the Table of Contents").

7. Choose OK or press ↵ to return to the document window.

WordPerfect inserts a hidden [Def Mark:TOC] code at the insertion point. When you generate the lists, WordPerfect will insert the table of contents below that code. (Before typing a title or creating a page heading, such as "TABLE OF CONTENTS," position the insertion point on or above the code.)

FORMATTING THE TABLE OF CONTENTS

The options in the Define Table of Contents dialog box let you specify the format of your table of contents, as summarized below:

Number of Levels: lets you choose how many levels are displayed in your table of contents, in the range 1 to 5.

Numbering Format: lets you choose a format for printing page numbers at each level in the TOC.

No Numbering	No page numbers
Text #	Page number follows the entry, separated by a space

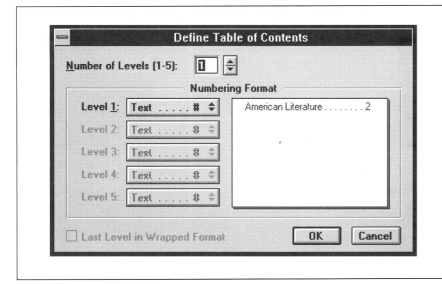

FIGURE 23.7:

The Define Table of Contents dialog box

Text (#)	Page number, enclosed in parentheses, follows the entry, separated by a space
Text #	Page numbers flush with right margin next to the entry
Text...#	Flush-right page numbers preceded by dot leaders (as in Figure 23.8)

Last Level in Wrapped Format: If this is on, WordPerfect word-wraps the last level in the TOC if it's longer than one line (you cannot choose a flush-right style for this level).

MARKING TABLE-OF-CONTENTS ENTRIES WITH STYLES

You can use the Styles feature to format section or chapter titles and headings, and include codes for the table of contents right in the styles. For example, you can mark all the chapter titles as TOC level-1 entries, all the main headings as TOC level-2 entries, all the subheadings as TOC level-3 entries, and so forth.

To do this, first create a paired style for whichever design element you want to format and include in the TOC (e.g., chapter titles or main headings). When you get to the screen for editing codes in the style, insert your formatting codes normally.

Then move the highlight in the Reveal Codes portion of the screen so that it is right on the [Comment] code that separates the style starting codes from the style ending codes. Press Shift+→ to select the [Comment] code.

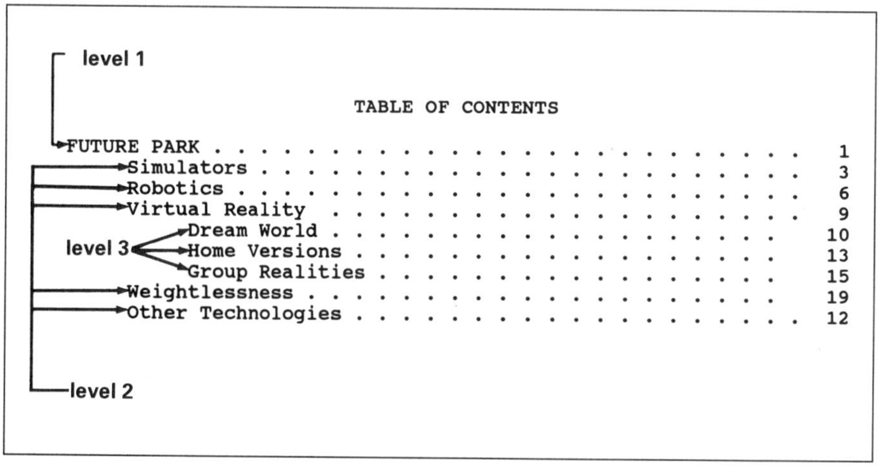

NOTE NOTE *See Chapter 14 if you need more information on creating or using styles.*

FIGURE 23.8:

A sample generated table of contents with dot leaders

Next, choose Tools ➤ Mark Text ➤ Table of Contents (or press F12 C), and enter the level for this style (e.g., *1* for chapter titles and *2* for main headings). Press ↵. You'll see the [Mark:ToC] code to the left of the [Comment] code and the [End Mark:ToC] code to the right. Save the style as you normally would.

While (or after) creating your document, use the styles to format the chapter titles, headings, and so forth. Then define the TOC and generate it, as described later.

MARKING INDEX ENTRIES

You can also mark entries for inclusion in an index. WordPerfect indexes offer two levels of entries: the index heading and the subheading, as shown in Figure 23.9. You can define your index entry at either or both of these levels.

To identify an index entry, follow these steps:

1. Move the insertion point to the word you want to include in the index, or, if you want to include a phrase (two or more words) as a single entry, select those words.

2. Choose **T**ools ➤ Mar**k** Text ➤ **I**ndex (or press F12 I). You'll see the Mark Index dialog box:

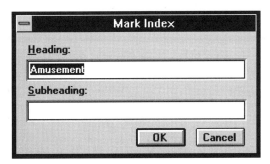

3. In the Heading text box, your selected word or phrase appears. You can either accept that heading or type a new one.

4. Enter a subheading in the Subheading text box if you wish.

5. Choose OK or press ↵ to use the displayed heading and subheading (if any).

```
                        INDEX

Amusement  1, 2
    engineers  1
Questor  1, 6                    ←index heading
Robotics  1, 9, 12
    entertainment  15
    industrial  10              ←subheadings
    home  11,14
Simulators  1, 15
Star Tours  1, 25
Theme parks  1, 12
Toontown  1, 16
Universal  1
Virtual reality  1, 10, 24
```

FIGURE 23.9:

A sample index illustrating a heading and subheadings

USING AN INDEX CONCORDANCE FILE

As an alternative to marking items individually in a document for inclusion in an index, you can simply make a file consisting of a list of all the words you want included. This word list is called a *concordance file*. When creating a concordance file, you must end each entry with a hard-return code [HRt]. Figure 23.10 shows a sample concordance file in the document window and Reveal Codes.

By default, each entry in the concordance file is a main heading. To convert an entry to a subheading, mark it as a subheading in the concordance file by following the steps in "Marking Index Entries." If you want the entry to be matched as both a heading and subheading, mark the entry twice: once as a heading and once as a subheading. After creating your concordance file, save it as you would any other WordPerfect document.

Word-Perfect can generate the index more quickly if the concordance entries are in alphabetical order—use the Sort feature (Chapter 17).

DEFINING THE INDEX

Before you generate the index, you must mark its location, define its format, and, if you plan to use a concordance file, specify the concordance file name. Follow these steps:

1. Move the insertion point to where you want the index to appear in your document. (Press Ctrl+End to move to the end of the document.)

2. If you want to start the index on a new page, choose Layout ➤ **P**age ➤ **P**age Break or press Ctrl+↵ to insert a hard page break.

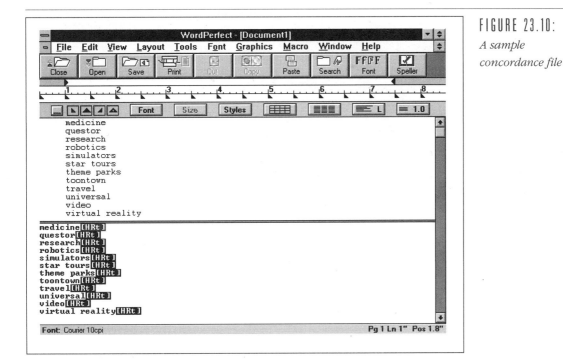

3. Choose **Tools** ➤ De**fi**ne ➤ **I**ndex. You'll see the Define Index dialog box, shown in Figure 23.11.

4. If you have created a concordance file, type its complete name in the Optional Concordance File text box, or click on the file-folder icon box at the right to get a list of files in the current directory.

5. Choose a format for the page numbers from the Numbering **F**ormat pop-up list. The choices are the same as those you saw when defining a table of contents. The sample index shown in the box reflects your choice.

WordPerfect inserts a [Def Mark:Index] code at the insertion point, marking the spot where the index will appear when you generate the lists (described in "Generating the Lists" later in this chapter). The index is alphabetized automatically. (Position the insertion point on or above the [Def Mark:Index] code before typing a title or creating a page heading, such as "INDEX.")

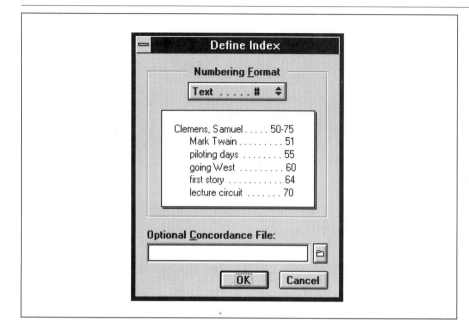

FIGURE 23.11:

The Define Index dialog box

MARKING GENERAL-LIST ENTRIES

General lists are lists of items that don't necessarily fit into the index or table-of-contents format. For example, you might want to mark words or phrases in text for inclusion in a glossary or bibliography. You can have up to five such general lists (lists 1–5).

WordPerfect can also automatically create lists of numbers and captions from graphics boxes. Figure 23.12 shows a sample list of figures.

You need not mark graphics boxes to generate a list for them. Instead, WordPerfect has predefined lists 6–10 as follows:

Only numbered and captioned boxes are included in lists 6–10. Also, only tables in Table boxes are included in list 7.

LIST NUMBER	CONTENTS
6	Numbers and captions from all Figure boxes
7	Numbers and captions from all Table boxes
8	Numbers and captions from all Text boxes
9	Numbers and captions from all User boxes
10	Numbers and captions from all Equation boxes

```
                         LIST OF FIGURES

Figure 1. Projected and Actual Cash Flow, 1991 . . . . . . .   1
Figure 2. Projected Cash Flow, 1992 . . . . . . . . . . . . .   3
Figure 3. Quarterly Sales for 1991  . . . . . . . . . . . . .   6
```

FIGURE 23.12:
A sample list of figures

To mark an item for inclusion in one of the general lists (1–5), follow these steps:

1. Select the word or phrase you want to put in a general list.
2. Choose **T**ools ➤ Mar**k** Text ➤ **L**ist (or press F12 L). You'll see the Mark List dialog box.
3. Choose the list you want (1–5) from the Number pop-up list and choose OK or press ↵. (If you're creating multiple general lists, it's up to you to remember which list is which; e.g., list 1 is the glossary, list 2 is the bibliography, and so forth.)

WordPerfect surrounds the word or phrase with [Mark:List,*x*] and [End Mark:List,*x*] codes, where *x* indicates the number of the list that will contain the word or phrase after you define and generate that list.

Defining a General List

After defining the items for your list, or if you're simply generating a list of graphics box numbers and captions using the predefined lists, you must define the list's location and format by following these steps:

1. Move the insertion point to where you want to create the list in your document.
2. If you want the list to appear on its own page, insert a hard page break by pressing Ctrl+↵.
3. If you are placing the list before numbered page 1 (e.g., in the document's front matter), move to the first numbered page and choose **L**ayout ➤ **P**age ➤ **N**umbering ➤ **N**ew Page Number (Alt+F9 N N) to ensure that page 1 is numbered properly, as explained earlier in "Defining a Table of Contents."

4. Choose **Tools** ➤ Define ➤ List.

5. Choose the list you're defining (1–10). The Define List dialog box appears, showing the format of your list (Figure 23.13).

If your document is lengthy and divided into several files, you can use the Master Document feature to generate a table of authorities for all the files.

6. Choose a numbering format for the page numbers in the generated list (see the table-of-contents sections if you need more information about each option).

7. Optionally, press Ctrl+↵ to have a new page start after the list.

You'll return to the document window. WordPerfect inserts a [Def Mark:List,*x·y*] code at the insertion point, where *x* is the list number and *y* is the number of the option you've chosen from the Define List dialog box. When you generate the list, as described later in this chapter, the list will be placed just below this code. (Position the insertion point on or above the [Def Mark:List] code before typing a title or creating a page heading, such as "LIST OF FIGURES," for the list.)

MARKING TABLE-OF-AUTHORITIES ENTRIES

A table of authorities (TOA) is a list of citations in a legal document (see Figure 23.14). It is typically divided into several sections, such as *Cases, Statutes,* and *Regulations,* with each section having a different format.

The document itself (typically a brief) generally contains two types of citations: a long form, which is usually the first reference in the document, and

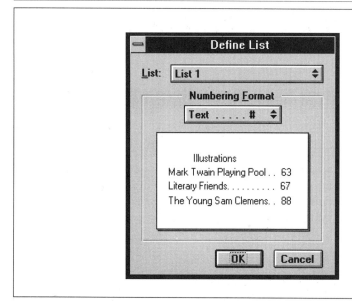

FIGURE 23.13:

The Define List dialog box

```
                    TABLE OF AUTHORITIES

Cases                                                    Page

Association of General Contractors v.
City and County of San Francisco
813 F.2d 922 (1987) . . . . . . . . . . . . . . . . . . 1, 9

City of Richmond v. Croson, 109 S.Ct. 706 (1989) . . . . .  1, 13

Fullilove v. Klutznick, 448 U.S. 448, 100 S.Ct 2758,
65 L.Ed. 2d 902 (1980) . . . . . . . . . . . . . . . . . 2, 13

Gregory Construction Co. v. Blanchard
691 F.Supp. 17 (W.D. Mich. 1988) . . . . . . . . .  12, 14, 15

Jackson v. Conway, D.C. Montana 1979, 472 F.Supp. 896 . . . 8, 11

London v. Coopers & Lybrand
C.A. Cal 1981, 644 F.2d 811 (1981) . . . . . . . . . . . . 12


Statutes

California Public Contract Code, Section 10115 . . . . . . . . 12
```

FIGURE 23.14:

A sample table of authorities

a short form, which is an abbreviated way of indicating subsequent references to the same authority. When using WordPerfect to generate a TOA, you initially mark all instances of the long form. Then you assign a short form to that authority, and from that point onward in the document, you can mark all references to the same authority by using the short form.

Marking the Long Form

To create the initial long-form TOA entry, follow these steps:

1. Select the long form of the citation, as in the example shown in Figure 23.15.

2. Choose **T**ools ➤ Mar**k** Text ➤ TOA **F**ull Form (or press F12 F). You'll see the Mark TOA Full Form dialog box.

3. Enter a section number (1–16), based on your own organization of the table. For example, you might use section 1 for cases, section 2 for statutes, and so forth. As with general lists, it's up to you to keep track of which section is which.

4. In the Short **F**orm text box, enter the short-form "nickname" that you want to use to identify the authority you selected in the document window. Be sure to assign each authority a unique short-form name, since each will identify a separate authority.

5. Choose OK or press ↵. You'll be taken to a screen for editing the long form of the authority.

6. As necessary, edit the existing long form to appear exactly as you want it to look in the table of authorities.

7. Choose **C**lose to return to the document window.

You've now defined how the authority will appear in the table of authorities, and have assigned the short-form nickname to that authority. Now you can start marking the references to that authority throughout the document.

Marking the Short Forms

After you mark the long form of the citation, mark all the subsequent occurrences of the short form. You can use the Search feature to help:

1. Move the insertion point to the top of the document (press Ctrl+Home).

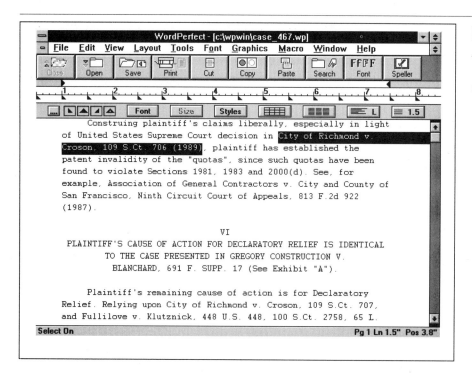

FIGURE 23.15:

A sample long-form TOA entry selected in the document window

The Search feature is optional; you can mark any short-form entry simply by selecting it and choosing Tools ➤ Mark Text ➤ TOA Short Form (or by pressing F12 S).

2. Choose **E**dit ➤ **S**earch (or press F2).

3. Type the short form (or part of the short form).

4. Choose **S**earch to start the search.

5. If the insertion point lands to the right of a valid short form, choose **T**ools ➤ Mar**k** Text ➤ TOA **S**hort Form (or press F12 S). (If this isn't a valid short form, press Shift+F2 to find the next one.)

6. Press ↵ to accept the suggested short-form name, or enter the correct short-form name and then press ↵.

7. Repeat steps 2–6 for each remaining short form in the document.

You've defined the long and short form of a single authority in a single section. You must repeat the general procedure for each authority in the document.

DEFINING THE TABLE OF AUTHORITIES

If you fail to indicate a new page number beyond the TOA page, WordPerfect will warn you later when you generate the lists. You can simply press any key to continue generating the lists, then make any changes or corrections later.

You define a table of authorities one section at a time. Follow these steps:

1. Position the insertion point where you want the table of authorities listed (usually at or near the beginning of the document).

2. To insert a hard page break, choose **L**ayout ➤ **P**age ➤ **P**age Break or press Ctrl+↵.

3. To ensure proper page numbers, move the insertion point to page 1 (beyond the TOA and any other front matter), and choose **L**ayout ➤ **P**age ➤ **N**umbering ➤ **N**ew Page Number (or press Alt+F9 N N) to mark that page as page 1.

4. Move the insertion point wherever you want the next section heading for the TOA to appear, and type the heading (e.g., *Cases, Statutes,* or *Regulations*). Typically this will be on or above the hard page break you entered in step 2.

5. Choose **T**ools ➤ De**f**ine ➤ Table of **A**uthorities. You'll see the Define Table of Authorities dialog box, shown in Figure 23.16.

6. Type the number of the section (1–16) that you want to define in the Section **N**umber text box.

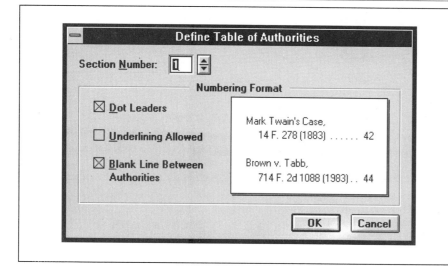

FIGURE 23.16:

The Define Table of Authorities dialog box

7. Choose the numbering format for the current section by marking the Dot Leader, Underlining Allowed, or Blank Line Between Authorities check box. A sample of the table of authorities, reflecting your selections, appears in the box to the right.

Dot Leaders	Places dot leaders in front of page numbers, which are flush with the right margin
Underlining Allowed	Retains any underlining from the original document entries
Blank Line Between Authorities	Puts one blank line between each authority

8. Choose OK or press ↵ to return to the document window.

Repeat steps 4–8 for each section in the TOA. WordPerfect inserts a [Def Mark:TOA,*x*] mark at the insertion point, where *x* is the number of the current section. When you generate the lists, as described later in this chapter, the citations for each section will be listed beneath each section's [Def Mark:TOA] code.

AUTOMATIC CROSS-REFERENCING

Suppose that somewhere in your document you refer to a table a few pages back. At the current insertion point, you want to type a cross-reference, such as "see the table on page 14." But perhaps you don't know the page number, or (more likely) you don't know what the page number will be after a few more hours (or days) of writing and editing.

WordPerfect can keep track of such cross-references automatically. The item referred to (the table on page 14 in the example) is known as a *target*. The place where you mention the target is known as a *reference*. (To keep the terms straight, just remember that a reference always points to its target.)

Your cross-references need not be to page numbers. As you'll see, you can also refer to an automatic paragraph number, a footnote or an endnote number, or a graphics box number.

Marking a Reference

To mark a reference in your document, follow these steps:

1. Move the insertion point to the place in your document where you want to reference the page number, note number, or graphics box number.

2. Type any introductory text as you normally would (e.g., *see page* or *as shown in*). Be sure to press the spacebar if you want a space between the last word and the number.

3. Choose **T**ools ➤ Mar**k** Text ➤ Cross-**R**eference (or press F12 R). The Mark Cross-Reference dialog box appears, shown in Figure 23.17.

4. Choose R**e**ference, **T**arget, or Re**f**erence and Target.

5. In the Tie Reference To box, select the item you are referencing from these options: Page Number, Paragraph/Outline, Footnote Number, Endnote Number, Figure, Table Box, Text Box, User Box, or Equation.

6. Type a name for the target—it can be up to 31 characters long and can contain spaces. Choose OK or press ↵ when you're finished.

7. If necessary, finish typing the introductory text for the reference (for example, type a] for a reference of the form "[see page 10]").

When generating references to graphics boxes, WordPerfect automatically inserts text from the caption number style defined for the referenced box type. For example, WordPerfect automatically inserts the word "Figure" before the referenced number of a Figure box.

You cannot exit this dialog box unless you've entered a target name.

When entering a target name, use something that's clear and easy to remember. For example, don't use *Fig 3* as a target name, because, if you later insert a figure in front of that one, it won't be *Fig 3* any more. Instead, use a descriptive name like *Quarterly Sales Fig.*

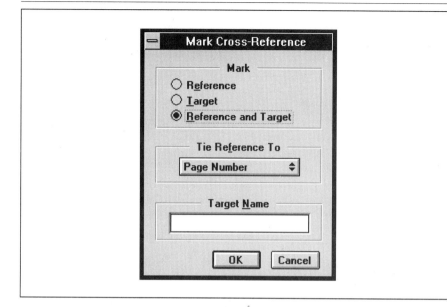

FIGURE 23.17:

The Mark Cross-Reference dialog box

After you enter the target name, you're returned to the document window. WordPerfect inserts the [Ref(*target*)] code at the insertion point, where *target* is the name you entered in step 6 above. Depending on the type of reference, the code appears for now as a question mark in the document window.

MARKING A TARGET

To identify a referenced target in your document, follow these steps:

1. Move the insertion point to the right of the target. (Open Reveal Codes to make sure that the insertion point is properly positioned just past the target.)

2. Choose **T**ools ➤ Mar**k** Text ➤ Cross-**R**eference (or press F12 R).

3. Choose **T**arget.

4. Enter the name of the target in the Target **N**ame text box, making sure to use the exact spelling you used when defining the reference (e.g., *Quarterly Sales Fig*), and choose OK or press ↵.

WordPerfect inserts a [Target(*target*)] code at the insertion point, where *target* is the target name you entered in step 4.

After you've marked your references and targets, you can replace all the question marks by generating the cross-references, using the same steps you use to generate lists (see "Generating the Lists" later in this chapter).

MARKING A REFERENCE AND A TARGET AT THE SAME TIME

As an alternative to marking references and targets independently, Word-Perfect lets you mark both of them at the same time. Follow these steps:

1. Position the insertion point where you want the referenced page, note, or graphics box number to appear, and type the introductory text.

2. Choose **Tools** ➤ Mar**k** Text ➤ Cross-**R**eference (or press F12 R).

3. In the Mark Cross-Reference dialog box, choose **R**eference and Target.

4. Make a selection from the Tie Re**f**erence To box.

5. If prompted, enter the name of the target.

6. If necessary, finish typing the introductory text for the reference.

PAGE X OF Y PAGE NUMBERS

By cross-referencing the last page of a document, you can set up "page x of y" page numbering for your page headers or footers, where x is the current page, and y is the last page. Follow these steps:

1. Move the insertion point to the last page of the document (press Ctrl+End).

2. Choose **Tools** ➤ Mar**k** Text ➤ Cross-**R**eference.

3. Choose **T**arget.

4. Choose Target **N**ame, and type an obvious name, such as *LAST PAGE*. Then choose OK or press ↵ to leave the dialog box.

5. Now you need to start typing the text of your page number. In this example, type **Page**, and then press the spacebar.

You may want to turn on Reveal Codes to help with cutting and pasting text later in these steps.

6. Choose **Layout** ➤ **P**age ➤ **N**umbering, then choose **I**nsert Page Number from the dialog box. The page number appears as ^B in the document window and as [Insert Pg Num:^B] in Reveal Codes.

7. Press the spacebar, type **of**, then press the spacebar again.

8. Choose **T**ools ➤ Mar**k** Text ➤ Cross-**R**eference.

9. Choose **R**eference (*LAST PAGE* should still appear under Target **N**ame).

10. Choose OK. A question mark appears in text; a [Ref<LAST PAGE>:Pg ?] code appears in Reveal Codes.

11. Move the insertion point back to the *P* in *Page* (so the highlight is just to the right of the [Target<LAST PAGE>] code in Reveal Codes).

12. Press F8 and then Ctrl+End to select the text and codes you just inserted.

13. Choose **E**dit ➤ Cu**t** or press Shift+Del to delete the selected text.

14. Move the insertion point back to the top of the document.

The Mark Text options are dimmed and unavailable when editing a page header or footer. But you can bypass this limitation by pasting the code into the header or footer.

15. Choose **Layout** ➤ **P**age, and then either Headers or Footers, depending on whether you want to place page numbers at the top or bottom of each page.

16. Choose A or B, and then **C**reate.

17. Chose **E**dit ➤ **P**aste, or press Shift+Ins, to insert the page number text and codes into the page header.

18. You can type any additional text, or use formatting options, to further refine the format of the header or footer.

19. Choose **C**lose to leave the header/footer editing screen.

At the document window, use Tools ➤ Generate to generate all the cross-references. To verify your new page numbering scheme, use Print Preview or print some pages. If you later insert or delete pages, remember that you'll need to make sure that the LAST PAGE reference is still at the bottom of the document, and then regenerate the references by using Tools ➤ Generate before printing.

GENERATING THE LISTS

After marking your reference list items or cross-references, you can generate all lists and referenced items in the document by following these steps:

1. Choose **T**ools ➤ **G**enerate (or press Alt+F12). You'll see this dialog box:

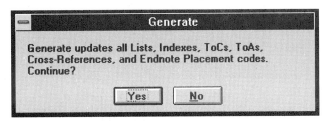

2. Choose **Y**es to proceed.

WordPerfect generates the lists and cross-references, giving you a progress report as it works. Then you'll be returned to the document window. You can scroll through the document to verify your work (though any generated references in headers, footers, notes, and so forth will be visible only on the Print Preview screen or printed document).

If your index is not acceptable, delete it before changing the definition and regenerating the index.

All reference lists in the document are generated whenever you go through these steps. Previously generated reference lists are replaced with new lists reflecting any changes in the content or pagination of the document.

Note that WordPerfect does not automatically update the lists when you add, delete, or change text in the future. If you make any changes to the document, you should repeat the steps above to regenerate all the lists before printing the document, to make sure all reference material is up to date.

Whenever you print a document that contains reference lists and has been edited since it was last generated, WordPerfect will remind you that the lists or indexes in the document may need to be generated for the lists to be current. You can cancel the print job and regenerate the lists or indexes before printing the document, or you can tell WordPerfect to print the document anyway.

EDITING A GENERATED REFERENCE LIST

When you generate reference lists, each list begins at the location of the [Def Mark:] code that was inserted in the document when you defined the list. At the end of each generated list, a new code appears: [End Def]. This code is important, because it marks the end of the material that will be replaced if the document is regenerated.

You can edit the contents of a generated reference list, refining it the same way you edit any WordPerfect text. However, your changes will be discarded if you regenerate the list in the future, because everything between a [Def Mark:] and [End Def] code is replaced with a newly generated list whenever you regenerate the document.

If you must edit text in a reference list, you're better off doing so at the source: within the main body of the text. That way, when you regenerate the list, the correction will be included in both the document proper and the generated list.

COMPARING DOCUMENTS

In the course of creating your correspondence, reports, or other written documents, you may have occasion to work with different versions of the same document. Later, you may need to see the differences between the two versions. If, for example, you have added, deleted, or moved material, you may need to see where the differences occur. Comparing documents can be especially useful if several people have worked on the same document.

If you compare documents manually, this can be a tedious and time-consuming process. However, WordPerfect can compare two versions of the same document, phrase by phrase, noting phrases that have been added, deleted, or moved. Once you have examined and noted the differences, you can then either completely restore the current document or selectively remove the markings that indicated the differences.

WordPerfect notes the differences between the two documents in three ways:

Because Word-Perfect will mark the differences in both files, you may want to make backup copies before you begin Document Compare.

Added phrases	Redline codes, which show as [Redln On] and [Redln Off] in Reveal Codes, mark any phrases that have been added. On a color monitor, these phrases are displayed in red.
Deleted phrases	Strikeout codes, which show as [Stkout On] and [Stkout Off] in Reveal Codes, mark any phrases that have been deleted. These phrases are displayed with lines through them.
Moved phrases	The message "THE FOLLOWING TEXT WAS MOVED" appears before a phrase that was moved, and "THE PRECEDING TEXT WAS MOVED" appears after a phrase that was moved.

1. Make sure that you've made backup copies of both versions of the documents you want to compare.

2. Choose **T**ools ➤ Do**c**ument Compare.

3. Choose **A**dd Markings. A dialog box appears showing the name of the version of the document that's on disk. If you want to compare the current file to another disk file, you can type in the name in the dialog box.

4. Choose **C**ompare to begin the comparison.

5. After you've looked at the results of the comparison, you may want to remove the markings from the current document. Choose **T**ools ➤ Do**c**ument Compare ➤ **R**emove Markings.

6. If you want to remove all the markings, choose OK or press ↵. If you want a version of the current document that contains the markings, mark the Leave **R**edline Marks check box, and then choose OK or press ↵.

In the next chapter, I'll conclude this part of the book with coverage of the Master Document feature, which lets you treat separate files as one file for purposes of referencing and consistency of style.

CHAPTER

24

Using Master Document to Work with Large Files

! f you write large documents, such as books with several chapters or reports with multiple large sections, you'll undoubtedly find it easiest to store each chapter or section in a separate file. This helps prevent any individual document from becoming so large that it is unwieldy to work with in a document window.

If you store chapters or large sections as separate files, you can use the Master Document feature to *link* these files into one large, master document. This lets you consistently apply or change a style, search and replace, and make formatting changes throughout all the separate files as though they were one large file. You can also generate automatic references, like a table of contents, an index, figure and table lists, tables of authorities, and cross-references for all the combined files at once.

When you link several files into a master document, WordPerfect also sequentially numbers all the pages, footnotes and endnotes, automatic (paragraph) numbers, and graphics boxes in the overall master document. This gives you all the advantages of automatic numbering, across many documents stored as separate files.

WHAT IS A MASTER DOCUMENT?

A *master document* is like any other WordPerfect document that you create in the document window, and it can contain text and hidden codes just like any other document. The only difference is that the master document contains links to other documents, which are referred to as *subdocuments*. Each sub-document, in turn, is also just a regular WordPerfect document that you've previously created and saved in the usual manner.

To get to the Master Document options, choose Tools ➤ Master Document. Master Document shares the Tools menu with the automatic-referencing features, because they are so often used to link separate files for referencing, as I'll discuss shortly.

BEFORE YOU USE MASTER DOCUMENTS

Before you use the Master Document feature for numbering pages, notes, or boxes, or for generating references, you need to be aware of the following:

◆ If you'll be using any front matter before page number 1, you should include a [Pg Num:1] code at the appropriate place to start numbering at page 1 (using Layout ➤ Page ➤ Numbering). None of the subsequent documents should contain [Pg Num:] codes, unless you want to interrupt the consecutive numbering sequence. For example, if each section in a report is numbered separately, such as *1-1, 2-1,* and so forth, you might want to put a page-numbering code at the start of each section to restart the numbering sequence.

◆ If you want each chapter or section to start on an odd-numbered page, you should include a [Force:Odd] code at the top of each chapter or section (also using Layout ➤ Page ➤ Numbering).

 *You can use Roman numerals to number front matter pages. Any material on these pages can also be marked for inclusion in reference lists.*

◆ Sequential numbering of footnotes, endnotes, graphic boxes, and automatic paragraph numbers throughout the files will not be accurate if subdocuments contain codes that activate a numbering change for any of these items.

◆ If you will be generating tables of contents, lists, or any other automatic reference lists, you may want to store the necessary [Def Mark:] definition codes in a separate file, perhaps named FRONTMAT.WP. Remember to use hard page breaks to separate various lists within the document.

◆ If you'll be generating back matter, such as an index, you may want to store the necessary [Def Mark:Index] code in a separate document, perhaps named BACKMAT.WP.

As an alternative to the last two options, you can store the generated lists within the master document itself by placing the [Def Mark:] codes above (for front matter) and below (for back matter) the subdocuments, and then generating the lists.

CREATING A MASTER DOCUMENT

TO CREATE A MASTER DOCUMENT,

start with a blank document window, and choose Tools ➤ Master Document ➤ Subdocument to define links to other documents.

To create a master document, follow these steps:

1. Start from a new, blank WordPerfect document window.

2. Choose **T**ools ➤ **M**aster Document ➤ **S**ubdocument. The dialog box shown in Figure 24.1 appears, allowing you to select a file for inclusion in the master document from the current directory.

3. Select the file that you want to link, just like you would select a file to open, except choose **I**nclude. (If you are unsure whether a file should be included, you can use the View option to preview the contents of any file.) After you've chosen a file, a comment indicating the position of the subdocument within the master document appears.

4. If you want to ensure that the next document starts on a new page, insert a hard page break (press Ctrl+↵).

5. Repeat steps 2 through 4 for each document you want to include in the master document, making sure to link the files in proper order (e.g., FRONTMAT.WP, CHAP1.WP, CHAP2.WP, and so forth). A subdocument link is placed at the current insertion point in the master document.

When you're finished, you'll see comments for each subdocument on the screen. If you inserted hard page breaks, you'll also see the double underlines used to signify those breaks in the document window (Figure 24.2).

> **NOTE** *The sub-document doesn't have to exist at the time you create your master document. You can type the name of a nonexistent file in the Include Subdocument dialog box, then choose Insert.*

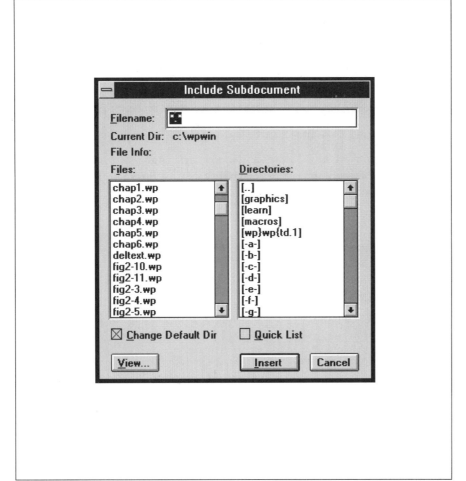

FIGURE 24.1:

*The Include
Subdocument dialog box*

GENERATING REFERENCES
FROM A MASTER DOCUMENT

If you've already positioned and defined reference lists that you want to generate from your subdocuments, you can use Tools ➤ Generate (Alt+F12) to generate them now. Optionally, you can position the insertion point where you want these lists to appear within the master document, insert hard page breaks where appropriate, and define the lists right in the master document. Then generate the references as you normally would. In this case, the generated lists will be part of the master document, rather than one of the subdocuments. You can print the lists and save them as described later in this chapter.

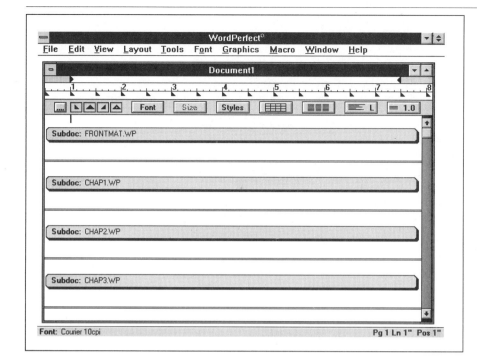

An example of several subdocuments in the document window

If the page or other automatic numbers are inaccurate in your generated lists, check to see whether one or more subdocuments contain codes that incorrectly restart numbering. Also, you may not have inserted hard page breaks everywhere that text needs to start on a new page.

EXPANDING THE MASTER DOCUMENT

TO EXPAND THE MASTER DOCUMENT,

choose Tools ➤ Master Document ➤ Expand Master.

> **NOTE** *When you generate references from a master document, WordPerfect automatically expands and condenses each document "behind the scenes" as necessary.*

You can edit and save subdocuments individually, just like any other WordPerfect files. But often, you'll want to work with all your subdocuments at once—to make global changes, for example. If you want to work with subdocuments as a whole within the master document, you must *expand* the master document. This expands the subdocuments, retrieving them into the document window for normal editing. Although it's not necessary to expand

If you are using a mouse, double-click on any of the subdocuments to expand all the subdocuments within the master document.

the master document to generate reference lists, it *is* necessary to do so for most other types of operations. Follow these steps:

1. With the master document in the document window, choose **T**ools ➤ **M**aster Document ➤ Expand Master. WordPerfect retrieves all the subdocuments in your master document (which could take some time) and places them in the normal document window.

2. If WordPerfect cannot find a subdocument, it displays this dialog box:

3. Choosing **S**kip enables you to ignore that document and proceed. Choosing **C**hange enables you to choose a different file. Choosing Cancel cancels the expansion.

Your retrieved subdocuments in the document window are essentially one large file, and you can edit this file like any other. Each subdocument is placed between a [Subdoc Start] code and [Subdoc End] code. Never move or delete the [Subdoc Start] and [Subdoc End] codes that surround a subdocument in an expanded master document.

EDITING A MASTER DOCUMENT

You can make any editing changes to any document within the master document, but keep four points in mind:

◆ Any codes outside of [Subdoc Start] and [Subdoc End] codes are part of the master document and will be saved as part of the master document only.

◆ Any codes inside [Subdoc Start] and [Subdoc End] codes are part of that subdocument and will be saved only as part of that subdocument when you condense the master document (see "Condensing a Master Document" later in this chapter).

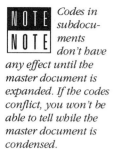

Codes in subdocuments don't have any effect until the master document is expanded. If the codes conflict, you won't be able to tell while the master document is condensed.

◆ As with single documents, later codes take precedence over earlier ones. For example, if you set the left and right margins to 2 inches each at the top of the master document, all the subdocuments will have 2-inch margins, unless one of the documents contains codes to set the margins differently. Those later codes will override the previous margin settings, and text below those codes will have the new margin settings (until those margins are overridden by subsequent margin codes).

◆ Any changes that you make within a subdocument are saved *only* if you condense and save the master document (discussed later).

Once the document is expanded, you can edit normally. You can also use Search to locate text or Search and Replace to make global corrections.

CHANGING A STYLE THROUGHOUT SUBDOCUMENTS

If you have used styles to format the text of individual files, and you are not sure that each document is using the most recent set of styles, you can use the Master Document feature to bring all the styles up to date. Normally, when you expand the master document, all styles in the subdocuments (and any styles that are defined within the master document) are combined in the Styles dialog box. If any two styles have the same name, WordPerfect uses the style in the document nearest the top of the master document.

If you know which document has the most recent "correct" set of styles, you can use that document to create an up-to-date style library for the first document in the master document, before expanding the master document. For example, let's suppose that a document named CHAP20.WP has the most recent, complete set of styles for the overall project. Follow these steps:

1. Use **File ➤ O**pen, as usual, to open the document that contains the most recent set of styles (CHAP20.WP in this example).

2. Choose **L**ayout ➤ **S**tyles to get to the Styles dialog box for that document.

3. Use the Save **A**s button to save the current styles list. (For purposes of illustration, let's say you name this style library LATEST.STY.)

4. Close the Styles dialog box, then close the current document (using **F**ile ➤ **C**lose).

5. Use **F**ile ➤ **O**pen to open the first document in your master document (for example, FRONTMAT.WP).

6. Retrieve the set of files you saved in step 3 (LATEST.STY in this example) into this document. Select **L**ayout ➤ **S**tyles, and click the **R**etrieve button in the dialog box. If asked about replacing existing styles, choose **Y**es.

7. Close the Styles dialog box, then select **F**ile ➤ **C**lose to close the current document.

Now you can create (or open) your master document, then expand it. Because the topmost subdocument now has the most recent set of styles, all documents beneath it will share these styles. When you condense the master document again, each document will inherit this style library.

PRINTING A MASTER DOCUMENT

To print the entire master document, you first need to expand it. Then print normally by using the Print dialog box. Every page of every document (and any hard page breaks) will be printed. If you want to print only a portion of the total document, you can first select the text you want to print, or use the Multiple Pages option in the Print dialog box.

CONDENSING A MASTER DOCUMENT

TO CONDENSE A MASTER DOCUMENT AND SAVE ALL YOUR CHANGES,

choose Tools ➤ Master Document ➤ Condense Master, and respond to prompts about saving subdocuments.

Once you're finished working with an expanded master document, you should *condense* it before saving it again. This procedure takes the subdocuments out of the master document, but retains the links to the subdocuments for future use. Follow these steps:

1. Choose **T**ools ➤ **M**aster Document ➤ **C**ondense Master. You'll see this dialog box:

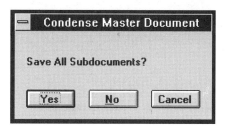

2. If you choose **N**o, WordPerfect will condense the master document right away, and any changes you have made to the subdocuments between their [Subdoc Start] and [Subdoc End] codes will be lost. If you choose **Y**es (the default), WordPerfect will ask whether you want to save the first subdocument:

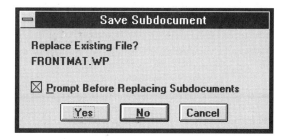

3. If you choose **Y**es, WordPerfect will save the subdocument and proceed to the next subdocument. If you choose **N**o, WordPerfect will allow you to save the subdocument under another name. The new name will replace the old one in the master document. If you want to save all the subdocuments, but don't want WordPerfect to pause and ask permission before saving each file, uncheck the **P**rompt Before Replacing Subdocuments option, then choose **Y**es.

If you do not choose to condense a master document, but choose to save the entire expanded master document under its own name (using File ➤ Save), you will see this dialog box:

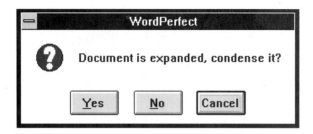

There is no need to save an expanded master document (it just wastes disk space and is best generated fresh each time you want to use it), so you should choose Yes. You'll then be given the same basic options described in the preceding steps for saving individual subdocuments before the master document is saved.

Keep in mind that you need only create a master document once, provided that you remember to save it with a unique file name. When you open an existing master document, all the links will still be in it, and you can then expand and condense subdocuments at will.

This chapter completes Part 7, in which you've learned many valuable techniques to help you manage larger projects. The next part takes you into more specialized, and in some ways more advanced, territories, such as interfacing with other programs and using advanced macro and merge commands.

PART EIGHT

Techniques for Power Users

This part of the book delves into the more sophisticated options that WordPerfect offers for power users. You'll learn how to share documents and data with other programs, including spreadsheets, database managers, and other word processing programs. Then you'll learn about some of WordPerfect's more widely used advanced macro and merge commands. Finally, you'll learn how to customize your keyboard layout, a particularly handy skill for authors and editorial teams who work together on diverse projects to produce a variety of documents.

CHAPTER 25

Interfacing with Other Programs

our WordPerfect package and the Windows environment include several tools that let you share documents and data with other programs. This chapter gives you the basic information you need to know to convert files to and from other formats, but it's your responsibility to know what formats you'll need and to keep track of the locations and names of files that you are importing or exporting. If necessary, refer to the documentation for the software whose data you are trying to import or export.

CONVERTING FILES TO AND FROM OTHER WORD PROCESSOR FORMATS

TO IMPORT A DOCUMENT FROM OR EXPORT A DOCUMENT TO ANOTHER WORD PROCESSOR,

choose File ➤ Open (to import) or File ➤ Save As (to export),

and select the format you want.

WordPerfect requires no special steps to convert most word processing formats to WordPerfect's format and vice versa. You simply choose the document to open or retrieve, and tell WordPerfect what the "foreign" word processor is (in some cases WordPerfect will already know). Exporting is equally as simple.

IMPORTING A FILE

To open (import and convert) a foreign word processing file, follow these steps:

1. If you are working on a document, save it by choosing **F**ile ➤ **S**ave (or pressing Shift+F3).

2. Choose **F**ile ➤ **O**pen (or press F4) to open a new window and bring in the foreign word processing document. You will see the Open File dialog box, shown in Figure 25.1.

3. Choose or type the name of the file you want to open, including the path if the file isn't on the current drive and directory. Then choose **O**pen or press ↵. If the file is not in WordPerfect 5.1 for Windows or WordPerfect 5.1 for DOS format, you'll see the Convert File Format dialog box:

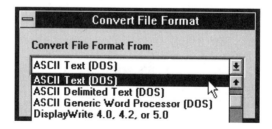

4. In many cases, WordPerfect will already have chosen the correct file format. If not, use the drop-down list button to scroll through the list of formats to select the correct one.

5. Choose OK. (You can also double-click on the correct format to choose it.) WordPerfect will convert the foreign format to WordPerfect for Windows format.

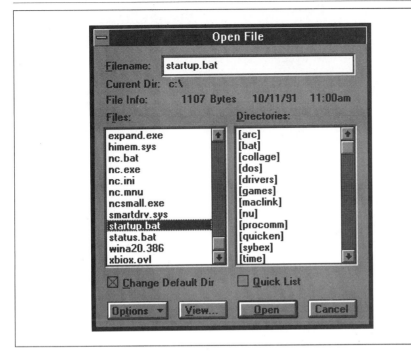

FIGURE 25.1:

The Open File dialog box

EXPORTING A FILE

Many word processors use a standard file-name extension. When converting a file to a different format, it is your responsibility to add the correct extension (if required).

Exporting a WordPerfect file to another word processor's format is equally as easy. Follow these steps:

1. To be safe, save the current document by choosing **F**ile ➤ **S**ave (or press Shift+F3).

2. Choose **F**ile ➤ Save **A**s (or press F3) to display the Save As dialog box.

3. Type a new name for the document based on the naming requirements (if any) of the word processing system you are converting to.

4. Use the **F**iles and **D**irectories list boxes to choose a different directory, if you want.

5. Scroll up or down the **F**ormat drop-down list to locate the word processing format.

6. When you have highlighted the format you want, choose **S**ave to save the document under the new name and format.

7. Choose OK.

CHOOSING AN INTERMEDIATE DATA FORMAT

Practically every program can export to ASCII text files, which WordPerfect can import. The drawback of an ASCII file is that it has no formatting codes, just text.

If WordPerfect does not have a conversion format listed to convert a particular file directly to or from WordPerfect format, try to find an intermediate data format common to both programs. For example, suppose you want to import text from a hypothetical program named *WonderWords* into WordPerfect format, but you see no option for WonderWords in the Convert File Format list box. Then you check the documentation for WonderWords and discover that it can export text to Navy DIF Standard format. If that's the case, your problem is solved, because you can use WonderWords to export text to Navy DIF format (which WordPerfect can import), and you can convert the Navy DIF file to WordPerfect format. Some other fairly standard formats include IBM Revisable Form Text (RFT), IBM Final Form Text (FFT), comma-delimited text (which I'll discuss later in this chapter), and ASCII text.

VIEWING AN ASCII TEXT FILE

TO LOOK INSIDE ANY ASCII FILE,

choose File ➤ Open, type or highlight the name of the file, and choose View to open the View window and see the contents of the file.

An ASCII text file is just text, stripped of all formatting codes. Each line of text can be up to 80 characters long (which would extend past the right default margin in WordPerfect), and each line has a carriage return (an [HRt] code in WordPerfect). At the end of the file, there may be one or more Ctrl+Z's, which look like this on the screen:

^Z^Z^Z^Z^Z^Z

To view an ASCII file, follow these steps:

1. Choose File ➤ Open (or press F4) to display the Open File dialog box.

2. Use the Directories list box to open the directory containing the ASCII file; the file name will be displayed in the Files list box.

3. Choose View. The View window opens to the right of the dialog box, as shown in Figure 25.2. You can use the View feature to view graphic images, spreadsheets and databases as well.

4. Select any file to view its contents.

5. Choose Cancel when you are finished.

IMPORTING DATA FOR SECONDARY MERGE FILES

Check the documentation of the program whose data you are exporting for information on exporting to delimited text files.

Many programming languages and database management systems, and some spreadsheets, let you export data to ASCII *delimited* text files (also known as CSV, for *comma separated value*), where each field is separated by a comma, and each record is terminated by a CR/LF (carriage return/line feed). Character strings (textual data) may be enclosed in quotation marks. You can use these ASCII delimited text files as secondary merge files. An example of a delimited file is shown in the View window in Figure 25.3.

CONVERTING DELIMITED FILES TO WORDPERFECT SECONDARY MERGE FILES

TO CONVERT A COMMA-DELIMITED FILE TO A WORDPERFECT SECONDARY MERGE FILE,

choose File ➤ Open and highlight the comma-delimited file. Choose Open, and from the Convert File Format dialog box, choose ASCII Delimited Text (DOS).

Suppose you have information in a database that you would like to use in WordPerfect. Export the data in the database as a comma-delimited file (CSV), and follow these steps to convert it to a WordPerfect secondary merge file:

1. Choose **File** ➤ **O**pen, or press F4. WordPerfect displays the Open File dialog box.

2. Highlight the name of the delimited file in the **Fi**les list box. Use the **D**irectories list box to find a different directory.

3. Choose **O**pen and you'll see the Convert File Format dialog box.

4. Highlight ASCII Delimited Text (DOS) in the list box, and choose OK or press ↵. WordPerfect converts the commas to secondary merge {END FIELD} commands, and the carriage returns to {END RECORD} commands, as shown in Figure 25.4.

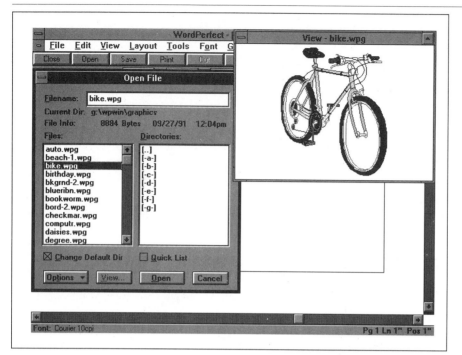

The File View window shows the contents of any file.

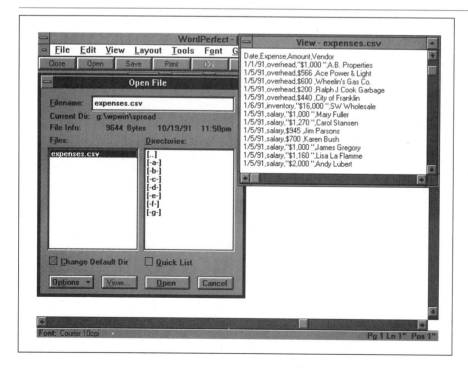

A sample ASCII delimited text file, which shows commas separating fields and shows each record on a separate line (a carriage return, which you don't see, breaks the line)

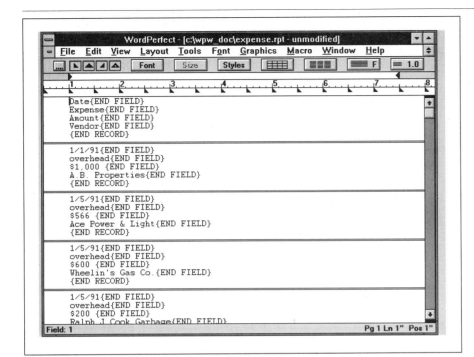

FIGURE 25.4:

The WordPerfect secondary merge file converted from a database comma-delimited file

CONVERTING IMPORTED DATES

Dates are sometimes stored in YYYYMDD format (e.g., 19911115 for 11/15/91).

When using text files as secondary merge files, the dates may be in the YYYYMMDD format. To convert this format to a more usable one, use the {MID} command in your primary merge file to isolate specific parts of the date. The {MID} command extracts a portion of a string from a larger string (called the *expression*), given a starting position (*offset*) and a length (*count*).

The first character in the string is counted as number *0*, the second character as number *1*, and so forth. In a date in YYYYMMDD format, the month starts at character 4 and is two characters long. The day starts at character 6 and is two characters long. The year starts at character 0 and is four characters long. Therefore, assuming that the date is in {FIELD}4~ of the secondary merge file, the series of {MID} commands next to *Date:* in the primary merge file shown in Figure 25.5 will display that date in MM/DD/YY format.

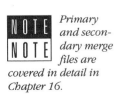

Primary and secondary merge files are covered in detail in Chapter 16.

When creating your primary merge file, you must use Tools ➤ Merge ➤ Merge Codes to choose the {MID} command and Tools ➤ Merge ➤ End Field (or Alt+Enter) to choose the {FIELD} command; you cannot simply type these commands at the keyboard. To show you how this works (because it's a bit tricky), here are the steps for inserting the first {MID} command shown in Figure 25.5:

1. Position the insertion point after *Date:* and press Tab.

2. Choose **T**ools ➤ **M**erge ➤ Merge **C**odes to display the Insert Merge Codes dialog box.

3. Highlight the {MID} command in the list box, and press ↵. You will see the Insert Merge Code dialog box.

4. Type **X** (or any other letter), and press Tab in the Expression text box.

5. Type **4** and press Tab in the Offset text box.

6. Type **2** in the Count text box.

7. Choose OK or press ↵ to go back to the first dialog box. Choose **C**lose to go back to the document window.

8. Move the insertion point to the letter *X* and delete it, being careful not to delete the tilde (~) after the *X*.

9. Choose **T**ools ➤ **M**erge ➤ **F**ield (or press Ctrl+F12 F), type **4** in the Enter Field text box, and choose OK or press ↵.

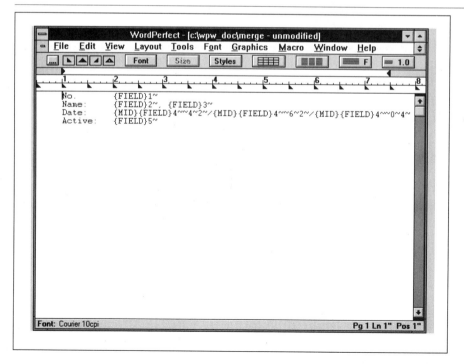

FIGURE 25.5:

{MID} commands used in a primary merge file to convert YYYYMMDD dates to MM/DD/YY format

Now use your mouse or press the End key to move to the end of the line, and type a slash (/), which separates the month from the day. To enter the {MID} commands for the day and the year, just repeat steps 2 through 9, adjusting the offset in step 5 and the count in step 6 accordingly, type another slash at the end of the line, and repeat steps 2 through 9 once more (again adjusting the numbers in steps 5 and 6).

INTERFACING WITH SPREADSHEETS

TO IMPORT OR LINK TO A SPREADSHEET,

choose Tools ➤ Spreadsheet, then choose either Import or Create Link, and choose options in the dialog box.

WordPerfect can import or link to PlanPerfect spreadsheets (versions 3.0 through 5.1), Lotus 1-2-3 (releases 1.0 through 3.1), Microsoft Excel (version 3.0), Quattro, and Quattro Pro. The differences between importing and linking are summarized below:

◆ If you *link* to the spreadsheet, changes made in your spreadsheet program to the spreadsheet file will be reflected in the WordPerfect document.

◆ If you *import* the spreadsheet, any subsequent changes to the spreadsheet are not reflected in the copy stored in your WordPerfect document unless you reimport the spreadsheet.

DDE links will be discussed later in this chapter.

There are two types of links available in WordPerfect for Windows: spreadsheet links and DDE (Dynamic Data Exchange) links. The differences between the two are summarized below:

◆ DDE links work with any Windows 3.0 application that supports DDE, but WordPerfect for Windows *and* the source application must both be running; spreadsheet links work with the spreadsheets listed above, and only WordPerfect must be running.

◆ DDE links update the linked information instantly; spreadsheet links update manually or whenever the WordPerfect document containing the linked information is opened.

◆ DDE links generally require considerably more memory and are usually run with Windows operating in 386 enhanced mode; spreadsheet links demand no more memory than normal (with the exception that some very large linked spreadsheets may tax your computer's memory).

◆ DDE links can link any type of information: tables, charts, other word processing documents, etc.; spreadsheet links can only link spreadsheets.

Regardless of whether you import or link, it's important to understand that only the results of formulas are imported, not the formulas themselves. You can edit the spreadsheet in WordPerfect as you would any other document (this has no effect on the underlying spreadsheet file). However, if you change some numbers in the spreadsheet and try to recalculate the math, nothing will happen, because there are no formulas in the imported spreadsheet.

To import or link a spreadsheet file, follow these steps:

1. Move the insertion point to where you want the spreadsheet to appear in the document.

2. Choose **T**ools ➤ Spr**e**adsheet.

3. Choose **I**mport (to import a copy of the spreadsheet without a link) or **C**reate Link (to link to the spreadsheet). Depending on your choice, you'll see either the Import Spreadsheet dialog box or Create Spreadsheet Link dialog box, shown in Figures 25.6 and 25.7.

4. Enter the full path, file name, and extension in the Filename text box for the file you are importing (for example, C:\123\LOAN.WK1 to import a 1-2-3 worksheet named LOAN.WK1 from the \123 directory of drive C).

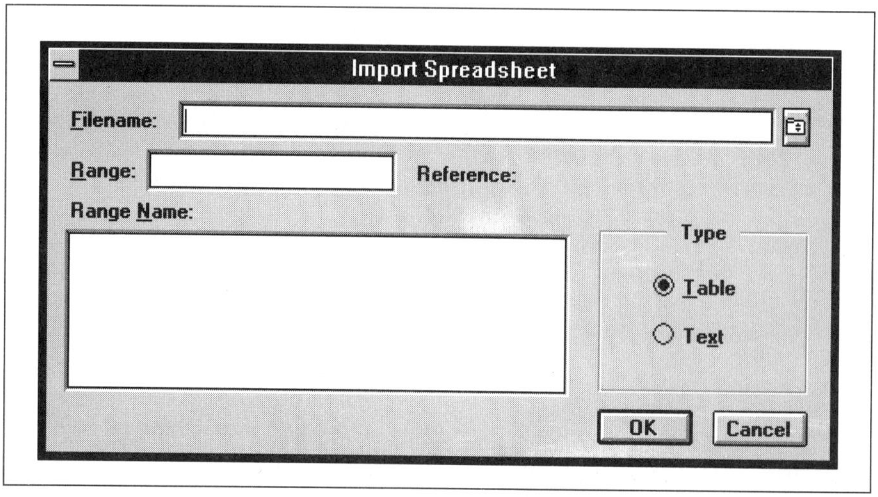

FIGURE 25.6:

The Import Spreadsheet dialog box

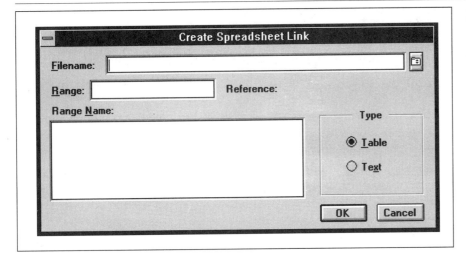

Optionally, you can click the file-folder icon to the right of the text box to display the Select File dialog box to locate the file, and then choose **S**elect to place the path and file name in the text box.

5. Optionally, choose **R**ange and Range **N**ame, and specify a range to import (described in more detail below).

6. Choose **T**ype, then either **T**able (to import the spreadsheet into a Word-Perfect table) or Te**x**t (to import the spreadsheet data as text in tabular columns).

7. Choose OK to import the spreadsheet or link to a spreadsheet.

WordPerfect displays the spreadsheet in the document window. The sections that follow describe the options available to you in the Import Spreadsheet and Create Spreadsheet Link dialog boxes.

IMPORTING A SPREADSHEET AS A TABLE OR AS TEXT

You can also change the font, margins, and paper size (or any combination thereof) to better format spreadsheet text that's too wide for the page.

If you import the spreadsheet into a table, WordPerfect will create the table automatically, and each cell in the spreadsheet will be copied to a cell in the table. If you import the cell as text, columns in the imported spreadsheet will be separated by [Tab] codes, and rows will be separated by [HRt] codes.

If the imported spreadsheet is too wide to fit between the current page margins, you'll see a brief warning near the bottom of the screen, and the table will be wider than the screen. Text beyond the right edge of the page will not be printed. To narrow columns, highlight the column with the mouse, then click on the column margin icon on the ruler and drag it to a new position.

If you import a spreadsheet as text, and it's too wide to fit on the page, some columns will wrap to the next line.

IMPORTING A RANGE

You can import a range from a spreadsheet, provided that you know the range coordinates you want or have already named the range in the spreadsheet program. Think of the range as a square part of the spreadsheet denoted by the upper-left cell location and lower-right cell location. To import a specific range, choose the Range option. The full size of the spreadsheet will be displayed next to the list box, showing you the upper-left and lower-right positions, separated by a colon. You will be able to edit with the WordPerfect editing keys or by typing entirely new range coordinates.

Optionally, you can scroll down the Range Name list box to choose from a list of range names in the file you are importing, and highlight the one you want to import. Choose OK or press ↵.

If you are importing to a table, the maximum number of columns you can import is 32. If you are importing as text, the maximum number of columns is 20.

MANAGING LINKED SPREADSHEETS

If you link rather than import a spreadsheet, you'll notice that your imported spreadsheet is surrounded by two link messages indicating where the link begins and ends (these messages are never printed). You can remove these messages from the screen and also control when the link is updated. Follow these steps:

1. Position the insertion point anywhere within the imported spreadsheet (between the [Link] and [Link End] codes in Reveal Codes).

2. Choose **T**ools ➤ Spr**e**adsheet ➤ **L**ink Options. You'll see this dialog box:

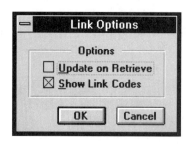

3. Choose any of the following options:

◆ To update the spreadsheet upon retrieval, mark the **U**pdate on Retrieve check box.

◆ To show the comment box indicating the name and range of the linked spreadsheet, mark the **S**how Link Codes check box.

4. Choose OK or press ↵.

EDITING THE LINK

If you link a spreadsheet to a document and need to change one of your previous settings, move the insertion point between the [Link] and [Link End] codes and choose Tools ➤ Spreadsheet ➤ Edit Link. You'll be taken to a dialog box that lets you change the file name and range settings for the current link.

IMPORTING SPREADSHEETS TO GRAPHICS BOXES

You can import a spreadsheet into a graphics box so that you can anchor it to a page and wrap text around it. To do so, double-click the box. You will see the Text Box Editor. Choose Tools ➤ Spreadsheet ➤ Import *or* Create Link. Follow the steps above to define the spreadsheet.

DYNAMIC DATA EXCHANGE (DDE) LINKS

TO CREATE A DDE LINK TO ANOTHER WINDOWS APPLICATION,

choose Edit ➤ Link ➤ Create to display the Create DDE Link dialog box. Choose one of the source applications, assign a link name, choose an update mode and storage type, and press ↵.

For you to establish a DDE link between WordPerfect and another Windows application, the application must support DDE, and both applications must be running.

Dynamic Data Exchange (DDE) is a standard means of linking data between Windows applications. Not all applications support DDE, but WordPerfect does. There are two sides to an active link involving WordPerfect: WordPerfect is the receiving side, and the other application is the source side. The link is the channel between the two. When the source information is changed, the linked information in WordPerfect is changed.

A typical use of a DDE link might be for the following scenario: You are creating an annual report in WordPerfect for a large corporation. End-of-year financials are being calculated in an Excel spreadsheet. Excel is also plotting the financial picture on a series of charts. You have linked the document containing the text of the annual report with the Excel spreadsheet and charts. Now, while the accountants make last-minute closing entries to the financial statements, you can run draft review copies of the report, knowing that the report contains up-to-the-minute financial data replotted on up-to-the-minute graphs, because the link updates the report whenever the financial data changes.

Creating a DDE Link

To create a DDE link to another Windows application (such as Excel), follow these steps:

1. Ensure that both WordPerfect and the other application (for this example, Excel) are running. If you want the link to be updated automatically whenever the spreadsheet changes, start the source application first (start Excel and open the spreadsheet), then switch to the Program Manager and start WordPerfect.

2. Once in WordPerfect, position the insertion point where you want the linked data to appear. Choose **E**dit ➤ **L**ink ➤ **C**reate to display the Create DDE Link dialog box, shown in Figure 25.8.

3. Displayed in the **S**ource File and Item list box will be all the currently active applications, including Excel, and the file names of all open files, including the Excel spreadsheet you want to link to. Highlight the Excel spreadsheet.

4. If you want to link only part of the source file, move the insertion point to the end of the file name in the text box, type a vertical line (|, next to the Backspace key on many keyboards), and type the name of the item or section. In this spreadsheet example, you would type a cell range, like *a10:d20*.

5. Choose **L**ink Name; the spreadsheet file name is the default, but you can change it to whatever you want.

6. Choose a mode in the Update Mode area: **A**uto will update whenever the spreadsheet is changed; **M**anual will update each time you choose the Update command (**E**dit ➤ **L**ink ➤ **U**pdate).

7. Choose a storage type: **T**ext for the spreadsheet; **G**raphics if you are linking to an Excel chart or a graphics program that supports DDE.

8. Choose OK or press ↵, and the spreadsheet will fill down the page from the insertion point, as shown in Figure 25.9.

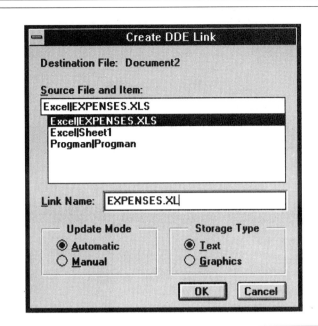

*The Create DDE Link
dialog box*

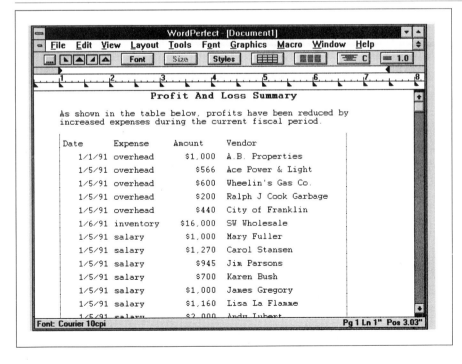

*A WordPerfect
document linked to a
spreadsheet*

Formatting the Linked Information

If you look at the linked spreadsheet in Reveal Codes shown in Figure 25.10, you will see the [DDE Link Begin:] code. What follows is based on the active or manual updates to the source file (the spreadsheet). Any formatting codes should be placed before the [DDE Link Begin:] code, or they will be erased when the data is updated.

Editing the DDE Link

You can change the DDE link at any time. Follow these steps:

1. Choose **E**dit ➤ **L**ink ➤ **E**dit to display the Edit DDE Link dialog box. The dialog box displays the following information:

Link Name — This list box contains the names of all the links in the document. Highlight the link you want to edit. The dialog box will display the remaining information about the link you highlight.

New Link Name — The current link name you assigned is displayed in the text box. Change the name if you want.

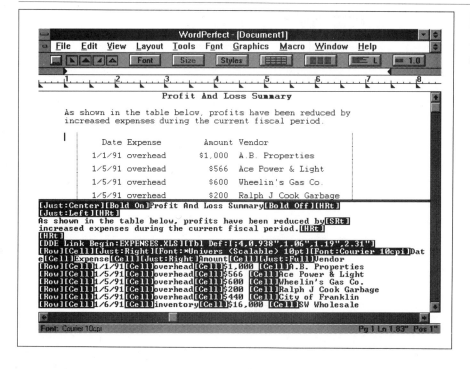

FIGURE 25.10:

Reveal Codes shows the [DDE Link Begin:] code.

Source File and Item	The current source file name and item name are displayed. Enter a different file name or item name, and the link will reflect the information in the new source.
Update	You can change the update method, if you want.
Current Link Info	Displayed are the current file name and item name, update method, and the date and time of the last update.

2. Choose OK or press ↵ to save the new information and return to the document window.

Pasting a DDE Link

Use the Paste Link command (instead of the Edit ➤ Paste command) to paste a portion of a source file into a WordPerfect document. Follow these steps:

1. Switch to the source file.

2. Choose **E**dit ➤ **C**opy to copy the portion of the source file you want to link to into the Windows Clipboard.

3. Switch to WordPerfect, and place the insertion point at the position where you want the link to begin.

4. Choose **E**dit ➤ **L**ink ➤ **P**aste Link. The portion of the source file you copied will fill in from the insertion point down.

CUTTING AND PASTING BETWEEN WORDPERFECT AND OTHER WINDOWS APPLICATIONS

TO CUT AND PASTE BETWEEN WORDPERFECT AND ANOTHER WINDOWS APPLICATION,

switch to the other application, highlight the information you want to copy, choose Edit ➤ Copy to copy it to the Windows Clipboard, switch back to WordPerfect, place the insertion point where you want the copied material, and choose Edit ➤ Paste.

The Windows environment makes it easy to move information between programs, because every Windows application uses the same Copy and Paste commands. Regardless of the application, copied information is copied to the

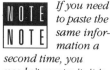

If you need to paste the same information a second time, you needn't recopy it; it is saved in the Clipboard until you clear it, copy something else to the Clipboard, or exit Windows.

Windows Clipboard, where it stays until something new is copied over it, the Clipboard is cleared, or you exit Windows. To copy or cut and paste between WordPerfect and another application, follow these steps:

1. In WordPerfect, click the Control-menu box and choose Switch To (or press Ctrl+Esc).

2. Choose Program Manager from the Task List, and double-click on the Windows application you want to start.

3. With the application running, open the file you want and select the text you want to cut or copy.

4. Choose Edit ➤ Copy (or Cut) to copy the highlighted information to the Windows Clipboard.

5. Click the Control-menu box, and switch back to WordPerfect.

6. Position the insertion point where you want the copied information to start, and choose Edit ➤ Paste. The information will be pasted at the insertion point from the Clipboard.

You can look in the Clipboard at any time: Just switch to the Program Manager, open the Main group, and double-click on the Clipboard icon.

CUTTING AND PASTING BETWEEN WORDPERFECT AND NON-WINDOWS APPLICATIONS

TO CUT AND PASTE BETWEEN WORDPERFECT AND A NON-WINDOWS APPLICATION,

highlight what you want to cut in the WordPerfect for Windows document, and choose Edit ➤ Cut to move it to the Clipboard. Minimize WordPerfect for Windows and start the DOS application. Press Alt+spacebar to put the application in a window. Click the Control-menu box, and choose Edit ➤ Paste.

To copy or cut material from WordPerfect for Windows and paste it in a non-Windows applications, follow these steps:

1. In WordPerfect for Windows, highlight the text you want, and choose Edit ➤ Copy (or Edit ➤ Cut) to copy the text to the Windows Clipboard.

To quickly minimize Word-Perfect for Windows, click on the Minimize button in the upper-right corner of the window.

See "Captured Text Screens" in Chapter 19 for more on interfacing with Windows applications.

2. Click the Control-menu box and choose **S**witch To. Double-click the Program Manager icon. WordPerfect for Windows will be minimized to an icon, and you'll see the Program Manager window.

3. Open the Non-Windows Applications group, and double-click on the DOS application.

4. Once the application is running, press Alt+spacebar to put the application in a window.

5. Position the insertion point or cursor where you want to paste the text.

6. Click the Control-menu box, and choose **E**dit ➤ **P**aste. The text will be pasted at the insertion point or cursor.

7. To pop back to the Windows Desktop, press Alt+Esc.

EXITING TEMPORARILY TO DOS

TO EXIT TEMPORARILY TO DOS,

minimize WordPerfect, and double-click the DOS Prompt icon in the Windows Main group.

If you need to use DOS for a few commands—but you do not want to save and close your document, exit WordPerfect, and exit the Windows environment—you can temporarily exit to DOS by double-clicking the DOS Prompt icon on the Windows Main group. Follow these steps:

1. Save all the documents you're working on in WordPerfect by choosing each document from the **W**indow pull-down menu and choosing **F**ile ➤ **S**ave (or pressing Shift+F3).

2. Press Ctrl+Esc to display the Task List. The dialog box lists all the applications that are currently running. Although you may not have any other applications running, you will always see Program Manager. Double-click on Program Manager to switch to the Program Manager window.

3. Double-click the DOS Prompt icon in the Main group, and you will exit to DOS.

4. When you are finished working in DOS, type **EXIT** to return to Windows. Then, double-click the WordPerfect icon at the bottom of the screen.

Be forewarned that loading a memory-resident program after temporarily exiting to DOS can prevent you from getting back into Windows and WordPerfect; you will lose any work not saved before you went to DOS.

IMPORTING DOS OUTPUT

If you want to use the output from a DOS command in your WordPerfect document, use the > redirection symbol at the end of the DOS command to send its output to a file. For example, the following command sends the output from the DIR command to a file named FILELIST.TXT:

DIR *.WP >C:\WPW_DOC\FILELIST.TXT

You can then use File ➤ Open (F4), or File ➤ Retrieve, or File ➤ File Manager options to read the file (C:\WPW_DOC\FILELIST.TXT in this example) into your WordPerfect document.

EDITING ASCII TEXT FILES

TO EDIT ASCII TEXT FILES WITH WORDPERFECT,

use File ➤ Open (F4) to open or File ➤ Retrieve to retrieve the file and File ➤ Save to save the file.

Many programs store their *source code* files as DOS text files (also called ASCII text files). This includes DOS batch (.BAT) files, dBASE command (.PRG) files, Paradox script (.SC) files, and others. You can edit such files with WordPerfect (with some degree of risk). To do so, start with a clear document window, choose File ➤ Open, choose the file you want, and choose Open or press ↵.

After making your changes, save the file by choosing File ➤ Save As, choose Format and scroll up the list to highlight ASCII Text (DOS), and choose Save or press ↵. Then choose Close to clear the document window. When asked if you want to save the file, choose No (you already saved it a moment ago).

There are risks, however:

◆ If you inadvertently save the text file in a WordPerfect format (or any other format), WordPerfect will add hidden codes to the file, rendering it unusable as an ASCII file. If that happens, you'll need to open the file as a WordPerfect document, then resave it as a DOS text file.

◆ WordPerfect will word-wrap lines that extend past the right margin, but most programs (including DOS) cannot execute a wrapped line. To prevent word wrap, you'll need to use a wide paper size and narrow margins whenever you edit text files.

If you do use WordPerfect to edit an executable DOS text file (such as a batch file or program), and that program no longer runs correctly, you should use some other editor to double-check the file. That editor will make any problems, such as invalid codes or incorrectly broken lines caused by WordPerfect's word wrapping, more apparent and easier to fix.

IMPORTING DOS TEXT FILES

File ➤ Open (F4) and File ➤ Retrieve can also be used simply to import a text file into a document. This is handy because many programs let you "print" (or save) reports to disk in ASCII (DOS) text format. Most often, these files are saved with the extension .PRN (or perhaps .TXT). You can retrieve such a file directly into WordPerfect.

For example, suppose you use the Paradox database management system and want your WordPerfect document to include a report that Paradox generates. First, run Paradox and use its Report, Output, and File commands to print a report to disk. When prompted, you could name this file something like C:\WPW_DOC\PDOX2WP.PRN so that it is stored in the \WPW_DOC directory.

After you exit Paradox and run WordPerfect, you can open the WordPerfect document in which you want to display the Paradox report, with File ➤ Open or File ➤ Retrieve. Then position the insertion point where you want the Paradox report to appear, choose File ➤ Retrieve, and choose the Paradox file.

You'll see the Convert File Format dialog box, described earlier. If you want to import the text file in its "natural" state (with a hard return at the end of each line), you can just choose OK.

CR/LF stands for carriage return/line feed, the ASCII equivalent of a Word-Perfect [HRt] code.

Optionally, if you want to be able to use WordPerfect's word-wrapping capabilities in the imported file, use the drop-down list to choose either *ANSI Text CR/LF to [SRt] (Windows)* or *ASCII Text CR/LF to [SRt] (DOS)*. Then choose OK. Choosing either of these options forces WordPerfect to ignore the single hard return at the end of any line that's wider than the margin, so that the imported text word-wraps properly within the document. A double hard return at the end of a line is considered the start of a new paragraph, and will be formatted accordingly when imported.

In the next chapter, I'll delve into advanced uses of macro and merge commands, introduced earlier in chapters 15 and 16.

CHAPTER

26

Advanced Macro and Merge Commands

HANDS-ON
....
LESSON 10

For a hands-on exercise in creating a complex macro, see Lesson 10 in Part 9.

WordPerfect offers two separate *programming languages,* which give you refined control over how macros and merges behave. These are called languages because they offer many features of more traditional programming languages, such as BASIC, C, and dBASE. The WordPerfect languages are unique, however, because they are specifically designed to work with WordPerfect macros and primary merge files.

The WordPerfect 5.1 for DOS macro programming language is *very* different from the WordPerfect for Windows macro programming language, although a conversion utility is provided to help you transform WordPerfect 5.1 macros into WordPerfect for Windows format (see Chapter 15). By contrast, the merge programming languages in both versions of WordPerfect are the same, so you can use WordPerfect 5.1 for DOS primary merge files with the WordPerfect for Windows program, without having to convert them first.

It's important to understand that you don't need to learn how to use the merge and macro languages to run WordPerfect; they will be of interest mostly to programmers. You can create many useful macros without programming simply by recording keystrokes, as described in Chapter 15. And you can create very sophisticated merges with just the basic merge commands presented in Chapter 16. You may, however, want to delve into the more advanced merge and macro commands if

◆ You want to automate the assembly of complex documents based on data in secondary merge files.

◆ You want to develop macros that repeat some sequence of steps many times over.

◆ You want to build custom *applications* that simplify and automate complex tasks for less experienced computer users.

◆ You want to develop utilities that enhance the capabilities of Word-Perfect, adding features that WordPerfect does not have.

Complete merge and macro language wizardry are not skills you learn overnight. Like all programming languages, thorough mastery of WordPerfect's two command languages requires a solid background in basic programming concepts (such as variables, looping, branching, and event handling), familiarity with all the commands and syntax of the languages, and knowledge of how to use WordPerfect features and shortcut keystrokes.

Unfortunately, there is not enough space to cover programming concepts and the entire merge and macro languages within this book. However, appendices J through L in the documentation that came with your WordPerfect package cover all the merge commands and introduce some basic merge programming concepts. Macro programming is covered in a separate volume, the *WordPerfect for Windows Macro Manual,* which you can order from Word-Perfect Corporation. You can also find in-depth treatments of merge and macro programming topics in any WordPerfect book that's dedicated to these subjects.

In this chapter, I'll present some practical merges and macros that demonstrate the merge and macro command languages and concepts in action. You'll find these examples quite useful, because you can use them to accomplish "real-life" tasks, and because they illustrate applications of these advanced commands.

Before looking at any examples, however, I'll cover some similarities and differences between the WordPerfect merge and macro languages. Then I'll discuss each of these powerful languages in more detail.

MERGES VS. MACROS

In some ways, the merge and macro programming languages are similar. The most important similarities are the following:

◆ Both languages have similar types of commands, and many commands have similar names in each language.

◆ Macros and merges can often be used to accomplish similar tasks.

◆ Both are well suited to repetitive jobs.

◆ You can start a merge from a macro and vice versa.

◆ Like all programming language commands, merge and macro commands must be entered in a specific format, or *syntax,* or they won't work properly.

◆ You edit merge and macro programs by using the normal WordPerfect document window.

There are many differences between macros and merge programs, however; these are some of the most important ones:

◆ Generally speaking, a macro records the results of entering keystrokes or taking certain mouse actions at your computer. Almost anything you can do in WordPerfect for Windows has a corresponding macro command, and the language includes hundreds of commands.

◆ A merge deals with text rather than keystrokes, combining text from several sources into a single document. Merge programming commands determine which text is merged in which order.

◆ You cannot use a macro programming command in a merge file, or vice versa. The two languages are completely independent of one another.

◆ When you record a macro program, WordPerfect converts your keystrokes and menu choices into a series of macro programming commands and stores them in a macro file. You can then play back the recorded macro, as described in Chapter 15. You cannot record merge programs this way. Instead, you must enter them in the normal document window, by typing text and choosing commands from the Insert Merge Codes dialog box, as explained in Chapter 16.

NOTE NOTE NOTE *In Lesson 10, you record a small macro, then use it to build a more sophisticated macro. You can edit a recorded macro just as you would any normal WordPerfect file.*

◆ WordPerfect macro files normally have a .WCM extension, whereas merge commands are stored in primary merge files, which can have any extension.

◆ You can type in macro programs in a free format. This means you can add tabs, indents, blank lines, page headers and footers, graphic lines, and other formatting features to make the programming commands easier to read. These codes do not affect your macro and are not inserted in the output of the macro. In a merge document, however, these keystrokes insert codes in the document, so you should put them in only if you want to see them in the final output document. As described later, you can use a {COMMENT} command to insert tabs and blank lines in merge documents, without inserting codes.

MERGE COMMANDS

Merge commands require you to use a specific syntax, or set of rules, when entering them. Many merge commands use *parameters,* or *arguments,* which require a tilde (~) to separate them and end the command. You enter all merge commands from the normal document window by choosing Tools ➤ Merge ➤ Merge Codes (or pressing Ctrl+F12 C) and choosing options from the Insert Merge Codes dialog box:

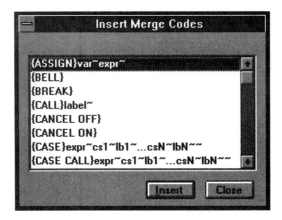

The dialog box shows the full syntax of each command, including parameters and tildes. When you double-click a merge command in the Insert Merge Codes dialog box, WordPerfect prompts you for all the information the command needs and inserts the tildes for you. You can then edit the arguments (but not the merge commands themselves) as normal text.

EXAMPLES OF SYNTAX

As an example, the command {ASSIGN} stores a value (i.e., a number or text) in a *variable.* Its syntax is

{ASSIGN}*variable~value~*

where *variable* is the name of the variable, and *value* is the value to store in the variable. (A variable is like a "placeholder" that stores information in memory. The text or number stays in memory until you exit WordPerfect.) The command below stores the number *10* in a variable named *HowMany:*

{ASSIGN}HowMany~10~

In the following example, the {FOR} command, which executes a series of commands a certain number of times, uses the general syntax

{FOR}var~start~stop~step~

where *var* is a variable, *start* is the starting value for *var, stop* is the ending value, and *step* is the increment.

Another frequently used command is {VARIABLE}, which accesses the contents of a variable. Its general form is

{VARIABLE}var~

Now, if you want to use the variable named *HowMany* for the *stop* value in the {FOR} command, you have to enter the command like this:

{FOR}LoopCount~1~{VARIABLE}HowMany~~1~

Notice the two tildes after HowMany. The first tilde ends the {VARIABLE} command, and the second marks the end of the "stop" portion of the {FOR} command. If one of the tildes is missing, the merge will not work properly. Be sure to check these tildes first if your merge doesn't seem to be working correctly. If you accidentally delete a tilde, you can just retype it in the document window, since tildes are normal keyboard characters.

Keep in mind that merge commands are not *compiled,* or translated, ahead of time. Therefore, if WordPerfect detects a syntax error midway through your primary merge file, the merge will begin as usual but will stop when the error is encountered. Subtle errors, like a missing tilde, can be even worse because instead of stopping, the merge may continue but will give incorrect results.

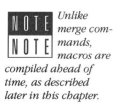 *Unlike merge commands, macros are compiled ahead of time, as described later in this chapter.*

TYPES OF MERGE COMMANDS

A thorough explanation of all WordPerfect's merge commands would require a hefty book of its own. However, you can get a good idea of the capabilities of the language just by studying the various categories of commands that are available to you:

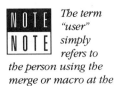 *The term "user" simply refers to the person using the merge or macro at the moment.*

CATEGORY	WHAT THE COMMANDS DO
User Interface	Communicate with the user by displaying a prompt, allowing input from the keyboard, or both
Flow Control	Change the flow of a merge execution
Merge or Subroutine Termination	End a merge or subroutine
External Condition Handling	Determine how to respond to a condition that occurs outside a merge (e.g., the user presses the Cancel key) or create a condition
Macro Execution	Start a macro from a merge
Variables	Assign a value to a variable, determine the state of a variable, or write out a variable
System Variables	Determine the value of system variables
Secondary Commands	Used in secondary merge files
Execution Control	Affect speed or visibility of execution on the user's screen
Programming Aids	Provide tools that can help you debug your merges when they aren't working properly

Table 26.1 lists commands in each of these categories. (Many commands, such as {BELL}, appear in more than one category.) You'll see examples of several of these commands in the next section.

USER INTERFACE

{BELL}	{CHAR}	{INPUT}	{KEYBOARD}
{LOOK}	{PROMPT}	{STATUS PROMPT}	{TEXT}

FLOW CONTROL

{BREAK}	{CALL}	{CASE}	{CASE CALL}
{CHAIN MACRO}	{CHAIN PRIMARY}	{CHAIN SECONDARY}	{ELSE}
{END FOR}	{END IF}	{END WHILE}	{FOR}
{GO}	{IF}	{IF BLANK}	{IF EXISTS}
{IF NOT BLANK}	{LABEL}	{NEST MACRO}	{NEST PRIMARY}
{NEST SECONDARY}	{NEXT}	{ON CANCEL}	{ON ERROR}
{PROCESS}	{QUIT}	{RETURN}	{RETURN CANCEL}
{RETURN ERROR}	{STOP}	{SUBST PRIMARY}	{SUBST SECONDARY}
{WHILE}			

MERGE OR SUBROUTINE TERMINATION

{BREAK}	{QUIT}	{RETURN}	{RETURN CANCEL}
{RETURN ERROR}	{STOP}		

EXTERNAL CONDITION HANDLING

{CANCEL OFF}	{CANCEL ON}	{ON CANCEL}	{ON ERROR}
{RETURN CANCEL}	{RETURN ERROR}		

MACRO EXECUTION

{CHAIN MACRO}	{NEST MACRO}

TABLE 26.1:

Categories of Merge Commands

VARIABLES			
{ASSIGN}	{CHAR}	{IF EXISTS}	{LEN}
{LOCAL}	{LOOK}	{MID}	{NEXT}
{SYSTEM}	{TEXT}	{VARIABLE}	

SYSTEM VARIABLES	
{DATE}	{SYSTEM}

SECONDARY COMMANDS		
{END FIELD}	{END RECORD}	{FIELD NAMES}

EXECUTION CONTROL	
{REWRITE}	{WAIT}

PROGRAMMING AIDS			
{BELL}	{COMMENT}	{STEP OFF}	{STEP ON}

TABLE 26.1:

Categories of Merge Commands (continued)

ASSEMBLING DOCUMENTS WITH ADVANCED MERGE COMMANDS

In Chapter 16 you learned to use numerous merge commands to create primary and secondary files for merging, and to merge text from the keyboard into an existing document. As you may recall, choosing Tools ➤ Merge ➤ Merge Codes (or pressing Ctrl+F12 C) takes you to a menu for accessing advanced merge commands, such as {IF BLANK} and {END IF}, which you can insert in your primary merge files.

You can also use the {IF} command with any of the operators shown below to make decisions within a primary merge, based on information in the secondary merge file:

OPERATOR	FUNCTION
=	Equal to
!=	Not equal to
>	Greater than
<	Less than
&	And
¦	Or
!	Not

By combining the {IF} command with the {DOCUMENT} command (which reads an entire document from disk into the primary merge file), you can decide which document to include while a merge is progressing. Such techniques are especially useful when you want to insert variable paragraphs in contracts, dunning notices, and other documents that must be customized for a particular situation.

Figure 26.1 shows a sample primary merge file that uses {IF} statements to build a dunning notice based on information in a secondary merge file. Depending on the value in a field named *Days_Late* in the secondary merge file, the primary merge file reads in a document named *UNDER30.WP, OVER30.WP, OVER60.WP,* or *OVER90.WP.*

Take a look at the second {IF}...{END IF} statement in the document, as shown below:

```
{IF}{FIELD}Days_Late~>29~&{FIELD}Days_Late~<60~{COMMENT}
    ~{DOCUMENT}OVER30.WP~{COMMENT}
~{END IF}{COMMENT}
```

The first line says, "If the Days_Late field contains a number that's greater than 29 *and* a value that's less than 60." Now if the Days_Late field satisfies the test, the {DOCUMENT}OVER30.WP~ command reads the OVER30.WP document into this primary merge file. The closing {END IF} command marks the close of the {IF} command. The first {IF}...{END IF} statement tests for Days_Late less than 30 (inserting UNDER30.WP), just in case you want to send a very gentle reminder to people whose accounts aren't yet late. The other two {IF}...{END IF} statements test for Days_Late between 59 and 90 (inserting OVER60.WP) and Days_Late greater than 89 (inserting OVER90.WP). The resulting merge file will contain one letter for each person in the mailing list, where the content of each letter depends on how late the person is in paying.

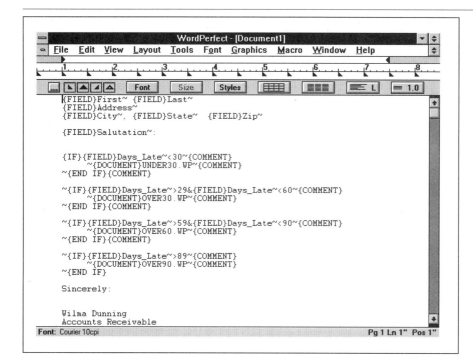

A primary merge file that assembles a document based on information in the secondary merge file

Using Comments to Control Spaces and Blank Lines

As with all merge commands, you must select {COMMENT} from the Insert Merge Codes dialog box; you cannot simply type the word {COMMENT} on the screen.

A comment (or programmer comment) is a block of text in a primary merge file that WordPerfect ignores. You use comments to write reminder notes to yourself (or other people) explaining the purpose of a particular set of commands and also to make your program easier to read and understand. Every comment in a primary merge file starts with a {COMMENT} command and ends with one tilde (~). In between the {COMMENT} and tilde, you can type text and enter tabs and hard returns.

As mentioned earlier, the tabs or hard returns you enter in a merge file will appear as extra spaces or hard returns in the merged file, unless you hide them in some way. You use a {COMMENT} command to hide them. In a primary merge file, comments are especially useful for structuring your {IF} and {END IF} commands in blocks (a common practice in most programming languages), without inserting hard returns or extra spaces in the primary merge file.

If you look at Figure 26.1, you'll notice that some {COMMENT} commands are used with each {IF} command. The {COMMENT} command at the end of the first {IF}{FIELD} line allows a hard return and tab to be inserted, which indents the command on the next line without showing the hard return and tab in the resulting merge. The tilde before the {DOCUMENT} UNDER30.WP line ends the first comment. Likewise, {COMMENT} commands are used after the lines containing the {DOCUMENT} and {END IF} commands to allow hard returns to be inserted in the primary merge file without printing blank lines on the final merged document. Ultimately, WordPerfect just interprets all these comments as if the four sets of {IF} and {END IF} commands had been strung together without any intervening tabs or hard returns.

MACRO COMMANDS

For extra convenience, add your macros to the Macro menu or Button Bar (Chapter 15), or assign them to keys on a keyboard layout (Chapter 27).

WordPerfect's powerful macro programming language adds a new level of sophistication and flexibility to the product, bringing you into a fascinating world where you can create Windows-style dialog boxes and pop-up menus, and link to applications and data files outside of WordPerfect itself. Once you master even the most basic macro programming techniques, you can create amazingly handy macros that will speed up your work and add new capabilities to WordPerfect.

CREATING MACRO COMMANDS

Macros are automatically saved in the directory specified by File ➤ Preferences ➤ Location of Files, usually C:\WPWIN\MACROS.

You can create a macro program by recording all or part of your final macro, then editing the macro document file, or you can create a macro program from scratch. Either way, you edit the macro just as you would any other Word-Perfect document.

Unlike merge commands, where the syntax is shown in a dialog box, the syntax for macro commands is given in the WordPerfect manuals and in books on macro programming, not on the screen. Therefore, when you type a macro programming command, you must type all parts of the command yourself, using the correct syntax, or rules, of the language.

One easy way to learn about the rules for creating macros and to find out which programming commands provide access to specific WordPerfect features is to record and edit a small macro that performs just one simple task.

For example, you could record a macro to create a horizontal line, by following these steps:

1. Choose **M**acro ➤ **R**ecord, or press Ctrl+F10.

2. Type **test** and press ↵ to name the macro.

3. Choose **G**raphics ➤ **L**ine ➤ **H**orizontal and press ↵ to create a horizontal line with all the default settings.

4. Choose **M**acro ➤ **S**top, or press Ctrl+Shift+F10 to stop recording the macro.

Now, you could edit this macro and find out exactly which macro programming command creates a horizontal graphic line, by following these steps:

1. Choose **F**ile ➤ **O**pen, or press F4.

2. Type **c:\wpwin\macros\test.wcm**, then choose **O**pen or press ↵ to open the macro file you just recorded. Your screen would resemble Figure 26.2.

*You can use the Quick List in the Open File dialog box to find your macros more easily. For example, to open the test macro described here, double-click Macros in the Quick List, then type **test.wcm** and choose Open or press ↵.*

Notice that the macro file in Figure 26.2 contains two commands. The first command

Application (WP;WPWP;Default;"WPWPUS.WCD")

specifies that WordPerfect is the application used in the macro. This command *must* appear at the beginning of your macro, or you are likely to have problems when you play the macro later.

The second command

GraphicLine
(
Operation:HCreate!
)

creates a horizontal line. Now that you know exactly which command creates graphic lines, you can look it up in the *WordPerfect for Windows Macro Manual*. You will discover that GraphicLine has nine parameters, many of which are optional, for defining the line.

Although you'll soon become familiar with many of the command names, parameters, and how to specify each one, you shouldn't forget this handy technique of recording a small macro. Keep in mind that after recording

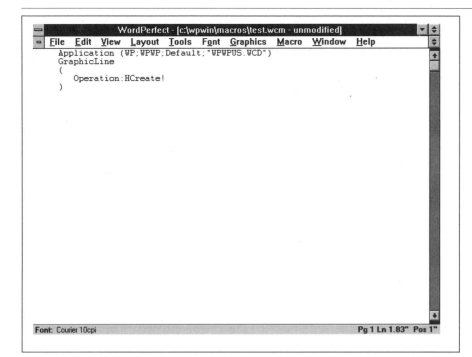

WordPerfect stores recorded keystrokes as macro programming language commands. This macro creates a horizontal line.

several small macros, each of which performs a specific task, you can use them as building blocks for more sophisticated programs by retrieving them into a larger macro file and editing them as necessary. (If you use this building-block trick, you should delete the extra APPLICATION commands that appear at the top of each retrieved macro file, since you need only one of these commands at the beginning of your macro file.)

COMPILING A MACRO

The first time you play a macro you will see a "Compiling macro" message in the lower-left corner of the document window and may notice a delay before anything happens. This message and delay indicate that the macro is being *compiled;* that is, it is being translated and condensed into a special internal format that WordPerfect can run more quickly. The compiled form of your macro is stored invisibly, at the beginning of the macro file, and is only recompiled if you edit and save the macro, then play it again. After a macro is compiled, it will play back much more quickly the next time you run it.

Although macro files look like normal WordPerfect documents on the screen, they actually contain two parts: an invisible, compiled version of the macro commands and a visible version that you can edit and print.

Although a compiler can't determine whether your program will actually accomplish the task you intend, it can detect typographical errors made when you incorrectly specify macro programming language commands. For example, if you delete the final parenthesis in the GraphicLine command shown earlier, close and save the TEST.WCM macro, then try to play it back again, you'll see the screen and message shown in Figure 26.3.

Notice that the compiler provides a description of the problem in the upper part of the dialog box and indicates the location of the problem in the lower part. In this example, it detected an error in line 5, character 1. When you see a message like this, you should choose Cancel Compilation, open the macro file and correct the problem, close and save the macro file, then run the macro again.

Sometimes the compiler's description of the problem doesn't provide an exact diagnosis of what is wrong, so you'll have to do some careful sleuthing to track down and correct the problem. Here are some tips:

◆ Since the compiler notes errors by line number, you can find problems more quickly if you add line numbers to the macro program file, then print it. To add line numbers, move the insertion point to the top of the macro file and choose **L**ayout ➤ **L**ine ➤ **N**umbering. Then open the **L**ine Numbering pop-up list, choose **C**ontinuous, and choose OK.

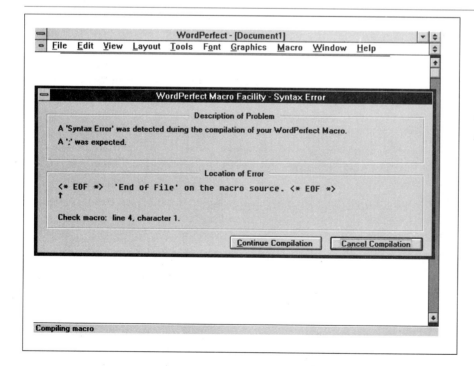

FIGURE 26.3:

The macro compiler can detect typographical errors. You must fix these errors before you can play the macro.

◆ Make sure you have an APPLICATION command at the beginning of your macro file. If this command is missing, the compiler will display misleading error messages, and you'll waste a lot of time trying to figure out what's wrong with perfectly written programming commands.

◆ Make sure that each command includes parentheses, braces, semicolons, colons, and quotation marks where they are needed and that you've spelled the command and parameter names properly.

◆ Close and save the macro document after making changes and before running it again.

◆ Consult the manual or your macro programming book frequently, and be sure to read a printed copy of your macro carefully before compiling it.

TYPES OF MACRO COMMANDS

The WordPerfect macro programming language has two basic types of commands: *programming* commands and *product* commands.

Programming Commands

Programming commands determine the flow of the macro and the contents of variables. These commands, which by convention are typed in uppercase, consist of a command name and any parameters the command may have. You'll see many examples of programming commands later in this chapter.

The programming commands for the macro language closely resemble the merge language commands, and can even be classified in similar ways. As with merge commands, you can get a good idea of the capabilities of the language just by studying the various categories of commands that are available to you:

CATEGORY	WHAT THE COMMANDS DO
User Interface	Communicate with the user by displaying a prompt or menu, allowing input from the keyboard, or both
Flow Control	Change the flow of a macro execution
Macro or Subroutine Termination	End a macro or subroutine

CATEGORY	WHAT THE COMMANDS DO
External Condition Handling	Determine how to respond to a condition that occurs outside a macro (e.g., the user clicks the Cancel button) or create a condition
Macro Execution	Start a macro
Variables	Assign a value to a variable, determine the state of a variable, or write out a variable
System Variables and Communication	Determine the value of system variables or define communication information such as which application or external program library to use
Execution Control	Affect speed or visibility of execution on the user's screen
Programming Aids	Provide tools that can help you debug your macros when they aren't working properly

Many commands, such as BEEP, appear in more than one category. This table also includes some product commands (see the next section) that behave like programming commands (they are in mixed case).

Table 26.2 lists programming commands in the categories above; boldfaced commands appear in examples in this chapter. If you compare this table with Table 26.1, you should see many similarities between the types of commands available in the merge language and the macro language.

Product Commands

The Word-Perfect for Windows Macro Manual documents programming and product commands in separate sections, and uses mixed case for product commands and uppercase for programming commands. Although the macro language compiler doesn't require you to type commands this way, your programs will be easier to debug if you stick with these conventions.

Macro product commands determine how the macro affects active applications, such as WordPerfect, and documents. There is a product command for nearly everything you can do in WordPerfect, and for this reason, I won't list all of them here. However, the examples in the following sections show many of these product commands and explain how to use them.

By convention, product commands are typed in mixed case, to distinguish them from programming commands, which are typed in uppercase. Their structure is also slightly different from programming commands, in that they include a *product prefix,* a command name, and any parameter names and values associated with the command. Take a look at this example:

```
WP.GraphicLine (
    Operation:HCreate!
)
```

WP is the product prefix, *GraphicLine* is the command name, *Operation* is a parameter name, and *HCreate!* is a value.

USER INTERFACE

BEEP	DEFAULTUNITS	**Display**	ENDPROMPT
GETNUMBER	**GETSTRING**	GETUNITS	MacroStatus-Prompt
MENU	PAUSE	**PauseKey**	**PROMPT**

FLOW CONTROL

ASSERTCANCEL	ASSERTERROR	ASSERTNOT-FOUND	CALL
CANCELOFF	CANCELON	CASE	**CASE CALL**
CHAIN	DLLCALL	ELSE	**ENDFOR**
ENDIF	ENDWHILE	ERROROFF	ERRORON
FOR	FOREACH	**GO**	**IF**
LABEL	ONCANCEL	ONCANCEL CALL	ONERROR
ONERROR CALL	ONNOTFOUND	ONNOTFOUND CALL	PAUSE
PauseKey	**QUIT**	**REPEAT**	**RETURN**
RETURNCANCEL	RETURNERROR	RETURNNOT-FOUND	RUN
UNTIL	WHILE		

MACRO OR SUBROUTINE TERMINATION

QUIT	**RETURN**	RETURNCANCEL	RETURN ERROR
RETURNNOTFOUND			

EXTERNAL CONDITION HANDLING

CANCELOFF	CANCELON	ONCANCEL	ONCANCEL CALL
ONERROR	ONERROR CALL	RETURNCANCEL	RETURN ERROR
RETURNNOTFOUND			

TABLE 26.2:

Categories of Macro Programming Commands and Product Commands with Programming Features

TABLE 26.2:

Categories of Macro Programming Commands and Product Commands with Programming Features (continued)

MACRO EXECUTION

CHAIN	RUN		

VARIABLES

ASSIGN	**FOR**	FOREACH	FRACTION
GETNUMBER	**GETSTRING**	**GetWPData**	INTEGER
MergeVariableGet	MergeVariableSet	NUMSTR	STRLEN
STRNUM	STRPOS	SUBSTR	

SYSTEM VARIABLES AND COMMUNICATION

APPLICATION	DLLCALL	DLLFREE	DLLLOAD
ENDAPP	**GetWPData**	NEWDEFAULT	

EXECUTION CONTROL

Display	SPEED	WAIT

PROGRAMMING AIDS

// (Comment)	**BEEP**	**Display**	SPEED

Commands in boldface have examples in the chapter.

Product commands within a single macro can come from several different applications, including WordPerfect, the Speller, the Thesaurus, the Macro Facility, and the File Manager. The two-character product prefix and period in front of the command name tell the Macro Facility which application you are working with. In the example above, the WP product prefix stands for WordPerfect.

You can also use the NEW-DEFAULT command to specify the default application.

However, since most macros deal with only a single application, adding a product prefix to each command can be a nuisance. Fortunately, the language designers thoughtfully provided a shortcut: If you use the APPLICATION programming command to specify the application you want, you can omit the product prefix. So, for example, if your APPLICATION command specifies WordPerfect as the default application, you can omit the product prefix and specify the GraphicLine command as it appears in Figure 26.2.

If you're ever unsure about which product command to use for a specific task, you can, of course, consult a detailed manual or book, or you can record a small macro, then edit it as described earlier.

DIALOG BOXES AND MACROS

As you know, many WordPerfect for Windows features are accessed through dialog boxes. When recording a macro, you can treat dialog boxes in either of two ways: The first method records the results of choosing options from a particular dialog box; the second method displays the dialog box for you to fill in when the macro is played back.

While recording a macro, you can choose options in a dialog box, then choose OK (or whatever button accepts the changes) to have WordPerfect translate your actions into a programming command that re-creates your choices exactly. For instance, if you choose Font ➤ Font, choose CG Times (Scalable) 12-point, then choose OK, WordPerfect inserts the following commands in your macro file:

```
Font
(
    Name:"CG Times (Scalable)";
    Size:12.0p;
    ForceInsert:Yes!
)
```

The check box appears only in the upper-right corner of a dialog box when you are recording a macro.

Alternatively, you can display a dialog box when the macro is run by using the following technique when recording your macro:

◆ Open a dialog box.

◆ Mark the check box in the upper-right corner.

◆ Close the dialog box by choosing OK, Close, or any similar button except Cancel.

892 MASTERING WORDPERFECT FOR WINDOWS **CH. 26**

All product commands that open dialog boxes end with the letters "Dlg," as in FontDlg, SearchDlg, and so on.

When you play the macro, it will open the dialog box for you to fill in. For example, in Figure 26.4, the check box in the upper-right corner is marked; this records a FontDlg() command, instead of a Font command, in the macro file.

Of course, you can also type the FontDlg() command directly in the macro document file, but the technique just described is handy when you don't know the name of the command that opens a particular dialog box.

Now that you know something about how the macro language works, you're ready to study some sample macros.

A MACRO TO ASSEMBLE DOCUMENTS

Figure 26.5 shows a macro that works very much like the merge example in Figure 26.1, except that instead of taking its data from a secondary merge file, it asks the user how many letters are being sent, then prompts for name, address, city, state, zip, salutation, and the number of days late on a customer's account before assembling the text of the dunning notice. Although you won't want to use this macro for a large number of letters, it can come in handy when you need to send out only a few letters. And of course, it's useful for demonstrating several basic principles that will help you develop advanced macros on your own.

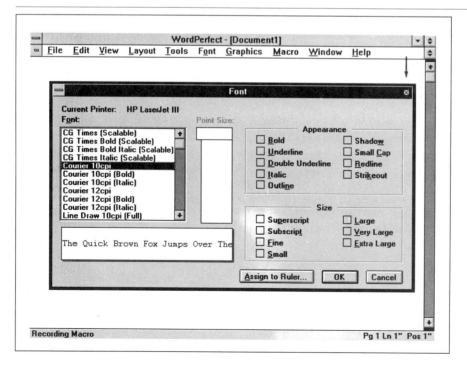

FIGURE 26.4:

To display a dialog box when you play a macro, mark the check box in the upper-right corner when you record the macro.

```
1     APPLICATION (WP; WPWP; Default; "WPWPUS.WCD")
2
3     //************************************************ Acct_age.wcm
4     // Assemble documents depending on lateness of payment.
5     // This macro is similar to the merge example in Figure 26.1.
6
7     //*** Show user what's going on behind the scenes.
8     //Display (State:On!)
9
10    //*** Find out how many letters there are.
11    GETNUMBER (HowMany;
12       "How many letters are you sending?" ; "How many?")
13
14    //*** For each letter, assemble the proper document.
15    FOR (Loop; 1; Loop <= HowMany; Loop + 1)
16
17       //*** Prompt user for information about the customer.
18       GETSTRING (First; "Enter first name." ; "First Name")
19       GETSTRING (Last; "Enter last name."; "Last Name")
20       GETSTRING (Add; "Enter address."; "Address")
21       GETSTRING (City; "Enter City."; "City")
22       GETSTRING (State; "Enter state."; "State")
23       GETSTRING (Zip; "Enter Zip Code."; "Zip Code")
24       GETSTRING (Salutation; "Enter Salutation." ; "Salutation")
25       GETNUMBER (DaysLate;
26          "How many days late is the payment." ; "DaysLate")
27
28       //*** Automatically fill in name, address, and salutation.
29       Type (First + " " + Last)
30       HardReturn()
31       Type (Add)
32       HardReturn()
33       Type (City + "," + State + "  " + Zip)
34       HardReturn()
35       HardReturn()
36       Type (Salutation + ":")
37       HardReturn()
38       HardReturn()
39
40       //*** Move to the bottom of the document
41       PosDocBottom()
42
43       //*** Retrieve the appropriate file, depending on DaysLate.
44       IF (DaysLate < 30)
45          FileRetrieve(Filename:"under30.wp")
46       ENDIF
47
48       IF ((DaysLate > 29) AND (DaysLate < 60))
49          FileRetrieve(Filename:"over30.wp")
50       ENDIF
51
52       IF ((DaysLate > 59) AND (DaysLate < 90))
53          FileRetrieve(Filename:"over60.wp")
54       ENDIF
55       IF (DaysLate > 89)
56          FileRetrieve(Filename:"over90.wp")
57       ENDIF
```

FIGURE 26.5:

A macro to assemble dunning notices. The line numbers, created using the Line Numbering feature, are shown for discussion purposes only and are not part of the macro.

```
58
59        //*** Move to bottom of the document and type the closing.
60        PosDocBottom()
61        HardReturn()
62        HardReturn()
63        Type ("Sincerely:")
64        HardReturn()
65        HardReturn()
66        HardReturn()
67        Type ("Wilma Dunning")
68        HardReturn()
69        Type ("Accounts Receivable")
70        HardReturn()
71
72        //*** Insert a page break at the end of the letter.
73        HardPageBreak()
74     ENDFOR
75
76     //*** If document isn't blank, move to the bottom of the document
77     //*** and delete the extra page break after the last letter.
78     GetWPData (
79        MacroVariable:Blank;
80        SystemVariable:DocumentBlank!)
81
82     IF (NOT Blank)
83        PosDocBottom()
84        DeleteCharPrevious()
85     ENDIF
```

FIGURE 26.5:

A macro to assemble dunning notices. The line numbers, created using the Line Numbering feature, are shown for discussion purposes only and are not part of the macro. (continued)

Notice that the figure has line numbers to the left of the macro text and commands. These are shown only to make this macro (and the one that follows) easier to understand as you learn about its inner workings. If you try to create these macros on your own, do not type the line numbers. Line numbers are *never* included in macros, although you can easily add them to your printed listing by using the Layout ➤ Line ➤ Numbering options described earlier.

Remember that the Macro Facility lets you create your programs in a free format, which means that you can add blank lines, indents, line numbers, page headers and footers, graphic lines, and other touches that make your programs easier to read and correct. The compiler ignores these formatting features, paying attention only to the actual text of the programming and product commands you enter.

SUMMARY OF THE MACRO

One way to learn macro programming is to read a few completed macros, thoroughly understand their logic and commands, type them, run them, and then try to write some macros on your own. To help you through this process, I'll discuss some sample macros step by step, first describing them in plain English, then discussing details of the commands used.

Here is an explanation of what's happening in the macro shown in Figure 26.5:

Line 1: Specifies that the WordPerfect application is used (WP).

Lines 3–5, 7, 10, 14, etc.: Contain comments to be read; WordPerfect ignores them.

Line 8: Changes made during macro playback will appear on the screen.

Lines 11 and 12: Find out how many letters the user wants to send.

Lines 15 and 74: Define a loop. The macro repeats (or "loops through") the commands between lines 15 and 74 as many times as there are letters to send.

Lines 18–24: Prompt for the first and last name, address, city, state, zip, and salutation information.

Line 25–26: Find out how many days late the payment is.

Lines 29–38: Automatically type the name, complete address, and salutation information into the document, inserting hard returns as needed to format the letter attractively.

Line 41: Move to the bottom of the current document.

Lines 44–46: If the payment is less than 30 days late, retrieve the file named "under30.wp" into the document.

Lines 48–50: If the payment is between 30 and 59 days late, retrieve the file named "over30.wp" into the document.

Lines 52–54: If the payment is between 60 and 89 days late, retrieve the file named "over60.wp" into the document.

Lines 55–57: If the payment is more than 89 days late, retrieve the file named "over90.wp" into the document.

Lines 60–70: Move to the bottom of the document, then automatically type the closing for the letter.

Line 73: Add a hard page break at the bottom of the document to separate the current letter from the next letter (if there is one).

Lines 78–80: Check to see whether the document is empty, which could happen if the user accidentally typed zero (0) as the number of letters to send. If the document is blank, the macro avoids trying to delete the last character (lines 82–85).

Lines 82–85: If the document isn't blank, move to the bottom of the document and delete the hard page break after the last letter.

ABOUT THE SAMPLE MACRO COMMANDS

Now that I've discussed the logic of how the macro operates, here's an explanation of the macro commands used (in order of appearance). Again, I've included line numbers so that you can refer to Figure 26.5 to see where these commands are used in the example.

Product identifiers reserved for WordPerfect include WPWP (WordPerfect), WPSP (Speller), WPTH (Thesaurus), WPMF (Macro Facility), and WPFM (File Manager).

APPLICATION (prefix; identifier; Default; filename) Tells the Macro Facility which application you are using and allows you to omit the product prefix for subsequent product commands. In line 1, the prefix is *WP*, the product identifier is *WPWP*, the word *Default* makes the WP product prefix the default, and the file name containing the product identifier is *wpwpUS.WCD*.

// comment Comments are notes to the macro programmer (or other programmers) about the purpose of various lines and subroutines. Everything between the // command and the next hard return is ignored by WordPerfect as it executes the macro. A comment can appear on a line by itself (lines 3–5, 7, etc.) or at the end of a line if you use the Tab key or spacebar to move the insertion point beyond the end of the command on that line.

A "subroutine" is a group of commands designed to do a specific job.

Display(State:state) Determines whether the screen displays changes made while the macro is running. Display(State:On!) shows changes, whereas Display(State:Off!) hides them. Macros typically run faster if Display is off; however, certain macros make a lot more sense to the user if they display changes on-screen, which is why Display is on in this example (line 8).

GETNUMBER (variable; prompt; title) Displays a dialog box containing the prompt and title indicated (lines 11–12 and 25–26). When the user types a number and presses ↵ or chooses OK, the number is placed in the variable. For example, the GETNUMBER command in lines 11 and 12 displays the following dialog box and stores the user's response in the variable *HowMany*.

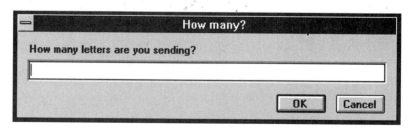

GETSTRING (variable; prompt; title) Works like GETNUMBER but is designed to store string or character information instead of numbers (lines 18–24). You can add an optional *LENGTH=numeric expression* parameter to limit the number of characters the user can type. For example, the GET-STRING command in line 18 displays the following dialog box and stores the user's response in the variable *First*.

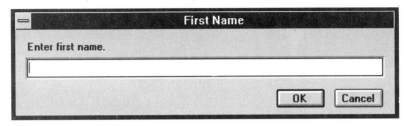

 You can use this command only with character strings and character variables. If you want to type out numeric variables, you must first convert them to string variables by using the NUMSTR command.

Type(expression) Types the character expression in the active document, beginning at the insertion point (lines 29, 31, 33, 36, 63, 67, and 69). This is the equivalent of typing text into the document window.

The expression can be a variable (line 31), text enclosed in quotes (lines 63, 67, and 69), or a combination of variables and text. To combine, or *concatenate,* variables and text, place a plus sign (+) between each variable or text string you are combining (lines 29, 33, and 36).

HardReturn() Inserts a hard-return code ([HRt]) in the active document at the insertion point, just as if you had pressed ↵ when typing in the document window (lines 30, 32, 34, 35, 37, 38, 61, 62, 64–66, 68, and 70).

 When comparing strings of text in an IF command, place quotes (") around the values being compared. When comparing numbers, you don't have to use quotes.

PosDocBottom() Moves the insertion point to the end of the active document, just as if you had pressed Ctrl+End in the document window (lines 41 and 60).

IF (test) Performs commands between the IF and closing ENDIF statements if the *test* is true (lines 44–46, 48–50, 52–54, and 55–57). If the *test* is false, the macro continues with the statement after ENDIF. The test can be simple expressions, like those in lines 44 and 55, or a more complicated expression involving two or more tests, as in lines 48 and 52. If you use complicated expressions as tests, be sure to include parentheses for grouping.

You can use the IF command with any of the following operators to make decisions within a macro:

OPERATOR	FUNCTION
=	Equal to
<>	Not equal to
>	Greater than
<	Less than
<=	Less than or equal to
>=	Greater than or equal to
AND	And
OR	Or
XOR	Boolean exclusive OR
NOT	Not

HardPageBreak() Inserts a hard page break at the insertion point, just as if you had pressed Ctrl+↵ in the document window.

GetWPData(MacroVariable:variable; SystemVariable:sysvariable)
GetWPData does for macros what the {SYSTEM} command does for merges: It provides information about the current state of WordPerfect or WordPerfect documents and stores it in a variable. You can then use the variable to decide whether you want the macro to perform certain actions.

For example, the command in lines 78–80 stores the value of the System-Variable named *DocumentBlank!* in the MacroVariable named *Blank*. If the document is blank, Blank contains the value TRUE; if the document contains text, Blank contains the value FALSE. This information is used in lines 82–85 to decide whether or not to delete the last character in the document. (You'll see more examples of this indispensable command in the next macro.)

DeleteCharPrevious() Deletes the command to the left of the insertion point, just as if you had pressed Backspace in the document window (line 84).

Trying to delete a character or search for text in a blank document will cause an error when the macro runs, so be sure to test for this condition!

A MACRO TO CONVERT TEXT TO UPPERCASE, LOWERCASE, OR INITIAL CAPS

The macro in the previous example is primarily designed to introduce you to the macro programming language, not to be added to your collection of the ten greatest macros ever written. However, the CONVERT.WCM macro in Figure 26.6 is sure to find its way to your Button Bar or Macro menu. This macro includes a handy initial caps feature that is missing from WordPerfect's built-in text conversion repertoire.

To use the CONVERT macro, follow these steps:

1. Select the text you want to convert.

2. Play the macro in the usual way. You will see this menu:

> **1 Convert To Uppercase**
> **2 Convert To Lowercase**
> **3 Convert To Initial Caps**

3. Choose an option.

This macro does not work correctly if you select multiple cells in a table, although it is just fine for converting selected text within a single cell.

The Convert To Uppercase and Convert To Lowercase options on the Macro menu work just like the Uppercase and Lowercase options on WordPerfect's Edit ➤ Convert Case pull-down menu: They convert selected text to uppercase or lowercase. The Convert To Initial Caps option, which has no equivalent in WordPerfect for Windows, converts the selected text from whatever case it was in originally to initial caps only. For example,

gUmby hITS a hoMer!

is converted to

Gumby Hits A Homer!

SUMMARY OF THE MACRO

As you can see, this macro is much more complex than the previous one, but it uses many of the concepts you've seen before. Here's what's happening:

Lines 6–8: Check to make sure you selected text before playing the macro.

```
1    Application (WP;WPWP;Default;"WPWPUS.WCD")
2    //**************************************************** Convert.wcm
3    // Convert selected text to uppercase, lowercase, or initial caps.
4
5    //*** Check to make sure text is selected.
6    GetWpData(
7       MacroVariable:SelectMode;
8       SystemVariable:SelectModeActive!)
9
10   // If no text selected, display warning dialog box and end macro.
11   IF (SelectMode=FALSE)
12      ASSIGN(Title; "Oops!")
13      ASSIGN(Message; "Please select text before running this macro!")
14      GO (ShowError@)
15   ENDIF
16
17   //*** Show menu of options.
18   MENU (Choice; Digit; ; ;
19      {
20         "Convert to Uppercase";
21         "Convert to Lowercase";
22         "Convert to Initial Caps"
23      })
24
25   //*** Delete // in front of Display command below to watch this
26   //*** macro do its thing (leave // in for faster performance.)
27   //Display (State:On!)
28
29   //*** Call a subroutine based on user's request.
30   CASE CALL (Choice;
31      {
32         1; ToUpper@;
33         2; ToLower@;
34         3; InitCaps@
35      };
36         AllDone@)
37
38   //*** All done, end macro.
39   LABEL (AllDone@)
40      QUIT
41
42   //*** Subroutines follow.
43   //*** Subroutine to convert selected text to lowercase.
44   LABEL (ToLower@)
45      CaseToLower()
46   RETURN
47
48   //*** Subroutine to convert selected text to uppercase.
49   LABEL (ToUpper@)
50      CaseToUpper()
51   RETURN
52
53   //*** Subroutine to convert to Initial Caps.
54   LABEL (InitCaps@)
55      //*** Cut selected text to a new document window.
56      EditCut()
57      FileNew()
58      EditPaste()
```

FIGURE 26.6:

A macro to convert selected text to uppercase, lowercase, or initial caps

```
59
60       //*** Put a caret (^) at end of the current document
61       //*** so we can later figure out when we're there.
62       PosDocBottom()
63       Type ("^")
64
65       //*** First onvert all the text to lowercase.
66       SelectAll()
67       CaseToLower()
68
69       //*** Move insertion point to top of document.
70       PosDocTop()
71
72       //*** Cap first letter of every word until caret (^) is found.
73       REPEAT
74          SelectCharNext()
75          CaseToUpper()
76          SelectMode(State:Off!)
77          PosWordNext()
78
79          //*** Define CurChar as character at insertion point.
80          GetWpData (
81             MacroVariable:CurChar;
82             SystemVariable:LeftChar!)
83       UNTIL (CurChar = "^")
84
85       //*** We're at last character in document (^). Delete it.
86       PosDocBottom()
87       DeleteCharPrevious()
88
89       //*** Select all the text and cut to Clipboard.
90       SelectAll()
91       EditCut()
92
93       //*** Close this window without saving anything.
94       CloseNoSave (Verify:No!)
95       Close (Save:No!)
96
97       //*** Paste modified text back into original position.
98       EditPaste()
99    RETURN
100
101   //*** Subroutine to show error message dialog box.
102   LABEL (ShowError@)
103      BEEP
104      PROMPT (Title; Message; 1; ; )
105      PauseKey (2)
106   QUIT
```

FIGURE 26.6:

A macro to convert selected text to uppercase, lowercase, or initial caps (continued)

Lines 11–15: If you haven't selected text first, the macro assembles a dialog box title and error message (lines 12 and 13), then goes to an error subroutine named *ShowError* (lines 102–106).

Lines 18–23: Display the menu shown earlier and wait for the user to choose one of the three options.

Lines 25–27: When using this macro to convert text to initial caps, you may be surprised at first when the text of your document seems to disappear. It's not really gone, of course; the macro has just switched temporarily to a new document (line 57), where it does the actual work of converting the selected text to initial caps. If this disappearing act proves bothersome, you can remove the // characters in front of the Display(State:On!) command in line 27, and you'll be able to watch everything the macro does. Warning: Removing this comment will slow down the macro considerably when you play it back.

Lines 30–36: Use a CASE CALL command (described below) to branch to one of four subroutines, depending on the user's menu choice. The subroutines are ToUpper (lines 49–51), ToLower (lines 44–46), InitCaps (lines 54–99), and AllDone (lines 39 and 40).

Lines 39–40: The AllDone subroutine simply exits the macro.

Lines 44–46: The ToLower subroutine converts the selected text to lowercase and returns.

Lines 49–51: The ToUpper subroutine converts the selected text to uppercase and returns.

Lines 54–70: The InitCaps subroutine is the trickiest one yet: It cuts the selected text to the Clipboard (line 56), opens a new (temporary) document (line 57), and pastes the selected text into the new document (line 58). Next, it inserts a caret (^) at the end of the new document so that the macro can later figure out when it's finished (lines 62 and 63). With that done, the macro selects all the text (line 66), converts it to lowercase (line 67), then returns to the top of the document (line 70).

Lines 73–83: With these preliminaries out of the way, the macro capitalizes the first letter of each word until it reaches the caret added earlier. This is handled by the commands between lines 73 and 83, which select the next character (line 74), convert it to uppercase (line 75), turn off the selection (line 76), move the insertion point to the next word (line 77), store the character at the insertion point in the *CurChar* variable (lines 80–82), then check to see whether there's any more to do. The REPEAT UNTIL loop is finished when *CurChar* is a caret (line 83).

Lines 86–99: Now that all the text has been converted to initial caps, the subroutine must replace the text in its proper position in the original document. To do this, it moves to the bottom of the temporary document (line 86), deletes the caret (line 87), selects all the text (line 90), cuts it and moves it to the Clipboard (line 91), and closes the temporary document without saving it and without asking

Opening a new document (line 57) leaves the insertion point unchanged in the original document. This lets the macro convert the selected text to initial caps in a "scratch pad" or temporary document, then pastes the text from the Clipboard to its proper position in the original document.

for the user's approval (lines 94 and 95). Finally, it pastes the text back into the original document (line 98).

Lines 102–106: The ShowError subroutine beeps a warning (line 103), displays a dialog box containing the title and message created in lines 12 and 13, waits for the user to press ↵ or choose OK, then exits the macro and returns to the document window. This subroutine isn't strictly necessary for this macro, since we can easily replace the commands in lines 12–14 with the commands in lines 103–106; however, the example here shows a general way to assign window titles and messages to variables, then pass control to an error-handling subroutine. The technique is most useful in complex macros where errors can occur in several places.

SOME NEW COMMANDS

I've covered many of the commands used in Figure 26.6, but several are new. They are explained in the sections that follow.

ASSIGN (variable; expression) Assigns values to WordPerfect variables. Values can be numeric, measurement, or character expressions (lines 12 and 13).

GO (label) Transfers execution to the LABEL command identified by the *label,* then continues from there. The GO command in line 14 transfers to the ShowError label in line 102 if the user forgets to select text before running the macro.

MENU (variable; mnemonic type; ; ; {option;...option}) Displays a pull-down menu of options, each of which has a corresponding number or letter (see lines 18–23). The mnemonic type Digit displays a number from 1 to 9 to the left of each option, and the mnemonic type Letter displays a letter from A to Z to the left of each option.

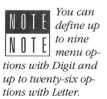 *You can define up to nine menu options with Digit and up to twenty-six options with Letter.*

You can choose any of the options by clicking on it or by typing the number or letter of that option. This assigns a numeric value to the *variable,* depending on which option you choose. For example, choosing the first option assigns *1* to the variable, choosing the second option assigns *2* to the variable, and choosing the third option assigns *3* to the variable. You can then use the variable in a CASE or CASE CALL statement to control the course of the macro.

You probably noticed some extra semicolons (;) in the MENU command. These indicate optional parameters for assigning a horizontal and vertical position to the menu. Horizontal menu positions are measured from the left side of the active application window to the left side of the menu, and vertical menu positions are measured from the top of the active application window to the top of the menu. Oddly enough, these positions must be specified in pixels or dots on the screen; however, since different screen types have different numbers of pixels, it's easiest to omit these positions (be sure to type the correct number of semicolons) and just let WordPerfect place the menu at the center of the screen.

CASE CALL (expression; {case; label;...case; label}; default) CASE CALL is sort of a glorified GO command, which branches to one of several locations, depending on the value of the *expression*. The value of the expression is compared with each *case*. When a match is found, execution branches to the *label* associated with that case. The *default* label handles situations where the expression doesn't match any of the cases listed. Figure 26.6 shows CASE CALL commands in lines 30–36. In line 30, for example, the expression being tested is the value in the Choice variable. If it's *1,* the case statement branches to the ToUpper label. If it's *2,* the statement branches to the ToLower label. If it's *3,* the statement branches to the InitCaps label. The default case of AllDone can't actually occur, but it must be included anyway, since the command syntax requires it.

After transferring to the appropriate LABEL command, execution continues until the macro encounters a RETURN command, then it resumes at the command following CASE CALL.

LABEL (label) Marks a place in a macro (lines 39, 44, 49, 54, and 102). Commands such as CASE, CASE CALL, GO, ONCANCEL, ONERROR, and ONNOTFOUND can send execution to a LABEL command. Your macro can contain as many labels as you need, as long as the names are unique. Label names must end with an "at" (@) character.

QUIT Stops the macro dead in its tracks (lines 40 and 106).

RETURN Marks the end of a subroutine and causes execution to resume with the command following a CALL or CASE CALL statement. If there isn't a CALL or CASE CALL to return to, the macro ends (see lines 46, 51, and 99).

EditCut() Removes any selected text and graphics from the document window and puts them in the Clipboard, just as if you had chosen Edit ➤ Cut (lines 56 and 91).

FileNew() Opens a new document window, providing that fewer than nine documents are currently open (line 57). If nine documents are already open, the command is ignored. This command is equivalent to choosing File ➤ New or pressing Shift+F4.

EditPaste() Pastes the contents of the Clipboard into the active document at the insertion point, just as if you had chosen Edit ➤ Paste (lines 58 and 98). This command replaces any currently selected text or graphics, just as it does when you use it from the document window.

SelectAll() Selects all text and graphics in the active window (line 90).

CaseToLower() Converts the selected text to lowercase, just as if you had chosen Edit ➤ Convert Case ➤ Lowercase (lines 45 and 67).

PosDocTop() Positions the insertion point at the beginning of text in the active document, just as if you had pressed Ctrl+Home (line 70).

REPEAT commands UNTIL (expression) Repeats the *commands* until the *expression* is true. The REPEAT loop in Figure 26.6 begins in line 73, causing the macro to repeat the commands in lines 74–82 until the variable *CurChar* is equal to the caret (∧) character (line 83). At that time, the macro stops executing the commands in the loop and continues with the command immediately after the UNTIL command.

SelectCharNext() Moves the insertion point one character to the right, and selects the codes and text between the previous position of the insertion point and the new position (line 74). This is the same as pressing Shift+→ in the document window and has no effect if the insertion point is at the end of the document.

CaseToUpper() Converts the selected text to uppercase, just as if you had chosen Edit ➤ Convert Case ➤ Uppercase (lines 50 and 75).

SelectMode(State:state) Turns the Select feature on or off. SelectMode (State:Off!) turns Select off (line 76), and SelectMode(State:On!) turns it on.

PosWordNext() Moves the insertion point to the beginning of the next word (line 77), just as if you had pressed Ctrl+→ in the document window. If the insertion point is at the last word of the document, this command moves the insertion point to the end of the word.

CloseNoSave(Verify:value) Discards the active document, without saving the document or closing the document window. CloseNoSave(Verify:Yes!) prompts the user to verify the discard, and CloseNoSave(Verify:No!) discards the document without asking permission (line 94).

Close(Save:value) Closes the active document window or text editor, just as if you had chosen File ➤ Close or pressed Ctrl+F4. Close(Save:Yes!) saves the contents of the window, whereas Close(Save:No!) discards the contents (line 95).

BEEP Causes the computer to beep (line 103).

PROMPT (title; message; icon; ;) Displays a dialog box with the specified *title, message,* and *icon* (line 104). You can set the icon as follows:

1	Displays a stop-sign icon
2	Displays a question-mark icon
3	Displays an exclamation-point icon
4 or greater	Displays the Important icon

If you leave this parameter blank, no icon is included in the box, but don't forget to include the semicolon (;).

The PROMPT command also lets you specify a horizontal and vertical position for the dialog box. But as with the MENU command described earlier, these values are in pixels, so it's easiest to position the dialog box in the center of the screen by leaving these parameters blank (again, be sure to include the semicolon as a placeholder).

Having studied the macros in this chapter, you may be ready to build a few on your own. Again, keep in mind that merge and macro programming is not something that you have to learn; simple merges like those covered in Chapter 16 and recorded-keystroke macros like those covered in Chapter 15 work just fine for most people.

In the next chapter, you'll learn ways to attach macros (recorded or otherwise) to specific keys, and how to build personalized or project-specific collections of macros.

CHAPTER 27

Customizing
the Keyboard Layout

**E**very key on your keyboard performs some action when pressed. When you press a letter or number key, that letter or number appears on the screen. When you press a movement key or function key, WordPerfect moves the insertion point or inserts a hidden code. The sum total of all possible actions that can be taken by pressing keys, or combinations of keys, is known as a *keyboard layout*.

ABOUT THE CUA AND WORDPERFECT DOS COMPATIBLE LAYOUTS

WordPerfect comes equipped with two unique keyboard layouts: the Common User Access (CUA) layout and the WordPerfect DOS compatible layout. In both layouts, certain keys and keystroke combinations perform the same function (for instance, F1 for Help). Other keys are assigned different functions.

The CUA keyboard assigns basic program tasks to function keys (such as F1 for Help, F3 for Save As, and F4 for File Open) to match the conventions of all Windows programs. It provides quick routes through common menu sequences (such as Alt+Shift+F7 for Print Preview) and displays often-used dialog boxes (such as Ctrl+F8 for the Font dialog box). It adds definitions for Ctrl+*letter* combinations, such as Ctrl+B for boldface and Ctrl+I for italic. (For a complete summary, see the template in the back of this book.)

The WordPerfect DOS compatible keyboard retains some keystroke compatibility with the DOS version of WordPerfect 5.1 (such as F6 for boldface, F10 for Save As, and F11 for Reveal Codes) and uses many of the CUA keystroke assignments (such as F1 for Help and Ctrl+F3 for Redisplay). For a complete summary, choose Help ➤ Keyboard ➤ DOS Keyboard Template.

The fact that there are two keyboard layouts to choose from should not intimidate you. In fact, if you are familiar with other Windows programs, you probably will prefer to use the CUA keyboard (it is the WordPerfect for Windows default). If you are upgrading from WordPerfect 5.1 and you are new to Windows, you can ease your transition into the Windows environment by initially selecting the WordPerfect DOS keyboard layout. Then, once you become more familiar with the Windows interface, you can switch to the CUA layout.

In addition to offering two distinct keyboard layouts, WordPerfect lets you create unique layouts that are designed to accommodate specialized word processing tasks. You may find this feature handy in these situations:

◆ You want to change some WordPerfect keystrokes to act like other programs you're familiar with.

◆ You want to be able to type special characters without using the WordPerfect Characters (Ctrl+W) key and having to remember special character codes.

◆ You share your computer with other users, and you want to create your own set of macros that can be executed with a single keystroke.

◆ You'd like to create unique keyboard layouts that organize WordPerfect features according to the needs of individual projects.

 *To preserve CUA keystroke compatibility with other Windows products, WordPerfect will not permit you to modify the CUA layout. You can, however, edit many of the key assignments for the WordPerfect DOS compatible keyboard.*

To change the roles played by various keys on your keyboard, you need to create a *custom keyboard,* define the roles played by the various keys on that keyboard, and then activate the keyboard. You can create any number of custom keyboards, each of which has a unique set of custom keys assigned to it. You can activate or deactivate a custom keyboard at any time.

When you create a custom keyboard, you can change the role of virtually any key or key combination (a process called *remapping*), except for the "hard-wired" keys: ↵, Print Screen, Scroll Lock, Pause/Break, Caps Lock, and Num Lock. You can also assign actions to key combinations, such as Ctrl and any letter, to execute a macro.

ACTIVATING A KEYBOARD

TO ACTIVATE AN EXISTING KEYBOARD,

choose File ➤ Preferences ➤ Keyboard, choose Select, move the highlight to the keyboard file name you want to activate, and choose Select to activate the keyboard.

The CUA keyboard is the default keyboard layout when you load WordPerfect for Windows. To activate the WordPerfect DOS compatible keyboard, follow these steps:

1. Choose **F**ile ➤ **P**references ➤ **K**eyboard. You'll see this dialog box:

2. Choose **S**elect to display the Select Keyboard File dialog box, shown in Figure 27.1.

3. Highlight WPDOS51.WWK in the Files list.

4. Choose **S**elect to activate the WordPerfect DOS compatible keyboard and return to the Keyboard dialog box.

5. Choose OK to return to the current document window.

When you return to the current document window, the WordPerfect DOS compatible keys go into effect. Notice also that WordPerfect changes the shortcut key listings in the pull-down menus to reflect compatibility with WordPerfect DOS.

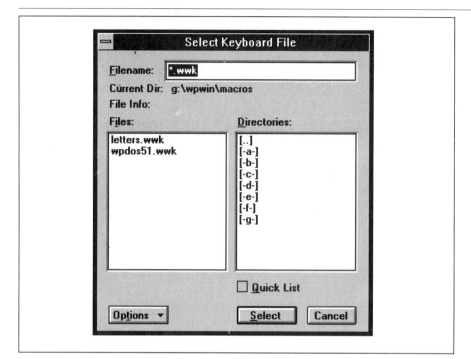

FIGURE 27.1:

The Select Keyboard File dialog box

EXPLORING A KEYBOARD

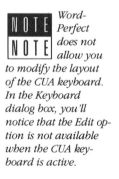 *Word-Perfect does not allow you to modify the layout of the CUA keyboard. In the Keyboard dialog box, you'll notice that the Edit option is not available when the CUA keyboard is active.*

To determine which key does what on the current keyboard, you can go through the basic steps required to edit the keyboard. After you've activated a keyboard, choose Edit in the Keyboard dialog box to display the Keyboard Editor dialog box, shown in Figure 27.2.

Although the Keyboard Editor dialog box appears to be complicated, it is simple to use. Take a look at the contents of the Change Assignment area in the lower-right corner of the dialog box. As the instructions indicate, you press a key to display a key assignment in the Current field. Until you press a key, the Current field displays "(Unassigned)." As soon as you press a key, WordPerfect lists the keystroke and its current assignment.

For example, if you press the F10 key when the WordPerfect DOS compatible keyboard is active, WordPerfect displays "F10" in the keystroke field and shows that this key is assigned to the command "FileSaveAsDlg (Command)" (see Figure 27.3).

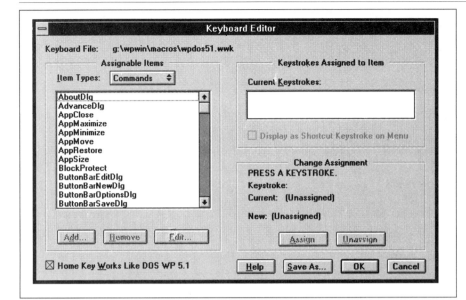

FIGURE 27.2:

*The Keyboard Editor
dialog box*

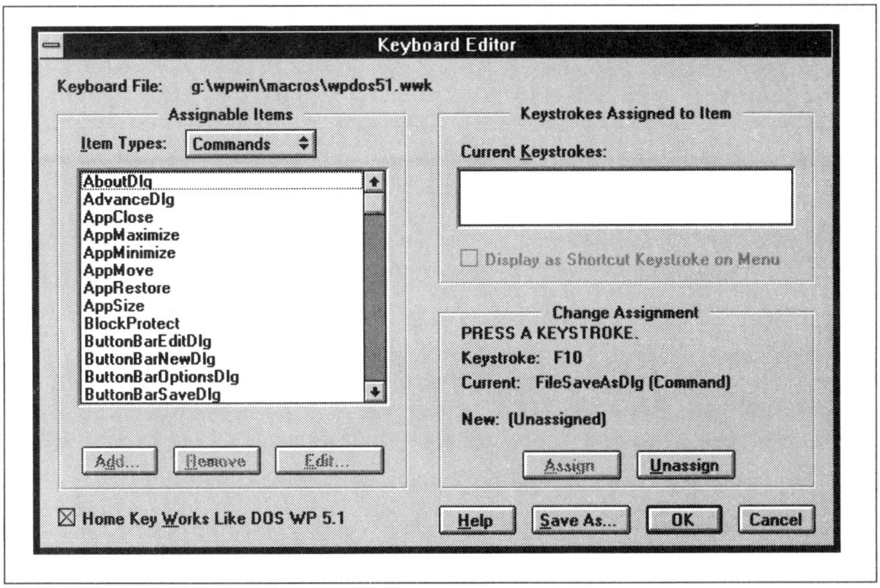

FIGURE 27.3:

*The Keystroke Editor
dialog box with F10
displayed*

FileSaveAsDlg is an assignable *command,* which describes the action that will be performed when the F10 key is pressed. WordPerfect displays a complete list of assignable commands on the list in the Assignable Items area of the dialog box. You may already have noticed that this command is comprised of three familiar words: File, Save As, and Dialog (Dlg). In this case, pressing F10 displays the Save As dialog box, just as if you had chosen File ➤ Save As to save a document to a file. In addition to commands, WordPerfect also allows you to assign submenus, macros, text, and user items to the keys on a keyboard. (Assigning these items to a keyboard is covered later in this chapter.)

 *On the Word-Perfect DOS compatible keyboard, F1 is Help and F3 is Undelete—the reverse of what you'd expect.*

You can use the preceding procedure to explore the WordPerfect DOS compatible keyboard. When you've finished viewing the descriptions, choose Cancel, then OK, to return to the current document window without affecting the current key assignments for the WordPerfect DOS compatible keyboard.

To try a key in the current document window, just press it (for example, press F10 to try the Save As key on the WordPerfect DOS compatible keyboard). For any commands that insert codes in the current document, you can also look behind the scenes to see what takes place by opening Reveal Codes.

To deactivate the current keyboard and return to the WordPerfect for Windows default keyboard, choose File ➤ Preferences ➤ Keyboard ➤ Default (CUA). (This erases any unsaved changes made to the key assignments for the current keyboard in the Keyboard Editor dialog box.) Then choose OK to return to the current document window.

CREATING A CUSTOM KEYBOARD

TO CREATE A CUSTOM KEYBOARD,

choose File ➤ Preferences ➤ Keyboard ➤ Create, and define the key assignments in the Keyboard Editor dialog box.

You can easily create your own keyboard by following these steps:

Each custom keyboard is stored as a file with the extension .WWK in the directory specified in File ➤ Preferences ➤ Location of Files ➤ Files (in the Macros/Keyboards/Button Bars area).

1. From the current document window, choose **File** ➤ **Preferences** ➤ **Keyboard** ➤ **Create**. You'll see the Keyboard Editor dialog box.

2. Choose **Save** As.

3. Type a file name (up to eight characters, with no extension) for the keyboard, and press ↵. The name will now appear as a keyboard file name in the Files list of the Select Keyboard File dialog box.

Now you can assign new actions to existing keystrokes or to new keystrokes, as described in "Assigning Actions to Keys" later in this chapter. You can activate the new custom keyboard at any time.

DELETING, RENAMING, AND COPYING KEYBOARDS

Custom keyboards are stored as files and therefore can be copied, renamed, or deleted just like other files. (Use a copy of an existing keyboard as your starting point to create a new custom keyboard that has some keys in common with it.) If you want a macro to choose a custom keyboard, be sure the macro uses the exact name of the file when it chooses the keyboard. That way, if the list of available keyboards changes (because you've added or deleted keyboards), the macro will still be able to locate the correct keyboard.

ASSIGNING ACTIONS TO KEYS

To assign a new action to a key or combination keystroke in a keyboard, follow these steps:

1. If you are starting at the current document window, choose **File ➤ Preferences ➤ K**eyboard to get to the Keyboard dialog box.

2. Choose **S**elect.

3. In the Files list, highlight the custom keyboard file name in which you want to add or change a key definition, then choose **S**elect.

4. In the Keyboard dialog box, choose **E**dit. The Keyboard Editor dialog box for that keyboard appears.

5. Press the key you want to redefine. For example, to assign an action to the Ctrl+Q combination, press Ctrl+Q. To prevent confusion, avoid changing shortcut keys that are predefined by WordPerfect. For example, since WordPerfect predefines Ctrl+B as the shortcut key for boldface, don't change the action of Ctrl+B.

6. In the Assignable Items list, highlight the command you want to assign to the selected keystroke. Optionally, to assign an item other than a command to the selected keystroke, choose the item from those listed in the **I**tem Types pop-up list:

   ◆ If you want the key to pull down a menu, choose **M**enus, then choose a menu name from the new list that appears in the Assignable Items area.

◆ If you want the key to type text, choose **Text** and choose **Add**. You'll see the Add Text dialog box. Type in a brief name and then type the text you want to attach to the selected key.

◆ If you want the key to activate a macro, choose the **Macros** option, and choose **Add**. You'll see the Import Macro To Keyboard dialog box. Highlight the name of a macro, then choose **Import** to select the macro to assign to the selected key. (More on this topic in a moment.)

7. Choose **Assign**. A complete description of your newly redefined key is listed in the Change Assignment area.

8. Choose **Save As**, then choose **Save**, to save a custom keyboard file.

9. Choose OK to complete the operation.

You may be curious about the New field in the Change Assignment area of the Keyboard Editor dialog box. Entries in this field tell you whether a key has been redefined from its original action. If you redefine a key, the entry for that key will appear in the New field. If you didn't actually change the key's original definition, the New entry will remain blank.

EDITING A CUSTOM KEYBOARD

See Chapter 15 for more information on recording macros.

The options in the Keyboard Editor dialog box let you manage the custom-key definitions within the current keyboard as follows:

Add	Lets you add text, macros, and user items to the list box in the Assignable Items area
Remove	Lets you remove text, macros, and user items from the list box in the Assignable Items area
Edit	Lets you edit text, macros, and user items that currently are displayed in the list box in the Assignable Items area
Home Key **W**orks Like DOS WP 5.1	Lets you redefine the Home key to operate exactly as it does in WordPerfect 5.1 for DOS (for example, as an accelerator key when used in conjunction with a movement key)
Assign	Lets you assign the currently highlighted item from the Assignable Items area to the keystroke listed in the Change Assignment area
Unassign	Lets you unassign the currently highlighted item from the Assignable Items area to the keystroke listed in the Change Assignment area
Help	Invokes the built-in Help feature (pressing F1 for Help while the Keyboard Editor dialog box is displayed does not invoke Help—it selects the F1 key for reassignment)
Save As	Lets you assign a unique file name to a custom keyboard layout
OK	Closes the Keyboard Editor dialog box and returns you to the Keyboard dialog box
Cancel	Discards all current changes and key assignments made in the Keyboard Editor dialog box, and returns you to the Keyboard dialog box

ASSIGNING MACROS TO SHORTCUT KEYS

If you are familiar with earlier versions of WordPerfect, you may miss the convenience of executing macros with Alt+*letter* combinations. One way around this, as mentioned in Chapter 15, is to assign macros to the Button Bars and the Macros menu.

As an alternative, you can assign macros to certain shortcut keys. But rather than use an Alt+*letter* combination (which is used for menus and dialog boxes in WordPerfect for Windows), you can use Ctrl+*letter* or Ctrl+Shift+*letter* combinations instead.

To help you get organized , I recommend that you first create and test the macros you want to assign to the keyboard. Then, if you haven't already done so, create a custom keyboard layout, as described earlier in this chapter. You need not assign any keys in this new keyboard, but you should give it a name so that it will be available when you want to start assigning macros to keystrokes.

CHOOSING MACROS TO ASSIGN TO KEYS

To get ready for assigning macros to keystrokes:

1. Choose **F**ile ➤ **P**references ➤ **K**eyboard.

2. If the custom keyboard to which you want to assign macros is not already selected, choose **S**elect and double-click the name of the keyboard to which you want to assign the macros.

3. Choose **E**dit.

4. In the **I**tem Types pop-up list, choose **M**acros.

5. Choose **A**dd. The Import Macro To Keyboard dialog box, shown in Figure 27.4, appears.

6. Choose any macro that you want to assign to a key, either by double-clicking its name or highlighting it and choosing **I**mport.

7. Repeat steps 5 and 6 to choose any additional macros that you want to assign to the keyboard.

When you have finished choosing macros to assign to the keyboard, you'll see the list of assignable macros in the Assignable Items list box.

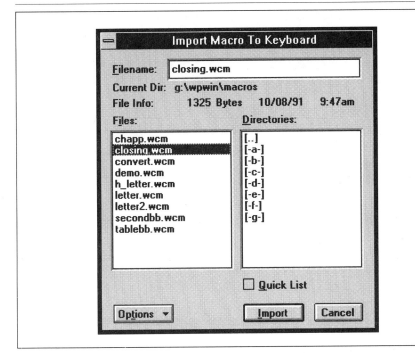

FIGURE 27.4:

The Import Macro To Keyboard dialog box

ASSIGNING THE MACRO KEYS

> **NOTE** *You can assign more than one keystroke combination to any given macro. The Current Keystroke list shows all the keystrokes currently assigned to the macro. To delete a previous assignment, click the keystroke combination you want to unassign, then choose the Unassign button.*

After you have chosen which macros you want to assign to the keyboard, follow these steps:

1. Press the keystroke combinations to which you will assign a macro. For example, press Ctrl+Shift+B to assign a macro to that keystroke combination.

2. If the keystroke combination you pressed already has an assignment, the assignment is displayed next to Current in the Change Assignment area of the dialog box.

3. If you don't want to change the current assignment, repeat steps 1 and 2 until you find an unused key combination.

4. In the Assignable Items list, highlight the name of the macro you want to assign to the keystroke combination.

5. Choose **A**ssign.

6. Repeat steps 1–5, as necessary, to continue to assign macros to keystrokes.

7. Choose OK when you've finished assigning macros.

8. Choose OK to save the current changes.

9. Choose OK from the Keyboard dialog box to return to the document window.

Don't forget that the shortcut keystrokes you assigned to the macros work only when the appropriate keyboard is active. If a keystroke combination doesn't work, use File ➤ Preferences ➤ Keyboard to activate the keyboard you need, as described earlier.

PART NINE

Hands-On Lessons

This part of the book presents ten hands-on lessons designed to teach you how to use many of WordPerfect's features right at your keyboard. Each lesson takes you step by step through the keystrokes required to produce a sample document or reach a specific goal. Though doing these lessons is optional, they help to illustrate features explained in the chapters, so you can see the features in action while using them. (Look at the bottom of each lesson page for a handy cross-reference to the appropriate chapter in the book.) If you're a beginning or an intermediate WordPerfect user, the lessons will help you quickly get up to speed.

Typing and Printing a Letter

In this exercise you'll type, print, and save your first document, a business letter, and then exit WordPerfect.

HANDS-ON

LESSON

1

BEFORE YOU BEGIN

Before you begin this lesson, start WordPerfect for Windows and get to a blank document window. You should also be familiar with the location of the Backspace, ↵, and other special keys. And, if you have a mouse, you should know how to move the mouse pointer and click options. If you need any help with these topics, refer to Chapter 1.

TYPING THE LETTER

Figure L1.1 shows a rough draft of a sample business letter. The sections that follow provide step-by-step instructions for creating, printing, and saving this document.

TYPING THE NAME, ADDRESS, AND SALUTATION

The blinking insertion point should be at the top of a blank WordPerfect document window. To type the short lines at the top of the letter, just type each line and press ↵ to end each one. If you make a mistake at any time while typing in WordPerfect, you can press the Backspace key to back up and make corrections.

Follow these steps:

1. Type **Mrs. Adrian Smith** and press ↵.

2. Type **123 Oak Ave.** and press ↵.

3. Type **San Diego, CA   92123** and press ↵.

4. Press ↵ again to add a blank line.

5. Type **Dear Mrs. Smith:** and press ↵.

6. Press ↵ again to add another blank line.

Refer to Chapter 1

```
Mrs. Adrian Smith
123 Oak Ave.
San Diego, CA  92123

Dear Mrs. Smith:

Thank you for your letter regarding our Hawaiian outer-island
tour packages. Currently, we offer two travel packages with no
overnight stays on Oahu.

If you have any additional questions, or wish to make a
reservation, please feel free to call me at (800) 555-1234 during
regular hours. The enclosed brochures describe these tour
packages in more detail.

        Best regards,


        Olivia Newton
```

FIGURE L1.1:

A sample business letter

The text on your screen should now look like Figure L1.2. In the next section, when you type paragraphs, you'll only press ↵ at the end of each paragraph.

TYPING THE BODY AND CLOSING

To type the first paragraph in the body, follow these steps:

1. Type the following paragraph as though it were one long line of text. Don't indent, and don't try to break the lines to match those shown below or those in the figure.

> Thank you for your letter regarding our Hawaiian outer-island tour packages. Currently, we offer two travel packages with no overnight stays on Oahu.

2. Press ↵.

Now follow these steps to add a blank line and type the second paragraph:

1. Press ↵ again to add a blank line.

2. Type the following paragraph, again as though it were one long line of text, without indenting or pressing ↵:

> If you have any additional questions, or wish to make a reservation, please feel free to call me at (800) 555-1234 during regular hours. The enclosed brochures describe these tour packages in more detail.

3. Press ↵.

Refer to Chapter 1

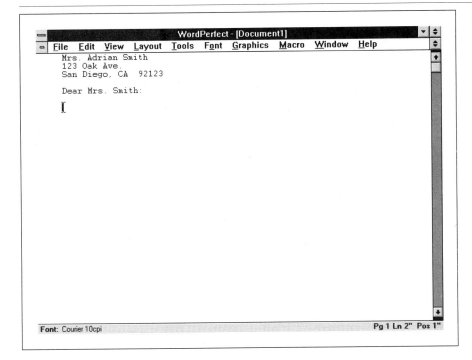

The sample business letter after the name, address, and salutation have been entered

Now you are ready to add the closing. Just to get a little practice indenting with the Tab key, which works much as it does on a typewriter, follow these steps:

1. Press ↵ to add a blank line.

2. Press the Tab key twice.

3. Type

   Best regards,

   and press ↵.

4. Press ↵ three times to add three blank lines.

5. Press the Tab key twice.

6. Type **Olivia Newton** and press ↵.

Your letter is complete now, and your screen should look something like Figure L1.3. Don't worry if you made mistakes; you'll learn how to correct them in Lesson 2. For now, print a copy of the letter.

Refer to Chapter 1

PRINTING YOUR LETTER

Make sure that your printer is turned on, is online, and has paper in it. Follow these steps to print your letter now:

1. Pull down the **F**ile menu. (To do so, you can move the mouse pointer to the File option on the menu bar, then click the left mouse button. Or, you can hold down the Alt key, press F, then release both keys.)

2. Choose **P**rint (move the mouse pointer to the Print option on the menu and click the left mouse button, or press P). You'll see the Print dialog box.

3. Choose the **F**ull Document option, if it isn't chosen already (move the mouse pointer to Full Document and click the left mouse button, or just press F).

4. Choose the **P**rint command button (move the mouse pointer to the Print button, near the lower-right corner of the dialog box, and click the left mouse button, or just press P).

You should see a printed copy of your document in just a few seconds. If your printer does not print, check Chapter 8 for additional information.

NOTE NOTE *Appendix B describes the many ways of using the menus in detail.*

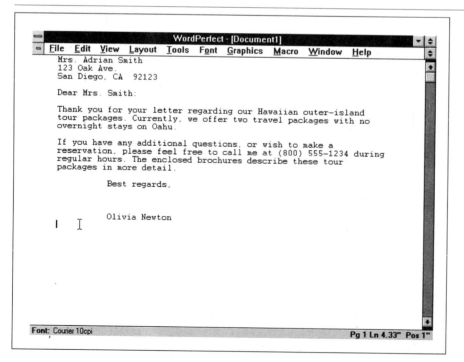

FIGURE L1.3:

The completed letter in the document window

SAVING YOUR LETTER
AND EXITING WORDPERFECT

You'll use this same letter in Lesson 2 to practice editing, so save the letter and exit WordPerfect:

1. Pull down the **F**ile menu, either by moving the mouse pointer to the File option on the menu bar and clicking the left mouse button or by holding down the Alt key and pressing F.

2. Choose E**x**it (move the mouse pointer to the E**x**it option and click the left mouse button, or press X). You'll see this prompt in a message box on the screen:

    Save changes to Document1?

3. Choose the **Y**es command button (move the mouse pointer to the **Y**es button and click the left mouse button, or press Y). You'll see a dialog box requesting a file name for this document.

4. Type the file name **smith.wp**.

5. Press ↵ or choose the **S**ave command button (by moving the mouse pointer to the button and clicking the left mouse button).

6. If a message like this appears:

    C:\WPWIN\SMITH.WP already exists. Do you want to replace it?

    either you or somebody else has already saved a file named SMITH.WP. If you're sure that that file is just a previous copy of this sample letter, you can choose **Y**es (either by moving the mouse pointer to the Yes command button and clicking the left mouse button or by pressing Y). If you're not so sure you want to replace the existing file, choose **N**o, then repeat steps 4 and 5 but type a different file name.

    You'll be taken back to Windows 3, and your work is now saved. Depending on how you started WordPerfect, the WordPerfect group window may still be open. If you want to close that window, click its Minimize button or press Ctrl+F4 (hold down the Ctrl key and press F4).

    You can now go to Lesson 2 for a lesson in opening and editing a document. Or, return to Chapter 1 for more information on typing, printing, and saving documents.

If you use a file name other than SMITH.WP to save the file now, you'll have to use that same name to open the file in later lessons.

Refer to Chapter 1

Editing a Document

Figure L2.1 shows the sample letter you created in Lesson 1, marked with some changes. In this lesson, you'll use some of the techniques described in Chapter 2 to make these changes.

BEFORE YOU BEGIN

If WordPerfect for Windows is not up and running on your computer, you need to get it running again, as described in Chapter 1.

OPENING THE LETTER

Before you can edit the sample business letter, you need to *open* it, which means to bring a copy back from disk into a WordPerfect document window. Follow these steps:

1. To open the SMITH.WP file you created in Lesson 1, first pull down the **F**ile menu (click the File option on the menu bar with your mouse, or press Alt+F).

2. Choose **O**pen (click that option, or press O). The Open File dialog box appears.

3. Type **smith.wp** and press ↵. If you prefer to use the mouse, you can use the scroll bar next to the list of file names to scroll down until SMITH.WP appears, then double-click on the name.

The letter appears on your screen, ready for editing, looking just as it did at the end of Lesson 1. The insertion point is at the top of the letter.

HANDS-ON
LESSON
2

Refer to Chapter 2

INSERTING THE DATE

> **NOTE**
> **NOTE**
>
> *The Num Lock key must be off for the arrow, Delete, and other special keys on the numeric keypad to work properly.*

In Lesson 1, you didn't insert the date at the top of the letter, so you can do that now (as well as insert a couple of blank lines). Follow these steps:

1. The insertion point should already be at the top of the document, but if you've moved it, press Ctrl+Home, or move the I beam to the upper-left corner of the screen and click the left button. This moves the insertion point just to the left of the *M* in *Mrs.*

2. Press ⏎ three times to insert three blank lines.

3. Move the insertion point back to the top line, by clicking in the upper-left corner of the document window or by pressing Ctrl+Home (or just ↑ three times).

4. Type the date (*August 1, 1992* is used in the example). As a shortcut to typing today's date, choose Date **T**ext on the **T**ools menu.

The date should now be at the top of the document, with a couple of blank lines beneath, as in Figure L2.2. If you'd like to experiment with adding and deleting blank lines, just move the insertion point to any blank line, press Delete to delete it, or press ⏎ to insert a new one.

DELETING A WORD

Exactly how text is formatted on your screen depends on the current font (described in Chapter 5). So don't worry if your letter doesn't look exactly like the example.

Refer to Chapter 2

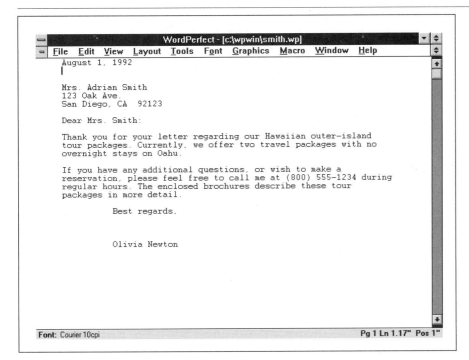

The letter, with the date inserted at the top

Exactly how text is formatted on your screen depends on the current font (described in Chapter 5). So don't worry if your letter doesn't look exactly like the example.

Now you'll delete the word *additional,* as marked in Figure L2.1. Follow these steps:

1. If you have a mouse, move the I beam anywhere inside the word *additional* in the second paragraph and click the left mouse button, or just press the ↓, →, ↑, and ← keys as needed until the insertion point is anywhere in the word *additional.*

2. Press Ctrl+Backspace (hold down the Ctrl key and press the Backspace key) once, or press Delete or Backspace as many times as necessary to delete the entire word and one blank space.

The word is deleted, and the paragraph is automatically reformatted to fill in the blank space that otherwise would have been left by the deleted word.

INSERTING A WORD

Now insert the word *business* by following these steps:

1. Move the insertion point to the letter *h* in the word *hours* (near the end of the first sentence in the second paragraph). You can move the I beam to the *h* in *hours* and click the left mouse button, or use the arrow keys to position the insertion point. The blinking insertion point should be right on the "stem" of the letter *h.*

Refer to Chapter 2

2. Make sure you are in Insert mode so that your new text is inserted at the insertion point. If you see the word "Typeover" in the status bar, near the lower-left corner of the screen, press the Insert key to switch to Insert mode.

3. Type **business** then press the spacebar to insert a blank space after the word.

Again, the paragraph is reformatted automatically to include the new word. If, for whatever reason, you end up with too many, or too few, spaces in front of or after a newly inserted word, you can use the arrow keys to move the insertion point wherever you need to insert or delete a space. Then press the spacebar to insert a space, or press Delete to delete one.

MOVING TEXT

Next you'll move the sentence at the end of the second paragraph to the start of that paragraph. This requires a basic cut-and-paste operation:

1. Select the last sentence in the second paragraph, beginning with the words "The enclosed brochures…," using any one of the following techniques:

   ◆ If you have a mouse, move the I beam anywhere inside the last sentence, then click the left mouse button three times rapidly.

   ◆ Use your mouse to move the I beam to the letter *T* that starts the last sentence. Then hold down the left mouse button, and move the mouse down slightly and to the right, until the entire sentence is selected.

   ◆ If you prefer to use the keyboard, use the arrow keys to move the insertion point to the letter *T* that starts the last sentence. Then press the F8 key, and type a period to extend the selection to the end of the sentence.

 *If you select the wrong text, just press F8 or click the left mouse button again to unselect it, then try again.*

Regardless of which method you use, the entire last sentence should be selected, as in Figure L2.3. When the correct text is selected, proceed with the steps below.

2. Pull down the **E**dit menu, either by clicking the Edit option on the menu bar with your mouse or by pressing Alt+E.

3. Choose Cu**t** by clicking that option or by pressing T. The selected text disappears.

Refer to Chapter 2

4. Move the insertion point to the *I* in *If* at the start of the second paragraph, by moving the I beam to the *I* with your mouse and clicking the left mouse button, or by pressing ↑ twice then Home (or whatever combination of arrow keys you need to press to position the insertion point so that it's just touching the left side of the letter *I* at the start of the paragraph).

5. Pull down the **E**dit menu again.

6. Choose **P**aste by clicking the Paste option or pressing P.

7. Press the spacebar to insert a blank space at the end of the sentence.

Figure L2.4 shows how your edited letter should look. Now you can print a copy.

PRINTING YOUR EDITED LETTER

The steps for printing the edited letter are exactly the same as for printing the letter the first time:

1. Pull down the **F**ile menu (click File on the menu bar, or press Alt+F).

2. Choose **P**rint, either by clicking that option or pressing P.

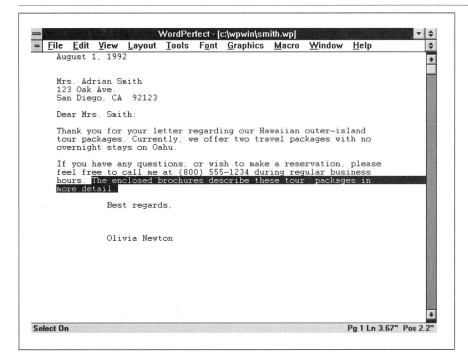

FIGURE L2.3:

The sentence to be moved is selected.

Refer to Chapter 2

FIGURE L2.4:

The edited letter in the document window

3. If it isn't already selected, choose **F**ull Document by clicking that option or pressing F.

4. Choose the **P**rint command button, either by clicking on it or pressing P.

In a few seconds, your letter will be printed.

SAVING YOUR CHANGES

The changes you've made in this lesson are visible on the screen and in the printed document, but have not been saved permanently to disk—they're only in the computer's memory (RAM). To save this copy of the letter, you must save the document again. You can also *close* the document window in the process, to clear it from the screen for the time being. Follow these steps:

1. Pull down the **F**ile menu again.

2. Choose **C**lose. You'll see a message like "Save changes to c:\wpwin\smith.wp?" followed by some command button options.

3. Choose **Y**es.

Refer to Chapter 2

The letter is cleared from the screen. But, unlike the previous lesson, this time you're still in WordPerfect and can work on a different document if you want. If, and when, you are ready to call it quits and turn off the computer, don't forget to first exit WordPerfect by choosing the Exit option on the File menu.

This concludes Lesson 2. Don't forget to read Chapter 2 for more information on basic editing techniques. Optionally, you can proceed to Lesson 3 right now for a hands-on lesson in using some general features of WordPerfect.

If you've had many difficulties with the first two lessons, you may want to read chapters 1–3 to get some more background, and perhaps refer to Appendix B for some Windows basics. Then try these lessons again.

Refer to Chapter 2

A Guided Tour of WordPerfect

Now that you've had a chance to learn some basic WordPerfect typing and editing skills, it's time to learn more about the WordPerfect for Windows interface and some general features.

BEFORE YOU BEGIN

Before you begin this lesson you should feel comfortable with basic menu selection techniques and the abbreviated menu sequence instructions described in Chapter 3. Also, you should be comfortable with the mouse and mouse terminology, such as click, double-click, and drag (as defined in Appendix B).

OPENING THE SAMPLE DOCUMENT

You can use the sample letter you created and edited in lessons 1 and 2 to try out some of the techniques in this lesson. To open that document, follow these steps:

1. If WordPerfect for Windows isn't currently running, start it now, as described in Chapter 1.

2. Choose **File ➤ O**pen (or press F4).

3. Type **smith.wp** and press ↵, or choose the name from the list of file names by double-clicking it.

MOVING AND SIZING WINDOWS

Like all Windows applications, WordPerfect lets you move and size the windows that applications and documents are displayed in. You can use the title bar and its buttons, or the Control-menu box, to manage the windows. If your windows are currently maximized to full-screen size, you may want to reduce their size a bit to experiment with moving and sizing them. You can use either the mouse or keyboard:

Refer to Chapter 3

◆ To use the mouse, simply click each window's Restore button.

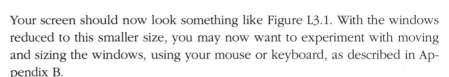

◆ To use the keyboard, press Alt+spacebar and choose **R**estore from the application window's Control menu. Then press Alt+- (hold down the Alt key and press the hyphen key), and choose **R**estore from the document window's Control menu.

Your screen should now look something like Figure L3.1. With the windows reduced to this smaller size, you may now want to experiment with moving and sizing the windows, using your mouse or keyboard, as described in Appendix B.

USING PRINT PREVIEW

The Print Preview screen gives you a bird's-eye view of how your document will look when printed, regardless of how you've sized your document window. Try it out:

1. Choose **F**ile ➤ Print Pre**v**iew (or press Shift+F5). You'll see the Print Preview screen, shown in Figure L3.2.

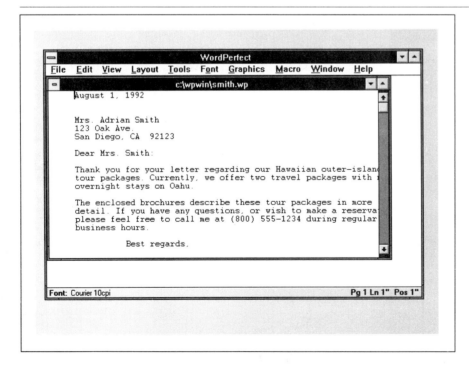

FIGURE L3.1:

Application and document windows reduced on the screen

Refer to Chapter 3

If the Button Bar appears on your Print Preview screen, you can use its 100%, 200%, and Full Page buttons rather than the menus to change magnification.

2. To zoom in, choose **View** ➤ **200%**.

3. To see the entire page, choose **Pages** ➤ **Full Page**. When viewing the full page, your text may be converted to thick lines. But even so, you get a good view of the overall page layout.

4. Print Preview is used only for viewing your document; you can't do any editing. When you're finished with Print Preview, just close it to get back to your normal document window: Choose **File** ➤ **Close** (or press Ctrl+F4); or click the Close button on the Button Bar, if it's available.

USING THE RULER

As you'll see in later lessons, the ruler provides a handy means of changing tab stops, line spacing, justification, and other formatting settings. To view the ruler,

◆ Choose **View** ➤ **Ruler** (or press Alt+Shift+F3).

The ruler appears near the top of the document window, as in Figure L3.3.

If you have a mouse, you can now try using one of the ruler buttons to change the line spacing in your letter:

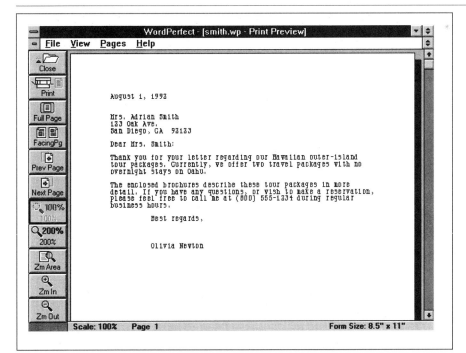

FIGURE L3.2:

The Print Preview screen at 100 percent magnification

Refer to Chapter 3

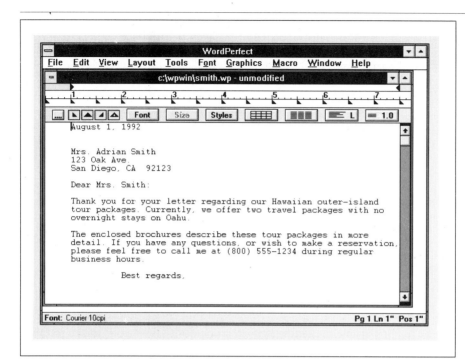

FIGURE L3.3:

The ruler displayed at the top of the document window

1. Move the insertion point to the top of the letter, by moving the I beam just to the left of the date and clicking the left mouse button, or by pressing Ctrl+Home.

2. Move the mouse pointer to the line-spacing command button on the ruler (which currently shows *1.0*).

3. Hold down the left mouse button, move the mouse pointer to the 2.0 option, then release the button.

The entire letter is now double-spaced. Before you make any other changes to the document, try undoing a change.

UNDOING THE MOST RECENT CHANGE

You just changed to double spacing in your letter, but you can undo the most recent change to a document by using the Undo option:

◆ Choose **Edit** ➤ **Undo** (or press Alt+Backspace).

Keep in mind that Undo undoes only your most recent change. If you've made additional changes since the one you want to undo, you may need to select

Refer to Chapter 3

menu options to go back to the previous settings or use Reveal Codes (discussed in a moment) to delete formatting codes.

VIEWING THE BUTTON BAR AND CREATING A BUTTON

The Button Bar offers a shortcut method for performing common tasks. You can create individual buttons that perform the same functions as a series of menu choices, so you need to click only one option rather than several. To view the Button Bar,

◆   Choose **View** ➤ **B**utton Bar.

The Button Bar appears beneath the menu bar in the application window, as in Figure L3.4.

Like menu options, some buttons may be dimmed and unavailable at the moment. For example, buttons for cutting, copying, and pasting text are only available when text is selected in the document. But you can use any of the available buttons to perform common tasks, or create your own buttons.

Try creating a button to switch to the Print Preview screen with a single mouse click:

1.   Choose **V**iew ➤ Button Bar **S**etup.

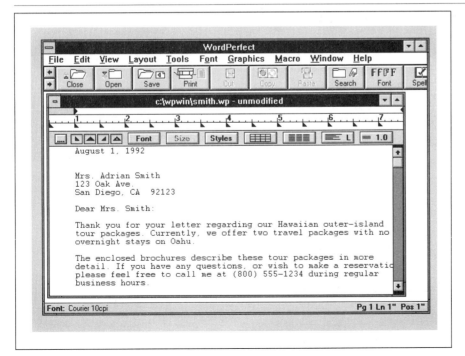

FIGURE L3.4:

The Button Bar is displayed beneath the menu bar after you choose View ➤ Button Bar.

Refer to Chapter 3

2. Choose **E**dit from the submenu. A dialog box with some instructions appears.

3. To create the button for Print Preview, just choose **F**ile ➤ Print Pre**v**iew. (Notice that the mouse pointer has changed to a hand holding a button.) The menu choices don't actually take you to the Print Preview screen. Instead, they simply add a Preview button to the Button Bar.

4. Choose the OK command button in the dialog box to return to normal editing.

You should see the new Preview button at the right edge of the Button Bar. You can scroll through buttons by clicking the ← and → buttons at the left edge of the Button Bar.

Now to switch to Print Preview, you don't need to use the menus. Just click the Preview button instead.

USING REVEAL CODES

Reveal Codes lets you see formatting codes that are normally hidden. The codes are hidden so that your document window looks more like a sheet of paper than a computer screen. But you can see the codes by using Reveal Codes. Seeing the codes can be handy for getting a behind-the-scenes look at your document and correcting formatting errors.

To activate Reveal Codes, do one of the following:

◆ Choose **V**iew ➤ Reveal **C**odes.

◆ Press Alt+F3.

◆ Drag one of the Reveal Codes bars from the top or bottom of the document window's scroll bar part of the way up or down the window.

Your screen is now divided into two sections: The top section shows the normal document window, and the bottom section shows the hidden codes, as in Figure L3.5.

If you scroll through your document by using the scroll bar at the right of the document window, or the ↑ and ↓ keys, you'll notice several codes embedded in your document:

[HRt]   Hard return, wherever you pressed ↵ while creating the document

[SRt]   Soft return, wherever WordPerfect has automatically word-wrapped a line

Refer to Chapter 3

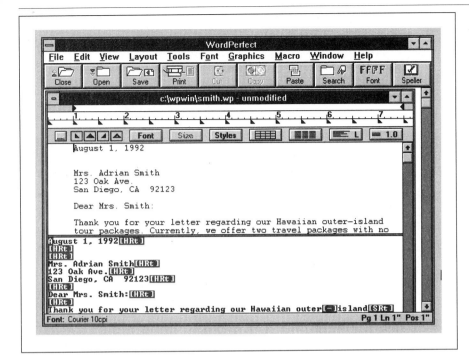

FIGURE L3.5:

Reveal Codes is active, so hidden codes are visible in the lower portion of the document window.

[Tab]	Tab, wherever you pressed Tab while typing or editing the document

If you use the arrow keys to move the insertion point, or click a character with your mouse, you'll notice that a small highlight in Reveal Codes moves wherever you move the insertion point. But in Reveal Codes, you can see when the insertion point is actually on a code rather than a space or character. As you'll see, this makes it easy to delete codes to help make formatting changes, which would be difficult with the document window only.

You'll see some examples of putting Reveal Codes to work throughout the book. For now, if you want to get rid of Reveal Codes, do one of the following:

◆ Choose **View** ➤ Reveal **C**odes (or press Alt+F3).

◆ Drag the Reveal Codes bar separating the two sections of the screen off the top or bottom of the document window.

For more information on Reveal Codes and other topics covered in this lesson, refer to Chapter 3. You'll also learn about some other useful features, including the built-in help system, Auto Code Placement, and more.

Refer to Chapter 3

If you want to try some more hands-on exercises first, you can go to Lesson 4. If you want to call it quits for now, you can exit WordPerfect by choosing File ➤ Exit. Choose No when asked about saving the current copy of the document, since you haven't made any changes to the text that are worth saving. You'll be taken back to Windows.

Refer to Chapter 3

Using Indents, Special Characters, and Fonts

In this lesson you'll get some hands-on experience in using some of the basic techniques described in Part 2, including indenting, changing the tab stops, and using special printer features.

BEFORE YOU BEGIN

Figure L4.1 shows the sample letter you created and edited in lessons 1 and 2 with some additions and changes, which you'll make in this chapter. If you've cleared the document window or exited WordPerfect, be sure to get Word-Perfect up and running again. Then use File ➤ Open to retrieve the SMITH.WP document.

SWITCHING TO FULL JUSTIFICATION

When you printed the SMITH.WP document, you may have noticed that it had an uneven right margin, because WordPerfect left-justifies text by default, which means that only the left margin is smooth. Switch to a smooth right margin now, by switching to full justification:

1. Make sure the insertion point is at the top of the document by pressing Ctrl+Home or by moving the insertion point to the upper-left corner of the document and clicking the left mouse button.

2. Choose **L**ayout ➤ **J**ustification ➤ **F**ull, or press Ctrl+F. The text in the document window immediately reformats to full justification, with a smooth right margin, as in Figure L4.2.

August 1, 1992

Mrs. Adrian Smith
123 Oak Ave.
San Diego, CA 92123

Dear Mrs. Smith:

Thank you for your letter regarding our Hawaiian outer-island tour packages. Currently, we offer two travel packages with no overnight stays on Oahu.

- Paradise Vacations' *Outer Islands Getaway*; offering three days each on Maui, Kauai, and Hawaii

- Heavenly Cruises' *Pristine Island Fun Pack*; offering three days each on Maui, Molokai, and Kauai, travelling by boat between islands

The enclosed brochures describe these tour packages in more detail. If you have any questions, or wish to make a reservation, please feel free to call me at (800) 555-1234 during regular business hours.

Best regards,

Olivia Newton

FIGURE L4.1:

The sample letter after making changes presented in this lesson

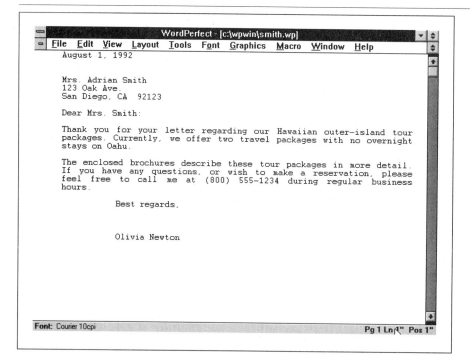

FIGURE L4.2:

The sample letter in the document window, with a smooth right margin

Refer to Chapters 4 and 5

To see what happened "behind the scenes," open Reveal Codes (choose View ➤ Reveal Codes or press Alt+F3). You'll see a [Just:Full] code near the upper-left corner of the document. (If you change your mind later and want to go back to the default left justification, you can just move the highlight to that code and press Delete.)

ADDING A BULLETED ITEM

Now add the first bulleted item to the letter. This time, leave Reveal Codes open, so you can see what's going on behind the scenes as you type.

1. Move the insertion point to the blank line that separates the first paragraph from the second one (so that the insertion point is above the letter *T* in the word *The*).

2. Press ↵ to insert another blank line.

3. Press the Tab key to indent.

4. Choose Font ➤ **W**P Characters, or press Ctrl+W. You'll see the WordPerfect Characters dialog box:

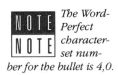

The Word-Perfect character-set number for the bullet is 4,0.

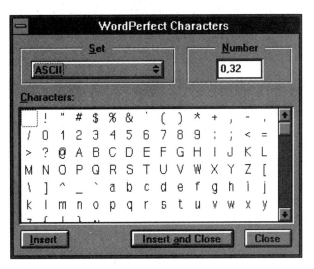

5. Open the pop-up list from the **S**et option, and choose the **T**ypographic Symbols option.

Refer to Chapters 4 and 5

6. Click the left mouse button to highlight the bullet character in the upper-left corner of the **C**haracters display box. The **N**umber text box will display 4,0 when you've highlighted the correct character:

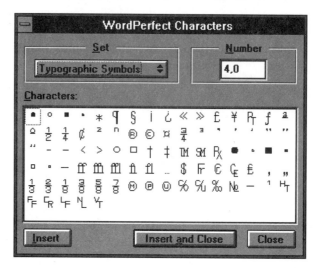

7. Choose Insert and Close, and the bullet will appear in your document.

8. To indent, press Ctrl+Shift+F7 or choose **L**ayout ➤ Pa**r**agraph ➤ **D**ouble Indent.

9. Start the text by typing **Paradise Vacations'** and then press the spacebar to insert a blank space.

10. Activate the italic print attribute by choosing Font ➤ **I**talic (or by pressing Ctrl+I). Notice that [Italc On] and [Italc Off] codes appear in Reveal Codes at the insertion point.

11. Type **Outer Island Getaway** and notice in Reveal Codes how that text stays between the [Italc On] and [Italc Off] codes.

12. Press → to move the insertion point past the closing [Italc Off] code to resume typing regular (unitalicized) text.

13. Type **;** (semicolon), press the spacebar, then type

   offering three days each on Maui, Kauai, and Hawaii

14. Press ↵ twice.

15. Press Tab to indent before typing the next bulleted item.

16. Type another bullet, this time using a shortcut method that is handy when you know the code of the character you want to type: Press Ctrl+W (or choose Font ➤ **W**P Characters), type **4,0** then press ↵.

Refer to Chapters 4 and 5

17. Press Ctrl+Shift+F7 or choose **L**ayout ➤ **P**aragraph ➤ **D**ouble Indent to indent.

18. Type

Heavenly Cruises' Pristine Island Fun Pack; offering three days each on Maui, Molokai, and Kauai, travelling by boat between islands

and then press ↵ to end that paragraph.

You may want to close Reveal Codes (by pressing Alt+F3) to get a better look at your document.

CHOOSING A PRINT ATTRIBUTE AFTER TYPING

In step 18 above, you didn't italicize the name of the travel package. But that's no problem, since you can just select it and choose the print attribute now. Follow these steps:

1. Using your mouse, move the I beam to the letter *P* in the word *Pristine*.

2. Hold down the left mouse button and drag the mouse to highlight "Pristine Island Fun Pack."

3. Release the left mouse button.

4. Activate italics by choosing **F**ont ➤ **I**talic or pressing Ctrl+I.

5. Click the left mouse button to unselect the text.

When you complete step 4, you'll see the text change to italic; notice that it is more slanted than the regular text. If you open Reveal Codes (press Alt+F3), you'll see the [Italc On] and [Italc Off] codes surrounding the text you selected in step 2.

CHANGING THE TAB STOPS

Currently, your document is using WordPerfect's default $1/2$-inch tab stops, and your bulleted items are indented accordingly. To change that amount of indentation, you'll need to change the tab stops. Follow these steps:

1. Move the insertion point above the first bulleted item (anywhere above the first bullet).

2. Choose **V**iew ➤ **R**uler or press Alt+Shift+F3. You'll see the ruler at the top of the window, as in Figure L4.3.

Refer to Chapters 4 and 5

3. Move the I beam over the Left Align tab button on the ruler, then drag the button until the status bar, in the lower-right corner of the window, indicates a Relative left tab of about 1.75". As you drag the button along the ruler, a vertical line extends from the tab icon on the ruler to the text of your document, to help you align your tab correctly (see Figure L4.4).

4. When you are satisfied with the tab-stop location, release the left mouse button. In the document window, the text to the right of each bullet moves in to the new tab stop, tightening the gap between each bullet and its text.

Now your document should look more like the example in Figure L4.1, shown at the start of this lesson. If you open Reveal Codes, you'll see that WordPerfect has inserted a [Tab Set] code, with the position of every tab stop, at the insertion point.

If you aren't happy with the new tab position and want to adjust it, simply drag the triangular tab icon along the ruler until it is positioned properly. To delete a tab stop, just drag the icon below the ruler and release the mouse button.

UNINDENTING THE CLOSING

In Lesson 1 you indented the closing of the letter (*Best regards* and *Olivia Newton*). Suppose you change your mind, and decide to align the closing at the

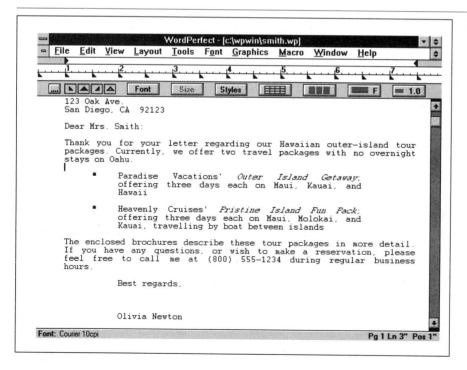

FIGURE L4.3:

The ruler, at the top of the document window

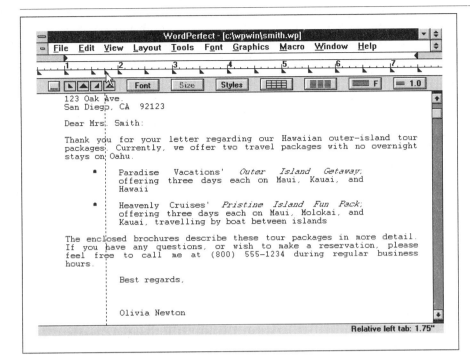

FIGURE L4.4:

A vertical line extends from the tab icon to the text in the document window to help you align the tab stop along the ruler

left margin. No problem—just delete the [Tab] codes that are pushing it out to the second tab stop:

1. If Reveal Codes is closed, open it by choosing **View ➤ Reveal C**odes or by pressing Alt+F3.

2. Press Ctrl+End to move the insertion point to the bottom of the document.

3. Press the ↑ key (or whatever key is required) to move the highlight to one of the [Tab] codes near the bottom of the document.

4. Press Delete twice to delete the two [Tab] codes.

5. Repeat steps 3 and 4 to delete the two [Tab] codes in front of *Best regards.*

Notice that you didn't do anything to the ruler here. You use the ruler just to set tab stops, not to align text. Hidden codes for indenting, such as [Tab], actually align the text at the tab stop.

You can choose Edit ➤ Undo to undo most editing changes right after you make them. But because it's been a while since you entered the tabs, you need to delete the hidden codes.

CHANGING THE FONT

You can use the Assign to Ruler option in the Font dialog box to add your favorite fonts to the Font button on the ruler. Later, you can bypass the lengthy font and point-size lists in the dialog box: Just click the Font or Size button on the ruler, and choose a font or size from the menus that appear.

Now let's take a look at what fonts your printer has to offer, and try one out on the letter. Follow these steps:

1. Press Ctrl+Home to move the insertion point to the top of the document (because you'll want to change the font for all the text in the letter).

2. Double-click the Font button on the ruler or choose Font ➤ Font (or press F9) to open the Font dialog box. If your printer has more than one font available, you'll see a list of fonts, like the one shown in Figure L4.5. You can move the highlight to or click the font you want. (The example in Figure L4.1 uses a Times font.)

3. If your printer has scalable fonts, you'll see a list of point sizes. Type a size in the Point Size text box (10 or 12 is "normal" print size), or click the size you want.

4. Choose OK or press ↵ to choose the font and point size.

The document window immediately reformats to show the text in the font you chose; in Reveal Codes, you can see that WordPerfect inserted a [Font] code, which includes the name and size of the font you chose.

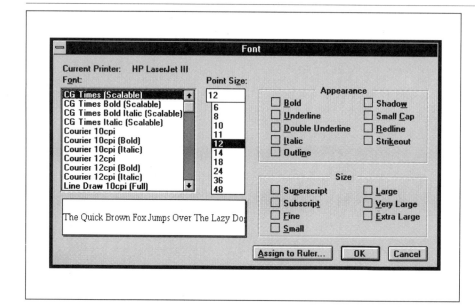

FIGURE L4.5:

The Font dialog box lists all the font names and point sizes available for the printer you have selected.

Refer to Chapters 4 and 5

PRINTING AND SAVING YOUR CHANGES

Now you can print and save your edited document, using the same steps you followed in previous lessons. To print, choose File ➤ Print, then choose OK or press ↵. To save your document and clear the screen, choose File ➤ Close, and choose Yes to reuse the existing file name and replace the old copy of the file. If you want to exit WordPerfect now, choose File ➤ Exit.

Refer to Chapters 4 and 5

Creating a Sample Table

In this lesson you'll create the table shown in Figure L5.1, using techniques presented in Chapter 6. You'll use this table again in Lesson 7, where you create a sample newsletter.

BEFORE YOU BEGIN

If you've exited WordPerfect, be sure to get WordPerfect up and running again, as described in Chapter 1. If you're already in WordPerfect, and there's a document on your screen at the moment, you can save that document and start with a new document window by choosing File ➤ Close. If you want to save that document, choose Yes and enter a file name. Otherwise, just choose No.

DEFINING THE TABLE

To define the number of columns and rows for the table shown in Figure L5.1, follow these steps:

1. If the ruler isn't visible in your current document window, choose **View ➤ Ruler**, or press Alt+Shift+F3. Notice the Tables button on the ruler.

2. Move the mouse pointer to the Tables button, hold down the left mouse button, and drag the mouse pointer until the icon displays a miniature 3x6 grid, then release the mouse button. If you don't have a mouse, choose **Layout ➤ Tables ➤ Create**, specify **3** for columns, press Tab, specify **6** for rows, then press ↵.

WordPerfect displays the empty table, ready for input, as shown in Figure L5.2.

Refer to Chapter 6

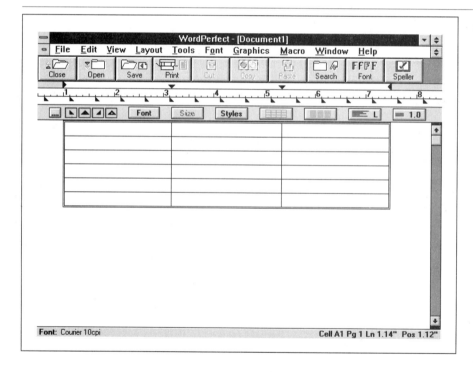

ENTERING THE TABLE TEXT

Now that you've defined the structure of the table, you're ready to type in text.
First, notice how the status bar, in the lower-right corner of the screen, shows the
current cell address as you move from cell to cell. Use that indicator to help position the insertion point properly when following the steps in this lesson.

Refer to Chapter 6

To enter the first column in the table, follow these steps:

1. Make sure the insertion point is in the first cell of the table (cell A1). If it isn't, use your mouse to move the I beam to that cell, then click the left mouse button. Or use the Tab, Shift+Tab, and arrow keys to move the insertion point to that cell.

2. Type **INSURANCE RATES** and press ↓.

3. Type **Model** and press ↓.

4. Type **30 watt** and press ↓.

5. Type **75 watt** and press ↓.

6. Type **100 watt** and press ↓.

7. Type **250 watt**.

Now you're ready to move to the top of the next column and add some more text:

1. Move the insertion point to cell B2 (the blank cell to the right of *Model*), using the mouse or keyboard.

2. Type **Premium** and press ↓.

3. Type **$.50** and press ↓.

4. Type **$.75** and press ↓.

5. Type **$1.49** and press ↓.

6. Type **$1.97**.

Column B is now complete, and you're ready to enter column C:

1. Move the insertion point to cell C2 (the blank cell to the right of *Premium*).

2. Type **Deductible** and press ↓.

3. Type **$25.00** and press ↓.

4. Type **$35.00** and press ↓.

5. Type **$70.00** and press ↓.

6. Type **$100.00**. The table on your screen should now look like Figure L5.3.

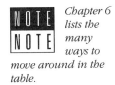

Chapter 6 lists the many ways to move around in the table.

Refer to Chapter 6

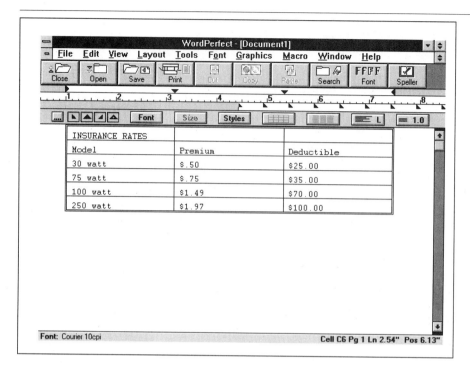

FIGURE L5.3:

The table after adding text

CHANGING THE APPEARANCE OF THE TABLE

If you compare the table you have now with the one shown in Figure L5.1 at the beginning of this lesson, you'll see that the basic structure and all the text are the same, but there are some important differences. In the next few exercises, you'll change the format of your table so that it matches the finished product shown earlier.

JOINING CELLS

If you select the wrong cells and need to start over, click the left mouse button, or press F8.

Your first task is to combine the three cells at the top of the table into a single cell. Follow these steps:

1. Move the insertion point to cell A1, which contains *INSURANCE RATES*.

2. Select the three cells across the top of the table, by dragging the mouse pointer across all three cells or by holding down the Shift key and pressing the End key twice.

3. Choose **L**ayout ➤ **T**ables ➤ **J**oin.

The three cells in the first row are now combined into a single cell, A1, which spans the width of the entire table.

Refer to Chapter 6

CENTERING AND BOLDFACING TEXT IN A CELL

Next, center and boldface the title, "INSURANCE RATES." Follow these steps:

1. Make sure your insertion point is still in cell A1. If it isn't, use the arrow keys to move to A1, or click in cell A1 with your mouse.

2. Choose **L**ayout ➤ **T**ables ➤ **C**ell. The Format Cell dialog box appears.

3. Choose **B**old in the Appearance options area.

4. Move the mouse pointer to the button under **J**ustification, hold down the left mouse button, drag the highlight to the **C**enter option, then release the mouse button. Optionally, press Alt+J, and press the ↑ and ↓ keys until Center appears on the button.

5. Choose OK or press ↵ to save your choices and leave the dialog box.

CHANGING THE LINE STYLES

Next, you'll add double lines at the tops of the cells in row 2 and change the double lines around the outside of the table to single lines. As you will see, WordPerfect offers many line styles, as well as shading, to help you create professional-looking tables. Follow these steps:

1. Using the arrow keys or your mouse, move the insertion point to cell A2, which contains the word *Model*. (The status bar will show "Cell A2.")

2. Select all the cells in the row, either by dragging the mouse pointer across all three columns or by holding down the Shift key and pressing the End key twice.

3. Choose **L**ayout ➤ **T**ables ➤ **L**ines. The Table Lines dialog box appears.

4. Move the mouse pointer to the button next to **T**op, hold down the mouse button, and choose **D**ouble. Or press Alt+T and use the ↑ and ↓ keys to choose **D**ouble.

5. Choose OK or press ↵ to leave the dialog box.

A double line now appears beneath cell A1. Next, you'll change the outside lines to Single:

1. Move the insertion point to cell A1, which contains "INSURANCE RATES."

2. Select all the cells in the table, either by dragging the mouse pointer to cell C6 (which contains *$100.00*) or by holding down the Shift key and pressing ↓ until the entire table is selected.

Refer to Chapter 6

3. Choose **L**ayout ➤ **T**ables ➤ **L**ines. The Table Lines dialog box reappears.

4. Choose **O**utside, then choose **S**ingle.

5. Choose OK or press ↵ to leave the dialog box.

Now the outside table lines are single lines, as shown in Figure L5.4.

JUSTIFYING COLUMNS AND CELLS

Now it's time to align the text and numbers in the columns. Your goal is to center the column headings in cells A2, B2, and C2, and to right-align numbers and text in the columns below the headings. To get started, follow these steps:

1. Move the insertion point to cell A3, which contains *30 watt*.

2. Select the cells in row 3, by dragging the mouse pointer across all three columns or by holding down the Shift key and pressing End twice.

3. Choose **L**ayout ➤ **T**ables ➤ Col**u**mn. The Format Column dialog box appears.

4. Choose **J**ustification, then choose **R**ight.

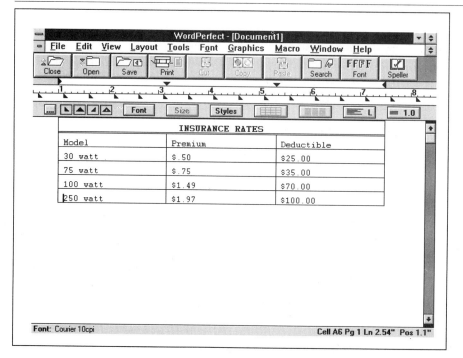

FIGURE L5.4:

The table after changing line styles

Refer to Chapter 6

5. Choose OK or press ↵ to leave the dialog box.

If your table widens after changing its format, try redrawing the screen by pressing Ctrl+F3.

Notice how the text and numbers in all three columns are now right-aligned. Next, center the column headings in cells A2, B2, and C2 by following these steps:

1. Move the insertion point to cell A2, which contains the word *Model*.

2. Select the entire row, by dragging the mouse pointer across all three columns or by holding down the Shift key and pressing End twice.

3. Choose **L**ayout ➤ **T**ables ➤ **C**ell. The Format Cell dialog box appears.

4. Choose **J**ustification, then choose **C**enter.

5. Choose OK or press ↵ to leave the dialog box.

The column headings are now centered. Notice that the new center alignment for this row overrides the right alignment you just chose for these columns in this row only. That's because options chosen from the Format Cell dialog box always override options chosen from the Format Column dialog box for the currently selected cells. Figure L5.5 shows how the table should now look on your screen.

ADDING SHADING TO THE TABLE

You can emphasize the low cost of insurance premiums in the table by shading cells B2 through B6. Follow these steps:

1. Move the insertion point to cell B2, which contains the word *Premium*.

2. Select the cells from cell B2 to B6 (which contains *$1.97*), by dragging the mouse pointer down to cell B6 or by holding down the Shift key and pressing ↓ four times.

Shortcuts for many table operations are available on the Tables Button Bar (choose View ➤ Button Bar Setup ➤ Select ➤ tables.wwb).

3. Choose **L**ayout ➤ **T**ables ➤ **C**ell. The Format Cell dialog box appears.

4. In the Cell Attributes area, choose **Sh**ading.

5. Choose OK or press ↵ to leave the dialog box.

The shading in column B will probably look like dots more than actual shading (it will look more like shading when you print the table).

Refer to Chapter 6

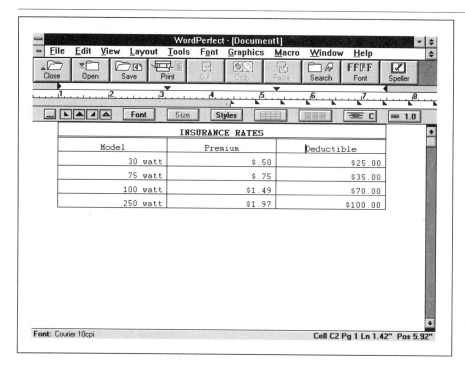

ADJUSTING COLUMN WIDTHS

Now the only remaining task is to narrow the columns so that the table looks better. Follow these steps:

1. Position the insertion point in cell A2 (which contains *Model*).

2. Choose **L**ayout ➤ **T**ables ➤ Col**u**mn.

3. Move the insertion point to the text box under **C**olumn Width by clicking in it with your mouse or pressing Alt+O.

4. Use the Delete or Backspace key to delete the current setting, and type **1.3** as the new column width.

5. Choose OK or press ↵.

6. Move the insertion point to cell B2 (which contains *Premium*).

7. Repeat steps 2–5, but change the width of this column to 1.2" in step 4.

8. Move the insertion point to cell C2 (which contains *Deductible*).

9. Repeat steps 2–5, but change the width of this column to 1.4" in step 4.

Your screen should now look like Figure L5.6.

Refer to Chapter 6

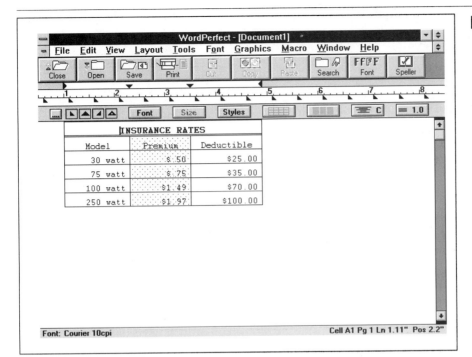

PRINTING THE TABLE

You can print your completed table as you would any other WordPerfect document. Just follow these steps:

1. Choose **File ➤ Print** (or press F5).

2. Choose **Print**.

A copy of the table is printed, and you're returned to the document window.

SAVING YOUR WORK

You'll use this table in Lesson 7 to create a sample newsletter, so you'll need to save a copy of it now. Follow these steps:

1. Choose **File ➤ Close** (or press Ctrl+F4).

2. When asked about saving the document, choose **Yes**.

3. Type **lesson5.wp** and press ↵.

Refer to Chapter 6

4. If you're asked whether you want to replace an existing copy of LESSON5.WP, choose **Yes**.

A copy of the table is saved to disk and cleared from the document window.

If you prefer to forge ahead with the hands-on lessons, continue with Lesson 6, which shows you how to create the styles you'll be using for the newsletter in Lesson 7.

Creating Some Sample Styles

In this lesson, you'll create and apply the three sample styles shown in Figure L6.1 for headlines, author bylines, and body text, and use them to help create the sample newsletter in the next lesson.

BEFORE YOU BEGIN

If you've exited WordPerfect, be sure to get WordPerfect up and running again, as described in Chapter 1. If there are one or more documents on your screen, you can save them and clear the screen by choosing File ➤ Close.

DELETING EXISTING STYLES

WordPerfect comes with some sample styles in a style library named LIBRARY.STY; these are the default styles that are normally loaded when you first start WordPerfect. You won't be using any of these styles in this document, however, so you can just delete them. Follow these steps to get started:

1. Choose **L**ayout ➤ **S**tyles or press Alt+F8. You'll see some existing styles, most likely the ones that came with your WordPerfect package, as shown in Figure L6.2.

2. Select the first style name, and choose **D**elete. You'll see the Delete Style dialog box:

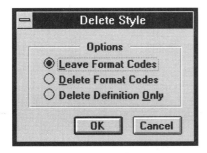

A Perennial Favorite ◄——— headline style

by Jo Brightman ◄——— byline style

Your life or your bulb's? That's what we asked ourselves when we designed the new Perennial Lightbulb. We know how important your life is, so we designed a bulb that never dies. Buy the Perennial and you'll never have to replace another lightbulb. A surefire winner at only $300 apiece, only from BulbCo -- the brightest idea in lights. ✿] body-text style

Insure it with ease

by G Ubetter

Now that we've got your attention, we'd like to tell you that Perennial Lightbulbs are guaranteed for a lifetime -- yours or theirs. As long as the bulbs remain intact. You drop one of our Perennials on the linoleum and your three hundred dollars aren't worth a filament. That's why we're offering insurance. Yep! We'll insure every one of these babies for a small premium, as shown in the accompanying table. ✿

Festival of Lights

by Les Pardee

Don't miss our Festival of Lights, for a firsthand look at all of our great products, including the new Perennial. There will be free refreshments at our offices, and the first 20 guests will get two years of Perennial insurance -- absolutely free! See you July 15. ✿

FIGURE L6.1:

The sample styles presented in this lesson

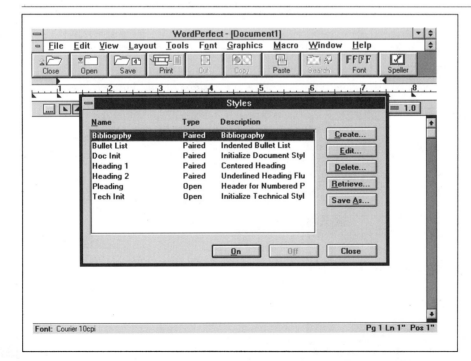

FIGURE L6.2:

The sample styles that come with WordPerfect

Refer to Chapter 14

Deleting the sample Word-Perfect styles in this lesson deletes them only from the current document; you'll still be able to use those styles in other documents.

For now, don't worry about the option buttons, just confirm the deletion by choosing OK or pressing ↵.

3. Repeat step 2 once for every style in your default library until none of the existing styles remains.

Now you can start creating a new set of styles.

CREATING THE HEADLINE STYLE

Now you're going to create a paired headline style that sets the font for article headlines. Follow these steps:

1. Choose **C**reate from the Styles dialog box, and you'll see the Style Properties dialog box:

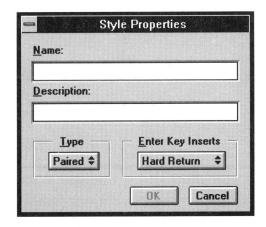

2. Type **Headline** in the **N**ame text box, and press Tab.

3. Type **Style for headlines** in the **D**escription text box.

4. Choose OK or press ↵. You're taken to the Style Editor screen.

5. Choose Font ➤ Font (or press F9). You'll see the Font dialog box.

6. Scroll through the list of fonts and highlight the font you want. Univers Bold (Scalable) 18pt is used in the example, but you must highlight a font from the options shown on your own screen.

Helvetica, Swiss, and Sans Serif are similar to the Univers font.

7. If you chose a scalable font in step 6, choose a point size by clicking on the size or by typing the size in the Point Si**z**e text box (18 points is used in the example).

Refer to Chapter 14

8. Choose OK or press ↵ to leave the Font dialog box.

9. Press → to move the insertion point past the [Comment] code.

10. Press ↵ to add the hard return [HRt] to be inserted when you turn off the style.

You can see the [Font:] code for your choice in the lower portion of the screen, as shown in Figure L6.3, although your font may be different. The [HRt] code is to the right of the [Comment] code and will ensure that any text after the headline starts on a new line.

Now follow these steps:

1. Choose **P**roperties to return to the Style Properties dialog box.

2. Choose **E**nter Key Inserts, and choose Style **O**ff.

3. Choose OK or press ↵ to return to the Style Editor screen.

4. Choose **C**lose to return to the Styles dialog box.

Choosing Style **O**ff in step 2 will cause pressing ↵ to automatically turn off the style when you apply the style later. Before you try out the style, however, create the next one.

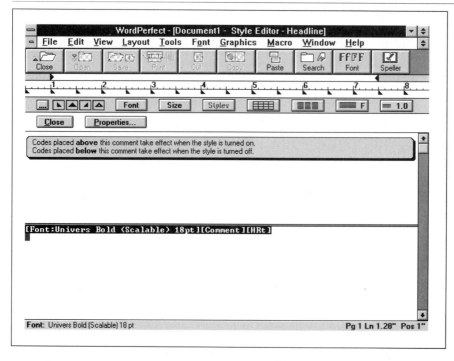

FIGURE L6.3:

The completed headline style on the Style Editor screen

Refer to Chapter 14

CREATING THE BYLINE STYLE

Now create the author byline style, which is almost identical to the headline style created above, except that it uses a different font. Follow these steps:

1. Choose **C**reate from the Styles dialog box to get back to the Style Properties dialog box.

2. Type **Byline** in the **N**ame text box, and press Tab.

3. Type **Style for author bylines** in the **D**escription text box.

4. Choose **E**nter Key Inserts, and choose Style O**ff**.

5. Choose OK or press ↵. You're taken to the Style Editor screen.

6. Choose Font ➤ **Fo**nt (or press F9). You'll see the Font dialog box.

7. Scroll through the list of fonts and highlight Univers Italic 12pt or some similar font from the list of available fonts.

8. If you chose a scalable font in the preceding step, choose **12** points as the point size by clicking on the size or typing the size in the Point Size text box.

9. Choose OK or press ↵ to leave the Font dialog box.

10. Press → to move the insertion point past the [Comment] code.

11. Press ↵ to add the hard return [HRt] to be inserted when you turn off the style.

12. Choose **C**lose to return to the Styles dialog box.

Now you have two styles in your current document, named *Byline* and *Heading*. Next, you'll create the body-text style.

CREATING THE BODY-TEXT STYLE

Now you'll create the style for defining the body text within each article, including the small special character that ends each article. To get started, follow these steps:

1. Choose **C**reate from the Styles dialog box to get to the Style Properties dialog box.

2. Type **Body Text** in the **N**ame text box, and press Tab.

3. Type **Style for body text** in the **D**escription text box.

4. Choose OK or press ↵. You're taken to the Style Editor screen.

5. Choose Font ➤ **Fo**nt (or press F9). You'll see the Font dialog box.

Refer to Chapter 14

Dutch Roman and Times Roman are similar to the CG Times font.

Special characters are covered in Chapter 5.

6. Scroll through the list of fonts, and highlight Times 12pt or some similar font from the list of available fonts.

7. If you chose a scalable font in the preceding step, choose **12** points as the size by clicking on the size or typing the size in the Point Size text box.

8. Choose OK or press ↵ to return to the Style Editor screen.

Now you've defined the codes to use when the style is turned on. The next step is to define the [Style Off] codes, which include a right-aligned special character and a hard return [HRt]. Follow these steps:

1. Press → to move past the [Comment] code.

2. Choose **Layout** ➤ **Line** ➤ **Flush Right** (or press Alt+F7).

3. Press Ctrl+W to display the WordPerfect Characters dialog box.

4. Use the special compass character in the Iconic Symbols set, which you can get to quickly by typing **5,6**.

5. Choose Insert **a**nd Close to leave the dialog box.

6. Press ↵ to insert a hard-return code [HRt]. Your completed style should now resemble Figure L6.4, although your font choice may be different.

7. Choose **C**lose to return to the Styles dialog box, where you can see that you now have three styles.

TRYING OUT THE HEADLINE STYLE

If you're ready to try out the headline style now, follow these steps:

1. Choose Close to return to the document window.

2. If Reveal Codes isn't open, choose **V**iew ➤ Reveal **C**odes (Alt+F3) to turn it on. This way you'll be able to see what's happening behind the scenes.

3. Choose **Layout** ➤ **S**tyles (or press Alt+F8).

4. Click on or move the highlight to Headline.

5. Choose **O**n or press ↵.

6. Type **A Perennial Favorite** and press ↵.

Your screen will now look like Figure L6.5. Notice the [Style On:Headline] and [Style Off:Headline] codes with the text between them, and see how pressing ↵ in step 6 automatically turned off the headline style, moving the insertion point past the [Style Off:Headline] code.

Refer to Chapter 14

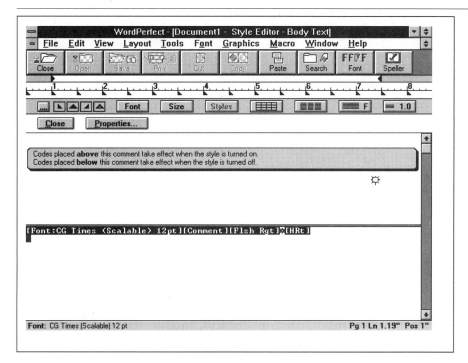

FIGURE L6.4:

The completed body-text style codes

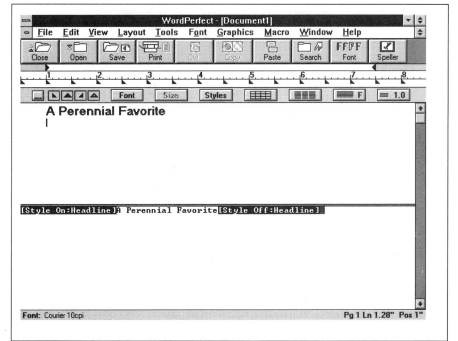

FIGURE L6.5:

The document and Reveal Codes after applying the headline style

Refer to Chapter 14

TRYING OUT THE BYLINE STYLE ON EXISTING TEXT

Applying a style to existing text is a lot like applying boldface or other formatting. You select the text, then apply the style.

Now try the byline style. This time, just for practice, you'll type the text first, then apply the style to it. You'll use the Styles button on the ruler rather than the menus. Follow these steps:

1. If you haven't already done so, display the ruler (choose **View** ➤ **R**uler or press Alt+Shift+F3).

2. Type

   by Jo Brightman

3. Press Home or use your mouse to move the insertion point to the *b* in *by*.

4. Select the entire byline, either by pressing Shift+End or by dragging the mouse pointer.

5. Click the Styles ruler button, and choose Byline.

6. Press ↵ to turn off the style at the end of the byline.

Notice how applying this style to existing text inserted the appropriate [Style On:Byline] and [Style Off:Byline] codes.

TRYING OUT THE BODY-TEXT STYLE

Test the body-text style now by following these steps:

1. Press Ctrl+End to make sure you're at the bottom of the document.

2. Click the Styles ruler button, and choose Body Text.

3. Type the following text without pressing ↵:

   Your life or your bulb's? That's what we asked ourselves when we designed the new Perennial Lightbulb. We know how important your life is, so we designed a bulb that never dies. Buy the Perennial and you'll never have to replace another lightbulb. A surefire winner at only $300 apiece, only from BulbCo -- the brightest idea in lights.

4. Press → to move past the [Style Off] code and turn off the style. Your screen will now look like Figure L6.6 (though your text may wrap differently, depending on the font you're using).

COMPLETING THE TEXT

Go ahead and type the two additional articles now, as shown in Figure L6.1 at the beginning of this lesson, using your styles to format the headings, bylines, and body text.

Refer to Chapter 14

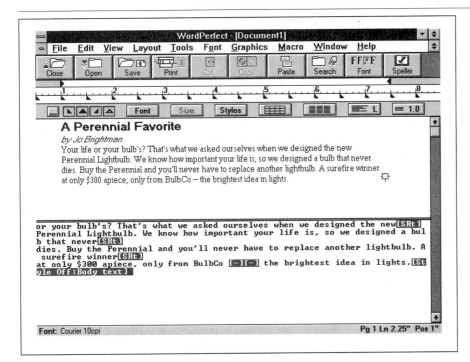

FIGURE L6.6:

*The document window
after applying the
body-text style to
some text*

When typing the text of each article, don't bother trying to break each line exactly as in the figure. Instead, let WordPerfect wrap the text in each paragraph. Press ↵ an extra time to insert a blank line above each article headline.

PRINTING AND SAVING YOUR WORK

If you wish, you can print a copy of your document now, and then save it. Follow the same steps presented in previous lessons:

1. If you want to print the document now, choose **File ➤ P**rint to display the Print dialog box, and press ↵ to start printing.

2. To save the document, choose **File ➤ S**ave.

3. Type **lesson6.wp** as the name of the file, then choose **S**ave or press ↵.

4. If you want to leave WordPerfect now, choose **File ➤ Ex**it or double-click on the Control-menu box. If you want to go straight to Lesson 7 and continue developing the newsletter, leave the current document on the screen.

Refer to Chapter 14

Now that you've created a few styles, you can go back and read Chapter 14 to learn more, or you can continue with the hands-on lessons. In the next lesson, you'll create a newsletter that uses the table from Lesson 5 and the text and styles you created in this lesson. You'll also learn about graphics, lines, and columns.

Refer to Chapter 14

Creating a Newsletter

In this lesson you'll use the table created in Lesson 5, the articles and styles created in Lesson 6, and the graphics and multi-column layout techniques presented in chapters 19 and 20 to create the one-page newsletter shown in Figure L7.1.

Newsletters are one of the most popular desktop publishing applications for WordPerfect, because they bring together three of the program's most dazzling features: styles, graphics, and multicolumn layouts. Once you've mastered the techniques shown here, you'll be able to adapt them to your own publications, including newsletters, fliers, memos, invitations, and any other documents requiring extra sparkle and pizazz.

BEFORE YOU BEGIN

If you've exited WordPerfect, be sure to get WordPerfect up and running again. Then use File ➤ Open to open the document you created in Lesson 6, LESSON6.WP. You should see the three short articles you created.

CREATING THE NAMEPLATE

We'll take it from the top by creating the nameplate, which consists of the shaded-text graphic with the name of the newsletter, the drop-shadowed blue ribbon, and the issue information followed by a horizontal line.

FIGURE L7.1:

The sample newsletter you'll create in this lesson

BulbCo
BLURBS

Volume 1, Number 1   June 1992

A Perennial Favorite

by Jo Brightman

Your life or your bulb's? That's what we asked ourselves when we designed the new Perennial Lightbulb. We know how important your life is, so we designed a bulb that never dies. Buy the Perennial and you'll never have to replace another lightbulb. A surefire winner at only $300 apiece, only from BulbCo -- the brightest idea in lights.

Insure it with ease

by G Ubetter

Now that we've got your attention, we'd like to tell you that Perennial Lightbulbs are guaranteed for a lifetime -- yours or theirs. As long as the bulbs remain intact. You drop one of our Perennials on the linoleum and your three hundred dollars aren't worth a filament. That's why we're offering insurance. Yep! We'll insure every one of these babies for a small premium, as shown in the accompanying table.

Festival of Lights

by Les Pardee

Don't miss our Festival of Lights, for a firsthand look at all of our great products, including the new Perennial. There will be free refreshments at our offices, and the first 20 guests will get two years of Perennial insurance -- absolutely free! See you July 15.

INSURANCE RATES		
Model	Premium	Deductible
30 watt	$.50	$25.00
75 watt	$.75	$35.00
100 watt	$1.49	$70.00
250 watt	$1.97	$100.00

Refer to Chapters 19 and 20

CREATING THE TEXT BOX

To create the shaded Text box, follow these steps:

1. Choose **View** ➤ Reveal **C**odes (or press Alt+F3) to turn on Reveal Codes. This will help you to keep track of the insertion point in relation to codes for existing styles.

2. Insert a blank line at the top of the document to get some room to work in above the existing [Style On:Headline] code. To do so, press Ctrl+Home twice, then ↵, then ←. The insertion point should be above the first article headline (on the [HRt] code in Reveal Codes).

3. Choose **G**raphics ➤ Text **B**ox ➤ **C**reate (or press Alt+F11). You'll see the Text Box Editor dialog box.

4. Choose the Box **P**osition button to open the Box Position and Size dialog box.

5. Open the **H**orizontal Position pop-up list and choose Margin, **F**ull to have the box fill the space between the left and right margins.

6. Open the **S**ize pop-up list and choose Auto **W**idth to set a height for the graphic box and let WordPerfect calculate the width automatically.

7. Choose H**e**ight, delete the existing measurement by pressing Delete, and type **2.25** (for inches) in the text box.

8. Choose OK or press ↵ to return to the Text Box Editor.

Now you're ready to type in the newsletter name. Follow these steps:

1. Press ↵ to insert a blank line.

2. Choose F**o**nt ➤ **F**ont (or press F9).

3. Move the highlight to the font you want, either by using the ↑ and ↓ keys or by clicking once with your mouse (the CG Times Bold Italic (Scalable) font was used in the example).

4. If you're using a scalable font, choose Point Si**z**e and type the point size you want (48 points was used in the example).

5. Choose OK or press ↵ to return to the Text Box Editor.

6. Choose **L**ayout ➤ Line ➤ **F**lush Right (or press Alt+F7) to align the text flush-right.

7. Type **BulbCo** and press ↵.

By default, Text boxes are anchored to the current page. Page-anchored graphics are placed at a particular spot on a page. Paragraph-anchored graphics float with the paragraph to which they're anchored. Character-anchored graphics float with the character to which they're anchored.

Standard fonts on a Hewlett-Packard LaserJet III printer were used for this newsletter. You may have to substitute other fonts from your own printer.

Refer to Chapters 19 and 20

The next line of the nameplate should be much larger, so again you'll choose a font and type the text:

1. Choose Font ➤ Font (or press F9).

2. Highlight the font you want; CG Times Bold Italic (Scalable) was used in the example.

3. If you're using a scalable font, choose Point Size and type in the point size (64 points was used in the example).

4. Choose OK or press ↵ to return to the Text Box Editor.

5. Choose Layout ➤ Line ➤ Flush Right (or press Alt+F7) to align the text flush-right.

6. Type **B L U R B S** and press ↵. Don't forget to include a blank space in between each letter, by pressing the spacebar, and to type the word in capital letters.

7. Choose Close to return to the document window.

The document window now displays the graphics box, as shown in Figure L7.2 (with Reveal Codes reduced in size slightly so that you can see the entire Text box).

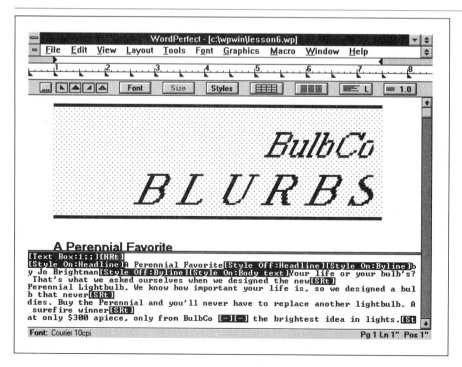

FIGURE L7.2:

The document window after creating the Text box for the nameplate

Refer to Chapters 19 and 20

DEFINING THE FIGURE BORDERS

To create a drop shadow, just use a thick or extra-thick line at the left and bottom edges or at the right and top edges of the graphic border.

Next, you'll create the blue-ribbon graphic in a Figure box. An ordinary Figure box has a border style with single lines at the left, right, top, and bottom. But adding a drop shadow will put a little more sizzle into your blue ribbon. To do this, you'll define some Figure options. Follow these steps:

1. Choose **G**raphics ➤ **F**igure ➤ **O**ptions. You'll see the Figure Options dialog box.

2. Open the **L**eft pop-up list (under Border Styles), and choose **T**hick for the left border.

3. Open the **B**ottom pop-up list, and choose **T**hick for the bottom border.

4. Choose OK or press ↵ to return to the document window.

In Reveal Codes you'll see a [Fig Opt] code, and any Figure boxes that you create to the right of that code will use the border style you've just defined.

CREATING THE FIGURE BOX

Now you're ready to define the blue-ribbon Figure box. Follow these steps:

1. The insertion point should be on the [HRt] code that follows the [Fig Opt] code. (If you moved the insertion point, be sure to put it on that code.)

2. Choose **G**raphics ➤ **F**igure ➤ **C**reate to display the Figure Editor.

3. Choose **F**ile ➤ **R**etrieve to choose a graphic from the disk.

4. Type **blueribn.wpg** and press ↵ (or double-click on *blueribn.wpg*) to retrieve that graphic (this step assumes you installed WordPerfect graphics files).

As discussed in Chapter 19, you can size and position a graphic in the document window with your mouse. But here you'll use menu options in the Figure Editor so that you can enter exact measurements.

5. Choose **F**ile ➤ Box **P**osition to open the Box Position and Size dialog box.

6. Open the **A**nchor To pop-up list, and choose **P**aragraph. The graphic is automatically placed at the left margin.

7. Open the **S**ize pop-up list and choose **S**et Both.

8. Choose **W**idth, press Delete to delete the existing entry, and type **.75** to set the width to 0.75 inches.

Refer to Chapters 19 and 20

9. Choose **H**eight, delete the existing entry, and type **.563** to set the height to 0.563 inches.

10. Choose OK or press ↵ to return to the Figure Editor.

11. Choose **F**ile ➤ **C**lose to return to the document window.

Figure L7.3 shows how the document window should look now. The Text box you created earlier may be scrolled up out of view.

ADDING NAMEPLATE TEXT

Helvetica and Swiss fonts are similar to Univers.

You've just about completed the nameplate—all that's left to do is to include the information about the newsletter issue and to draw the horizontal dividing line below it. Follow these steps:

1. Choose **F**ont ➤ **F**ont (or press F9).

2. Highlight the font you want (a Univers 12-point font was used in the example).

3. If you are using a scalable font, choose Point Si**z**e and choose or type the point size you want (12 points is used in this example).

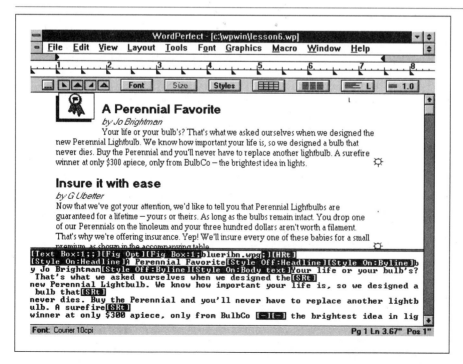

FIGURE L7.3:

The document and Reveal Codes portions of the screen, with the blue-ribbon Figure box in place

Refer to Chapters 19 and 20

4. Choose OK or press ⏎.

5. Press ⏎ to add a blank line above the text.

6. Type

   Volume 1, Number 1

7. Choose **L**ayout ➤ **L**ine ➤ **F**lush Right (or press Alt+F7).

8. Type **June 1992** and press ⏎.

ADDING THE HORIZONTAL LINE

The next task is to define the horizontal line:

1. Choose **G**raphics ➤ **L**ine ➤ **H**orizontal (or press Ctrl+F11). For this line, you can just use the default settings.

2. Choose OK or press ⏎ to return to the document window.

3. Press ⏎ twice to allow some space beneath the horizontal line.

The nameplate is now complete. Although you can see the nameplate in a true-to-life form in the document window, you might want to switch to the Print Preview screen, where you can look at it at various sizes. Follow these steps:

1. Choose **F**ile ➤ Print Pre**v**iew from the menus, or press Shift+F5.

2. Choose **V**iew ➤ 100%, or click the 100% button. Move the scroll box upward until the nameplate appears at the top of the screen, as shown in Figure L7.4.

3. If you want to experiment with other viewing sizes, choose size options from the **V**iew menu, page options from the **P**ages menu, or use the buttons.

4. Choose **F**ile ➤ **C**lose or click the Close button when you're finished viewing the newsletter.

If the buttons aren't visible, choose View ➤ Button Bar. Try experimenting with the 100%, 200%, Full Page, and Zoom buttons.

DEFINING THE NEWSPAPER-STYLE COLUMNS

The newsletter consists of three newspaper-style columns, with vertical lines, a table, and, of course, the text of the articles. To create multiple columns, you must define and activate the columns. Follow these steps:

1. Position the insertion point before the headline of the first article in the newsletter, with the [Style On:Headline] code highlighted in Reveal Codes.

Refer to Chapters 19 and 20

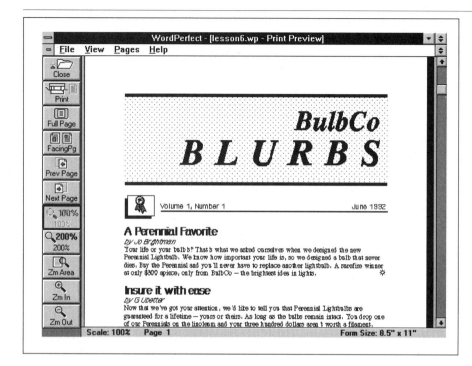

FIGURE L7.4:

The completed nameplate on the Print Preview screen

2. If you haven't done so already, open the ruler by choosing **View ➤ R**uler or pressing Alt+Shift+F3.

3. Move the I beam to the Columns button on the ruler, and pull down the Column menu by holding down the left mouse button.

4. Choose 3 Columns from the menu to define and activate three evenly-spaced newspaper-style columns.

NOTE
NOTE
You can easily change the column margins later by using the Define Columns dialog box or the column-margin icons on the ruler. For now, however, the default settings are fine.

The Columns button on the ruler provides a quick, convenient way to define up to five evenly-spaced newspaper columns. When you choose a three-column format, as in step 4, the text reformats into three evenly-spaced columns in your document window. WordPerfect predefines the left and right margins for each column, with an initial distance between columns of 1/2 inch. For example, column 1 ends at 2.83" and column 2 begins at 3.33", 1/2 inch to the right.

Refer to Chapters 19 and 20

With the highlight still on the first [Style On:Headline] code in the document, you may want to jot down the the current Ln measurement shown on the status bar (about 4.46 inches, depending on your fonts) for use in the following steps.

ADDING THE VERTICAL LINES

Defining vertical lines is similar to defining horizontal lines. Follow these steps:

Place the insertion point exactly where you want the vertical line to begin, then choose Specify from the Vertical Position pop-up list. This way, you won't have to type a measurement for the starting position of the line, because WordPerfect automatically begins the line at the insertion point.

1. Choose **G**raphics ➤ **L**ine ➤ **V**ertical (or press Ctrl+Shift+F11).

2. Open the **H**orizontal Position pop-up list, and choose **B**etween Columns. Leave the **R**ight of Column option set at 1 to place the line to the right of column 1.

3. Open the **V**ertical Position pop-up list, and choose **S**pecify.

4. The **P**osition text box should indicate 4.46 inches (or whatever number you jotted down earlier), which is exactly what you want; if it doesn't, type this measurement into the box. This will set the top of the vertical line even with the first line of text in the first column and calculate the length of your line automatically.

5. Choose OK or press ↵ to return to the document window.

The line appears in the document window, placed just to the right of the first column. Next, use the same basic steps you just used to create the second vertical line, but with a different horizontal position:

1. Choose **G**raphics ➤ **L**ine ➤ **V**ertical (or press Ctrl+Shift+F11).

2. Open the **H**orizontal Position pop-up list, and choose **B**etween Columns.

3. Choose **R**ight of Column, and type **2** to place the line to the right of column 2.

4. Open the **V**ertical Position pop-up list, and choose **S**pecify.

5. The **P**osition text box should again indicate 4.46 inches (or whatever number you jotted down earlier), setting the vertical line even with the first line of text in the second column.

6. Choose OK or press ↵ to return to the document window.

Refer to Chapters 19 and 20

Now you can use the scroll bar to view the page in the document window, or you can switch to the Print Preview screen to check your progress. If you switch to Print Preview, don't forget to choose File ➤ Close or click the Close button to return to the document window.

DEFINING THE TABLE BOX

The last graphic you need to create is the Table box, which appears at the bottom of the page between columns 2 and 3. By default, WordPerfect places a thick horizontal line above and below a Table box. Follow these steps:

1. Make sure the insertion point is just to the right of the second [VLine] code, right on the first [Style On:Headline] code for the first article in Reveal Codes.

2. Choose **G**raphics ➤ **T**able Box ➤ **C**reate.

3. Choose OK or press ↵ to open the Text Box Editor.

4. Choose **F**ile ➤ **R**etrieve.

5. Type **lesson5.wp** and press ↵ to choose the table you created in Lesson 5.

6. Choose **Y**es when asked whether you want to insert the file in the current document.

7. Choose Box **P**osition to open the Box Position and Size dialog box. By default, the graphics box is anchored to the current page.

8. Open the **V**ertical Position pop-up list, and choose **B**ottom to place the graphic at the bottom of the page.

9. Open the **H**orizontal Position pop-up list, and choose Column, **F**ull to have the graphic fill the space between the left and right margins of the columns you chose in the next step.

10. Choose **C**olumns and type **2-3** to place the graphic across columns 2 and 3.

11. Choose OK or press ↵ to return to the Text Box Editor.

12. Choose **C**lose to return to the document window.

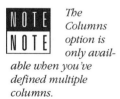
The Columns option is only available when you've defined multiple columns.

Refer to Chapters 19 and 20

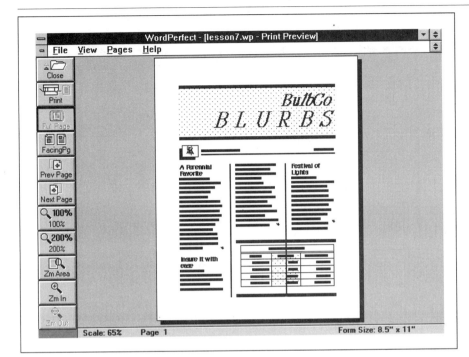

FIGURE L7.5:

A full-page view of the Print Preview screen after defining the Table box

Once again you may want to check your progress by using the scroll bar in the document window or the Full Page button on the Print Preview screen. Your Print Preview screen should look like Figure L7.5 (the small text is represented as horizontal bars at this magnification on most monitors). If you use Print Preview, don't forget to choose File ➤ Close or click the Close button when you're ready to return to the document window.

EDITING THE GRAPHIC LINE

You can also shorten (or lengthen) lines visually, by using your mouse.

Whoops! Do you see a problem? The vertical line between column 2 and column 3 is too long and cuts right through the table near the lower-right corner of the document. At this point, you could print the page and measure how long the line should be. (For the example, I determined that the line should be about three inches long.) Here's how to edit that line:

1. In the document window, scroll down to where you can see the vertical line between columns 2 and 3.

2. Move the I beam to the vertical line in the second column. The I beam will change to the arrow when you have positioned it properly.

Refer to Chapters 19 and 20

3. Double-click the left mouse button. You'll see the Edit Vertical Line dialog box:

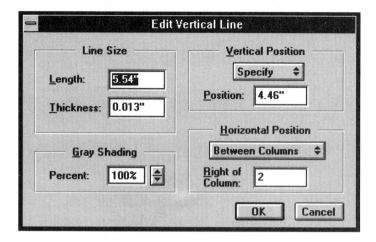

4. Choose **Length**, and type **3.0** (or whatever measurement seems right for you).

5. Choose OK or press ↵ to return to the document window.

Once again you can scroll through the document to make sure that the line no longer intersects the table, or choose File ➤ Print Preview (Shift+F5) to take a look at the revised line. If you use Print Preview, remember to choose File ➤ Close or click the Close button to return to the document window.

CHANGING THE BODY-TEXT STYLE

Suppose now that you decide you want to end each article with a small graphic rather than the compass character you defined earlier. This will be easy because you created a style to format all the articles, so you just need to change the style. Follow these steps:

1. Choose **Layout** ➤ **S**tyles (or press Alt+F8).

2. Highlight the body-text style.

3. Choose **E**dit in the Styles dialog box to open the Style Editor.

4. Press the → key three times to move the insertion point to the compass character, as shown in Figure L7.6.

Refer to Chapters 19 and 20

5. Press Delete to delete that character.

6. Choose **G**raphics ➤ User Box ➤ **C**reate to create a User box (which, by default, has no borders).

7. Choose the **F**igure Editor, and choose OK or press ↵.

8. Choose File ➤ **R**etrieve, type **fatpencl.wpg**, and press ↵.

9. Choose File ➤ **B**ox Position to open the Box Position and Size dialog box.

10. Open the **A**nchor To pop-up list and choose **C**haracter, because you want this graphic to "stick to" its neighboring character.

11. Open the **S**ize pop-up list and choose Auto **W**idth.

12. Choose H**e**ight and type **.125** to make the graphic very small.

13. Choose OK or press ↵ to return to the Figure Editor.

14. To print the graphic a little more clearly at this size, choose **E**dit ➤ **O**utline (or choose Outline in the Button Bar).

15. To align the graphic a little better on the printed line, press Insert until the percentage indicator in the status bar (near the lower-right corner of the screen) reaches 1%. Then press ↓ four times to move down the graphic within its box.

16. Choose File ➤ **C**lose to return to the Style Editor. The graphic appears where the compass used to be; in Reveal Codes, it appears as the code [Usr Box:1;fatpencl.wpg].

17. Choose **C**lose twice to return to the document window.

MOVING TEXT TO A NEW COLUMN

Your printed document may not look exactly like Figure L7.1, because your printer may not have the same fonts. You may find that the words *Festival of* are at the end of column 2 rather than at the top of column 3. You can force text to a new column by moving the insertion point to the start of the text that you want to bump over to the next column and by pressing Ctrl+↵ to insert a hard page break ([HPg]).

If you need to bump the article heading over to column 3, follow these steps:

1. Choose **E**dit ➤ **S**earch, or press F2, type **Fest**, then choose **S**earch (or press ↵). This moves the insertion point to the article heading.

2. Press ← until the highlight is on the [Style On:Headline] code for the article headline.

Refer to Chapters 19 and 20

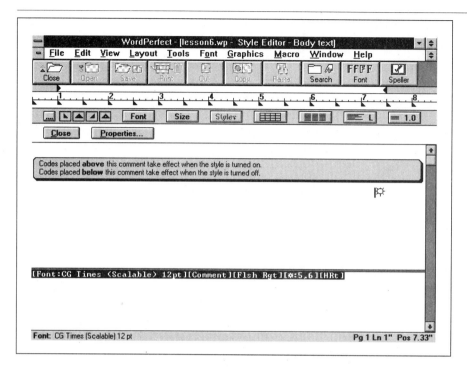

The insertion point is to the left of the compass character, highlighting [:5,6] in the Reveal Codes portion of the screen.*

3. Press Ctrl+↵. This inserts a hard page break, which forces text to the next column.

Again, you can use Print Preview to check your work, or just scroll through the document. It should now look something like Figure L7.1, shown at the start of this lesson.

PRINTING AND SAVING YOUR DOCUMENT

Now you're ready to print and save your document. Follow these steps:

1. Choose **F**ile ➤ **P**rint (or press F5).

2. For the highest-quality graphic output, open the **G**raphics Quality pop-up list and choose **H**igh.

3. Choose OK or press ↵ to print the full document. Be patient—it takes a while for most printers to print high-quality graphics.

4. When the printing is finished, choose **F**ile ➤ Save **A**s.

5. Type **lesson7.wp** and press ↵.

Refer to Chapters 19 and 20

6. If you want to call it a day and leave WordPerfect, choose **File ➤ Ex**it or press Alt+F4. If you prefer to stay in WordPerfect, clear the screen by choosing **F**ile ➤ **C**lose (or pressing Ctrl+F4).

Congratulations! You've just created a sophisticated WordPerfect document with columns, lines, and graphics. To learn more about the features used here, see chapters 19 and 20. Or, if you prefer, dive into the next hands-on lesson to learn how to create macros.

Refer to Chapters 19 and 20

Creating Some Handy Macros

Macros are terrific time-savers because they let you capture keystrokes—much as tape or video recorders capture sound and images—then play them back with push-button ease. In this lesson, you'll create several very handy macros that you can use right away to make working with WordPerfect faster and easier.

BEFORE YOU BEGIN

If you've exited WordPerfect, be sure to get WordPerfect up and running again. If your screen isn't clear at the moment, clear it by choosing File ➤ Close (or pressing Ctrl+F4), then choose Yes or No when asked about saving changes, depending on whether or not you want to save the current document. Optionally, just choose File ➤ New to open a new document window.

SIG: A MACRO TO CLOSE CORRESPONDENCE

Suppose you usually end all correspondence this way:

Fred Stevens
Vice President, Marketing
MegaMamaToid Corp.

The following steps store those keystrokes in a macro named *SIG*. But, of course, you can store your own name, address, title, or whatever you commonly use to end a letter or memo.

1. Press ↵ a couple of times to move to the beginning of a new line.

2. Choose **M**acro ➤ **R**ecord, or press Ctrl+F10. A dialog box appears that asks for the name of the macro, plus an optional description and abstract.

3. Type **sig** and press Tab to give your macro a name.

4. Type **Letter Signature** and press ↵ to give the macro a description (don't provide an abstract).

5. If you see the message

   Replace existing macro?

   someone has probably done this lesson before. It's probably safe to choose **Yes** and erase the old macro. Notice the "Macro Recording" message in the status bar, indicating that your actions are now being recorded.

6. Type your signature, using whatever text you wish. For this example, you can type

   Fred Stevens
   Vice President, Marketing
   MegaMamaToid Corp.

   Remember to press ↵ at the end of each line. Your screen should now look something like Figure L8.1.

7. Choose **Macro ➤ S**top or press Ctrl+Shift+F10 to finish the macro. The "Macro Recording" message disappears, and your macro is recorded.

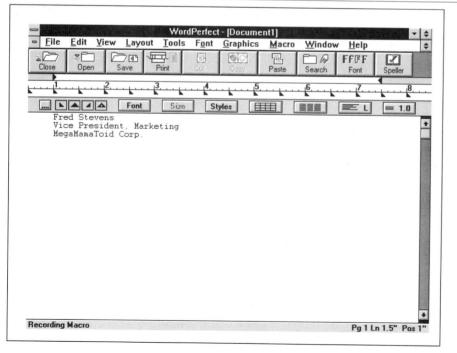

FIGURE L8.1:

The screen, just before ending macro recording

Now when you're at the end of a document, where you would normally type your signature, you can use the SIG macro. To try it now, follow these steps:

1. Choose File ➤ Close to clear your screen now without saving the current document. Choose **No** when asked whether you want to save the changes to the current document.

2. Type your usual letter closing, such as **Sincerely yours,** and press ↵ three times to insert some blank lines.

3. Choose **Macro** ➤ **P**lay or press Alt+F10.

4. In the Play Macro dialog box, type **sig** and press ↵, or double-click SIG.WCM.

Your signature will be typed automatically at the insertion point.

NEWLET: A MACRO TO START A NEW LETTER

WordPerfect for Windows makes it easy enough to begin a new document: Just choose File ➤ New and a fresh document window appears. Unless you specify new margins and tabs, each new document opens with 1-inch margins at tabs spaced every $1/2$-inch. These settings may be fine for the bulk of work you do, such as writing manuscripts or reports.

But suppose you need to make certain margin and tab-setting changes for your correspondence. Instead of 1-inch margins all around, you want 1.5-inch margins, and only one tab, at the 5-inch mark. Changing these settings for each letter you write can be time consuming; a better way is to create a macro that performs the steps for you.

To create the NEWLET macro, follow these steps.

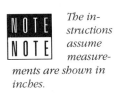

The instructions assume measurements are shown in inches.

1. Choose File ➤ New to start a new document.

2. Choose **Macro** ➤ **R**ecord, or press Ctrl+F10.

3. Type **newlet** and press Tab.

4. For the description of the macro, type **Start a New Letter** and press Tab.

5. It may be helpful to provide additional information and description for the macro, so include a sentence or two in the abstract. Type

   Create a new letter using custom margins of 1.5 inches and one tab stop.

Refer to Chapter 15

6. Press ↵ when you're finished. The "Macro Recording" indicator appears in the status bar. From here on, everything you do will be recorded. Remember: If you make a mistake, you can stop the macro and start over.

7. Choose **Layout ➤ M**argins. The Margins dialog box appears.

8. Type **1.5"** in both the Right and Left text boxes. Press ↵ when you're finished.

9. Choose **Layout ➤ Line ➤ T**ab Set. The Tab Set dialog box appears.

10. Choose Clear Ta**b**s. All tabs are removed.

11. In the Position box, type **3.5"**, then choose OK to accept the changes.

12. Stop macro recording by choosing **Macro ➤ S**top or pressing Ctrl+Shift+F10.

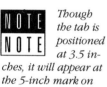 *Though the tab is positioned at 3.5 inches, it will appear at the 5-inch mark on the ruler, because the tab is set relative to the 1.5-inch left margin.*

The macro is now ready to be played back. You may want to test it now to make sure it works the way you anticipate.

1. If the ruler isn't already displayed, choose **View ➤ R**uler or press Alt+Shift+F3.

2. Turn on Reveal Codes by choosing **View ➤** Reveal **C**odes or pressing Alt+F3.

3. Use the Backspace key to remove the codes that were inserted when you recorded the NEWLET macro. There should be only two codes: one for left/right margins and one for tabs.

4. Turn off Reveal Codes by choosing **View ➤** Reveal **C**odes or pressing Alt+F3.

5. Choose **Macro ➤ P**lay. The Play Macro dialog box appears.

6. Type **newlet** in the Filename text box and press ↵, or double-click its name.

It takes a few moments for WordPerfect to process the macro. Once the macro is played, the new margin and tab settings will take effect. You will be able to see those changes in the ruler. The left and right margin controls should be positioned at the 1.5" and 7" marks, and a single tab should rest under the 5" mark.

Feel free to make changes to the macro so that the margin and tab settings are the way you want them. For example, you can readily change the left and right margins to read 0.5" or include changes to the top and bottom margins as well. You can also include any other formatting changes you like and have them recorded in the macro.

Refer to Chapter 15

You are finished with the temporary document that you opened for this macro. Close it by choosing File ➤ Close or pressing Ctrl+F4. Choose No when asked whether you want to save the changes you've made.

TRPOSE: A MACRO TO TRANSPOSE CHARACTERS

One of the most common typing mistakes is swapping two letters or numbers around, such as typing *hte* instead of *the*. It's annoying to have to switch the two misplaced characters using the ordinary editing keys. But you can create a macro that does this job for you.

You can call this one *TRPOSE,* to remind you that the macro *transpose*s letters. Follow these steps:

1. Press ↵ to start on a new line.

2. Type the misspelled word **hte** and press ↵.

3. Move the insertion point to the letter *h*.

4. Choose **M**acro ➤ **R**ecord, or press Ctrl+F10.

5. Name the macro by typing **trpose**, then press Tab.

6. Type **Transposes two letters** as the description of the macro. Press ↵ to start macro recording.

7. If WordPerfect indicates that this macro already exists, choose **Y**es to verify the replacement.

8. Hold down the Shift key and press → to select the current letter.

9. Choose **E**dit ➤ Cu**t** (or press Shift+Del) to cut the current character.

10. Press → to move one character to the right.

11. Choose **E**dit ➤ **P**aste (or press Shift+Ins). The two characters are transposed.

12. Choose **M**acro ➤ **S**top or press Ctrl+Shift+F10 to stop recording keystrokes.

To see just how handy this macro can be, intentionally mistype another word, then use the new TRPOSE macro to transpose the letters. Follow these steps:

1. Press End to move to the end of the current word.

2. Press the spacebar to insert a blank space.

3. Type the misspelled word

smiple

Refer to Chapter 15

4. Press ← five times to move the insertion point between the letters *s* and *m*.

5. Choose Macro ➤ **P**lay, type **trpose**, and press ⏎. The macro will transform *smiple* into *simple*.

ATTACHING A MACRO TO A BUTTON

You can quickly and easily turn any macro into a button. You can then run the macro simply by clicking on its button (the Button Bar cannot be activated by using the keyboard).

The Trpose macro is a good candidate for use as a button on the Button Bar because it's one you are likely to use often. Follow these steps:

1. Choose **V**iew ➤ Button Bar **S**etup ➤ **E**dit. You'll see the Edit Button Bar dialog box:

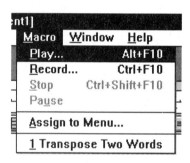

2. Choose **A**ssign Macro to Button.

3. Select the file TRPOSE.WCM in the file list, and choose **A**ssign.

4. This is the only macro you want to assign to the Button Bar at this time, so you're ready to save your changes. In the Edit Button Bar dialog box, choose OK.

The new button appears at the end of the current Button Bar. To try it out, simply move the insertion point to the first of any two characters that you want to transpose. Then click your new Trpose button.

Refer to Chapter 15

TRWORD: A MACRO TO TRANSPOSE WORDS

Another common mistake is transposing two words, such as typing *important really* instead of *really important*. You can create a macro named *TRWORD* that reverses their order. Follow these steps:

1. Press End to move to the end of the current line.

2. Press the spacebar to insert a blank space.

3. Type the words

   cat black yelped

4. Move the insertion point to the *c* in *cat*.

5. Choose **M**acro ➤ **R**ecord, or press Ctrl+F10.

6. Name the macro by typing **trword**, and press Tab.

7. Type **Transpose two words**, and press ↵.

8. If WordPerfect indicates that this macro already exists, choose **Y**es to verify the replacement.

9. Press Shift+Ctrl+→ to select the current word and the blank space that follows it.

10. Choose **E**dit ➤ **Cut** (or press Shift+Del).

11. Press Ctrl+→ to move one word to the right.

12. Choose **E**dit ➤ **P**aste (or press Shift+Ins) to insert the cut.

13. Choose **M**acro ➤ **S**top or press Ctrl+Shift+F10 to stop recording.

Be forewarned that this macro is not perfect. If you transpose two words that have a comma or period at the end, it will also transpose the punctuation mark. And if you transpose the two words at the end of a paragraph, the first word will end up at the beginning of the next paragraph.

You can try the macro now by positioning the insertion point at the first character of any word that has another word to the right of it, then choosing Macro ➤ Play and choosing TRWORD.WCM to reverse the order of the words.

Refer to Chapter 15

ATTACHING A MACRO TO THE MACRO MENU

Earlier in this lesson you attached the macro to transpose letters to a button on the Button Bar. You can also attach a macro to the Macro menu. Follow these steps:

1. Choose **Macro ➤ A**ssign to Menu. The Assign Macro to Menu dialog box appears.

2. Choose **I**nsert to insert a new macro.

3. Type **trword.wcm**, and press Tab to move the insertion point to the Menu Text entry box.

4. Type **Transpose Two Words**, and press ↵.

5. Choose OK to return to the document window.

WordPerfect appends "Transpose Two Words" to the bottom of the Macro menu. Pull down the menu to make sure the menu assignment worked. To run the macro, just choose Transpose Two Words as if it were a regular Word-Perfect menu option.

```
Macro  Window  Help
Play...            Alt+F10
Record...          Ctrl+F10
Stop         Ctrl+Shift+F10
Pause
─────────────────────────
Assign to Menu...
─────────────────────────
1 Transpose Two Words
```

STARTMEM: A MACRO THAT PAUSES
FOR INPUT FROM THE KEYBOARD

In many cases, you might want a macro to perform a few keystrokes, then wait for you to type something, then perform a few more keystrokes. One example would be if you were typing a memo where you wanted the macro to automatically type the lines shown below, pausing after each line to let you fill in the missing information:

DATE:
TO:
FROM:
SUBJECT:

Refer to Chapter 15

If you want your macro to wait for you to make an entry before playing back other keystrokes, you need to insert a *pause* in your macro. Follow these steps to create the STARTMEM macro:

1. Choose **File** ➤ **C**lose to clear the document window, or press Ctrl+F4. Answer **N**o if asked whether you want to save changes.

2. Choose **M**acro ➤ **R**ecord, or press Ctrl+F10.

3. Type **startmem** to name the macro. Press Tab.

4. Type

   Start a memo with pauses

   to describe the macro. Press ↵ to start macro recording.

5. If WordPerfect indicates that this macro already exists, choose **Y**es to verify the replacement.

6. Type **DATE:** and press the Tab key. Press ↵ twice.

7. Repeat step 6, but type **TO:**, **FROM:**, and **SUBJECT:** instead of *DATE:*.

8. Choose **M**acro ➤ **S**top or press Ctrl+Shift+F10 to stop recording keystrokes.

You're only halfway done with the STARTMEM macro. If you were to play it back now, it would type the Date, To, From, and Subject lines without giving you time to enter your own text.

To complete the macro, follow these steps:

1. Choose **File** ➤ **O**pen, or press F4. The Open File dialog box appears.

2. Use the Directories list box to locate the Macros directory. Select it and press ↵ (or double-click on it).

3. Use the Files list box to locate the STARTMEM.WCM macro. Select it and press ↵ to open it.

4. Refer to Figure L8.2 to modify the macro so that it will pause after each memo heading. You'll add a special macro command, PauseKey(0), after each heading and beneath each Tab( ). This command pauses the macro and waits for you to press the ↵ key. The macro resumes operation after you press ↵.

5. When you are finished editing the macro, choose **File** ➤ **C**lose, or press Ctrl+F4. Choose **Y**es to save the changes you've made.

Be sure to type the Pause-Key(0) command exactly as it appears. Although you can insert a space between PauseKey and (0), you must type PauseKey as one word.

Refer to Chapter 15

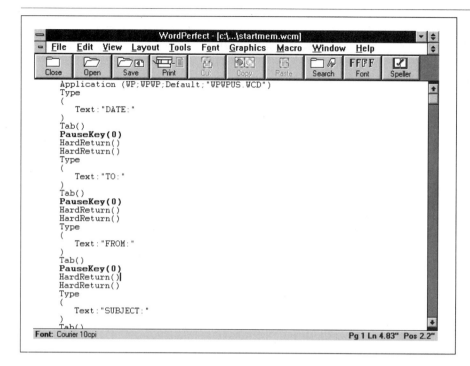

```
WordPerfect - [c:\...\startmem.wcm]
File   Edit   View   Layout   Tools   Font   Graphics   Macro   Window   Help

Close   Open   Save   Print   Cut   Copy   Paste   Search   Font   Speller

Application (WP;WPWP;Default;"WPWPUS.WCD")
Type
(
    Text:"DATE:"
)
Tab()
PauseKey(0)
HardReturn()
HardReturn()
Type
(
    Text:"TO:"
)
Tab()
PauseKey(0)
HardReturn()
HardReturn()
Type
(
    Text:"FROM:"
)
Tab()
PauseKey(0)
HardReturn()|
HardReturn()
Type
(
    Text:"SUBJECT:"
)
Tab()

Font: Courier 10cpi                          Pg 1 Ln 4.83" Pos 2.2"
```

FIGURE L8.2:

How to modify the STARTMEM macro so that it pauses after each memo heading

You run a macro that has a pause in it the same way you run any other macro. When the macro reaches the point where you entered the pause, it will stop and wait for you to take action. Type in your entry, and then press ⏎ to play back the rest of the keystrokes.

To try your new macro now, follow these steps:

1. Choose File ➤ Close, then No, to clear the current document window.

2. Choose Macro ➤ Play, or press Alt+F10.

3. Type **startmem** and press ⏎.

4. The macro will type **DATE:** and enter a tab, then wait for you to type something.

5. Type the date and press ⏎.

6. The macro will type **TO:** and enter a tab, then pause, as shown in Figure L8.3.

7. Type the recipient's name and press ⏎.

Refer to Chapter 15

8. The macro will type **FROM:** and enter a tab, then pause.

9. Type your name and press ↵.

10. The macro will type **SUBJECT:** and enter a tab, then pause.

11. Type a subject for your memo and press ↵.

With the heading information complete, you can now start typing the body of your memo. (You can change the tab stops above to align items better if you wish.)

Now that you've created several macros on your own, you can explore macros in more detail by reading Chapter 15. Then you might want to tackle the power macro in Lesson 10.

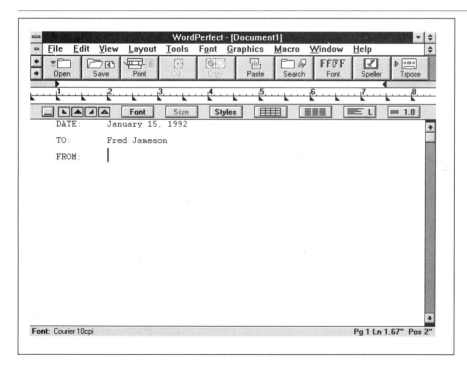

FIGURE L8.3:

The macro types the initial keystrokes, then pauses.

Creating Form Letters and Mailing Labels

In this lesson you'll create some sample form letters and mailing labels by merging primary and secondary merge files.

BEFORE YOU BEGIN

Before you begin this lesson, you need to start WordPerfect and get to a blank document window. You should have completed at least the first few lessons so that you know the basics of creating, editing, saving, and printing a document.

CREATING A SECONDARY MERGE FILE

Suppose that you want to write a form letter to everyone in your Rolodex, and each card in the Rolodex has a name and address on it, in this form:

Marie Abzug
ABC Corporation
123 Ocean Way
Los Angeles, CA 91234
(213)555-0134

To write a form letter to each person, you first need to create a secondary merge file with the information on each card broken into *fields* and *records*. Each record represents a single Rolodex card; each field represents some unit of information that's repeated on most, or all, of the cards. For this lesson, you'll divide the information on each card (i.e., in each record) into the nine fields shown in Figure L9.1.

FIELD NAME	EXAMPLE
LastName	Abzug
FirstName	Marie
Company	ABC Corporation
Address	123 Ocean Way
City	Los Angeles
State	CA
ZipCode	91234
Phone	(213)555-0134
Salutation	Ms. Abzug

FIGURE L9.1:

The nine fields for the secondary merge file

DEFINING THE FIELD NAMES

You don't have to define field names, but it makes the merge procedure easier in the long run.

The first step in creating your secondary merge file is to define the field names you'll be using. You need to start from a blank document window, then follow these steps:

1. Choose **Tools** ➤ **Merge** ➤ **Merge Codes** (or press Ctrl+F12 C).

2. Move the highlight to {FIELD NAMES}name1~...nameN~~. Choose **Insert** or press ↵.

3. Type **LastName** for field 1 and choose **Add**.

4. Type **FirstName** for field 2 and choose **Add**.

5. Type **Company** for field 3 and choose **Add**.

6. Type **Address** for field 4 and choose **Add**.

7. Type **City** for field 5 and choose **Add**.

8. Type **State** for field 6 and choose **Add**.

9. Type **ZipCode** for field 7 and choose **Add**.

10. Type **Phone** for field 8 and choose **Add**.

11. Type **Salutation** for field 9 and choose **Add**.

Refer to Chapter 16

12. Instead of entering field 10, just choose OK or press ↵ to stop entering field names.

13. Choose **C**lose to close the Insert Merge Codes dialog box.

After you leave the dialog box, you'll see the list of field names followed by a double line, as shown in Figure L9.2.

REFINING THE FIELD NAME LIST

If you want to make the field names easier to read, you can move the insertion point to the start of each name, then press ↵ and Tab to place each on a separate line and indent it. You can also move the insertion point to the second tilde (~) after the Salutation~ field name and press ↵. (The text will appear to wrap incorrectly at first, because there are no blank spaces for WordPerfect to use for wrapping. But don't worry about that.) That way, the field names stand out clearly, and you can read them at a glance, as shown at the top of Figure L9.3 later in the chapter.

You can also make any corrections, such as correcting a misspelled field name, with the usual editing keys. When you're finished, just make sure that all the field names and tildes are in place, as at the top of Figure L9.3 (above the first page break).

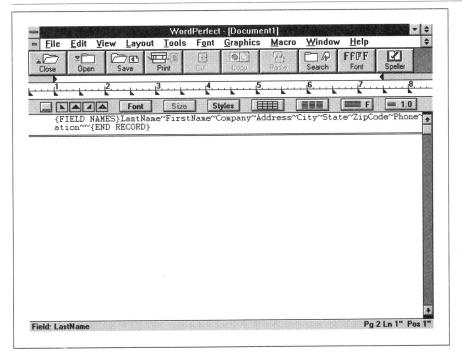

FIGURE L9.2:

The screen after defining field names for the secondary merge file

Refer to Chapter 16

ADDING THE NAMES

Had you not defined field names earlier in this lesson, a field number rather than a name would appear at the bottom of the screen, making it harder to keep track of which field WordPerfect is expecting data for at the moment.

Now you're ready to add the first person's record (i.e., Rolodex card) to the secondary merge file. Make sure the insertion point is below the double line (press Ctrl+End), then follow the steps below. As you type, notice that the lower-left corner of the screen displays which field WordPerfect is expecting next.

1. Type **Abzug** for LastName and press Alt+Enter.

2. Type **Marie** for FirstName and press Alt+Enter.

3. Type **ABC Corporation** for Company and press Alt+Enter.

4. Type **123 Ocean Way** for Address and press Alt+Enter.

5. Type **Los Angeles** for City and press Alt+Enter.

6. Type **CA** for State and press Alt+Enter.

7. Type **91234** for ZipCode and press Alt+Enter.

8. Type **(213)555-0134** for Phone and press Alt+Enter.

9. Type **Ms. Abzug** for Salutation and press Alt+Enter.

10. Choose **T**ools ➤ **M**erge ➤ End **R**ecord (or press Alt+Shift+Enter) to mark the end of the first record.

Figure L9.3 shows how this record should look on your screen, below the field names. The double line beneath the record is a hard page break, which Word-Perfect automatically places at the end of each record.

The insertion point is now positioned so that you can start typing the second record; in the lower-left corner of your screen, you can see that Word-Perfect is expecting an entry for the LastName field. You'll add this record next:

Izzy Hartunian
XYZ Corporation
2345 Salamander Rd.
San Diego, CA 92067
(619)555-9320

Follow these steps:

1. Type **Hartunian** for LastName and press Alt+Enter.

2. Type **Izzy** for FirstName and press Alt+Enter.

3. Type **XYZ Corporation** for Company and press Alt+Enter.

4. Type **2345 Salamander Rd.** for Address and press End Field Alt+Enter.

Refer to Chapter 16

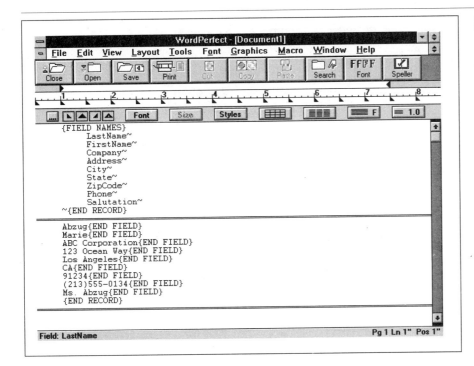

5. Type **San Diego** for City and press Alt+Enter.

6. Type **CA** for State and press Alt+Enter.

7. Type **92067** for ZipCode and press Alt+Enter.

8. Type **(619)555-9320** for Phone and press Alt+Enter.

9. Type **Mr. Hartunian** for Salutation and press Alt+Enter.

10. Choose **T**ools ➤ **M**erge ➤ End **R**ecord (or press Alt+Shift+Enter) to
mark the end of the second record.

Figure L9.4 shows how your screen should look now, with the second record
added to the secondary merge file.

The third record, shown below, presents a bit of a switch, because this
person has no company affiliation:

Wilbur Watson
123 Apple St.
Encinitas, CA 92024
(619)555-1234

Refer to Chapter 16

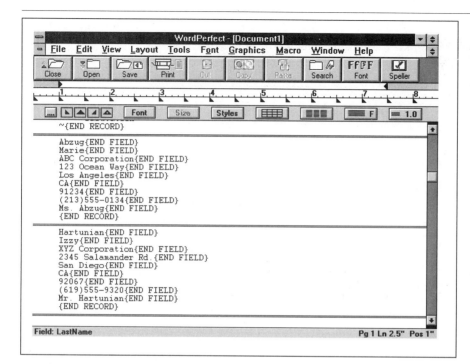

FIGURE L9.4:

*The second record
added to the secondary
merge file*

Because you've defined your field names with a company name in each record, you must include the Company field in every record of the secondary merge file. To do so, press Alt+Enter when you get to the Company field, to indicate that the field is empty. Follow these steps:

Glance at the bottom of the screen to see what field information is expected, so you don't accidentally type information in the wrong field.

1. Type **Watson** for LastName and press Alt+Enter.

2. Type **Wilbur** for FirstName and press Alt+Enter.

3. Press Alt+Enter to leave the Company field empty.

4. Type **123 Apple St.** for Address and press Alt+Enter.

5. Type **Encinitas** for City and press Alt+Enter.

6. Type **CA** for State and press Alt+Enter.

7. Type **92024** for ZipCode and press Alt+Enter.

8. Type **(619)555-1234** for Phone and press Alt+Enter.

9. Type **Mr. Watson** for Salutation and press Alt+Enter.

10. Choose **Tools ➤ Merge ➤ End Record** (or press Alt+Shift+Enter) to mark the end of the record.

Refer to Chapter 16

SAVING THE SECONDARY MERGE FILE

Your secondary merge file should now look like Figure L9.5 (the field names and first record have scrolled off the top of the screen). The file contains only three records, but yours can contain any number of fields and records. You don't need to do anything else with this file right now, so you can save the completed secondary merge file and clear the screen.

Follow these steps:

1. Choose **File ➤ C**lose (or press Ctrl+F4).

2. Choose **Y**es.

3. Type the file name **namelist.scd** (though you can use any valid file name), and press ↵.

4. If asked for permission to replace a previous NAMELIST.SCD file, choose **Y**es (this may happen if you or someone else has already taken this lesson).

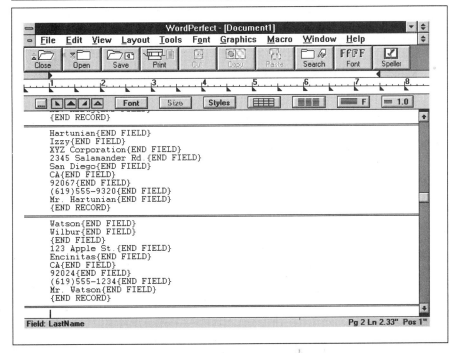

Using .SCD as the extension will remind you that this file is a secondary merge file.

Now you've created a secondary merge file, which you can use over and over again in the future to print form letters, mailing labels, envelopes, and so forth. You need never retype any of that information. But to use the information, you must create a primary merge file, described in the next part of this lesson.

FIGURE L9.5:

The secondary merge file on the screen

```
WordPerfect - [Document1]
File  Edit  View  Layout  Tools  Font  Graphics  Macro  Window  Help

Close  Open  Save  Print  Cut  Copy  Paste  Search  Font  Speller

    Font    Size    Styles         F   = 1.0

{END RECORD}

Hartunian{END FIELD}
Izzy{END FIELD}
XYZ Corporation{END FIELD}
2345 Salamander Rd.{END FIELD}
San Diego{END FIELD}
CA{END FIELD}
92067{END FIELD}
(619)555-9320{END FIELD}
Mr. Hartunian{END FIELD}
{END RECORD}

Watson{END FIELD}
Wilbur{END FIELD}
{END FIELD}
123 Apple St.{END FIELD}
Encinitas{END FIELD}
CA{END FIELD}
92024{END FIELD}
(619)555-1234{END FIELD}
Mr. Watson{END FIELD}
{END RECORD}

Field: LastName                                    Pg 2 Ln 2.33" Pos 1"
```

Refer to Chapter 16

CREATING A PRIMARY MERGE FILE

Creating a primary merge file is much like creating any other document in WordPerfect. However, you need to tell WordPerfect where to place information that will come from the secondary merge file, and you need to include the usual blank spaces and punctuation between each piece of information. In this section, you'll create a form letter.

Follow these steps from a blank document window:

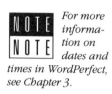

For more information on dates and times in WordPerfect, see Chapter 3.

1. Enter the current date at the top of the letter by choosing **Tools** ➤ **Date** ➤ **Code** (or pressing Ctrl+Shift+F5).

2. Press ↵ twice.

3. To place the first name at the insertion point, first choose **Tools** ➤ **Merge** ➤ **Field** (or press Ctrl+F12 F).

4. Type **FirstName** and press ↵.

5. Press the spacebar to add a blank space.

6. Choose **Tools** ➤ **Merge** ➤ **Field** (or press Ctrl+F12 F).

7. Type **LastName** and press ↵.

8. Press ↵ to move to the next line.

9. Choose **Tools** ➤ **Merge** ➤ **Field** (or press Ctrl+F12 F).

The question mark after the field name prevents an extra blank line from appearing in your merged output when the corresponding field is empty in the secondary file.

10. Type **Company?** and press ↵.

11. Press ↵ to move to the next line.

12. Choose **Tools** ➤ **Merge** ➤ **Field** (or press Ctrl+F12 F).

13. Type **Address** and press ↵.

14. Press ↵ to move to the next line.

15. Choose **Tools** ➤ **Merge** ➤ **Field** (or press Ctrl+F12 F).

16. Type **City** and press ↵.

17. Type a comma and press the spacebar so that there will be a comma and a blank space after the city in your printed letter.

18. Choose **Tools** ➤ **Merge** ➤ **Field** (or press Ctrl+F12 F).

19. Type **State** and press ↵.

20. Press the spacebar twice to add a couple of blank spaces.

21. Choose **Tools** ➤ **Merge** ➤ **Field** (or press Ctrl+F12 F).

22. Type **ZipCode** and press ↵.

Refer to Chapter 16

23. Press ↵ twice to move down a couple of lines.

24. Type **Dear** and then press the spacebar to add a blank space.

25. Choose **Tools ➤ Merge ➤ Field** (or press Ctrl+F12 F).

26. Type **Salutation** and press ↵.

27. Type a colon (**:**) to end the salutation.

28. Press ↵ twice to add a couple of blank lines.

Your screen should look like Figure L9.6 (though the date at the top of your screen will probably be different). As you can see, it looks kind of like a "skeleton" for the start of a letter (which is exactly what it is).

As a convenience, just so you don't have to repeat all those steps in the future when creating new form letters, you can save your work right now:

1. Choose **File ➤ S**ave, or press Shift+F3.

2. Type the file name **startlet.prm** and press ↵.

3. If asked for permission to replace a previous STARTLET.PRM file, choose **Yes**.

Using the .PRM extension will remind you that this file is a primary merge file.

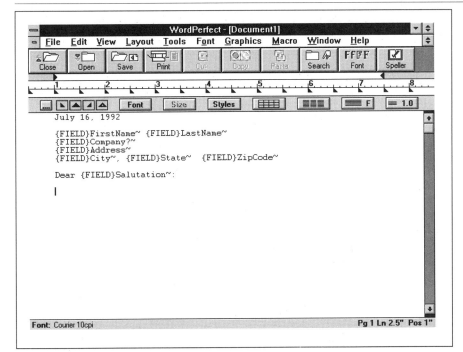

FIGURE L9.6:

The start of your primary merge file

```
July 16, 1992

{FIELD}FirstName~ {FIELD}LastName~
{FIELD}Company?~
{FIELD}Address~
{FIELD}City~, {FIELD}State~  {FIELD}ZipCode~

Dear {FIELD}Salutation~:
```

Refer to Chapter 16

Now it's time to create a complete form letter. Follow these steps:

1. Type this paragraph and letter closing:

Just a brief reminder that the next annual meeting of cave dwellers is just a few weeks away. Please call if you can volunteer any time to this momentous occasion.

Sincerely,

Wanda K. Doorknob

2. Press ↵ after typing the last line.

SAVING THE PRIMARY MERGE FILE

Your letter should now look like Figure L9.7. Save it as LETTER1.PRM:

1. Choose **File ➤ Save As** (or press F3).

2. Type **letter1.prm** (replacing the current file name), and press ↵.

3. If asked for permission to replace a previous LETTER1.PRM file, choose **Yes**.

MERGING THE PRIMARY AND SECONDARY FILES

Now you have a secondary merge file named NAMELIST.SCD and a primary merge file named LETTER1.PRM that can merge information from that file into a form letter. Follow these steps to merge the two files:

1. Choose **File ➤ Close** (or press Ctrl+F4) to start at a blank document window before beginning. Choose **Tools ➤ Merge ➤ Merge** (or press Ctrl+F12 M).

2. Type **letter1.prm** in the Primary File text box, and press Tab.

3. Type **Namelist.scd** in the Secondary File text box, and press ↵.

4. When the merge is complete, a letter appears on your screen. You can press Page Up and Page Down to scroll through the completed, merged letters. Notice that each letter is addressed to one person from your secondary merge file. Each will be printed on a separate page, as indicated by the hard page break line between letters.

5. To print the letters, choose **File ➤ Print** (or press F5).

6. Choose **Full Document**, then **Print**.

Refer to Chapter 16

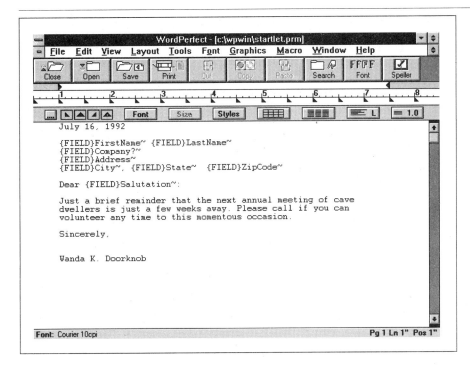

FIGURE L9.7:

The completed primary merge file, a form letter

7. There is no need to save this sample merged file after printing the letters, so choose **File ➤ C**lose (or press Ctrl+F4).

8. Choose **N**o to clear the screen and stay in WordPerfect.

Figure L9.8 shows one of the completed form letters. As you can see, WordPerfect has filled in the skeleton at the top part of the original LETTER1.PRM primary merge file ({FIELD}FirstName~, {FIELD}LastName~, and so forth) with the contents of the corresponding fields from the NAMELIST.SCD secondary file.

PRINTING MAILING LABELS

Now you'll create and print mailing labels, which requires adding a paper size for printing on labels rather than on standard 8.5" × 11" paper. First, you have to find out whether there's already a label size available for you to use. Follow these steps:

1. Start from the document window (clear or otherwise).

2. If you've installed multiple printers, select the printer you want to use for printing labels: Choose **File ➤ S**elect Printer **➤ W**ordPerfect, highlight the printer of your choice, and choose **S**elect or press ↵.

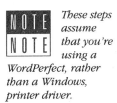

These steps assume that you're using a WordPerfect, rather than a Windows, printer driver.

Refer to Chapter 16

```
July 16, 1992

Marie Abzug
ABC Corporation
123 Ocean Way
Los Angeles, CA  91234

Dear Ms. Abzug:

Just a brief reminder that the next annual meeting of cave
dwellers is just a few weeks away. Please call if you can
volunteer any time to this momentous occasion.

Sincerely,


Wanda K. Doorknob
```

3. Choose **L**ayout ➤ **P**age ➤ Paper **S**ize.

You'll see the Paper Size dialog box, shown in Figure L9.9, except that the options available on your screen will depend on the formats that have already been set up for your printer.

Refer to Chapter 16

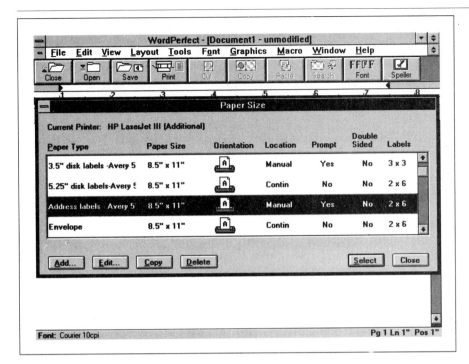

What you do next depends on what's currently available for your printer:

◆ If you see a label paper type that's suitable for your needs, choose Close and skip to "Creating a Primary Merge File for Labels."

◆ If you do not see a label paper type that's suitable for your needs, continue with the section below.

CREATING A LABEL PAPER SIZE

Chapter 7 describes paper sizes in detail.

To create a paper size for printing labels, follow these steps:

1. Choose **A**dd in the Paper Size dialog box.

2. Choose **L**abels from the Paper **T**ype list.

3. Choose **C**ontinuous from the Paper Location list.

4. Choose **L**abels. The Edit Labels dialog box appears.

5. Enter the appropriate size for your labels, as discussed in Chapter 7.

6. Choose OK from the next two dialog boxes, then Close to return to the document window.

Now you have a label paper size to experiment with, which you'll use in a moment to print some sample labels.

CREATING A PRIMARY MERGE FILE FOR LABELS

The name and address format on a mailing label or an envelope is identical to that of the heading on a letter. So, rather than go through all the steps to insert the merge codes in a new primary merge file, you'll just modify the format you already created earlier in this lesson. Follow these steps:

1. Choose **F**ile ➤ **O**pen (or press F4).

2. Type **startlet.prm** and press ↵.

3. Press Delete three times to delete the date and the two blank lines beneath.

4. Press ↓ to move to the {FIELD}City~ line.

5. Press End to move the insertion point to the end of the line.

6. Press Shift+Ctrl+End and then Delete to delete all text below the insertion point.

Your label format should look like Figure L9.10, which is a good layout for printing mailing labels.

This procedure places the appropriate codes for defining how information in the final document should be arranged after the merge. This approach is a shortcut to individually placing each field in the document window, since you went through those steps when creating the primary merge file for the form letter. The same basic arrangement of fields will work fine for labels.

CHOOSING A LABEL SIZE

Now you need to tell WordPerfect to print each name and address on a separate label, rather than on a separate page, by choosing a label paper size. Follow these steps:

 Placing the label format in Document Initial Codes ensures that your labels will be formatted properly after you merge the primary and secondary files.

1. Choose **L**ayout ➤ **D**ocument ➤ Initial **C**odes (or press Ctrl+Shift+F9).

2. Choose **L**ayout ➤ **P**age ➤ Paper **S**ize.

3. Use the ↑ and ↓ keys to move the highlight to the label format you want.

4. Choose **S**elect.

5. Choose **C**lose to return to the document window.

6. Choose **F**ile ➤ Save **A**s (or press F3).

Refer to Chapter 16

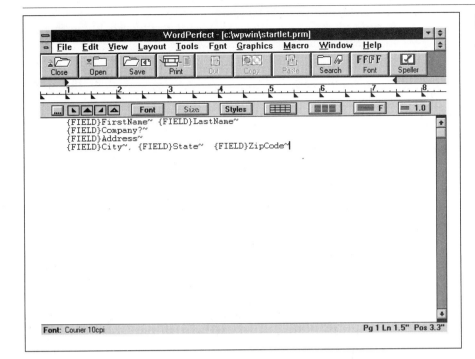

7. Type **labels.prm** and press ↵ (though you can use any file name you want).

8. If asked for permission to replace a previous LABELS.PRM file, choose **Yes**.

Now you've completed the primary merge file for printing labels and have saved it with the file name LABELS.PRM. Before you can print labels, you need to merge that file with the NAMELIST.SCD secondary merge file that you created earlier in this lesson, so there will be a properly formatted label for each record in that file.

MERGING AND PRINTING THE LABELS

To merge the LABELS.PRM primary merge file with the NAMELIST.SCD secondary merge file that you created earlier, follow these steps:

1. Choose **File** ➤ **Close** (or press Ctrl+F4) to clear the document window.

2. Choose **Tools** ➤ **Merge** ➤ **Merge** (or press Ctrl+F12 M).

3. Type **labels.prm** in the Primary File text box, and press Tab.

Refer to Chapter 16

4. Type **namelist.scd** in the Secondary File text box, and press ↵. Your screen will like Figure L9.11. Don't worry that the labels don't appear in their final format in the document window. They will print properly.

5. To view the labels, choose **File** ➤ Print Pre**v**iew (or press Shift+F5). When you're ready to return to the document window, choose **File** ➤ **C**lose.

6. If you want to print the labels now, choose **File** ➤ **P**rint (or press F5), select **F**ull Document, and choose **P**rint or press ↵.

7. There is no need to save the merged file, so choose **File** ➤ **C**lose, and choose **N**o to clear the document window without saving the file.

Now that you've created a secondary merge file and have merged it with a couple of sample primary merge files, you should read Chapter 16 to learn all about merging.

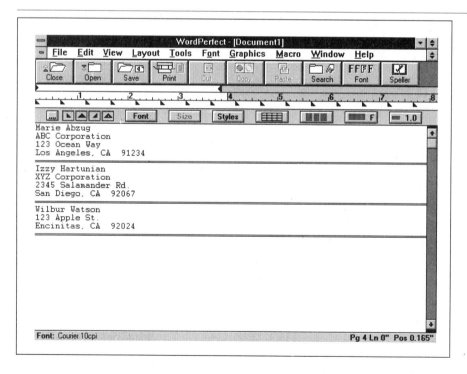

FIGURE L9.11:

The document window just after merging

Creating a Power Macro

This lesson will give you some hands-on experience in recording and editing a complex macro that recalculates all the tables in a document.

BEFORE YOU BEGIN

If you've exited WordPerfect, be sure to start WordPerfect again to get to a blank document window. You should already be familiar with creating, naming, and running recorded-keystroke macros, as described in Chapter 15 and Lesson 8. Finally, you should create a few tables with math calculations, as described in Chapter 18 and Lesson 5, because the macro you create in this lesson requires some tables to work with.

If you've already completed the table in Lesson 5, you can use it as a starting point for your sample tables. Figure L10.1 shows a table that's similar to the one you created in Lesson 5, with these extra features and changes, which you can incorporate now:

1. Add one row at the bottom and one column at the right to hold totals and extended price information.

2. Include the following formulas: column subtotal (+) in cells C7 and D7, and multiply Price by Quantity in cells D3, D4, D5, and D6 (see the notations in Figure L10.1).

3. Change the table titles from "INSURANCE RATES" to "ORDER FORM," from "Premium" to "Price," and from "Deductible" to "Quantity." Type **Extended Price** in cell D2 (optional).

4. Remove dollar signs ($) from the cells in column C.

5. Add dollar signs in front of the numbers in cells D3 through D6 and fine-tune other formatting features as necessary (optional).

Refer to Chapter 26

FIGURE L10.1:

A sample table containing math calculations

column				
row	**A**	**B**	**C**	**D**
1	ORDER FORM			
2	Model	Price	Quantity	Extended Price
3	30 watt	$.50	25	$12.50	← **B3*C3**
4	75 watt	$.75	35	$26.25	← **B4*C4**
5	100 watt	$1.49	70	$104.30	← **B5*C5**
6	250 watt	$1.97	99	$195.03	← **B6*C6**
7	Totals		229	$338.08

column subtotal (+)

After creating one table, you can copy it into several places in your document, or create additional tables from scratch.

HOW THE SAMPLE MACRO WORKS

Before creating your macro, you should understand something about what it does. Figure L10.2 shows the finished macro. I've added line numbers to make it easier to explain this macro; actual macros *never* contain line numbers. (You can, however, add line numbers to *printed* copies of your macros, which will make the macros much easier to correct if you make typing errors when creating or editing them. You'll add line numbers to the macro later in this lesson.)

In a nutshell, the macro starts at the very top of the document, then searches for and recalculates the formulas in every table in the document.

Take a look at how the macro does its job:

Line 1: The Application command tells the Macro Facility that the macro commands in this file pertain to the WordPerfect application.

Line 6: The Display command turns on the screen display so that you can see what's happening as the macro makes changes in the document window. This command is optional, and you can omit it if you want the macro to run faster.

Line 9: The PosDocVeryTop command moves the insertion point to the very top of the document, before any text or codes.

The // followed by text in lines 3, 4, 8 and several of the other lines is a comment. Comments are ignored when you play back the macro.

Refer to Chapter 26

```
1      Application (WP;WPWP;Default;"WPWPUS.WCD")
2
3      //*** Recalc.wcm
4      //*** Recalculates all the tables in a document.
5
6      Display (STATE:On!) //This command is optional.
7
8      //*** Move to top of document.
9      PosDocVeryTop()
10
11     //*** When search for a [Tbl Def] code fails, we're done.
12     OnNotFound (AllDone@)
13
14     //*** Main loop of the macro.
15     Label (NextTable@)
16
17     SearchText
18     (
19        SearchString:"";
20        SearchDirection:Forward!;
21        SearchScope:Extended!
22     )
23     TableCalculate()
24     PosLineDown()
25     Go (NextTable@)
26
27     //*** No more tables, so end macro.
28     Label (AllDone@)
29     Quit
30
```

FIGURE L10.2:

*A power macro to
recalculate all tables in
a document*

*Your
macro can
contain as
many
labels as you need, as
long as the label
names are unique.
Labels must end with
an "at" (@) character.*

Line 12: When a search fails to find the specified text or codes, it sends the macro program a "not found" signal. The ONNOTFOUND command detects this signal and handles it by jumping to a label. Therefore, when the search in lines 17–22 fails, the macro jumps to the label named *AllDone* (line 28).

Line 15: The NextTable label starts the main loop that searches for the next [Tbl Def] code, recalculates the table, and moves down a line. The GO command in line 25 returns to the NextTable label unless the search fails, in which case the ONNOTFOUND command takes over.

Lines 17–22: The SearchText command searches for the next [Tbl Def] code. Using SearchText in a macro is like choosing **E**dit ➤ **S**earch from the pull-down menus or pressing the F2 key and filling out the Search dialog box. SearchString (line 19) tells the macro what to search for, SearchDirection (line 20) specifies the search direction, and SearchScope (line 21) specifies how much of the document to search. In this case, the macro searches for a [Tbl Def] code in the forward direction and throughout the entire (extended) document. Although the [Tbl Def] code isn't visible in Figure L10.2 or in the

Refer to Chapter 26

document window, you can see it in Reveal Codes, where line 19 looks like this:

SearchString:"[Embedded:Tbl Def]";[HRt]

Line 23: The TableCalculate command recalculates the formulas in the current table.

Line 24: The PosLineDown command moves the insertion point down one line, past the [Tbl Def] code.

Line 25: The GO command tells WordPerfect to go back to the Next-Table label in line 15 to repeat the search and recalculation steps.

Line 28: The macro jumps to the AllDone label when the search fails (i.e., when no more [Tbl Def] codes exist in the document).

Line 29: The QUIT command stops the macro and returns you to the document window.

CREATING AND TESTING THE MACRO

You'll create this macro in three major steps:

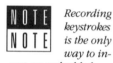
Recording keystrokes is the only way to insert an embedded code in a SearchText command.

1. Record the results of keystrokes that search for a table, then move down one line. This will save some typing and will insert the embedded [Tbl Def] code.

2. Edit the macro: Add line numbers, comments, and commands that repeat the search throughout the document.

3. Print, save, and test the final macro.

CREATING THE RECORDED MACRO

You'll name the macro *RECALC.* If you already have a macro with that name on your computer, you'll have to use a different name or rename the existing macro. Then, follow these steps:

1. Choose **File ➤ O**pen (or press F4) to open the document containing your sample tables.

2. Choose **Macro ➤ R**ecord, or press Ctrl+F10.

3. Type **recalc** in the **F**ilename text box.

4. Type **Recalculate a table** in the **D**escriptive Name text box.

5. Choose **R**ecord or press ↵. If you're prompted to replace the existing macro (and want to do so), choose **Y**es; otherwise, choose **N**o and type a different name in the **F**ilename text box.

Refer to Chapter 26

Now you're ready to enter macro commands. Follow these steps:

1. Choose **E**dit ➤ **S**earch, or press F2.

2. Choose **C**odes. You'll see the Codes dialog box shown in Figure L10.3.

3. Highlight the Tbl Def code in the Codes dialog box.

4. Choose **I**nsert or press ↵.

5. Choose **S**earch or press ↵.

6. Choose **L**ayout ➤ **T**ables ➤ **C**alculate, or press Ctrl+F9 A.

7. Press the ↓ key.

8. Choose **M**acro ➤ **S**top, or press Ctrl+Shift+F10.

TESTING THE RECORDED MACRO

WordPerfect's Macro Facility automatically saved your recorded macro in the default macros directory (normally C:\WPWIN\MACROS) and named it RECALC.WCM. You're now ready to give it a quick test.

1. Change a few of the numbers in the first table, so you can see the effects of the macro when you play it back. For example, if you're using the

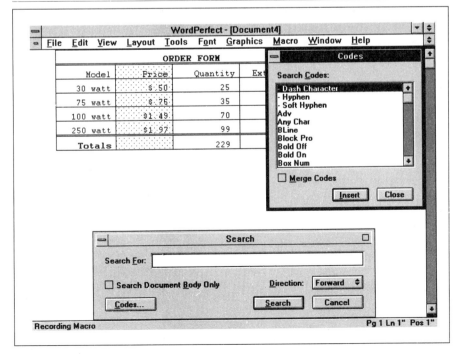

FIGURE L10.3:

The Codes dialog box lets you insert hidden codes in the search string.

Refer to Chapter 26

table shown in Figure L10.1, change some of the quantities or prices.

2. Press Ctrl+Home twice to move to the very top of the document.

3. Choose **Macro ➤ P**lay, or press Alt+F10.

4. Type **recalc** and choose **P**lay or press ↵. WordPerfect will recalculate the formulas in the first table almost instantly.

EDITING THE MACRO

Technically speaking, macro files are not normal WordPerfect documents, because they contain both invisible compiled macro commands and visible text and codes that you can edit and print.

Although the recorded macro is quite handy in its own right, your ultimate goal is to create a macro that automatically positions the insertion point at the top of the document and then recalculates every table in the document. To achieve that goal, you must edit the RECALC.WCM macro file, which is just a normal WordPerfect document. Follow these steps:

1. Choose **File ➤ O**pen, or press F4.

2. Double-click the Macros directory name.

3. Type **recalc.wcm** and choose **O**pen or press ↵.

4. Choose **View ➤** Reveal **C**odes (or press Alt+F3) to open Reveal Codes. Your screen should resemble Figure L10.4.

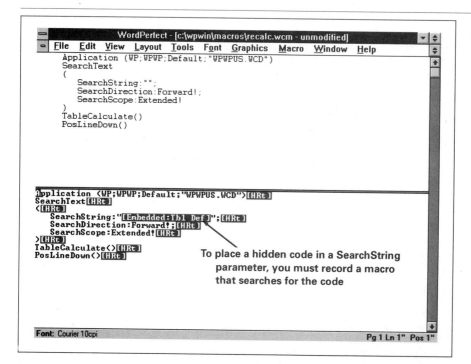

FIGURE L10.4:

The recorded-keystroke macro, with Reveal Codes open

Refer to Chapter 26

The macro programming language commands you see are the result of searching for a [Tbl Def] code (lines 2–7), recalculating the table (line 8), and moving the insertion point down by one line (line 9). The Application command in line 1 is added automatically to any macro you record while in WordPerfect; every macro you create, whether from scratch or by recording keystrokes, needs an Application command.

You're now ready to add line numbers to the macro; these will appear when you print the document or view it with Print Preview. Follow these steps:

1. Press Ctrl+Home to move to the top of the document.

2. Choose **Layout** ➤ **Line** ➤ **Numbering**.

3. Open the **Line** Numbering pop-up list, and choose **Continuous**.

4. Choose OK or press ↵.

Although the Macro Facility lets you type programs in a free format, you must still obey all the rules of the macro programming language. Incorrectly typed commands and extra or missing characters (e.g., parentheses, braces, semicolons, or colons) will prevent your macro from being played back.

Next, you'll add comments, blank lines, and the extra commands you need to make the macro recalculate all tables in the document. Keep in mind that you can type macros in a free format, which means that tabs, indents, blank lines, spaces, page headers and footers, and other formatting features are ignored and should not cause any problems when you play the macro.

Feel free to use these formatting features to make your macros easier to read, correct, and enhance. Also, be sure to include lots of comments so that you or someone else can easily figure out what the program is doing later on. (To save you some typing time, this lesson includes only a few comments.)

To insert the comments and commands in your document, follow these steps:

1. Press ↓ to move the insertion point to the beginning of the second line.

2. Press ↵.

3. Type //*** **Recalc.wcm** and press ↵.

4. Type //*** **Recalculates all tables in a document.** Press ↵ twice.

5. Type **Display(State:On!) // This command is optional.** Press ↵ twice.

6. Type //*** **Move to top of document.** Press ↵.

7. Type **PosDocVeryTop( )** and press ↵ twice.

8. Type //*** **When the search for a [Tbl Def] code fails, we're done.** Press ↵.

9. Type **ONNOTFOUND (AllDone@)** and press ↵ twice.

Refer to Chapter 26

10. Type //*** **Main loop of the macro.** Press ↵.

11. Type **LABEL (NextTable@)** and press ↵ twice.

12. Press **Ctrl+End** to move the insertion point to the bottom of the document.

13. Type **GO (NextTable@)** and press ↵ twice.

14. Type //*** **No more tables, so end the macro.** Press ↵.

15. Type **LABEL (AllDone@)** and press ↵.

16. Type **QUIT** and press ↵.

PRINTING, SAVING, AND TESTING THE FINAL MACRO

On the Print Preview screen, each line-numbered page of a multipage document begins with line 1, even if you chose Continuous numbering. The document will print correctly, however.

You've now completed the program text. Before printing or saving the macro, you might want to compare it with Figure L10.2. If you discover typing mistakes, just edit them as you would any text. With that finished, you can preview, then print, your document:

1. Choose **File ➤ Print Preview**, or press Shift+F5. Choose **File ➤ Close** after viewing the macro.

2. Choose **File ➤ Print** or press F5.

3. Choose **Print** or press ↵ to print the full document. Notice the line numbering on your printout.

Now that you have a printout, you can close and save the macro:

During compilation, your macro program is checked for errors and condensed into a format that will run more quickly when you play the macro.

1. Choose **File ➤ Close** (or press Ctrl+F4).

2. Choose **Yes** when asked whether you want to save the changes.

Now comes the moment of truth. With any luck, you typed your macro correctly and the macro will work perfectly the first time.

Before testing the macro, change some numbers in *each* table of your sample tables document, just so the changes will be obvious when you run the macro.

Now, test the macro:

1. Choose **Macro ➤ Play**, or press Alt+F10.

2. Type **recalc** and choose **Play** or press ↵. After a short delay, the macro will recalculate each table, one by one, until all tables are recalculated.

Refer to Chapter 26

If you made a typing error, the macro compiler will display a screen like the one shown in Figure L10.5. Choose Cancel Compilation or press ↵ to stop the compilation. Then open the macro file again, fix your macro by editing it, close and save the macro, then try playing it back again.

Now that you've had a chance to create, edit, and use some macros, you can delve further into advanced macro techniques by reading Chapter 26 and explore ways to add macros to your keyboard in Chapter 27.

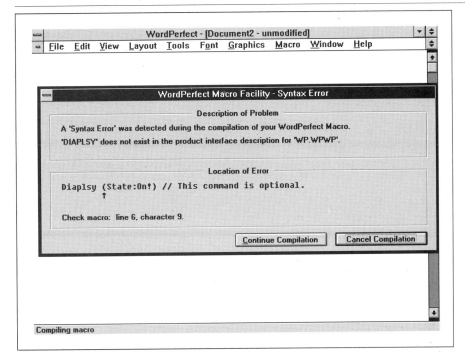

FIGURE L10.5:

This compilation error indicates that the Display command was misspelled as "Diaplsy," which isn't a valid macro programming language command.

Refer to Chapter 26

APPENDIX A

Installing WordPerfect on Your Computer

Before you can use WordPerfect for Windows, it must be *installed* on your computer. You need only install WordPerfect once, not each time you plan to use it. So if you or somebody else has already installed WordPerfect on your computer, you can go straight to Chapter 1 and start using the program.

BEFORE YOU INSTALL WORDPERFECT

WordPerfect for Windows is designed to be run from Microsoft Windows version 3.0 or higher, so you must install Windows before installing WordPerfect for Windows. If the Windows program is not installed on your computer, you should follow the instructions in your Windows manual for installing the program, then return to this Appendix.

Before installing WordPerfect for Windows, you should also make sure that your hard disk has about 8MB of available space. You can find out how much space is available by typing the directory command at the DOS prompt (C>), like this:

DIR C:

Then press ↵.

At the end of the listing, you will see a message indicating the number of bytes free: This number should be at least 7300000. If it isn't, you'll need to delete some existing files or see your computer dealer about adding a larger hard disk to your computer.

If you previously installed WordPerfect 5.1 for DOS, and you don't want to reinstall fonts, see "Reusing WordPerfect 5.1 for DOS Fonts" later in this Appendix before deleting any WordPerfect for DOS files.

ANSWERING PROMPTS AND SWAPPING DISKS DURING INSTALLATION

> NOTE
> *The examples and lessons in this book assume that you have installed the entire WordPerfect program and chosen all the default answers.*

During the installation, you may be asked to make some decisions about what to install. For a standard installation, just press ↵ to accept the default choices. Be sure to install the Windows (CUA) keyboard.

The installation program will also tell you when to swap disks and exactly which disk to place in drive A (or drive B). Swap the disks as instructed, then press ↵ to proceed with the installation. If you accidentally put the wrong disk in the drive, the program will beep and ask you to insert the correct one.

INSTALLING WORDPERFECT FOR THE FIRST TIME

If you are installing WordPerfect for Windows for the first time, it's easiest to follow the basic installation procedure, which installs all features WordPerfect offers:

1. Start your computer and get to the DOS command prompt (typically C>). If necessary, exit Windows by choosing E**x**it from the Program Manager menu's **F**ile and choosing OK.

> NOTE
> *If you want to install WordPerfect in a nonstandard directory, choose Custom (option 2); if you are a network supervisor and want to install WordPerfect on a network drive, choose Network (option 3).*

2. Insert the WordPerfect for Windows disk labeled *Install/Program 1* in drive A or B.

3. At the DOS prompt, type **A:INSTALL** (or **B:INSTALL**) and press ↵.

4. You'll see an initial screen asking whether you want to continue. Press ↵ or choose **Y**es.

5. You will see the main menu for installation, shown in Figure A.1. Choose Basic by pressing 1 or B to perform a standard installation in C:\WPWIN and C:\WPC.

NOTE NOTE *This book assumes you've installed the Windows (CUA) keyboard, so be sure to press ↵ (or choose Yes) when asked whether you want to install it.*

6. When prompted "Install from what location: a:\", press ↵ if the Install/Program 1 disk is in drive A, or type **B:** if the installation disk is in drive B.

7. The screen will show the amount of disk space required for Word-Perfect installation, the amount that will remain after installation, and will ask you whether you want to continue. Press ↵ or choose **Yes**.

8. Installation begins. Follow all the on-screen instructions carefully, and swap disks whenever you're prompted, as described in the next section. If asked whether you want to install a certain feature or certain files, choose the default answer by pressing ↵.

9. During installation of the Button Bar, you may be asked which video display monitor you are using, so the program can install appropriate Button Bar graphics for your computer screen (see Figure A.2). Use the arrow keys to move the triangle pointer to the appropriate video display option, then press ↵ to mark the option. When you've marked all options that apply, press F7 to continue. (If you accidentally choose a monitor that you don't have, no harm will result. It's easy to un-mark a marked option: Move the triangle pointer to the option and press ↵ again.)

```
WordPerfect Installation Options              Installation Problems?
                                                   (800) 228-6076

▶ 1 - Basic      Install standard files to default locations, such as c:\wpwin\,
                 c:\wpwin\graphics\, and c:\wpc\.

  2 - Custom     Install standard files to locations you specify.

  3 - Network    Install standard files to a network drive.  Only a network
                 supervisor should use this option.

  4 - Printer    Install additional or updated WordPerfect printer files.

  5 - Interim    Install Interim Release program files.  Use this option only
                 if you are replacing existing WordPerfect for Windows files.

  6 - Copy       Install every file on a diskette to a location you specify
                 (useful for installing all the Printer .ALL files).

  7 - Language   Install additional WordPerfect Language Modules.

  8 - README     View WordPerfect for Windows README files.

Selection: 1                                   (F1 for Help; Esc to exit)
```

FIGURE A.1:

The main menu for installing WordPerfect

```
Button Bar Picture Selection                    Installation Problems?
                                                     (800) 228-6076

  ▶ 1 - Hercules (HERC)
    2 - EGA                          ┌─────────────────────────────┐
    3 - VGA                          │ Different Button Bar picture files │
    4 - MVGA                         │ are available for each type of │
    5 - Super VGA or 8514            │ video display hardware shown. │
                                     │ Select one or more types of │
    6 - All of the above             │ pictures that you want available │
                                     │ your computer.  Then press F7 to │
                                     │ install them. │
                                     │ │
                                     │ When you select a picture type, it │
                                     │ is marked with a diamond (♦). │
                                     │ │
                                     │ Each type of picture file you │
                                     │ select requires approximately 300K │
                                     │ of disk space. │
                                     └─────────────────────────────┘

  Enter Select; F7 Install selected picture types; F1 Help;
  Esc Skip picture file installation

  Selection: 1
```

FIGURE A.2:

Choose one or more video display options to help the installation program locate appropriate Button Bar pictures for your monitor.

10. You'll also be asked to choose one or more printers from a list like the one shown in Figure A.3. As in the previous step, you can move the triangle pointer to a printer name and press ↵ to mark it. After marking each printer name, press F7 to continue.

 You can reuse WordPerfect 5.1 DOS printer fonts with WordPerfect for Windows, as described later.

11. You may be asked whether you want to view the WordPerfect for Windows README files, which provide information that wasn't available when the user manual was printed. You can press Escape to bypass the README files, or you can press ↵ or choose **Y**es to see the screen shown in Figure A.4. Choose options from this screen to view the README files; press Escape when you're finished.

12. When you're informed that the installation procedure is complete, press any key to exit to the DOS command prompt.

13. Remove any floppy disks, then reboot your computer by pressing Ctrl+Alt+Del.

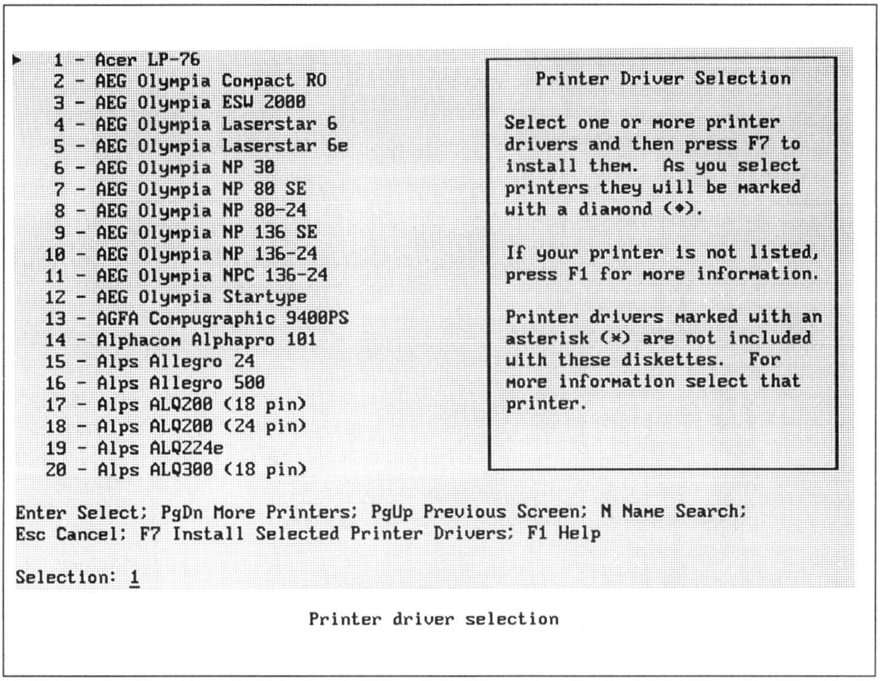

```
▶  1 - Acer LP-76
   2 - AEG Olympia Compact RO
   3 - AEG Olympia ESW 2000            Printer Driver Selection
   4 - AEG Olympia Laserstar 6
   5 - AEG Olympia Laserstar 6e     Select one or more printer
   6 - AEG Olympia NP 30            drivers and then press F7 to
   7 - AEG Olympia NP 80 SE         install them.  As you select
   8 - AEG Olympia NP 80-24         printers they will be marked
   9 - AEG Olympia NP 136 SE        with a diamond (♦).
  10 - AEG Olympia NP 136-24
  11 - AEG Olympia NPC 136-24        If your printer is not listed,
  12 - AEG Olympia Startype          press F1 for more information.
  13 - AGFA Compugraphic 9400PS
  14 - Alphacom Alphapro 101         Printer drivers marked with an
  15 - Alps Allegro 24               asterisk (*) are not included
  16 - Alps Allegro 500              with these diskettes.  For
  17 - Alps ALQ200 (18 pin)          more information select that
  18 - Alps ALQ200 (24 pin)          printer.
  19 - Alps ALQ224e
  20 - Alps ALQ300 (18 pin)

Enter Select; PgDn More Printers; PgUp Previous Screen; N Name Search;
Esc Cancel; F7 Install Selected Printer Drivers; F1 Help

Selection: 1

              Printer driver selection
```

FIGURE A.3:
The Printer Driver selection screen lets you choose printers to use with WordPerfect for Windows.

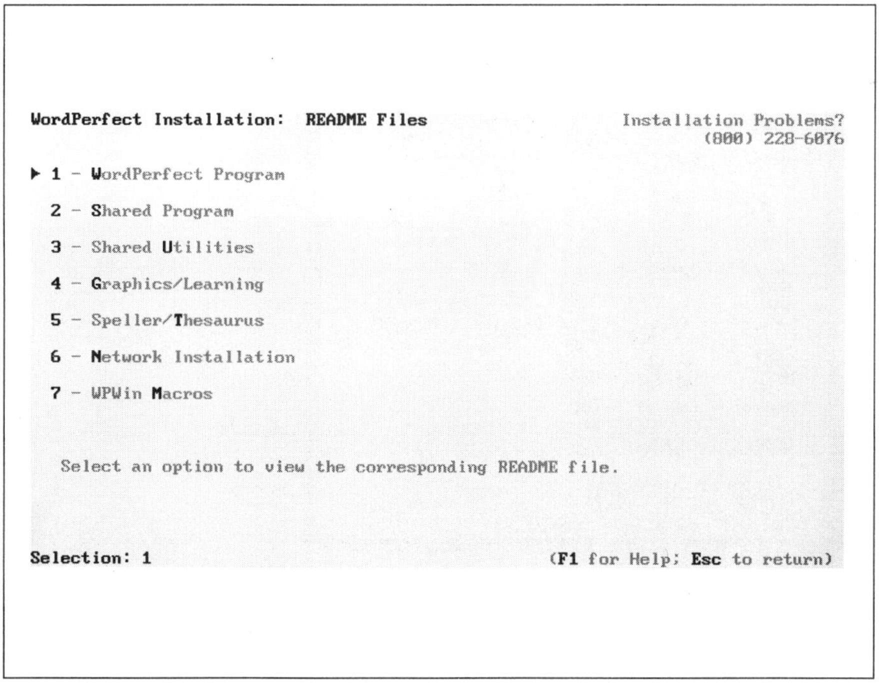

```
WordPerfect Installation:  README Files        Installation Problems?
                                                   (800) 228-6076
▶  1 - WordPerfect Program

   2 - Shared Program

   3 - Shared Utilities

   4 - Graphics/Learning

   5 - Speller/Thesaurus

   6 - Network Installation

   7 - WPWin Macros


    Select an option to view the corresponding README file.


Selection: 1                      (F1 for Help; Esc to return)
```

FIGURE A.4:
You can view README files on various topics by choosing options from this menu.

RUNNING WORDPERFECT
FOR THE FIRST TIME

After installation is complete, you can run WordPerfect for Windows. Follow these steps:

1. Run Windows 3 in the usual manner.

2. If the WordPerfect group window isn't already open, double-click the WordPerfect group icon. Your screen will resemble the one shown in Figure A.5.

3. Double-click the WordPerfect application icon in the WordPerfect group window.

4. Type your license number in the start-up window. You only need to type the license number the first time you start WordPerfect for Windows. The license number is printed on the Certificate of License Registration card that came in your WordPerfect package.

5. Choose OK or press ↵.

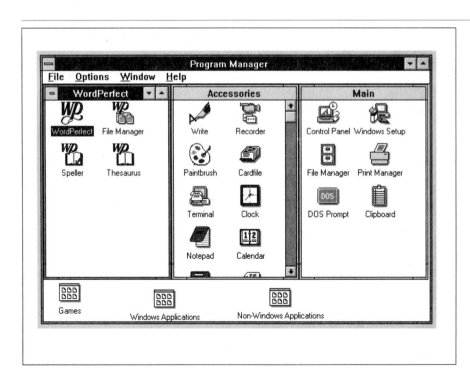

FIGURE A.5:

The WordPerfect group window

REUSING WORDPERFECT 5.1 FOR DOS FONTS

WordPerfect for Windows can reuse your old WordPerfect printer drivers and fonts, which is good news if you've been using WordPerfect 5.1 with fonts supplied by a third-party font manufacturer. After installing WordPerfect for Windows, you can go through the rather time-consuming task of reloading fonts directly from the font manufacturer's disks, or you can complete the following steps for reusing your WordPerfect 5.1 printer fonts with WordPerfect for Windows:

> **NOTE** *If you previously copied the .ALL files from WordPerfect 5.1 to your hard disk, you may also want to copy these from the \WP51 directory to the \WPC directory.*

1. Copy the printer resource (.PRS) files from your old WordPerfect 5.1 directory to the new \WPC directory that was created when you installed WordPerfect for Windows. For example, the following DOS command copies all printer drivers from the \WP51 directory on drive C to the \WPC directory on drive C:

   COPY C:\WP51*.PRS C:\WPC

2. If you used DOS to complete step 1, run Windows and WordPerfect for Windows again.

3. Choose **File** ➤ Se**l**ect Printer from the WordPerfect for Windows pull-down menus. You'll see the Select Printer dialog box.

4. Choose **W**ordPerfect.

5. Choose **A**dd in the Select Printer dialog box.

6. Choose **P**rinter Files (*.prs).

7. Choose whatever driver you want to install from the Add Printer dialog box, then choose **A**dd. You'll return to the Select Printer dialog box.

8. Repeat steps 5–7 to add more drivers, if necessary.

9. Double-click the name of the printer you want to use for future printouts. If you want to use a different printer later, just choose **File** ➤ Se**l**ect Printer and double-click the new printer name.

DOING A PARTIAL INSTALLATION

If you change or add monitors, printers, or networks, or if you want to update your current version of WordPerfect to a more recent interim release provided by WordPerfect Corporation, you can do a partial installation of WordPerfect.

See your Windows manual for information on setting up Windows to work with different printers, monitors, keyboards, mice, or networks.

To perform a partial installation, you need to start from the DOS prompt of your WordPerfect directory. For example, to do a partial installation from the standard C:\WPWIN directory, follow these steps:

1. Start from the DOS prompt (C>).

2. Type **CD C:\WPWIN** and press ↵. (If you installed WordPerfect on a different drive or directory, type that drive or directory name and press ↵.)

3. Type **INSTALL** and press ↵ again.

4. Press ↵ or choose **Y**es when asked whether you want to continue. You will see the main installation menu (shown earlier in Figure A.1).

5. Follow the instructions and answer the prompts on the screen.

Here is a brief description of each installation menu option:

If you reinstall an existing printer, you'll lose any additional fonts and paper sizes that may already have been created for that printer. You will need to redefine them.

Custom	Lets you install WordPerfect files on the drive and in the directories of your choosing.
Network	Used by the network supervisor to install WordPerfect for use on a network.
Printer	Lets you install the driver for a new printer or several printers. You'll need to have handy the Printers disks from your WordPerfect package after choosing this option (you'll then see instructions for installing the printer driver).
Interim	Lets you install Interim Release files provided by the WordPerfect Corporation Software Subscription Service. Choosing this option displays the menu shown in Figure A.6. Choose one or more options to selectively update your WordPerfect files. (You can use ↑ or ↓ to move from option to option on this menu. As you do so, a brief explanation of the option appears in the box near the bottom of the screen.)
Copy	Decompresses and copies all the compressed files from installation disks to another disk (or other disks).
Language	Lets you install modules for foreign languages

After you choose an option, you'll see instructions for completing the installation, like the instructions presented during the basic installation.

```
WordPerfect Interim Release Installation        Installation Problems?
                                                    (800) 228-6076

▶ 1 - WordPerfect Program                   Select an option to update the
                                            corresponding set of files.
  2 - Shared Programs

  3 - Shared Utilities

  4 - Graphics/Learning

  5 - Language Module

  6 - Printer

  7 - Exit Install

   ┌──────────────────────────────────────────────────────────────┐
   │ The WordPerfect Program option installs the updated WordPerfect for │
   │ Windows program files.                                         │
   └──────────────────────────────────────────────────────────────┘

Selection: 1                              (F1 for Help; Esc to return)

          WordPerfect Interim Release Installation screen
```

The WordPerfect Interim Release Installation screen lets you install interim releases of WordPerfect for Windows.

TECHNICAL OPTIONS AND TROUBLESHOOTING

This section provides some technical information that will be of interest mainly to technical support personnel responsible for installing and setting up Word-Perfect, and to advanced users who are familiar with memory usage, Windows 3, and DOS. It may also help solve some problems in getting WordPerfect to load properly.

MEMORY USAGE

Check your Windows and DOS manuals for details on fine-tuning your memory usage.

You must have an 80286, 80386, or 80486 computer to use WordPerfect for Windows, and you need at least 2MB of memory to run the program. In addition, Windows must be configured to run in standard or 386 enhanced mode.

If WordPerfect can't fit the entire document into memory, the part that doesn't fit into memory spills into overflow files named WP}WP{.TV1 (for text above the insertion point) and WP}WP{.BV1 (for text below the insertion point) in Document 1. If two documents are being edited, the overflow files for the second document have the same name, but with *2* as the last character. WordPerfect can create overflow files for up to nine documents.

When you start up WordPerfect, the program creates a temporary sub-directory, named WP}WP{TD.1, for storing overflow files and temporary buffers. This subdirectory is just below the directory where WPWIN.EXE is located, unless you indicate a different location by using the /D start-up option, as described later.

You can use RAM drives with WordPerfect, although you won't gain much by doing so. A RAM drive lets you use a portion of your computer's extended memory as if it were a hard drive. RAM drives are faster than hard drives because the information is always stored in memory; however, information stored in a RAM drive is lost when you reboot or turn off your computer. If you use a RAM drive, be sure to use the /D start-up option to direct the overflow files, Speller, or Thesaurus to that drive, and also be sure to indicate that drive in the File ➤ Preferences ➤ Location of Files option for the Speller or Thesaurus.

> **N O T E**
> **N O T E** *A RAM drive lets you use a portion of your computer's extended memory as if it were a hard drive. RAM drives are faster than hard drives because the information is always stored in memory; however, information stored in a RAM drive is lost when you reboot or turn off your computer.*

Tips for Conserving Memory

Although Windows 3 manages the memory that WordPerfect uses, you can control the amount of memory available for running WordPerfect by trying one or more of the following techniques. I've divided these sections into three categories, corresponding to things you can try in DOS, in Windows, and in WordPerfect. If all else fails, you should see your computer dealer about adding memory to your computer: The more memory your computer has, the better.

Conserving Memory in DOS Try the following DOS techniques, before you start Windows and WordPerfect for Windows, to increase the amount of memory available to WordPerfect:

◆ Remove any TSR (terminate-and-stay-resident) programs before you start Windows.

◆ Reduce the settings in your FILES= and BUFFERS= lines in your CONFIG.SYS file (but don't reduce FILES= to less than 20).

Conserving Memory in Windows Another way to make more memory available to WordPerfect for Windows is to switch to the Windows Program Manager and try the following techniques:

◆ Reduce the number of programs currently running by closing as many applications windows as possible.

◆ In the Windows Control Panel, set the Wallpaper option in the Desktop dialog box to None.

◆ Delete the Windows Clipboard contents (open the Clipboard application in the Program Manager's Main window and choose **E**dit ➤ **D**elete).

◆ If you are using 386 enhanced mode, run each non-Windows applications in full-screen mode rather than in a window.

◆ Minimize Windows applications to icons by clicking the Minimize button.

Conserving Memory in WordPerfect Try these techniques to free up memory while you're using WordPerfect for Windows:

◆ Reduce the number of open WordPerfect documents by saving and closing one document before opening or creating a new one.

◆ Unselect any selected soft keyboards: Choose **F**ile ➤ **P**references ➤ **K**eyboard, choose **D**efault (CUA), then click OK or press ↵.

◆ Turn off hyphenation (choose **L**ayout ➤ **L**ine ➤ **H**yphenation), or choose the Internal hyphenation dictionary (**F**ile ➤ **P**references ➤ **E**nvironment).

◆ Choose a printer whose .PRS file has only a few fonts.

◆ Do not print in the background.

START-UP OPTIONS

Normally, to start WordPerfect, you just double-click the WordPerfect icon from within the WordPerfect group window. This section presents some optional start-up switches that you can use when starting WordPerfect from the File ➤ Run option on the Windows Program Manager menu.

Follow these general steps:

1. Start Windows in the usual way.

2. Choose **F**ile ➤ **R**un from the Program Manager menu.

3. Type **WPWIN**, followed by any of the start-up switches discussed below. For example, type **WPWIN /m-d:\macros\startup.wcm** to start WordPerfect and run the macro named *startup*.

4. Choose OK or press ↵ to start WordPerfect with the options you specified in step 3.

The following switches start WordPerfect with certain features enabled or disabled. All these switches are optional.

/D-*drive:\directory*	Redirects overflow files and temporary buffers to a drive other than the default drive where the WPWIN.EXE file is located.
filename	Automatically retrieves the specified file from the current directory at start-up. You can also type a complete path name with the file name, as in WPWIN D:\MYMEMOS\MEMO.WP.
/M-*macroname*	Automatically loads and executes the specified macro from the current directory at start-up. You can also type a complete path name with the macro name, as in WPWIN D:\MACROS\STARTUP.WCM.
/NB	Disables the Original Backup option. This is useful when you do not have enough file space to save two copies of the same file.
/NT-*network #*	Tells WordPerfect which network software you are using, such as Novell or Banyan. Each supported network has an assigned network number (*network #*), as described in Appendix M of the WordPerfect documentation.
/PS-*path*	Instructs WordPerfect to use the Setup options stored in the .SET file in the specified path. This is generally used on a network to have WordPerfect use Setup options from a network drive rather than the local drive where WPWIN.EXE is located.
/SA	Forces WordPerfect to start up in standalone mode and ignores the network environment file (.ENV) if it exists.
/U-*username*	Provides the correct user initials to Word-Perfect and allows multiple users to run WordPerfect on a network.
/X	Restores all Preferences options to their original (default) values for this session only. If you exit WordPerfect, then restart it without the /X option, any changes you made to the default preferences will take effect again.

You can also exit Windows and type a SET WPWIN command at the DOS prompt. In this case, the SET command remains in effect until you reboot your computer and issue another SET WPWIN command.

Start-up options can be combined. For example, WPWIN/X/D-F: temporarily restores all Preferences settings to their defaults and redirects overflow files to drive F.

To run start-up options automatically, you can modify the AUTO-EXEC.BAT file to place the start-up command in the DOS environment. For example, if you want to be able simply to double-click the WordPerfect application icon to start WordPerfect, but you want to use the /NB and /D start-up options, put the command

SET WPWIN=/NB/D-F:

in your AUTOEXEC.BAT file.

APPENDIX B

A Windows Primer

! f you're new to computers or just new to Windows, this appendix will be your best starting point, even if you're primarily concerned with learning WordPerfect for Windows. The reason for starting here is that Windows and all Windows applications (programs designed for use with Windows) share certain features, such as dialog boxes, windows, and menus. And the techniques for using these features are the same for all Windows products. That is, they all share a Common User Access (CUA). Therefore, many of the basic skills you'll need to use WordPerfect for Windows are actually contained in this appendix.

I'll begin with a basic discussion of what Windows 3 is all about, then help you get "up and running" so that you can use Windows, and WordPerfect for Windows, effectively.

ABOUT WINDOWS 3

Windows 3 is a graphical environment for using your computer. Windows offers several advantages over its predecessor, DOS, including the following:

◆ Pointing and clicking with a mouse replaces awkward commands and the keyboard-oriented approach to interacting with your computer.

◆ Graphical icons present more information on the screen than is possible with the text-based DOS product, making it easier to find and use features.

◆ The screen is graphical at all times in Windows, so you can see fonts, lines, and graphics as you create and change them. This takes the guesswork out of determining how your final printed document will look.

◆ Several programs can be active at once, and you can easily exchange information between programs; this is not possible with plain DOS alone.

This last feature of Windows, called *multitasking,* is perhaps its most powerful, because it lets you use multiple programs easily. For example, if you're creating a business document that uses business graphics, you can easily use Word-Perfect for Windows to create the text, and you can also easily "drag" a bar chart or other graphic image from a spreadsheet or graphics program into your document.

Furthermore, unlike DOS, you don't need to wait for one program to finish a job before using another. For example, if you're printing a lengthy document and want to run another program, you can just run that other program. The document will keep printing while you continue to be productive with whatever it is you need to do.

STARTING WINDOWS 3

*To start Windows automatically when you first turn on your computer, make **WIN** the last command in your AUTOEXEC.BAT file.*

Depending on how your computer is configured, Windows 3 may appear on your screen when you turn on the computer. In this case, you'll see the Microsoft Windows version 3.x introductory screen briefly, followed by the actual Windows program. The exact appearance depends on how Windows has been configured, but typically you'll see the Program Manager window with some icons in it, as in Figure B.1. (The background on your screen may not look like the crinkled paper shown in the illustration, and different icons may appear within the window, but don't worry about that.)

If Windows 3 does not appear automatically when you first start your computer, follow these steps to start your system and Windows:

See "Changing the Wallpaper" later in this appendix if you'd like your screen to show the "crinkled paper" Desktop.

1. If you have not done so already, start your computer and printer as instructed in whatever directions came with your computer.

2. When the computer's self-test is done, you'll see either the DOS command prompt (typically C>) or perhaps a DOS shell.

3. If a DOS shell (other than Windows 3) appears, exit that shell (typically by pressing the key labeled F3). This should take you to the DOS command prompt (typically C>).

If you have trouble locating keys such as ↵, refer to Chapter 1.

4. Type **WIN** and press ↵.

At this point, you should see the Windows 3 screen, looking something like Figure B.1. If you see a message such as "Bad command or file name" instead, then either Windows hasn't been installed yet or it requires an unusual start-up procedure on your computer. If you share a computer and can't get Windows started, your best bet is to ask an experienced user exactly how to start Windows on your computer.

If Windows 3 is not yet installed on your computer, see your User's Guide for installation instructions.

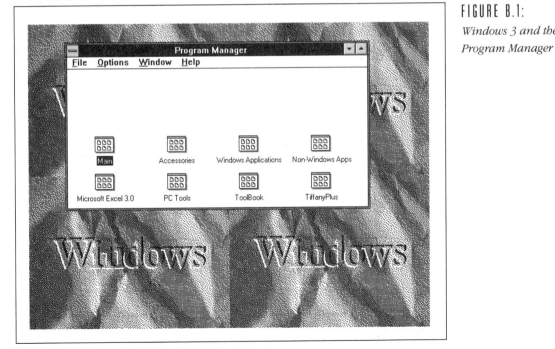

FIGURE B.1:

Windows 3 and the Program Manager

THE DESKTOP AND WINDOWS

When Windows is running, the entire screen is called the *Desktop,* based on the notion that the computer screen acts like a miniature desktop on which you do work. A *window* is any framed area on the Desktop. For example, Figure B.1 shows the entire Desktop, with the Program Manager window displayed on top. As you'll soon see, you can arrange windows on the Windows Desktop just as you'd arrange papers and other items on your actual desk.

ABOUT YOUR MOUSE

Perhaps the most important tool for managing windows and other items on the Windows Desktop is the mouse (or a trackball, which is similar to a mouse). As you move the mouse on your desktop or mouse pad, the arrow-shaped *mouse pointer* on your screen moves in the same direction. If Windows is running right now, you can see this for yourself simply by moving your mouse or trackball.

To position the mouse pointer in an area on the screen, simply move the mouse in the direction you want to go until the pointer points to whatever item you want it to point to.If you run out of room on your desktop or mouse pad, lift the mouse and put it down again where you have more room, then continue moving the mouse.

Here are some terms used to describe basic mouse operations; I use these terms throughout this book and show many examples of these operations in this appendix.

Click or single-click	Position the mouse pointer, then press and release the left mouse button.
Right-click	Position the mouse pointer, then press and release the right mouse button.
Double-click	Position the mouse pointer, then press and release the left mouse button twice in rapid succession (as quickly as you can).
Drag	Position the mouse pointer, hold down the left mouse button, move the mouse pointer to its new destination, then release the mouse button. (This is also called *clicking and dragging* in some computer literature, but that term can be misleading since you don't actually click the mouse button after positioning the mouse pointer; you just hold it down.)

ABOUT YOUR KEYBOARD

Though using the mouse is the most natural and intuitive means of interacting with Windows, virtually all operations can be performed from the keyboard. Many operations require *combination keystrokes,* which are indicated as *key + key.* That is, when you see two key names separated by a plus sign (+), it means you should hold down the first key, press the second key, then release both keys. For example, the keystrokes Ctrl+Tab mean "hold down the Ctrl key, press the Tab key, then release both keys."

If you are not already familiar with the computer keyboard and don't know the location of the function keys, ↵, Tab, and other special keys, see Chapter 1 for a keyboard map pointing out the location of these keys.

MANAGING WINDOWS

To use this appendix as a reference to Windows buttons and icons, just scan the left margin for whatever icon or button you're curious about.

Learning to use Windows effectively is largely a matter of learning how to open, close, size, and position windows and icons at will. Most windows have certain elements in common, such as various buttons, icons, scroll bars, and other items identified below (see Figure B.2). I'll describe the purposes of these elements and how to use them in the sections that follow.

OPENING A WINDOW

The Program Manager window is generally the first window to appear when you start Windows, so I'll use that window as the starting point in describing general techniques for managing windows. Each *icon* in the Program Manager window represents a window that's currently closed. To open a window,

◆ Double-click the icon or name of the icon that you want to open.

If you prefer to use the keyboard rather than the mouse,

1. Hold down the Ctrl key and press Tab until the name of the window you want to open is highlighted.

2. Press ↵.

For example, if you double-click the Main icon in the Program Manager window (or use Ctrl-Tab and ↵), the Main window will open and your screen will look something like Figure B.3.

Notice that the window name, *Main* in this example, appears in the window's title bar, and the Main window has its own set of icons. You could

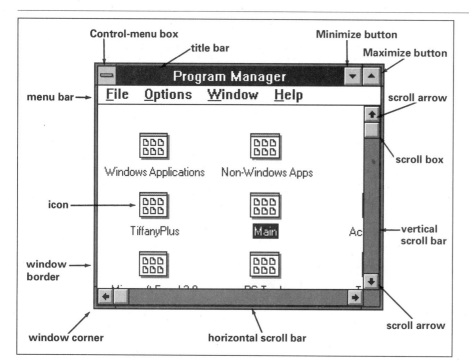

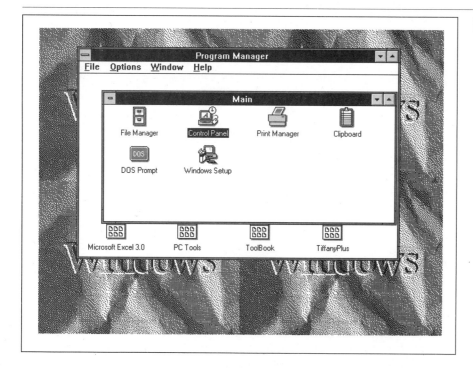

On keyboards that share the arrow and other special cursor keys with the numeric keypad, the Num Lock key must be off for those keys to work properly.

open any of these windows by double-clicking whichever icon you wish. However, to open one of these *program item icons* with the keyboard, you use the arrow keys, rather than Ctrl and Tab, to highlight the icon you want, then press ↵. I'll discuss the different types of icons in more detail a little later.

TYPES OF WINDOWS

There are actually two main types of windows you'll encounter when using the Windows program (and WordPerfect for Windows): *application windows* and *document windows*. An application window contains a running application (program). The Program Manager window is an example of an application window. A document window is opened up by an application window, and is, in a sense, a part of the application window that opened it. A document window has the same menu bar as the application window that holds its icon; therefore, a document window has no menu bar of its own. The Main window is an example of a document window.

For the most part, you'll use the same techniques to open, close, resize, and move both application and document windows. A few differences are worth noting, however. The most important ones are listed below:

◆ You can place application windows anywhere on the Desktop, but document windows can (usually) only be moved within the application window that holds them.

◆ Similarly, an application window can be sized however you wish, from very small to the size of the entire screen. A document window, however, can only be sized to fit within its application window. That is, it can be quite small, but its maximum size is determined by the size of its application window, not the entire screen. Furthermore, some document windows (those with narrow borders) can't be sized at all; they can only be moved, opened, or closed.

◆ Although document windows lack a menu bar, they have their own title bar, Control-menu box, and Maximize and Minimize buttons. When working with a document window, be sure to use the appropriate document-window title bar, Control-menu box, and buttons, and not those in the application window.

CLOSING A WINDOW

When you've finished using a window, you can close it to get it out of the way.

1. Click the Control-menu box in the upper-left corner of the window you want to close. You'll see this menu:

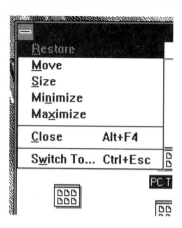

2. Click the **C**lose option.

 *Remember, a plus sign separating two keys signifies a combination keystroke.*

If you're using the keyboard rather than the mouse, you can press Alt+− to open the Control-menu box for a document window; you can press Alt+spacebar to open the Control-menu box for an application window. Then press **C** to choose Close.

Either way, the window closes, shrinking back to its original icon size. To try this out for yourself, go ahead and close the Main window if you've opened it: Position the mouse pointer on the Control-menu box in the Main document window, at the left of the title bar that contains the title *Main,* and click the left mouse button. Then move the mouse pointer down to the Close option on that menu, and click the left mouse button again. Or, press Alt+− and press C.

 As a shortcut for closing most windows, double-click the window's Control-menu box.

SIZING A WINDOW FROM ITS BORDERS

There are many ways to control the size, shape, and position of windows. It's important to know how to do this in case a newly opened window overlaps or completely hides some other window you need to access.

You can change the size of most windows by dragging any of the four sides or four corners of the window with your mouse.

The borders of windows that can be sized are fairly thick; the borders of windows that cannot be sized are like thin pencil lines.

1. Move the mouse pointer to any side or corner of the window border you want to resize. The pointer will change to a two-headed arrow when it's properly placed.

2. Drag the corner or side until the window is the size you want. If you drag a side, the window size changes only on that side. If you drag a corner, the two adjoining sides of the corner change size at the same time. An outline shows the size and shape of the window as you drag.

3. Release the mouse button when the window is the size you want.

To try this for yourself, use your mouse now to reduce the size of the Program Manager window on your screen. Depending on how small you size the window, scroll bars may appear along the left and right borders of the window.

If you reduce the size of the window enough, some of its icons may seem to disappear. You can use the scroll bars (described shortly) to view other icons or rearrange the icons in the window to bring them back into view using techniques described under "Using Icons" a little later in this appendix. Or, you can just increase the size of the window so that all of its icons are visible, as described next.

USING THE KEYBOARD TO SIZE A WINDOW

To size a window using the keyboard, either press Alt+– (for a document window) or Alt+spacebar (for an application window) to open the window's Control-menu box. Press S to select Size, then use the arrow keys to size the window. Press ↵ when the window is sized to your liking.

MAXIMIZING THE SIZE OF A WINDOW

If a particular window is too small to show all the information you need to see, or if you just want to get rid of distractions, you can expand the window to full-screen size. This is called *maximizing* the window. Here's the technique:

 ◆ Click the Maximize button (the one with an upward-pointing arrow) in the upper-right corner of the window you want to enlarge.

To try this, click the Maximize button in the upper-right corner of the Program Manager window. Regardless of its previous size, the window now fills the entire screen, as in Figure B.4. Notice, however, that the title bar, menu bar, and various buttons still appear near the top of the window.

To maximize a window from the keyboard, open the Control-menu box for that window, and press X to choose the Maximize option.

RESTORING A WINDOW TO ITS PREVIOUS SIZE

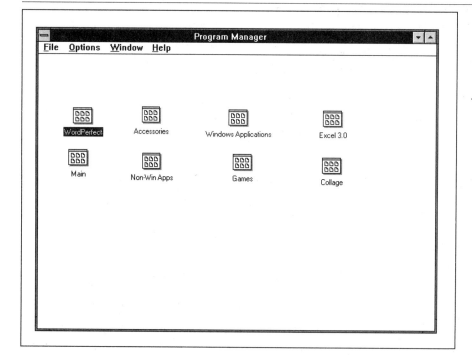

When you've maximized a window using the Maximize button, the button itself changes to the Restore button, with both up- and down-pointing arrows, as you can see in the upper-right corner of Figure B.4. Use the Restore button to return the window to its previous size:

◆ Click the Restore button (which has the double arrows) in the upper-right corner of the window.

Try this technique now to return the Main window to its previous size.

If you're using the keyboard, you can restore the window to its previous size by opening the Control-menu box (press Alt+spacebar or Alt+−) and pressing R to choose Restore.

FIGURE B.4:

The Program Manager window has been maximized to full-screen size.

Shrinking a Window to an Icon

 As an alternative to closing a window, you can shrink it to an icon to get it out of your way. This is called *minimizing* the window.

◆ Click the Minimize button (the one with a downward-pointing arrow) near the upper-right corner of the window you want to close.

If you're using the keyboard, you can minimize a window by opening its Control-menu box and pressing N to choose Minimize.

The window will shrink to the size of an icon, as shown in Figure B.5. *Application* icons appear on the Desktop near the bottom of the screen, and *document* icons just return to their original icon size within their application windows. To see how this works, click the Minimize button in the upper-right corner of the Program Manager window to shrink it to an icon in the lower-left corner of the Desktop.

Reopening a window that's been minimized to an icon is the same as opening any other window: You just double-click its icon. If you're following

FIGURE B.5:

Minimized windows appear as icons.

Program Manager window reduced to an icon

along, go ahead and double-click the Program Manager window to reopen it.

Reopening a minimized (or closed) document window from the keyboard is the same as opening it for the first time: Press Ctrl+Tab until the document you want is selected (highlighted), then press ↵. To reopen a minimized application window, press Alt+Escape until the icon name you want to reopen is highlighted. Then press Alt+spacebar to open its Control-menu box, and press R to choose Restore. (Optionally, you can use the Task List, described later.)

CLOSING A WINDOW VS. MINIMIZING IT

Although closing and minimizing both shrink an application window into an icon, some important differences exist between the two procedures:

♦ When you *close* an application window, the program running in that window stops running.

♦ When you *minimize* an application window, the program continues to run, even though its window is reduced to the size of an icon.

Keep in mind that these differences apply only to *application* windows, not document windows. When you close or minimize a document window, the result is the same: The window shrinks back to an icon within its application window (a document window does not contain a running program). You can use whichever method is most convenient at the moment.

But getting back to application windows, you might ask why you would want to minimize an application window rather than close it. To answer this question, let's assume you want to use three different programs during your current Windows session: WordPerfect for Windows, Excel, and ToolBook. Furthermore, you want to share information between them, or at least be able to flip back and forth from program to program freely.

In this case, it's more convenient to minimize the programs not currently in use than to close them. First, when you minimize the program, whatever work you're doing at the moment is minimized with the program. This is much simpler than saving your work and closing (exiting) the program. Second, when you simply minimize the program, its icon remains available near the lower-left corner of the screen, as shown in Figure B.6. When you later want to go back to that program, you just have to double-click its icon. The program, and whatever work you were doing when you minimized it, appears instantly on your screen. This is always much simpler and quicker than starting the program from scratch with the Program Manager and reopening whatever work you were doing before you closed the program.

You can easily flip back and forth between programs in this manner all day long if you wish. At the end of the day, or when you've finished working with your Windows programs, *then* you'll probably want to save all your work and close all the open windows before exiting Windows and turning off the computer. But up until that time, you'll probably find it more convenient to simply shrink running applications to icons and reopen them from icons as needed.

MOVING A WINDOW

You can control the position of a window just as easily as you can control its size. To move a window, follow these steps:

NOTE *Most document windows can only be moved within the application window that holds them.*

1. Move the mouse pointer to the title bar of the window you want to move.

2. Drag the window to wherever you want it on the Desktop.

3. Release the mouse button.

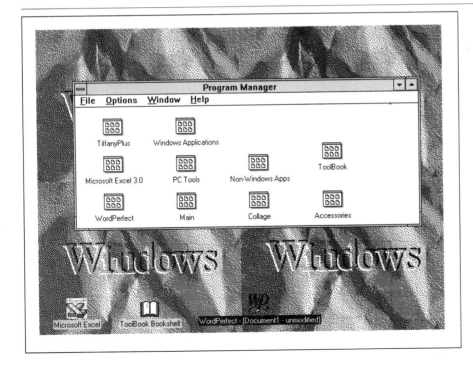

FIGURE B.6:

Excel and ToolBook are still running and readily available, but they are out of the way because they're minimized.

You can practice this technique now by dragging the Main document window to a new position inside the Program Manager window. If you position the window such that the Control-menu box or Minimize and Maximize buttons are obscured, you can just reposition the window to bring whatever box or button is obscured back into view when you need one of them.

To move a window using the keyboard, open that window's Control-menu box (using Alt+− or Alt+spacebar), press M to choose Move, use the arrow keys to position the window, then press ↵.

USING SCROLL BARS

Some windows and dialog boxes (explained below) have *scroll bars*, which are used to view text or icons that can't be seen at the moment. Earlier I showed the elements of a window with a scroll bar, which includes the scroll bar itself, a scroll box, and two scroll arrows. Here are some techniques for using a scroll bar to bring hidden text or icons into view:

◆ Drag the scroll box to a position in the scroll bar corresponding to the general location where you want to work.

◆ Repeatedly click the left or right scroll arrow (on a horizontal scroll bar) or the top or bottom scroll arrow (on a vertical scroll bar) to scroll by small increments in the direction of the arrow.

◆ Move the mouse pointer to a scroll arrow and hold down the left mouse button until the information you want comes into view, then release the button.

◆ Click to the left or right of the scroll box (on a horizontal scroll bar) or above or below the scroll box (on a vertical scroll bar) to scroll horizontally or vertically a full window at a time.

You can try these techniques by resizing the Main or Program Manager window to a very small size by dragging one of its corners. When the window is too small to display all its icons, the scroll bars will appear (after you release the mouse button). Then use the scroll bars to scroll through the various icons inside the window.

You can also use the following keys to scroll through a window when scroll bars are visible:

TO MOVE	PRESS
Up, down, left, or right	↑, ↓, ←, →

TO MOVE	PRESS
Page up or down	Page Up, Page Down
Page left or right	Ctrl+Page Up, Ctrl+Page Down
Start of line	Home
End of line	End
Top of text	Ctrl+Home
End of text	Ctrl+End

ACTIVATING A WINDOW

You'll often have several document and application windows open on your Desktop at once. But only one window—the one you're currently working with—can be *active* at any given time.Furthermore, you can only use (i.e., move, size, open, close) the active window. To activate a window so that you can use it,

◆   Click anywhere in the window you want to activate.

The active window will always be displayed in the foreground. That is, it will either partially or fully cover any windows or icons beneath it. Also, the title bar of the active window is also colored differently, or shown in reverse video, and if several document windows are open, only the active window shows the Control-menu box and the Maximize and Minimize buttons. So you can easily see at a glance which window is active at the moment.

If the window you want to activate is not visible, because it's covered by a larger window or maximized window, there are a few techniques you can use to uncover the hidden window:

◆   Move the window that's covering the one you want by dragging its title bar out of the way.

◆   Minimize whatever window is covering the one you want using that window's Minimize button.

◆   Size the window that's covering the one you want so that part or all of the hidden window is visible.

◆   Press Ctrl+Escape to open the Task List. Then double-click the name of the program that you want to activate. This brings the window for that application to the foreground.

Use the Task List to switch out of a full-screen DOS application that you started from within Windows.

The last option works only for application windows, not document windows. To activate a document window when several are active, press Ctrl+Tab until the document window you want is in the foreground. This technique cycles through all the open and closed document windows in the current application window.

USING MENUS

In a restaurant, a menu is a list of meals to choose from. On your computer screen, a menu is a list of features or *commands* to choose from. Application windows have a menu bar just beneath the title bar. For example, looking back at Figure B.1, you can see the Program Manager menu bar with the options File, Options, Window, and Help.

When you choose an option from the menu bar, a *pull-down* menu usually appears. For example, Figure B.7 shows the Window pull-down menu, which appears after clicking Window on the menu bar.

Much of your work with Windows and Windows applications (including WordPerfect for Windows) will involve choosing options from menus. There are several ways to choose menu options; you can use whichever techniques work best for you.

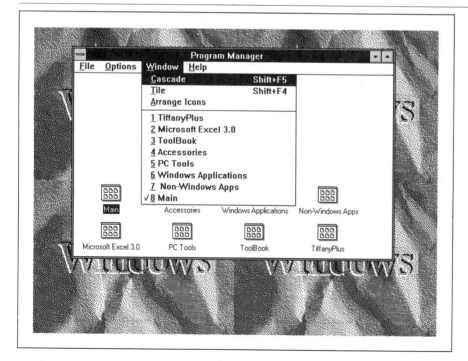

FIGURE B.7:

The Window pull-down menu

CHOOSING MENU OPTIONS WITH THE MOUSE

Perhaps the easiest way to work with menus is to choose menu options with your mouse. Here's how:

◆ Click the option you want to choose.

This technique works for options on the menu bar as well as options within a pull-down menu.

CANCELING MENUS WITH THE MOUSE

If you inadvertently choose an item from the menu bar, and a pull-down menu appears, you can close the pull-down menu without making a selection:

◆ Click the menu name or any empty space outside the menu.

To see how this works, click the Window option on the Program Manager menu bar, then click an empty area of the screen to cancel the selection.

CHOOSING MENU OPTIONS WITH THE KEYBOARD

You can also choose menu options using the keyboard:

1. Hold down the Alt key and press the underlined letter of the option you want.

2. Release both keys.

For example, to open the Window pull-down menu, hold down the Alt key, press W, then release both keys. Once a pull-down menu is displayed, you can choose any option from that menu by pressing the underlined letter, without the Alt key. For example, after pulling down the Window menu, you can choose Tile by pressing T.

Here is another way to use the keyboard to choose items from menus:

1. Press and release the Alt key. This highlights the first item on the menu bar.

2. Use the arrow keys to highlight the option you want to choose. Press ↑ or ↓ to move *within* a menu. Press ← or → to move *across* the menu bar.

3. Press ↵ when the option you want to choose is highlighted.

Again, this method works for both menu bar options and pull-down menu options.

CANCELING MENUS WITH THE KEYBOARD

If you want to leave a pull-down menu without making a choice,

◆ Press and release the Alt key, the F10 key, or the Escape key twice.

If a menu selection opened a window, and you want to leave that window without making a choice,

◆ Click the Cancel button in the window, or close the window by double-clicking its Control-menu box or by pressing Alt+F4.

MENU SYMBOLS

A few sample menus from Windows are shown in Figure B.8. Notice that the menus use several symbols, which are described below.

SYMBOL	MEANING
...	An ellipsis after the name indicates that choosing the menu option will take you to a *dialog box* (described below), where you will be asked for additional information.
Dimmed (grayed)	A dimmed option is currently unavailable, most likely because it is not applicable at the moment.

FIGURE B.8:

Sample menus

SYMBOL	MEANING
Check mark (✓)	A check mark next to the name indicates that an option is currently active ("on"). Check marks are used to mark lists of *toggle* options that can be either on or off. Options in the list are often related, and sometimes you can check more than one option.
Triangle	A right-pointing triangle to the right of the name indicates that choosing the option presents another, cascading menu of additional commands you can choose.
Shortcut key	A key name (such as Del) or combination keystroke (such as Shift+F4, Ctrl+O, or Alt+Esc) appears next to a command name when you can use a keyboard *shortcut* to activate a command, instead of opening the menu and choosing menu options.

The optional shortcut keystrokes are handy when you become proficient with your keyboard and want to choose frequently used commands by pressing a key or two, rather than by choosing options from menus.

You'll see some menus and menu options in action in the sections that follow.

USING ICONS

You've already seen how to open a window by double-clicking its icon and how to shrink a window to an icon by closing it or using the Minimize button. Windows 3 actually uses three basic types of icons, as shown in Figure B.9 and described below:

◆ *Document icons* represent minimized document windows. These appear within an application window. All document icons look the same—like a collection of papers with the upper-right corner folded in, as you can see in Figure B.9.

◆ *Program item icons* appear within the Program Manager document windows when opened (as in the Accessories window shown in Figure B.9), and each represents an application or document you can start up from the Program Manager.

◆ *Application icons* appear after you start up an application and use the Minimize button. Application icons appear at the bottom edge of your Desktop, outside the window borders, and they resemble the program item icons that start the application.

MOVING ICONS

You can easily move icons using the same dragging technique used to move an entire window:

1. Move the mouse pointer to the icon you want to move.

2. Drag the icon to wherever you want it to appear.

3. Release the mouse button.

You can move a document icon, or program icon, anywhere within its window, but not outside the borders of that window. You can move an application icon to any position on the screen.

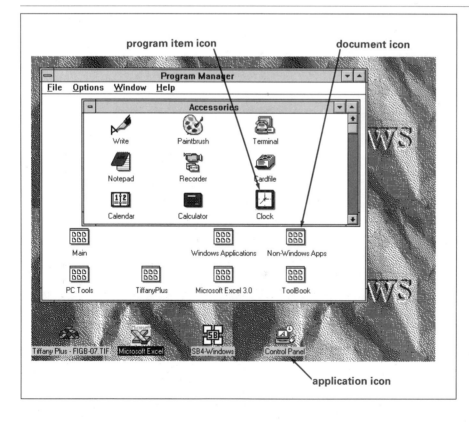

FIGURE B.9:

Three types of icons

REARRANGING ICONS

After resizing a window you might not be able to see all the icons in it, or they may be too disorganized to satisfy your desire for a tidy computer desktop. These problems are easily solved by rearranging the icons:

You can choose the Auto Arrange command from the Program Manager's Options menu to have Windows automatically rearrange program item icons whenever you resize their document window.

1. Choose the **W**indow option on the Program Manager menu bar (by clicking that option or by pressing Alt+W).

2. Choose the **A**rrange Icons option from the menu that appears (by clicking that option or by pressing A).

The icons within the window will rearrange themselves to fit within the new window size as best as they can. If the window is too small to display all its icons, you can use the scroll bars to see the hidden icons, or you can enlarge the window with the resizing techniques described earlier.

REARRANGING DOCUMENT WINDOWS

In addition to rearranging icons, you can also rearrange document windows within their application window. This is handy when you've opened many document windows, some of which might overlap or completely cover another window or icon.

1. Choose the **W**indow option on the application window's menu bar.

2. Choose the **C**ascade or **T**ile option from the menu that appears.

Rearranging application windows is described under "Switching among Applications" later in this appendix.

The Cascade option arranges the document windows so that each window's title bar is visible, making it easy to activate any given window by clicking its title bar—that window "jumps" to the foreground. The Tile option arranges the open windows in smaller sizes using a tile-like setup, so you can see every open window at once.

Figures B.10 and B.11 illustrate the difference between the two options. Figure B.10 shows several cascaded windows; Figure B.11 shows the same windows tiled.

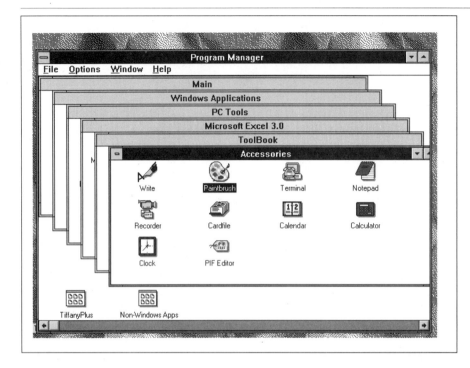

FIGURE B.10:
Multiple cascaded windows

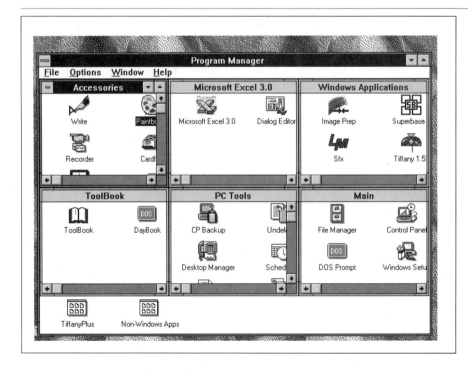

FIGURE B.11:
Multiple tiled windows

USING THE CONTROL-MENU BOX

 The Control-menu box, which appears in the upper-left corner of most windows, contains several alternatives for sizing and moving a window and for performing other tasks. To view those options, do either of the following:

◆ Click the Control-menu box for the window you want to work with.

◆ Press Alt+spacebar to open the Control menu for an application window, or press Alt+– to open the Control menu for a document window.

NOTE *The Control menu will also appear if you single-click a minimized icon.*

As an example, Figure B.12 shows the Control menu for the Main window. After the Control menu appears on the screen, you can choose any available (undimmed) option as described in "Using Menus" above.

Here is a list of the most common Control-menu options:

Restore: restores a maximized or minimized window to its previous size.

Move: lets you move the window using the arrow keys rather than the mouse.

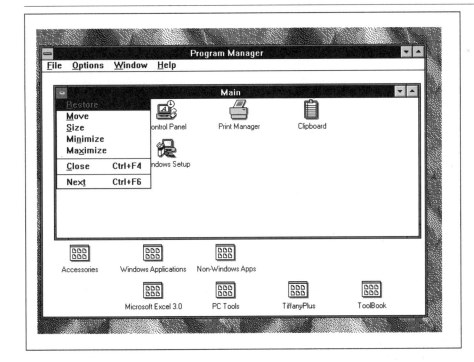

FIGURE B.12:

The Control menu for the Main window

Size: lets you change the size of the window using the keyboard rather than the mouse.

Minimize: shrinks the window to an icon (same as the Minimize button).

Maximize: enlarges the window to its maximum size (same as the Maximize button).

Close: closes the window (exits Windows if chosen from the Program Manager window).

Switch To...: takes you to the Task List, which lets you switch to any application (program) that's currently running. The Task List is described in "Switching among Applications" below. (This option is available only in application windows, such as the Program Manager.)

Next: takes you to the next available document window if several document windows are open. (This option is only available for document windows.)

RUNNING APPLICATIONS

 Certain DOS-based programs such as CHKDSK /F and Norton Utilities' SD.EXE, that change the file allocation table, undelete files, or perform disk compaction or optimization, should not be run inside Windows. Be sure to exit Windows before running these programs.

In the Windows world, a program is known as an *application*. WordPerfect for Windows, Microsoft Excel, the Windows Clock accessory, and the Program Manager are all examples of applications. Windows 3 lets you run more than one application at a time, and it lets you switch among running applications at will.

Applications that were designed to use the Windows 3 graphical environment are called *Windows applications,* and those developed to run under MS-DOS are called *non-Windows applications,* or just DOS applications. WordPerfect 5.1, which was developed before Windows was available, is an example of a non-Windows application. You can run both Windows and non-Windows applications within Windows 3. Non-Windows applications usually run in a full-screen window (temporarily obscuring Windows applications), unless you are using *386 enhanced mode*. (Modes are explained in "Windows Operating Modes" at the end of this appendix.)

STARTING AN APPLICATION

To start an application, you just open its window by double-clicking its icon.

1. Open the Program Manager window if it isn't already open.

2. Open the group (document) window containing the application you want to start by double-clicking it. Typical group windows include Windows Applications, Non-Windows Applications, Games, Main, and Accessories.

3. Double-click the icon for the application you want to run.

From the keyboard, you need to press Ctrl+Tab until the group window you want is highlighted, then press ↵ to open that window. Within that window, use the arrow keys to highlight the name of the program you want to start, then press ↵.

Every Windows application that you start appears in its own application window. So, aside from the fact that you can start using that application once it's open, you can also move, size, shrink, or close its window—all those things described in "Managing Windows" earlier in this appendix.

NOTE
NOTE

Starting an application is sometimes called launching, or opening, an application.

SWITCHING AMONG APPLICATIONS

When several applications are running, you can easily switch from one to another simply by activating the application's window. Remember, the active window always appears in the foreground with its title bar highlighted.

Windows 3 offers several ways to switch from one application to another, and you can choose whichever way is most convenient. If the application is currently running in an open application window, use either of these techniques:

◆ Click anywhere in the application window you want to activate.

◆ Press Alt+Escape repeatedly until the open window you want is active.

If the application you want to switch to is currently running as a minimized application icon, do either of the following:

◆ Double-click the icon.

◆ Press Alt+Tab until that icon is highlighted, then release the Alt key.

As an alternative, you can use the Task List, shown in Figure B.13, to switch among application windows. Here are the steps for using the Task List:

1. Double-click anywhere on the Desktop (outside all windows) to open the Task List at that position on the Desktop. Or, press Ctrl+Escape, or choose Switch To from any application window's Control-menu box.

Pressing Ctrl+Escape lets you choose which running application you want to switch to; pressing Alt+Escape cycles through all running applications.

2. Double-click the application name you want from the list shown in the Task List box (or click the application name, then click the Switch To button).

Here's the keyboard method for using the Task List. This is especially handy if you are working from within a non-Windows application:

1. Press Ctrl+Escape to display the Task List.

2. Press ↑ or ↓ to highlight the application you want.

3. Press ↵ to choose the application.

If you are running Windows in 386 enhanced mode (see "Windows Operating Modes" later in this appendix), and a full-screen non-Windows application is covering the screen, you can switch between full-screen and windowed mode for that application by pressing Ctrl+↵.

REARRANGING APPLICATION WINDOWS

Notice that the Task List window also contains three command buttons labeled Cascade, Tile, and Arrange Icons. These arrange open application windows

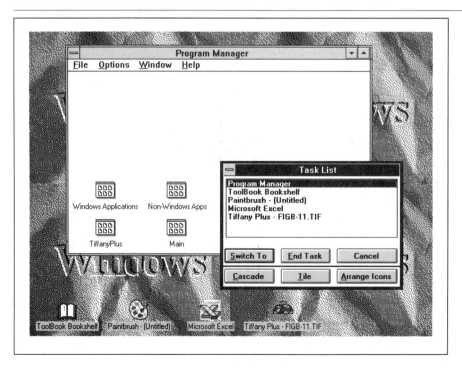

FIGURE B.13:

The Task List lets you switch to any application on the list.

and icons like their counterparts for document windows on the Window pull-down menu.

EXITING APPLICATIONS

After you're finished using a Windows application and no longer need to leave it running, you can exit in one of four ways:

◆ Double-click the application's Control-menu box.

◆ Click the application's Control-menu box, then click Close.

◆ Click the application's **F**ile menu, then click **E**xit (sometimes Exit will be on a Settings or an Options menu if the application doesn't have a File menu).

◆ Go to the Task List, highlight the name of the application you want to exit, then click the End Task command button.

If you are running a non-Windows application from Windows, you'll need to go to that application (using the Task List), then exit it normally. For example, to exit WordPerfect 5.1 (for DOS) after starting it from within Windows, you still select File ➤ Exit or press Exit (F7), just as though you'd started that program from DOS.

If you've accessed the DOS command prompt from within Windows *without* actually exiting Windows (by clicking the DOS Prompt icon in the Main window), type **EXIT** and press ↵ to return to Windows.

Remember, closing an application terminates that application, so it is no longer running and no longer in memory. If you simply want to shrink the application to an icon, so it's out of the way but still running and readily available, click the Minimize button to the right of that application window's title bar.

USING DIALOG BOXES

A *dialog box* appears whenever you choose a menu option that requires additional information or when an application needs to display some information or warnings. You complete a dialog by filling in the missing information or clicking a command button to carry out the command.

Any dialog box can contain a number of elements, including command buttons, drop-down lists, scroll bars, and more (see Figure B.14). You'll have many opportunities to use all the features described in this section when you start using WordPerfect for Windows. But for now, I'll point out some of these features and summarize the many techniques available for using them.

MOVING WITHIN A DIALOG BOX

Some dialog boxes offer many options, and you may need to move around within the dialog box to make choices. The current option within a dialog box is highlighted, outlined with a dashed line, or both. To move from one option to the next, you can do either of the following:

◆ Move the mouse pointer to the option you want.

◆ Press Tab (to move forward) or Shift+Tab (to move backward) to move to the item you want.

If the option you want has an underlined letter, you can choose the option by holding down the Alt key and typing the underlined letter in the option name.

If you're an experienced DOS user, your natural inclination may be to press ↵ to move from one option to the next within a dialog box. However, pressing ↵ usually closes a dialog box. So you may need to make an extra effort to remember to press Tab instead of ↵, or try to remember to use your mouse whenever a dialog box appears.

TIP *If the insertion point is not currently in a text box or list, you can choose an option by typing the underlined letter, without holding down the Alt key.*

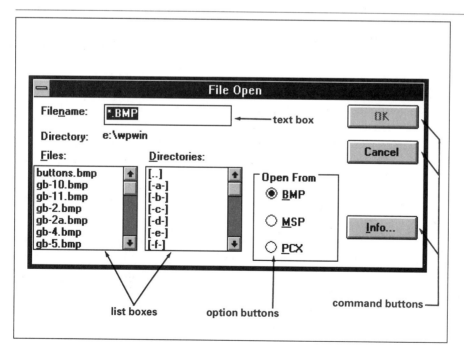

TEXT BOXES

A text box is a rectangle in a dialog box where you type information. The sample dialog box shown previously in Figure B.14 has a text box next to the Filename option. When you move the mouse pointer to an empty text box and click the left button, a flashing vertical bar called an *insertion point* appears at the far-left side of the box. Text you type will begin at the insertion point.

If the box already contains text when you move to it, all the text will automatically be selected (highlighted) and any text you type will replace it. Sometimes, however, you'll want to unselect the text (remove highlighting) to prevent the entire contents from being replaced. Here's how:

◆ Click the mouse pointer anywhere inside the highlighted text box before you type anything.

If necessary, you can move the insertion point without typing text first. Click where you want the insertion point to appear, then add or delete text at the new position of the insertion point.

If you make a mistake when typing text or just want to erase some characters, use either of these techniques:

◆ Press the Backspace key to delete the character to the left of the insertion point.

◆ Press the Delete key to delete the character to the right of the insertion point.

You can also select just a part of the existing text:

1. Move the mouse pointer to the first character you want to select.

2. Drag the mouse across the text you want to select. Or, double-click a word to select that word.

Now you can type new text, which will replace the existing text, or you can press the Delete key to delete the text.

LIST BOXES

A list box, available in some dialog boxes, contains a list of available choices. For example, a list box appears beneath the Files and Directories options in the sample dialog box shown in Figure B.14.

If a list contains more choices than will fit within the box, scroll bars appear to help you move quickly to the item you want. Most list boxes let you select only one item, but some let you select more than one. Selected items are highlighted within the list box.

Selecting One Item

To select one item from a list box, follow these steps:

1. If a scroll bar appears with the list, click the scroll arrows until you see the item you want.

2. Click the item you want to select, then click the command button you want. Or double-click the item to select the item and complete the command.

Sometimes it's faster to use the keyboard to select a list box item:

1. Use the arrow keys (↑ or ↓) to move to the item you want. Or, type the first letter of the item you want. The first item that starts with that letter will be highlighted.

2. Press ↵ to choose the item and complete the command.

Selecting More Than One Item

For applications that let you choose more than one item from a list box, the selection process works like a toggle switch, activating (turning on) or canceling (turning off) a selection:

◆ Click each item you want to select. To cancel a selection, click the item again.

If you're using the keyboard, use the arrow keys to move the highlight to any item you want to select, then press the spacebar to select that item.

OPTION BUTTONS

Option buttons present a number of mutually exclusive options, much like the buttons on your car radio let you choose only one station at a time. The currently selected option button contains a black dot, unselected buttons are empty, and unavailable options are dimmed. In the sample dialog box shown in Figure B.14, three option buttons appear under the Open From option. To choose an option button, do either of the following:

◆ Click the option button you want.

◆ Press the Tab and arrow keys until the option button you want is turned on (contains the black dot).

Check Boxes

☒
☐ Check boxes let you choose from a list of options that you can switch on and off. The sample dialog box in Figure B.15 shows check boxes under the Terminal Modes and CR → CR/LF options, and next to the Blink and Show Scroll Bars options.

You can select as many check boxes as necessary. When an option is selected, you'll see an *X* in the check box; otherwise, the box will be empty.

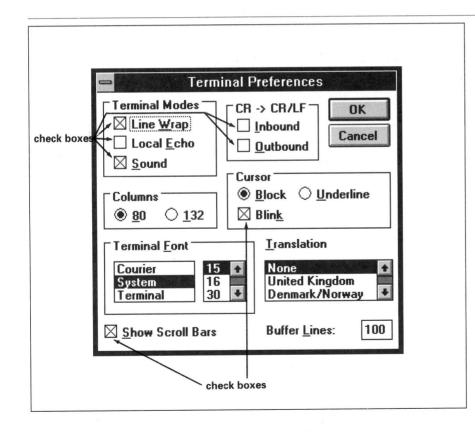

FIGURE B.15:

A sample dialog box with check boxes

To use a check box, do either of the following:

◆ Click the box you want to check or clear (clicking a checked box clears the selection; clicking an empty box selects it).

◆ Press the Tab key until the check box option you want is selected (the option is surrounded by a dotted box), then press the spacebar to select or unselect the check box.

DROP-DOWN LIST BOXES

When a dialog box is too small for a regular list box, you'll see a drop-down list box instead. The Pattern and Wallpaper options shown in Figure B.16 contain drop-down list boxes, with the drop-down list under the Wallpaper option already open.

Initially, the drop-down list box will appear as a rectangular box with only the currently selected option visible. After you select the box, the drop-down list opens up to reveal a list of selections. Here's how to open and use

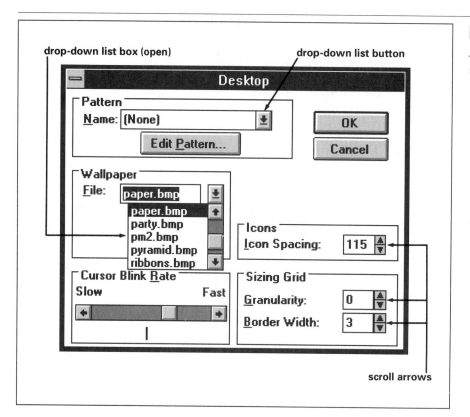

FIGURE B.16:

A sample dialog box with a drop-down list

a drop-down list box:

1. Click the underlined down arrow to the right of the text box to open the drop-down list box.

2. Click the up or down scroll arrow or drag the scroll box to move to the item you want.

3. Click the item you want.

If you're using the keyboard, follow these steps:

1. Press Tab or Shift+Tab until the option with the drop-down list is selected.

2. Press Alt+↓ to open the drop-down list.

3. Use the arrow keys to highlight the option you want.

4. Press Alt+↑ or Alt+↓ to select the highlighted option.

SCROLL ARROWS

Scroll arrows are similar to scroll bars, except that they do not have a scroll bar. Scroll arrows are generally used to choose some number within a specified range; they appear next to the Icon Spacing, Granularity, and Border Width options in the dialog box shown in Figure B.16. To use scroll arrows, do either of the following:

◆ Click on the upward-pointing arrow to increase the number in the accompanying box or the downward-pointing arrow to decrease that number.

◆ Press the Tab key until the option is selected, then type a new number, or edit the existing number using the same techniques used for text boxes.

COMMAND BUTTONS

Command buttons cause an immediate action. Most dialog boxes have an OK button, which saves whatever settings or choices you've made in the dialog box, then closes the dialog box. The Cancel button, which also appears in most dialog boxes, closes the dialog box without saving any changes or settings. There may be other buttons as well.

To choose a command button, do one of the following:

◆ Click the command button you want.

◆ Press Tab or Shift+Tab until the button you want is selected (its frame will be darker), then press ↵.

◆ If the button has an underlined letter in its name, you can choose it by holding down the Alt key and typing the underlined letter in the button name.

 If the command button has a dark border, you can select it by pressing ↵.

In addition to the command name, some command buttons will include special markings, as explained below:

SYMBOL	MEANING
...	An ellipsis after the button name indicates that the command button opens another dialog box or lets you provide more information.
>>	The double greater-than sign after the button name means that the command button expands the dialog box to show you some new options.
Dimmed (grayed)	Dimmed or grayed buttons are currently unavailable, most likely because using them does not make sense at the moment.
Dark border	The dark border around a button indicates the default button. You can choose the default button simply by pressing ↵.

Using Pop-Up Lists

Some command buttons display a pop-up list of options when chosen. Often (though not always), these buttons can be identified by their up- and/or down-pointing triangles, as shown at left. To use a pop-up list:

1. Move the mouse pointer to the command button, then hold down the left mouse button. The pop-up list appears.

2. Keeping the mouse button pressed, move the mouse to scroll the highlight to the option you want.

3. Release the mouse button.

To use the keyboard rather than a mouse:

1. Hold down the Alt key and type the underlined letter in the command button.

2. Release the Alt keys. The current option is outlined on the button.

3. Use the ↑ and ↓ keys to scroll through options on the button. Press another Alt+key combination or click on another button to move to another button.

CANCELING A DIALOG BOX

Sometimes you'll want to cancel a dialog box without choosing any of the options. Here are three ways to cancel a dialog box:

◆ Double-click the Control-menu box.

◆ Press the Escape key.

◆ Click the Cancel command button if there is one.

Again, you'll have many opportunities to try out all the features described so far when you start using WordPerfect for Windows. For now, just remember that when you need a quick reminder of how to use these features, you can refer to this appendix.

MOVING A DIALOG BOX

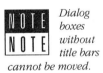

Dialog boxes without title bars cannot be moved.

Occasionally a dialog box will cover something you need to see. You can move a dialog box out of the way just as you move any other window: Simply drag its title bar as you would a window. Optionally, open the dialog box's Control menu (if it has one) by clicking its Control-menu box, or press Alt+spacebar, choose Move, position the dialog box with the arrow keys, and press ↵.

USING MESSAGE BOXES

System message boxes appear when an application cannot complete a command or needs to alert you about something. The message box will typically describe the problem and may recommend actions for you to take. In cases where you need to make a choice, you'll see some combination of OK, Cancel, and Retry buttons, as in the sample message box shown below:

To respond to the message, you can do one of the following:

◆ Click the command button you want.

◆ Press ↵ to choose OK, press Escape to choose Cancel, or press Alt+R to choose Retry.

Sometimes an inactive application has a status or an error message for you. Typically, a beep will sound and the application's title bar or icon will flash to let you know about the message. For instance, you might hear from the Print Manager if you're printing a document and the printer runs out of paper. To receive the message,

◆ Click the flashing application window or icon.

After reading the message, correct any error conditions (for example, replace the printer paper), then click the appropriate command button.

GETTING HELP

With Windows, help is just a click or keyword search away. Most applications included with Windows 3 and nearly every Windows program you use, including WordPerfect for Windows, will provide online help. Some Help screens even include practice exercises to speed up the learning process. Try using online help whenever you're not sure how to do something, and you don't have a book, manual, or resident expert handy.

STARTING HELP

The Help option on the application's menu bar provides one of the easiest ways to get help and lets you access the categories described above. Some applications also provide a Help command button, which you can click for quick access to Help topics. Here's how to start Help from the menu bar:

1. Click Help on the menu bar (or press Alt+H).

2. Click the Help category you want (or press the underlined letter).

Figure B.17 shows the Help menu for the Program Manager window, accessed by clicking Help in that window's menu bar.

The Help categories available from that menu are summarized below:

Index	Provides an alphabetical list of all Help topics available for the application
Keyboard	Provides tables of key combinations for using your keyboard with the application

T.I P

Once a Help window is open, press the F1 key to access the Help Index category in a single step.

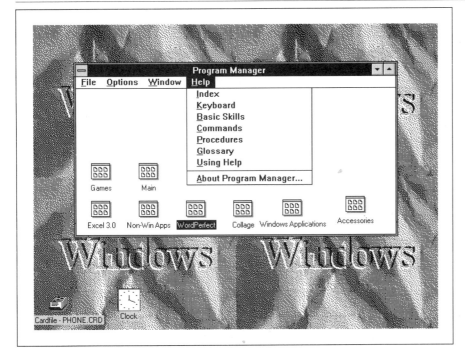

Help categories on the Help menu for the Program Manager window

Basic Skills	Introduces you to basic features and techniques for using basic skills
Commands	Lists all commands you can use with the application
Procedures	Provides a "how-to," step-by-step approach to using application features
Glossary	Presents a list of keywords, and offers a definition of a word when you move the mouse pointer to that word and hold down the left mouse button
Using Help	Explains how to use Windows Help
About (application name)	Gives the application name, version number, copyright, and other useful information

To choose a Help category, just click it with your mouse, or press the underlined letter.

FINDING INFORMATION

When you choose a Help category, a Help window appears on the screen. A typical Help screen appears in Figure B.18. Notice the five Help buttons and the underlined topics, all of which can be used to find information.

Help Buttons

The five command buttons will assist you in moving around the Help system. To use a Help button, click the button you want, or type the underlined letter shown on the Help button. Buttons will be dimmed if they aren't available at the moment. The buttons are listed here:

Index: displays the Help Index for the application.

Back: moves back to the last topic displayed. Each time you click the Back button, you'll move back one topic at a time until you reach the Help Index.

Browse <<: displays the previous topic in a related series of topics. Each time you click the Browse << button, you'll move back one topic in the series until you reach the first topic.

Browse >>: works like Browse <<, except that it displays the next topic in the series until you reach the last topic.

Search: lets you search for Help topics based on keywords or phrases. The next section explains how to use the Search button.

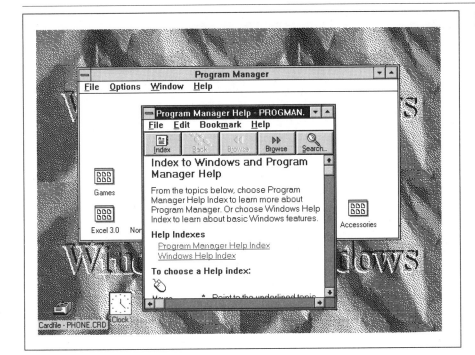

Searching for Keywords

The Search button provides one of the most efficient ways to search for information because it lets you select a keyword or phrase. The sample Search window shown in Figure B.19 summarizes the basic techniques.

Here's how to use the Search feature:

1. Open Help as described above and click the Search button.

2. Type a word or short phrase in the Search For text box. As you type, the list box just below the Search For text box will highlight the word or phrase that most closely matches what you typed. Alternatively, you can scroll through the entries by using the scroll bar, then click the entry you want.

3. Click the Search command button. A list of related topics will appear in the Topics Found list box at the bottom.

4. Click the topic you want from the Topics Found list box, then click the Go To command button.

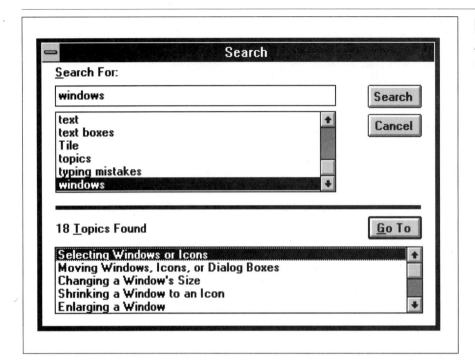

The next time you press the Search button, the Search For box will contain the keyword you previously searched for.

Selecting Underlined Topics

You can get immediate information about underlined topics on a Help screen. Looking back at the sample Help screen in Figure B.18, you'll see two types of underlining: unbroken and broken. *Unbroken* underlining indicates a topic that has its own Help screen. *Broken* underlining is typically used for definitions, as when you choose Glossary from the Help menu. Here's how to get information about an underlined topic:

1. Move the mouse pointer to an underlined topic. Its arrow-shaped pointer will change into a hand pointer to indicate that information is available for the topic.

Topics containing more information are underlined and displayed in green on color monitors.

2. If the topic has an *unbroken* underline, click the topic. A new Help screen will display information about that topic. If the topic has a *broken* underline, press and hold the left mouse button while you read the definition from a pop-up window. Release the mouse button after you've read the information.

If you prefer to use your keyboard rather than the mouse, you can just press Tab or Shift+Tab until the topic you want is highlighted, then press ↵ to select that topic (or hold down ↵ to view a topic that has a broken underline).

Printing Help Topics

Sometimes you'll want to print a copy of the current Help screen so that you can refer to it later. Here's how:

1. Click the **F**ile menu on the current Help screen (or press Alt+F).

2. Click the **P**rint Topic option (or press P).

EXITING HELP

When you've finished using Help, you can close the Help window by double-clicking its Control-menu box or by selecting Exit from its File pull-down menu (or press the shortcut key Alt+F4). If you just need to see what's behind the Help screen, resize or move the Help window as you would any other window. This can be handy for keeping the Help screen nearby as you learn to use a new application or feature.

ENDING YOUR WINDOWS SESSION

When you're finished using Windows, you should be sure to end the session properly. It's best to follow the procedures below rather than just turn off your computer:

1. Exit any applications you are currently running (see "Exiting Applications" earlier in the appendix). This is important because if you forget to do so, you might lose much of the work you've accomplished in the current session.

2. Click the Program Manager's File menu to open it (or press Alt+F).

3. Click **E**xit Windows (or type X). The Exit Windows dialog box shown below will appear:

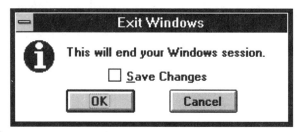

After exiting all applications, you can double-click the Program Manager's Control-menu box to immediately bring up the Exit Windows dialog box.

4. If the Save Changes check box is empty and you want to save the current Desktop layout, click the **S**ave Changes box (or press S). If the **S**ave Changes box contains an *X* and you *don't* want to save the layout, click Save Changes or press S to clear the box.

5. Click OK or press ↵ to exit Windows and return to the DOS prompt (typically C>) or the DOS shell you were running when you started Windows. If you change your mind (before exiting), press Escape, or press Tab then ↵, to choose Cancel.

WINDOWS OPERATING MODES

You may have heard about different *modes* for running Windows. These modes are related to the type of microprocessor and the amount of memory installed in your personal computer.

Real mode is useful if you need maximum compatibility with applications developed for previous versions of Windows. Here are some features and limitations of this mode:

You can find out what mode you are using by clicking on Help in the Program Manager menu bar, then clicking the About Program Manager option. Click the OK button after noting the mode.

◆ Requires an 80286 processor and 640K RAM

◆ Is compatible with Windows 2.*x* applications

◆ Runs Windows applications only (no DOS applications)

◆ Shares information between Windows applications only

◆ Uses only conventional memory (RAM)

To start Windows in real mode, enter **WIN /R** at the DOS command prompt, rather than just the WIN command.

Standard mode is the normal operating mode for AT-class computers and Windows 3 applications. This mode

◆ Requires an 80286 or higher processor and at least 1MB RAM

◆ Runs Windows 3 and full-screen DOS applications

◆ Shares information between Windows and DOS applications

◆ Accesses conventional and extended memory

NOTE *You cannot use standard mode if you're using upper memory blocks in DOS 5 (from 640K to 1MB).*

To run Windows in standard mode, enter **WIN /S** at the DOS command prompt.

386 enhanced mode provides full access to Windows capabilities. This mode

◆ Requires an 80386 or higher processor and at least 2MB RAM

◆ Runs multiple Windows 3 and DOS applications

◆ Shares information between DOS and Windows applications

◆ Uses conventional, extended, and virtual memory

Virtual memory is unique to 80386 and higher processors. When applications use up all available memory, Windows automatically starts using available disk storage as memory. To start Windows in 386 enhanced mode, enter **WIN /3** at the DOS command prompt.

Note that all the switches, /R, /S, and /3, are entirely optional. If you start Windows without a switch, by simply entering WIN at the DOS command prompt, Windows automatically examines your system and starts in whatever mode is most appropriate for your computer.

CHANGING THE WALLPAPER

You can change the Windows Desktop to any of several different appearances (the "crinkled paper" appearance is generally used throughout this book). If you'd like to configure Windows to show this same Desktop appearance on your own computer, follow these steps:

1. Start Windows.

2. Open the Main window by double-clicking the Main icon in the Program Manager window.

3. Open the Control Panel window by double-clicking its icon.

4. Open the Desktop window, again by double-clicking.

5. Click the drop-down list button next to *File:* under Wallpaper to see your options, as shown in Figure B.20.

6. Use the scroll bar in the window to scroll down the list until the paper.bmp option appears.

7. Click on paper.bmp to choose it.

8. Click the Tile option button.

9. Click the OK command button to leave the dialog box.

10. Double-click the Control-menu box in the Control Panel window, then in the Main window, to close both windows.

When you exit Windows using the Exit Windows option on the File pull-down menu, choose the Save Changes check box (so it contains an *X*) before clicking the OK button. This will ensure that your new wallpaper design appears in future Windows sessions.

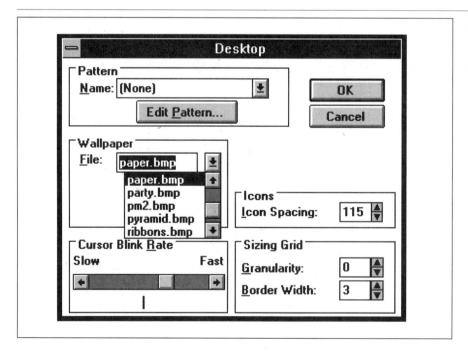

FIGURE B.20:

The Desktop window with Wallpaper options

SUMMARY OF MOUSE
AND KEYBOARD TECHNIQUES

Table B.1 lists basic mouse and keyboard techniques for managing windows, icons, and applications. Table B.2 summarizes mouse and keyboard techniques for working with dialog boxes. You may want to make copies of these tables and keep them nearby as you learn to use Windows and WordPerfect for Windows—they're sure to come in handy from time to time.

The basic information presented in this appendix is enough to get you up and running with Windows now, and pave the way for using WordPerfect for Windows. For more information on the many features available to you in Windows, refer to the Windows *User's Guide* or SYBEX's *Mastering Windows 3.0,* by Robert Cowart, SYBEX, 1990.

TABLE B.1:

Mouse and Keyboard Techniques for Windows, Icons, and Applications

IF YOU WANT TO	MOUSE	KEYBOARD
Arrange application icons	*Click minimized icon* ➤ Switch To ➤ Arrange Icons	Ctrl+Esc Alt+A
Arrange document icons	Window ➤ Arrange Icons	Alt+W A
Cascade open application windows	*Click Control-menu box* ➤ Switch To ➤ Cascade	Ctrl+Esc Alt+C
Cascade open document windows	Window ➤ Cascade	Shift+F5
Choose options on menu	Click option	Alt+*underlined letter*
Close application window	*Click Control-menu box* ➤ Close	Alt+F4
Close document (group) window	*Click Control-menu box* ➤ Close	Ctrl+F4
Exit non-Windows application	Usual DOS technique	Usual DOS technique

IF YOU WANT TO	MOUSE	KEYBOARD
Exit Windows application	File ➤ Exit or *click Control-menu box* ➤ Close	Alt+F4
Maximize window	Click Maximize button	*Control menu* ➤ Ma**x**imize
Minimize window	Click Minimize button	*Control menu* ➤ Mi**n**imize
Move window	Drag title bar	*Control menu* ➤ **M**ove
Open Control menu for application window	Click Control-menu box	Alt+spacebar
Open Control menu for document window	Click Control-menu box	Alt+−
Open Control menu for full-screen DOS application		Alt+spacebar
Open document (group) icon	Double-click icon	Ctrl+Tab then ↵
Open minimized application window	Double-click icon	Alt+Esc ↵ or Alt+Tab
Open program item icon	Double-click icon	→ ← ↑ ↓ then ↵
Restore window	Click Restore button	*Control menu* ➤ **R**estore
Run application (program)	Double-click icon	→ ← ↑ ↓ then ↵
Size window	Drag border or corner	*Control menu* ➤ **S**ize
Switch between full-screen/window (non-Windows application)	*Click Control-menu box* ➤ Settings ➤ Window/Full Screen	Alt+↵
Switch to running application	Click window or double-click icon	Ctrl+Esc or Alt+Esc
Tile open application windows	*Click Control-menu box* ➤ Switch To ➤ Tile	Ctrl+Esc Alt+T
Tile open document windows	Window ➤ Tile	Shift+F4

TABLE B.1:

Mouse and Keyboard Techniques for Windows, Icons, and Applications (continued)

IF YOU WANT TO	MOUSE	KEYBOARD
Choose button, check box	Click option	Move to item, press spacebar
Choose highlighted list item	Click item	Press spacebar
Choose highlighted list item (drop-down list)	Click item	Alt+↑ or ↓
Exit (cancel) dialog box	Click Cancel button	Esc or Alt+F4
Exit dialog box, save choices	Click OK button	↵
Highlight first item in a list		Home
Highlight last item in a list		End
Move to area	Click option	Tab or Shift+Tab
Move to option	Click option	→ ← ↑ ↓ or Alt+*letter*
Open drop-down list	Click drop-down list button	Alt+↓
Scroll in list	Scroll bar	→ ← ↑ ↓ PgUp PgDn

TABLE B.2:

Summary of Dialog Box Techniques

APPENDIX C

Hidden Codes

Every time you perform an action in WordPerfect, such as entering a hard return or setting line spacing, the program inserts a hidden code in your document. These codes are hidden to prevent the document window from becoming cluttered (to see them, choose View ➤ Reveal Codes or press Alt+F3). The following table lists all the codes and their meanings (some are given in a generic form):

CODE	MEANING
[x:m,n]	WordPerfect character (x = character; m = character set number; n = character number)
–	Soft hyphen
[–]	Hyphen character
[Adv]	Advance text
[BLine Off]	Baseline placement off
[BLine On]	Baseline placement on

CODE	MEANING
[Block Pro]	Block protection
[Bold Off]	Bold off
[Bold On]	Bold on
[Box Num]	Caption in graphics box
[Cell]	Table cell
[Center]	Center text
[Center Pg]	Center page vertically
[Cndl EOP]	Conditional end of page
[Cntr Tab]	Centered tab
[Col Def]	Column definition
[Col Off]	End of text columns
[Col On]	Beginning of text columns
[Color]	Print color
[Comment]	Document comment
[Date]	Date/Time function
[Dbl Indent]	Double indent
[Dbl Und Off]	Double underline off
[Dbl Und On]	Double underline on
[DDE Link Begin]	Start of Dynamic Data Exchange link
[DDE Link End]	End of Dynamic Data Exchange link
[Dec Tab]	Decimal-aligned tab
[Decml/Algn Char]	Decimal character/thousands separator
[Def Mark:Index]	Index definition
[Def Mark:List]	List definition
[Def Mark:ToA]	Table-of-authorities definition
[Def Mark:ToC]	Table-of-contents definition
[Dorm HRt]	Dormant hard return
[DSrt]	Deletable soft return
[Embedded]	Embedded code for macro

CODE	MEANING
[End C/A]	End centering/alignment
[End Def]	End of index, list, or table of contents
[End Mark]	End of marked text
[End Opt]	Endnote options
[Endnote]	Endnote
[Endnote Placement]	Endnote placement
[Equ Box]	Equation box
[Equ Opt]	Equation box options
[Ext Large Off]	Extra-large print off
[Ext Large On]	Extra-large print on
[Fig Box]	Figure box
[Fig Opt]	Figure box options
[Fine Off]	Fine print off
[Fine On]	Fine print on
[Flsh Rgt]	Flush right
[Font]	Font
[Footer A]	Footer A
[Footer B]	Footer B
[Footnote]	Footnote
[Force]	Force odd/even page
[Ftn Opt]	Footnote options
[HdCntrTab]	Hard centered tab
[HdDecTab]	Hard decimal tab
[HdRgtTab]	Hard right tab
[HdSpc]	Hard space
[HdTab]	Hard left tab
[Header A]	Header A
[Header B]	Header B
[HLine]	Horizontal line

CODE	MEANING
[HPg]	Hard page break
[Hrd Row]	Hard row (tables)
[HRt-SPg]	Hard return/soft page break
[HRt]	Hard return
[Hyph Ign Wrd]	Hyphenation ignore word
[Hyph Off]	Hyphenation off
[Hyph On]	Hyphenation on
[HyphSRt]	Hyphenation soft return
[HZone]	Hyphenation zone
[Indent]	Indent
[Index]	Index entry
[Insert Pg Num]	Insert page number
[Italc Off]	Italic off
[Italc On]	Italic on
[Just Lim]	Word-spacing justification limits
[Just:Center]	Center justification
[Just:Full]	Full justification
[Just:Left]	Left justification
[Just:Right]	Right justification
[Kern Off]	Kerning off
[Kern On]	Kerning on
[Lang]	Language
[Large Off]	Large print off
[Large On]	Large print on
[Line Height Adj]	Line height (leading) adjustment
[Link]	Spreadsheet link
[Link End]	End of linked spreadsheet
[Ln Height]	Line height
[Ln Num Off]	Line numbering off

CODE	MEANING
[Ln Num On]	Line numbering on
[Ln Spacing]	Line spacing
[L/R Mar]	Left and right margins
[Mar Rel]	Left margin release
[Mark:List]	List entry
[Mark:ToC]	Table-of-contents entry
[New End Num]	New endnote number
[New Equ Num]	New Equation box number
[New Fig Num]	New Figure box number
[New Ftn Num]	New footnote number
[New Tbl Num]	New Table box number
[New Txt Num]	New Text box number
[New Usr Num]	New User box number
[Note Num]	Footnote or endnote note number
[Open Style]	Open style
[Outline Lvl Open Style]	Open outline style
[Outline Lvl Style Off]	Paired outline style off
[Outline Lvl Style On]	Paired outline style on
[Outline Off]	Outline off
[Outline On]	Outline on
[Outln Off]	Outline text appearance off
[Outln On]	Outline text appearance on
[Ovrstk]	Overstrike
[Paper Sz/Typ]	Paper size and type
[Par Num]	Paragraph number
[Par Num Def]	Paragraph-numbering definition
[Pg Num]	New page number
[Pg Num Style]	Page number style (accompanying text)

CODE	**MEANING**
[Pg Numbering]	Page number position
[Ptr Cmnd]	Printer command
[Redln Off]	Redline off
[Redln On]	Redline on
[Ref]	Reference (cross-reference)
[Rgt Tab]	Right-aligned tab
[Row]	Table row
[Select]	Beginning of selected text
[Shadw Off]	Shadow off
[Shadw On]	Shadow on
[Sm Cap Off]	Small caps off
[Sm Cap On]	Small caps on
[Small Off]	Small print off
[Small On]	Small print on
[SPg]	Soft page break
[SRt]	Soft return
[Stkout Off]	Strikeout off
[Stkout On]	Strikeout on
[Style Off]	Style off
[Style On]	Style on
[Subdoc]	Subdocument (master document)
[Subdoc End]	End of subdocument (expanded master document)
[Subdoc Start]	Beginning of subdocument (expanded master document)
[Subscpt Off]	Subscript off
[Subscpt On]	Subscript on
[Suppress]	Suppress page format
[Suprscpt Off]	Superscript off
[Suprscpt On]	Superscript on

CODE	MEANING
[Tab]	Tab
[Tab Set]	Tab set
[Target]	Target (cross-reference)
[T/B Mar]	Top and bottom margins
[Tbl Box]	Table box
[Tbl Def]	Table definition
[Tbl Off]	Table off
[Tbl Opt]	Table box options
[Text Box]	Text box
[ToA]	Table of authorities entry
[Txt Opt]	Text box options
[Und Off]	Underlining off
[Und On]	Underlining on
[Undrln]	Underline spaces/tabs
[Unknown]	Non-WordPerfect 5.1 for Windows code
[Usr Box]	User box
[Usr Opt]	User box options
[VLine]	Vertical line
[Vry Large Off]	Very large print off
[Vry Large On]	Very large print on
[W/O Off]	Widow/orphan off
[W/O On]	Widow/orphan on
[Wrd/Ltr Spacing]	Word and letter spacing

Symbols

A

Selections from The SYBEX Library

OPERATING SYSTEMS

The ABC's of DOS 4
Alan R. Miller
275pp. Ref. 583-2

This step-by-step introduction to using DOS 4 is written especially for beginners. Filled with simple examples, *The ABC's of DOS 4* covers the basics of hardware, software, disks, the system editor EDLIN, DOS commands, and more.

The ABC's of DOS 5
Alan Miller
267pp. Ref. 770-3

This straightforward guide will haven even first-time computer users working comfortably with DOS 5 in no time. Step-by-step lessons lead users from switching on the PC, through exploring the DOS Shell, working with directories and files, using essential commands, customizing the system, and trouble shooting. Includes a tear-out quick reference card and function key template.

ABC's of MS-DOS
(Second Edition)
Alan R. Miller
233pp. Ref. 493-3

This handy guide to MS-DOS is all many PC users need to manage their computer files, organize floppy and hard disks, use EDLIN, and keep their computers organized. Additional information is given about utilities like Sidekick, and there is a DOS command and program summary. The second edition is fully updated for Version 3.3.

The ABC's of SCO UNIX
Tom Cuthbertson
263pp. Re. 715-0

A guide especially for beginners who want to get to work fast. Includes hands-on tutorials on logging in and out; creating and editing files; using electronic mail; organizing files into directories; printing; text formatting; and more.

The ABC's of Windows 3.0
Kris Jamsa
327pp. Ref. 760-6

A user-friendly introduction to the essentials of Windows 3.0. Presented in 64 short lessons. Beginners start with lesson one, while more advanced readers can skip ahead. Learn to use File Manager, the accessory programs, customization features, Program Manager, and more.

DESQview Instant Reference
Paul J. Perry
175pp. Ref. 809-2

This complete quick-reference command guide covers version 2.3 and DESQview 386, as well as QEMM (for managing expanded memory) and Manifest Memory Analyzer. Concise, alphabetized entries provide exact syntax, options, usage, and brief examples for every command. A handy source for on-the-job reminders and tips.

DOS 3.3 On-Line Advisor
Version 1.1
SYBAR, Software Division of SYBEX, Inc.
Ref. 933-1

The answer to all your DOS problems.

The DOS On-Line Advisor is an on-screen reference that explains over 200 DOS error messages. 2300 other citations cover all you ever needed to know about DOS. The DOS On-Line Advisor pops up on top of your working program to give you quick, easy help when you need it, and disappears when you don't. Covers thru version 3.3. Software package comes with 3½" and 5¼" disks. **System Requirements:** IBM compatible with DOS 2.0 or higher, runs with Windows 3.0, uses 90K of RAM.

DOS Instant Reference
SYBEX Prompter Series
Greg Harvey
Kay Yarborough Nelson
220pp. Ref. 477-1
A complete fingertip reference for fast, easy on-line help:command summaries, syntax, usage and error messages. Organized by function—system commands, file commands, disk management, directories, batch files, I/O, networking, programming, and more. Through Version 3.3.

DOS 5 Instant Reference
Robert M. Thomas
200pp. Ref. 804-1
The comprehensive quick guide to DOS—all its features, commands, options, and versions—now including DOS 5, with the new graphical interface. Concise, alphabetized command entries provide exact syntax, options, usage, brief examples, and applicable version numbers. Fully cross-referenced; ideal for quick review or on-the-job reference.

The DOS 5 User's Handbook
Gary Masters
Richard Allen King
400pp. Ref. 777-0
This is the DOS 5 book for users who are already familiar with an earlier version of DOS. Part I is a quick, friendly guide to new features; topics include the graphical interface, new and enhanced commands, and much more. Part II is a complete DOS 5 quick reference, with command summaries, in-depth explanations, and examples.

Encyclopedia DOS
Judd Robbins
1030pp. Ref. 699-5
A comprehensive reference and user's guide to all versions of DOS through 4.0. Offers complete information on every DOS command, with all possible switches and parameters—plus examples of effective usage. An invaluable tool.

Essential OS/2
(Second Edition)
Judd Robbins
445pp. Ref. 609-X
Written by an OS/2 expert, this is the guide to the powerful new resources of the OS/2 operating system standard edition 1.1 with presentation manager. Robbins introduces the standard edition, and details multitasking under OS/2, and the range of commands for installing, starting up, configuring, and running applications. For Version 1.1 Standard Edition.

Essential PC-DOS
(Second Edition)
Myril Clement Shaw
Susan Soltis Shaw
332pp. Ref. 413-5
An authoritative guide to PC-DOS, including version 3.2. Designed to make experts out of beginners, it explores everything from disk management to batch file programming. Includes an 85-page command summary. Through Version 3.2.

Graphics Programming
Under Windows
Brian Myers
Chris Doner
646pp. Ref. 448-8
Straightforward discussion, abundant examples, and a concise reference guide to graphics commands make this book a must for Windows programmers. Topics range from how Windows works to programming for business, animation, CAD, and desktop publishing. For Version 2.

Hard Disk Instant Reference
SYBEX Prompter Series
Judd Robbins

256pp. Ref. 587-5

Compact yet comprehensive, this pocket-sized reference presents the essential information on DOS commands used in managing directories and files, and in optimizing disk configuration. Includes a survey of third-party utility capabilities. Through DOS 4.0.

Inside DOS: A Programmer's Guide
Michael J. Young

490pp. Ref. 710-X

A collection of practical techniques (with source code listings) designed to help you take advantage of the rich resources intrinsic to MS-DOS machines. Designed for the experienced programmer with a basic understanding of C and 8086 assembly language, and DOS fundamentals.

Mastering DOS (Second Edition)
Judd Robbins

722pp. Ref. 555-7

"The most useful DOS book." This seven-part, in-depth tutorial addresses the needs of users at all levels. Topics range from running applications, to managing files and directories, configuring the system, batch file programming, and techniques for system developers. Through Version 4.

Mastering DOS 5
Judd Robbins

800pp. Ref.767-3

"The DOS reference to keep next to your computer," according to PC Week, this highly acclaimed text is now revised and expanded for DOS 5. Comprehensive tutorials cover everything from first steps for beginners, to advanced tools for systems developers—with emphasis on the new graphics interface. Includes tips, tricks, and a tear-out quick reference card and function key template.

Mastering SunOS
Brent D. Heslop
David Angell

588pp. Ref. 683-9

Learn to configure and manage your system; use essential commands; manage files; perform editing, formatting, and printing tasks; master E-mail and external communication; and use the SunView and new Open Window graphic interfaces.

Mastering Windows 3.0
Robert Cowart

592pp. Ref.458-5

Every Windows user will find valuable how-to and reference information here. With full details on the desktop utilities; manipulating files; running applications (including non-Windows programs); sharing data between DOS, OS/2, and Windows; hardware and software efficiency tips; and more.

Understanding DOS 3.3
Judd Robbins

678pp. Ref. 648-0

This best selling, in-depth tutorial addresses the needs of users at all levels with many examples and hands-on exercises. Robbins discusses the fundamentals of DOS, then covers manipulating files and directories, using the DOS editor, printing, communicating, and finishes with a full section on batch files.

Understanding Hard Disk Management on the PC
Jonathan Kamin

500pp. Ref. 561-1

This title is a key productivity tool for all hard disk users who want efficient, error-free file management and organization. Includes details on the best ways to conserve hard disk space when using several memory-guzzling programs. Through DOS 4.

Up & Running with DR DOS 5.0
Joerg Schieb

130pp. Ref. 815-7

Enjoy a fast-paced, but thorough introduction to DR DOS 5.0. In only 20 steps, you can begin to obtain practical results: copy and delete files, password protect your data, use batch files to save time, and more.

Up & Running with DOS 3.3
Michael-Alexander Beisecker
126pp. Ref. 750-9

Learn the fundamentals of DOS 3.3 in just 20 basic steps. Each "step" is a self-contained, time-coded lesson, taking 15 minutes to an hour to complete. You learn the essentials in record time.

Up & Running with DOS 5
Alan Simpson
150pp. Ref. 774-6

A 20-step guide to the essentials of DOS 5—for busy users seeking a fast-paced overview. Steps take only minutes to complete, and each is marked with a timer clock, so you know how long each one will take. Topics include installation, the DOS Shell, Program Manager, disks, directories, utilities, customization, batch files, ports and devices, DOSKEY, memory, Windows, and BASIC.

Up & Running with Your Hard Disk
Klaus M Rubsam
140pp. Ref. 666-9

A far-sighted, compact introduction to hard disk installation and basic DOS use. Perfect for PC users who want the practical essentials in the shortest possible time. In 20 basic steps, learn to choose your hard disk, work with accessories, back up data, use DOS utilities to save time, and more.

Up & Running with Windows 286/386
Gabriele Wentges
132pp. Ref. 691-X

This handy 20-step overview gives PC users all the essentials of using Windows—whether for evaluating the software, or getting a fast start. Each self-contained lesson takes just 15 minutes to one hour to complete.

Up & Running with Windows 3.0
Gabriele Wentges
117pp. Ref. 711-8

All the essentials of Windows 3.0 in just twenty "steps"—self-contained lessons that take minutes to complete. Perfect for evaluating the software or getting a quick start with the new environment. Topics include installation, managing windows, using keyboard and mouse, using desktop utilities, and built-in programs.

Windows 3.0 Instant Reference
Marshall Moseley
195pp. Ref. 757-6

This concise, comprehensive pocket reference provides quick access to instructions on all Windows 3.0 mouse and keyboard commands. It features step-by-step instructions on using Windows, the applications that come bundled with it, and Windows' unique help facilities. Great for all levels of expertise.

SPREADSHEETS AND INTEGRATED SOFTWARE

1-2-3 for Scientists and Engineers
William J. Orvis
371pp. Ref. 733-9

This up-to-date edition offers fast, elegant solutions to common problems in science and engineering. Complete, carefully explained techniques for plotting, curve fitting, statistics, derivatives, integrals and differentials, solving systems of equations, and more; plus useful Lotus add-ins.

The ABC's of 1-2-3 (Second Edition)
Chris Gilbert
Laurie Williams
245pp. Ref. 355-4

Online Today recommends it as "an easy and comfortable way to get started with the program." An essential tutorial for novices, it will remain on your desk as a valuable source of ongoing reference and support. For Release 2.

The ABC's of 1-2-3 Release 2.2
Chris Gilbert
Laurie Williams
340pp. Ref. 623-5

New Lotus 1-2-3 users delight in this book's step-by-step approach to building trouble-free spreadsheets, displaying graphs, and efficiently building databases. The authors cover the ins and outs of the latest version including easier calculations, file linking, and better graphic presentation.

The ABC's of 1-2-3 Release 2.3
Chris Gilbert
Laurie Williams
350pp. Ref. 837-8

Computer Currents called it "one of the best tutorials available." This new edition provides easy-to-follow, hands-on lessons tailored specifically for computer and spreadsheet newcomers—or for anyone seeking a quick and easy guide to the basics. Covers everything from switching on the computer to charts, functions, macros, and important new features.

The ABC's of 1-2-3 Release 3
Judd Robbins
290pp. Ref. 519-0

The ideal book for beginners who are new to Lotus or new to Release 3. This step-by-step approach to the 1-2-3 spreadsheet software gets the reader up and running with spreadsheet, database, graphics, and macro functions.

The ABC's of Excel
on the IBM PC
Douglas Hergert
326pp. Ref. 567-0

This book is a brisk and friendly introduction to the most important features of Microsoft Excel for PC's. This beginner's book discusses worksheets, charts, database operations, and macros, all with hands-on examples. Written for all versions through Version 2.

The ABC's of Quattro Pro 3
Alan Simpson
Douglas Wolf
338pp. Ref. 836-6

This popular beginner's tutorial on Quattro Pro 2 shows first-time computer and spreadsheet users the essentials of electronic number-crunching. Topics range from business spreadsheet design to error-free formulas, presentation slide shows, the database, macros, more.

The Complete Lotus 1-2-3
Release 2.2 Handbook
Greg Harvey
750pp. Ref. 625-1

This comprehensive handbook discusses every 1-2-3 operation with clear instructions and practical tips. This volume especially emphasizes the new improved graphics, high-speed recalculation techniques, and spreadsheet linking available with Release 2.2.

The Complete Lotus 1-2-3
Release 3 Handbook
Greg Harvey
700pp. Ref. 600-6

Everything you ever wanted to know about 1-2-3 is in this definitive handbook. As a Release 3 guide, it features the design and use of 3D worksheets, and improved graphics, along with using Lotus under DOS or OS/2. Problems, exercises, and helpful insights are included.

Lotus 1-2-3 2.2 On-Line Advisor
Version 1.1
SYBAR, Software Division of
SYBEX, Inc.
Ref. 935-8

Need Help fast? With a touch of a key, the Advisor pops up right on top of your Lotus 1-2-3 program to answer your spreadsheet questions. With over 4000 index citations and 1600 pre-linked cross-references, help has never been so easy to find. Just start typing your topic and the Lotus 1-2-3 Advisor does all the look-up for you. Covers versions 2.01 and 2.2. Software package comes with 3½" and 5¼" disks. **System Requirements:** IBM compatible with DOS 2.0 or higher, runs with Windows 3.0, uses 90K of RAM.

Lotus 1-2-3 Desktop Companion SYBEX Ready Reference Series
Greg Harvey
976pp. Ref. 501-8

A full-time consultant, right on your desk. Hundreds of self-contained entries cover every 1-2-3 feature, organized by topic, indexed and cross-referenced, and supplemented by tips, macros and working examples. For Release 2.

Lotus 1-2-3 Instant Reference Release 2.2 SYBEX Prompter Series
Greg Harvey
Kay Yarborough Nelson
254pp. Ref. 635-9

The reader gets quick and easy access to any operation in 1-2-3 Version 2.2 in this handy pocket-sized encyclopedia. Organized by menu function, each command and function has a summary description, the exact key sequence, and a discussion of the options.

Lotus 1-2-3 Tips and Tricks (2nd edition)
Gene Weisskopf
425pp. Ref. 668-5

This outstanding collection of tips, shortcuts and cautions for longtime Lotus users is in an expanded new edition covering Release 2.2. Topics include macros, range names, spreadsheet design, hardware and operating system tips, data analysis, printing, data interchange, applications development, and more.

Mastering 1-2-3 (Second Edition)
Carolyn Jorgensen
702pp. Ref. 528-X

Get the most from 1-2-3 Release 2.01 with this step-by-step guide emphasizing advanced features and practical uses. Topics include data sharing, macros, spreadsheet security, expanded memory, and graphics enhancements.

Mastering 1-2-3 Release 3
Carolyn Jorgensen
682pp. Ref. 517-4

For new Release 3 and experienced Release 2 users, "Mastering" starts with a basic spreadsheet, then introduces spreadsheet and database commands, functions, and macros, and then tells how to analyze 3D spreadsheets and make high-impact reports and graphs. Lotus add-ons are discussed and Fast Tracks are included.

Mastering Enable/OA
Christopher Van Buren
Robert Bixby
540pp. Ref 637-5

This is a structured, hands-on guide to integrated business computing, for users who want to achieve productivity in the shortest possible time. Separate in-depth sections cover word processing, spreadsheets, databases, telecommunications, task integration and macros.

Mastering Excel on the IBM PC
Carl Townsend
628pp. Ref. 403-8

A complete Excel handbook with step-by-step tutorials, sample applications and an extensive reference section. Topics include worksheet fundamentals, formulas and windows, graphics, database techniques, special features, macros and more.

Mastering Excel 3 for Windows
Carl Townsend
625pp. Ref. 643-X

A new edition of SYBEX's highly praised guide to the Excel super spreadsheet, under Windows 3.0. Includes full coverage of new features; dozens of tips and examples; in-depth treatment of specialized topics, including presentation graphics and macros; and sample applications for inventory control, financial management, trend analysis, and more.

Mastering Framework III
Douglas Hergert
Jonathan Kamin
613pp. Ref. 513-1

Thorough, hands-on treatment of the latest Framework release. An outstanding introduction to integrated software applications, with examples for outlining, spreadsheets, word processing, databases, and more; plus an introduction to FRED programming.

Mastering Freelance Plus
Donald Richard Read
411pp. Ref. 701-0

A detailed guide to high-powered graphing and charting with Freelance Plus. Part I is a practical overview of the software. Part II offers concise tutorials on creating specific chart types. Part III covers drawing functions in depth. Part IV shows how to organize and generate output, including printing and on-screen shows.

Mastering Quattro Pro 2
Gene Weisskopf
575pp, Ref. 792-4

This hands-on guide and reference takes readers from basic spreadsheets to creating three-dimensional graphs, spreadsheet databases, macros and advanced data analysis. Also covers Paradox Access and translating Lotus 1-2-3 2.2 work sheets. A great tutorial for beginning and intermediate users, this book also serves as a reference for users at all levels.

Mastering Quattro Pro 3
Gene Weisskopf
618pp. Ref. 841-6

A complete hands-on guide and on-the-job reference, offering practical tutorials on the basics; up-to-date treatment of advanced capabilities; highlighted coverage of new software features, and expert advice from author Gene Weisskopf, a seasoned spreadsheet specialist.

Mastering Smartware II
Jonathan Paul Bacon
634pp. Ref. 651-0

An easy-to-read, self-paced introduction to a powerful program. This book offers separate treatment of word processing, data file management, spreadsheets, and communications, with special sections on

data integration between modules. Concrete examples from business are used throughout.

Mastering SuperCalc5
Greg Harvey
Mary Beth Andrasak
500pp. Ref. 624-3

This book offers a complete and unintimidating guided tour through each feature. With step-by-step lessons, readers learn about the full capabilities of spreadsheet, graphics, and data management functions. Multiple spreadsheets, linked spreadsheets, 3D graphics, and macros are also discussed.

Mastering Symphony (Fourth Edition)
Douglas Cobb
857pp. Ref. 494-1

Thoroughly revised to cover all aspects of the major upgrade of Symphony Version 2, this Fourth Edition of Doug Cobb's classic is still "the Symphony bible" to this complex but even more powerful package. All the new features are discussed and placed in context with prior versions so that both new and previous users will benefit from Cobb's insights.

Teach Yourself Lotus 1-2-3 Release 2.2
Jeff Woodward
250pp. Ref. 641-3

Readers match what they see on the screen with the book's screen-by-screen action sequences. For new Lotus users, topics include computer fundamentals, opening and editing a worksheet, using graphs, macros, and printing typeset-quality reports. For Release 2.2.

Understanding 1-2-3 Release 2.3
Rebecca Bridge Altman
700pp. Ref. 856-4

This comprehensive guide to 1-2-3 spreadsheet power covers everything from basic concepts to sophisticated business applications. New users will build a solid foundation; intermediate and experienced users will learn how to refine their spreadsheets, manage large projects, create effective graphics, analyze data-bases, master graphics, more.

Understanding PFS: First Choice
Gerry Litton
489pp. Ref. 568-9
From basic commands to complex features, this complete guide to the popular inte-grated package is loaded with step-by-step instructions. Lessons cover creating attrac-tive documents, setting up easy-to-use data-bases, working with spreadsheets and graphics, and smoothly integrating tasks from different First Choice modules. For Ver-sion 3.0.

Up & Running with Lotus 1-2-3 Release 2.2
Rainer Bartel
139pp. Ref 748-7
Start using 1-2-3 in the shortest time pos-sible with this concise 20-step guide to the major features of the software. Each "step" is a self-contained, time-coded les-son (taking 15, 30, 45 or 60 minutes to complete) focused on a single aspect of 1-2-3 operations.

Up & Running with 1-2-3 Release 2.3
Robert M. Thomas
140pp. Ref. 872-6
Get a fast start with this 20-step guide to 1-2-3 release 2.3. Each step takes just 15 minutes to an hour, and is preceded by a clock icon, so you know how much time to budget for each lesson. This book is great for people who want to start using the program right away, as well as for potential 1-2-3 users who want to evaluate the program before purchase.

Up & Running with Lotus 1-2-3 Release 3.1
Kris Jamsa
141pp. Ref. 813-0
A 20-step overview of the new 3.1 version of 1-2-3. The first twelve steps take you through the fundamentals of creating, using and graphing worksheets. Steps 13 through 15 explain the database, and the balance of the book is dedicated to 3.1's powerful WYSIWYG capabilities.

Up & Running with Quattro Pro 3
Peter Aitken
140pp. Ref.857-2
Get a fast start with this 20-step guide to Quattro Pro 3. Each step takes just 15 minutes to an hour, and is preceded by a clock icon, so you know how much time to budget for each lesson. This book is great for people who want to start using the program right away, as well as for potential Quattro Pro 3 users who want to evaluate the program before purchase.

WORD PROCESSING

The ABC's of Microsoft Word (Third Edition)
Alan R. Neibauer
461pp. Ref. 604-9
This is for the novice WORD user who wants to begin producing documents in the shortest time possible. Each chapter has short, easy-to-follow lessons for both keyboard and mouse, including all the basic editing, formatting and printing functions. Version 5.0.

The ABC's of Microsoft Word for Windows
Alan R. Neibauer
334pp. Ref. 784-6
Designed for beginning Word for Win-dows users, as well as for experienced Word users who are changing from DOS to the Windows version. Covers every-thing from typing, saving, and printing your first document, to creating tables, equations, and graphics.

The ABC's of WordPerfect
Alan R. Neibauer
239pp. Ref. 425-9
This basic introduction to WordPefect consists of short, step-by-step lessons—for new users who want to get going fast. Topics range from simple editing and for-matting, to merging, sorting, macros, and more. Includes version 4.2

Mastering WordPerfect
Susan Baake Kelly

435pp. Ref. 332-5

Step-by-step training from startup to mastery, featuring practical uses (form letters, newsletters and more), plus advanced topics such as document security and macro creation, sorting and columnar math. Through Version 4.2.

Mastering WordPerfect 5
Susan Baake Kelly

709pp. Ref. 500-X

The revised and expanded version of this definitive guide is now on WordPerfect 5 and covers wordprocessing and basic desktop publishing. As more than 200,000 readers of the original edition can attest, no tutorial approaches it for clarity and depth of treatment. Sorting, line drawing, and laser printing included.

Mastering WordPerfect 5.1
Alan Simpson

1050pp. Ref. 670-7

The ultimate guide for the WordPerfect user. Alan Simpson, the "master communicator," puts you in charge of the latest features of 5.1: new dropdown menus and mouse capabilities, along with the desktop publishing, macro programming, and file conversion functions that have made WordPerfect the most popular word processing program on the market.

Mastering WordStar Release 5.5
Greg Harvey
David J. Clark

450pp. Ref. 491-7

This book is the ultimate reference book for the newest version of WordStar. Readers may use Mastering to look up any word processing function, including the new Version 5 and 5.5 features and enhancements, and find detailed instructions for fundamental to advanced operations.

Microsoft Word Instant Reference for the IBM PC
Matthew Holtz

266pp. Ref. 692-8

Turn here for fast, easy access to concise information on every command and feature of Microsoft Word version 5.0—for editing, formatting, merging, style sheets, macros, and more. With exact keystroke sequences, discussion of command options, and commonly-performed tasks.

Practical WordStar Uses
Julie Anne Arca

303pp. Ref. 107-1

A hands-on guide to WordStar and MailMerge applications, with solutions to common problems and "recipes" for day-to-day tasks. Formatting, merge-printing and much more; plus a quick-reference command chart and notes on CP/M and PC-DOS. For Version 3.3.

Teach Yourself WordPerfect 5.1
Jeff Woodward

444pp. Ref. 684-7

Key-by-key instructions, matched with screen-by-screen illustrations, make it possible to get right to work with Word-Perfect 5.1. Learn WordPerfect as quickly as you like, from basic editing to merge-printing, desktop publishing, using graphics, and macros.

Alan Simpson's Mastering WordPerfect 5.1 for Windows Companion Disk

If you want to use the sample documents, styles, and macros presented in this book without keying them in yourself, you can send for a companion disk containing all the files (excluding the files that already came with your WordPerfect package). You can use each file as it is, or as a starting point in creating your own document, style, or macro.

To purchase the disk, complete the order form below and return it with a check, international money order, or purchase order for $20.00 U.S. currency (plus sales tax if you are a California resident) to the address shown on the coupon. Or, we can bill you later. Sorry, we cannot accept credit cards.

If you prefer, you can return the coupon without making a purchase to receive free, periodic newsletters and updates about Alan Simpson's latest books.

. . . .

Alan Simpson Computing
P.O. Box 945
Cardiff-by-the-Sea, CA 92007
Phone: (619) 943-7715
Fax: (619) 943-7750

☐ Please send the companion disk for *Mastering WordPerfect 5.1 for Windows*

☐ No disk, thanks, but please send free newsletters from Alan Simpson Computing

_____
NAME

_____
COMPANY

_____
ADDRESS

_____
CITY, STATE, ZIP

_____
COUNTRY   P.O. NUMBER (IF APPLICABLE)

Check one:

☐ Payment enclosed
($20.00, plus sales tax for California residents),
made payable to *Alan Simpson Computing*

☐ Bill me later

☐ No charge (newsletters only)

Check one disk size:

☐ 5¼ " disk

☐ 3½ " disk

. . . .

FREE BROCHURE!

Complete this form today, and we'll send you a full-color brochure of Sybex bestsellers.

Please supply the name of the Sybex book purchased.

_____

How would you rate it?

_____ Excellent   _____ Very Good   _____ Average   _____ Poor

Why did you select this particular book?

_____ Recommended to me by a friend

_____ Recommended to me by store personnel

_____ Saw an advertisement in _____

_____ Author's reputation

_____ Saw in Sybex catalog

_____ Required textbook

_____ Sybex reputation

_____ Read book review in _____

_____ In-store display

_____ Other _____

Where did you buy it?

_____ Bookstore

_____ Computer Store or Software Store

_____ Catalog (name: _____)

_____ Direct from Sybex

_____ Other: _____

Did you buy this book with your personal funds?

_____ Yes   _____ No

About how many computer books do you buy each year?

_____ 1-3   _____ 3-5   _____ 5-7   _____ 7-9   _____ 10+

About how many Sybex books do you own?

_____ 1-3   _____ 3-5   _____ 5-7   _____ 7-9   _____ 10+

Please indicate your level of experience with the software covered in this book:

_____ Beginner   _____ Intermediate   _____ Advanced

Which types of software packages do you use regularly?

_____ Accounting   _____ Databases   _____ Networks

_____ Amiga   _____ Desktop Publishing   _____ Operating Systems

_____ Apple/Mac   _____ File Utilities   _____ Spreadsheets

_____ CAD   _____ Money Management   _____ Word Processing

_____ Communications   _____ Languages   _____ Other _____
                                                                        (please specify)

Which of the following best describes your job title?

_____ Administrative/Secretarial   _____ President/CEO

_____ Director   _____ Manager/Supervisor

_____ Engineer/Technician   _____ Other _____
                                                        (please specify)

Comments on the weaknesses/strengths of this book: _____

_____

_____

_____

_____

Name _____

Street _____

City/State/Zip _____

Phone _____

PLEASE FOLD, SEAL, AND MAIL TO SYBEX

SYBEX, INC.
Department M
2021 CHALLENGER DR.
ALAMEDA, CALIFORNIA USA
94501

SYBEX ®

SEAL

FEATURE	MENU SELECTIONS	SHORTCUT	PAGE
Line Numbering	Layout ➤ Line ➤ Numbering	Shift+F9 N	794
Line Spacing	Layout ➤ Line ➤ Spacing	Shift+F9 S	96
List Entry*	Tools ➤ Mark Text ➤ List	F12 L	822
Location of Files	File ➤ Preferences ➤ Location of Files	Ctrl+Shift+F1 L	450
Macro (play)	Macro ➤ Play	Alt+F10	516
Macro (record)	Macro ➤ Record	Ctrl+F10	512
Margin Release	Layout ➤ Paragraph ➤ Margin Release	Shift+Tab	107
Margins	Layout ➤ Margins	Ctrl+F8	100
Master Document	Tools ➤ Master Document		839
Merge Codes	Tools ➤ Merge ➤ Merge Codes	Ctrl+F12 C	545
Merge Documents	Tools ➤ Merge ➤ Merge	Ctrl+F12 M	554
Move (Cut) Text*	Edit ➤ Cut	Shift+Del	40
New Document	File ➤ New	Shift+F4	57
Open Document	File ➤ Open	F4	27
Outline On/Off	Tools ➤ Outline ➤ Outline On or Outline Off		784
Page Numbering	Layout ➤ Page ➤ Numbering	Alt+F9 N	244
Paper Size	Layout ➤ Page ➤ Paper Size	Alt+F9 S	277
Paragraph Number (insert)	Tools ➤ Outline ➤ Paragraph Number	Alt+F5	778
Paragraph Numbering (define)	Tools ➤ Outline ➤ Define	Alt+Shift+F5	776
Password	File ➤ Password		408
Paste	Edit ➤ Paste	Shift+Ins	40
Print Document	File ➤ Print	F5	301
Print Preview	File ➤ Print Preview	Shift+F5	71
Redisplay		Ctrl+F3	188
Redline	Font ➤ Redline		146
Replace	Edit ➤ Replace	Ctrl+F2	350
Reveal Codes	View ➤ Reveal Codes	Alt+F3	74
Right Justification	Layout ➤ Justification ➤ Right	Ctrl+R	106
Ruler	View ➤ Ruler	Alt+Shift+F3	66
Save Document	File ➤ Save	Shift+F3	404

Requires that text be selected